Zinacantan

Evon Z. Vogt

Zinacantan

A Maya Community in the
Highlands of Chiapas

The Belknap Press of Harvard University Press

Cambridge, Massachusetts

1969

To the Zinacantecos

Mi chalekil-ch'ambekon,
Mi chalekil-ʔich'bekon,
   Ti yo hset' ʔune,
   Ti yo hhuteb ʔune,
     Tavamikoe,
     Tavermanoe.

Will you take this in good grace,
Will you receive this in good grace,
   This lowly little bit,
   This humble amount,
     From your friend,
     From your brother.

Haʔ chahtaik ʔo ta k'oponel,
Chahtaik ʔo ta tiʔinel,
   ʔOyuk ʔavokol ʔun,
   ʔOyuk ʔavik' tiʔ ʔun,
     Kolavalik hutuk.

For this reason I speak to you,
For this reason I pray to you,
   If you have been kind,
   If you have done favors,
     Thank you a little.

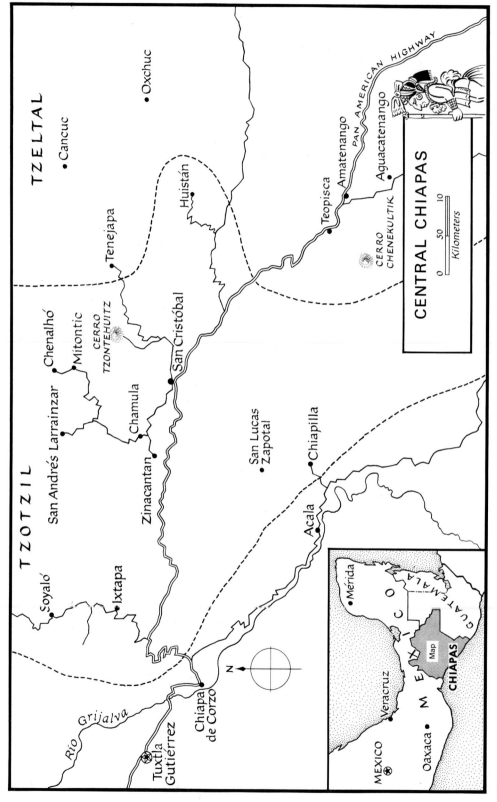

Map 1

Preface

Zinacantan is one of twenty-one *municipios* (municipalities) in the highlands of Chiapas, Mexico, where Tzotzil is spoken.* Tzotzil is a Mayan language, and Zinacantan is located (see Map 1) near the western border of the contemporary Mayan Indian habitat, which extends southeastward through the highlands of Guatemala and northeastward into the peninsula of Yucatán and contains a total of more than two million descendents of the Ancient Maya who once inhabited these same regions.

The name "Zinacantan" derives from the preconquest epoch when Aztec traders named the region and its people "Tzinacantlan," meaning "place of bats" in their Nahuatl language (Peñafiel 1885: 180; Becerra 1930: 293). According to Fray Tomás de la Torre (Ximenez 1929–31), one of the Dominican missionaries who arrived in Chiapas in 1545, the aboriginal patron deity of the Zinacantecos was a stone bat believed to have been found by their ancestors before there was a sun above the earth and was worshiped as a god. There is now no trace of this deity except for the Aztec name of the municipio.

The contemporary municipio of Zinacantan, covering an area of 117 square kilometers, lies just to the west of the Ladino town of San Cristóbal Las Casas, along both sides of the Pan American Highway (see Map 2), and contains a population of approximately 8000. About 400 people live in the ceremonial center of Zinacantan, the others in fifteen scattered hamlets. Hence the settlement pattern is typically Mayan with ceremonial center and outlying hamlets. Zinacantan Center contains three Catholic churches, the *Cabildo* (town hall), a government school, a few stores, and a plaza where markets are held during important fiestas. In and around this ceremonial center are located a series of sacred mountains and waterholes that figure importantly in the religious life.

The topography is rugged, consisting of limestone and volcanic mountains

*For ease in distinguishing them, Spanish words have been italicized at first mention; thereafter they appear in regular type. Tzotzil words have been set in small capital letters throughout, although family and given names and names of places found on Ladino maps have not.

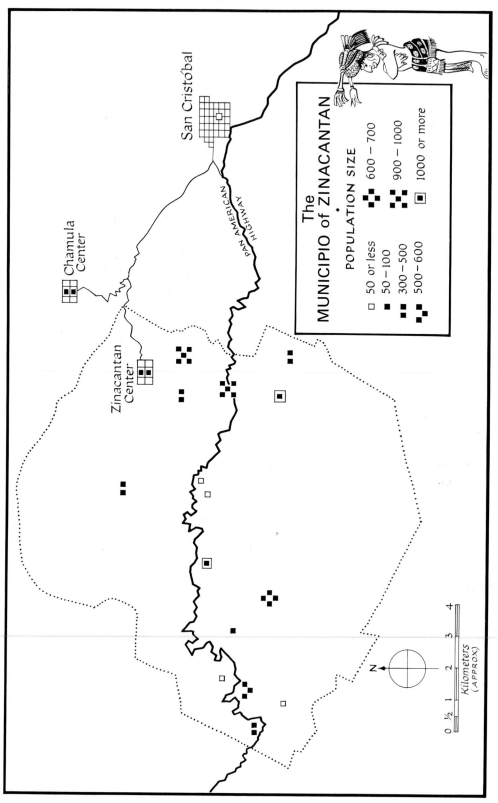

The
MUNICIPIO of ZINACANTAN

POPULATION SIZE

50 or less
50 – 100
300 – 500
500 – 600
600 – 700
900 – 1000
1000 or more

San Cristóbal

Chamula Center

Zinacantan Center

PAN AMERICAN HIGHWAY

N

Kilometers (APPROX)

0 ½ 1 2 3 4

Map 2

covered with magnificent stands of pine and oak trees. The altitude is high, with the ceremonial center situated at 2135 meters; some of the outlying hamlets are as high as 2450, others as low as 1500 meters.

Like the inhabitants of each of the other Indian municipios, the Zinacantecos speak a distinct dialect, possess distinctive styles of dress, and have local customs that differ from those of their neighbors. These customs are currently a blend of ways of life inherited from Ancient Maya ancestors and of Spanish patterns acquired over the centuries since the conquest.

The basic purpose of this book is to provide the first general ethnographic description of this Zinacanteco way of life that has been evolving in the remote highlands of Chiapas for at least a thousand years. While their Ancient Maya ancestors probably participated in Classic Maya civilization that flourished in the first millenium A.D. and developed a form of hieroglyphic writing, the knowledge of this writing was not transmitted to the Zinacantecos, who are essentially a nonliterate people. Except for a handful of younger men who have recently been taught to read and write in Spanish by the Mexican government schools, or in Tzotzil by the members of our Harvard Chiapas Project, there has been no one in Zinacantan to record or study their intricate and complex ways of life.

Ethnographic field work began in Zinacantan in 1942–43 when Professor Sol Tax, of the University of Chicago, led an expedition of nine Mexican students from the Escuela Nacional de Antropología e Historia into the highlands of Chiapas. This field party spent about six weeks in Zinacantan during the months of December and January and made preliminary observations which are available in microfilm (Tax 1943) and in one short article (Tax 1944). From 1940 to 1950 the Summer Institute of Linguistics maintained two missionary-linguists in one of the hamlets of Zinacantan, and they produced three technical articles, two on the language (Nadine Weathers 1947, 1950) and one on agricultural practices (Kenneth Weathers 1946).

Apart from these early observations, Zinacantan was an "unstudied" culture until I initiated the Harvard Chiapas Project in 1957; therefore, I feel a deep obligation to provide (whatever else I do) an ethnographic account of this unique and fascinating way of life before its patterns become eroded and altered by the process of "modernization" that is now underway in southern Mexico. But no ethnography is purely descriptive; some interpretation of the ethnographic facts occurs in almost every chapter of the book, and I have added three chapters at the end to summarize some of the most important theoretical problems posed by the description of Zinacantan. My emphasis, however, is upon the ethnographic description of

Zinacantan; more theoretical and methodological topics are treated in detail in a number of specialized monographs and technical articles that have already appeared (see Bibliography) or are currently in preparation by various members of the Project.

The Harvard Chiapas Project

My long-range field study in the highlands of Chiapas was initiated in the summer of 1957 and has been in continuous operation since that time. It was Dr. Alfonso Caso, the Director of the Instituto Nacional Indigenista of Mexico, who first interested me in this region when he graciously invited me to attend a series of field trips and meetings of his staff in the summer of 1955. I had previously worked with the Indians of New Mexico, especially the Navahos and Zunis, and was looking for a new field site in Mexico. My initial trip to Chiapas was made in the company of Dr. Gonzalo Aguirre Beltrán, now the Director of the Instituto Indigenista Interamericano, Dr. J. Luis Gómez Pimienta, and the late Dr. Manuel Gamio. We traveled together by automobile from Mexico City to San Cristóbal Las Casas. From the moment I first entered the highlands of Chiapas I knew that I had discovered the type of exciting field situation in which I wanted to work. I returned to Chiapas in the winter of 1956 to make further preparations, and again in the summer of 1957 when the then Director of the Tzeltal-Tzotzil Center of the Instituto Nacional Indigenista, Professor Alfonso Villa Rojas, suggested that I begin my field work in Zinacantan and was instrumental in introducing me to this municipio.

The project goals have been to undertake a series of basic ethnographic studies utilizing both traditional and new methods, and then to investigate in detail the trends of social and cultural change in the Chiapas highlands. I have been interested not only in contemporary processes of change but also in utilizing the ethnographic data to make inferences about the Ancient Maya and to project forward and make predictions about the future of these Indian cultures as they become more significantly linked to the modern world.

The field studies have been concentrated in the Tzotzil-speaking municipios of Zinacantan, Chamula, and Huistán, and in the Ladino town of San Cristóbal Las Casas. The project has been organized for field operations in three phases. Phase 1, from 1957 to 1960, involved my work and a series of graduate students in field research. This phase has continued and has provided field experience for twenty-four graduate students, most of whom spent at least fifteen months in the field. I have managed to spend twenty months doing field work in Chiapas, almost wholly in Zinacantan, during summers and leaves-of-absence from teaching at Harvard. Phase 2 began in the summer of 1960 when undergraduate students were added in connection with the Columbia-Cornell-Harvard-Illinois Summer Field Studies Program. This program has involved six undergraduates each year drawn from the participating universities, who have done field research in Chiapas each summer. Phase 3 was initiated in 1963–64 with a research plan to obtain aerial photographic coverage of the highlands of Chiapas. The photographs were taken in February and March 1964 and have provided us with excellent coverage of the 6400 square miles occupied by the Tzotzil and Tzeltal. I am now utilizing the photographs for studies of settlement patterns, land-use, markets, and communications networks in an aerial photography laboratory that has been established in William James Hall at Harvard.

Pre-field training for the students includes a seminar in research methods which I teach with the assistance of experienced students who have returned from Chiapas; and also an intensive course in Tzotzil, taught by the most fluent member of the Project who is in residence at Harvard. These Tzotzil teachers are normally graduate students, but are sometimes undergraduates who have become fluent in the language.

In our field operations we first tried the procedure of building or renting houses in Zinacantan, either in the ceremonial center or in the outlying hamlets, and living as neighbors of the Indian families. This phase was necessary at first when we knew no Indians and no Tzotzil, and the Indians were as frightened of us as we were of them. We soon discovered that this mode of operations led to less exposure to Indian life than I had anticipated. When we lived in the ceremonial center, occupied in part by Ladinos, we spent a great deal of time visiting and coping with them rather than the Indians. Furthermore, since it is impolite in Zinacanteco society to go visiting just for the sake of seeing people, we soon found, even when living in a separate house in an outlying hamlet (where there are no Ladinos), that we were observing and interviewing very limited numbers of Indians and then only at certain times during the day.

As our command of Zinacanteco customs and of the Tzotzil language increased, we began to develop good rapport with an increasing number of families who came to regard us less as threatening intruders and more as friendly, or at least harmless, observers of their way of life. We were able to work out a different, and more effective, pattern of field work. We now maintain a base of operations in San Cristóbal. We have rented some old ranch buildings at the edge of town where the field directors and married students can headquarter and where we can offer the hospitality of meals and overnight lodging to any number of Indians who arrive. Unmarried students are based in various hotels or small boarding houses in San Cristóbal.

We alternate our field work activities between interviewing Indian informants at base headquarters and participating in Zinacanteco life by living with Indian families in their villages. The work at headquarters provides a situation for uninterrupted and intensive interviewing. The informants are paid a daily wage equivalent to the amount they can earn on the local labor markets, and they are more secure in working with us than they would be in the crowded conditions in their own homes. On the other hand, living in the hamlets places us on a 24-hour-a-day basis with Indian families and provides a total immersion in Zinacanteco life. We eat and sleep as the Zinacantecos do and join them in their various work activities. We also make an effort to select an Indian family that will provide maximum field data on the problem of interest to the student. For example, if a student is studying curing ceremonies, we place him in the house of a shaman. If one is studying the ritual in the ceremonial center, he lives with a cargo-holder. If another is studying politics, we place him in the house of the Indian president—so that he can observe what happens at night as well as at the Cabildo during the day. After several days or weeks (depending upon how long the hosts and the students can gracefully accommodate to each others' presence), the student returns to headquarters in San Cristóbal to write up his field notes. He usually brings an informant back from the field to work for a few days in San Cristóbal on more intensive interviewing about what has perplexed him about the patterns of behavior observed in the Indian villages. Then the student returns to the field for another period of time. The results have been very productive in providing a range of intensive data on all aspects of Indian life.

In our accommodation to Zinacanteco life we have stressed the use of the maximum amount of Tzotzil that it is possible for the student to learn in the training course at Harvard and in his early weeks in the field. We have also made certain that each student acquires a Tzotzil name so that he can be easily identified and related to by the Zinacantecos. In my own case, since it was not possible to translate "Evon" into Tzotzil, I assumed the name of "Juan," following a suggestion of Professor Norman McQuown that "Evon" is closest to English "John"—hence in Spanish, Juan, which easily translates into Tzotzil as SHUN.

In the process of field work over the years, we have also managed to train a series of Zinacanteco informants who can now write out texts for us in

Tzotzil with interlinear translations in Spanish. Two of them have become very competent in transcribing interview data from tape recorders and using the touch system on typewriters. They can type in both Tzotzil and Spanish, and have learned to footnote when they come to a difficult passage to translate. One of these men was brought to Cambridge in 1965 and 1968 to help teach the Tzotzil course and to be available for interviews for students. The experiment was very successful and very exciting for the students. We hope to repeat it in the future.

The students' projects are tailored to fit their own interests, providing they also contribute to the total project and do not repeat something that has been done before. During the first few weeks we insist that students keep full daily journals that are read and criticized by the field director. We then shift to a more specialized format for recording the data, one geared to the problem under investigation. This format might be behavior observations recorded in special ways, formal interviews, conversations or texts like myths recorded on the tape recorder, and so forth. Strong emphasis is placed upon a hard focus on a delimited problem area so that the student does not wander aimlessly in his research.

Students give progress reports at occasional formal seminars, lasting two or three days. But most of the field direction is provided in long individual conferences held every two or three days throughout the field season. These may take place on the trail into some remote hamlet; driving on the road in the project vehicle; at base headquarters; or in a Zinacanteco house where the student has been visited by the field director. At the end of the season each student is asked to produce the rough draft of his final report before he leaves Chiapas. These drafts are reworked after having been commented on by the field director; copies are later placed in the central file, along with the indexed field notes, at Harvard.

In our publication program each student is encouraged to publish on the specialized topic that he researched in the field. A number of student papers, some by undergraduates, have appeared in Evon Z. Vogt (editor), *Los Zinacantecos,* which was published in Spanish in 1966 by the Instituto Nacional Indigenista in Mexico. Other students and younger colleagues have published specialized books or monographs—Cancian (1965a), Colby (1966), and Jane F. Collier (1968), for example. Still others are in active preparation by Robert M. Laughlin, Daniel Silver, John D. Early, and Victoria R. Bricker. The complete Project bibliography, including technical articles, appears at the back of this volume. It will be noted that there have been some joint publication efforts, but most of the publication has been by individual students and colleagues. I should add, however, that each manuscript is subjected to intense and constructive criticism by other field workers. I have been unable to produce any manuscripts without having to rewrite, correcting errors in my data or analysis, at least three times. All of this means extra work but results in more precise ethnographic statements than would have been possible if the Indian cultures were being studied by a single field worker.

Acknowledgments

The Harvard Chiapas Project is sponsored by the Laboratory of Social Relations and the Peabody Museum of American Archaeology and Ethnology at Harvard University, and by the Instituto Nacional Indigenista in Mexico. The research funds have been provided by the National Institute of Mental Health of the United States Public Health Service (Grants No. M-1929 and MH-02100); the Carnegie Corporation of New York under a grant (B-3204) for the Columbia-Cornell-Harvard-Illinois Summer Field Studies Program, which was later supported by the National Science Foundation (Grant GY-120); the American Philosophical Society (Grant No. 2295), and a Ford Foundation Grant-in-Aid. I have also received support from the National Science Foundation (GS-262, GS-976, GS-1524) to undertake, in collaboration with Professors Norman A. McQuown and A. Kimball Romney, an aerial survey of the Tzotzil and Tzeltal zone in the highlands of Chiapas. The aerial survey work was done under contract to Harvard University by the Itek Corporation (Vidya Division) of Palo Alto, California, and by the Compañía Mexicana de Aerofotos, S.A., of Mexico, with the sponsorship of the Instituto Nacional Indigenista of Mexico.

Over the years I have become obligated to many persons and institutions in the United States and in Mexico for assistance of many types on the Project. At Harvard I have received strong support from the two sponsoring institutions of the Project, and I would like to express my gratitude to the former director of the Laboratory of Social Relations, the late Professor Samuel A. Stouffer, and to its present director, Professor Robert F. Bales, and to the Director of the Peabody Museum, Professor J. O. Brew. I have also had many stimulating conversations concerning the project and our data with my colleagues in the Peabody Museum, especially Professor Gordon R. Willey, Professor and Mrs. John W. M. Whiting, and Dr. and Mrs. William R. Bullard, all of whom have visited us in Chiapas, as well as the late Professor Clyde Kluckhohn, and Drs. H. E. D. Pollock and Tatiana Proskouriakoff.

During the last few years the highlands of Chiapas have attracted many other anthropologists from other institutions who have also undertaken long-range field work in the area. Special mention should be made of the University of Chicago, Stanford University, and the work of the late William R. Holland of the University of Arizona. Our Harvard Project has profited both intellectually and logistically from close cooperation with the personnel from these other universities. From the University of Chicago and Stanford University projects I would like to mention especially Sol Tax, Norman A. McQuown, Robert M. Adams, A. Kimball Romney, Julian Pitt-Rivers, Calixta Guiteras-Holmes, Duane Metzger, Gerald Williams, John Hotchkiss, Brent Berlin, and Nicholas A. Hopkins who, among many others, made genuine contributions to our Harvard Project.

My colleagues on the Board of Directors of the Columbia-Cornell-Harvard-Illinois Summer Field Studies Program, Professors Joseph B. Casagrande, Charles Wagley, Marvin Harris, and the late Allan R. Holmberg, maintained a deep and continuing interest in our Chiapas Project, and Casagrande and Wagley have both visited us in the field. Duane Metzger in 1960, Frank Cancian in 1962, and George A. Collier in 1964 and 1966 have served as field directors for the Program in Chiapas.

The detailed plans for the project were formulated at the Center for Advanced Study in the Behavioral Sciences in Palo Alto, California, where I served as a Fellow during the academic year 1956–57. I would like to express my appreciation to the Center, and especially to its former Director, Dr. Ralph W. Tyler, and its Assistant Director, Mr. Preston Cutler, for the opportunities they provided for my preparations for the project, including a travel grant to visit Chiapas in 1956. I am also indebted to Professor David C. McClelland of the Department of Social Relations at Harvard for a small grant that permitted the project to begin in the summer of 1957.

In Mexico, I would first of all like to express my appreciation to the Instituto Nacional Indigenista from which I have received continuous intellectual stimulation and logistic support, especially from Dr. Alfonso Caso and Dr. Gonzalo Aguirre Beltrán. The Instituto Nacional Indigenista personnel at the Centro Coordinador Tzeltal-Tzotzil in San Cristóbal Las Casas have been unfailingly helpful over the years. I would especially like to mention the assistance of the former Director, Professor Alfonso Villa Rojas; the former Sub-Director, Dr. Francisco Alarcón, who likewise provided the Project with many crucial services; and the former administrative officer, Sr. Enrique Leal de la Peña, who supervised the construction of a field house for the Project in the Zinacanteco hamlet of Paste⁷.

In San Cristóbal Las Casas we have also had the good fortune to enjoy the warm hospitality and close cooperation of Sr. Don Leopoldo Velasco Robles, formerly Presidente Municipal of San Cristóbal and Diputado a la XLVIII Legislatura del Estado de Chiapas; of Don Manuel Castellanos, the former director of the office of Asunto Indígenas of the state government of Chiapas, and recently appointed Sub-Director del Centro Coordinador Tzeltal-Tzotzil; of the late Doña Roberta Montagu; and the late Dr. Frans Blom and his widow, Doña Gertrudes Duby Vda. de Blom who valiantly continues to manage the famous "Casa Blom" with its magnificent library on Chiapas. We are also indebted in various ways to the Bishop of the Diocese of San Cristóbal Las Casas, Samuel Ruiz García, to Monseñor Eduardo Flores, and to Padre Juan Bermúdez who serves as parish priest for Zinacantan. Others who have been kind enough to help us on many occasions include Professor Prudencio Moscoso Pastrana, Sr. Mariano S. Trujillo Robles, Sr. Jorge Sarquis Asís, and Sr. Fernando Hernández Velasco.

In Zinacantan we have deeply appreciated the hospitality, friendship, and cooperation of the Indian and Ladino population with whom we have been working all these years. I should especially mention Don Belizario Lievano, the Secretario Municipal, and Doña Elisea Suárez, among the many Ladinos who have helped us; and Mariano Hernández Zárate, Juan de la Cruz ʔAkov, José de la Cruz ʔOk'il, Antonio López Tsintan, Andrés Gómez Rodríguez, Antonio Montejo Cruz, Manuel Pérez Con Dios, Pedro Pérez Con Dios, Antonia González Pakanchil, Juan Vásquez Shulhol, Mariano Pérez ʔOkots, Guillermo Pérez Nuh, and Juan Hernández Min, among the many Zinacantecos who have helped us. Special mention must be made of Domingo de la Torre Pérez and José Hernández Peréz, who have been working for the Project for many years and have been trained to read and write both Tzotzil and Spanish and to use typewriters and tape recorders with a facility that is rare indeed.

Meanwhile, in the City of Mexico, I have never failed to enjoy warm hospitality, have a stimulating conversation with, and receive additional help on countless matters from Dr. Alfonso Caso and Dr. Aguirre Beltrán, at the offices of the Instituto Nacional Indigenista; from Dr. Ignacio Bernal, the new Director of the Museo Nacional de Antropología; and from Dr. Alberto Ruz Lhuillier, Director del Seminario de Cultura Maya.

The assistance of my secretaries over the years, especially Gloria A. de Caetano, Patricia B. de Hume, Nora M. de Sacerdote, Roberta Huber, and Carol W. Shweder, in typing and assembling the manuscript is gratefully acknowledged. Symme H. Burstein of the Peabody Museum produced the original drafts of the maps.

I am indebted to Barbara Metzger, Olga Linares de Sapir, and Elena Uribe Castañeda for research assistance, and to Sally Price for her splendid editorial work on earlier versions of the manuscript. A later draft profited from the editorial work of Eleanor A. Gossen. The final version was improved by the sensitive editing of Mrs. Philip C. McLaughlin of the Harvard University Press.

Robert M. Laughlin and Victoria R. Bricker provided needed editorial assistance in standardizing the spelling of Tzotzil words throughout the volume. Judith E. Merkel kindly assisted in the translation of many of the myths and prayers. Brent Berlin graciously provided the data on the scientific identification of plants grown and used by the Zinacantecos.

Most of the photographs were taken by Frank Cancian, John D. Early, and Mark L. Rosenberg, and I appreciate their permission to use them. I would also like to express my appreciation to Richard Kroeck who served as the project director of the aerial photography work for the Itek Corporation.

The Master of Leverett House at Harvard, Dr. Richard T. Gill, graciously provided a small study for me in which I could work on this manuscript without the usual academic interruptions.

I am eternally grateful to my wife, Catherine C. Vogt, who has accompanied me on almost all of my field trips to Chiapas and who has not only managed our household and family affairs with care and affection but has cheerfully provided hospitality for field workers, Indian informants, visiting anthropologists, and friends in San Cristóbal. At Harvard she has also worked as a research assistant and has played a major role in condensing and organizing the ethnographic data available on the ceremonial life of Zinacantan.

Finally, I would like to add that the Project would have been impossible without the remarkable work of my students and younger colleagues (listed in Appendix I) who have done field research with me in Chiapas.

Evon Z. Vogt
Cambridge, Massachusetts
June 1967

Contents

Illustrations

Maps (drawn by Samuel H. Bryant)

Tables

Part I / Geographic and Cultural Setting

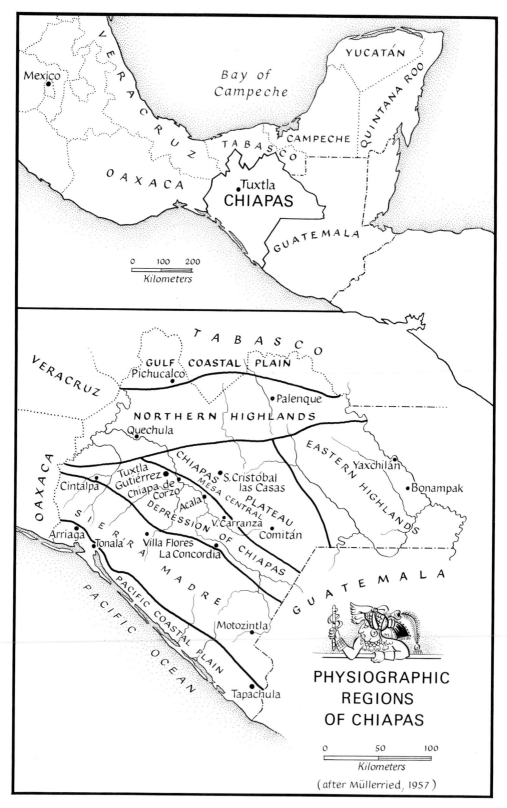

PHYSIOGRAPHIC
REGIONS
OF CHIAPAS

0   50   100
Kilometers

(after Müllerried, 1957)

Map 3

1 / The Highlands of Chiapas

Between the isthmus of Tehuantepec and the Cuchumatan mountain massif on the Guatemalan border lies the Mexican state of Chiapas. Near the geographical center of the state of Chiapas are "Los Altos de Chiapas," a highland region that is the present habitat of three important Mayan-speaking groups: the Tzotzil, the Tzeltal, and the Tojolabal. Zinacantan, located near the western edge of this region, is one of the most important Tzotzil municipios. An acquaintance with this highland habitat is essential to the following presentation of Zinacanteco culture.

Physiographic Setting

The state of Chiapas has seven distinct physiographic regions (Müllerried 1957): (1) a narrow coastal plain along the Pacific on the southwest; (2) the Sierra Madre de Chiapas, a mountain range which rises sharply above and parallels the Pacific coastal plain; (3) the great Central Depression of Chiapas through which flows the Grijalva River; (4) the Chiapas plateau (or highlands) in the center of the state; (5) the Eastern highlands dropping off to the tropical rain forest area of the Usumacinta River valley; (6) the Northern highlands; and (7) a small portion of the large Gulf coastal plain which extends on through Tabasco to the coast of the Gulf of Mexico (see Map 3).

The Tzotzil, Tzeltal, and Tojolabal are concentrated in the Chiapas plateau, or Meseta Central de Chiapas (Tamayo 1949a, I: 393–395). The communities of these three Mayan groups correspond closely to the area covered by this physiographic region.

This highland mass is about 220 kilometers in length along its principal axis which runs northwest to southeast from the vicinity of Pichucalco to the Guatemalan border, and from 50 to 100 kilometers in width. In physiographic shape, it has three basic parts: a broad base at an elevation of some 1500 meters above sea level; terraced margins or flanks at an elevation of approximately 2000 meters; and a summit, for the most part between 2100 and 2500 meters, but with a few peaks reaching over 2700 meters near San Cristóbal Las Casas. The highest peak, Tzontehuitz, just north of San Cristóbal, reaches to 2910 meters and on clear days provides a magnificent panorama of vast stretches of this highland mass as it drops off to the lowlands in all directions. The descent into the lowlands is much more precipitous in a southwesterly direction where the terraced margins are narrow, and the descent from the summit to the Grijalva River in the Central Depression in many places involves a drop of 2000 meters with only some 15 kilometers of travel. The elevation of the Central Depression varies from 800 meters down to 400 meters at its lowest point near the town of Chiapa de Corzo (Hill 1964). In other directions the margins and the base are much broader and the descent into the lowlands is much more gradual, but the trip is still rugged since the routes of travel must pass over precipitous ridges and across broken limestone terrain.

Geology and Soils

The highlands of Chiapas have a complex geological history, as is evident in the schematic profile adapted from Müllerried (see Figure 1). The core is a massive upfaulted block capped by strata of Cretaceous and Tertiary limestone. The originally horizontal strata have been much broken by faulting and by volcanic intrusions which occurred in the upper Tertiary and Quaternary. On the southwestern side this mountain mass rises abruptly (as mentioned above) as a fault scarp overlooking the Central Depression of Chiapas (West 1964: 67). The summit of the plateau is extensively scarred with sinks, and there are many caves that are of ritual importance to the Indians. Fault-line scarps have divided the area into ridges and basins, many of which drain internally. These upland basins are important for human settlement in the highlands. In the largest of these enclosed valleys lies the Ladino town of San Cristóbal Las Casas; many of the smaller ones are the locations of ceremonial centers for the dispersed Indian communities.

The soils derived from these limestone and volcanic features are generally fertile, both for natural flora and for domesticated plants. They tend, however, to erode badly when overgrazed by livestock, and much of the surface is made up of slopes too rugged and too rocky for cultivation.

Surface drainage is slight on the plateau summit. The enclosed basins

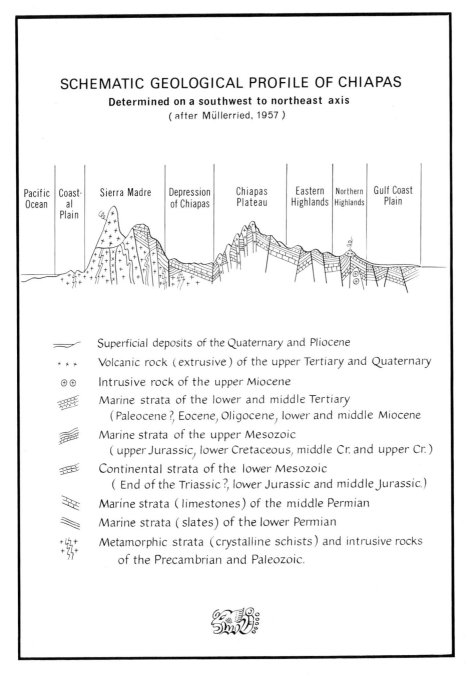

SCHEMATIC GEOLOGICAL PROFILE OF CHIAPAS

Determined on a southwest to northeast axis

(after Müllerried, 1957)

| Pacific Ocean | Coast-al Plain | Sierra Madre | Depression of Chiapas | Chiapas Plateau | Eastern Highlands | Northern Highlands | Gulf Coast Plain |

Superficial deposits of the Quaternary and Pliocene

Volcanic rock (extrusive) of the upper Tertiary and Quaternary

Intrusive rock of the upper Miocene

Marine strata of the lower and middle Tertiary
(Paleocene?, Eocene, Oligocene, lower and middle Miocene

Marine strata of the upper Mesozoic
(upper Jurassic, lower Cretaceous, middle Cr. and upper Cr.)

Continental strata of the lower Mesozoic
(End of the Triassic?, lower Jurassic and middle Jurassic.)

Marine strata (limestones) of the middle Permian

Marine strata (slates) of the lower Permian

Metamorphic strata (crystalline schists) and intrusive rocks
of the Precambrian and Paleozoic.

1. Schematic geological profile of Chiapas

drain into sinks (*sumideros*), where water disappears into limestone fissures, to reappear as springs and streams at lower elevations. A few of the basins, like that of Zinacantan Center, have permanent streams that provide water, but the outlying Indian settlements are usually situated near those water-holes which can be relied upon in the dry season. Below the plateau rim, surface drainage becomes more pronounced with decreasing altitude, and deep valleys have been carved into the skirts of the plateau on all sides. Springs are increasingly numerous at lower elevations, providing ample water for Ladino settlements. The scattered Indian settlements that pre-dominate on the plateau give way to Ladino hamlets and towns, inter-spersed with large plantations (*fincas*) and cattle ranches (Adams 1961). Large streams and rivers appear on both sides of the plateau—the Grijalva River and its branches on the south and west, the Lacantu, the Jatate, the Tlacotalpa, the Tzaconeja, and their various branches on the north and east.

Climate

Like most of Mexico, the Chiapas highlands have a marked wet and dry season. Over 90 percent of the precipitation falls between May and October, and the winters are dry. The heavy summer rains make these highlands among the wettest uplands in Mexico; at San Cristóbal Las Casas, with an elevation of 2128 meters, the mean annual rainfall is 1171 millimeters. Total rainfall decreases westward into the Central Depression, and Tuxtla receives only 941 millimeters per year (Hill 1964: 3). On the other hand, certain areas north and east of San Cristóbal exceed these figures markedly (Tamayo 1949b). Summer rains are mostly of convectional origin and are sometimes accompanied by hail. The strong, cold northeast winds (*nortes*) of the winter bring copious rains to the northern slopes of the Chiapas highlands, but by the time these winds reach the area of San Cristóbal and Zinacantan, they bring only slight drizzles, which may last for several days. One interesting feature of the summer rainfall pattern is a marked *canícula* (dry period) in late July and early August, when the precipitation slacks off for several days. June and September are the wettest months, with San Cristóbal's mean precipitation reaching almost 250 millimeters during each of these months.

On the plateau summit the climate is cool. During the winter dry season the days are sunny and warm, the nights quite cold, with frost in December and January. The hottest season occurs in the spring before the rains arrive in May. During the summer rainy season it is cool most of the time, and the sky is generally overcast with either rain clouds, fog settling in the valleys in the early mornings, or clouds condensing and pouring up over the plateau rim.

Flora and Fauna

The flora found in the Chiapas highlands is now being systematically investigated by the botanist Dennis Breedlove, who describes the plant cover as follows:

> The vegetation of the central highlands of Chiapas can be separated into associations by elevation. On the highest peaks and ridges, elevation 8,000 to 9,400 feet, is a cloud forest characterized by many genera of thick leaved, evergreen trees. The trees range in height from 50 to 150 feet. The understory is dense, consisting of many ferns, shrubs and vines. Many epiphytic ferns, mosses, bromeliads and orchids are one of the more striking features of this forest. (The predominant species are: *Drimys granadensis, Magnolia sharpii, Rapanea Juergensenii, Clethra lanata, Clethra oleoides, Gaultheria odorata, Quercus acatenangensis, Oreopanax xalapensis, Oreopanax capitatus, Symplocos limoncillo, Viburnum jucundum, Pinus ayacahuite, Chiranthodendron pentadactylon.*)
>
> Interfingering with this forest on the north and east slopes of the highlands is a temperate forest of tardily deciduous trees. The trees range in height from 50 to 100 feet. The understory is moderately dense with many kinds of shrubs, subshrubs and vines. The trees have broader crowns than those in the cloud forest and the trees are spaced further apart, but epiphytes are still very common. The elevational range of this association is 3,500 to 8,200 feet. (The predominant species are: *Liquidambar styraciflua, Quercus candicans, Quercus sapotefolia, Quercus segoviensis, Clethra suaveolens, Cornus disciflora, Garrya hartwegii, Ceanothus coeruleus, Viburnum hartwegii, Nyssa sylvatica, Pinus chiapensis, Pinus montezumae, Saurauia veraguensis, Cleyera theaeoides, Ostrya guatemalensis, Carpinus caroliniana, Cupania dentata, Brunellia mexicana.*)
>
> On the dryer south and west slopes of the highlands a sparser, less variable, temperate forest occurs. The trees range in height from 50 to 125 feet. The trees are spaced very far apart and the understory is poorly developed with often only grassy patches between the trees. There are very few epiphytes. The elevation ranges from 4,000 to 8,400

feet. (The predominant species are: *Quercus rugosa, Quercus corrugata, Quercus mexicana, Quercus crassifolia, Pinus oaxacana, Pinus oocarpa, Pinus michoacana, Arbutus xalapensis, Buddleia skutchii, Crataegus pubescens, Rhamus nelsonii, Vernonia leiocapa, Ternstroemia tepezapote.*) On the moist north and east sides of the highlands, below 3,500 feet elevation, the temperate deciduous forest is replaced by a tropical evergreen rain forest. The trees range in height up to 250 feet.

On the dry south and west sides of the highlands the vegetation is variable according to exposure. In canyons and on sheltered slopes without intensive cultivation, there is a tall tropical deciduous forest. On exposed slopes and on recently fallow, sheltered slopes, one finds a scrubby thorn forest. (Personal Communication, May 23, 1966)

According to native informants, the forests formerly had many deer, coyotes, rabbits, and several varieties of foxes and cats. There may have been at one time many jaguars and ocelots, considering the importance of these animals in the belief system. But these animals have been largely hunted off, and today, except for birds and small animals like skunks, raccoons, and opossums, one may travel for days in the highlands without seeing wild animals; even the nearby lowlands appear to have few animals compared to their former populations. There continues to be a rich terminology covering animal life, including reptiles, insects, and birds. Acheson (1962) elicited 143 terms for different varieties of mammals, reptiles, and insects and 90 terms for different birds that are clearly recognized by the Zinacantecos.

Highland-Lowland Contrast

Perhaps the physiographic feature of overriding importance for this highland Chiapas habitat is the proximity and accessibility of adjoining lowlands. Although the Zinacantecos live in the highlands, they now cultivate most of their maize in the adjacent lowlands of the valley of the Grijalva River. Furthermore certain key items in their cultural inventory— such as copal incense, bamboo staffs for their shamans, and certain types of gourd containers in everyday use—also come from the lowlands.

Local Ladinos classify the lands of central Chiapas into the usual distinction of Hot Country (*Tierra Caliente*), extending up to about 900 meters; Temperate Country (*Tierra Templada*), which lies between 900 and 1800 meters; and Cold Country (*Tierra Fría*), which is the country above 1800 meters. On this geographic scale, most Zinacantecos live in Cold Country, but farm in Hot Country. A few Zinacantecos in the lower hamlets live below 1800 meters, in Temperate Country, and some of the important farming operations are found in this zone, but the important contrast to the Zinacantecos is between the highlands above 1800 meters and the lowlands below 900 meters. In effect, the Zinacantecos, as well as many of their neighbors in other municipios, are both "Highland" and "Lowland" Mayas.

The economic and social implications of this dual environment will become clear in the course of this book, but I shall anticipate a few of the major points. Many students of the Maya classify them into "Highland Maya" and "Lowland Maya." The Highland Maya are those societies inhabiting the highlands of Guatemala and the highlands of Chiapas, while the Lowland Maya are those who occupy (or occupied in the past) the lowlands of Tabasco, Chiapas, Veracruz, and the Yucatán Peninsula in Mexico, the Petén and the Pacific Coast in Guatemala, and the lowlands of British Honduras. It has long been recognized that one of the important geographic facts in the development of cultural richness and social complexity, and, indeed, the development of "high civilization" in Ancient Middle America, has been the fundamental symbiosis between highland and lowland environments in close proximity. Thus, for example, the Ancient Aztecs established their capital at Tenochtitlán in the Valley of Mexico, where in *Tierra Fría* they could exploit a rich highland environment, but they also had access to an amazing variety of products from the tropical lowlands by way of active trade and tribute from regions they controlled by conquest. In the Maya area there were no conquest states of the same scale, but systematic trade between societies in the highlands and those in the lowlands served to enrich the economic life of both. In most of the Maya region the interaction between the two ecological zones seems to have been (and continues to be) between different sociopolitical units. But in the case of Zinacantan both the highland and lowland ecological niches are being exploited by one Maya society. This ecological adaptation has not, of course, led to the same kind of "high civilization" found in Ancient Middle America; ecological symbiosis between highlands and lowlands is clearly only one important factor in Middle American cultural development. But it is evident that without its dual environment, contemporary Zinacantan could not begin to produce sufficient maize for its basic needs and that its economic life would be much impoverished without the tropical products available to them from the lowlands of the Grijalva River valley.

This dual environment has far-reaching effects on the social life of Zinacantan, especially in that the women and small children remain at home in their highland hamlets while the men spend months of their time engaging in maize cultivation in the lowlands and in traveling to and from their fields in *Tierra Caliente*. The whole theme of travel to and from the lowlands also appears in prayers and petitions (for example, in petitions for a bride), and even in myths that describe how Zinacantecos encounter adventures with various demons while traveling on the trails. Further, many of the most important sacred places that figure in Zinacanteco ritual are located in the lowlands. The adaptation to the two ecological zones obviously has had a major impact on the Zinacanteco way of life.

2 / Tzotzil Prehistory and History

The prehistoric origins of the contemporary Tzotzil are only partially understood, but a number of inferences based upon archaeological and linguistic research in the Maya area can be made which indicate the probable course of events in their cultural history before the Spanish conquest. The period since the conquest is still under investigation, but enough is known to sketch some of the major developments during the Colonial period. The more recent impact of "modernization" in the form of highways, schools, clinics, and other community development programs is well documented. This chapter will sketch what is known of the cultural history of the Tzotzil and place the municipio of Zinacantan within its historical framework.

Maya Origins

The present evidence from comparative linguistics suggests a point of dispersal for the Maya in the area that is now the Department of Huehuetenango in northwestern Guatemala, where a proto-community can be postulated for approximately 2600 B.C. (McQuown 1964). There is definite evidence from the linguistic data that subsistence was based upon cultivated maize. The community probably had a relatively small population, on the order of 5000. It may have had various dialect groups within it, but the dialect were not very differentiated, and hence it is likely that it was an integrated unit of some type (Vogt 1964a).

From this proto-community, various Maya groups emigrated and ultimately reached the habitats that comprise the contemporary distribution of the Maya peoples: Guatemalan highlands, peninsula of Yucatán, Chiapas highlands, and one outlying area in northern Vera Cruz, where the Huastec are found.

McQuown (1964) infers that a number of movements out from the proto-community took place in the direction of the Usumacinta River drainage basin: Huastec, Yucatec, Chontalan, and Tzeltalan. The latter were the remote ancestors of the contemporary Tzeltal and Tzotzil, and it is postulated that their movements into the Usumacinta drainage took place at about 750 B.C. and that they occupied the lowlands for over a thousand years before moving westward into the Chiapas highlands between A.D. 500 and 750. If these inferences are correct, the ancestors of the contemporary Tzeltal and Tzotzil may have participated in the development of Maya Classic civilization, most probably on the western margins of the Petén, before moving into the highland of central Chiapas where the differentiation between Tzeltal and Tzotzil has occurred (Vogt 1964a).

Highland Chiapas Prehistory

The major archaeological work in the heartland of Tzotzil and Tzeltal occupation has been undertaken by Robert M. Adams and his students. Adams' 1961 paper summarizes the findings on changes in territorial organization and settlement patterns and provides a provisional chronology. More recently, Culbert has published his findings on the ceramic history and has added estimated dates for the phases in the cultural chronology (see Table 1).

Table 1. Archaeological phases of the Chiapas highlands

Cultural period	Phase	Estimated dates
Late Postclassic	Lum	A.D. 1250–1524
Early Postclassic	Yash	A.D. 1000–1250
Late Classic	Tsah	A.D. 700–1000
Early Classic (discontinuity)	Kan	A.D. 300–700
Late Preclassic	Sak	300 B.C.–A.D. 100

Source: Culbert 1965: 4

The Sak phase is barely present in the Chiapas highlands. Culbert reports that Sak ceramics were encountered by excavation at only one site near Teopisca (1965: 79); he agrees with Adams (1961: 342–344) that the highlands appear to have been sparsely inhabited in Preclassic times.

During the Kan and Tsah phases which followed, equivalent to the Classic period, there was a marked influx of population in the highlands.

It is still difficult to judge precisely when this influx occurred, but Adams' best estimate is that it coincided with the latter part of the Early Classic, A.D. 500 to 700. Culbert is inclined to an earlier date, about A.D. 300, but adds that "penetration of the Highlands proper by the Kan tradition may not have occurred earlier than A.D. 400 to 500" (1965: 81). At any rate, Adams and Culbert agree that the Kan phase represents the arrival of new settlers in the highlands, rather than an expansion of population from the earlier Sak phase, and that the new phase is a tradition of ultimately Maya origin. The influx is significantly close to McQuown's (1964) lexicostatistic reckoning for the appearance of the ancestral Tzeltalans in the Chiapas highlands—that is, A.D. 500 to 750. Culbert adds, on the basis of his more recent analysis, that there is "an apparent parallel between the patterns of linguistic and ceramic divergence within the Highlands. Both sets of data suggest a relative uniformity of culture patterns in the region during the Classic period, followed by increasing divergence that eventually resulted in the establishment of two separate zones" (1965: 82). He also believes that, although it is probable that the spread of Classic ceramics in the highlands can be correlated with the advent of the parent Tzotzil-Tzeltal group in the region, all hypotheses about the origin of the group must be considered extremely conjectural, since lexicostatistic data are preliminary and the archaeological considerations are derived from fragmentary evidence (Culbert 1965: 82). I concur, but since there is increasing evidence from the lowlands of some type of disturbance in Maya culture at the end of the Early Classic (600 A.D.)—a disturbance that seems to bring non-Mayan influences into the western borders of the Maya lowland (Willey 1964)—it is conceivable that the Tzeltal migration into the Chiapas highlands was in some way significantly related to these developments. Whether these influences reaching the sites in the Usumacinta drainage correlated with a Pipil, or other non-Mayan invasion, as Willey (1964) and others have suggested, is not yet clear, but it is significant that the settlements established in highland Chiapas by the presumed ancestors of the present Tzeltal-Tzotzil are predominantly what Adams (1961: 344) calls "headlands settlements." He suggests that they entered the highlands from the Ocosingo region on the northern flank of the plateau, a route that would also correspond with McQuown's inference that they were previously living in the Usumacinta drainage. Upon arrival in the highlands they selected headland sites for the location of their ceremonial centers, and perhaps for dwelling areas as well. An argument could be made that the importance of sacred mountains in their mythology and ceremonialism could have influenced their selection of headland locations in the earlier Kan phase, especially since not all of them seem to offer defensive advantages.

By the time of the succeeding Tsah phase (Late Classic) the data are much more adequate, and Adams finds that the settlements were "regularly placed in highly defensible locations on steep ridge-lines, bluffs, hilltops, or even sharp andesitic pinnacles" (1961: 347). The general picture that emerges is one of relatively small, independent communities, located in defensible locations, suggesting that they were under outside pressures, either Pipil or perhaps Chiapanec, since the Chiapanecos were by this time well settled along the Grijalva River. But although the situation reflects possible external threats, there is no evidence, at least in ceramics, of "a significant penetration of the region by groups involved in inter-regional trading relationships"; rather, the data suggest that the Chiapas highlands "remained an isolated and backward region not directly influenced by any of the major Mesoamerican centers" (1961: 348).

The most common type of settlement during this phase was a symmetrical arrangement of descending terraces of crude masonry, in the form of a truncated cone, which crowned a hilltop. The summit typically contained a platform mound that seems to have been the focus of ceremonial activity. There may have been levels in the system (as we find today) since at least at some sites "small mounds were placed on the crests of outlying terraced hills" (1961: 349). It is still unclear whether the encompassing unit of significant settlement was concentrated around these hilltops, as Adams thinks, or whether the hilltop settlements were merely ceremonial centers. In the latter case, the terraces would have formed house sites for the ritual specialists and the bulk of the population would have lived in a more dispersed sustaining area. Many of the locations do appear to have been selected with military considerations in mind, and Adams' suggestions may prove to be correct: that there may have been more nucleation during the Late Classic with people living in relatively compact settlements on headlands and utilizing adjacent valley bottoms for agriculture.

By the time of the Yash phase in the Early Postclassic, the patterns of settlement had changed. Most of the widely distributed inaccessible headland sites had been abandoned, and settlements shifted to sites around the larger upland basins, such as the valley of San Cristóbal. The extent to which these were politically important "regional groupings," as Adams (1961: 352) describes them, is not yet clear. It does seem evident that the groupings are larger than in the previous Tsah phase, but whether they were larger in scope than the present municipios, such as Zinacantan with its outlying hamlets, is debatable. Both the archaeological manifestations and the ethnohistoric data appear to be in line with a hypothesis that the settlement patterns and the levels in the political structure were not greatly different in scope from the contemporary municipio arrangement.

Unfortunately, we have not yet been able to undertake archaeological field work in Zinacantan. An attempt was made by Edward E. Calnek in 1960 to secure permission to do so, but it was rejected by the authorities in Zinacantan. Therefore, our data are restricted to survey work around the edges in various adjacent municipios and to excavations that had been carried out nearby. Of particular possible relevance to the prehistory of Zinacantan were the test excavations undertaken in 1961 by Adams, Calnek, and Donald McVicker at the large site on the summit of Cerro Ecátepec located at the southwestern corner of the valley of San Cristóbal, especially since this site is within ten kilometers of contemporary hamlets of Zinacantan. But, except for the ceramic data and some information on the tombs (Culbert 1965: 19–25), the results have not yet been published. Other relevant excavations are the four sites investigated by McVicker (1965) near Ixtapa, and the work of the New World Archaeological Foundation at Chiapa de Corzo and other sites along the Grijalva River (Lowe 1959). However, all the data from archaeology and early postconquest reports indicate that Zinacantan Center was located in the same valley where it is today, and that it controlled a number of outlying hamlets, some of which were probably in their present locations. There is some suggestive evidence of prehistoric terracing on the slopes of a major sacred mountain, now called KALVARIO, "Calvary," at the edges of the valley of Zinacantan. The best guess seems to be that the central focus for aboriginal ceremonialism (probably with some type of platform or pyramidal mound) is precisely where the ancestral gods are believed to gather for their meetings today. We see no evidence of the old platform mound, but it could have been destroyed in the process of building the present shrine.

The extent of central Mexican influence upon Zinacantan in the Post-classic period has been a focus for recent ethnohistoric research (see especially Calnek 1962). For, although the archaeological data indicate little penetration of the Chiapas highlands from central Mexico, we know from Sahagún that amber, quetzal feathers, and skins from the hinterland of Zinacantan did reach the Aztec capital (Anderson and Dibble 1959: 21–23) and that the Zinacantecos were described as "sensible people and many of them traders" (Díaz 1912: 305). But Sahagún's account emphasizes the dangers to the Aztec merchants who carried on the trade, and describes the careful disguises needed to penetrate Zinacanteco territory. We also know that major Aztec campaigns against the Chiapanecos in the Grijalva lowlands were followed in the highlands by only an apparently temporary conquest of Comitán and the establishment of a temporary garrison at Zinacantan (Adams 1961: 359). On the other hand, Calnek (1962) adduces evidence from his more recent ethnohistoric research that highland Chiapas was probably occupied by Toltec or Toltec-influenced invaders during the Postclassic period. He argues that the patterns observed at the time of the conquest were shaped out of a merging of central Mexican and Mayan cultures which took place about two centuries earlier. He concedes, however, that the Chiapas highlands must still be regarded as a marginal, backward area from the point of view of central Mexican influence, compared to Yucatán or highland Guatemala, and that much more research is needed to clarify the extent of central Mexican influence in Chiapas.

The Spanish Conquest*

Although present evidence suggests that the highlands of Chiapas were not subjected to heavy Toltec or Aztec influence in the pre-Columbian period, the Spanish conquest in the sixteenth century and subsequent developments during the seventeenth, eighteenth, and nineteenth centuries did have an important impact upon the Indian cultures of the region.

The first Spanish penetration of the Chiapas highlands occurred in 1523 and 1524. A reconnaissance ordered in 1523 by Gonzalo de Sandoval, leader of the Spaniards stationed in Coatzacoalcos, led to the discovery of the sierras of Quechula, the Zoques, Chiapa de Corzo, the "Quilenes" or Tzotziles, and Copanaguastla. All of these lands and peoples were divided by Sandoval among his men. These first *encomenderos* of Chiapas chose to remain in Coatzacoalcos rather than settle on their grants, and their attempts to exact tribute from their nominal tributaries were so unsuccessful that they soon sent to Mexico for reinforcements to help them subdue the area. Cortés responded by sending them Luis Marín and thirty men with orders to help pacify and settle Chiapas (Díaz 1939: 319, 363).

The combined forces (of which Bernal Díaz was a member) set out from Coatzacoalcos in 1523, cutting through forest to Tepuzuntlan and then proceeding up the Grijalva in canoes to Quechula. From here they went on to Ixtapa and Chiapa and captured the latter. Marín then sent word to the neighboring towns to come to him and surrender. Díaz (1939: 372) reports that among the first to arrive were representatives of Zinacantan,

---

*In this section, and the following section on "Highland Chiapas History," I have drawn materials from my article, "Chiapas Highlands" in the *Handbook of Middle American Indians,* vol. 7 (in press).

Copanaguastla, Pinola, Gueyguistlan, and Chamula, all of whom had been enemies of the Chiapanecos. Thus here, as in the Valley of Mexico, local hostilities played into the Spaniards' hands and gave them an early victory. Only an instance of insubordination—a treasure-seeking soldier's private foray against Chamula—made further fighting necessary. After a battle at Chamula and another at Gueyguistlan, in which they were aided by Chiapaneco warriors and Zinacanteco bearers, the Spaniards gathered, divided the spoils (Bernal Díaz was given Chamula in *encomienda*), and returned to Coatzacoalcos.

Once again, and this time against the express orders of Cortés, no Spanish settlement was left in Chiapas from which to maintain the peace. Pineda (1888: 30) reports that ten or fifteen Spaniards did remain in the region. Where they lived is unclear, but when the Indians resisted control, they fled to Comitán and from there sent to Mexico City for help. In response, late in 1526 Cortés commissioned Diego de Mazariegos to reconquer the Indians in Chiapas. Mazariegos' mission (1527–28) put an end to massive armed resistance to Spanish rule in Chiapas for nearly two centuries. In March of 1528 Mazariegos founded the capital, Villa Real, at Chiapa, and the conquest of Chiapas was essentially completed.

Highland Chiapas History

The Spanish settlement at Chiapa was only temporary, however, for the *ayuntamiento* (municipal government) named by Mazariegos soon decided to move Villa Real into the highlands where the climate was more pleasant. The town was moved to the site of the present city of San Cristóbal Las Casas, which became the capital of Chiapas and the base for Spanish operations in the highlands.

Land and laborers were allotted to the Spaniards for their support by means of the encomienda (royal grant of land and Indians) and some of them moved out onto their grants to supervise better their operation and the collection of tributes. In 1536 only forty Spaniards were living in Villa Real, but the "others on their estates" (Remesal 1908: 21) were sufficiently numerous to have required an increase in the number of *regidores* (councilmen) in the *cabildo* (town hall) from six to nine. Spaniards held in encomienda the towns of Chiapa, Zinacantan, Pinola, and Chamula (Trens 1957: 40), and undoubtedly many other Indian towns. These early years saw the *villa* (town) raised by royal decree to the status of *ciudad* (city) and the church elevated to the status of cathedral. The first bishop was appointed in 1537, but as he died en route and a new appointment had to be made, none reached Chiapas until 1544. The clerical population grew quite slowly; a small group of monks called *Mercedarios* established a monastery in Ciudad Real in the early years, but aside from these, there were only five priests in the whole province when the first bishop arrived.

At the same time the bishop, Bartolomé de las Casas, arrived, a group of seventeen Dominican friars came from the monastery in Guatemala. Because of his views on the treatment of Indians, Las Casas was poorly received by the encomenderos in Ciudad Real. The resentment against him made it difficult for the Dominicans to carry on their own work; consequently, they soon moved their headquarters to Chiapa de Corzo and established other convents in Zinacantan, Copanaguastla, and Soconusco (Ximenez 1929: 356). A year later, the encomenderos of Ciudad Real, alarmed by the bad opinion of them that by this time had reached the Court in Spain, decided to seek the favor of the clergy, and invited the Dominicans to build a convent in Ciudad Real (Trens 1957: 142). The friars came in from Zinacantan in 1546 and, with money and Indian labor contributed by the Spanish community, built a church and monastery there. From the convents they went out by twos to preach, administer the sacraments, and found new, congregated communities on the Spanish model. Churches went up in these towns, many being completed within seven or eight years of the friars' arrival in Chiapas (Remesal 1908: 52). On the invitation of the bishop of Chiapas of that period, Franciscan monks from Guatemala joined the other friars in 1577; they founded their first monastery in Ciudad Real and a later one in Huitiupan.

By 1616 Thomas Gage found some four hundred Spanish families in Ciudad Real (Gage 1908: 85). The earliest complete census with a breakdown by ethnic identity seems to be that of 1778 (Trens 1957: 221–224). In that year, there were 7499 *blancos* (whites) and *mestizos* (mixed bloods) in Chiapas and 51,279 *indios* (Indians). While the Ladinos (as the blancos and mestizos came to be called in Chiapas) were spread far and wide across the state (with the result that few Indian communities were far from a settlement of Spaniards), there were still no resident Ladinos in nearly half of all Chiapas towns, and, in all but four towns, the Indian population was substantially larger than the non-Indian. About half of the Ladino population lived in Ciudad Real and Comitán, and no other Spanish-speaking community even approached these in size. Ladino settlements were more frequent at lower altitudes, suggesting that the interests of the Spaniards were, except for the political control points of Ciudad Real and Comitán, better served where they could engage in raising sugar cane and cattle, and in trading these items, as well as cacao and cotton, in Mexico and Gautemala.

Barbara Metzger, in an interesting interpretation of the history of Indian-Ladino relationships in the highlands of Chiapas (1960), suggests that the major issues can be grouped under two headings: exploitation and acculturation. The first includes the perennial problems of land, labor, tribute, taxes, and trade; the second consists of the varied efforts to integrate the Indian population into a Spanish-dominated society—religious conversion, congregation, political control, education, and so on.

The earliest relationships between Spaniards and Indians in Chiapas, and perhaps the dominant ones throughout the centuries, have been exploitative in nature. The forms were the familiar ones found elsewhere in New Spain in this period: slavery and the encomienda system. Despite efforts on the part of both the Crown and the local Dominicans under the leadership of Bishop las Casas, the encomiendas persisted until they were finally abolished, beginning in 1720. But, as McBride (1923: 61) points out, the abolition of the encomienda did not return the lands to the original owners. Rather, in most cases the Indians remained on the *haciendas,* bound to the land by long-established custom. The absorption of Indian lands by Ladinos, already a serious problem by the middle of the 19th century, was given added impetus by the Ley Lerdo (1856), calling for the sale of lands of religious and civil corporation. The stripping of the Indian communities of their communal lands proceeded apace under this law, as Ladinos rather than Indians snapped up the best lands. The number of haciendas in Chiapas increased from 518 in 1877 to 1076 in 1910—the greatest percentage increase in the nation during this period (Cosio Villegas 1956: IV, 210). It was not until the *ejido* system was put into effect by the Mexican Revolution that this trend was reversed, and even then it was not until Cárdenas came to power in the 1930's that much land was actually distributed. The struggle continues today in the highlands of Chiapas, but with the aid of the Instituto Nacional Indigenista (hereinafter INI) the Indian communities are finally making real progress in increasing their landholdings.

The labor problem has been closely associated with the land problem. As Ladino landowners gained control over more and more of the cultivable land, they established claims to the labor of the people who lived on it as well. Indians who were bought out by Ladinos in the sales of lands in the nineteenth century chose to enter into the service of the new owner rather than leave their land. This service, called *baldiaje,* consisted of unremunerated labor on the owner's land for as many as four days a week

(Trens 1957: 597). At the bottom of the inseparability of the Indians and their land was probably a deep-rooted and often supernaturally sanctioned attachment to the land which their ancestors had known and worked. Supporting this traditional attachment was undoubtedly an increasing shortage of suitable land on which to settle as the *hacendado's* holdings increased. In addition, the initiative and responsibility required to move and set up a new operation may have further deterred the Indians from leaving. Debt peonage was also established as a means of controlling the Indian labor force on the haciendas. Another arrangement was used on the coffee fincas which were established in Soconusco in the 1880's and by the early 1900's were beginning to seek Indian labor in the Chiapas highlands (Pozas 1952). On fincas, debt servitude in the form of advance payment of wages, rather than extension of credit on goods, was later established as a means of attaching the Indian worker to his employer.

Exploitation was not restricted to the encomenderos and hacendados, but also came to be practiced by the clergy and public officials (Trens 1957). The over-all record of Spanish exploitation of the Indians in highland Chiapas appears to have had an important effect upon the course of acculturation. Despite over four hundred years of efforts to integrate the Indian population into the Ladino-dominated society, the exploitative measures have led to a complex set of reactions in these corporate Indian communities. Those which have been able to maintain at least minimal control over their land bases have selectively incorporated certain Ladino patterns into their cultural systems but have remained strongly Indian.

The history of Ladino efforts to transform the Indian cultures may be viewed in terms of political control, religious conversion, congregation of dispersed Indian settlements, and education.

The structure of Spanish political control in Chiapas underwent a number of changes over the centuries.* From the time of Mazariegos up to 1790, the province was governed by alcaldes mayores appointed by the Audiencia and approved by the Consejo de las Indias (Trens 1957: 131). Under the alcaldes were tenientes, one in each important town. In 1790, the alcaldías were replaced by the intendencia. The intendente, governing all of Chiapas, remained accountable to some extent to the Audiencia, and subdelegados replaced the tenientes in function (Paniagua 1876: 20). After independence, Chiapas became a state in Mexico and sent delegates to the national legislature. Governors and state legislatures were elected periodically and/or established by military coup.

*See Glossary for explanations of the terms used in this discussion.

Within this framework, local ayuntamientos have been a fairly stable unit. The ayuntamiento dates back to the early period of settlement, when these local organizations were set up in accordance with the Laws of the Indies to maintain order and administer justice. The ayuntamiento consisted of a gobernador, four alcaldes in charge of the administration of justice, six to eight regidores with responsibility for the collection of tributes, for cleanliness, and for general welfare, and finally an unspecified number of aguaciles or mayores to assist the regidores, maintain the cabildo building, and attend to the needs of travelers. The gobernador was appointed by the jefe principal of the province; the others were elected on the first of January of each year under the supervision of the alcalde mayor and the local teniente. Other positions were later added in compliance with the state constitution of this century, but in a number of places they have remained distinct from the traditional set in one way or another. It is quite clear that what we observe today in Chiapas Indian municipios represents a complex adjustment and retailoring of these formal Spanish governmental positions in response to local Indian political patterns and needs. In many municipios all the positions are filled by Indians except for that of the secretary, which continues to be filled by a Ladino on the grounds that the Indians cannot read, write, or keep records properly. In fact, the secretary's basic political function, as Aguirre Beltrán (1953: 120-121) points out, is to provide the point of control by Ladinos of the Indian municipios.

Over the centuries there have been many Indian revolts in Chiapas against Spanish political control, but two stand out—the "Tzeltal revolt" of 1712 (Klein 1966) and the "Cuzcat rebellion" of 1869-70 (Pineda 1888; Molina 1934). The revolt of 1712 was preceded by years of unrest in which rumblings of rebellion were perceived but not suppressed. Discontent and especially ill-feeling toward the greedy and unscrupulous bishop appointed in 1706 were widespread among the Indians. In 1712, one Sebastián Gómez and his niece claimed that the Virgin Mary appeared near Cancuc, and a chapel was built on the spot for the worship of both the Virgin and the girl, as her interpreter. Many Indians came on pilgrimages to the chapel, and it was here in Cancuc that plans for the revolt took shape. Thirty-two Tzeltal towns, plus Huistán and a few other Tzotzil-speaking villages, were ultimately involved, and the Indians sacked a number of Ladino settlements before they were finally stopped with the aid of military reinforcements from Guatemala.

The rebellion of 1869-70 was also foreshadowed by rumors of war for some years. In 1867, Pedro Díaz Cuzcat, the fiscal of Chamula, and a woman, Agustina Gómez Checheb, made a clay figure, adorned it with ribbons, and set it up in the hamlet of Tzajalhemel on the road to Chenalhó. They sent word to the neighboring hamlets that it had descended from heaven and that they must bring it offerings in order to induce it to stay. Many Indians came with gifts, and the idol spoke to the worshipers from its box (in which Cuzcat was hidden) through Agustina Gómez, its interpreter. When the priest in Chamula succeeded in taking the figure away, Cuzcat and Agustina made several more figures for the box and claimed that she had borne them and so was "mother of God." Several women were appointed to serve her and were baptized by Cuzcat with names of saints. A group of Chamula men formed a council for Cuzcat, and they decided that he should appoint a "saint" for each hamlet to execute his orders and carry the news of the idols' miracles. These communications through the "saints" led to the amassing of firearms. Cuzcat was arrested and sent to the state officials in Chiapa, but was soon released on the grounds that the constitution permitted freedom of religion. His return was a triumphal march, and when he spoke to the assemblage he declared that Indians no longer needed to worship images representing people of another race. He suggested that the Indians choose someone among them to be crucified on Good Friday in order that they might have a Lord of their own to worship. The proposal was accepted and carried out on Good Friday of 1868. Cuzcat was arrested again and jailed, but his place was taken by Ignacio Fernández Galindo, a Ladino from Mexico City, who began to lead the revolt. Finally, in June 1869, the priest of Chamula once again seized the idol, and Galindo led more than a thousand Indians in pursuit. They killed the priest and began to terrorize the Ladinos in the area. Galindo led a party of Indians to San Cristóbal and demanded that Cuzcat be freed. The Ladino leader agreed to exchange Cuzcat for Galindo, and Cuzcat was escorted home. But when Galindo did not return to Chamula, Cuzcat led his men into San Cristóbal, and the ensuing series of military encounters here and elsewhere in the area lasted until October 1870, when the last of the rebels were subdued.

The two revolutions shared a number of features. Both used Catholic religious symbols as rallying points and/or a camouflage for the conspiracy. Neither was easy to suppress, but in both the Ladinos were able to make use of the abstinence of some Indian towns from the cause to augment their own armed forces.

Efforts to settle the Indians in towns apparently have achieved even less success. Resettlement became an issue about 1540 when, at the instigation of Bishop Las Casas, the King decreed that Indians should be settled in towns in order to receive instruction in religion and in civilized manners (Trens 1957: 134). The Dominicans did the actual building of these communities, founding many by "taking the Indians from the rocky mountains where they used to live." Often after a town was settled, the Indians moved back to their hamlets as soon as the priests left, and the friars had to start over again. In 1577, the King decreed that Indians be forbidden to return to their old homes by "whatever measures should be necessary" (Remesal 1908: 49, 50–51). A look at Indian Chiapas today is enough to show that, although orderly towns were established, living in them did not become the rule. With a few exceptions, noted above, the ancient dispersed settlement pattern continues today.

The education of the Indians has always been a concern of the Ladinos in Chiapas. During the Colonial period teachers were placed in certain towns to give primary instruction at the expense of the community. However, by 1838, most municipios still had no schools. A state normal school for Indians was established in 1847, but it was not until after the Revolution that steps were taken to improve the amount and quality of instruction for Indians.

One of the dominant themes in the political history of central Chiapas since Mexican Independence was achieved from Spain in 1821 was a continuing struggle between Federalist and Centralist factions (Locke 1964). After Independence, San Cristóbal remained the capital of Chiapas. But as early as 1833 this position was disputed. Throughout Mexico at this time the conservative upper-class oligarchy, the high-ranking clergy, the principal army chiefs, and the wealthiest property owners, most of whom were Spanish, favored a strong central government. San Cristóbal was controlled by this faction, but it faced Federalist rivals in Tuxtla Gutiérrez, the major town in the nearby lowlands of the Central Depression of Chiapas. In 1833 Joaquín Miguel Gutiérrez became governor of Chiapas and, as leader of the Federalist faction, moved the capital to Tuxtla Gutiérrez. The following year, when Centralist Santa Anna gained national power, he sent troops to occupy the state of Chiapas, and the capital was returned to San Cristóbal where it remained during his regime.

The Federalists regained power as the Liberal Party, led by Ignacio Comonfort and Benito Juárez, took over in 1855. But San Cristóbal continued as a stronghold of conservatism, and its leaders refused to recognize the new governor, Angel Corzo, who set up the capital in Chiapa de Corzo in 1858. Corzo moved the capital of Tuxtla, and, with the aid of Tuxtla, Chiapa de Corzo, Comitán, and other towns, moved with troops into the highlands and put down the rebellion by the conservative San Cristóbal leaders.

The leaders in San Cristóbal next turned, with other conservatives, to the radical solution of handing national power over to Maximilian II. Governor Angel Corzo returned the capital to San Cristóbal temporarily in hopes of gaining its support for his attempt to restore order to the state. But when pro-French imperialist forces began threatening the Chiapas government, Governor Corzo moved back to Tuxtla again to avoid a surprise attack. Juan Ortega and his pro-French imperialist followers attacked San Cristóbal and took over the town. The Liberals, aided by troops from Oaxaca, retaliated and soon defeated Ortega. Porfirio Díaz, then an important general, declared Chiapas in a state of war against the French, and in 1866 Chiapanecos had to fight the French who had advanced close to their borders. Along with the rest of the nation, Chiapas celebrated the decisive victory against the French in 1867, and the new governor, Pantaleon Domínguez, moved the capital to its ancient site at Chiapa de Corzo and later to San Cristóbal where it remained until 1892.

In 1867 Porfirio Díaz gained control of the national government and began a strong rule designed to bring peace and prosperity to Mexico through industrialization and science. But the still isolated, church-controlled society of San Cristóbal resisted Díaz' innovations. The issue came to a head during the regime of Emilio Rabasa who was an adherent of Positivism and a friend of many of the *científicos* who worked with Díaz. Before he became a political leader, he was director of the Instituto de Ciencias, a preparatory school in San Cristóbal, where he attempted to initiate reforms in the school program, substituting the positivistic for the metaphysical approach. This antagonized the Church hierarchy by refuting their teachings and threatening their control over state education. At the same time, the new programs of Díaz threatened the position of the conservative elite of San Cristóbal, composed mainly of *finqueros* and *hacendados* with vast landholdings in the nearby lowlands. This elite maintained town houses in San Cristóbal and depended heavily upon Indian labor drawn from the highland Indian municipios.

There are many local legends in San Cristóbal explaining why Rabasa moved the capital to Tuxtla following his inauguration as governor in 1891—including one that the blue bloods of San Cristóbal snubbed him and failed to attend his inaugural ball. But as Locke (1964) has demonstrated, the facts were much more complex. The permanent removal of the capital to Tuxtla reflected the political and economic unwillingness of the elite in San Cristóbal to cooperate with the trends of change during the Díaz regime.

An even greater impact upon San Cristóbal and the outlying Indian municipios came with the Mexican Revolution (1910 to 1920). Losing the capital to Tuxtla was a blow to the economic and social structure of San Cristóbal, but the Revolution and its aftermath have had an even greater lasting effect. Many of the elite families migrated from San Cristóbal to Mexico and elsewhere following the losses of their large holdings of land (Lowenthal, 1963), permitting the rise to power of middle class families engaged in commerce with the Indians; and the Indians eventually managed to regain, through the ejido program, much of the land previously held by the hacendado families.

To the Indians themselves, the movements of troops during the Revolution was a rather mystifying set of events about which they relate colorful legends (Binderman 1960). But more important from the Indian point of view is the fact that the Revolution provides a kind of mythological charter for the gains they made in control of land.

Zinacanteco History

Specific mentions of Zinacantecos in the early postconquest period emphasize the importance of both their trade and their religious rituals. The trading of salt derived from wells at Salinas and from near Ixtapa was apparently prehispanic (McVicker 1965; Miles 1965: 280), and continued vigorously during the Colonial period. Ximenez describes Zinacantan as a pueblo that "had an infinite number of gods; they worshipped the sun and offered sacrifices to it; to the rivers, the fountains, the heavily-foliaged trees and to the high mountains they offered incense and gifts" (1931: 359).

By the early nineteenth century (1812 to 1830), the Zinacantecos had expanded their commercial activity to trade in cacao, coffee, and tobacco. They brought cacao and coffee to the Chiapas highlands from points as distant as Soconusco and Tabasco, and purchased tobacco in the Lacandon territory, trading it all the way to the Pacific coast.

The exact territorial extent of Zinacantan in early Colonial times is not known, but there is evidence that it included Ixtapa, San Felipe, San Lucas, and Totolapa (Zabala 1961a: 21–22).

In 1572 at least two types of Indian authorities existed in Zinacantan: twelve cantores (who were later converted into the mayordomos) are mentioned, and two alcaldes (Zabala 1961b: 147). In 1592 there is mention of alcaldes and regidores, as well as principales, described as political authorities. There were also aguaciles indios, who carried their *varas de justicia* (staffs). Zabala thinks these officials subsequently became the mayores (who still serve as policemen), the mayordomo reyes, and the mesoneros in the contemporary cargo system.

In 1639 there was a *cargo* (religious position) called regidor pescador, but no further mention is made of this position in later documents. In 1704, a maestro de coro, a sacristan, and a cantor existed, positions which were later organized into sacristanes. At this same time, the alcaldes and regidores were in charge of collecting taxes in the community and transmitting them to Ciudad Real (Zabala 1961b: 147–149). In 1743, the alcaldes were again mentioned as the officials who issue orders, which the regidores were in charge of carrying out. The alcalde mayor or teniente was Spanish, and was appointed by the government in Ciudad Real. The alféreces, mentioned for the first time in 1800, appear to have had direct political control of Zinacantan. In 1812, two additional cargos were noted—a pair of alcaldes de monte—which made a total of four alcaldes. This same year there were also twenty-two mayordomos, whose duty was to look after the church.

In the first decade of the nineteenth century the hierarchy in Zinacantan was described as having been headed by alcaldes, who were followed in rank order by: gobernador, regidores, principales, mayores, aguaciles, fiscales, and sacristanes (Zabala 1961b: 150). It is still unclear where the post of alférez fitted into the system.

In 1592, the community became called El Pueblo de Santo Domingo Zinacantan, indicating that Santo Domingo was the patron saint in these early years after the conquest. A shift in patron saint took place sometime between February 12, 1776, when Santo Domingo Zinacantan is last mentioned, and May 16, 1792, when San Lorenzo Zinacantan is first mentioned (Zabala 1961b: 150). It is unclear why the change took place, but Santo Domingo still functions as an important saint and the alférez of Santo Domingo still occupies a prominent position in the cargo system (see Chapter 11 for a description of the contemporary system).

The three most important recent historical events in their impact upon Zinacantan have been: the ejido program stemming from the Mexican Revolution; the construction of the Pan American Highway through the Chiapas highlands; and the establishment of El Centro Coordinador Tzeltal-Tzotzil of INI.

When the Mexican constitution was prepared in 1917, it included an article, number 27, providing for state action to regulate the use and distribution of property, the division of large estates, the protection of small properties, and the donation of lands to communities needing them. To

carry out these provisions the ejido was created.* The word "ejido" originally referred to the communal lands outside (at the "exit" of) a medieval
Spanish village (Simpson 1937). Originally, the ejido program was specifically designed to give land to deprived Indian "pueblos, ranches, hamlets
and communities," but now any "nucleus of population" of twenty or more
people is eligible. The petitioners (*agraristas*) are responsible for organizing
an assembly, signing an appeal for land, and selecting an executive committee to represent them.

In Zinacantan, an attempt to secure ejido land was made first in 1925,
but little is remembered of this petition and many of the documents
involved are no longer to be found in the government files (Edel 1962:
12). The petition that did succeed was prepared at a meeting of some 210
men of Zinacantan on November 4, 1934. This was the year that Lázaro
Cárdenas became president of Mexico, and his efforts greatly increased
the scope of the program that had been official for almost three decades.

In 1933, several Zinacanteco hamlets submitted petitions, but that of
1934 was the first coordinated effort. The petition was sent to Tuxtla
Gutiérrez, where the governor duly remitted it to the Mixed Agrarian
Commission for action. Even so it was not until 1937 that an engineer
was dispatched to take a census of the inhabitants to determine who was
eligible for land, and to survey the lands already held by the municipio
and the lands within the seven-kilometer radius (the legal distance established by the law) that might be available for distribution. It took another
three years to get action, but finally, on September 10, 1940, two engineers
came to Zinacantan to divide the land and distribute ejido plots among
the Zinacantecos. There was enormous resistance from the Ladino landowners, but the redistribution finally took place and the members of the
ejido received provisional certificates to 12,070 hectares of land, which more
than doubled the area of the municipio.

Although the Zinacantecos are now using it, there were a series of
complex struggles with the Ladino landowners over the Indians' rights to
the land. In the case of the large Ladino ranch San Nicolás, in the valley
of Zinacantan, it was quite clear that the portion given the Zinacantecos
consisted of the least desirable land and that the best land was kept by
the landowner (see Map 4).† There have been several attempts on the part

---

*I am grateful to Matthew Edel for the excellent data he collected on the ejido in the
summer of 1962.

†Map 4 gives the hamlets and haciendas as they are spelled on Ladino maps; the Tzotzil
names of the hamlets according to the Zinacantecos are given in parentheses.

THE EJIDOS OF ZINACANTAN
(from Edel, 1966)

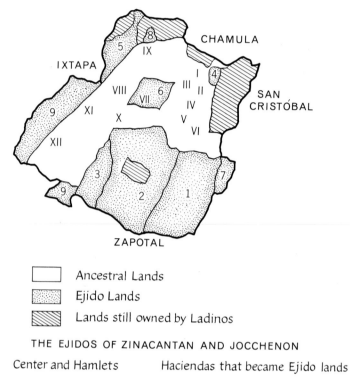

ZAPOTAL

	Ancestral Lands
	Ejido Lands
	Lands still owned by Ladinos

THE EJIDOS OF ZINACANTAN AND JOCCHENON

Center and Hamlets	Haciendas that became Ejido lands
I Zinacantan Center (Hteklum)	1 Guadalupe Xucun
II Vochovo (Vo'ch'oh Vo')	2 San Antonio
III Patosil (Pat'Osil)	3 San Isidro
IV Nachig (Na Chih)	4 San Nicolás
V Paste (Paste')	5 Tierra Colorado
VI Elambo ('Elan Vo')	6 Yalentaib, El Pig
VII Yalentaib (Yaleb Taiv)	7 La Lagunita
VIII Navenchauk (Nabenchauk)	8 Santa Rita Agil
IX Salinas ('Ats'am)	9 Ejido of Jocchenon
X Apaz ('Apas)	
XI Sekemtik (Sek'emtik)	
XII Jocchenon (Hok' Ch'enom)	

Map 4

of the Zinacanteco agraristas to acquire more of this land for the ejido. Additional tension is created by the fact that the Ladino-held portion includes BANKILAL MUK'TA VITS, one of the most important sacred mountains for the Zinacantecos—the one in which their CHANULETIK (animal spirit companions) are believed to be kept by the ancestral gods. Similarly, there was much difficulty when the father of the Catholic priest who serves Zinacantan had much of his land taken away from him and placed in the ejido; for a time the priest refused to say Mass during the important fiestas. Another long series of boundary disputes with the owners of a ranch on a terrace south of Zinacantan continued until 1961. As the population of Zinacantan expands and the Indians learn better how to utilize Mexican law, new pressures to acquire even more of the remaining Ladino holdings within the legal seven-kilometer radius of existing Zinacanteco settlements may well arise.

The second major development in recent years has been the construction of a segment of the Pan American Highway, which is now paved and in good condition all the way from Tuxtla through San Cristóbal and on to the Guatemalan border. The ancient wagon road which connected Tuxtla with San Cristóbal passed through Ixtapa and Zinacantan Center on its way. The first funds for the construction of the Pan American Highway were allocated in 1931, but it was not until 1950 that asphalt surfacing was completed to San Cristóbal. The new route bypasses Zinacantan Center, and instead passes by or through the hamlets of Hok' Ch'enom, Nabenchauk, and Na Chih. The road to Zinacantan Center from San Cristóbal has a gravel surface and is passable in all seasons, but generally is in rough condition, requiring almost an hour to traverse the ten-kilometer distance. By comparison, motor vehicles can drive the ninety kilometers between San Cristóbal and Tuxtla on the paved highway in a little over an hour.

The completion of the highway has vastly improved the transportation network for the bulk of Zinacanteco population, which lives either along the Pan American route or within an hour's walk of it. Zinacantecos now ride buses or passenger trucks to San Cristóbal and Tuxtla regularly. Much of the maize from the lowlands, once carried on human backs or on horses and mules, is now transported by truck from the rented plots along the Grijalva River to the junction of the roads at Chiapa de Corzo and from there into the highland hamlets. The highway has also permitted the development of a flower-growing industry (Bunnin 1963), which supplements maize-growing for many households. The flowers are transported by bus or truck to Tuxtla and sold there in the market. Within the past few years, four groups of Zinacantecos have formed cooperatives and purchased their own vehicles. One is a large truck that operates between San Cristóbal and Zinacantan Center. The other three are pickup trucks (two owned by Zinacantecos in Na Chih and one by Zinacantecos in Hoyihel), which do a brisk business in human passengers and maize along the Pan American Highway.

The third major development in recent history was the formal establishment in 1950 of El Centro Coordinador Tzeltal-Tzotzil. The national agency is headed by Dr. Alfonso Caso in Mexico City. Its headquarters in highland Chiapas is located on the northern edge of San Cristóbal.

INI's program has had the goal of teaching the Indians to become literate in Spanish, bringing modern medicine and new agricultural crops and technology into the Indian communities, integrating them into the national life by building roads to hitherto isolated villages, and generally assisting them to improve their economic situation vis-à-vis the local Ladinos. The program has influenced Zinacantan mainly through the establishment of schools in isolated hamlets, the building of a clinic in Zinacantan Center with a full-time male nurse who treats illnesses and dispenses medicine, the establishment of an experimental farm in the valley of Zinacantan, and the building and improvement of roads within the municipio. INI has also assisted the Zinacantecos by providing legal advice in their political struggles with the Ladinos. A notable feature of the program has been to train *Promotores Culturales* (Cultural Promoters), Indians who are given special training courses at the Centro and then employed as schoolteachers and community developers in the hamlets.

Indian-Ladino Relations

The Chiapas highlands today are fundamentally bicultural, with Indian and Ladino segments. This bicultural system has been described by Aguirre Beltrán (1953) and Pitt-Rivers (1967) and more specifically for Zinacantan by Colby and van den Berghe (1961), and by Colby (1966). A superordinate minority of Ladinos, concentrated mainly in San Cristóbal and Teopisca, are living among a subordinate majority of Indians dispersed in the rural hinterland. The differences between the groups are cultural rather than racial; hence Indians can and do become Ladinoized by learning Spanish, changing clothes, and moving into town, but the process is neither easy nor rapid. Interethnic concubinage is frequent, but intermarriage is rare. Ritual kinship ties, made possible by common membership in the Catholic Church, are frequent, but these are unequal and one-directional, since

Indians frequently ask Ladinos to become godparents, but Ladinos seldom reciprocate. The division of labor is complementary: the Indians serve as peasants, unskilled laborers, or servants; the Ladinos as merchants, artisans, clerks, and professionals. Ladinos generally treat Indians with the condescending kindness accorded a backward child, and the Indians, though latently ambivalent and sometimes hostile to Ladinos, outwardly accept their subservient status. Rigid rules of etiquette help to maintain the social distance, but formal segregation is minimal. Contacts are frequent, especially in the economic sphere, but seldom equalitarian (Colby and van den Berghe 1961: 785).

The three main focuses of interethnic integration are *religious,* through shared formal membership in the Catholic Church (though the priests are all Ladinos, and.*compadrazgo*—ritual kinship—is mainly one-directional); *political,* since power is monopolized by the Ladinos in the towns of San Cristóbal and Teopisca, whence it extends to the rural Indian municipios through the appointment of a Ladino secretary, who is often the real power in the Indian community (Aguirre Beltrán 1953: 119–121); and *economic,* since the Indians produce the food surplus, charcoal, wood, and other needed commodities to keep the Ladinos fed and warm. San Cristóbal and Teopisca, on the other hand, are major distributive centers for manufactured products (such as textiles and metal tools) and major producers of services in the form of hospitals, prisons, barbershops, and so forth. "It is clear that, if Indians and Ladinos ceased to have trade relations, neither group could subsist in its present state" (Colby and van den Berge 1961: 779).

Part II / Material Culture and Economics

3 / Subsistence Activities

When Zinacantecos speak of ʔISHIM, they are using a Tzotzil variant of a proto-Mayan word ʔISHIʔM that still occurs in all Mayan languages (Kaufman 1964: 99) and designates "cultivated maize." The Mayas have been maize-farmers par excellence for some 4500 years, and the Zinacantecos are no exception. Not only does the overwhelming bulk of daily calories come from maize, but a proper meal without this grain in some form is inconceivable to Zinacantecos. They are aware that other people, such as anthropologists, serve meals without maize. But a Zinacanteco hostess would not dream of serving a "civilized" meal without tortillas or *atole,* whatever else she might be serving. And Zinacanteco men, who spend long periods away from home working their fields in the lowlands, invariably take maize foods with them—either *pozol* for the trail or for midday nourishment in the fields, or toasted tortillas for their morning and evening meals.

Maize

Maize, like humans, is believed to have "inner souls" (CH'ULEL) which are found in the ear and in the "heart" of each maize kernel just as they are found in the "heart" of a person. (The term SYOL refers to a small heart-shaped unit in the center of the kernel.) It follows that maize is handled with extreme care; kernels that are dropped on the ground are carefully picked up, and great care is exercised to avoid spilling atole while it is being transported or served. On one occasion when some atole was spilled on the muddy floor of our project Land Rover, one of the Zinacantecos riding in the back lapped it up with his tongue! Maize is often referred to as the halo (SHOHOBAL), literally, "sunbeam [of the gods]." The eighteenth-century Spanish chronicler Francisco Vásquez dramatized the Mayan view of maize which is still held, perhaps to a lesser extent, by those Indians' descendants in Zinacantan. "Everything they did and said so concerned maize that they almost regarded it as a god. The enchantment and rapture with which they look upon their milpas is such that on their account they forget children, wife, and any other pleasure, as though the milpa were their final purpose in life and source of their felicity" (Vásquez 1714, translated in Thompson 1954: 234).

Although maize is the focus of their food-producing activities, Zinacantecos grow, gather, buy, and consume a variety of other foods. They cultivate not only beans and squashes (those other members of the important trinity of aboriginal Mesoamerican food crops), but also chilis, chayotes, and fruit trees such as peaches and apples. They keep and eat chickens and pigs and gather a variety of wild plants and animals for food. In markets they purchase fish and fruits from the lowlands, as well as beef, liquor, coffee, sugar, and wheat bread, especially for ritual occasions. The principal condiment is salt, considered important both for nourishment and for ritual protection.

The Maize Cycle. The annual agricultural cycle for the production of maize is well adjusted to the winter dry season, summer rainy season climatic pattern of southern Mexico. The fields are prepared for planting in the late winter and spring (when the brush and/or stubble can be burned); the main planting occurs either just before or during the onset of the summer rains in May; the maize grows and matures during the rainy season, and is harvested and transported home in the fall or early winter after the dry season sets in again. Once the maize is safely stored away in granaries, it is available for processing into the various types of maize foods consumed by the Zinacantecos.

Zinacantecos are currently cultivating maize on three types of land which are differently controlled and differently situated geographically (Cancian 1965a): small plots owned individually by Zinacanteco men and located in or near their house compounds in the highlands; plots of ejido land, ordinarily 4 hectares, some located in the valley of Zinacantan near the ceremonial center and at high elevations at Yaleb Taiv and P'ih, but more often located at lower elevations in temperate country; and larger plots rented from Ladino landowners in the lowlands along both banks of the Grijalva River.

The farming operations in or near the house compounds are relatively small-scale; many are almost like garden plots, with a few rows of maize planted around the house or on a small parcel of land nearby (see Figure 2). These small plots of land usually are inherited from fathers, and,

2. Farming operations near house compounds in the highlands

although they are now controlled by individual men, the ownership rights are limited by two kinds of considerations. They can be purchased or sold among Zinacantecos (usually by the square meter in the present scarce land situation), but by custom they can never be sold to a non-Zinacanteco—whether Indian or Ladino. Furthermore, there is a belief that these lands really "belong" to one's patrilineal ancestor and that the present owner is merely a "caretaker" or "user" who will ordinarily pass these rights along to his patrilineal descendants. Since the plots are small and the yield is not great (compared to farming in the lowlands), an interesting system of fertilizing, as well as careful cultivation, is employed to increase production. The portable sheep corral is moved at intervals of approximately two weeks from place to place within the house compound so that the manure adds substantial fertility to the soil. Even with these measures, most Zinacanteco families could never subsist on the very limited amount of maize produced on these small plots. The yield is at best supplemental to farming operations on the ejidos or in the lowlands.

Considerably more maize is currently cultivated on the 12,070 hectares of ejido land which the Zinacantecos acquired in the early 1940's (Edel 1962). With the exception of a small 78-hectare parcel in the valley of Zinacantan and a larger 813-hectare block (providing the land base for the hamlet of Yaleb Taiv) at high elevation between Na Chih and Naben-chauk, these lands are located on benches or in valleys below 1500 meters and hence have a longer growing season. Although much of the land taken from Ladino owners is of poor quality, the ejido appropriation doubled the area controlled by Zinacantan and provided an average of 4 hectares of land for some 866 ejido members. These parcels are assigned by the Comisariado Ejidal. The ejido member who receives rights to land may use the plot during his lifetime; later, one of his sons may inherit these rights. A member sometimes illegally rents out parts of his ejido parcel that he does not care to farm. Rental charges to other Zinacantecos are usually one *fanega* (see Table 2) of corn per hectare per year. But the parcel may never be divided or sold, and if it goes unused, it may be reassigned to another individual by the Comisariado. Although some of the parcels are contiguous, a man's ejido holdings may be scattered between two different areas. Farming operations on the parcels are similar in technique to lowland farming, except that the elevation is higher and the yield somewhat less.

Table 2. Maize measures by volume

Unit of measurement	Volume contained
caldera	1 metric liter
tasa	1.67 metric liters
cuartilla	5 *calderas*
almud	3 *cuartillas*
litro	4 *cuartillas* (or *doble decalitro*)
fanega	12 *almuds* (or *fanega chica*)[a]
fanega-litro	12 *litros*

[a] This *fanega chica* weighs approximately 130 kilos, calculating with average maize from Chiapas.

Even more Zinacanteco maize is cultivated on rented lands in the low-lands along both sides of the Grijalva River (see Stauder 1966). On a clear day a Zinacanteco can stand on the rim of the escarpment and see all the way to his lowland fields near the shimmering river. But the land lies 1500–1800 meters below him and at least a hard six-hours' walk away for a Zinacanteco traveling with mules or horses to carry his heavier burdens. Zinacantecos claim that they once owned all this land located between ʔITSʼINAL MUKʼTA VITS (Junior Large Mountain), called Cerro Chenekultik by the Ladinos, and the present town of Chiapa de Corzo, but that the Ladinos came to grow cattle, maize, and sugar cane and took over the land. Whether or not the Zinacantecos did, in fact, control all this land is not yet clear from our historical researches, but Ladinos do own the lands now and Zinacantecos must therefore make arrangements to rent in order to farm maize in the lowlands.

Over the years a rental system has evolved in Zinacantan that is now universally followed in acquiring rights to farm in the lowlands. In some cases an individual Zinacanteco may enter into rental arrangements, but more commonly a group of patrilineally related Zinacanteco men and sometimes even a group of unrelated men band together under a *respon-sable,* one of their kinsmen who knows enough Spanish to deal with the Ladino landowners. He approaches the landowner, discusses rental terms for the rest of the group, and makes an agreement with the Ladino. When the time comes for the landowner to collect his rent, the responsable is responsible for seeing that it is paid; the landowner usually does not collect from each renter individually, but from the group as a whole. The respon-sable apportions each share, and acts as "the middleman and captain for the group" (Stauder 1961: 31).

The renting arrangement is ordinarily two fanegas (see Table 2 and Figure 3) of maize due to the landowner at harvest for every almud of seed maize planted. But this is only for every almud theoretically planted; in actual practice the rent is calculated on the area of the land. By the area the landlord can tell how many almudes should be planted. Since it would be extremely difficult for him to check the actual number of grains seeded, this is a handy way of arriving at the rent. The system of fixed rent places all the risk on the Zinacantecos. If the harvest is bad, legally they still must pay the same amount as if it had been a good harvest. If it is a bad year, the Zinacantecos can ask the landowner to reduce his rent, to take only one fanega per almud planted; but this reduction is voluntary on the part of the landlord (Stauder 1961: 24–25).

3. Measures of maize, left to right: *tasa, cuartilla, caldera*

Once rental arrangements have been made, the fields of a renting group in the lowlands are usually laid out in such a way as to give each man an equal part, both in area and in quality of land. This is important so that all members of the renting-group can go to and return from the lowlands together for each farming operation. Stauder describes the twelve men in one renting-group dividing their newly rented land near Chiapilla into twelve nearly equal parts:

> The rows of corn would run uphill, up a steep "cerro" that rises on their land. And it would be good, for laboring purposes, to let each man work a row from the beginning—the bottom of the hill. Dividing the land into squares would be confusing. Also some of the men would be likely to get better or worse land than others. But if the land were divided into long strips, no other markers would be needed except eleven stones. Also, long strips would give each man an equal sampling of the different levels of terrain. . . . They decided that each man should have a strip of land 20 *brazadas* in width. A *brazada* is the length between the finger-tips of a man's arms outstretched perpendicular to his body. They found a stick this size, and measured off each person's piece. The length of the strips, they decided, should be about 200 *brazadas*. This, they calculated, would give each man land enough to plant about one and one-half *almudes* of corn. The three strips at one end of the field, however, had their length impeded by the hill, which curved in too steeply for them. To compensate for the shortness of these strips three men were given pieces of 30 *brazadas'* width. The Chiku?s figured then that their shares were equal, and they could go and return together to Hot Country. (1961: 33–34)

Family working-groups within the renting-groups work their parcels together, and their strips of land are always contiguous. These field plans are sketched in Figure 4, reproduced from Stauder's report (1961: 33a).

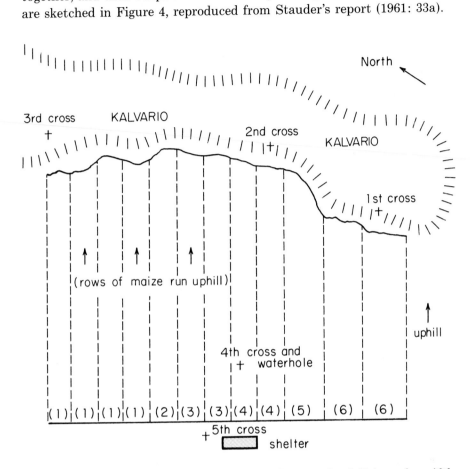

(1) Land of Mikel and his three sons. Each has a strip of 20 brazadas width, but the four work the whole 80-brazada piece together.

(2) Land of Telesh, 20 brazadas wide, that he works alone.

(3) Land that Petul works with his son Manvel. Their two strips of 20 brazadas are combined to make a 40-brazada-wide strip.

(4) Land that Pil and his son Manvel work. Each has a strip of 20 brazadas, but together they work the whole 40-brazada strip.

(5) Land that Marian works alone, a 30-brazada-wide strip to compensate for its shorter length.

(6) Land that brothers Shun and Petul work together. Each has strip of 30 brazadas, to compensate for shorter length; combined, they have 60 brazadas.

4. CHIKUʔETIK division of rented land

Although the immediate boundaries of the Zinacantecos' rented parcels are usually marked and clearly recognized in the field plans, fencing of some kind must be provided to keep Ladino livestock out of the fields. This problem is handled in various ways: sometimes the Ladino landlord has already constructed fences which keep his animals under control; in other cases, the landlord furnishes barbed wire and the Zinacanteco renters cut the fence posts (while they are clearing the land) and erect the fence around the parcel to be worked by the renting-group.

The small highland plots in or near house compounds are always fenced, sometimes with barbed wire, but more commonly by pole and brush fences, described in Chapter 4. These fences are necessary, even though sheep are generally herded all day by the women, and horses and mules are usually tethered until the maize is harvested, for there is always the chance that livestock will get into the fields and consume part of the growing maize.

The Zinacantecos always construct a shelter near their fields in the lowlands. During the dry season, when the men are cutting down the timber on a new field, they sometimes camp out in the open. But by the time the rainy season begins, they need a shelter for cooking and sleeping. The most common type has a pitched roof of cane leaves or palm frond on posts, and no walls.

The technology used in Zinacanteco farming operations is still fundamentally aboriginal Mesoamerican Indian in character. While Zinacantecos utilize a limited number of steel tools (such as axes, machetes, billhooks, and hoes) produced in modern factories or by blacksmiths in San Cristóbal and purchased from Ladino merchants, these are essentially more efficient replacements for aboriginal tools (Figure 5a–d). Farming techniques in both

5. Farming tools

a. hoe used for weeding fields

b. axe, billhook, machete

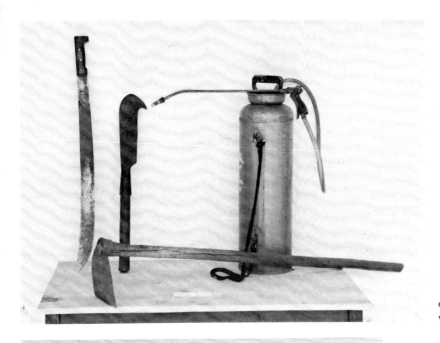

c. machete, billhook,
weed-killer, hoe in front

d. pickaxe, planting stick

highlands and lowlands follow the patterns of swidden agriculture developed and perfected centuries ago. There is as yet little use of the medieval European plow drawn by horses, mules, or oxen found in many other areas of Mesoamerica, including some of the nearby Indian villages in highland Chiapas. Nor is there any use of irrigation, except by the INI experimental field station. Rather, the pattern is one of cutting down the trees and brush, burning them when dry, and then planting with a pointed digging stick. Fields are planted for varying periods of time, depending upon elevation and quality of the soil, and then allowed to grow into brush again.

The length of the cycle from the first cutting and burning through the fallow period to another cutting and burning differentiates small-scale highland farming from farming at lower altitudes, whether on ejido or rented land. In the small highland parcels fertilized with sheep manure the cycle is very long; certain parcels can apparently be farmed every year for a generation or more. Eventually they must be allowed to lie fallow and grow back into brush again, judging from the abandoned fields and houses found in various parts of the municipio. In the lowlands, on the other hand, where fertilization is not practiced, the cycle is much shorter; some parcels can be farmed for only three years before the fields must be moved to allow the old parcels to lie fallow for several years and recharge their rapidly declining fertility, and to stop their susceptibility for heavy and rapid weed growth.

This difference in cycle calls for different types of operations in the preparation of the fields. In small highland plots the maize stubble is cut, raked into piles, and burned. The topsoil is then turned over with a hoe (ʔASALUNA) which works the sheep manure into the soil and prepares the ground for planting. This preparation is done in February and March.

In the lowlands the fields are prepared either by burning the stubble, in the case of an old field, or by cutting, drying, and burning the trees and brush of new fields. The cutting takes place between December and March. Large trees must be cut in December, to give them a chance to dry before they are burned in April, but the small growth can wait until March. An axe (ʔEK'EL) is used for felling large trees; a machete (MACHITA) and billhook (LUK) for cutting the branches and smaller growth.

The Zinacantecos often hire Chamula workers (paid in maize or pesos at an average rate, in 1962, of 5 pesos a day plus meals) to help them with the hard work of cutting as well as for weeding and harvesting later in the year Land with large trees is the hardest of all, but here weed growth is sparser, so that only one weeding is necessary (as opposed to two for fields with smaller growth).

Burning takes place in April, after the brush is well dried and before the first rains arrive, and is an easy operation. It ordinarily requires only one match and one day for a parcel of land. If the forest is thick, a firebreak must be cleared of brush at the boundaries to stop the fire from burning into adjacent properties. Even this is not necessary when only small growth has been cut and dried. Throughout April and sometimes into early May smoke from the burning on thousands of small Indian fields fills the Chiapas atmosphere. The smoke persists until the rains arrive in May and signal the time for planting.

In the highlands maize is planted in March on the small parcels in or near the house compounds. In the lowlands, where the temperatures are higher, it is not planted until the onset of the rainy season in May, following the K'IN KRUS ceremonies in the hamlets (see Chapter 20). Compared to the operations which prepare the fields, planting is considered a delicate task and is accompanied by extensive ritual activity. The largest and best seed for planting is carefully selected at harvest time and stored separately in a burlap bag in the house or hung from the rafters. After planting, the cobs from the seed maize are hung up on trees, for they are believed to be exhausted from having had to carry the burden of the maize.

Planting in the larger fields in the lowlands is preceded by a ceremony, called SLIMUSHNAIL CHOBTIK ("alms for the milpas"), which involves the offering of candles, incense, liquor, and special prayers by a shaman, as well as a ritual meal. These offerings are for YAHVAL BALAMIL, "The Lord of the Earth" and the ruler and sender of the clouds, wind, and rain. The ceremonial circuit typically includes the corners and center of the field, and the prayers emphasize rainmaking. The chicken feet (from the fowl for the ritual meal) are dipped into the seed maize carried by each of the workers in order to make the crop grow well.

The planting (ʔOVOL) is done by making a hole in the soil with a planting stick (BARETA). The stick is cut from hawthorne (CH'ISH) or from ʔISBON (a kind of dogwood) and has a metal tip which the Zinacantecos purchase from blacksmiths in San Cristóbal. Formerly, the seed was carried in containers made of armadillo shells (as it still is in neighboring municipios like Huistán and Chenalhó), but it is now more commonly carried in a net bag (K'OSH NUTIʔ) or a leather bag (MORAL).

The planter carries the seed in the bag draped from his left shoulder and works with the planting stick in his right hand. He makes a hole about 8 centimeters deep with the stick, then reaches into the bag for the proper number of seeds and drops them into the hole with his left hand. In the highlands, the planter is often assisted by his wife who follows him, drops in the bean seed, and then covers up the hole with her foot (see Weathers 1946: 316). In the lowlands, the planting is done entirely by the men who cover up the holes themselves using either their feet or the digging stick. In the highland parcels the holes are four sandal lengths apart and each hole receives four or five grains of maize and two or three bean seeds. In the lowlands, each hole receives a standard six grains.

In the larger lowland fields it takes one man about three days to seed an almud of maize. The planting operations thus last from three to five days. The maize shoots begin to show in eight days, and are finished showing in fifteen days. At this point, about June 1, reseeding is done. If only one or two shoots have emerged, two to four more grains are put in; if three or four show, the farmer does not bother to reseed the hole. Often it is necessary to reseed a second time about mid-June if the holes are not producing at least three growing maize shoots. Since rent is charged by area planted, it pays to plant as much as the land will bear.

The *milpas* (maize fields) must be kept weeded, for it is believed that if weeds are allowed to grow the "souls" of the maize plants will move to a "clean" *milpa* to grow. The number of times a field must be weeded during the growing season varies. A new field needs to be weeded only once if it has been made in heavy brush where large trees were felled and dense weeds have not yet grown up. Other fields must be weeded at least twice, usually once in June and once in July. The first weeding, preceded by another milpa ceremony, begins about the 15th to 20th of June in the lowlands and is the longest and most difficult of all the farming operations. It takes a man about twelve to fifteen days of hard labor to clean a plot of maize seeded with one almud—approximately a hectare. This means that if a Zinacanteco has more than two almudes planted, he requires the help of either sons, younger brothers, paid Chamula workers, or occasionally paid Zinacanteco workers to finish this weeding in time. The second weeding begins about mid-July; ordinarily it takes less time since fewer weeds appear after the first weeding.

The weeding is performed with a hoe (Figure 5a) which each man carries in his net bag when traveling to the lowlands for the weeding operation. The metal part of the hoe is purchased in San Cristóbal, for about 15 pesos. Smaller blades work better on rocky ground, and Zinacantecos can choose from three sizes, from 18 to 20 centimeters in breadth. Zinacantecos then cut a handle about 1½ meters long from a lowland tree called TUSHNUK' TE?. They split one end of this stick with a billhook, insert the split end into the holder of the hoe, and fasten it by driving an oak wedge into the split. When it comes time to leave the handle, the head of the hoe is knocked

6. Weeding the maize fields in the lowlands

against a rock, the wedge flies out, and the metal part of the hoe can easily be transported home for work and safekeeping there (Stauder 1961: 17–18).

Zinacantecos always weed barefooted, proceeding from left to right across the field, and uphill, even when it is a very slight slope, since this means less bending of the back. The working-group, whether composed of a father and his sons, a group of brothers, or the owner or renter of the field plus his paid Chamula workers, always hoes together. The leader positions himself on the left and sets the pace for the others (Figure 6). Stauder reports:

> They all work smoothly, bending forward from the hips, pulling and not chopping, their strokes two feet long, about two inches deep, until a rock or stump impedes. They all hoe with their right feet forward on the earth; their right hands forward on the hoes, they are deft and sure, in upturning the green, prolific weeds within a fraction of an inch of the tiny corn shoots, never uprooting one, or cutting through a bean plant or squash vine. They pull the weeds neatly into the middle of the rows, leaving the ground around the corn and beans bare and clean. Each man hoes over all the earth between the two rows of corn he works between, himself; doing it exactly, never reaching into his neighbor's row nor missing any of his own. (1961: 15–16)

7. Zinacanteco farmer

Work begins shortly after dawn; there is a stop for pozol at about nine o'clock, and a meal at high noon. The farmers continue working until four P.M., "slowly hoeing down the mountains of Middle America" (Stauder 1961: 18). Then they stop to rest (Figures 7, 8) look over the horses, and gather wild plants to supplement the evening meal of toasted tortillas and beans.

The second weeding, begun in July, is ideally finished by August 10, the time of the important fiesta of the patron saint, San Lorenzo. Often it is not, however, and many Zinacantecos must return to the lowlands to continue their work after the fiesta. Usually also by the time of San Lorenzo, fresh ears of maize can be picked and taken home for food. Often even earlier in the summer very small ears of maize (YI) are ready to be eaten.

There is predictably a very rich vocabulary in Tzotzil referring to the various stages of maize farming and maize growth. For example:

8. Farmer in maize field

ʔOVOL   maize planting
LAVUSHTIK   nails (referring to first appearance of maize shoots)
SHKUNLAHET   leaves touching the ground
ʔAVEN   replanting
TSOʔ KOKTIK ʔECH'EL   above the calves
BA ʔAK'IN   first weeding
CHAʔ-LOM ʔAK'IN   second weeding
S-HOLOVAL KAKANTIK   knee-high
S-HOLOVAL HCHUKBENALTIK ʔECH'EL   above the waist
S-HOLOVAL HNEKEBTIK ʔECH'EL   above the shoulders
SH-HASHET TA HOLTIK   rustling about the head
SHIMUKETOTIK   buried (beneath the maize)
HPAHTSAHEL   maize that has reached full height
BALALIK   in flower
CHLILIH HUHUNTIK   (flowers of maize tassel) have burst open
CHLILIH SHA   (the flowers) have burst open
CHYIAN HUHUNTIK   a few young ears of maize
HYIANEL   *jilotes,* young ears of maize
MUK'TIK MEʔ YI(TIK)   large young ears of maize
ʔAHAN   ear of maize
ʔOCH K'ON   ripening
CHK'ANUT SHA   yellowing now
K'AN-POCHANIK   yellow husks (i.e., husks bursting)
PAK CHOBTIK   doubling the maize stalks
K'AHOH   harvesting the maize
MAH ʔISHIM   flailing the maize

Similarly, different types of ears are given special names. Ears with a middle section that lacks grains are called MAYOLETIK. Two ears joined together within one husk is called MEʔ (mother); one that has a large ear with a number of little ears at its base is called TOT (father); and one that has the top wrapped with much silk is called CH'O (mouse).

In the Autumn, when the maize is ripe, Zinacanteco farmers return again to the lowlands to "double" the stalks. (If beans are to be planted at this time, there is another weeding, but only for the beans, since it is too late to help the maize much.) The stalks are broken a little above the middle. The top half is bent down almost to the ground, and the full ears are left to harden on the stalk. This process serves three purposes: it cuts off the food supply so that the maize begins to dry; it prevents the rain from rotting the mature ears of maize; and, finally, beans planted at this time are

9. Use of the
maize husker

given more sun, so they will grow between the rows of maize. The operation takes a man two to three days per almud.

In the highlands maize is harvested in October, but in the lowlands harvesting begins in November and continues into December and January. The Zinacantecos harvest the maize using a husker (HATOBAL) (Figure 9) made of deer bone and carried on a cord tied to their belts. Figure 10 shows the size of the husker.

← 15. 25 cm →

10. Maize husker

11. Shelling maize by pounding with a stick

The sharp end of this instrument is inserted through the end of the husks and pulled upward, thus starting the separation. The farmer peels the husks down the sides, using both hands at once. The ear is then removed with a sharp twist, leaving the husks on the stalks. The ears are placed in bags and carried to the threshing ground where the flailing is done by one of two methods: either the ears are placed in a net bag with holes of a size that allow the maize kernels but not the cobs to come out as the bag is pounded with a pole (Figure 11), or a platform is constructed and a net of cowhide stretched underneath, parallel to the ground, so that the kernels fall to the ground while the cobs stay in the net when the ears are pounded with a pole on the platform (Figure 12).

The shelled maize is heaped in piles, and small wooden crosses are stuck in the tops of the piles. Then the landlord collects his rent. He will have

12. Shelling maize with the use of a cowhide net; note wooden cross and special ears protecting the pile in foreground from evil spirits

measured the land by then, with a long rope, counting the brazadas, and from this, he can calculate the almudes that should have been planted and the fanegas due him. Since the owner does not care about each man's share, the responsable has to see that each man pays his proportion of the rent to the central heap of maize which the landlord then either hauls away or asks to have delivered to him.

Now the Zinacantecos know how good the year has been. They have tried their utmost by reseeding to be certain that each clump of maize had at least three or four stalks, and they have performed the necessary weeding operations and the necessary ceremonies to the Earth Lord to keep the proper amount of rain falling. If an average of five ears grew in each hill of stalks and the ears grew to ample size, the year was a good one and they should have more than the average of eight fanegas of maize for every almud planted on approximately one hectare of land. After the landlord takes away his two fanegas, there are still six fanegas per hectare left for the Zinacanteco farmer. An average family consumes about five fanegas of maize each year. Thus, average to good years leave supluses to be sold in the market.

For each hectare, a Zinacanteco puts out an average of 360 pesos for seed, Chamula labor, food for himself and laborers, and transportation. If his own time is calculated at 5 pesos a day, or 160 pesos for thirty-two days of working time, his maximum expenses would have been 520 pesos per hectare planted. But if he can sell the surplus at 620 pesos or better, his net earnings will be 100 pesos per hectare farmed in the lowlands.

One major operation remains to be performed, for the piles of shelled maize are at least six hours walking distance from home and 1500 – 1800 meters below the highland villages. Some maize is still carried, especially short distances, on Zinacanteco backs. (In pre-Columbian times, before the horse and mule, transporting maize must have been a major task.) For carrying maize, the Zinacantecos sometimes use burlap bags (KOSHTAL or the larger LONA) supported by a tumpline (PEK') across the forehead (Figure 13), but more commonly it is carried either by horses or mules which struggle up the escarpment with loads of 6 to 10 almudes (Figure 14). Zinacantecos never use burros, for burros do not keep the fast, steady pace of a group of Zinacantecos traveling to and from the lowlands. They say burros are for Ladinos! But horses and mules can keep up, and before the modern roads reached into Zinacantan and into the towns along the Grijalva River, the bulk of the maize was transported home on these pack animals. Many families own one or more horses or mules, and those who do not often rent them from other families. They are owned and cared for

13. Men carrying maize with a tumpline

exclusively by men and are ordinarily kept tethered with long ropes, either to trees or to pegs on grassy slopes. They require constant care, for their grazing locations must be changed and they must be led to water at least once each day. Since the pasture is better in the lowlands than in the highlands, many men keep their animals there permanently and maintain a system of rotating duty in which each man in an extended family takes a turn of three or more days living at the lowland fields and caring for the horses or mules. The system functions throughout the year, so there is always someone on hand to keep watch on the fields.

In recent years an increasing amount of the maize has been transported by Ladino trucks which haul it from the nearest point on the road along the Grijalva River to the road junction near Chiapa de Corzo and then up the Pan American Highway to the hamlets in Zinacantan. Here it is dumped off at the end of the road and must be carried by animal or by tumpline on human backs to each Zinacanteco's house. The truckers charge about 10 to 15 pesos a fanega for hauling the maize from towns such as Chiapilla to hamlets such as Paste'; the cost is correspondingly less to less distant and more conveniently located hamlets.

Once the maize is home, some further division of the harvest may be necessary. Each family unit which shares a single maize supply takes its share to its granary and places it in storage. The granary may be a separate structure, either an abandoned house or a special building erected for the purpose, or, in the case of poorer families with only one house, the maize may be stored in a bin in the corner. In any case, it is always "protected" ritually by erecting a small wooden cross (KRUS ʔISHIM) on the shelled maize in the bin. This cross is decorated with flowers and is surrounded with several unhusked ME? and TOT ears of maize. These symbolic "fathers" and "mothers" are believed to keep an evil spirit (PUKUH) from entering the bin and eating the maize. The family eats some of the maize, and the men sell the surplus in the market (see Chapter 6).

Making Tortillas. The most important maize food consumed by the Zinacantecos is the tortilla (VAH). An adult male ordinarily eats about six to ten tortillas at each of his three daily meals when he is at home. So while the man's part in the maize cyle is largely finished (except for eating!), the woman's work has just begun.

There are three basic processes in the production of tortillas: boiling the maize kernels in lime water to make *nixtamal* (PANIN); grinding the nixtamal on *metates* (CHO?) to make dough (PICH'BIL ʔISHIM); and patting out and cooking the tortillas on a *comal* or griddle (SEMET).

The women bring the maize from the granary in baskets. They first pour it into another container, letting the wind remove the chaff. Then they fill cooking pots (of the type made by the Chamulas) half full of maize. Water is poured into another pot that has lime (TAN) in it and stirred until the lime dissolves. (This lime is made by Zinacanteco men in hamlets of Paste? and ʔElan Vo? by heating limestone in a hot fire; the powdered lime is then slaked by mixing it with water, made into lumps, and dried in the sun. The lime is stored in the house underground to preserve its strength, and pieces are broken off as needed. In other hamlets, lumps of lime are purchased from Chamulas who process it for sale.) The lime water is added to the pots with maize, placed on the fire to boil until the kernels become soft, then put in a corner to cool.

Before this soft maize (*nixtamal*) is ground, it is lifted out by handfuls, placed in other pots, and washed in clean water. (Figure 21). The kernels then are again lifted out by handfuls and placed either directly on the metate to be ground, or sometimes kept temporarily in other pots.

The nixtamal for tortillas is ordinarily ground two or three times (Figure 15). The metates in use in Zinacantan are three-legged types, made of basalt by the Chamulas and sold in the market in Chamula or in San Cristóbal. They are approximately 40 cm. long, 28 cm. wide, and 11.5 cm. high at

14. Men and animals loaded with maize

the highest point (nearest the grinder); the *manos* (K'OB CHO?) are also of basalt and approximately 38 cm. long. Near the household cooking fire, the *metates* are placed on a board (?EK'EN) which raises them about 30 cm. off the ground and makes it easier for women to grind in a kneeling position. Typically there is a metate on each end of the board so that women can grind facing each other and visit as they work. While the making and washing of nixtamal requires little time and effort, the grinding process is long and arduous. Women awake in the morning between 5 and 6 A.M. to start making tortillas, and it is often 8 A.M. before they have produced enough for the day's meals. It is easy to understand why hand maize-grinders have become so popular in many hamlets and why in larger settlements like Zinacantan Center there is now much use of a gasoline-powered grinder where the women take the nixtamal for the first grinding.

15. Grinding maize for tortillas

These machines do the first grinding well, but the metates are normally used later to produce the desired texture.

As soon as a woman has enough nixtamal ground into dough, she begins to pat out tortillas and to cook them. (Figure 16). The patting is done in three ways: traditionally, a small piece of the dough is patted back and forth between the two hands and revolved in such a way as to make a perfect round flat cake (this produces the characteristic hand-patting sound so familiar in the early morning all over the highlands of Middle America); alternatively, the dough is patted out on a piece of plastic placed on a small round stool—this being a universal technique in Yucatán where the patting is done on banana leaves; and a few families have recently purchased wooden tortilla presses, made by Ladinos in San Cristóbal and sold in the market for about 15 pesos.

16. Patting out tortillas

The cooking of tortillas is done on a slightly concave, round clay or metal comal, about two feet in diameter, that is propped up over the fire on three stones (Figure 17). One or two of the "stones" may be old pots turned upside down, but they still symbolize the famous "three hearthstones" of a Maya home. Before being placed on the fire, the comal is rubbed by hand with small wet lime lumps or with a brush dipped in lime water, which produces a thin film of dried white lime on the comal once it is heated. The tortillas are cooked for about thirty seconds on each side and placed in a dry gourd container used to keep them warm until served or to store the surplus for meals later in the day. Zinacanteco tortillas are approximately 18 cm. in diameter and 0.15–0.3 cms. thick.

Once the cooking begins, a remarkably efficient set of operations is in process, for a woman may simultaneously be grinding additional maize, stopping to pat out tortillas when more are needed, and cooking tortillas on the comal. All of the materials and instruments are within reach of her kneeling position at the metate, and she can shift easily from one activity to another, while her husband and sons either wander around the compound or sit by the fire, warming themselves, and waiting hungrily until she has produced enough to feed them their morning meal.

A longer process is used for the large toasted tortillas (K'OSHOSH), which last for several days and can be carried in large baskets to the lowlands by the men to eat while they are away farming. Toasted tortillas are larger, about 20 cm. in diameter and 0.3 cm. thick. They are made from maize which has been boiled twice, first with lime, then rinsed and boiled without lime. After being cooked on the comal, these toasted tortillas must be propped up around the fire and allowed to dry out for at least ten minutes. Immense quantities must be made during the farming season to keep the men supplied with food while they are away.

Two other types of maize foods made from the ground dough are important. *Pozol* (ʔUCH'IMOʔ) is a ball of dough taken by the men to the lowlands. A small piece is broken off and added to water in a bowl or open gourd, and the mixture is drunk (see Figure 18). The dough is prepared in the same manner as for toasted tortillas. It sours after a day or two, but while it lasts it provides nourishment on the trail and in the fields.

Atole (ʔUL) is highly prized by the Zinacantecos and always served on festive occasions. It is made by soaking the maize in water for four or five days before grinding, then boiling the maize dough in water and adding *panela,* a type of brown sugar made by the Ladinos in the lowlands and sold in cylindrical cakes in San Cristóbal (see Benderly 1961). It is a heavy, sweet gruel, with a number of differently seasoned varieties, tasty and highly nourishing.

17. Cooking tortillas on a comal

Types Grown. Zinacantecos grow several varieties of maize including hybrids, but the most important from their point of view are classified into four categories based on color—yellow (K'ON), red (TSAH), white (SAK), and black (ʾIK')—and two based on shape—round grains (BOLA) and flat grains (PACHA). Before they started growing real maize (ʾISHIM), they had, according to their tales, an early type of maize (SHIMOʾ), which grew only in the lowlands, produced only one or two ears, and required four weedings. The gods then told the Zinacantecos to abandon SHIMOʾ and to grow ʾISHIM, which produces more ears and only requires one or two weedings.

Ritual Uses. Maize is important not only in the diet but also in the ritual life of the Zinacantecos. Perhaps the most important ritual occurs in the type of divination known as SAT ʾISHIM (literally, "grains of maize") in which thirteen grains of each of the four basic colors of maize are tossed into a bowl of salt water to determine how many parts of the "inner soul" are missing from a sick person (see Chapter 20). Regardless of what types of maize a Zinacanteco family may be growing for food, it always keeps on hand at least one ear of each of these four colors. Another ritual use of maize accompanies childbirth; right after parturition, two cobs are placed against the woman's belly and her stomach is tightly bound in cloths for a week or more until she feels well.

Maize kernels serve as counters in various ritual procedures. For example, when the principales are collecting money for hamlet ceremonies, or a regidor is collecting money for an important fiesta in Zinacantan Center, kernels of maize are moved from one bag to another to indicate how many heads of household have paid. Similarly, when the money for a given ceremony has been collected and the men calculate the total available for ceremonial paraphernalia, they move kernels of maize from one pile to another to keep track. Kernels are also used by the mayordomos, mayordomos reyes, and mesones in counting the numbers of coins on the necklaces for the saints (see Chapter 21).

It is tempting to view these counting procedures as ritual survivals of Ancient Mayan practices for calculating amounts of tribute paid for the support of priests, rulers, and their ceremonial centers. It is possible that the contributions were originally paid in maize, and that, although they are now paid in Mexican pesos, kernels are still used in the counting. On the other hand, Zinacantecos without formal training in the Mexican schools are not able to add. For unacculturated Zinacantecos the only way to arrive at the total of, for example, 8 plus 5 Mexican pesos is to count out a pile of 8 kernels and then count up 5 more to arrive at 13!

18. Mixing *pozol* for noonday meal; note figure-eight shape of gourd for carrying water

Beans

Next to maize, the most important domesticated food plant grown by the Zinacantecos is beans, a crucial source of protein in a diet that is very short on meat.

In the highlands, several varieties of beans, planted in the same holes with the maize, grow at the base of the maize stalks. These include two varieties of *Vigna sinensis,* called MUK'TA ʔIK'AL CHENEK' and ʔIKAL KAN-TELA CHENEK', and a variety of *Phaseolus lunatus* L., called either PUTASH CHENEK' or SHVET' CHENEK', by the Zinacantecos. More important are the crops of *Phaseolus lunatus* L., called SHLUMIL CHENEK', that are planted in two rows between the rows of maize in September when the stalks are bent over in the lowland fields.

The SHLUMIL CHENEK' are planted with the digging stick, and six seeds are dropped into each hole. The holes are about 45 cm. apart, two almudes can be seeded per hectare. The crop is harvested in the late autumn and, in good years, yields a fanega per almud planted. The bean pods are pulled off the plants by hand and threshed either by hand or by pounding with a stick.

The beans are transported to the highland villages, sometimes by truck but more commonly by pack horse or mule. Surpluses are sold in the market (see Chapter 6); the rest are kept stored in large jars or in large sacks in the house. Although they are mainly eaten boiled, beans are also used for special dishes such as the bean tamale (CHENEK'UL VAH) that must be served at weddings (see Chapter 9) and at change of office ceremonies for the mayordomos. These are made by grinding both maize and boiled beans finely. The maize dough is placed on a table and spread out until it forms a thin layer, and the bean paste is spread evenly on top. Salt is sprinkled over the whole mass, which is rolled up so that it looks something like a large jellyroll. It is cut into pieces, four fingers to a handspan wide, and each piece is wrapped in a leaf. The tamales are then piled crisscross in a huge pot and one of the women spits rum liquor on three sides of the pot "to cure anything that might have happened to it since it was put away." The tamales are boiled on the fire while the two special cooks dance with orange branches and geraniums in their hands "so that the tamales will cook properly" (Fishburne 1962: 60–61).

Squash

The third most important cultivated food plant is squash. Sometimes squash is planted in the same holes with the maize, but more are planted at the edges of the maize fields. One important species, called MAIL by the Zinacantecos, has a hard rind variety as well as a smoother, softer one. Both are eaten boiled.

Two closely related plants, both varieties of *Lagenaria siceraria* (Mol.) Standl., are rarely eaten, but the gourds are of crucial importance for containers. The *tecomate* (TSU) has a figure-eight shape (see Figure 19). The larger ones are used to carry water while traveling or working in the fields; smaller ones serve as whistles in curing ceremonies to summon a lost "soul" (see Chapter 20) or for babies' rattles. A special variety, from a tree called TSIMAʔ, is used to make rattles for the dances of the Alféreces (see Chapter 21). The round *toles* (HAY) are used for plates and bowls for the storage and serving of food. Tortillas can be kept warm in them, and they can be used for serving boiled beans, atole or pozol.

19. Figure-eight-shaped gourd for carrying water

Other Cultivated Food Crops

Other native Middle American plants cultivated by the Zinacantecos include chilies and chayotes. The chilies are planted in both highlands and lowlands. The most important of the many varieties are BAK ʔICH (which is green, but turns red), SAKIL ʔICH (which is white and short), and PUH ʔUT ʔICH (which is white and long). Besides salt, chilies are the most important condiment for dishes of beans, squash, and meat.

Chayotes (CH'UM TEʔ) are grown in mats with their long vines climbing over woodwork lattices especially constructed for them in the highland house compounds. They are ripe in late October and are eaten boiled. Zinacantecos also cultivate and eat cabbages and potatoes in the highland hamlets. The hamlets at lower elevations also cultivate coffee, avocado, and banana trees.

Although the Zinacantecos have not taken up the growing of cereal crops such as wheat, as have some of their Indian neighbors (for example, in Huistán, Amatenango, and Aguacatenango), they have enthusiastically started apples, pears, quince, and especially peaches, and occasionally figs, plums, and passion fruit, and many house compounds now possess one or more fruit trees. Most of the fruit is eaten ripe, but some is sold in the market.

Hunting and Gathering

Hunting animals for food is currently unimportant for the Zinacanteco diet. An occasional rabbit is shot, and hunters from the hamlets close to the lowlands bring back deer from time to time. But the Chiapas highlands have been populated so densely for such a long period that almost all forms of edible mammals have long since been hunted off. However, rats, mice, and doves are caught in traps.

On the other hand, there is relatively full exploitation of edible wild plants, insects of various types, snails, and iguanas. While working in the lowlands, men chew on the stems of a purple flowery plant (VALAPOHOV) to quench thirst, and they season their beans with KULANTU (coriander). In the highlands various types of greens are collected by the women and cooked for meals, including NAPUSH, BOTIL NICHIM, and ʔUNEN MU. At least sixteen types of mushrooms have Tzotzil names and are collected for food, the most common being CHECHEV, YUY, and MONIʔ. One type (YISIM CHIH) closely resembles a poisonous variety of mushroom and extreme care must be exercised to collect the edible species; in 1964 an entire Chamula family died from eating the poisonous species. The mushrooms are eaten either roasted on the coals or boiled.

The most commonly eaten insect is the larvae (MUM) of a wasp found under the ground. The mud "case" is heated by the fire until the larvae ooze out. Two types of snails are collected—large, black land snails (TONTOB), which are not considered very good eating, and small snails (PUY) that live in the lowland rivers and are considered a delicacy. Another lowland delicacy is the iguana ('INATAB), whose meat is sometimes substituted for the chicken required in ceremonies for the lowland maize fields. Finally, like their Maya ancestors, Zinacantecos are fond of honey ('AHA-POM) from wild bees (CHANUL POM) which they collect mostly in December and January.

Domesticated Animals

If the ancestors of the Zinacantecos had domesticated animals or fowl in pre-Columbian times, they must have had only dogs and turkeys. Most Zinacanteco houses still have one or more dogs, and there are a few turkeys (Figure 20). But much more important now are the domesticated animals which came with the Spanish: chickens, pigs, cows, sheep, horses, and mules.

Almost all Zinacanteco households maintain a flock of about a dozen chickens (KASHLAN) that are owned and tended by the women. These are red, white, or black, but the favored color is black, since only black chickens can be used in curing ceremonies. Some families have coops for the chickens, others keep them inside the house, but most chickens roost in trees in the house compound. They lay their eggs in old pots kept partly filled with grass at the edge of the house, under the overhang of the roof. The women feed them, mainly on maize kernels, twice a day.

Chickens are killed by pulling the head loose from, but not off, the neck. The feathers are plucked after the chicken has been dipped in hot water. The entrails are removed with a knife, and the chicken is cut into pieces and boiled. Although ordinarily served in a broth with chile, the pieces of chicken are served cold with tortillas when the Zinacantecos are on pilgrimages to their mountaintop shrines. (These crucial functions of the chicken in the ceremonial life of Zinacantan lead me to suspect that the chicken has replaced the aboriginal turkey which was probably once used in a comparable manner.)

Pigs are a minor item in the economy of Zinacantan. In fact, most pork consumed is purchased in the market in San Cristóbal. The one or two pigs

20. Turkeys in Zinacanteco house patio in early morning

kept by some households are an economic investment. Zinacantecos may purchase a small pig from a Ladino, fatten the animal on maize, and then sell it in a Ladino market. Pigs are rarely butchered in Zinacantan.

Except for a few head recently acquired by Indians in the hamlet of Hoyihel, the Zinacantecos do not own cattle. They do, however, purchase bulls from Ladinos to provide beef for major fiestas in Zinacantan Center and for weddings.* The purchase is made either in the lowlands or in San Cristóbal. The butchering takes place most commonly at the location of the sale, and the beef is carried to Zinacantan Center (or to a hamlet in the case of a wedding) to be cooked and eaten.

Zinacanteco sheep are owned and tended entirely by the women, especially the younger girls. They are never butchered for mutton, but are kept purely for their wool which the women shear, card, spin, and weave into clothing. (For details see Chapter 5.)

* As elsewhere in Middle America, Zinacantecos classify foods in "hot" and "cold" categories that are conventionally established and have little to do with temperature. Cows are regarded as having "cold" meat, while bulls have "hot" meat; the Zinacantecos prefer the latter.

Horses and mules are owned by the men, but are almost never ridden, except for the ritual "horse races" during the fiestas of San Lorenzo and San Sebastián in Zinacantan Center. Rather, they are used mainly to transport heavy burdens. Unlike the Ladinos, Zinacantecos have no personal brands for their horses and everyone uses the "B" of the communal branding iron. This iron may be borrowed from the Senior Alcalde by presenting him with a bottle of liquor. Finally, almost every Zinacanteco household has cats or dogs, but since they are kept only as household pets they are described in Chapter 4.

The Zinacanteco Diet

There are marked variations in the Zinacanteco diet, based on the ritual or nonritual purpose of the meal, the family's relative wealth, and the season of the year.

An ordinary meal for a Zinacanteco man at home consists of tortillas and a bowl of beans seasoned with salt and chili. He eats the beans by scooping them up with a piece of tortilla. Depending upon the season of the year this monotonous diet may be varied by the addition of other cultivated plants, such as cabbage, squash, or chayote, or wild plants or mushrooms. If the Zinacanteco is working in the lowlands, the diet is ordinarily even more monotonous and modest. His fresh tortillas will last only a day and his pozol only a few days; thereafter he will have to eat toasted tortillas and beans, supplemented by greens, as long as he stays. Ritual meals provide a really important addition to the diet, for either chicken, pork, or fish (and, on some large ceremonial occasions, beef) seasoned with chili must be served along with rum, coffee, and rolls, and frequently atole as well.

Poor families eat many more ordinary meals, and when they do serve ritual meals, the main dish is much more likely to be pork or dried fish than chicken. On the other hand, rich families more frequently approach the level of ritual meals in their daily diet—more chicken and more eggs are served and larger and more stable supplies of beans are available.

Eggs may be eaten but are also sold, especially to Ladinos, to add to the family's cash income. When eaten, eggs are most frequently fried dry on a comal or in a frying pan. For ritual occasions, they are served hard-boiled, for example in the ritual meals eaten by cargoholders during the Fiesta of San Sebastián.

Chicken serves as the main dish in ritual meals that are invariant parts of ceremonies, and as sacrificial offerings to the ancestral gods (TOTILME?-

ILETIK) in curing ceremonies. These sacrificial offerings are called "substitutes" (K'ESHOLIL). For a female patient, the offerings must be black hens; for a male patient, black roosters. In a large curing ceremony two chickens are sacrificed: one is left at KALVARIO or another sacred mountain, and one is killed over the patient after he has been placed in bed in his house. The chicken left at the mountain is never eaten, but the chicken killed in the house is later eaten by the patient. Some shamans kill the chickens by extracting and cutting the jugular vein with a knife and then use the blood in the ceremony. (For further details see Chapter 20.) If a family does not own the necessary chickens, they may be purchased from a neighbor; the price of chickens in 1962 was 15 to 25 pesos, depending on size.

The seasons add to dietary variation. In the spring Zinacantecos consume enormous quantities of mangoes and melons, late summer brings the season of fresh green corn, the ripening of squashes, and a variety of fruits, like highland peaches and apples, and lowland pineapples and melons.

But even the basic daily diet of tortillas and beans, supplemented by cultivated or wild greens contains high food value. Robert S. Harris, who has spent many years researching this basic Middle American diet, finds it highly nutritious. He writes: "The data on the nutrient content of Mexican foods are interesting. The exceptional quantities of calcium, iron, caroten, thiamin, and protein found in Mexican foods suggest that it may be possible to nourish the Mexican people without the use of dairy and meat products. It is clearly evident that the foods of Mexico are, in general, more nutritious than the foods of the United States" (1946: 947). These findings are confirmed by Aguirre Beltrán (1956) who summarizes the dietary data and provides an excellent bibliography on the subject. It is also possible, according to surveys conducted by the Food and Agriculture Organization of the United Nations, that soaking the maize in lime increases the availability of niacin in the Mexican diet and therefore helps to explain the low incidence of pellagra in Middle America—as compared, for example, to many parts of Africa where the maize is not so treated (FAO Nutritional Studies No. 9, 1953). It is evident that the Zinacantecos are living well on a basic diet that has supported Maya culture for some 4500 years.

4 / Houses

The basic dwelling unit in Zinacantan is a rectangular, single-roomed house (NA) with a hearth for cooking food and heating the interior and a "house cross" just outside the door. Many terms used for the human body also apply to house parts—a wall is CH'UT (stomach), a foundation rock YOK (foot), a corner CHIKIN (ear), and so forth—reflecting the Zinacanteco belief that a properly constructed and dedicated house has a "soul" (CH'ULEL) much like a person's. Indeed, the house's soul is even more powerful than the person's, since the house consists of so many elements derived from the Earth Lord (woods, mud, thatch, and so on).

In this chapter I shall describe the types of houses, stages of construction, furnishings, and auxiliary structures such as granaries, sweathouses, and fences surrounding the house compound. For in the Zinacanteco view, the term NA encompasses not only the actual house, but the entire compound with these smaller buildings, a small maize field, some chayote vines, a few fruit trees, and a surrounding fence of some kind. The house dedication ceremonies serve to incorporate the unit into the sacred belief system as it acquires its "soul" and becomes a living part of Zinacanteco culture.

Types

Zinacantecos classify their house types by the four kinds of wall construction; the four kinds of roofing materials; and the three architectural forms of the roof. In more general terms, Zinacantecos recognize three historical house types. The oldest type they remember is a VAKASH NA (literally, "cow house"), which has a gable roof with a gradual pitch. In fact, its shape

This chapter utilizes especially the field data collected by James Warfield in the summer of 1963 (see Warfield 1963 and 1966). I have made minor stylistic changes in quotations from Warfield (1963), and have translated most of his Tzotzil terms into English.

resembles that of *toritos*, the firework-spouting, reed-mat frameworks carried by men in fiestas to impersonate bulls. The walls are generally of split logs or sometimes of flat boards, and the back wall of the house is often rounded. Not many of these houses exist today, but informants report that many people lived in them a generation or two ago. The most common type of house is the CHUKAL NA with a very steep hip roof of thatch and walls of wattle and daub (see Figure 21). The third type, which is becoming increasingly popular, approaches Ladino patterns in size and style of construction. This is the hip-roofed house with tile roof and adobe walls.

While Zinacantecos commonly characterize the changes in their housing types in terms of these three basic types, the actual situation is really more complex. The four types of walls are wattle and daub (PAK'BAL); dried mud brick or adobe (SHAMITAL); split logs or branches (HIT'BAL); and flat boards (TENEL TE?AL). There are four types of roofing materials. The several varieties of thatch (HOBEL) are tall grasses that grow in bunches; tile (TESHA) is bought from Ladinos in San Cristóbal or in Chiapa de Corzo; wood slat shingles of pine (*tejamanil* or K'ALB'IL TE?AL) are cut by Zinacantecos in the mountains, or more commonly purchased from Ladinos in San Cristóbal or from Chamulas; and LAMINA comes in two varieties, both purchased from Ladinos in San Cristóbal: laminated tarpaper (LAMINA KARTON) and a laminated metal (LAMINA TAK'IN). By far the most common roofs are of either thatch or tile. Three roof forms are in use in Zinacantan. These are the gable roof (VAKASH); the steep hip roof (CHUKAL); and the shed roof (KUCHOMAL). The last-named is used mainly on animal shelters.

Construction

Since flat land for fields is at a premium in the generally rugged terrain of Zinacantan, plots allocated for house-building tend to be restricted to hillsides. The first problem in building is the construction of the terrace on which the house will be erected. Figure 22 illustrates the most common technique: an area half the size of the intended base of the house is dug out of the slope, and the earth from this excavation is then used to build the second half of the terrace. This provides an area of level land large enough for both the house and patio. The houses are never placed directly against the hillside, but are set forward a meter or more from the rear bank of the terrace. This narrow space in the rear of the house is often used as a storage place for firewood.

Thatch Roof Houses. In a thatch roof house with wattle and daub walls, the structure is essentially post and beam; the walls are non-load-bearing. Warfield describes the process of constructing the walls as follows:

21. Typical thatch roof house; woman in foreground is placing maize kernels in lime-water to soften

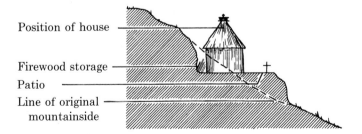

Position of house

Firewood storage

Patio

Line of original
    mountainside

22. Construction of a common type of Zinacanteco house

The weight of the roof is carried by a number of heavy timber posts (ʔOY) 15 to 20 cms. in diameter. These are usually of cypress (ʔOK'IL TEʔ) or oak (TULAN) . . . The structural posts are supported by the earth at the bottom and are notched at the top . . . to carry beams which support the roof. The beams . . . are lashed with chayote vines to the posts. If the beam is not continuous, two beams may be ship-lapped and lashed together with the joint occurring above the post . . . This heavy timber frame gives lateral support to the entire building.

To the heavy timber frame, the lighter wall framework is added. The vertical framework consists of posts approximately 5 cms. in diameter. These posts may be spaced as often as every 45 cms. or may be as far apart as a meter. The posts are set into the ground and lashed to the roof beams for stability. Wattle made from horizontal hardwood or bamboo poles (SHUL) are lashed then to the posts. The wattles are very light, being only 1.3 cm. to 2.5 cm. in diameter. They are usually 15 to 23 cms. on center and are lashed with chayote vines.

It is to the framework illustrated in Figure 23 that the mud wall is attached (Figures 24, 25). Stones are placed within the framework between the bottom wattle to prevent the mud wall from absorbing ground water. The mud plaster, a mixture of mud and dried pine needles (SHAK TOH), is laid between the interior and the exterior SHUL from the outside. Pine needles are used both because they are plentiful in the highlands of Chiapas and because their resin acts as a preservative and makes them less likely to rot than other materials. Once the

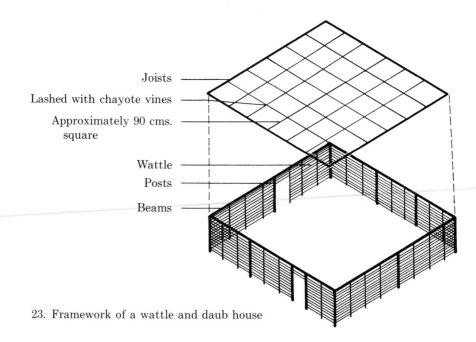

Joists
Lashed with chayote vines
Approximately 90 cms. square
Wattle
Posts
Beams

23. Framework of a wattle and daub house

24. Carrying mud for wattle and daub wall construction

25. Wattle and daub wall construction

framework has been filled, the mud walls are smoothed on both the inside and the outside with a spoon. Because the posts which support the roof are heavy, it is sometimes necessary to die the mud plaster into the posts and to leave some wood exposed on the inside face. An alternate method is to thicken the wall around the posts. If the exterior is to be plastered with mud or lime, finger holes are pressed into every 8 or 10 cms. of the surface. This enables the plaster to grip more easily. Usually, the wall varies from 10 to 15 cms. in thickness throughout its length. Each wall is completely filled with mud before another wall is begun. Many times, the mud is not carried to the roof beams. In these instances, an open space between 15 and 23 cms. is left at the top of the wall for smoke to escape. (163: 12–14)

In the process of constructing the walls some provision must be made for doors. Some houses have only one door, but more commonly there are two on opposite sides of the house. Normally, the door (MAK NA) is constructed of a single piece of wood, making it very narrow (about a half meter); important doorways consist of two planks that meet in the middle. Ordinarily the doors constructed of a flat board have an extended nub on one top and one bottom corner. This nub (SHCHU?) fits into holes provided at the top and bottom of the door frame, enabling the door to pivot. Usually there is no handle in the door, which is opened from the inside by pulling a rope, and from the outside merely by pushing when it is not locked.

Several means for locking or barring the door are utilized. In some cases locks are purchased in San Cristóbal, but these are used primarily for locking from the outside when the family goes away. More commonly the door is barred (by setting a wooden pole diagonally across the interior face of the door; by setting vertical posts on each side of the door and placing the pole horizontally between the two posts and the door; or by setting heavy wood or metal rods into holes to prevent the door from opening).

Thatch is an efficient material for roof construction for non-load-bearing walls, as its roof framing is easily adapted for use with the post and beam construction system. Warfield describes the framing as follows:

For the ceiling framing, joists (TS'AM TE?) are run in both directions to form a grid composed of squares 90 cms. on a side. The joists rest upon the wall beams which are in turn supported by the structural posts, as illustrated in Figure 23. The joists are lashed for stability at every crossing. The actual structural framework of the roof consists of six heavy timber rafters (CHUK) and a series of joists as illustrated in Figures 26, 27. The horizontal wattles are then added to this frame as on the gable roof. The vertically inclined rafters are 8 to 10 cms.

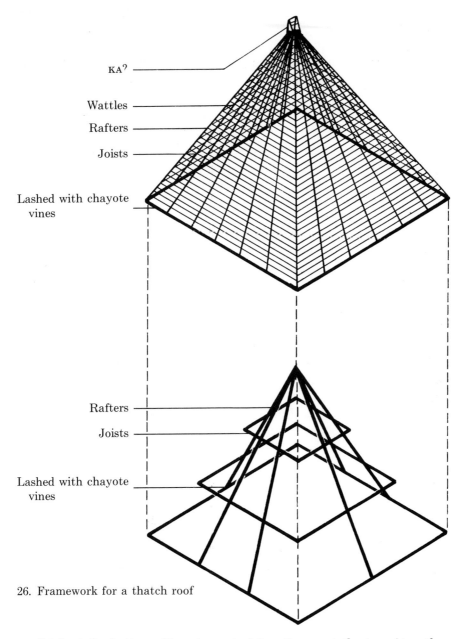

KA?

Wattles

Rafters

Joists

Lashed with chayote vines

Rafters

Joists

Lashed with chayote vines

26. Framework for a thatch roof

thick at the bottom. They taper to 2.5 or 5 cms. at the top. Atop the frame, another smaller structure called a KA? is added. KA? is Tzotzil for "horse," a name which comes from the Spanish use of *caballo* for a carpenter's horse. This is the exact form of this top structure. Through the open ends of the KA?, the smoke from the interior fire is supposed to escape. [The framing which carries the thatch is illustrated in Figures 26 and 28.] (1963: 21)

27. Constructing framework for thatch roof

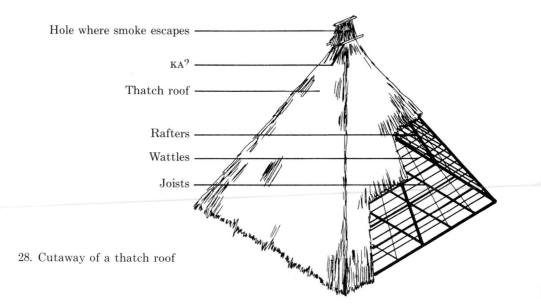

Hole where smoke escapes ————————————

KAʔ ————————

Thatch roof ————————

Rafters ————————

Wattles ————————

Joists ————————

28. Cutaway of a thatch roof

Once the framing is completed, the thatch is laid:

> . The laying of the thatch is begun at the bottom and is done in units called *manojos*. These bunches are . . . usually about 90 to 120 cms. long and about 8 cm. in diameter at the neck. This is the length of the thatch when it is picked from the mountains. They are laid in parallel rows and are lashed to the wattles with chayote vines. They are overlapped to provide additional rain protection. Only about 30 cm. of each bunch is left exposed. This means that over any one area of the roof, there are at least three thicknesses of thatch. The last bunches of thatch are laid over the joists at the peak. . . They are then tacked and held in place by long poles. . . On some houses, the first row of thatch is allowed to hang down as much as 60 cms. This provides additional insulation by protecting the upper part of the wall from rain and wind. (Warfield 1963: 20)

Many houses also have a porch (YUT KORAL) which is especially useful for storage of firewood and other items—such as pots (Figure 29)—during the rainy season. In some houses it is made by supporting a large overhang by columns; in others, the porch is incorporated in the rectangular floor plan (Figure 33).

Tile Roof Houses. In a tile roof house with adobe walls, the walls are load-bearing; that is, the walls support the load of the roof structure in addition to their own weight (Figure 30). Usually, the mud brick wall is built upon a stone foundation. Stones are plentiful in the mountains of Zinacantan and provide a strong, economical base for the house. The adobe walls are laid on top of the foundation, and mud mortar is used to bond the adobe together. The adobes are made in a number of hamlets in Zinacantan; they are also sometimes purchased and transported from San Cristóbal, where they are made by Ladinos. Although these walls are sometimes covered with mud or lime plaster, they are usually left exposed on both the interior and exterior of the house.

In these adobe houses, the load over the door is carried by a heavy timber resting on wooden blocks which transfer the load of the lintel to the adobe wall below. Windows are sometimes added to the walls of these adobe houses, but this practice is still quite rare.

The tile roof is constructed as follows:

> The ceiling framing rests on the mud brick walls of the adobe house. It is of heavy, rough cut timber construction, the joists being approxi-

29. Cooking pots stored under eaves of thatch roof house

30. Modern tile roof house

mately 10 cms. by 15 cms. All of the ceiling joists are of pine. . . The beams are usually spaced about 90 cms. on center. Some Indian builders actually attempt to build on a one meter module. A roof overhang of about 30 cms. is usually provided to protect the adobe wall. When it is necessary to join beams perpendicularly, a morticed joint. . . is usually used.

The roof structure for the tile roof is also of heavy timber construction. The total weight of this framing system is transferred to the ceiling joists and to the mud brick wall by Member A on Figure 31. The tile roof and its framing transfer their load through both A *and* B. The frame which carries the tile rests on the structural roof frame. (Warfield 1963: 18–19)

Shingle Roof Houses. The roof of wood shingles is less common in Zinacantan than, for example, in Huistán or in Ladino towns, where it is commonly used by families who cannot afford tile. Warfield describes the construction process as follows:

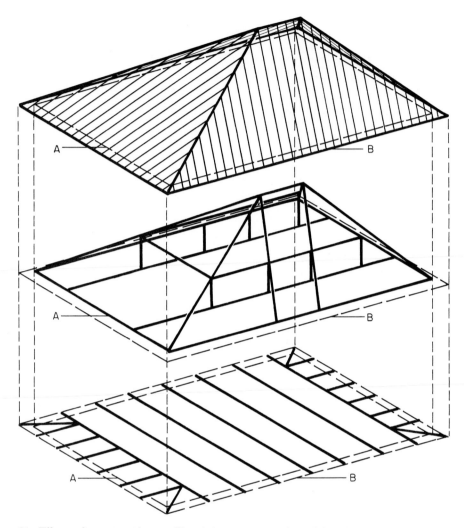

31. Tile roof construction: ceiling joists, structural roof framing, and framing to receive roofing

Perpendicular to the longitudinal joists, the rafters are erected about 46 cms. on center. In this type of construction, also, there is some attempt to balance the roof framing with the posts below, which are usually held to one meter intervals. The rafters are of rough cut lumber or of logs and are usually only 2.5 to 5 cms. thick and about 10 cms. wide. The rafters need not be of heavier wood because of the lightness of the shingle roof. Onto the rafters pieces of wood slats are added perpendicularly. These wood slats are the same shingles used for the roofing. The slats are about 60 cms. on center and, with the rafters, form a grid system of framing . . .

To these wood slats the roofing is added. The shingles are very thin slats of pine, a soft wood and therefore easy for the Indians to cut themselves. The slats are about 10 cms. wide and 120 cms. in length. The roof is begun at the bottom and the slats are overlapped in order that they might shed water more effectively. The roofing is held to the structure by perpendicular wood slats above and below. . . The K'ALBIL TE? roofing is sandwiched between these slats and pegged by wooden nails (LAVUSH TE?). These nails are about 15 cms. long, 0.6 cms. in diameter, and pointed at one end. 5 to 8 cms. of the nail is left exposed both above and below the roofing.

On the majority of houses, the wood slat roof is capped with tile in order to prevent water from entering the house at the peak. (Warfield 1963: 22–23)

Laminated Roof Houses. Both laminated tarpaper and laminated metal are bought in San Cristóbal. Since this roofing material is sold in large sheets (80 centimeters by either 1 or 2 meters), it needs very little supporting framework. The sheets are secured to the frame by nails, driven through a bottlecap to prevent the head of the nail from passing through the roofing.

Furnishings

Although Zinacanteco houses contain no interior walls or partitions, they are conceptually divided into "rooms" or living spaces. These are defined by the location of the hearth and associated objects that are owned and used by the women, and by the location of the interior house altar and associated objects owned and used by men. The house altar is nearly always constructed against the wall opposite the hearth. If the hearth is located on the right as one enters through the main door, the altar is found against the wall on the left; if the hearth is to the left, the altar is to the right. Some altars are constructed against the middle of the wall; others are located in corners but with one edge against the wall opposite the hearth. In houses without interior altars, the men's possessions still tend to be clustered in the living space opposite the hearth (Figures 32, 33).

The hearth, with a fire that almost never dies (except when the members of the household are away for extended periods of time), is a focal point for women's work, as well as for family interaction, since men and children sit by the fire for warmth and also eat near the fire. This hearth always contains three stones (ʔOSHYOKET) to support the comal, with the largest stone (ME ʔ YOKET) located closest to the grinding table. Its position is fixed, while the two smaller stones can be moved depending upon how the women decide to place the burning logs and the cooking pots.

32. House of ʔAntun Peres Shulubteʔ in ʔApas

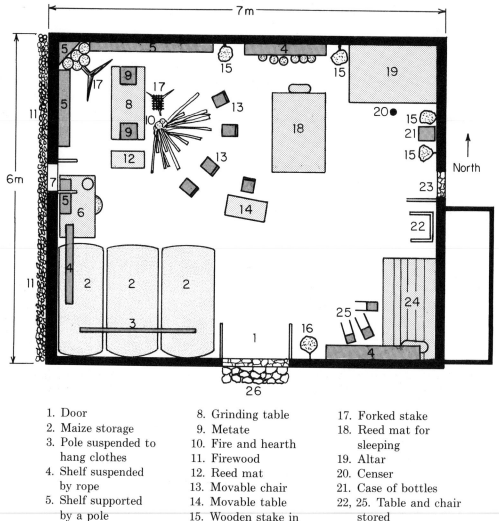

1. Door	8. Grinding table	17. Forked stake
2. Maize storage	9. Metate	18. Reed mat for
3. Pole suspended to	10. Fire and hearth	sleeping
hang clothes	11. Firewood	19. Altar
4. Shelf suspended	12. Reed mat	20. Censer
by rope	13. Movable chair	21. Case of bottles
5. Shelf supported	14. Movable table	22, 25. Table and chair
by a pole	15. Wooden stake in	stored
6. Table and chair	adobe wall	23. Door
7. Window	16. Metal hanger	24. Plank bed
		26. Stoop

33. House of Petul Peres K'obyosh in Nabenchauk

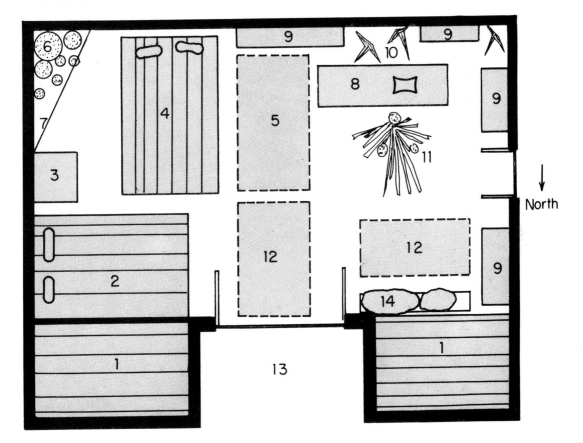

North

1. Plank bed
2. Bed of Chep and wife
3. Altar
4. Bed of Petul and wife
5. Pot storage
6. Reed mat of Petul's sons
7. Clothesline
8. Grinding table
9. Table
10. Forked stake
11. Fire and hearthstones
12. Reed mat for visitors
13. Porch
14. Maize storage

The lengths of firewood, which have been dried outside under the eaves, are brought into the house by the women and placed on the hearth like the irregular spokes of a wheel. As their ends burn (near the center of the wheel), the logs are simply pushed further into the fire (see Figures 34, 35). During the night the fire dies down, but at dawn the women rekindle it quickly by blowing on the coals in the ashes.

Each house has at least one small wooden table and a series of small wooden chairs. These small chairs and tables are very well adapted to Zinacanteco life. They do not take up as much living space as large ones would, and the chairs can be moved easily and stored when not in use. Their size also allows the man to sit near the fire, where he can stay warm on cold nights and chilly mornings. The table is ordinarily used only for ritual meals, but the chairs are used by the men, while the women sit or kneel on *petates* on the ground. Both the tables and the chairs are constructed in Chamula, in San Cristóbal, or by Ladinos in Hteklum, and sold to the Zinacantecos. The chairs are made of pine; few nails are used and most of the joints are morticed. The seat of the chair is between 23 and 30 cms. from the floor, and the top of the backrest is never more than 60 cm. high. The chairs, though small, are of very sturdy construction and last for years. The tables vary considerably in size. The tops range from 45 by 30 cms. to as large as 90 by 60 cms. When not in use, chairs and tables are stored in out-of-the-way places in the house.

34. Zinacanteco domestic furniture

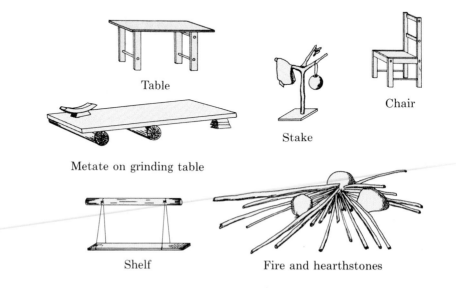

Table

Metate on grinding table

Stake

Chair

Shelf

Fire and hearthstones

35. House interior

A number of tables serving various functions are constructed by the Zinacantecos themselves. Most of these are built into the wall or floor and are not movable. In many cases, legs for the tables are poles driven into the ground or a single timber post embedded in the earth. Sometimes the tabletop is partially supported by stakes driven into the wall. One of the most important tables in the house is that used for an altar. A common building technique for the altar is to support the back by wall-stakes and the front by legs. In almost every case a baldachin is erected above the altar. Still another type of table is the grinding table. This is a heavy timbertop table, about 60 by 150 cms., which is raised about 30 cms. above the ground and leveled by logs or stones beneath. It is constructed next to the hearth and holds the metates and other cooking equipment.

Zinacantecos sleep either on reed mats, called *petates* (POP) on the floor, or on wood plank beds (TEM) that are usually built into the side of the house. The wood planks are raised above the ground by legs; forked limbs are often used for this purpose with the planks resting upon a short beam which spans the distance between the forks.

Some objects are stored on shelves or hung on hooks. Shelves (KAHANAB) are constructed in two ways: a board may be suspended by rope from the ceiling joists, and steadied by its contact with the wall, or a wood plank may be supported by wooden stakes driven into the wall.

Another common means of providing storage in the mud-wall houses is to drive stakes into the walls and hang net sacks from them. Similarly, a forked stake (CHIKIN TE? or PECHECH TE?) is often used for hanging items such as pots, lanterns, or bags. And the function of the grill (KUSHANOB TOH) near the fire is to hold flaming *ocote* for additional light at night.

Ceiling joints are used in a variety of ways. Poles are suspended from them in a manner similar to the suspended shelves and are used for hanging clothes. Clotheslines of rope or wire (CH'OHONETIK) are sometimes connected to the joists for hanging clothes and blankets. Above the fire, a long pole with crooked ends is suspended by ropes. This BA K'OK', adjustable in height, is used to hold pots above the fire and to dry strips of beef.

The House Compound

The exterior space, defined by fences, geographic barriers, or the use of land, is almost as important to Zinacanteco architecture as the area within the house. That most closely connected with the house is the patio, a flat yard of exposed earth (?AMAK') in front of the house. The patio is of ritual importance because it contains the house cross which functions as the domestic group shrine (see Chapter 7). This cross is made of CH'UL TE?, a type of cedar which withstands the weather well. It is made by Ladino carpenters in San Cristóbal or Zinacantan Center who use the leftover wood for a small cross which is placed on top of the house.

The house cross has no regular orientation, except that it is placed so that the arms are parallel to one side of the house. It marks not only the physical entrance but also the ritual entrance to the house's "soul." At its dedication ceremony the owner of a new house prays:

> Cross of the door of my house,
> Cross of the door of my wealth,
> Of my heart's repose,
> Of my eyes' awakening . . .
>
> (Laughlin, quoted in Warfield 1963: 79–80)

The patio is of social significance because often guests are entertained there rather than inside the house. It is the place where the women weave cloth, the men plait palm for hats or perform other small tasks, and the children play. Wood is stored under the eaves next to the patio; looms are hung from poles. Grass-filled baskets or old pots in which chickens lay eggs are kept along the edge of the house. There may be a small coop—open at the sides and roofed with thatch or tile—for the chickens. If there is a pig, it is kept in a pen at the side of the patio.

The maize may be stored in a bin inside the house or in an especially constructed granary at the edge of the patio. The granaries are like small houses with wattle and daub walls and thatched roofs. Sometimes the doorway is placed above the level of the ground and reached by ladder; this technique helps protect the maize from rodents and chickens.

The sweathouse (PUS) is commonly found beside the house or at the edge of the patio. When constructed beside the house, it is usually a lean-to structure with wattle and daub walls and a thatched roof. More commonly now it is tunneled into the bank of earth, either above or below the terrace which has been dug out of the slope for the construction of the house. Sweathouses can accommodate two to three people, either sitting up or lying down. Lava rocks are placed at the back of the structure and heated by a fire of oak wood. The burning pieces of wood are removed, leaving coals and hot rocks, and water is sprinkled on the rocks to make steam. *Chamarras* are placed over the door to keep the heat in. Then two to three persons (men, women, and/or children) undress and enter the sweathouse. They first sit down and fan the air with palm leaves to make the heat circulate; then they lie down with their feet to the hot rocks for a period of 15 to 30 minutes.

These sweat baths were formerly used on many occasions—for example, when men returned exhausted from work in the lowlands. Now they are used mainly in two contexts: a woman who has given birth invariably takes a series of three sweat baths with the midwife at intervals after the birth (see Chapter 9); and, following a major curing ceremony, the patient takes one or more sweat baths with the shaman, who returns to visit him for this purpose (see Chapter 20).

Beyond the patio there is ordinarily a larger space enclosed by a fence. This area (YUT MOK or "inside the fence") normally contains, besides the structures and objects in or around the patio, some chayote vines, frequently a number of fruit trees, and perhaps a plot of red geraniums—as well as a small plot of maize and squash. The movable sheep corral is ordinarily placed just outside this area in a larger plot of land devoted principally to maize cultivation.

The house compound is frequently enclosed by one of four types of fences (Warfield 1963: 29–31). The most common is the HIT'BIL MOK, made of tree limbs or flat boards; the CHANTE? MOK is made of long, thin poles; the SUKBIL MOK is the simplest, being constructed of limbs from a hawthorn tree piled between two wooden poles; and finally, the LATSBIL TON MOK is constructed of field stones that are piled up and usually not bonded together. The most common type of gate is made of removable poles which rest in the gateposts.

Durability and Cost of Houses

Zinacanteco houses must withstand heavy summer rains and strong September winds, and provide shelter on cold winter nights. The walls and roofs that are now constructed vary in cost, durability, and construction man-hours.

The house with adobe walls and tile roof performs best on all counts. It lasts at least thirty-five to forty years, but is costly to build. In 1963, a 10-meter-square house of this type cost approximately 3100 pesos and took at least twelve working days to build, with the help of professional Ladino masons and carpenters, usually from San Cristóbal, as well as a working force of four to seven helpers, either neighbors or members of the family, who were paid 5 pesos a day plus food. Zinacantecos prefer such houses, and many of the new ones being built are of this type, if their owners can afford them.

The next most durable house has wattle and daub walls with a steep thatched roof. The walls endure about twenty-five years, while the roof lasts about fifteen, after which the thatch must be replaced. The cost of such a house 10 meters square is much less (approximately 900 pesos in 1963), and it can be built by Zinacantecos alone in about twenty-four working days with four to seven men.

Of the common types still found in Zinacantan, the least satisfactory—in beauty (from a Zinacanteco point of view), maintenance, and perform-ance—is the VAKASH NA, with walls of split logs or branches and a gable thatched roof. It cost less than 600 pesos in 1963, and could be built in less than a week with the aid of four working men, even fewer if the house was small.

Floors of all types of houses are of exposed earth, packed hard by con-tinuous use. Mud tracked into the house during the rainy season does not upset the Zinacanteco housewife; it merely dries and adds surface to the floor. (This advantage first became evident to me when my family lived in the Harvard project field house in the hamlet of Paste?. We had unfortunately had the floors made of tile, which meant that my wife had to mop them almost daily when the children tracked in mud.) Warfield writes:

> In a climate where there is considerable amount of rain during many months of the year, the earth floor is most practical. Mud and dirt are constantly being tracked into the house, yet they soon become a part of the floor. This not to imply that the earth floor is necessarily dirty, for debris is regularly swept from the house. In addition to water being tracked into the house from the outside, there are a number of times throughout the day when the earth floor becomes wet . . . Before ritual meals there is a washing of the hands and no attempt is made to keep the water from dripping onto the floor. Often times, the excess water is even emptied onto the floor. This is followed by the washing of the mouth, where water is spat upon the earth floor. During the drinking rituals, every drink of liquor is followed by spitting on the floor and emptying the excess liquor from the glass. In the preparation of food, also, women often empty water from bowls and pots onto the floor around the fire.
>
> In all cases, the earth floor quickly absorbs the moisture . . . Similarly, leaks from the roof are not a critical problem in Zinacanteco houses. Also, because the floor is of earth, no special provisions need be made for the fire. (1963: 66)

As soon after marriage as a Zinacanteco is financially able to, he builds his own house and moves out of his father's. Land is usually given to him by his father, so that the new house is located near that of his father, often within the same house compound.

Houses are built during January, February, March, or April. Since this is the peak of the dry season, builders can work more hours per day and mud construction dries more quickly. Also, these are the months during which farming is less demanding, allowing more time for the construction work.

There are usually two ceremonies during the construction of a new house: one (HOL CHUCH) is performed at the midpoint in construction; the second (CH'UL KANTELA) comes at the completion of the construction. (See Chapter 20 for details on these ceremonies.)

5 / Clothing

Perhaps the most striking feature of Zinacanteco material culture is clothing, especially that of the men. Zinacanteco costumes present a sharp contrast with the type of clothing worn by Ladinos in the Chiapas highlands and elicit much comment by tourists and newly arrived anthropologists in this remote part of Mexico. The reaction is expressed colorfully by Robert Laughlin, who wrote about his first encounter with Zinacantecos:

> No one who has seen a Zinacantecan striding jauntily down the Pan American highway forgets that first impression, both ridiculous and awesome. He stands on great elevated sandals; a straw platter, streaming long pink and purple ribbons, is perched at a rakish angle on his head. Around his neck a blue checkered scarf dangling four pink pom poms . . . a white smock with elegant red pin stripes, and a pair of gleaming white, short shorts from which protrude smoothly muscular chestnut legs. When, rounding a curve on the highway, I caught sight of the first of these, my immediate startled reaction was, "Good Lord, who let *it* out?" The next apparition pierced through my daze, provoking the astonished question, "What does *it* think?" (1960: 2)

Zinacanteco Costumes*

Men's Clothing. The clothing styles are best visualized with the help of photographs (Figures 36, and 37). Men wear woven short pants (VESHAL) of white cotton, belted at the waist by a red and green wool sash (SHINCHAIL). A short pull-over shirt (MOKITEIL), also woven of white cotton, has

---

*I am grateful to Susan Tax who studied clothing styles and weaving in Zinacantan and whose field report (1959) was utilized in this chapter.

38. New ribbons on hats for the Fiesta of San Lorenzo

sleeves reaching below the elbow and may or may not be tucked into the sash at the waist. A *chamarra* (POK' K'U?UL) of red and white striped cotton is worn over the shirt, and covers the pants at the top of the thigh. For cold weather, there is a red and white wool chamarra (TSOTS HERKAIL or TSOTS K'U?UL) which is worn on top of the cotton one. A large black wool blanket (CHAMAROIL) is worn over all in very cold weather and used on trips for both wear and sleeping. A blue (or gray) and white checkered kerchief (POK') with red wool tassels (NICH POK') at the corners is worn around the neck, or may be tied in various ways around the head, especially in cold, windy weather. The materials for the kerchief are purchased in San Cristóbal, and the tassels are then dyed and attached by the men. The hat (PISHALAL) is of white palm (SHAN), woven in strips and then sewn into thick layers, with some rows of dyed black palm on the underside of the brim. The crown is low and rounded and supports multicolored ribbon streamers, primarily rose and purple, with occasional white, green, blue, or yellow ones (see Figure 38). The hat is held in place by a buckskin

37. Men's clothing

strap that fits snugly around the back of the head. Heavy sandals (VARACHIL) made of leather with soles cut from used automobile tires are purchased in San Cristóbal for everyday use. Over their left shoulders the men carry one of two types of bags: a net bag (NUTI?) on a leather cord, or a more expensive bag (MORAL) of tooled leather with a small pocket sewn on the front. For rainy weather, a few Zinacantecos still wear raincoats of palm leaves (SHAN ?ASHIBAL), but most have now purchased rubberized ponchos sold in San Cristóbal. They are also beginning to wear rubberized rain hat covers (FORO) that fit over their palm platters and keep the ribbons dry. When not needed, the rain hat cover is carried in the leather or net bag, and the poncho is carried folded, with the rubber side turned in, and draped over the top of the bag.

This is an extraordinary costume and much more colorful than that of the women. In this respect Zinacantecos are like birds—the males have brighter plumage than the females. However, when a Zinacanteco goes to work his fields in the lowlands, and sometimes when he travels to market in lowland towns such as Tuxtla Gutiérrez, he commonly wears long trousers and a cotton shirt, purchased from Ladino stores, in order to protect himself from the mosquitoes and other insect pests. Many Zinacanteco men are now in the process of changing to this Ladino style of clothing, even for everyday wear, in the highlands (see Chapter 25), and a few shift to some type of Ladino-style hat for work in the lowlands.

Women's Clothing. The women wear a pull-over blouse (SK'U? ?ANTS) of store-bought white cotton cloth, made from a simple rectangle with an opening cut for the head, and decorated at the seams with red yarn stitching. When a woman has a nursing baby, the side seams are left partly open. The skirt (TSEK), of home-woven cotton dyed dark blue, is a wide tube of cloth folded around the body to a pleat in front and bound at the waist with a sash identical to that of the men. A home-woven black wool skirt is worn occasionally, in cold weather or when the woman is menstruating. A red and white cotton shawl (POK' MOCHEBAL) is used as a carrying cloth or for protection from the sun; it is fastened with colorful yarn tassels in front and is a regular part of the costume (Figure 39). For cold weather, there is a wool and cotton shawl (TSOTS MOCHEBAL) of black or gray wool and white cotton. This is also sometimes worn folded up on top of the head as a protection from the sun, especially when the woman is herding sheep. For decoration, women usually wear strings of beads and purple or rose-colored ribbons around their necks. For rainy weather, they now usually hold pieces of inexpensive plastic over their heads and shoulders. Small babies are carried in large white cloths or rebozos of red and white cotton. Zinacanteco women always go barefooted.

39. Women's clothing

Children's Clothing. Boys dress like adult men, with the exception of the very young who wear, instead of short pants, a shirt (KAMISHAIL or TS'IL K'U?UL) of red and white striped or plain white cotton, long enough to cover their genitals.

Small girls dress like adult women. However, for a girl's baptism, her godparents present her with a special blouse (SHELA K'U?UL), with an intricate pattern of red, green, orange, and purple wool woven into the white cotton. The girl may continue to wear this special blouse for some years, but she usually outgrows it by the age of five or six.

Ritual Clothing. For ritual occasions special items of clothing are added to the costume, especially the men's, to designate particular ceremonial statuses. The most common addition are heavy sandals purchased for 25 to 35 pesos from the Chamulas who make them. These sandals (CHAK SHONOBIL) with their high heel-guards are worn by many of the men during fiestas, but are *de rigueur* for those serving in the priestly cargo-system in the ceremonial center.

Another item of clothing worn by all cargoholders (except the mayores) and by the shamans on ritual occasions is the SHAKITAIL, a large, full-length, black wool chamarra or ceremonial robe with red, rose, or purple silk cloth decoration around the square neck and ribbons in front (see Chapter 11). In addition, the three upper levels of the cargoholders and the ritual advisers (TOTILME?ILETIK) wear turbans (TSAHAL POK' or TS'IL POK), woven of red cotton with thin black horizontal thread running through, wrapped around their heads. The three upper levels of the cargoholders also wear large black hats.

Staffs of various types constitute a more specialized item of ritual costuming. The senior alcalde and junior alcalde (see Chapter 22), the two highest ranking cargoholders, carry silver-headed canes, with multicolored ribbons attached, under their left arms. The four regidores carry in their left hands a long plain wooden staff (VARA). The presidente and sindico carry silver-headed canes without ribbons. Shamans carry bamboo staffs (BISH) in their left hands (see Figure 40). The mayordomos reyes and mesoneros wear policemen's clubs (TS'ARAM TE?) at their belts, and the mayores carry small policemen's clubs in their shoulder bags. When dancing, the alféreces use special rattles, previously decorated with feathers from the macaw, but now with painted hen feathers.

The costuming for rituals becomes even more elaborate during change-of-office ceremonies. For example, the alféreces who are changing office wear long capes with white collars (see Figure 41), blue or green velvet knee pants, and long red stockings (knitted by a Zinacanteco man in

40. A shaman always carries his bamboo staff

Zinacantan Center). There are many specialized roles in the major fiestas of the Christmas and Easter seasons, and of San Lorenzo and San Sebastián, that require elaborate and very special costuming (described in Chapter 22).

On ritual occasions most of the elaborate costuming is worn by the men, but some women shamans carry bamboo staffs, and the old women who serve as incense-bearers and who dance with the mayordomos during Holy Week and at flower-changing ceremonies wear a special chamarra called a CHILIL. Except for these instances, women appear in special ritual costuming only at their weddings (see Chapter 9).

Clothing Manufacture

In the manufacture of wearing apparel there is a clear-cut division of labor by sex, with the bulk of the work being done by the women. The Zinacanteco men make palm hats and dye and arrange yarn for the tassels on their kerchiefs and thread for the tassels on their chamarras; they also make, paint, and generally maintain the special masks, headgear, and other items of costuming needed in the large fiestas. Otherwise, clothing in Zinacantan is women's work from beginning to end—from owning, herding, and shearing the sheep to washing the clothing when it is soiled.

Weaving Hats. The palm strips for the hats are purchased in San Cristóbal from Ladinos who import the material from the lowlands. Some Ladinos specialize in the dyeing of palm, and the black strips are purchased from them. The strips are braided by the men while they sit and talk in their homes or on their terraces, or while they are traveling. They often braid palm strips while walking to and from San Cristóbal or Zinacantan Center, or while riding in trucks or buses. Braiding palm is a time-filling activity; like the women's looms the work is portable and can be done almost any time and any place. At one all-night K'IN KRUS procession (see Chapter 20), I remember seeing a Zinacanteco light his oil lamp and begin braiding palm at 4:30 A.M. during a lull in the ceremony.

Once the braided strips are finished, some men sew their own hats, but generally the strips are taken to a hat-sewer (HTS'IS PISHALAL). There then remains only the purchase and addition of the multicolored ribbon streamers (SHELAIL PISHALAL) and the buckskin strap (KAMOSA) to hold the hat in place. Not counting the labor for the braiding, a good hat costs 5 pesos for the white palm, 3.50 pesos for the dyed black palm, 7 to 10 pesos for its sewing, 8 to 12 pesos for the ribbons, and 5 pesos for the buckskin strap, for a total of 28.50 to 35.50 pesos. Zinacanteco men like to have at least

41. An alférez during his change-of-office ceremony; note peacock feather in his hat, velveteen britches, cape, and high-backed sandals

one new hat a year, and preferably two, one for each of the major fiestas of San Lorenzo and San Sebastián, so hat-making is going on almost constantly—with special intensity before the fiestas. The hats are not ordinarily made for sale, although a few are produced for a tourist shop in San Cristóbal, and some are even for sale in fashionable arts and crafts shops in New York and Boston.

The men also use the red (or pink) yarn for the tassels on their kerchiefs. The yarn threads must be carefully pulled apart to make the tassels look fluffier and more impressive. They spend hours rolling multicolored threads together on their knees to make the tassels (SHOKON K'U?UL) for the edges of their chamarras.

Weaving Cloth. The women use cotton and wool for their weaving. White and red cotton thread is purchased in San Cristóbal; the wool is generally procured within the municipio. Many women own their own sheep; others buy the wool at a rate of one liter of maize for the fleece of one animal.

The herds of sheep are owned and cared for entirely by the women. At night they are kept in small rectangular corrals, constructed of vertical planks, that can be taken apart periodically and moved to new locations. During the day the herds (never more than about thirty animals) are let out to graze and are taken to water, herded by one of the women or a couple of the small daughters (Figure 42). The lambs are born in the spring, usually in February, and most of the male lambs are castrated when they are one year to a year and a half old, leaving only one or two rams in each herd.

Women shear the sheep three times a year (November, March, July), with scissors purchased in San Cristóbal. They wash the fleece in water with suds made from soaproot (CH'UPAK'), and then either leave the wool white or dye it black, using a mixture of water, black earth, and a plant called CH'A TE?. The wool from the black sheep must also be dyed, for the natural color tends to fade and turn brown if it is not. Red yarn is either purchased in San Cristóbal or more commonly made by using store-bought red dye on the white wool. Green yarn is generally purchased, but is occasionally prepared at home with store-bought dye.

The wool is carded with two carding combs (KALASH), and then spun using a spindle (PETET) that rests in a gourd (see Figure 43). The carding combs are generally of metal and are purchased in San Cristóbal; the spindle is made in San Andrés Larrainzar and traded in from there. Most women also own a revolving winding frame (PISOB NO) which stands about two feet high and holds the skeins of yarn as they are being wound into balls. This frame is also used to wind the cotton skeins purchased in San Cristóbal.

42. Sheep are herded by women of all ages

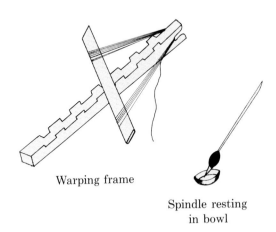

Warping frame

Spindle resting
in bowl

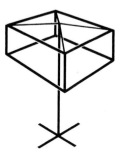

Winding frame

Carding comb
for wool

43. Implements for carding wool

After the thread of yarn is wound, it is ready to be measured on the warping frame (KOMEN). This is notched most of the way down its trunk to allow a number of positions for the cross-bar around which the thread of yarn is strung. For example, the warp of a man's shirt must be shorter than that for men's pants, so the cross-bar is moved up toward the head. As the thread is wound on to the frame, not only the length of the warp but also one of the sheds is set by simply crossing each thread as it is brought around the cross-bar.

Next, the cotton thread is starched by dipping it in boiling water mixed with maize dough. It is then strung, still wet, on to the two bamboo poles that are the head and foot of the loom (see Figure 44). The thread is spread out along the poles and stretched out to dry. A wooden comb drawn lengthwise up and down the warp is used to separate the threads, which are then fastened more securely to the head and foot and laced on with twine.

All Zinacanteco weaving is done with only two sheds. The one which has been fixed on the frame is held open by the shed roll (YAKAN); the second is fixed by the attachment of the heddle (ʔOLINAB TEʔ). If the first shed has separated threads 1, 3, 5, 7, 9, and so forth, on the top of the shed roll, from threads 2, 4, 6, 8, 10, and so on, underneath the roll, the heddle does exactly the reverse—it picks up the even-numbered threads and leaves the odd-numbered ones underneath. This is done by catching

44. Zinacanteco loom

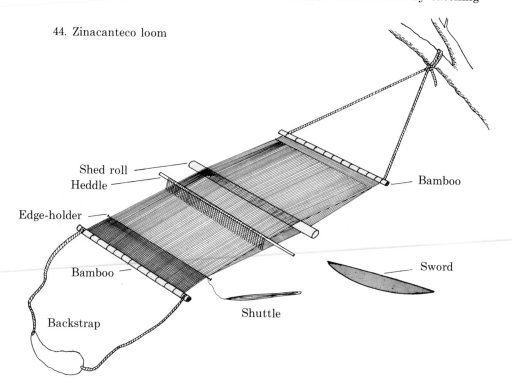

Shed roll

Heddle

Edge-holder

Bamboo

Backstrap

Bamboo

Shuttle

Sword

each even-numbered thread with the heddle thread; thus the even-numbered threads are all raised at once when the weaver pulls up the heddle. Exactly the same procedure is followed with wool except that it is not starched.

A shuttle stick is prepared in advance with the warp thread wound lengthwise around the stick, and the weaver is ready to begin weaving. The actual weaving is simply the process of passing the shuttle through each shed alternately. The weaver sits on her knees, the back-strap passing behind her, holding the loom taut (see Figures 45, 46). First, the weaving sword is passed through the shed held by the shed roll and pulled hard toward the weaver to open the shed all the way down to the end. The sword is left in, turned on its side to hold the shed open, and the shuttle is inserted from one side. Then the shed is changed by moving the shed roll toward the top of the loom and pulling up on the heddle which is closer to the weaver. The sword is reinserted in the shed and pulled forward, holding the shed apart while the shuttle is inserted, this time in the reverse direction. Each time a new weft thread is inserted and the shed changed, the sword is brought down hard to tighten the fabric. A woman usually weaves an inch or two of material at one end of the loom then switches ends for the entire remainder of the textile. This is primarily to facilitate the work of ending the textile, for were she to weave all the way to the end, the end pole would hinder the last rows. Pre-weaving at the far end also helps to set and maintain the width of the textile.

The final three or four inches of weaving become very difficult, for the warp has been woven tight and there is not much slack for the insertion of the sword or shuttle. Thus, a set of smaller, narrower sticks is generally used in the final stages. In the final two inches even the smaller sticks will not fit, and it is necessary to take each weft thread gradually across the warp with a metal needle. These last few rows near one end of the textile, are evened out as much as possible with the wooden comb, the heddle is removed by cutting its threads, the end sticks are removed—and the textile is completed.

Using the back-strap loom and cotton thread, women weave the men's pants, shirts, and chamarras, as well as their own skirts and shawls. From wool, they weave their black skirts, and heavy wool shawls (which have some cotton in them), as well as the men's woolen chamarras, the large blankets, and the black SHAKITAIL. The woolen sashes used by both men and women are woven on small looms by specialists who make a surplus and sell them.

Like hat-weaving for the men, textile-weaving on the back-strap loom

45. The backstrap loom in action

46. Closeup of backstrap loom

is a time-filler for the women. Since the loom is portable, it can be carried along while they are herding sheep. It can also be easily set up in a few minutes on the terrace in front of the house. While women normally do some weaving each day, the peak activity precedes the two major fiestas (San Lorenzo and San Sebastián) when every Zinacanteco would like to have a new outfit to wear.

Symbolic Significance

Zinacantecos are especially interested in clothes and appear to attach an extraordinary amount of social significance to them. Their styles readily indicate who is a Zinacanteco, as opposed to a Chamula, a Huisteco, or a Ladino. The rare marriages between Zinacantecos and people from other municipios always entail a change of costume for one of the couple. The style of clothing differentiates between men and women and indicates who is a shaman or a cargoholder serving in a specified ceremonial role. Since the population is relatively large, one person cannot know personally more than a fraction of his fellow Zinacantecos, but he can easily identify his role from the clothing that is worn.

There is strong emphasis upon having new and clean clothing—an emphasis expressed not only in the desire of both men and women to have new clothing for the important fiestas, but also in ritual sequences in curing ceremonies. A special clothes-washer is always appointed to wash the clothes of the patient in a particular river (NINAB CHILO?) that runs past KALVARIO, the major sacred mountain near Zinacantan Center. These freshly washed clothes are later incensed by holding them over the smoke of burning copal. The patient is then dressed in these clean, incensed clothes before he goes with the shaman to visit the ancestral gods on the mountaintops. There is a strong belief that the ancestral gods will punish a person who goes about in dirty clothes.

Sacred objects as well as people have clothing in Zinacantan, and the emphasis upon new and clean clothes applies equally to them. The saint statues in churches are clothed elaborately; their clothes must be washed and incensed periodically and new ones provided when the others become too old. The crosses at mountain and cave shrines are "clothed" in pine boughs and other types of plants, and these must be renewed for each new ceremonial occasion (see Chapter 18).

Clothing patterns and styles are reminiscent of those that we know (or infer) for the Ancient Maya who are shown in painted wall murals and on stelae wearing elaborate headgear, capes, and jewelry. It is obvious that the contemporary Zinacanteco costumes are derived in part from aboriginal elements and in part from Spanish Colonial styles. It seems likely that some elements, such as the high-backed sandals, are survivals from the aboriginal past (see Figures 47, 48). Other styles appear to be functional substitutions for aboriginal elements, such as the multiribboned streamers on the men's hats, which are probably the contemporary version of the feathered headdresses worn by the ancient Maya men.

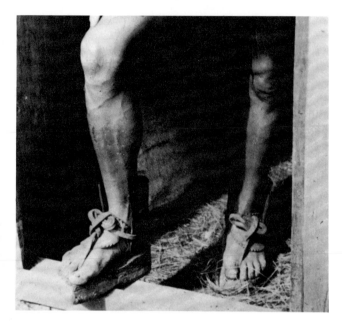

47. Zinacanteco in ceremonial high-backed sandals; for fiestas the legs are rubbed with brilliantine

48. Ancient Maya high-backed sandal carved in stone at Bonampak

6 / Trading and Other Economic Activities

Although Zinacantecos have more of a subsistence economy than the Ladinos of nearby San Cristóbal, they have been involved in marketing and trade with other Indians for centuries and with Ladinos since the Conquest. There is good historical evidence that they traded goods to the Aztec merchants in prehispanic times (Anderson and Dibble 1959: IX,21); they have certainly been salt merchants since early Colonial times, and perhaps before; and they enjoy a well-deserved and long-standing reputation for their astuteness in trade and marketing. Most of the traveling they do now to San Cristóbal, Tuxtla Gutiérrez, Chiapa de Corzo, and even other Indian towns, such as Chamula and San Andrés Larrainzar, is to transact business in the market.

Markets and Stores

We know little as yet of the aboriginal markets of preconquest times. There is one site on the trail between Zinacantan Center and Ixtapa, marked by a cross shrine called "Market Cross," where in former times Zinacantecos reportedly met peoples from the lowlands to engage in trade. There undoubtedly was also active trade on important ceremonial days in Zinacantan Center, as well as in the ceremonial centers of nearby towns.

Today the most important locations for marketing and trade are in Zinacantan Center—in small stores owned both by Ladinos and Indians and in large open-air markets that function on certain ceremonial days —and in Na Chih, where a small market is active two days a week. Beyond the borders of the municipio the most important markets are in the Ladino towns of San Cristóbal, Tuxtla Gutiérrez, Arriaga, and Chiapa de Corzo, and in the neighboring Tzotzil towns of Chamula and San Andrés Larrainzar.

Zinacantan. Daily trade in Zinacantan Center takes place on a relatively small scale in eighteen small stores—eight owned by Ladinos, and ten by Indians. Not all of the daily buying and selling takes place here, since Zinacantecos are constantly buying chickens, red geraniums, and so on, from one another; but these stores do carry on a small but brisk trade, mainly in rum, beer, soft drinks, candles, copal incense, cigarettes and matches, kerosene, and a few food items such as coffee, cookies, candy, sausages, brown sugar, and rolls. Several of the stores also have battery-powered record players with loudspeakers and play Mexican records for a small price. The bulk of the trade involves items needed for ritual activity rather than subsistence items needed for daily food which are still produced mainly within the Zinacanteco households.

Much more important trade, which does involve foodstuffs, occurs in Zinacantan Center on important fiesta days—especially during the fiestas of San Lorenzo and San Sebastián. Stands serving both food and drink (hard and soft) are set up, and hundreds of Ladinos and Indians from other municipios arrive to sell a variety of products in the open-air market to the well over 5000 people who attend the high points of the fiestas. These products include rum, chicha, beer, soft drinks, ice cream, highland fruits in season (such as peaches and apples), lowland foods (such as bananas, mangoes, avocados, zapotes, sugar cane, and pineapples), fresh ears of maize, tortillas, salt, chickens, and even horses, mules, and tanned buckskin.

Since the construction of the Pan American Highway through the hamlet of Na Chih between Tuxtla Gutiérrez and San Cristóbal, a small open-air market has developed on two days of the week beside the highway, where trails from Paste? and Pat ?Osil feed into the center of Na Chih. On Tuesdays and Thursdays women who have ridden the buses or trucks up from Chiapa de Corzo trade lowland products (fruits, baskets, and so forth) to Zinacanteco men who have brought maize from these three important hamlets. Some Chiapaneco men come, as well as some Zinacanteco women, but the basic exchange is between Chiapaneco women and Zinacanteco men.

Chamula. Since Chamula borders Zinacantan and the two ceremonial centers are only two hours' walk apart, there is heavy traffic between these municipios. Chamula's land area is relatively small for its population (approximately 40,000), and the result has been the development of numerous small home industries in Chamula (Pozas 1959; Arhuz 1963) which produce many items used by the Zinacantecos: rum, chicha, manos and metates, cooking pots, small tables and chairs, violins, harps, and guitars, high-backed sandals, black ceremonial robes, and so forth. The Zinacantecos purchase some of these from Chamulas in the San Cristóbal market; but in many cases they either go directly to the hamlets in Chamula where they are made or do their trading at the large markets that take place each Sunday in Chamula, and more especially on important fiesta days in the Chamula ceremonial calendar.

The Zinacantecos mainly sell surplus maize and salt in the Chamula markets, since the Chamulas with scarce land often need maize and have no salt sources of their own. There is some exchange of products between Zinacantan and other Indian municipios, especially Larrainzar, and the Zinacanteco salt merchants also sell their product in many other municipios.

San Cristóbal. The most important market town for the Zinacantecos is San Cristóbal, where the main market is in full operation every day of the year. There is an increase in activity immediately preceding important ceremonial days, but any morning between approximately 8 A.M. and noon this market, next to the Church of La Merced, is teeming with hundreds of Indians and Ladinos engaged in a complicated variety of marketing operations.

The major products Zinacantecos sell in this market are maize, beans, and salt. The maize and beans are surplus from their farming operations; the salt is sold by those who specialize in this trade. A special area of the market is devoted to the sale of maize, and two types of Zinacantecos are active in selling it: producer-venders and middlemen. Large numbers of producer-venders come in from the various hamlets of Zinacantan to pour their maize out in piles on burlap sacking or to sell it directly from the large burlap sacks. There are now nine Zinacanteco middlemen who work almost permanently reselling maize in the market, and three occasional middlemen. These purchase maize from those Zinacanteco producers who find it expedient to sell early in the day so that they can attend to other matters; they buy early maize in the lowlands and bring it to San Cristóbal; they "buy futures" to be delivered at San Cristóbal, Na Chih, or other locations at harvest time; or sometimes they buy from Ladino retailers when their prices are low. They make enormous profits, as much as 40 pesos a day (Capriata 1965), but they continue to grow maize themselves and to dress as Zinacantecos. Capriata's conclusion about this apparently paradoxical behavior is that, by keeping up their personal maize farming and their Zinacanteco dress, the middlemen are able to maintain a role definition as being good Zinacantecos and hence continue their rapport with fellow Zinacantecos who furnish the basic maize supplies for resale.

Minor items sold by Zinacantecos in the San Cristóbal market include eggs, flowers, and fruit, especially peaches. There is usually a row of Zinacanteco women selling toasted tortillas, and, as a side line, offering eggs, fruit, or mushrooms for sale.

Elsewhere in San Cristóbal, especially in the barrios of Santa Lucía and San Antonio, Zinacantecos sell reeds for the sticks used to construct skyrockets (*cohetes*) to the *coheteros* who live in these neighborhoods (Goldberg 1961).

The major items purchased by the Zinacantecos in San Cristóbal, either in the large market, or in various stores are generally for ceremonies, houses, farming and woodgathering activities, food, or clothing. For their ceremonies, they purchase rum, candles, skyrockets, incense, cigarettes, and musical instruments. For their houses, they buy kerosene and small kerosene lamps, locks and flashlights, metates, comales, cooking pots (made in Chamula), water jugs (made in Amatenango), and furniture, mainly small tables and chairs (also made in Chamula). For their farming (and for woodgathering), they purchase axes, machetes, hoes, and billhooks. For food, they buy coffee, rolls, brown sugar, fish products, pork, sometimes beef—all important for ritual meals—as well as candy and fruits, especially mangos, bananas, pineapples, and melons. For clothing, they purchase cotton thread and cotton cloth, palm for men's hats, men's sandals, net and leather shoulder bags, rubberized ponchos, kerchiefs, colored ribbons, and the large black hats worn by the upper-level cargoholders.

Other Ladino Towns. Tuxtla Gutiérrez, Arriaga, and Chiapa de Corzo are market towns whose importance to Zinacantecos has increased since the construction of the Pan American Highway and the improvement of bus and trucking service along this route. Many Zinacantecos now take their surplus maize to the large markets in Tuxtla and Chiapa for sale. A few highland fruits, especially peaches, are also sold there. The Indians not only sell peaches from their own trees, but also those purchased from neighbors. The fruit is then transported on horseback to the highway and trucked down to the lowlands.

Even more important has been the development of a whole new industry as a result of the highway and its rapid transit connection to Tuxtla: the growing of flowers for sale (Bunnin 1966). The major flower-growing villages are Nabenchauk, Pat ?Osil, and Zinacantan Center, which have the proper combination of temperature range, soils, and access to the highway to stimulate the industry. The major types of flowers grown and sold are small and large daisies, lilies, calla lilies, carnations, and gladiolas. Some Zinacantecos both grow and sell the flowers; others merely sell them. The flowers are carried to bus and truck stops on the highway at Na Chih and Nabenchauk whence they can be transported to Tuxtla within about two hours. Since they are highly perishable, the enterprise is risky, but, given relatively quick sales in the Tuxtla market, it is profitable. The Zinacantecos in the industry have detailed knowledge of the types of flowers that will sell quickly at different fiesta seasons in Tuxtla. Bunnin discovered that flower-growers, in contrast to flower-sellers, are average maize producers who fill spare time by cultivating plots of flowers. The sellers, on the other hand, tend not to produce much maize and in many cases might have emigrated from the community if they had not taken up the flower business. By engaging in flower-selling, they are able to lead in many respects a normal life in Zinacantan and at the same time spend extensive amounts of time in the Ladino world in Tuxtla.

Arriaga is important as an outlet for Zinacanteco fruit, especially peaches. Located on the Pacific coastal plain of Chiapas, it is a profitable place to purchase fish products for resale in Zinacantan. It is also the farthest that the vast majority of Zinacantecos have ever wandered from home.

Purchased Food

Although the bulk of the Zinacanteco diet comes from foods which the Zinacantecos produce, a number of crucial items are purchased either from Ladinos or from Indians in other municipios.

POSH. The most important is a clear sugar-cane rum called POSH (a word that also means medicine). This is produced either legally by the Ladinos in their *aguardiente* distilleries, or illegally by the Chamulas in homemade stills. It is distilled from panela, a type of brown sugar produced from sugar cane. The principal Ladino distillery is at Puhiltik, near Soyatitán. The Chamula stills are located in various hamlets within easy travel distance from Zinacantan, and there are now a few stills in Zinacantan itself.

The rum is manufactured in ingenious homemade stills improvised from various pots, kegs, metal coils, and bamboo tubes. Since this is a "bootleg" operation, our project field workers have not yet been allowed to visit one of these stills, but we have data on selected aspects of the operation. The rum, made from brown sugar purchased in the market in San Cristóbal, is of excellent quality, and regularly undersells the legal aguardiente produced by Ladino distilleries. For example, a liter of strong Chamula rum can be purchased for 6 pesos, while the current price of a liter of legal aguardiente in San Cristóbal is 7.50 pesos. The strongest liquor from the still is known as K'ISHIN POSH (strong liquor), while the liquor of lesser proof is called SIKIL POSH (weak liquor). POSH can be purchased by the *garrafón* (a heavy, glass jug which contains 17 to 20 liters), or it may be sold, transported, and presented to others in a standard set of smaller quantities.

Cuarta   small beer bottle (one-half pint)
Media   large beer bottle (2 cuartas, or a pint)
Límite   4 cuartas (or a quart)
Litro   5 cuartas (or a liter)

These smaller containers are pictured in Figure 49. The bottles, from left to right, are cuarta, media, límite, and litro. In front of the row of bottles are a large and a small shot glass of the sizes most commonly used by drink-pourers for serving rum.

A typical Chamula establishment that manufactures POSH not only is prepared to sell the product to take home, but also is set up as an Indian cantina for drinking parties. A trusted client may order a liter of "strong liquor" to be served to a group of his relatives or friends and be provided with a shot glass and small chairs on which to sit in the patio (if the weather is good) or inside the house (if it is raining). For a small additional fee the proprietor may often be able to provide harp and guitar music by members of the family to add to the gaiety of the occasion. The stills were interestingly described in a recent text written by one of our Zinacanteco informants. He writes:

> To prepare POSH in Chamula, they buy a large metal drum in San Cristóbal, and a wooden cask. If they don't have a cask, they use an old pot instead. They use the drum as a container to boil the chicha water, and the cask, or the old pot, to hold the panela. They pour cold water on the panela. But first, before putting in the panela, they put in what is called *madre del trago* which is a kind of yeast they buy in San Cristóbal. Sometimes they use sour maize dough, but this is not good for the smell of the rum. They also buy two meters of *culebra* (cooking coil made of thin copper pipe that can be bought at a hardware store). This is a special coil used only for rum. They wind it inside another pot, which serves as a cooler only. This coil is attached to the metal drum also. The rum comes from the vapors of the chicha. These vapors come up out of the drum and there is a bamboo tube which is connected to the copper coil which is curled inside the cooling pot. There is an opening in the cooling pot where

49. Liquid measures, left to right: *cuarta, media, límite, litro,* and two sizes of shot glasses

a little piece of the coil comes out and this is where the rum drips out. Where the coil is attached to the drum and where it goes through the cooling pot, they put some starch to secure both parts well and to prevent the vapors of the chicha from escaping or the air from coming in.

When they use four bundles of panela, they can produce one garrafón of rum. If they use five bundles, they get a stronger liquor. But if they use only two bundles, they can obtain only a half-garrafón of liquor. When the metal drum is small, they can produce 40 liters, but they can produce more if they have a larger drum and a larger pot where they can put more panela. Also, they perforate one of the lower corners of the drum, which they keep closed by means of one peg, while the chicha is boiling. When they finish making rum, they remove this peg so they can remove the chicha that is not strong enough anymore to produce liquor. This is what is called *supia*. In the first distilling of the rum, it takes eight days before the chicha is well fermented and ready to boil, but after this, it takes only a day and a night for it to be ready. The same fermentation lasts for five or six additions of panela. But after that, more yeast has to be purchased. The liquor is much better when it is regularly produced by one of these stills, because the drum and the pots retain the smell of the rum. If the pots are not used for a time, then it takes eight days again for the chicha to get ready to boil. It takes about a *tercio* [load carried by one person] of dry wood to produce one garrafón of rum.

Figure 50 is a drawing produced by the same informant explaining the operation of the typical Chamula still.

Chicha. Zinacantecos purchase *chicha* (YAKIL VO?—meaning "intoxicating water") especially from the Chamulas, although they produce a type themselves that is drunk during the fiestas of San Sebastián and Carnaval. The Chamula variety is made from sugar cane grown in the lowland communities of Magdalena and Santa Marta. The Chamulas purchase the juice of the sugar cane and bring it home in wooden barrels. The chicha produced in Zinacantan is made by specialists, who are engaged by particular cargoholders. It is brewed from brown sugar in large pots of water, to which is added either a charred ear of maize or a charred piece of sugar cane. This "mother of the chicha" (ME? YAKIL VO?) starts the fermentation process. It stays at the bottom of the pot and the manufacturers keep adding more panela and more water to produce more chicha. Small chunks of pineapple are added, and the chicha is ready to serve.

Salt. The frequently mentioned word ?ATS'AM is a Tzotzil variant of the proto-Mayan word for salt: ?AATZ?AM (Kaufman 1964: 100). Salt is of

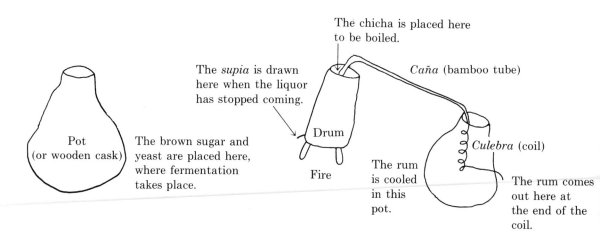

50. Diagram of a Chamula still

51. Zinacanteco salt-seller in the San Cristóbal market

crucial physiological importance to people who live in the tropics and who sweat as much as the Zinacantecos in their daily work. But more than this, salt has also taken on ritual significance. Not only does it invariably accompany meals, but it is also utilized in a variety of ritual contexts. Salt is rubbed on the patient's head in curing ceremonies; and salt water is used for divination and is held in the curer's mouth when he sucks on a patient. An important ritual takes place in the Hermitage of Esquipulas every other Sunday morning when the mayordomo from Salinas ('ATS'AM) arrives with gifts of ritual salt from the sacred salt well and presents them to the ranking members of the religious hierarchy and civil officials (see Chapter 22). Zinacantecos, however, generally use the salt, not from Salinas, but from Ixtapa, where it is produced and sold in cylindrical cakes. Many Zinacantecos are salt venders, buying the cakes in Ixtapa, carrying them on mules to the highlands, and reselling them in 5-centavo to 2-peso blocks in the markets of Zinacantan Center, San Cristóbal, Chamula, and elsewhere (Figure 51).

Other Foods. Next to rum, Zinacantecos probably spend most money for meat (beef, pork, fish). They also spend much for beer and various types of soft drinks, including the more expensive Coca Cola and the less expensive types bottled in San Cristóbal.

Some coffee trees are owned by the Zinacantecos, particularly on their ejido lands. A number of families, especially in the hamlets at lower elevations, pick enough coffee to sell; but most Zinacantecos purchase it at small stores in Zinacantan Center or in San Cristóbal.

The two other important types of food purchased from Ladinos in Zinacantan Center or San Cristóbal are KASHLAN VAH and brown sugar. KASHLAN VAH is a type of wheat bread, baked in round loaves and slightly sweetened, that is used in all Zinacanteco ritual meals. Brown sugar (see Benderly 1961) is used to sweeten coffee and atole.

Finally, there are a number of lowland products that are imported and sold in Zinacantan, or that the Zinacantecos buy in the lowlands. Dried shrimp and various types of dried fish are much used as an alternative to chicken or pork in Zinacanteco ceremonies. Lowland fruits, especially mangoes, melons, bananas, oranges, and pineapples, are in demand.

Economic and Social Aspects of Trading

The marketing and trading patterns, which have evolved over time and have involved the Zinacantecos in various economic transactions outside their tribal boundaries, have a number of critical economic and social functions. The transactions are a means of exchanging goods between the highlands and the lowlands, the Indians and the Ladinos in this bicultural society, the outside industrial world and the local peasant world, and various Indian towns that specialize in different products.

The highland-lowland exchange in central Chiapas represents in microcosm the kind of economic transaction that is of crucial importance in many parts of Middle America; some suggest that it is a major reason for the relative economic "richness" of aboriginal life in the region. Unlike, say, the Plains Indians, who lived largely on buffalo meat and perhaps a little maize grown during the summer, the Zinacantecos have long depended upon a dual environment. Indeed, the Zinacanteco lives in the cool, pine-covered forests of the highlands, but can enjoy mangoes in season in larger quantities and less expensively (100 for 3 pesos!) than even the twentieth-century American with his supermarkets. Furthermore, since basic subsistence crops such as maize and beans are harvested at different seasons at different altitudes, their year-round availability is highly dependent on these highland-lowland exchanges. The important fiesta days attract merchants busily transporting and buying and selling goods between the two ecological zones.

The Indian-Ladino exhange is also fundamental to the economic system, with the Indians generally providing the basic foodstuffs and labor for the Ladinos, and the latter providing mainly ritual and decorative products for the Indians (Aguirre Beltrán 1953). The Zinacantecos bring in maize, beans, and salt, and the Ladinos provide them with rum, ribbons, candles, cohetes, beef, pork, and even Catholic priests—all for ritual.

The exchange between the outside industrial world and the local peasant world is of course also involved in the Ladino-Indian transactions, in that the hardware stores and blacksmith shops where the Indians purchase hoes, machetes, flashlights, kerosene lamps, and metal locks are owned by Ladino merchants.

Finally, current economic transactions continue a pattern of trade among various Indian municipios specializing in the production of different goods that was probably aboriginal. Amatenango produces the water-jugs (*cántaros*) which are used with tumplines throughout the Chiapas highlands for carrying water from the waterholes to the Indian houses; Tenejapa grows and sells peanuts; Chamula, more diversified than the other municipios, produces everything from guitars to metates for sale; and so forth. Zinacantan specializes in surplus maize and salt for export to other municipios.

More than purely economic signals are transmitted in this vigorous trade between Ladinos and Indians and among Indians of various municipios. All transactions between Indians and Ladinos in the market, and to some extent in stores, are characterized by bargaining, the vender asking a higher price than he expects to receive and the buyer naming a lower price than he expects to pay. This continues until a mutually agreed-upon price is reached or the bargaining is given up without a transaction. However, careful study of marketing (see especially Zubin 1963) reveals that much bargaining takes place where the price is really set and the bargaining has no relation to the ecomonic outcome, for example, in the maize market between Zinacanteco venders and Ladino buyers. The Ladinos appear to be expressing symbolically their superiority over the Indians by engaging in aggressive bargaining behavior, even when both parties realize that the economic outcome will not be affected. The messages being communicated are loaded with expressions of Ladino superiority and Indian inferiority in a social situation. In general, the marketing behavior tends to express the basic patterns of social stratification in highland Chiapas.

The social aspects of economic transactions that occur directly between members of two Indian municipios are even more complex. Bargaining, to be sure, often takes place, but for many types of transactions there is also a pattern of requests accompanied by the presentation of rum, chicha, or beer and by ritual drinking that appears to be necessary to seal the bargain. For example, a Zinacanteco buying ceremonial high-backed sandals from a Chamula sandal-maker does not simply bargain for a price and order the sandals. He presents chicha and goes through a formal petition, requesting that the sandals be made. The sandal-maker accepts the chicha; they drink ritually together and in the process arrange details, such as the price and the time when the sandals will be ready. It is possible that this type of trade, surrounded by ritual talk and drinking, was characteristic of preconquest trade between the various Tzotzil and Tzeltal communities in the Chiapas highlands.

Much importance is placed upon economic transactions by the Zinacantecos. They are admirably astute in knowing the current price for every product they purchase, trade for, or have owned for years, and can make a visiting ethnographer feel entirely incompetent by asking, "How much was your flashlight?" or "How much did you pay for the jacket you are wearing?" The ethnographer usually has only the vaguest memory of the price he paid for these items, often purchased years before in New York or Chicago. But, unless he can produce an exact price, he will be considered incredibly stupid by the Zinacanteco questioner.

Loans

Since Zinacantecos participate in a money economy, we might ask how they acquire the requisite number of Mexican pesos to purchase the goods they do buy, not only for daily household use, but more especially for ceremonial activity—whether for small, less costly domestic ceremonies or for very expensive cargo positions when they serve in the religious hierarchy.

A few Zinacantecos save money and store it away in their houses; others keep on hand surpluses of maize which they can sell when the prices are favorable in the markets of San Cristóbal or Tuxtla. But much more common is a complicated set of loaning and borrowing patterns (Trosper 1966). When a Zinacanteco needs money, he goes to another Zinacanteco, most frequently a *compadre* (see Chapter 10), bearing a bottle of rum of suitable size. He goes through the proper etiquette of arriving and entering the house of the potential lender, then presents the bottle. If the potential lender accepts the bottle, he is obligated to give the loan. For this reason, there is a patterned hesitance (if not outright refusal) to accept the bottle, unless the motives of the visitor can be ascertained. If the bottle is accepted, ritually patterned drinking begins and the visitor completes his request for the loan, stating in detail why he needs the money. The loan is made, or promised for a future date, and more drinking takes place. There are some possible variations in the pattern. For example, a potential borrower may arrive at the house of the potential lender with two bottles of rum and ask for 200 pesos. The lender may choose to accept only one bottle and lend only 100 pesos. It is not considered good form to ask for the return of loans granted to pay for curing ceremonies or for the expenses of a cargo until the lender has some emergency need for cash. For example, if a time is approaching when the lender is going to be installed in one of the positions in the cargo system, it is quite proper for him to go to the borrower and ask for the return of the pesos.

A test of this procedure occurred during 1959–60, when Robert Laughlin was in the field and had loaned out some 5,000 pesos to various Zinacantecos. He discovered that near the end of his field trip, he could quite properly go to his various debtors and say, "I am about to leave for New York by plane. The cost of the ticket is almost 4,000 pesos for myself and wife and baby and now I need the money." He managed to collect all but about 500 pesos.

Loans to non-kin and for purposes other than curing ceremonies, funerals, or cargos are more likely to be due on a fixed date, and the lender will generally ask that interest be paid on the loan. The rates of interest are high by our standards, varying from 5 to 10 percent per month!

Most Zinacantecos are scrupulously honest about their loans. I have repeatedly had the experience of offering to pay a Zinacanteco for a day's work, only to be told, "Don't you remember that I borrowed 20 pesos from you last year . . . you don't owe me money . . . I still owe you 10 pesos."

Of course some men are notoriously bad about repaying loans, whether to fellow Zinacantecos or to visiting ethnographers. Therefore, the failure to repay loans frequently ends up in court, with the Presidente receiving requests for the arraignment of bad debtors (see Chapter 12).

Although few Zinacantecos borrow money from regular banks in San Cristóbal or Tuxtla, increasing numbers are acquiring funds by loans through the recently established federal warehouse system of the Mexican government. This system was established to provide a guaranteed price for producers and to establish a nationwide network of maize distribution, to protect the consumer from extreme price fluctuations (Young 1962).

It was established in 1959 with CONASUPO (Compañia Nacional de Subsistencia Populares, S.A.) as the parent organization. The federal government supports CONASUPO, allocating a certain sum in its annual budget to be spent in the purchase of maize. The money is deposited in the Banco Nacional de México, which serves as the banker and cashier of the operation. When CONASUPO buys maize, it is stored in the warehouse of ANDSA (Almacenes Nacionales de Depósito, S.A.). The system includes two loan banks, BANJIDAL and BANGRICOLA (the Banco Nacional de Crédito Ejidal, and Banco Nacional de Crédito Agrícola, respectively). These banks are responsible for certifying the maize producers and for buying the maize on behalf of CONASUPO. They have the additional job of loaning money to maize producers—BANJIDAL to ejido holders and BANGRICOLA to free producers or private landholders.

A maize producer who wishes to sell to the warehouse system must report to the appropriate bank before he plants his crop. If he wishes to borrow money, he can do so by going to the BANGRICOLA where his land serves as security for the loan, if he owns land. If he is an *ejidatario,* he goes to the BANJIDAL and the loan is made on the basis of the crop as security. In either case he must purchase obligatory crop insurance at a rate of 25 pesos per hectare of land planted by digging stick. In the case of the non-ejido farmer, the bank will not grant the loan until there is proof of ownership (a difficult step for most Indians), and an inspector must visit the site to certify the quality of the land. The maximum loan for land planted by digging stick is 350 pesos per hectare.

After the harvest, the producer sells his maize to CONASUPO by delivering it to one of the warehouses of ANDSA, receives a guaranteed price of 800 pesos a ton, and repays his loan. Despite the large amount of paperwork involved in all these transactions and the various deductions (for burlap bags, taxes, and so on) made from the guaranteed price, increasing numbers of Zinacantecos are utilizing the system—both for loans and for good maize prices.

The Economic System

Zinacantecos are engaged in an economic operation in which their own land and labor produce the basic necessities for their style of life (maize and beans to eat, houses to live in, clothes to wear). But they are also enmeshed in a complicated set of economic relations with Indians in other municipios and, more importantly, with Ladinos, for which they need

Mexican pesos to add to the basic necessities and to purchase an array of products that have become integral parts of their social and ceremonial life.

As Cancian describes so clearly (1965a), a large part of Zinacanteco resources is allocated not to the sheer necessities of food, housing, and clothing but to the "purchasing" of prestige by serving in positions in the cargo system and to defraying the costs of domestic rituals, such as curing ceremonies. Most Zinacantecos could meet their obligations for the basic necessities either by farming land that they own or rent or (if they control no land) by working as laborers. But to add to the basic necessities (for example, to buy a flashlight rather than using a pine-pitch torch) and to pay for domestic rituals and, more importantly, for the high costs of serving in the cargo system, Zinacantecos need surplus cash. Various alternatives are open for the production of this surplus cash. Salt-sellers make some profit and maize resellers make more. The flower-growers and sellers have been able to add to their cash income. A few Zinacantecos make small profits on their small stores in Zinacantan Center and in the hamlets. Owners of "talking saints" take in some income, until the "saint" is confiscated by the officials. Working for INI, on roads, or on coffee fincas is another possibility, but wages are still low and possibilities for surplus cash limited.

The most lucrative possibility is to become a large, entrepreneur-type maize- and/or bean-grower—either on lands that are controlled, via inheritance or ejido membership, or that are rented in the lowlands from Ladinos. Many successful operators have been able to borrow money from the Mexican government banks, hire laborers (mainly Chamulas), and plant up to 10 or 15 hectares of land in the lowlands. In good years the surpluses are such that they can not only supply family food with ease, but hold the surpluses in maize and beans for the best possible price in the market in late summer. The surplus cash controlled by these large operators is impressive by Zinacanteco standards: it can be converted into rapid movement through the cargo system and an achievement of power and prestige that reaches well beyond the potential for men without land or entrepreneurial skill.

To date, most of this surplus continues to be poured into the ritual system (either in cargos in Zinacantan Center or in domestic ceremonies at home). To be sure, new houses are often built of adobe brick and tile roofs and are of larger size; a man might own two flashlights rather than one; and the family may eat chicken or beef more often. But these costs are minor compared to the cost of 5,000 to 14,000 pesos for prestigeful cargo positions in Zinacantan Center.

Hence, while surpluses are being made by a segment of Zinacantecos, the expenditures tend to shift the cash from the private to the public sector quite rapidly via the costs of ceremonial life. The surplus is going up in smoke, in the form of fireworks, and down in drink, in the form of rum. The system has not really reached a point in which surpluses go into capital resources; furthermore, it is difficult to imagine what these capital resources might be since the milpas are too steep for tractors and the houses too scattered for efficient use of power maize-grinding mills (except in the Center and the more compact hamlets). The most likely immediate prospect is the purchase of more trucks (four are owned by Zinacantecos now) so Zinacantecos will not have to pay Ladinos high rates for transport of maize and people. Beyond this, the economic system is likely to continue at its present level of balance between subsistence farming and marketing economy for at least another generation or two.

Part III / Social Structure

7 / Social Groupings

The fifteen hamlets of Zinacantan are subdivided into three basic social units of ascending size: the domestic group living in one or more houses in a compound; the SNA, consisting of two or more domestic groups; and the waterhole group, composed of two or more SNAS.

The Domestic Group

The basic unit of Zinacanteco social structure is the domestic group that is composed of kinsmen, living together in a house compound and sharing a single maize supply. Interestingly enough, this social unit does not have a generic name in Tzotzil. One can designate a particular domestic group by saying "the house of" or "the houses of" and naming a particular man. But there is no way to talk in Tzotzil about domestic groups in general. Despite this, each domestic group is symbolized by a KRUS TA TIʔ NA, meaning literally "cross at the edge of the house." It might also be translated as "door cross" or "entrance cross," but since this cross is invariably erected on the terrace outside the door of the principal house of the domestic unit, I shall refer to it as "house cross" to indicate its relation to the dwelling house or houses of the domestic group.

The relation between the domestic group and the house cross is so close that a count of all these crosses in Zinacantan would indicate (within a small margin of error) the total number of functioning domestic groups in the municipio. The exact composition of these groups varies as the unit moves through a developmental cycle and responds to a number of economic and social pressures, but the closest economic cooperation, most of the socialization of the young, and the overwhelming number of daily interactions occur within this domestic unit.

Whenever a Zinacanteco constructs a house in a new compound and moves into it with his own maize supply, he erects a house cross on the terrace in front of the house. When a young married man moves out of his father's house and constructs his own nearby, he likewise erects a house cross. Henceforth, everyone entering or leaving his house in a ceremonial context must stop and pray at the cross on the terrace. The house cross serves as "a doorway" to the "soul" of the house, as well as a means of communication between the domestic group and the rest of the social system, between this small house compound tucked away in a maize-field and the outside world. On all ceremonial occasions, from domestic rituals such as curing, baptismal, or wedding ceremonies to a municipio-wide fiesta (K'IN), such as those for San Lorenzo or San Sebastián, the house cross is decorated in special ways with pine boughs and flowers, prayers are said in front of it, and copal incense is burned in a censer. (See Chapter 4 for a description of the cross and Chapter 17 for further details on rituals involving it.)

The house cross represents the smallest unit within the patrilineage. The symbolic focus for the domestic group living in one or more houses, it mirrors the unity of this group and provides a means of relating it to other parts of the social structure. It is the Zinacanteco form of the household shrines which appear throughout the Maya area, both in contemporary communities and in the prehistoric past. Many other contemporary Maya communities, especially among the neighboring Tzotzil and Tzeltal municipios of highland Chiapas and among the Mam-speaking groups in the northwest highlands of Guatemala, also erect house crosses on the terraces outside houses. Some of the Maya communities and municipios in highland Guatemala and the lowlands of Yucatán maintain altars inside the houses (LaFarge 1947; Bunzel 1952; Wisdom 1940; Redfield and Villa Rojas 1934). In prehistoric sites, for example, there is evidence of shrines, both inside the houses and in the patios of their compounds (Smith 1962). All of these data stress the importance of some kind of altar or shrine representing the domestic group throughout Mayan societies.

I have purposely defined the domestic group rather loosely as a group of kinsmen who live together in a compound and share a single maize supply. To understand the structure and dynamics of these Zinacanteco domestic groups, it is necessary to construct a model which takes account of what these units should be like in the minds of the Zinacantecos, as well as the many empirical variations observable in the field. One way of looking at the domestic group is to regard it as a segment of a patrilineage. Patrilocal residence and patrilineal inheritance of land ideally construct domestic units each generation that are composed of fathers and their married sons, who live with the fathers in the same houses, or in houses in the same compound. And, in fact, most Zinacanteco domestic groups are patrilocal extended families living in one or more houses constructed around a common terrace and sharing a single house cross. On the other hand, at any given point in time, many Zinacanteco domestic units are found to be "nuclear" families or combinations of widows and young unmarried sons, or even, rarely, matrilocal extended families, again with one or more houses in a compound.

The domestic group may also be looked at as a small group of kinsmen that must contain both men and women, since each sex controls technological skills that are required for the successful operation of any domestic unit. To simplify the Zinacanteco view, men are required to grow and bring home the maize supply and women are required to make the tortillas. By the most common arrangement a married couple provides this union of technological specialists, and one of the most important symbols of the marriage relationship is that a wife (and never anyone else) is expected to serve maize foods to her husband. But other combinations also provide maize-growers and tortilla-makers: widowed mothers with young unmarried sons; widowed fathers with unmarried daughters; women with illegitimate children; two old sisters, one widowed and one unwed, with an unmarried son of the widow; and so on. In general, the domestic group is composed of one or more related adults of each sex occupying at least one house in a compound and sharing a single maize supply and a common house cross. Normally the group consists of a large patrilocal extended family occupying several houses in a compound, sharing a common maize supply and house cross, and engaging in close economic and social cooperation.

The Developmental Cycle of the Domestic Group. If Zinacanteco domestic groups are examined on a flat time-scale, most of them seem to consist of patrilocal extended family units forming segments of localized patrilineages. But there is a great deal of variation in the system. My most complete data are for one of the large hamlets, Paste⁷, with a 1960 population of 1086, where I have done intensive field work. Paste⁷ has 246 married couples, who reside in the compounds of the husband's parents, wife's parents, or others, as shown in Table 3.

Table 3. Residences of married couples in Paste⁷

Residence type	Number of couples	Percentage
Patrilocal	199	81
Matrilocal	41	17
Neolocal	6	2

If the domestic unit is viewed as one stage in a developmental cycle (Fortes 1958), however, the observed variation assumes a regularity that reflects the two crucial structural features of the system: the technological need for both sexes, and the rules of patrilocal residence and patrilineal inheritance.

When the eldest son is married, after a long and expensive courtship (see Chapter 9), he ordinarily possesses neither a house nor land of his own. Following the rule of patrilocal residence, he moves his wife into his father's house and continues to work with the father on his lands and to share his maize supply. However, no young Zinacanteco really likes this arrangement. From the start he looks forward to having a house of his own, a desire shared by his wife who typically has difficulties adjusting to working under the general supervision of her mother-in-law. He works hard to pay off the debts of his courtship and marriage, to acquire a parcel of farming land of his own (either from the father's holdings, from the ejido, or from rental arrangements with Ladinos in the lowlands), and to accumulate enough resources to construct his own house. When, after a few years, he succeeds in reaching this happy state, he builds his house, either on a plot of land across the terrace from his father's house, or on a nearby plot of land his father gives him. When the house is ready, he moves his small nuclear family into it and begins to function independently and to form the nucleus for the gradual growth of a new extended family.

After a few years, the second son of the father marries, lives at first in the father's house, then moves into another house. This process of fission ordinarily continues until it reaches the youngest son, who inherits the house (because he has stayed at home, cared for the aging parents for a longer period of time, and paid for the funeral expenses of the father when he dies). Meanwhile, the daughters in the family marry and move out to live with their husband's families.

The sons ordinarily do not move very far away. If they stay in the same compound, the houses are literally next door to each other. If they move to houses constructed on lands given them by the father, but farther away, they are still by our standards close by. A move of 200 or 300 meters is regarded as a distant move by the Zinacantecos! In these cases, there is still much cooperation in farming, herding, carrying water, and gathering wood; the men still travel to and from the lowlands together and rent their lands as a unit from the same Ladino landlord, while the women pool their sheep for more convenient daily herding and fetch wood, and often water, together. But the families cook and eat separately, and the group does not have the corporate character of those in which the sons are still living in the same house or compound with the father and are still sharing the same maize supply and house cross.

If a man's wife dies before he does, he is expected to remarry soon; in fact, the widower states (as a regular part of the funeral ceremonies) whom he intends to marry while his wife's body is being carried out of the house to be taken to the cemetery! This is important to Zinacantecos, for some woman must make his tortillas. Occasionally, elderly men do not remarry; their tortillas may be made by an unmarried daughter, or by the wife of the youngest son, if he is still in the father's house. But more frequently the men die before their wives do, leaving a substantial population of elderly widows in Zinacantan. In these cases, the widow finds it difficult to remarry. She stays on in her husband's house and her maize may be provided either by her youngest married son, or often by a still unmarried son. Such cases result in what may be called "remnant" domestic families, in the sense that they persist for some years near the end of the normal developmental cycle of the domestic unit. They contain related individuals of both sexes, so that maize-growing and tortilla-making (and other tasks) can be carried out, but they are not reproductive units.

When the eldest sons' sons reach marriageable age and begin to import their wives to their fathers' houses, new patrilocal extended families are formed which persist until the next generations break off—and so the cycle is started all over again.

A number of factors may alter this model developmental cycle in Zinacantan. Daughters sometimes marry men who have no possibilities of acquiring rights to land from their patrilineal kinsmen; such men are brought to live on and work lands belonging to the wives' patrilineages. Or a father may have daughters only, and hence need a son-in-law in his house to help him with maize-farming. These situations account for most of the cases of matrilocal residence. Land at times has been scarce in the past (especially before the acquisition of the ejidos in 1940), and is becoming so again with the growth of population. This means not only that there are insufficient lands for farming, but also that house plots close to the father's house are scarce. Therefore, even though both he and his father would prefer that the son construct his house next door, the son may be forced to build farther away. Family quarrels (especially between older and younger brothers over rights to land) can lead one of the brothers to move farther away, perhaps even to another hamlet.

Viewed in terms of a developmental cycle, most variations in domestic groups are understandable as systematic changes in structure and dynamics. A good example is provided by the ʔAKOVETIK, who live in the waterhole group of BIK'IT VO? in the hamlet of Paste? and with whom various of our field workers have lived over the past ten years. When we first knew this patrilineage, in 1958, it was headed by Dionisio de la Krus ?Akov, an old man in his late sixties. Dionisio had six living children—four sons and two daughters. He and his wife lived in the central house with Maruch I, an unmarried daughter; Maruch II, married to Manvel de la Krus (different lineage), who had no land of his own; Marian, a son who had recently married; and Romin, the youngest son, still unmarried. The oldest sons, Chep and Shun, had left the father's house, built their own houses, and set up their own house crosses on plots approximately 20 to 30 meters from Dionisio's house (see Figure 52).

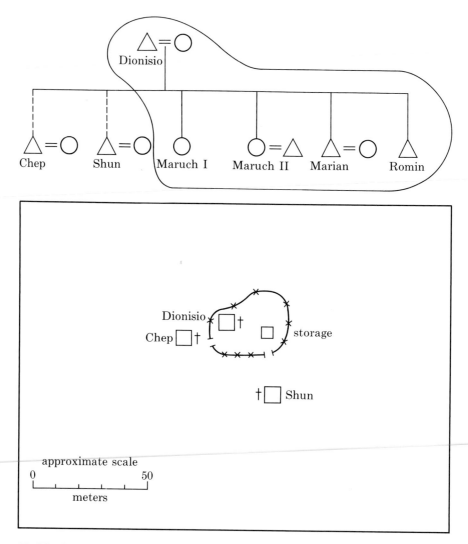

52. The ?AKOVETIK in 1958

By 1964, Dionisio's wife had died and the unmarried Maruch I remained with her father to make his tortillas and care for him. Maruch II and her husband, as well as Marian and his wife, had been given plots of land for new houses and had moved out and set up their own house crosses. Romin, the youngest son married in 1960. He and his wife remained in the father's house until 1962, when Romin also received a plot, built his own house, and set up his own house cross (see Figure 53). Although the ʔAKOVETIK continue to cooperate in lowland farming, and in sheepherding, horse-tending, wood-gathering, and water-fetching, all but one of the younger generation is starting a new branch of the lineage, while Dionisio and the unmarried daughter form a "remnant" domestic group.

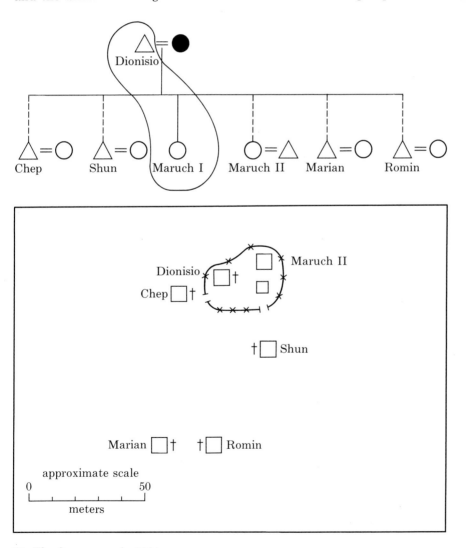

53. The ʔAKOVETIK in 1964

Additional examples of domestic groups in various stages of the cycle come from ʔApas, where we also have good data on household composition. Figure 54 displays a patrilocally extended family with the father and mother still living. (The numbers under the male and female symbols indicate approximate age.)

Figure 55 depicts a three-generation household with the widowed mother of the father still living.

Figure 56 shows the more complex case of a three-generation household with an elderly widow and her son who has been married twice and has children from both marriages living at home.

The family of Figure 57 is one in which both parents have died and two sisters live with a younger brother.

A case of matrilocal residence is diagramed in Figure 58, in which a widow's daughter and son-in-law have moved in with her.

The Zinacanteco type of relationship between the domestic groups, represented symbolically by house crosses and developing in cycles, is not an isolated phenomena in the Maya area. La Farge, in his study of Santa Eulalia in the Cuchumatan area of northwest Guatemala, writes:

> The ancestral or house-crosses tie in closely with the patriarchal social organization and with what appears to be a conceptually related ancestor-worship. . . .
>
> There can be no doubt that the name [of the cross which is KURUS KO-MAM] means "cross of our fathers."
>
> Such a cross is made by the patriarchal head of the house . . . and is placed by him on the house altar, where it is the central object. Images or pictures of saints or other such things are entirely secondary and subordinate. . . . Until the great family breaks up, generally at the time of the death of the patriarch, the married adults usually do not make crosses of their own; and, even after the breakup in many cases, the new households may continue for some time to depend solely upon the original cross of their fathers. In time, as the new households grow into patriarchies themselves, they will acquire crosses of their own; but allegiance to the original one will continue in vanishing form for a generation or so. If a son continues in his father's house he will use his father's cross, and in this way one may be handed down through many generations. (1947: 114)

The Structure and Functions of the Domestic Group. One of the prime functions of a Zinacanteco domestic group is of course reproduction and the socialization of the young. Some reproduction takes place outside the

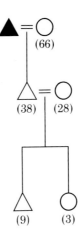

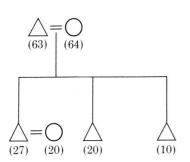

54. A patrilocally extended family

55. A three-generation household

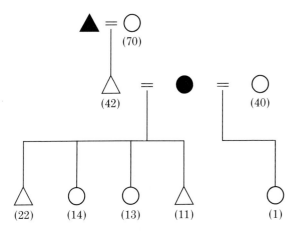

56. A complex three-generation household

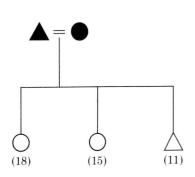

57. An orphaned household

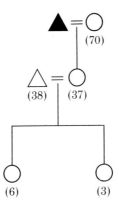

58. A case of matrilocal residence

structural boundaries of this domestic unit, and some socialization of the young is accomplished by other units in Zinacanteco social structure (such as the working-groups of men in the lowlands who teach young boys to farm) and by recently introduced institutions, (such as the Mexican government schools). Reproductive and socialization activity, most of which is carried on in the domestic groups, is treated in detail in Chapter 9.

Another set of prime functions are the economic and social activities that are most effectively carried on through cooperation among kinsmen. This cooperative activity more commonly involves a group of related women or a group of related men working together on their respective tasks. Thus, a group composed of a father and his sons normally forms the core of a working-group for house-building, for farming maize in the lowlands, for the management of their horses and mules, while one composed of a mother, her daughters-in-law, and her unmarried daughters forms the core of a working group for herding the sheep, cutting and fetching wood, cooking for domestic ceremonies, and so on. There is much sharing of utensils, tools, and ritual equipment within the domestic group; for example, if one of the houses does not have the proper gourd containers or all four colors of maize required for a curing ceremony, they are freely borrowed from another house. Finally, the domestic group is the crucial structural unit that provides the necessary people for all the roles needed in domestic ceremonies. The shaman may have to be imported if none of the men in the group is one. But all of the ritual assistants, as well as the women to do the cooking for the ceremony, are normally selected from the domestic group, and all the members of the domestic group normally attend the domestic ceremonies, such as curing, baptism, or weddings. The result is that the bulk of daily, face-to-face interaction in Zinacanteco society takes place within the context of these domestic groups.

Structurally, the most crucial relationships are between a father and his sons and between brothers. All are members of the same patrilineage and form a core of relationships for the control and inheritance of lands and houses and for the exercise of jural authority. The relationship between mother-in-law and daughters-in-law is also important, especially since they are left alone to manage the house, the children, the sheep, and to perform daily tasks while the men are away farming. The relationship between a father and his sons is usually warm and close, but there is considerable strain between older and younger brothers, especially over the inheritance and control of land. The mother-daughter relationship is likewise warm and close, and married daughters frequently run home to their mothers after marital disputes, especially in the early years of marriage. When this happens, the daughter's husband must appear with a bottle of rum, present it to his parents-in-law, and give long explanations and reassurances that his wife will be better treated at his father's home before the wife and the parents are persuaded that she should return. On the other hand, the mother-in-law's relationship with daughters-in-law is (predictably) filled with stress. The daughter-in-law is under pressure to perform well in a new situation for which she has been given little preparation. While sons spend most of their lives working under their father's supervision, the daughters move away from their parents' home at marriage. They come to know the mother-in-law slightly, if at all, before the wedding takes place. They must spend years working in situations in which an older woman who is not their mother initiates action and gives the orders for daily tasks.

Daily Life in the Domestic Group. A typical day in a Zinacanteco household begins before dawn, when the woman awakens, gently blows the smoldering embers in the hearth into a fire, and starts grinding maize for the day's tortillas. The daughters and daughters-in-law help her with the early morning tasks, bringing wood for the fire, boiling a pot of beans, grinding maize on a second metate, or patting out tortillas.

Although the whole household is awake by sunrise, the men and small children may linger on their petates (reed mats), for they have no such urgent chores during the early morning hours. Or the men may attend to their horses or mules, look over the crops growing in their compound, or watch the sunrise. But the air is chilly, and soon they gather around the fire to warm themselves and to visit leisurely. By seven or eight o'clock enough tortillas have been made to start the morning meal. The men, seated in a semicircle of tiny chairs, accept a gourdful of water from a kneeling woman and rinse their hands and mouths. The woman then presents them with tortillas, beans, and sweetened coffee, announcing each food as she places it before them. A tiny dish of salt is always set down after the food, and each man sprinkles a little on his beans or greens before he takes a bite. Torn pieces of tortillas are used to scoop up the beans, and the women replenish the supply throughout the meal by expertly tossing freshly cooked ones into the gourd container in front of the men (see Figure 59). When the men have finished, they hand each container back to the women, who finish any bits of food the men may have left. The women nibble as they cook and finish their informal "meals" after the men have departed; in contrast to the men, they tend to see food as "a continuous stream of tidbits" throughout the day (Strodt 1965: 3).

After breakfast the men, if working at home, may cultivate the maize, beans, or squash in their compound, repair a fence, or perhaps go to

59. Eating tortillas and beans

Zinacantan Center to perform some economic or ritual task. One of the women or girls lets the sheep out of the corral and leads them out to graze, taking her backstrap loom along so that she can keep busy weaving while she watches the animals on a nearby hillside. Other women and young girls either go to the waterhole to wash clothes and fetch water for household use or set off to find firewood. At the waterhole, they may spend the morning rubbing the wet clothes on smooth rocks; later they will spread them out to dry on rocks, bushes, or the ground near their house. On the return, each woman is bent forward under the weight of her waterjug, which a tumpline across her forehead supports and keeps in place on her back.

Every couple of days, the household supply of firewood must be replenished. The women and girls arm themselves with billhooks and ropes and walk over trails and rock-strewn milpas to a wooded field, perhaps an hour and a half away. Here the group scatters and each woman or girl finds young trees to cut down or large broken branches to split for firewood. When the pieces are cut, split lengthwise, stripped of bark, and fashioned into appropriate lengths, each worker carefully piles her pieces together, binds them with a rope, and attaches her tumpline. She hoists her heavy load onto her back with the help of a friend and adjusts the tumpline on her forehead, and the single file of barefoot women begins the hike back home, perhaps stopping along the path to gather a few greens for the midday meal.

A nursing baby always accompanies his mother on water and wood trips, either jogging along on her back supported by a large cloth which she ties in front, or, if the baby is older, sitting astride the waterjug or pile of wood that his mother is carrying. After being weaned, small children are carried and entertained by slightly older sisters, not yet strong enough to bear heavy loads of water or wood.

At noon the men and women reassemble for the midday meal, unless of course the men have been working in the lowlands or are too far away to return to eat. Both menu and procedure are similar to the morning meal, with men being formally served as they sit on their tiny chairs, and the kneeling women nibbling on bits of food as they prepare it and after the men have left.

During the afternoon the men and grown boys continue the morning's planting, hoeing, or other work in the fields or around the house. Their wives and sisters are more likely to do less strenuous tasks than they did in the morning—weaving, cooking, caring for the children, or even just chatting with each other. At sundown, the third meal of the day is served, followed by a period of quiet visiting around the hearth. By about 8 P.M. the family has normally gone to sleep, to recharge their energies for another strenuous day that will begin before the sun comes up again.

This "typical" day is divided very differently for men and women. Aside from meals, they work separately and at very different tasks; and even during meals, the male-female division between formality and informality, sitting on chairs and kneeling, being served and serving, and so on, is quite explicit. While doing their tasks, men are likely to spend long hours of uninterrupted work—hoeing all morning, seeding a field for hours at a time, or other continuous activities. Women, on the other hand, constantly switch from one chore to another, nursing the baby, sweeping the house, preparing maize dough, fetching a jugful of water, and generally spending very few hours of uninterrupted work—except, in a sense, when they gather firewood or do the wash. Even in these activities, however, they have many more opportunities to stop work every little while to visit, nurse a baby, collect greens, and so forth, than the men have as they work steadily in their fields (Rakoff 1965: 16–17).

The daily routine of the Zinacanteco household as just described is broken on numerous occasions. The unusual timing of meals during fiestas, the all-night rituals of curing ceremonies, the long periods for drinking and leisurely visiting on Sundays, the hours of walking or riding trucks or buses on market days, and the altered meal patterns for men when they work in the lowlands are all adaptations to meet the requirements of special kinds of days. These activities are each described in more detail elsewhere. In general, the sharpest break from ordinary daily patterns occurs during ceremonial activities, and Zinacanteco life rhythmically ebbs and flows between the two patterns.

The SNA

Zinacanteco domestic groups are embedded in two other crucial social structural units—the SNA and the waterhole group—which in turn are grouped into hamlets.

Just as Tzotzil has no generic name for the domestic group, so also it lacks an abstract way of designating the larger unit which I have chosen to call SNA. SNA means literally "the house of," and it is never used in its unpossessed form.* A Zinacanteco may say "SNA SHUN ʔAKOV," meaning "the house of John Waspnest," and in this context it will be understood as designating the domestic group headed by John Waspnest. A Zinacanteco who hears "SNA ʔAKOVETIK" (the houses of the Waspnests) knows from the context that a larger unit of social structure is being designated. For the purposes of this monograph, I have adopted the term sna to refer in the abstract to the grouping that is composed of one or more localized patrilineages; the sna is thus an extension of the patrilocally extended domestic group described above. Genealogical connections can be traced in these localized patrilineages, since they reach back no more than four generations. The members of a patrilineage live on adjacent lands which they have inherited from their ancestors. A patrilineage possesses some jural authority, in that important decisions for lineage members are made by the senior males. In addition to control of land, some patrilineages also own ritual paraphernalia used in ceremonies in Zinacantan Center. For example, the small drum used in the Fiesta of San Sebastián is owned

*Because sna is a "coined" word, which I have used to refer to a particular lineage-based social unit, henceforth it will be treated typographically as an English word.

by a patrilineage in ʔElan Voʔ, and a patrilineage in the VOM CH'EN waterhole group of Pasteʔ owns the ritual jousting target and lance used during the same fiesta, as well as the masks worn by the masked dancers who perform during the Christmas season.

The sna takes its name from the localized patrilineages. If it contains only one lineage, the unit is simply called by the name of that lineage. If it contains two or more lineages, it takes its name from the predominant one. Thus, SNA ʔOK'ILETIK, "the house of the Coyotes," contains not only the Coyote lineage, but also two smaller lineages that have settled next to the Coyotes and intermarried with them. From the data now available, it appears that the predominant lineage is usually the one which first settled on the land now controlled by the sna.

The snas vary in size from those containing one localized patrilineage, only four or five houses (Figure 60) and less than fifteen people to large ones with seven patrilineages and over one hundred and fifty people living in more than forty houses (Figure 61). But, whatever the history and number of patrilineages in a sna, its present boundaries and composition are made operationally clear by the K'IN KRUS ceremony, performed each year in May and in October for the ancestral gods and the Earth Lord.

Each sna maintains a series of cross shrines: some are erected on hills and designated as KALVARIO, which defines them as means of communication with the assembled ancestral deities of the lineage making up the sna; others are erected in caves and defined as means of communication with the Earth Lord. All of the shamans who live in the sna assemble in rank order to perform the ritual at the K'IN KRUS ceremonies. If a small sna does not have a shaman among its members, it imports one from a neighboring sna to perform the ceremonies. Small snas may also have only one, rather than two, mayordomos.

The K'IN KRUS ceremony has four basic parts. First, a formal ritual meal is eaten in the house of the outgoing senior mayordomo, who serves each year as the host. The expenses are shared by the outgoing junior mayordomo. Seated in rank order at the table (oriented east-west) are the senior male members of the predominant lineage of the sna, the shamans, and the four mayordomos (two leaving office and two assuming office). Chicken is always served and the meal is accompanied by the ritual drinking of rum. Second, a long prayer is recited over the candles, flowers, and incense by the shamans, who pray in rank order using censers with burning copal. Third, an all-night ceremonial circuit proceeds counterclockwise around the lands belonging to the sna; stops are made at various cross shrines, decorated with pine boughs, red geraniums, and other plants,

60. Aerial view of small sna in Paste?

61. Aerial view of large sna in Paste?

for offerings of violin, harp, and guitar music, candles, rum, incense, and appropriate prayers to the ancestral gods of the sna and to the Earth Lord. The ceremony concludes the following morning with a closing ritual meal back at the house of the mayordomo.

The K'IN KRUS ceremony occurs near the time of Santa Cruz in May. But since it is also repeated at the end of the rainy season in October, it probably has little to do with the Christian concept of the cross. Christ and the crucifixion are not mentioned, though the term KALVARIO (calvary) is used to designate ancestral shrines. Rather, the ceremonial circuit appears to be a symbolic expression of the rights of sna members to the lands which they have inherited from their patrilineal ancestors. By including rituals for these ancestral patrons, their ceremony not only pays appropriate respect to them, but also links together the descendants as common worshipers and members of the same sna. In this way the ceremony symbolizes the unity of the sna as a structurally significant unit in Zinacanteco society.

Patronymics

Beyond about four generations, the precise names of ancestors are forgotten, and exact genealogical connections generally can no longer be traced by informants. Through the generations, however, there survives an important system of patronymics that is still functionally important in Zinacanteco society.

Each Zinacanteco possesses three names: a first name, such as ROMIN (Domingo), SHUN (Juan), or MARUCH (María), all borrowed from Spanish; a so-called Spanish surname, like LOPIS (López), ʔERNANTIS (Hernández), TERATOL (De la Torre); and an Indian surname, for example, ʔAKOV (Waspnest), ʔOK'IL (Coyote), or CHOCHOV (Acorn). Both surnames are inherited patrilineally and retained throughout life, even by women after they are married and living patrilocally. The first name is given a child at the baptismal ceremony.

A man might be named Romin Peres Tanhol, but since the Indian surname Tanhol can combine with only one Spanish surname (Pérez), he may be identified simply as Romin Tanhol. Zinacantan now has sixteen Spanish surnames which combine with approximately seventy Indian surnames. (See Appendix III, Table 1, for a complete list of these names and their combinations.)

Zinacantecos now utilize a limited set of personal first names—twenty-seven for men, sixteen for women (see Appendix III, Table 2). With eight thousand Indians now living in Zinacantan, the total list of first names and surnames is very limited, and the problem of taking an accurate census is formidable. One sna in the hamlet of Paste? had, in 1960, seventeen men named Marian Lopis Chiku?, and in a few cases the men were full brothers living in the same domestic group! Zinacantecos themselves have trouble differentiating people, and the use of kin terms does not identify well enough for them. There is therefore a proliferation of nicknames; these are never used for direct address (except in joking contexts), but are nearly always used for reference. For example, one man with a squash-shaped head is called TSU (Squash), a guitar player is refered to as VOB (Guitar), and so on.

The meaning of the Spanish surnames is obscure, since they appear to have lost whatever functions they may once have had. It may well be that they are the vestiges of patrilineal units of the type described for Oxchuc by Villa Rojas (1947), who calls them "patrilineal clans" or by Siverts (1960) who calls them "phratries." Guiteras-Holmes (1961) and Pozas (1959) describe "clans" designated by the Spanish surnames for Chenalhó and Chamula. I shall use the term "phratry" to describe these Spanish surname groups in Zinacantan and reserve the term "patriclan" for the Indian surname groups, for it is clear that the Indian surnames are still functionally important designations of exogamous units. The Zinacantecos say that one should never marry a person of the same Indian surname, regardless of whether or not a close genealogical connection can be traced. This means that, while a man can marry some classes of relatives who are close from our point of view, other more "distant" classes are prohibited. Thus, a Zinacanteco may, and sometimes does, marry a mother's sister, or, more frequently, a mother's sister's daughter or a mother's brother's daughter, for these women do not possess his Indian surname and are not members of his own patriclan.

The Waterhole Group

The "waterhole group" is the next unit of ascending size in Zinacanteco social structure. Like the sna, it has no generic name in Tzotzil, but a particular waterhole group can be described by reference to the name of the waterhole (vo?) around which it lives.

Waterhole groups vary in size from two to thirteen snas, depending largely upon the amount of water available for household use and for watering livestock. This availability of water varies seasonally. During the summer rainy season the larger waterholes contain an ample supply and the smaller ones have enough to support many households; but in the winter dry season, many of the smaller waterholes dry up completely, so that the same number of households must depend upon fewer sources of water. This seasonal cycle in the availability of water leads to a corresponding cycle in the size of many of the waterhole groups. During the dry season, the groups are fewer and larger and draw their water from the major waterholes, while they are smaller and more numerous in the rainy season and draw their water from many waterholes. For example, in the hamlet of ʔApas there are eight waterhole groups drawing water from eight waterholes in the rainy season; in the dry season the same households regroup into four large waterhole groups drawing water from the four major waterholes that normally contain water the year around (Meadow 1965). Similarly, in the hamlet of Pasteʔ the waterhole called KORAL BURO regularly dries up in the winter season, and the members of this wet season waterhole group subdivide, with approximately half the households joining the waterhole group of SHUL VOʔ and half joining that of BIK'IT VOʔ.

The major waterholes typically have multiple openings: one is for household water; one is used for washing clothes; and a third supplies water for the livestock. Some maintain water in all the openings, even in the height of the dry season, but those that retain water in only one portion force their users to draw water for all three purposes from a single opening.

The waterholes are highly sacred, and myths are told about each of them, describing the circumstances under which the ancestors found the water and the way in which the waterhole acquired its distinctive name. The following myth is about one of the important waterholes in the hamlet of Pasteʔ.

"Little Waterhole"

There went a man, he went looking for soaproot, in the mountains, by "Little Waterhole." He went to look at "Little Waterhole." There, he heard a music-band, and so he went to see, he went to see what he heard, where the music was. But suddenly, it started to rain. Not knowing if the rain would go on, he went to sleep at the foot of a tree; he waited for the rain to pass. A thunderbolt came, and the man was hit by the bolt. The thunder passed, but the tree was destroyed; where it was standing, the thunder had passed. Still, the music was playing, and the man heard where it was. He went to see where it was, and then he saw that there was the water. It was a very small well.

When he saw it, he returned home. "There is a well," he said. "Where?" the others asked. "Over there let's go see it," he said. They went to look at the water, but it wasn't little, it was a big well. They saw how big it was and were frightened and cornets played at them. There was a cave there, and they went in, into the ground. Then they returned home. "Well, I only speak now so you know where the water is. I am going to die," the man said. "There I remained, one with the ground, there, in the ground," he said. In three days the man died. He said just before he died, "You can drink the water, I will look over it, but you mustn't lose its name, it is 'Little Waterhole.'"

Each waterhole group maintains a series of cross shrines. One of these shrines is at the side of the waterhole; another, on a high hill above, is designated as the KALVARIO for the whole waterhole group. At this KALVARIO the waterhole group's ancestral gods are believed to assemble and hold meetings to survey the affairs of their descendants and to wait for the semiannual offerings of white candles in the K'IN KRUS for the waterhole. This ceremony ordinarily precedes by a few days the various K'IN KRUS ceremonies for the snas that comprise the waterhole group.

The K'IN KRUS for a waterhole is performed by all the shamans living in the waterhole group. It follows the pattern of the ceremonies for the snas, except that before the ceremony the men all clean out the waterhole and repair the fences and crosses, and during the ceremonial circuit ritual is performed at the waterhole and at the KALVARIO, for both the waterhole and the ancestral gods who found it in mythical times. This ceremony appears to express the rights which members of the waterhole group have to draw water from their waterhole and their obligations to care for it properly. Control of rights to water is crucial for human and animal life in the Chiapas highlands, especially during the long dry season from October to May when supplies of water are strictly limited. Just as the K'IN KRUS ceremony for a sna expresses rights in land, so the K'IN KRUS ceremony for a waterhole group expresses rights over water. Because it includes rituals for the deities associated with the waterhole, the ceremony links together the snas that compose a waterhole group, and hence symbolizes its unity as another structurally significant segment of Zinacanteco society.

The waterhole group also holds some jural authority; men who refuse to contribute to either the expenses of the semiannual K'IN KRUS ceremony or to the labor of cleaning out the waterhole may be fined by the shamans or even excluded from using the waterhole. During the 1960 K'IN KRUS ceremony for the waterhole of VO⁷ TA PASTE⁷, I observed the highest ranking shaman holding court on the cases of three young men who had refused to pay their two-peso share of the ritual's cost. The event was handled much like the Presidente's listening to cases brought before the Cabildo in Zinacantan Center; it was finally resolved when the delinquents agreed to contribute.

The Hamlet

The next unit of ascending size in the social structure, and the largest subdivision of the total municipio, is the hamlet (*paraje* or PARAHEL). Although occasionally, the term PARAHEL is used to describe waterhole groups, it usually is restricted to the eleven official hamlets used by the Mexican government as a basis for taking censuses and keeping other official records, or for the fifteen hamlets which send principales to Zinacantan Center. Each of these hamlets has a special name, each slightly different customs, and the people in each are believed by the Zinacantecos to have distinctive characteristics.

The hamlet is composed of one or more waterhole groups. Two principales are ordinarily selected each year from each hamlet to represent the Presidente.* They are classified as senior (BANKILAL) and junior (⁷ITS'INAL), and it is their duty to carry out orders that come from the ceremonial center. In addition, they are expected to report hamlet affairs and problems to the Presidente each Sunday in Zinacantan Center.

Those hamlets which have government schools also have a *Comité de Educación* (school committee) composed of a president, secretary and *primer vocal*. One of the three is supposed to be on duty whenever school is in session, during which period he is responsible for rounding up children in the morning and looking after the school building and property. This office lasts for a year, after which three new men are selected to serve. If a K'IN KRUS ceremony is performed for the school (as it is in Paste⁷), the members of the school committee are expected to serve as hosts for the ritual.

Hamlet unity is ritually expressed by two annual ceremonies performed by all the shamans living within it. New Year (⁷ACH' HABIL) and End of Year (SLAHEB HABIL) can be conceived of as symbolizing the unity of the hamlet and its relationship to the tribal ancestral gods in the ceremonial center. Significantly enough, the two principales serve as the mayordomos

---

* Except for Chaynatik, Hoyihel, Yaleb Taiv, P'ih, Potovtik, and ⁷Ats'am which have only one principal each, and Na Chih which has three.

and play host for the ritual meals which begin and end the ceremonial circuit. This circuit does not include sacred places within the hamlet, but is rather a pilgrimage to offer candles and prayers to the saints in the churches and to the tribal ancestral gods in the sacred mountains around the ceremonial center. Just as the principales are required to report to the Presidente, the shamans must pay their respects to the tribal gods.

While all have these common features of social structure and ceremony, the variations in detail of cultural patterns and beliefs from one hamlet to another have led me to realize that, just as the Tzotzil and Tzeltal municipios have become differentiated over time from a proto-Tzotzil-Tzeltal community, so also the hamlets within a municipio have become differentiated in culture. Some variation may be attributed to differential acculturation to the Ladino style of life, but some is due to the fact that the hamlets are quite isolated from each other both geographically and socially. Most communication among Zinacantecos from different hamlets occurs in Zinacantan Center and in the market in San Cristóbal; for this reason market behavior and ritual behavior that occur in the cermonial center are constantly standardized. But the patterns of behavior and belief that are activated mainly at the hamlet level display more variation.

Patterns of Endogamy and Exogamy

One of the principal reasons each hamlet is so socially isolated is that it tends to be a strongly endogamous unit. When a Zinacanteco seeks a mate, he must not marry his mother, a *comadre,* or a girl with the same Indian surname. The third prohibition prevents marriage with sisters, or, as I pointed out above, any other woman who belongs to his patriclan. Men tend to seek spouses as close to home as the three incest rules permit. For example, in Paste?, where we now have precise data on 246 married couples, 120 wives were reared in the waterhole group of their husband; another 75 wives were reared in different waterhole groups but within the hamlet of Paste?. In short, 80 percent of the marriages took place within the hamlet. Almost all of the remaining 20 percent married men from the neighboring hamlets of ?Elan Vo? and Na Chih.

These data on snas, waterhole groups, and hamlets raise some intriguing questions concerning the ancient social structure of Zinacantan. I think it is quite possible that the sna unit was originally a localized patriclan and the waterhole group a localized phratry. The contemporary structure in which most snas contain more than one localized lineage and most waterhole groups contain two or more snas could have resulted from two complicating historical and demographic factors. When, in order to escape serfdom, Zinacantecos fled from lands that had become part of Ladino *latifundios* (large, rural estates; see Guiteras-Holmes 1961: 68–69), they probably attached themselves to already existing settlements, thereby complicating the social structure. Furthermore, there has been a marked demographic growth in Zinacantan in recent decades. The resulting land pressure has made it impossible for many lineages to expand through the generations onto adjacent lands as their members would have elected to do had lands been available.

If, however, we can assume that the contemporary waterhole group was originally a phratry, designated perhaps by an aboriginal equivalent of the Spanish surname, and that the contemporary sna was originally a patri-clan, designated by an Indian surname, then we would have had a functionally consistent social system that worked in one of two ways. First, if the phratry were the basic exogamic unit, each phratry living around a waterhole could have exchanged women with other phratries living around adjacent waterholes (see Figure 62.) Or, if on the other hand the patriclan were the basic exogamic unit—as the sna is today with its Indian surname—a series of exogamic patriclans living in a phratry around a waterhole could have exchanged women (see Figure 63). In either case, all marriages would have been kept within the local hamlet unit.

Unfortunately, there are few data that permit us to choose between these possibilities. The first is attractive in that it provides a hypothetical function in the past for the Spanish surname group that now appears to have none. But the fact that 50 percent of the marriages in Paste⁷ still occur *within* waterhole groups provides a strong indication that the basic exogamic unit was the patriclan, designated by the Indian surname, as it is today.

Calnek's 1749 census data (1962) indicate that intermarriage within Spanish name groups—especially the larger units such as Pérez and Hernández—was common in Zinacantan two centuries ago, but never exceeded 15 to 20 percent of all marriages, and this incidence could have occurred by chance. The same data show no cases of marriage within the Indian surname group.

This sounds as if the situation two centuries ago was much like it is today. If both patriclans and phratries were localized, it must have been at some time period before 1749. But, Calnek adds: "There is a small, but apparently significant, body of evidence suggesting marriage of daughters within the Spanish name group of the mother. Unfortunately, the indigenous name group of the mother is not known in these cases" (personal communication, December 26, 1961).

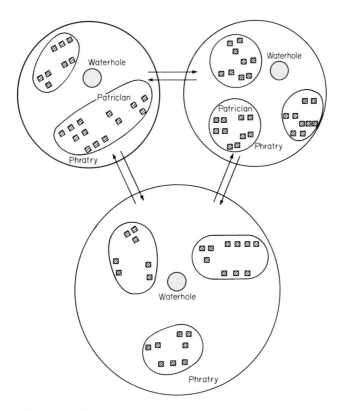

62. Schematic model of exchange of women among phratries

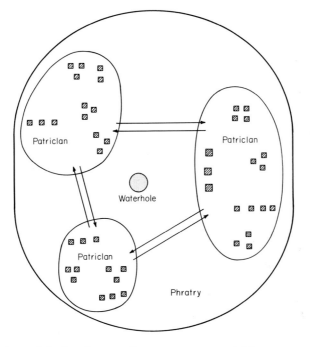

63. Schematic model of exchange of women among patriclans

Whether the system followed some kind of alliance rules between some phratries but not others is impossible to tell. Comparative evidence from another Tzotzil municipio (Chenalhó), and Tzeltal communities (Cancuc and Oxchuc) does suggest that by 1749 Zinacantan may have already been in the process of changing from a strongly patrilineal system to the somewhat more bilateral system that is now most apparent (Barbara Metzger 1959). On the other hand, it may well have been that Zinacanteco social structure was formerly quite similar to what it is today—with two or more localized lineages living together in the typical sna. In this event, the most important mystery is still unsolved: what is the meaning and function of the Spanish surnames in the system?

Victoria R. Bricker has suggested that "Spanish surnames may not mean anything except that they were assigned to the Indians when the Spaniards baptized them. Their only function may be Hispanization. They became *legal* surnames for the Indians, but were not sociologically important, since marriage rules are still based on the *Indian* surname" (personal communication, November 7, 1966).

There is evidence from Landa (Tozzer 1941: 98–99) that the Ancient Maya did in fact have a double surname system, but it is not known whether or not it carried down to the common people or whether it bears any relation to the Spanish surnames found today. It is interesting that the Spanish surname is combined with, and only with, a selected list of Indian surnames. This could be associated with some sort of "clan" or "phratry" which existed in preconquest times with each unit having taken on a single Spanish name. However, there are other possible explanations. The Indians may have been baptized en masse, with everyone present at one time given the same Spanish name. It is also possible that people from several unrelated lineages living on the same hacienda may all have been given the owner's surname as a means of distinguishing them from the Indians working on other haciendas. This remains in the realm of speculation, for only if the Spanish surnames replaced Maya patronyms on a one-to-one basis could we talk about them as "vestiges" of patrilineal units, and at present we have no way of knowing this.

An even more intriguing mystery is posed by a comparison of Calnek's 1749 data with contemporary names; at least 100 Indian surnames have been lost. Calnek lists a total of 19 Spanish names, combining with 176 Indian names. The continuity in Spanish surnames is very marked: 15 of the 19 Spanish surnames reported in 1749 still exist in Zinacantan. Four have disappeared (Alarcón, Alvaro, Díaz, and Gutiérrez), and only one (Martínez) has been added. On the other hand, a comparison of the lists of Indian surnames shows that not only has there been a loss of over 100 names, but that 27 new Indian names have been added since 1749.* Nine of the 27 are clearly either Spanish names, now functioning as Indian surnames (for example, MANTUHANO), or are Spanish loan words (such as VOTASH, derived from "botas"). The other 18 are new Indian names, like SHULUB TE? (Edward C. Calnek, personal communication, December 26, 1961).

I have no data to determine what happened to the more than 100 eighteenth-century Indian names which are now no longer used. It may be that these family lines migrated or died out because of various pressures of Colonial life. Perhaps a clue could be found in the historical records of the three Ladinoized towns that are probably offshoots of Zinacantan: San Felipe, San Lucas, and Ixtapa. The astonishing reduction in names has certainly contributed to the current problems Zinacantecos face in trying to distinguish among 8000 people with a more restricted set of names than they had with a substantially smaller population two hundred years ago.

The comparison with 1749 census rolls suggests a possible solution to the problem of how Spanish names came to function as Indian surnames. Let us assume that at given times in the past, pressures were placed upon Zinacantecos to use the Spanish rather than the Tzotzil naming system. One can imagine a young Zinacanteco working on an hacienda being given his father's Spanish name and his mother's father's Spanish name at time of baptism—in the Spanish tradition. He might have later moved from the hacienda back to a more traditional setting in Zinacantan; in the next generation, shifts to the traditional Zinacanteco naming system would have passed both his surnames (say, Gómez Rodrigo) on to all of his children, thereby starting another lineage. The incidence of Spanish names functioning as Indian surnames is slowly increasing. I can find only four clear-cut examples in the 1749 data: Gómez Rodrigo, Hernández Gerónimo, Hernández Marín, and Hernández Zárate—all but the third still important in Zinacantan today—but now there are at least seven such combinations, as shown in Table 1 of Appendix III.

It is also interesting to speculate about the origins of the Indian surnames. There appear to be at least four possible sources: calendrical names from the old Maya calendar, geographical place names, plant and animal

---

* I say at least 100 Indian surnames have been lost, because Calnek reports that 30 percent of the entries in the 1749 Census are illegible because of damage to the manuscript. It is possible that the 27 new Indian names are not new, but were listed in the illegible part of the manuscript.

names, and individual idiosyncrasies that provide stimuli for nicknames.

Baroco has collected some notes on the use of calendrical names in the sixteenth century in Chiapas from a book of baptismal and marriage records for the years 1557 to 1584 (1958). He has been unable to identify precisely the community that bore these calendrical names, but concludes that it was probably near Comitán; it is therefore not certain whether the names are from a Tojolabal, Tzeltal, or Tzotzil community, though Baroco thinks it was probably Tzotzil. At any rate, at least six of the contemporary Indian surnames in Zinacantan may have some relation to these ancient calendrical names.

There are strong indications that geographic place names have provided a few of the Indian surnames. For example, K'A'MOK (old fence or corral) could have been derived from a place where there was such a structure. Animal and plant names are common. For example: 'OK'IL (coyote), 'OKOTS (lizard), TONTOB (snail), and SHUT (type of wild beans), and CHOCHOV (acorn). Even more common are special characteristics of individuals, which probably provided the stimulus for nicknames that later became established as regular Indian surnames. For example, HILI'AT (long penis), HOL CH'O (rat head), MANI' (hooked nose). (The last-named may be derived from an ancient calendrical name, but the evidence is tenuous.)

There are interesting data from contemporary Zinacantan that nicknames and place names are in use which may eventually become established as regular Indian surnames. For example, a small man in Paste' is commonly called López Chicharrón (pig cracklings) rather than his true name, López TSINTAN; another is called Jiménez VOB (guitar) rather than Jiménez MANI' because he plays the guitar. In Nabenchauk the people who live by the cemetery are commonly called MUK'ENAL (cemetery). Another group of people in the same hamlet are called 'ACH'ELTIK (swamp), since they live by a muddy, humid place. Recent field data from Victoria R. Bricker (personal communication, November 7, 1966) on nicknames indicates that they often come to be applied to other members of the family. Of the 103 nicknames collected by Mrs. Bricker, 32 (30 percent) apply to other members of the family as well. It seems highly probable that this has been a source of new Indian surnames.

8 / Settlement Patterns

Zinacantan is a classic example of an ancient type of Maya settlement pattern: a ceremonial center with a sustaining area of outlying hamlets in which the bulk of the population lives. During Classic Maya times in areas like the Petén in Guatemala, the major ceremonial centers contained pyramids, stelas, so-called "palaces," causeways, plazas, and other ritual structures. In the outlying hamlets smaller pyramids and other structures typically served as minor ceremonial centers for the population in each hamlet. The hamlets in turn were subdivided into "cluster groups," "clusters," and "house groups" that were probably the residential aggregations of successively smaller units in a kin-based system of patriclans, patrilineages, and patrilocal extended families (Bullard 1960; 1964; Vogt 1964b).

Contemporary Zinacantan has a ceremonial center (HTEKLUM) and fifteen outlying hamlets. Approximately 400 people (including 51 Ladinos) live in the center; the other 7600 live in the hamlets (see Map 5). The Mexican municipio political structure has been imposed upon the ancient pattern so that the cermonial center is now the municipio's administrative center (*cabecera*), where political as well as religious officials serve their tours of duty; pyramids and temples have been replaced by Catholic churches; and there is a Cabildo and a handful of small Ladino stores. Life in the hamlets has changed less. There are Catholic-looking crosses by waterholes and on hills and mountains, but they function as a means of communicating with the ancient ancestral deities and the earth god. Three of the hamlets now have Catholic chapels. Otherwise, the basic settlement pattern seems to have changed little since the time of the Conquest.

The continuity of this type of settlement pattern from the prehistoric past into the present and the continuing predominance of the pattern in contemporary Maya communities raises the intriguing question of its determinants. Since the pattern is the predominant one found in both highlands and lowlands, and in both ancient and modern Maya communities, it can be argued that the Maya have long had a model of a preferred

Map 5

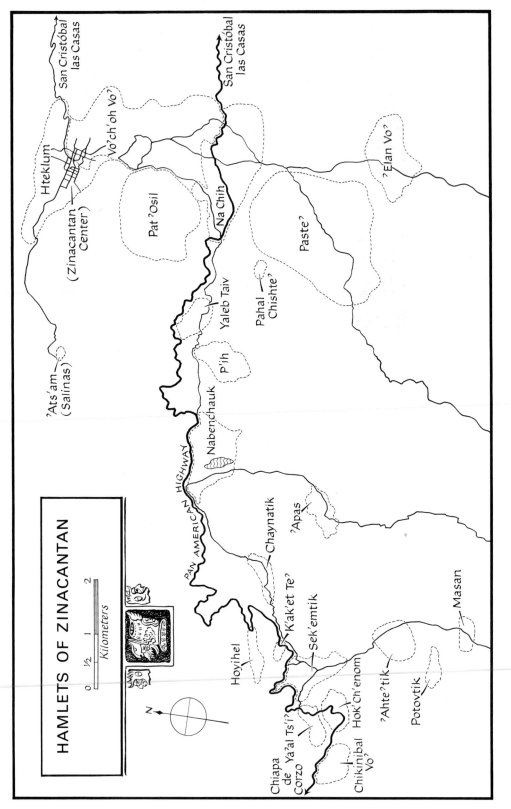

HAMLETS OF ZINACANTAN

Kilometers

0   ½   1   2

N

San Cristóbal las Casas

San Cristóbal las Casas

ʔAts'am (Salinas)

Hteklum

Voʔchʔoh Voʔ

(Zinacantan Center)

Pat ʔOsil

Na Chih

ʔElan Voʔ

Pasteʔ

Pahal Chishteʔ

Yaleb Taiv

Pʔih

Nabenchauk

PAN AMERICAN HIGHWAY

Chaynatik

ʔApas

Kʔakʔet Teʔ

Sekʔemtik

Hoyihel

Chiapa de Corzo

Yaʔal Tsiʔ

Chikinibal Voʔ

HokʔChʔenom

ʔAhteʔtik

Potovtik

Masan

type of settlement pattern and have implanted it on the landscape as geographical and political conditions permit. On the other hand, some critical ecological features, such as the relative availability of household water during the dry season, may account for the similarities observed in both highlands and lowlands. Further research on this question of "cultural" versus "ecological" determinants is currently underway as part of the Harvard Chiapas Project.

Zinacantan Center

Zinacantan Center is quite literally the center of the Zinacanteco universe. Not only is the ceremonial and political life of the municipio focused here, but there is even a small mound near the center which is called MISHIK' BALAMIL ("the navel of the world").

The center is located in a well-watered valley at 2200 meters and is surrounded with a series of impressive mountains. The streets are now laid out in a grid pattern—a feature found only in the center, not in any of the hamlets (Map 6). There are three Catholic chapels: San Lorenzo (by far the most important), San Sebastián (connected by a straight trail, resembling an ancient causeway, with San Lorenzo), and the Hermitage of Señor Esquipulas, near San Lorenzo. Across the street from the churchyard of San Lorenzo is the Cabildo, with jail attached, where the civil officials headquarter and carry out their duties. There is also a federal school, an INI clinic, and a series of small stores.

To the east at the upper end of the valley, one Ladino ranch, called San Nicolás, remains. Part of the lands of this ranch were taken over by the Zinacanteco ejido, and in turn part of the ejido was taken over by INI for an agricultural experiment station (see Figure 64).

Even more important to Zinacantecos are the sacred places in and around Zinacantan Center, especially the sacred mountains, waterholes, and cross-shrines (see Map 8). These sacred places symbolically represent "tribal" as opposed to "hamlet" gods; because of them the presence of Zinacantecos is required in the ceremonial center, even when they are not serving in a cargo or civil position and have no legal business to settle with the Presidente.

A special problem arises in connection with the distinction between Zinacantan Center and the hamlet of Voʔch'oh Voʔ (see Map 5). The western border of the hamlet of Voʔch'oh Voʔ is just across a small stream (NINAB CH'ILOʔ) from the land plots and houses that are regarded as part of Zinacantan Center. To the outsider, this valley section of the hamlet (which continues on across the mountains to the south and east) might

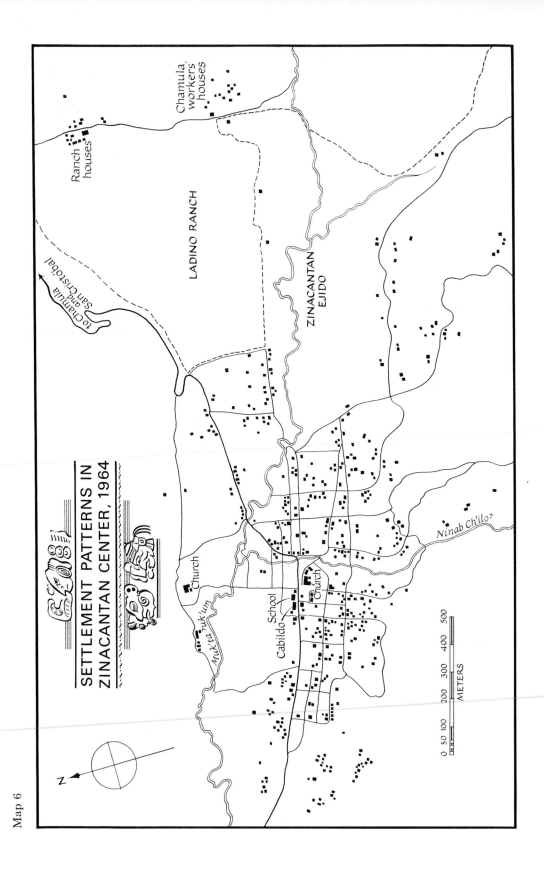

SETTLEMENT PATTERNS IN
ZINACANTAN CENTER, 1964

Ranch
houses

Chamula
workers'
houses

LADINO RANCH

to Chamula
and San Cristóbal

ZINACANTAN
EJIDO

Church

Muk'ta 'uk'um

Cabildo

School

Church

Ninab Ch'ilo?

0 50 100   200   300   400   500
              METERS

N

Map 6

64. Aerial view of Zinacantan Center

appear to be a part of Zinacantan Center, especially since many of the sacred waterholes and mountains are either in Voʔchʼoh Voʔ or beyond it to the east. Furthermore, many of the cargoholders serving their year in office live in houses that they own or rent in Voʔchʼoh Voʔ. But Zinacantecos still make a clear conceptual distinction between Zinacantan Center proper and this bordering hamlet. What may have happened is that the population of Voʔchʼoh Voʔ expanded from the hills to the south and east, began to settle in the valley bottom, and kept on expanding until they reached the borders of the ancient sacred ceremonial area of the center. Alternatively, it is possible that residents of Zinacantan Center acquired plots of land and moved away from the heart of the settlement in search of peace and quiet.

Movement between Center and Hamlets

Of the approximately three hundred and fifty Zinacantecos who live in the center, about two hundred are permanent residents—many own farmlands in the valley or nearby; a few own small stores or work for INI; others earn their living largely by engaging in ritual activity (as shamans, musicians, or sacristans, who are given food and drink in connection with performance of ceremonies). The approximately one hundred fifty others are temporary residents in Zinacantan Center—important cargoholders and their families who either own or have rented houses there for their year in office. These annually installed cargoholders provide a changing population that moves between the hamlets and the center. Other ceremonial movements that link the center with the hamlets are the coming of the many cargoholders' assistants to the center for important rituals; the daily arrival of curing parties to visit the temples and the sacred mountains in their ceremonial circuits; the arrival of mayores to collect water from the seven sacred waterholes for bathing the patients and the chickens in curing ceremonies; the arrival of groups of shamans to perform the Year Renewal ceremonies—three times a year for the whole municipio, twice a year for most of the hamlets; and the importation of ritual paraphernalia from the hamlets to the center.

In addition, the large fiestas such as those for San Lorenzo and San Sebastián bring an estimated 4000 to 5000 Zinacantecos into Zinacantan Center to watch the ceremonies and to engage in the drinking, dancing, and other social activities accompanying these affairs.

Although ceremonial life plays a more profound role in linking the center and the hamlets, important political functions provide additional links: the Sunday reports of the Principales to the Presidente at the Cabildo, the meetings of the members of the Ejido Committee in front of the town hall, and the daily disputes brought to the Presidente and his assistants for litigation. For municipal works, such as building and repairing religious and civil buildings, Nabenchauk traditionally provides the lumber, Paste? supplies the lime, and the other hamlets provide the porters to carry these materials to the center.

Finally, there are economic links that involve movement of personnel between the hamlets and the center. These are less important now than the links between the hamlets and the town of San Cristóbal. Nevertheless, on important fiesta days there is a large market beside the church of San Lorenzo where there is a brisk sale of such products as chicha from Chamula, salt from Ixtapa, lowland fruits from Ixtapa and San Lucas, and peanuts from Tenejapa. An especially important motivation for attending these markets is the expectation that young men will at this time purchase nets full of food, bread, and so on, for the families of their fiancées.

The Contemporary Hamlets

Zinacantan has fifteen hamlets that are recognized officially by Zinacantecos in that each has at least one, and normally two, principales, whose duty it is to represent the Cabildo in their hamlets and vice versa. One or both normally report to the Presidente each Sunday in the center; they carry official messages to their hamlets, collect "taxes" to help defray the expenses of major fiestas, and also have some ritual duties, especially at the Year Renewal ceremonies (described in Chapter 20). In addition, each hamlet is named; its borders are clearly known to its inhabitants; and each is said by the Zinacantecos to have special characteristics. In population (according to the 1960 census) they range from 121 (Chaynatik) to 1227 (Nabenchauk).

According to the Mexican Census, taken every decade, the municipio of Zinacantan has only eleven hamlets. The other four recognized by Zinacantecos are small and are included for convenience with larger, neighboring hamlets. Table 4 lists these hamlets in order of size and indicates which smaller hamlets the Mexican Census has included in the eleven. It also provides data on the population, elevation, special ceremonial characteristics and possessions, and number of principales for each of the fifteen.

Nabenchauk. Nabenchauk, the largest hamlet, is concentrated in a beautiful mountain valley which contains a number of springs and water-holes and is surrounded by precipitous limestone hills (Figure 65). The

Table 4. The hamlets of Zinacantan

Name	Translation	1960 population	Approximate elevation in meters	Number of principales	Special Ceremonial characteristics or possessions
Nabenchauk	lake of the lightning	1227 (including 12 Ladinos)	2300	2	chapel dedicated to Virgen de Guadalupe
Paste?	chunk of wood	1086	2350	2	1 saint; jousting target and lances; torito painters; sacred candleholder and censermaker.
Na Chih	house of the sheep	915	2300	3	none known
Vo?ch'oh Vo?	five waterholes	914	2200–2350	2	waterhole from which water is drawn for curing ceremonies
?Apas	?	704	2150	2	chapel dedicated to Señor Esquipulas
Sek'emtik	?	672 (including 11 Ladinos)	1900	2	serves as minor ceremonial center
?Ats'am (Salinas)	salt	433 (including 20 Ladinos)	1700	1	chapel dedicated to Virgen del Rosario
?Elan Vo?	?	400 (including 20 Chamulas)	2200	2	T'ENT'EN
Pat ?Osil	backland	347	2300	2	trousers used by capitanes
Hok' Ch'enom	?	300	1700	2	none known
Chaynatik	?	121	2400	1	none known
Yaleb Taiv	fallen frost	included in census with Chaynatik	2400	1	none known
P'ih	alert, or clever	included in census with Chaynatik	2400	1	none known
Hoyihel	?	included in census with Sek'emtik	2000	1	none known
Potovtik	place of guayaba fruit	included in census with Sek'emtik	1600	1	none known

65. Aerial view of Nabenchauk

valley drains into a lake at the southwest corner, and the lake in turn drains out through a fissure in the limestone, or so-called *sumidero*. This lake, believed to be "the lake of the lightning," inspired the name for the hamlet. During the dry season the sumidero carries off much of the accumulated water and the lake is small, but during the summer rainy season, it expands to cover a substantial area. The houses are therefore concentrated on the eastern, upper side of the valley and on the steep hill to the west to avoid being flooded during the rainy season. The Pan American Highway now skirts the northern edge of the valley as it passes from Tuxtla to San Cristóbal, giving Nabenchauk a major means of transportation for people and maize, either to the market in San Cristóbal or to Tuxtla. It also makes possible the sale of flowers from the flower-growing industry (see Bunnin 1963). The flowers are sold locally by small boys who hold up bunches of gladiolas, daisies, and carnations, attempting to flag down passing cars to sell their products; or they are transported by bus or truck to the markets in San Cristóbal, or, more frequently, in Tuxtla.

The hamlet contains a school, a small chapel dedicated to the Virgen de Guadalupe, a couple of small stores, which sell rum, candles, cigarettes, kerosene, and other miscellaneous items, and a Cabildo where an Agente Municipal copes with local problems of law and order. Nabenchauk has been an *agencia* (agency) for some years, and hence has its own civil officials. There has been constant pressure over the past fifteen years for Nabenchauk to become independent of Zinacantan Center, and this political pressure has been important in the formation of two major factions that are constantly contending with each other for power and influence within the hamlet.

The Catholic chapel, a relatively recent construction, was the result of the Catholic hierarchy's move against Protestant missionary activity. In the 1940's a Protestant missionary and his family lived in Nabenchauk for a few years and attempted to convert the people. Although the people of Nabenchauk liked and admired him personally, they rejected his efforts to convert them. And when the Catholic hierarchy stepped into the situation, the missionary was evicted from the hamlet and a chapel constructed and dedicated to the Virgen de Guadalupe. The presence of the chapel has added two positions (Junior and Senior Mayordomo of the Virgen de Guadalupe) to the cargo system of Zinacantan (see Chapter 11). These mayordomos are especially active ceremonially during the annual Fiesta de la Virgen de Guadalupe (December 12), but they also perform flower changes in the Chapel and are responsible for the safe transport of the Virgin when she is taken to Zinacantan Center for the fiestas of San Lorenzo, San Sebastián, Esquipulas, and Cuarto Viernes.

Paste?. Paste?, located in high terrain south of the Pan American Highway, is almost as large as Nabenchauk, and much more dispersed (see Map 7). Elevations range from 2100 to 2400 meters, with an average of 2350. The name of the hamlet derives from the name of its largest waterhole VO? TA PASTE?, located on the southern border where the land begins to fall off in a descent of over 1800 meters into the lowlands of the Grijalva River. Two explanations for the origin of the name are given: some say the earlier settlers around the waterhole were noted for working with wood products; others attribute the name to the presence of a sacred tree beside the waterhole, placed there by the ancestral god who found the waterhole in the mythological past.

Paste? is noted for having a relatively large number of special items of ceremonial paraphernalia and ritual specialists whose services or products are needed in cargo ceremonies in Zinacantan Center. The jousting target (K'OLTISHYO) and lances (VARETIK) used for the jousting in the Fiesta of San Sebastián are kept by a lineage in one of the waterhole groups; the same lineage is called upon to paint the reed mat bull that is used in the dance with the masked dancers (MAMALETIK) and unmasked transvestite dancers (ME?CHUNETIK) during the Christmas season; this localized lineage is therefore referred to as PINTOLETIK (Painters). In another waterhole group lives a specialist in the making of the sacred candleholders and sacred censers for ceremonies in Zinacantan Center. Finally, one of the houses in Paste?, although not involved with ceremonial in Zinacantan Center, owns and maintains a small saint figure that is important in the K'IN KRUS ceremony for the waterhole of VO? TA PASTE?.

Na Chih. Na Chih, with a population of 915, is located in a mountain valley between Vo?ch'oh Vo? on the north and Paste? on the south. Its valley, unlike that of Nabenchauk, is open to the west and drains into a precipitous barranca that carries the water down into the lowlands through the neighboring municipio of Ixtapa. The dispersal of houses is somewhere between the more compact pattern found in Nabenchauk or ?Apas and the more scattered pattern found in Paste? (see Figure 66).

The hamlet contains a large government school and a number of small Indian-owned stores, selling the usual rum, soft drinks, cigarettes, candles, and other items. Since Na Chih is bisected by the Pan American Highway, it is more profoundly affected by this transportation artery than any other Zinacanteco hamlet. The highway has hazards as well as advantages. Since it is straight for over a mile at this point, cars roar through the hamlet at high speeds, and not infrequently strike sheep, mules, horses, and even children on the highway. A few years ago, after two children were killed, the people of Na Chih moved to "encapsulate" this section of the Pan

66. Aerial view of Na Chih

American Highway into their rituals in order to cancel out the "evil." Cross shrines were erected where the highway enters and leaves the hamlet, and a special ceremonial circuit is now performed each year at which the shamans say prayers and make offerings to the ancestral gods, attempting to offset the hazards of this modern invasion of their hamlet by the twentieth century transportation system. (See Chapter 24 for an analysis of this process of "encapsulation.")

Voʔch'oh Vo. This hamlet of 914 people is located in the upper or eastern end of the valley of Zinacantan, and extends over the hills that separate it from Na Chih to the south. The portion located in the valley has a relatively compact settlement pattern (like Nabenchauk), but the house compounds are more dispersed in the higher elevations toward Na Chih. Perhaps because it is so close to Zinacantan Center, it has no important stores, and no school, chapel, or other special ceremonial features, except for its sacred waterhole.

ʔApas.* ʔApas is substantially smaller than the four large hamlets described above, and is one of the most compactly settled hamlets (see Figure 67). It is about an hour by trail southwest of Nabenchauk and at least 150 meters lower in elevation. Its houses are located on a relatively flat bench, wedged in between a rim of limestone mountains to the south and a series of precipitous barrancas on the north. The site contains twelve waterholes, providing ample water for the population and livestock. Surplus drainage flows into the barrancas and from there into the lowlands toward Chiapa de Corzo. Although there are no stores of consequence, there is a federal schoolhouse and a recently constructed Catholic chapel devoted to Señor Esquipulas.

ʔApas also performs two Year Renewal ceremonies, for the New Year and Middle of the Year, at which all of the shamans perform, and for which the two principales serve as hosts. Since the hamlet has a Catholic chapel and four cargo positions attached to the saints in the church, the people also perform ceremonies for the major saint, Señor Esquipulas. A very unusual cemetery (with small thatched roofs erected over the graves) is maintained at the edge of the trail leading in from Nabenchauk.

ʔApas is subdivided into waterhole groups (seven in the rainy season, four in the dry season) and about twenty snas. Instead of holding separate K'IN KRUS ceremonies for each waterhole and sna, as is done in the more dispersed areas of Pasteʔ, the hamlet has only one K'IN KRUS ceremony which makes a circuit and presents offerings at all of the crosses associated

---

*For data on ʔApas, I am especially indebted to George A. Collier, who wrote his PhD dissertation on this hamlet, and to Richard Meadow, who worked with ʔApas data for his Freshman Seminar paper (May 1965).

67. Aerial view of ʔApas

with all of the waterholes. This produces a highly compressed and abbreviated ceremonial structure. Ritually, the entire hamlet is treated as a single group, and the same ceremony that serves for the waterhole also serves the functions provided for in most neighborhoods of Paste? by the separate K'IN KRUS ceremonies for snas.

Of great importance to the social organization of ?Apas is the seasonal cycle from the rainy to the dry season. In the rainy season there are seven waterhole groups drawing water from seven dependable waterholes. But in the dry season, the number of waterholes with a dependable water supply is reduced to four and a regrouping places all of the residents within four larger waterhole groups. This cycle is similar to the situation in KORAL BURO in Paste? where the waterhole dries up during the dry season and the lineages living there take water from SHUL VO? or BIK'IT VO?, and participate in the K'IN KRUS ceremonies of these waterhole groups.

Sek'emtik. Sek'emtik is a sizable hamlet slightly smaller than ?Apas, distributed in several units along both sides of the Pan American Highway in the rugged terrain between Nabenchauk and Hok' Ch'enom (see Map 5). It contains three features of importance to the ceremonial life of the hamlets extending from Sek'emtik to the western edge of the municipio border: a major sacred mountain called K'UK CH'EN (named after K'UK TE?, a tree which grows around this particular type of rock formation) which is alternatively called MUK'TA VITS, and a nearby KALVARIO, both of which are visited by ritual parties from as far away as Hok' Ch'enom. It also contains a large cemetery where, until recently, people from this western zone of the municipio were buried. These features suggest that within this western zone of Zinacantan, Sek'emtik may have once served as a ceremonial center in much the same respect that Zinacantan Center now serves for the entire municipio.

?Ats'am. ?Ats'am (salt), called *Salinas* in Spanish, is one of the most interesting and distinctive hamlets. It is located at the bottom of a very precipitous barranca west of Zinacantan Center and near the route of the ancient wagon road that connected Ixtapa with the center and San Cristóbal. It is relatively small, even including the houses located further downstream (at Tierra Blanca), and the houses are compactly located in a small space that is wedged between the walls of the barranca (see Figure 68).

The most distinctive feature of ?Ats'am is a sacred salt well located just east of the Catholic chapel. The opening to the well consists of a treetrunk from an oak (TULAN) tree with a hole chiseled through the center. This meter-high log is called a HOM (canoe). The salt water is pulled out in small buckets and boiled in an open oven in the Mayordomo's house, leaving the much-prized salt which is delivered to the cargoholders in the

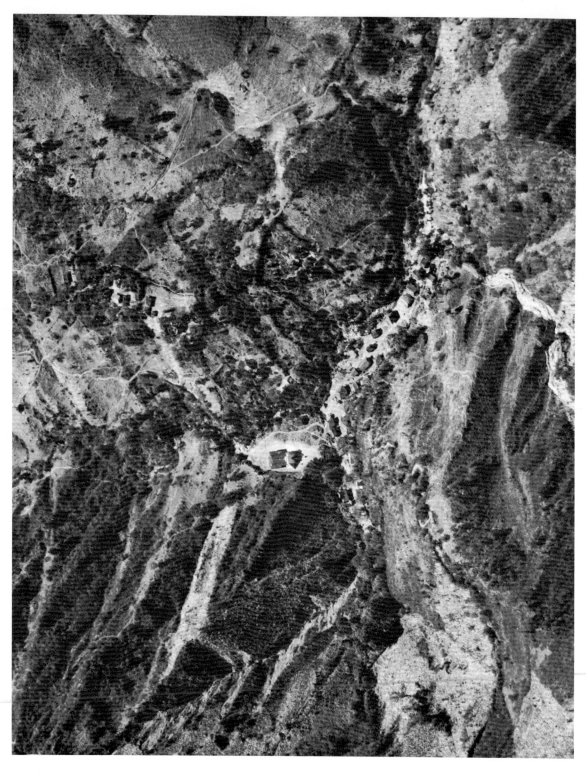

68. Aerial view of ʔAtsʼam

Hermitage of Esquipulas on alternate Sundays. The nearby chapel contains the Virgen del Rosario and other statues which are cared for by the Mayordomo. There is also a Mayor who makes the trip to Zinacantan Center with the gift of salt. During the Fiesta of the Virgen del Rosario in October, an elaborate ritual is performed in which the mayordomos reyes and mesoneros go to ʔAts'am with special offerings for the salt well (see Chapter 22).

ʔElan Voʔ. This small hamlet of four hundred persons (including some Chamulas who have moved into the municipio at the eastern edge) has only one major waterhole. The hamlet is located east of Pasteʔ and borders the municipio of San Cristóbal. Its most distinctive ceremonial feature is the sacred T'ENT'EN, a small slit drum of the type that the Aztecs called *Teponaztli,* made of cedar wood (CH'UL TEʔ). The drum, which appears to be one of the most sacred objects in all of Zinacantan, is illustrated in Figure 69. Its ownership and care rest with one patrilineage; the drum is kept in an altar in their house and is brought into Zinacantan Center to be played only during the Fiesta of San Sebastián.

69. The sacred T'ENT'EN   Slits

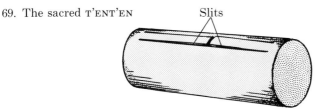

Pat ʔOsil. Pat ʔOsil is a dispersed hamlet of three hundred and forty-seven people, located on the ridge between Zinacantan Center and Na Chih and west of the upper portion of Voʔch'oh Voʔ.

Hok' Ch'enom. A hamlet of three hundred, Hok' Ch'enom is the farthest removed from Zinacantan Center. In Spanish this hamlet along with Sek'emtik is often referred to as *La Milpería* (the cornfields). It is located along both sides of the Pan American Highway as the road climbs into the highlands toward Nabenchauk. It is at an elevation considered as "Temperate Country," and the people grow bananas, mangoes, and other tropical fruits.

Chaynatik. This small hamlet is located between Nabenchauk and Na Chih at the highest elevations (generally over 2400 meters) at which people live within the municipio.

Yaleb Taiv and *P'ih.* These two hamlets, included by the Mexican Census with Chaynatik, are composed of families from Chamula, who were peons attached to these two former *fincas.* When the fincas were confiscated by the ejido program, the Chamula families were given lands and remained. These families are now in the process of becoming acculturated to Zinacanteco customs. While the old men still dress as Chamulas and serve cargos in Chamula Center, the younger generation has shifted to Zinacanteco clothes, and at least one of the young men has recently served as mayor in Zinacantan Center.

Hoyihel and *Potovtik.* These two hamlets are included by the Mexican Census with Sek'emtik.

Other Settlements. In addition to the fifteen hamlets which have their own principales, there are a few settlements, sometimes including several hundred people, which function much as independent hamlets, except that they have no principales of their own. Chikinibal Vo? and Ya?al Ts'i? share principales with Hok' Ch'enom; Masan and ?Ahte?tik with Potovtik; and K'ak'et Te? with Sek'emtik.

An Illustration: Paste?

I shall now present in detail the settlement patterns of one of the larger, more dispersed hamlets, Paste? (with a population of 1086)* where I have done extensive field work. Table 5 contains the same numbers and letters used in Map 7 showing the settlement pattern.

By far the largest waterhole group, and the one which gives its name to the entire hamlet, is VO? TA PASTE?, which included approximately five hundred and twenty-three persons in 1960. This waterhole is located in a depression rimmed by limestone hills near the southern edge of the hamlet and only about a kilometer from the escarpment which drops off into the lowlands in the central valley of the Grijalva River.

A myth told about the discovery of the waterhole explains its name. The original settlers in the hamlet were said to have been seeking water when they saw a large tree, a kind of oak called CHIKIN?IB. "There's a tree," they said, "let's go look for water over there." They began to dig near the large tree, and worked all day. The next day at dawn they returned to dig again and saw that the tree was gone. In its place they saw what looked like a person, but when they approached they realized it was a cut-off tree of a kind of oak called TULAN. They continued to

---

*A higher total population figure was reported in a number of the preliminary papers that utilize Paste? data. The discrepancy results from the fact that I originally included several domestic groups that belong to neighboring hamlets. The more recent use of aerial photographs has permitted more precise interviewing and mapping of the various waterhole groups and snas that properly belong in the hamlet of Paste?, and I now believe my new data is more accurate than the Mexican Census of 1960 which reports a population of 1276 for Paste? and must have included domestic groups that in fact belong to neighboring hamlets.

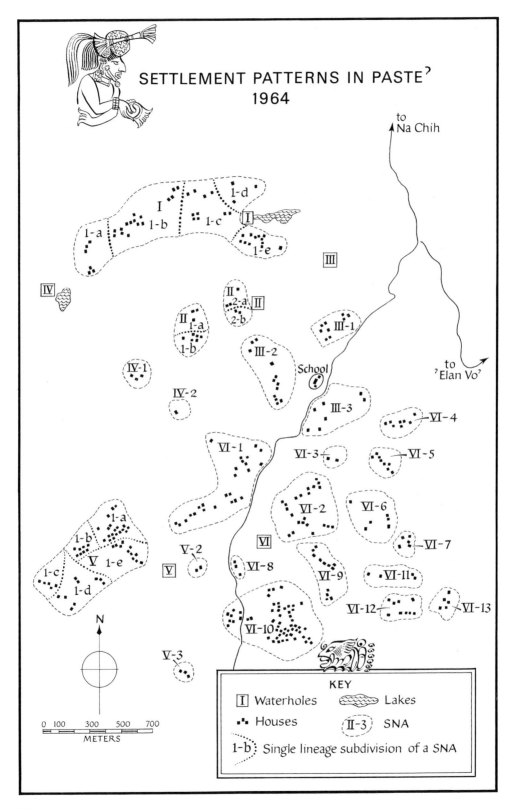

SETTLEMENT PATTERNS IN PASTE'
1964

to Na Chih

to 'Elan Vo'

School

KEY

| ☐ Waterholes | 〰️ Lakes |
| • Houses | ⬭ SNA |

1-b ⋯ Single lineage subdivision of a SNA

N

0 100 300 500 700
METERS

Map 7

work, digging for water, until they found the waterhole they now use. The first tree that showed them the location of the water was an ancestral god, an old man named Marian Peres Shulubte?. This ancestor had transformed himself into a tree to indicate where the water would be found; then he disappeared and in his place grew a large TULAN tree. It is under this tree that the shamans still sit in rank order for the K'IN KRUS for the waterhole (see Chapter 20). And this is why the waterhole is referred to as VO? TA PASTE?, "waterhole where he [the ancestor] makes a tree."

This waterhole contains two subdivisions (see Figure 70). To the west is CH'ENTIKAL VO?, with one opening excavated in the side of a hill and now walled with a cement retaining wall constructed with INI assistance. This is used by SNA CHIKU?ETIK and SNA LANTUETIK for drawing household drinking water during the rainy season. Another opening, called ?UK'UNAHEBAL VO?, "waterhole for washing clothes," is used by the same people. To the east are three openings around the large sacred tree mentioned in the myth, and these are all called CH'ISHAL VO? (thorny waterhole). This waterhole is used by all the rest of the snas in this waterhole group, and the three openings provide separate water for household drinking, watering animals, and washing clothes during the rainy season. During the dry season, CH'ISHAL VO? goes dry and all the domestic groups in this waterhole group have to use the large CH'ENTIKAL VO?, which seldom goes

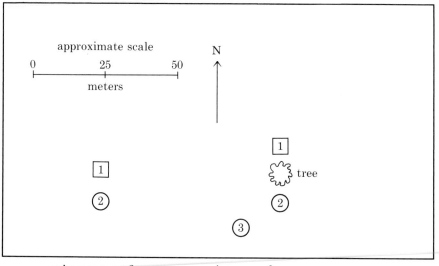

CH'ENTIKAL VO?
1. Household water
2. Laundry

CH'ISHAL VO?
1. Household water
2. Laundry
3. Water for animals

70. VO? TA PASTE?

dry. Because all the households in this waterhole group share the water in CH'ENTIKAL VO', they share in the common K'IN KRUS ceremony for this set of waterhole openings (see Appendix V).

The waterhole group has grown to include half the population of the hamlet, with thirteen snas of varying sizes. At one extreme there is the large SNA CHIKU'ETIK with at least one hundred and eighty-five persons and containing not only the predominant LOPIS CHIKU' lineage but five small lineages that have settled nearby and intermarried with the CHIKU'ETIK. At the other extreme, there are small snas composed almost entirely of one lineage, for example, SNA VASKISETIK, which has only twenty-six persons. VO' TA PASTE' includes twelve shamans—eleven men and one woman as of July 1961—which makes a relatively high ratio of one shaman to forty-six persons.

The VOM CH'EN waterhole group is located west of VO' TA PASTE' in the direction of Nabenchauk. The waterhole is also located in a depression and contains two openings, one with water the year around, and one smaller one (used for laundry) that dries up each year. In the mythological past, some people are said to have passed by the waterhole unmolested, while others would be stopped by an ancestral god, one of the first men who came to live in the hamlet. The people started talking among themselves about this extraordinary situation, asking why the waterhole let some people go past but not others. They decided to have a meeting and find out what was going on. About fifty men assembled and went to explore the waterhole. Two of the men fell inside as they approached, and the others were afraid to go any closer. Instead, they left and brought back candles which they lighted as offerings and began to pray. As they prayed, the waterhole began to bark like a dog—"vom, vom"—which is why it is called VOM CH'EN. (When I protested that dogs do not bark like this, but make sounds like "bow, wow!" or "arf, arf!," my informants laughed and said that any fool knows a dog's bark sounds like "vom, vom!")

Note from Table 5 that most of the waterhole is included in one large social group—SNA MENTISETIK—with 142 people. The name of the sna comes from the predominant MENTIS PATISHTAN lineage that settled first around the waterhole. This sna is sometimes called PINTOLETIK, since the second most important lineage, PERES 'ASIENTO, controls the ceremonial paraphernalia and ritual skills that are important in Zinacantan Center; the name PINTOL comes from the fact that men in this PERES 'ASIENTO lineage are the ones who paint the designs on the side of the petate bull that dances with the masked dancers; they also own and repaint each year the masks used by some of these as well as the jousting target, lance, and staffs used in the Fiesta of San Sebastián.

Table 5. Social groups in Paste?

Waterhole group	Snas	Major lineages	Number of persons[a]
I. SHUL VO?[b]			179
	1. VASKISETIK	a. VASKISETIK	(179)
		b. KOMIS ROTRIKOETIK	
		c. PERES BUYUMETIK	
		d. RUISETIK	
		e. BULUCHETIK	
II. KORAL BURO[c]			81
	1. LOPISETIK	a. LOPISETIK	(46)
		b. PULANOETIK	
	2. TSINTANETIK	a. TSINTANETIK	(35)
		b. BULUCHETIK	
III. BIK'IT VO?			128
	1. ?AKOVETIK	a. ?AKOVETIK	(30)
	2. MENTIRAETIK	a. MENTIRAETIK	(62)
	3. ?OK'ILETIK	a. ?OK'ILETIK	(36)
IV. PAHAL CHISHTE?			10
	(two isolated domestic groups)[d]		(10)
V. VOM CH'EN[e]			165
	1. MENTISETIK	a. MENTISETIK	(142)
		b. PERES TANHOLETIK	
		c. VASKISETIK	
		d. KULANTROETIK	
		e. PERES ?ASIENTOETIK	
	2. MARTINESETIK	a. MARTINESETIK	(14)
	3. CHECHEVETIK	a. CHECHEVETIK	(9)
VI. VO? TA PASTE?			523
	1. LANTUETIK	a. LANTUETIK	(49)
	2. SHIMENESETIK	a. SHIMENESETIK	(41)
	3. KITSETIK	a. KITSETIK	(7)
	4. TSINTANETIK	a. TSINTANETIK	(32)
	5. ?AKOVETIK	a. ?AKOVETIK	(27)
	6. CHOCHOVETIK	a. CHOCHOVETIK	(34)
	7. ?AMALISHETIK	a. ?AMALISHETIK	(18)
	8. KRUSETIK	a. KRUSETIK	(10)
	9. RUISETIK	a. RUISETIK	(58)
	10. CHIKU?ETIK	a. LOPIS CHIKU?ETIK	(185)
	11. VASKISETIK	a. VASKISETIK	(26)
	12. KUNULBAKETIK	a. KUNULBAKETIK	(25)
	13. MANI?ETIK	a. MANI?ETIK	(11)

[a] Numbers in parentheses represent the populations of the various snas.

[b] This entire waterhole group celebrates a single K'IN KRUS twice a year. The ceremony is performed both for the waterhole and for the five lineages which compose the waterhole group's only sna. Since there is a single ceremony, informants more commonly speak of the whole unit as SNA VASKISETIK than as SHUL VO?.

[c] This waterhole dries up in the winter. When this occurs, SNA LOPISETIK fetches water from BIK'IT VO?, and SNA TSINTANETIK from SHUL VO?. For ceremonial purposes, each sna performs its own K'IN KRUS.

[d] The other domestic groups that fetch water from PAHAL CHISHTE? belong to the neighboring hamlet of Na Chih.

[e] Like SHUL VO?, the five lineages in SNA MENTISETIK live close together and celebrate K'IN KRUS as a unit.

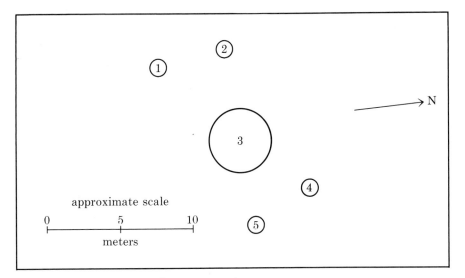

1. Household water—rainy season only
2. Water for animals—rainy season only
3. Water for households and in dry season for animals
4. Laundry
5. Water for households and animals—rainy season only

71. BIK'IT VO?

While the residents of MENTISETIK ordinarily consider themselves as a single group for the purposes of performing and sharing expenses for the waterhole's K'IN KRUS ceremony, they are often subdivided by informants into five smaller units (MENTISETIK, PERES TANHOLETIK, VASKISETIK, KULANTROETIK, and PERES ?ASIENTOETIK which are recorded as a, b, c, d, e in Table 5) that more nearly coincide with localized patrilineages. This case, along with that of SHUL VO?, indicates that the sna unit can be thought of on different levels of contrast. Thus, one may speak of SNA MENTISETIK when talking about the unit that performs K'IN KRUS together for the VOM CH'EN waterhole. But if a Zinacanteco is asked "How many different groups are there in MENTISETIK?," his response will include all five subdivisions. The other two snas are very small, containing only one lineage each—SNA MARTINESETIK and SNA CHECHEVETIK. They are spatially isolated from the large SNA MENTISETIK (see Map 7). Vom ch'en has relatively few shamans (only three men in July 1961 for a ratio of one shaman to fifty-five persons).

The BIK'IT VO? waterhole group is located north of VO? TA PASTE?. The waterhole (the myth about it was given in Chapter 7) contains one large and four small openings (see Figure 71). In the rainy season, all five openings are used with the functions being divided among those for household water, livestock, and laundering clothes. But in the dry season, only No. 3 is left with water for household use and animals, and No. 4 for laundry.

This waterhole group contains three snas: SNA MENTIRAETIK with sixty-two persons; SNA ʔOKʼILETIK with thirty-six; and SNA ʔAKOVETIK with thirty. The names of the groups translate respectively as "Liars" (loan word from Spanish), "Coyotes," and "Waspnests," There is only one shaman (a woman) in this waterhole group.

The SHUL VOʔ waterhole group is located at the northern edge of the hamlet near Na Chih. Above the waterhole is an impressive limestone rock formation, with one large rock resting above another. In the myth told about this waterhole a large horn, the size of a man, used to come out on top of the rock three times a week. The people heard about it and went to see it, but they became lost inside the rock and did not return. This is when the people started to have their KʼIN KRUS ceremony. The rock was alive at that time. But then a lightning bolt came out of the waterhole below it and killed the rock (an ancestral god in disguise). This is why the rock is called SHUL TON, meaning "rock that had a horn coming out of it."

The hundred and seventy-nine persons in SHUL VOʔ, like the MENTISETIK in VOM CHʼEN, constitute a single unit for performing and sharing the expenses of the KʼIN KRUS ceremony. Also like the MENTISETIK in VOM CHʼEN, the VASKISETIK in SHUL VOʔ can be subdivided into five sna units (VASKISETIK, KOMIS ROTRIKOETIK, PERES BUYUMETIK, RUISETIK, and BULUCHETIK) which more nearly approach localized patrilineages. Since VASKISETIK is the most important lineage, it provides the name for the whole unit when the people talk about the group as a whole as SNA VASKISETIK.

The cases of MENTISETIK in VOM CHʼEN and VASKISETIK in SHUL VOʔ suggest that, when a settlement pattern is very compact, the separate KʼIN KRUS ceremonies performed by residents of more dispersed waterhole groups are conveniently compressed into a single ceremony. At this ceremony, offerings are made to the cross shrines for the waterhole as well as for the ancestors from whom each lineage inherited its lands. The ceremonial organization becomes very similar to the situation in more compact hamlets, such as ʔApas in which the KʼIN KRUS ceremony is performed for the entire hamlet. Shamans must be imported for the KʼIN KRUS ceremonies in SHUL VOʔ, because apparently none live in this waterhole group.

KORAL BURO is a small and not very reliable waterhole located over a ridge to the south of SHUL VOʔ. According to the mythological account of its discovery, a Zinacanteco wandering through the woods encountered a corral full of burros belonging to the Earth Lord. Others went, but could not see the corral, since the man had seen it in his dream. But he insisted the corral was there and suggested that it would be a good place to live. He asked for gifts of candles to light in the cave above the waterhole, and in this way performed the first KʼIN KRUS for the waterhole. People have continued to live there, but nobody has seen the burros which belonged to the Earth Lord. There is an important specialist living in KORAL BURO who makes the bull candleholders for the Hermitage of Esquipulas, as well as the special censers used by the Mayordomo Reyes in the Fiesta del Rosario in ʔAts'am.

KORAL BURO usually dries up during the dry season; when this occurs, the small snas of LOPISETIK with forty-six people and TSINTANETIK with thirty-five have to carry their water from BIK'IT VOʔ and SHUL VOʔ respectively. Hence, SNA LOPISETIK joins in the K'IN KRUS for BIK'IT VOʔ and SNA TSINTANETIK in the K'IN KRUS for SHUL VOʔ. KORAL BURO has one shaman.

The PAHAL CHISHTEʔ waterhole is located over the ridge to the southwest of SHUL VOʔ. Most of the families using it belong to the hamlet of Na Chih, but two domestic groups totaling ten persons, including one female shaman, belong to Pasteʔ.

Although the snas and the waterhole groups are fundamental units in the settlement pattern and social organization of Pasteʔ, the hamlet, dispersed as it is, has a number of cohesive beliefs and functions that make it into a coherent unit in the social system of Zinacantan. It is clearly an administrative unit for various civil functions. Two principales (junior and senior), appointed each year, are in charge of reporting on hamlet affairs to the Cabildo in Zinacantan Center each Sunday; they also carry orders and messages from the Cabildo back to the hamlet. The hamlet is also considered a unit when the national census is taken every decade. The elementary school established by INI is attended by a few children from all the waterhole groups, and a three-man school committee is appointed each year to help with the management of school affairs. The unity of the hamlet of Pasteʔ is ritually expressed by two annual Year Renewal ceremonies performed by all the fifteen male shamans living in the hamlet, and it is the duty of the principales to serve as the hosts for these ceremonies. Finally, it is clear that all residents of Pasteʔ feel themselves to be members of the hamlet. If a man is asked where he lives, he first answers that he lives in Pasteʔ and only later mentions his waterhole group or sna.

In collaboration with the hamlet of Elan Voʔ, a large cemetery is maintained along both sides of the road that runs from the Pan American Highway into Pasteʔ. Most people who die in Pasteʔ are buried in this cemetery, but a few are carried to the cemetery called MUKENAL TSELEH located on the high ridge between Zinacantan Center and Na Chih. The cemetery at the edge of Pasteʔ is only about two generations old. It was established one year when many people died in a severe famine and it was too difficult to carry all the bodies to MUKENAL TSELEH.

9 / The Life Cycle

The beliefs and customs of key points in the Zinacanteco life cycle—birth, socialization, marriage, and death—provide understanding of the way of life in Zinacantan.

Birth

Zinacantecos believe that conception is caused by the mixing of men's with women's semen. The seminal fluids are called HPVERSATIK (from the Spanish *fuerza* or "force"), or SCHINAMIL HPATIK (the brains of our back), and they are believed to come from the spine. Though not thought to be reservoirs of semen, the testes of men are believed responsible for erections. Some informants say that just one coitus is necessary for conception; others say two or three are necessary. The embryo is formed in the uterus and fed by the placenta. During the first month, the fetus is believed to be of the consistency of atole; by the second month it has arms, legs, a head, and an indication of where the eyes will form. It begins to move in the third or fourth month, and by the fourth month the fetus is believed to be fully formed, though small. Children are born from the eighth to the tenth month, but generally during the ninth. In the last month, women stop carrying heavy loads, weaving, and having sexual relations, as it is feared the father may break his child's limbs if he lies on his wife at this time.

In the sixth or seventh month of pregnancy, the wife's family selects the midwife, and the husband's mother presents two liters of rum to request her services. The midwife is expected to visit the pregnant mother every eight to ten days before the birth occurs, and to massage lightly the

For some of the field data in this chapter I am especially grateful to Jane Fishburne Collier, Robert M. Laughlin, Francesca Cancian, Merida Blanco, Nancy Chodorow, Mary Anschuetz, and Carolyn Pope.

woman's stomach. A woman's husband should assist at the birth, and she may also be aided by her husband's mother, father, sisters, and brothers. The woman kneels on a petate on the floor, while her husband stands behind her pulling her sash tight. One of the other male relatives sits on a chair facing her, seizing her by the shoulders to support her during each labor pain. All the participants (except the mother) are served rum often during both the period of labor and the birth. As soon as the baby is born, the midwife takes over. The umbilical cord is tied a handspan from the baby, then cut with the point of a heated machete. The cord and the afterbirth are wrapped in rags and buried in the patio either the same day or after an interval of three days. If the first child is a girl, a piece of the father's pants or shirt is buried with them so that the next child will be a boy. The midwife cleans the new baby with a dry rag, and washes the mother's hair. If the baby does not cry right away, but appears dead, black chicks are held close to its ear in the belief that the peeping will awaken the infant. While the baby is being washed, three rounds of rum are served to all present. Within an hour after birth, a ritual symbolizes the sex identity of the new baby. The midwife holds the infant, and objects that will be used in later life are placed in both of its fists. Both sexes are given sacred salt and both are presented with three small red chilis. If the infant is a boy, he is presented with a digging stick, hoe, and billhook (which he will use to farm maize when he grows up), as well as an axe and a splinter of ocote so that he will know how to go out with a torch to meet his father coming home in the dark. A girl is presented with a mano (which she will use to grind maize) and various parts of the back-strap loom that she will use when she grows up. The baby is then given to the mother, and both are wrapped up in blankets and virtually hidden from view.

The day after the birth, the midwife comes to take the first of three sweat baths with the mother. They enter the sweathouse together, and the midwife washes the mother with myrtle and laurel leaves. The mother is then helped back into bed, and the midwife is offered a ritual meal during the course of which five bottles of rum are served and all of the women present bow to the midwife. While this is going on, the mother and baby are ignored as they lie under the blankets in the corner.

The second day after the birth, the baby is formally presented to everyone in the house who embrace it, kiss it, and blow in each of its ears. For four to five days no one talks much to the mother and visitors are not welcome. If people do talk to her, punishment will come in the form of MAHBENAL, or sickness from the ancestral gods.

The mother must take two more sweat baths with the midwife, who returns every two days after the birth for this purpose. The midwife is given a meal each time, but this is not accompanied by the ritual drinking that follows the first sweat bath.

The mother continues to be treated delicately for about three weeks, during which time she must observe certain food restrictions—for example, she must eat only "hot" foods like chicken and beef. She does not wander out of the house, except to relieve herself or take the sweat bath with the midwife. Nor does she do any labor, such as grinding maize. Even when the mother starts working again, she continues to keep the baby wrapped up and hidden from view. This careful shielding of the infant is intended to keep the soul in its body. The mother also binds its wrists and ankles to keep in the soul. This treatment continues until the baptismal rite takes place and the soul is thereby more firmly fixed in the infant's body.

Socialization

From birth to weaning (at the birth of the next child, or at two to three years of age), a Zinacanteco is referred to as an ʔUNEN (baby) and addressed affectionately as NENE (Figure 72). From the age of about three to adulthood (defined by marriage) a boy is referred to as a KREM, the girl as a TSEB. For only the early stage of this period—ages three to four—are there terms of address, apart from names: a boy is addressed as TSUK, a girl as CHIN (Blanco and Chodorow 1964: 8). After marriage the man becomes a VINIK, the woman an ʔANTS. At forty-five or fifty, a man becomes MOL (respected old man) and the woman MEʔEL (respected old woman). As Francesca Cancian points out (1963), the social marker between baby and child is clear—weaning and cessation of the nearly constant carrying—and the social marker between child and adult status is likewise clear— marriage. Other markers fluctuate with individual circumstances. Further, there is a fundamental difference in treatment of a child aged three to about nine, as compared to one older. Blanco and Chodorow summarize three named stages in childhood, as shown in Table 6.

In the first stage children are "small boys" and "small girls," In the second, considered "big boys" and "big girls," the boys join their father in farming activities in the lowlands, while the girls learn to weave, grind maize, and cook. The terms for the third stage, which mean "full-grown boy or girl," indicate that they may work on their own, without being given orders, and that they look like "men" and "women."

72. Zinacanteco baby

Table 6. The stages of childhood

Age	Male	Female
2 or 3 to 9 or 10	BIK'IT KREM	BIK'IT TSEB
9 or 10 to 12 or 13	MUK'TA KREM	MUK'TA TSEB
12 or 13 onward	SVA'LEH KREM	SVA'LEH TSEB

73. Older sister aids mother in caring for the younger siblings

Babies. The fundamental fact about a Zinacanteco baby during its first three or four months of life is that it interacts almost exclusively with its mother and receives almost constant care, love, and affection. It is seldom, for more than a few minutes, separated from the mother or some other female in the household (Figure 73). It is either nursing (whenever it cries and wishes the breast), wrapped in a rebozo and carried on the mother's back, or asleep beside the mother in bed. There continues to be great concern for the infant's soul during this period, for it is believed that it is very loosely attached within the body. When a Zinacanteco mother gets up from a spot on the ground away from home where she has been sitting with her baby for some time, she almost invariably brushes the ground with the rebozo in which she carries the baby in order to gather up any parts of the infant's soul that might have left the body at that location. Until (and to a lesser extent, after) the baptism, great care is exercised, since the early period of a Zinacanteco life is an extraordinarily delicate one.

After about four months, the infant's interaction expands to include the other household members, all of whom cuddle and play with it. By the age of one to one and a half, the infant crawls and/or walks about freely, and the totally nurturant treatment begins to change. He no longer spends most of the day tied to the back of his mother or another female, but is allowed to walk on his own. However, the caretakers are still careful to watch a walking baby so that he will not fall and lose his soul. He now knows how to crawl and walk among the axes and machetes without hurting himself. Severe scoldings or other forms of punishment are extremely rare. Francesca Cancian reports that, with the exception of one very hostile mother, she never saw an unweaned child struck unless it bit its mother's nipple while nursing (1963: 60). (In such a case, the mother would lightly slap the baby's head.)

By the time an infant is walking competently, expectations increase, and he is scolded for failure to comply. He is expected to keep clear of the fire and out of puddles and to notify an older member of the household when he needs to urinate or defecate. (Before the children are toilet-trained, both sexes wear skirts so that they can urinate and defecate easily. If the skirts get wet, they are not changed but allowed to dry on the child.) He is expected not to bother the mother when she is very busy with her tasks and not to play with food, especially maize. There is little pressure to master the basic skills of walking, talking, and learning to urinate and defecate outside, and little or no pride on the part of parents over the speed which children learn them. Rather, the interaction consists of the repetition of words and phrases in a playful, affectionate tone that helps the infant learn.

In brief, the Zinacanteco child's first two to three years are an almost wholly nurturant period, when everybody loves him and shows it. He is protected against attacks from his older siblings; food is plentiful and he can either nurse or eat what and when he wants (Figures 74, 75).

Children. This nurturant phase ends when a new baby is born to the mother, and the older child must be completely weaned. At first the adults make an effort to give the displaced child extra attention and cater to his tantrums.

They help him master his aggression against the baby and his mother by encouraging him "playfully" to hit his mother and the baby (the blows to the baby are usually intercepted by the mother). This system seems to work. By the time the new baby is about half a year old and ceases to spend all its life sleeping on his mother's back or nursing, the older child has learned to behave in a predominantly nurturant way to the baby. Manifest aggression to younger siblings reappears when the baby gets older. (Francesca Cancian 1963: 61–62)

74. Zinacanteco child eating beans

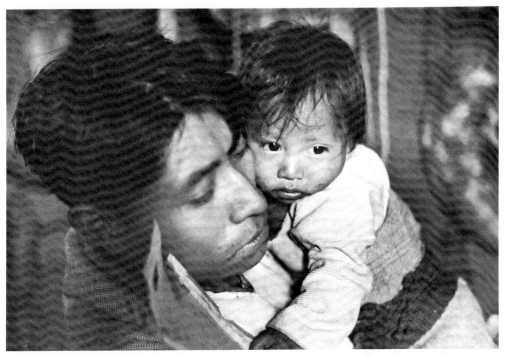

75a. Zinacanteco parents are very affectionate

75b. Infant watching mother make tortillas

76. Small Zinacanteco boys

Life becomes more trying for a boy or girl between three and nine. Other household members can be expected to offer little affection, many commands to perform errands, and a general attitude of "don't bother me." This shift from baby to young child clearly means losing affection and attention, and moving into a position of being ordered around constantly. The situation is especially difficult for a boy, since his father may be away farming maize in the lowlands and he is too young to go along. Hence, he spends his time in a predominantly female environment, with the young sisters paying more attention to each other and to the new baby, and the older sisters and mother busy running the household. He may be called upon to perform small tasks, such as bringing in the chickens or playing with the baby, but most of the time he is expected to amuse himself (Figure 76).

While the girls are performing chores that lead directly into the skills needed for an adult woman's role—weaving, cooking, tending children, and fetching water and wood (Figure 77)—the boys' chores are primarily feminine work and do not prepare them adequately for the heavy farming work (Blanco and Chodorow 1964: 24–25).

During this period children spend most of the day in small groups playing together (Figures 78, 79); they play house or store and a kind of hide-and-seek. Boys often play with tops, slingshots, or homemade bows and arrows; they also imitate the rituals of the cargoholders, constructing small models of ritual objects and practicing the dance steps. (I have observed two small boys pretending to be the dancers who perform during the Christmas season for hours at a time, following the interesting performance of these ritual figures in December and January.) Girls, on the other hand, have toy looms for make-believe weaving, and little metates and pots for making toy tortillas and carrying water. Many adult skills are learned through these games.

Adolescence. While between the ages of three and nine, boys and girls often play together in groups, the period between about nine and adulthood is characterized by rigid separation of the sexes. The boys begin to accompany their fathers to the lowlands to farm and to the markets to buy and sell. By the age of twelve to fourteen, boys are "formed"; they may walk to the lowlands alone, and are able to take down loads of toasted tortillas for the farming parties and bring back maize. When not working, and at home, groups of related boys wander around together, watching the approach of strangers or cars; they sometimes go to San Cristóbal together to buy and sell in the market and watch the crowds.

77. Young girl learns ancient technique of water-carrying

78. Zinacanteco child

But adolescence does not last long in Zinacantan. By the age of sixteen or seventeen the boys are beginning to think about becoming engaged, and they work hard at farming, wage labor, or trading to accumulate their share of the money needed for the courtship, which often lasts two years. Between the ages of eighteen and twenty-two, most boys move from the status of KREM to VINIK by getting married and, in effect, becoming adults ready to assume positions in the religious hierarchy and to farm their own land as soon as they can acquire it. By the age of seven or eight most girls have begun to make substantial contribution to the work of the household, and by ten or eleven almost all of them are busy helping the adult women—grinding maize, making tortillas, fetching wood and water,

79. Zinacanteco children

herding sheep, helping tend the younger children, sweeping the house, and so on. They also begin to learn to weave at this time, since one of the essential qualities for a Zinacanteco wife is to be able to weave good clothes for herself and her husband. By the age of fifteen or sixteen the girl is usually engaged, and by seventeen or eighteen married and moved from the status of TSEB to ʔANTS. Children are born; she helps her husband with his cargo duties; and she begins to run her own household as soon as a separate house is constructed.

Learning Rituals. There appears to be little formal instruction in Zinacantan about the sacred values of the culture or about the ritual procedures and prayers learned and performed by any competent adult. Sacred stories about the gods and their activities are sometimes told around the hearth at night by the father; these stories are often repeated during the lonely nights in the lowlands while the men are away from their wives and younger children for weeks at a time. Experiences involving beliefs about the soul and animal spirit companion are shared in conversation. But even more learning appears to take place when a shaman comes to diagnose an illness or returns to perform a curing ceremony; small children hear and observe the proceedings as a matter of course. When the children are very small, they sleep through the all-night ceremonies, but as they become older, they stay awake longer and longer and may be called upon to help with the ceremonies. The boys are pressed into duty as assistants for the shaman—to help carry the candles or the pine boughs or to serve as drink-pourer. The girls are expected to make tortillas, and to help kill and cook the chicken for the ritual meals that accompany the ceremonies. The children are similarly involved during a K'IN KRUS for a sna or waterhole group, and from an early age they are taken to ceremonies in the ceremonial center.

Schools. To date, only a small proportion of Zinacanteco children attend formal schools—whether run by the state, the federal government, or INI—but there is currently an increase in attendance. For example, in Paste?, a hamlet of 1086 people where we have good data on formal schooling, an INI school constructed in 1952 had 33 pupils, all boys, by 1958. By 1965 the number of pupils had increased to 72, including 28 girls.

There are a number of reasons for the slight attendance. Perhaps the most important is that Zinacanteco parents simply do not see the importance of formal schooling for their way of life. It is of course important, especially for men, to know enough Spanish to deal with the Ladinos in the renting of land in the lowlands and in the markets in San Cristóbal and Tuxtla Gutiérrez. But, with the Republic of Mexico still a vague concept and Mexico City a somewhat mythical place somewhere between Chiapas and New York City, there is no strongly felt need to learn the language of the Ladinos and to participate in the national culture. Further, as Colby points out, when Zinacantecos do learn to read, there is little for them to read in Spanish that is readily available and has any vital significance for them (1961). He suggests that INI consider publishing items such as almanacs with information about such critical matters as the Catholic ceremonial calendar, weather, and maize production. On the other hand, the labor of both boys and girls is needed in the fields and houses. At about the very time Zinacanteco parents are willing to send them to school (age seven to eight), the children begin to be economically useful at home. In addition, the parents have a special concern that the girls will be sexually molested by the boys if they go to school.

The children who do go to school are taught, mainly by rote, the elements of reading, writing, and arithmetic, and something of the history of Mexico. They ordinarily stay in school only about three years—with the result that they may be able to read and write haltingly in Spanish and will know something about the Mexican republic and its institutions. Among adult Zinacantecos, we have discovered only three or four men who can read and write Spanish well, and there are at most only one or two women who are literate.

Problems in Socialization. The major problems in Zinacanteco socialization appear to occur between the ages of three, after weaning, and nine, when boys are old enough to accompany their fathers to the maize fields and girls to be of genuine help in the household. I have noted how the treatment of children, especially the boys, shifts drastically from a stage of care and affection to one of being ordered around. There is evidence of fairly intense sibling rivalry, or at least ambivalence, between older and younger brothers at the adult status. Some of this undoubtedly has to do with struggles between brothers for land and other inherited property, but the evidence seems to indicate that the treatment of boys between ages three and nine exacerbates this tension point in the system. For girls, the situation is different. They appear to have fewer problems at an early age, since they learn useful work gradually. Sisters are separated at the adult stage by patrilocal residence, and there is little evidence of the type of rivalry that is common between brothers. While a younger brother spends his life, so to speak, in a struggle for status within a system that has led his older brother to resent him in the first place, a girl's role is quite different—she moves after marriage and has the problem of getting along with her husband's parents.

In general, observers studying socialization in Zinacantan have been impressed with the obedience training built into Zinacantecos by their parents—and in the absence of systematic patterns of rewards and punishments. It appears that the strong values placed upon work and obedience by the culture are of crucial importance in the socialization process. Blanco and Chodorow conclude that

> these values of work and obedience determine the way children behave. Parents are erratic in their encouragement of work learning in young children, occasionally providing them with half-sized hoes, bags, or water jugs, while often discouraging them from initiation of their own chores. Also, children are not immediately rewarded for obeying chore commands; despite both of these things, they comply to chore com-

mands and perform chores. Since parents give most chore commands, learning and doing this work is synonymous for the children with obeying their parents. Zinacanteco children, by their willingness to work, demonstrate that work and obedience are values in their culture. (1964: 33)

Courtship and Marriage*

When a Zinacanteco boy reaches seventeen or eighteen, he begins to think of marrying. If he has an older brother, who ideally marries first, his courtship may be delayed for a year or two while the family struggles to pay off the expenses of the previous wedding. Occasionally a father suggests that his son start looking for a wife and sometimes even suggests a particular girl. It is always the boy, however, who selects the girl he wishes to marry. In theory, he has a wide range of choice; he may marry any woman who does not come within the range of incest prohibitions— that is, his mother, his comadre, or a woman with the same Indian surname. In practice, since most marriages are endogamous within hamlets, and many even within waterhole groups, the available girls close to home who do not belong to his patrilineage may be few, especially in the smaller hamlets. Since the girls have very little freedom, and are constantly accompanied, after the age of ten, by their mothers, older female relatives, or at least age-mates, the boy often selects a girl to marry (ordinarily his age or a year or two younger) with whom he has rarely spoken but has only seen along the paths or at fiestas.

The courtship and marriage which follow the boy's selection involve complicated social and economic transactions as well as long, complex rituals. The patterns focus on taking the wife away from her domestic group and installing her permanently in her husband's; but there are also important by-products, such as the establishment of many new compadrazgo and affinal kin ties, and the definition of the new couple as full adult members of the community.

The Initiation of a Courtship. As soon as a boy has selected the girl he wishes to marry, he presents a bottle of rum to his parents and asks them to help him with the expenses of the courtship. If they accept the bottle, they must agree to go to ask for the girl and to help the boy with

---

*This section draws especially upon field data collected by Jane Fishburne Collier and upon her monograph *Courtship and Marriage in Zinacantan, Chiapas, Mexico* (1968), as well as the analysis of courtship by Robert Laughlin in his PhD Thesis (1963).

the courtship. However, if the father completely disapproves of his son's choice, he may refuse the rum and try to persuade his son to look for a more suitable girl.

When the boy and his parents have agreed on the girl, they begin collecting the money (between 100 and 200 pesos) they will need for a formal petition (HAK'OL). They also select two or more petitioners (H HAK'OLETIK) to help the father ask for the girl. These petitioners are always respected men and must be good speakers, since the petitions are long and arduous. The petitioning group always includes the boy's father, mother, and older brothers; the brothers of his father and mother often come, and occasionally even his older sisters' husbands or other relatives.

The boy's parents present a bottle of rum to each of the petitioners and request their assistance. They arrange the day and time, but do not announce the name of the girl, for her father might hear of the plans and arrange to be away from home to avoid giving away his daughter. Once the petitioners have agreed to serve, they assume several obligations: they must accompany the boy on all important ritual occasions during the courtship and advise him if asked; they may even help him financially. More generally, they must see that the boy fulfills all his obligations and that the marriage successfully takes place. The boy respectfully calls each of them TOT (father) for the rest of his life.

As the date of the petition draws close, the boy spends a great deal of time trying to discover the future plans of the girl's father and find out about his house and the habits of all the people who live in it. He will later use this information to plan the best time and strategy for entering the girl's home. The boy's mother prepares a basket of gifts, including chocolate, brown sugar, and several rolls of bread, while his father purchases a garrafón of Chamula rum (17 to 20 liters, worth about 50 pesos) and prepares four special bottles of rum to be presented with the basket of gifts.

Other helpers include a drink-pourer (HP'IS VO²), often a younger brother of the boy, and a bottle-filler (HCH'OL VO²). The latter is a woman, usually an older sister of the future groom, who pours the rum from the large garrafón into the bottles which the drink-pourer serves. On the appointed day the petitioners and their wives gather at the boy's house, in the afternoon if the girl's house is far, and after dark if she lives nearby. They are served rum and a meal with meat and are told the name of the prospective fiancée. The boy then presents them with a bottle of rum and asks them to be persistent and to keep asking until the girl's father accepts.

The group leaves for the girl's house with the boy's mother or some other older woman carrying the basket of bread, and the boy carrying the garrafón. Arriving at the girl's house well after dark, they stop quietly and wait while several young men, acting as helpers, surround the house to prevent the father from escaping out the back door. One of the petitioners then approaches quietly and calls to the people inside, usually using trickery to get the door open. He may ask to borrow some ocote to use as a torch to light his way or an axe or some money. Once the door is open, all the petitioners, their wives following, force their way inside. Taken by surprise, the girl's family tries to run out the back door but are stopped by the helpers. The petitioners then kneel in front of the girl's father, place the four bottles of rum at his feet, and begin their request. The woman who has carried the basket of bread deposits it near the rum and joins the other women who are kneeling before the girl's mother. At this point, the drink-pourer begins to serve rounds of rum.

Outside the house the bottle-filler, the helpers, and the boy settle down for a long wait, often building a fire to keep warm. During this period one or two of the petitioners may come outside to rest by the fire, while the others remain, kneeling. In the house, the pleading continues, the women talking to the mother, and the petitioners trying to persuade the father. The phrases are traditional and both sides talk at once, without listening to each other. The only person who is silent is the girl, who sits apart with her eyes downcast and her rebozo drawn bashfully over her mouth. She has nothing to say about whether the potential suitor is accepted, and few people pay any attention to her.

A typical dialogue (adapted from J. F. Collier (1968: 152), goes as follows:

The petitioners:

> May your head speak,
> May your heart give advice.
> > Take my words, Father,
> > Accept what I say, Mother.
> I speak for the good of your mud,
> I speak to benefit your earth [metaphorical ways of referring to the
> > girl].
> Do not cut my child's heart.

The father of the girl replies:

> Your child is a devil,
> He drinks too much.

I won't give my daughter to suffering,
I won't give my child to beating.
With difficulty I reared her,
With patient words I trained her.
Get Out!
Leave!
Take your water [rum] away.

The petitioners try again:

Don't scold me,
Don't give my heart sadness.
May your head not scold,
May your heart not scold.
I speak for my child who works well,
I speak for my child who doesn't drink.
Don't give us cause for crying,
Don't give us cause for shouting.
My words of truth have been heard,
Here in this house of poverty and wealth.
Beloved Father,
Beloved Mother,
Answer my words,
Reply to me now.

And so on through the long night, as the drink-pourer periodically serves more rum liquor. Although he offers a glass to the girl's parents on every round, they do not accept. For the moment the girl's father accepts the liquor and drinks, he has agreed to give his daughter away, and the courtship formally begins.

When the father finally succumbs, he says:

I answer your words,
Your child may come to the house of poverty and wealth,
We will be fine wherever we are, coming and going.
There will not be any scolding between us,
There will not be anything bad between us.
So now you have your child.

A man usually accepts the first proposition for his daughter, for if he delays, the girl might elope and he would not receive the gifts that accompany a normal courtship. The amount of difficulty and length of time the petitioners spend in convincing the father are taken as indications of the probable future relations between the families. If the father gives in unwillingly, the courtship will probably be long, expensive, and unpleasant. If, on the other hand, he accepts readily, the courtship is likely to be short and the marriage will almost certainly take place.

After the girl's father has accepted, and the petitioners have moved from the floor to chairs, the father may send for relatives to join the party for the rest of the night. He then tells the petitioners he is ready to meet his future son-in-law. The petitioners bring in the boy who enters carrying a liter of rum and a glass to serve it with. He kneels before his future father-in-law, begins calling him TOT, and asks his pardon for having entered the house:

> My mud,
> My earth has entered.
>> Do not give me cause for crying,
>> Do not give me cause for screaming.
> If I obey your words, Father, My Lord,
> If I follow your knowledge, Father, My Lord,
>> Now I will work,
>>> I will descend to the lowlands,
>>> I will ascend from the lowlands
>>>> With my Father,
>>>> With my Lord.

The girl's father answers the boy who remains kneeling:

> If you accept my words,
> If you obey my words,
>> My advice coming,
>> My advice going,
>>> We will go to the lowlands together.
> You are my child,
> You will become a man.
>> It seems good to me,
>>> That we descend,
>>> That we ascend,
>>>> Coming,
>>>> Going.
> We will do the beams of the gods [that is, maize],
> We will do the shadow of the gods.

Adaptation from J. F. Collier 1968: 153

The boy arises and pours the girl's father a drink, and proceeds to serve the girl's relatives, kneeling before each one. The drink-pourer then serves rounds of liquor to everyone until the large jug is empty and all are drunk. The petitioners depart, leaving the boy to spend the night helping his future parents-in-law to bed, offering more rum if they awaken during the night, and soothing their hangovers with additional drinks in the morning. When they are on their feet and relatively sober, he may return home.

A day or two after the petition the boy brings to the girl's house a large net containing such fruits as oranges, bananas, and mangoes, as well as sugar cane, fresh maize, and two bottles of rum (or one of rum and one of chicha). He presents the fruit to her father, and together they drink the liquor. Afterwards the boy eats a meal with them, and then goes home.

Two or three days later, the boy and two of his petitioners go to the girl's house to ask her father to name the "giver" (H?AK'VANEH) of the bride. The boy must then go to the giver's house with two of his petitioners, bearing exactly half the gifts they took on the petition to the girl's father. They drink with him, and thereafter he attends every important occasion during the courtship.

Following the formal petition, a boy uses kin terms to address his future wife's family. He calls the girl's father TOT, her mother ME?, and uses appropriate addresses for the other close relatives. The boy is the only one who enters into the web of kinship at this time. This appears to be an expression of the fact that the early phases of courtship are a trial period. If the engagement does not work, the only kin tie that must be severed is that between the boy and his fiancée's family.

The Bride Price. A year or more elapses before the next major ceremony—"entering the house" (?OCHEL TA NA). During this period the ties between the two groups are gradually cemented by the boy's payment of a bride price. As one informant expressed it, "poco a poco va pagando, poco a poco va quitando" little by little he pays, little by little he removes [her] (J. F. Collier 1968: 156). The bride price is an important symbol in insuring the good intentions of the suitor with his future in-laws. When troubles between the young couple do occur before or after the marriage and the case is taken to the Presidente, the difficulty is resolved by an adjustment in the bride price: in cases of elopement, the girl's irate father will still demand payment from his son-in-law; if the girl's family has broken off the engagement, the boy will demand reimbursement for the gifts he has given them.

The payments take three forms: large gifts during certain fiestas; work the boy does for his father-in-law; and smaller gifts every two or three weeks. Supposedly these amounts are specified, but Jane Collier found variations in practice which she attributes to three main factors. If the two families live nearby, the bride price is likely to be lower because the families already have strong ties, and after marriage the girl's parents will retain close contact with their daughter. If the girl's family is large, more rum is required to make them all drunk and more gifts must be divided among them. Finally, and most important, if the girl's family is rich, they can expect and demand a higher price for their daughter.

The prestations involving major amounts of goods occur during the important fiestas. For the largest, San Lorenzo (August 10) and San Sebastián (January 20), the procedure replicates the behavior at the original petition. The boy, his family, and the petitioners all go to the girl's house, bearing the same kind of presents they took for the original petition. This time they go in the morning, but the ritual speeches and drinking of rum, and the presentation of gifts are all similar. The boy must also stay to see that his parents-in-law get to bed safely, and he must relieve their hangover with drink the next morning.

Each fiesta requires appropriate gifts:

San Juan (June 24): a net of bananas and other fruit purchased in Chamula, costing 20 to 50 pesos, plus two bottles of rum. The girl's family reciprocates by serving a meal with chicken or beef.

San Lorenzo (August 10): a net of fruit given in the market by the church, followed by three rounds of rum and three rounds of chicha presented by the boy and his petitioners. The boy also offers the girl a necklace and/or a ring, and the party then makes a formal visit to the girl's house (described above), bearing the additional gifts.

San Mateo (September 20): a net of fruit and two bottles of rum.

Todos Santos (November 1). On this day the dead are thought to return to the homes of the living where food is set out for them. The engaged boy must provide some of this food to feed the dead of his fiancée's family—a net of fruit, some meat, and several bottles of rum. He also spends the day in the cemetery cleaning the graves of her relatives— removing dead pine needles, adding fresh ones, and lighting candles for the dead.

San Sebastián (January 20): the procedure is the same as that followed for San Lorenzo.

Cuarto Viernes (during Lent): a net of fruit.

Semana Santa (Holy Week): a basket of bread with brown sugar and chocolate, plus some fish and atole rather than rum, which is not supposed to be drunk at this time.

Sagrado Corazón (a movable date): a net of fruit.

This completes the annual cycle, for the next fiesta is San Juan, and if the courtship goes on, the gifts are repeated for the second year.

In addition to these major prestations, the boy and/or his mother is expected to visit the girl's family every two or three weeks, bearing small gifts of maize or beans and some tortillas and rum. They pay short visits and are usually fed.

The third part of the bride price is work supplied by the boy. Each time he goes for a visit, he asks his future father-in-law if he can be of service and is either put to work in the fields or asked to help build or repair a house. He may also be called upon to be an assistant in a curing ceremony or to serve as a drink-pourer in the courtship of one of his future brothers-in-law. Usually the boy does not work more than about fifteen days before the house-entering ceremony occurs. In addition to paying for the bride, these visits are important in setting up carefully controlled situations in which the boy and girl and their two family groups become acquainted. Each side watches for small cues to see how the courtship is proceeding. If the girl or her relatives grudgingly accept the prestations, the boy and his family have time to consider breaking the engagement. If, on the other hand, all is going well, the courtship proceeds to the next stage, the house-entering ceremony.

The House-Entering Ceremony. Between one and two years after the original petition, the girl's father, who has kept a careful account of the boy's expenditures and labor, may decide that the boy has invested enough in the girl, and suggest that he begin to think about the house-entering ceremony. If the girl's father does not take the initiative, the boy's family themselves may decide they have spent enough. The boy and all his petitioners go to the girl's father, bearing more gifts of bread, brown sugar, and chocolate, and a garrafón of rum, and ask him to set the date. He often refuses, and a second or even third visit to make the request may be necessary.

Once the date is set, the girl's side asks an old woman to accompany the girl; they also appoint a ritual adviser, an older man who knows the ritual and who will act as the ceremonial leader; and they invite all their close relatives. Finally, they prepare the food that will be served and purchase the rum they will offer the boy's family. The boy's family also has many responsibilities. They must be prepared to give each member of the girl's family two rolls of bread, three gourds of coffee, and several glasses of rum. In addition, the boy must take a burlap bag containing maize, beans, and meat, as well as a blanket.

The ceremony ordinarily takes place on a Sunday or important Saint's Day. The boy's group includes all the petitioners and their wives, as well as a drink-pourer and a bottle-filler. In addition, some younger helpers are often taken along. Before arriving at the girl's house, the group stops to allow each of the petitioners to put on his black ceremonial robe (SHAKITAIL) and wrap his head in a red "turban," while each of their wives puts on a ceremonial poncho (CHILIL).

When the boy's group is heard outside, the girl's ritual adviser goes to the door, where he greets them with a prayer and a round of rum served by his drink-pourer. The boy's group is ushered into the house and seated; they then offer a round of rum. Meanwhile, the boy and the helpers remain outside preparing the portions of coffee and bread, the men serving men and the women serving women from the girl's side to ask pardon for having entered the house. This is followed by another round of rum.

On the second round of bread, coffee, and drinks, the petitioners ask the girl's father to make everyone compadres and allow the boy to enter the house. He complies and immediately the boy's group and the girl's group begin calling each other KUMPARE and KUMALE in a permanent compadrazgo relationship. The petitioners then bring in the boy, who is carrying a liter of rum, and two helpers, one carrying the burlap bag of maize, beans, and meat, and the other the blanket. The petitioners tell the girl's father that the boy is now his son. The boy serves drinks, and the girl's father seats him with the girl's relatives.

On the third round of coffee served in gourds to the girl's family by the petitioners, the girl's father is asked to name the "embracer" (HPETOM) of the wedding. When the embracer has been named, the girl and the old woman accompanying her rise and go to the boy's side where they go through bowing and releasing behavior. By this act, the girl acknowledges that the boy's parents are now her parents-in-law, and she begins to address them as TOT and ME? and to use the proper reference terms.

The girl's relatives set up a table in front of the boy's group and serve a ritual meal, while the boy's parents and the petitioners and their wives sit along the sides. The petitioners then go to ask the man named as embracer if he will serve. While they are gone, the boy is served a meal with the girl's relatives.

Singing as they walk, the petitioners carry a basket of bread and four bottles of liquor to present to the potential embracer. Entering his house on a ruse to prevent his escape, they place the gifts at his feet and make their request: "Will you take the souls of our children under your care?" The chosen embracer answers by telling them that he cannot serve, that he doesn't know the proper words to speak. But the petitioners plead with him again:

> Carry for us the souls of our children,
>> So give the two pines,
>> So give the two candles,
>>> Beneath the feet,
>>> Beneath the hands,
>>>> Of Father San Lorenzo,
>>>> Of Father Santo Domingo.
> You will plant firmly [the candles, and by extension, the souls]
>> You will carry their backs,
>> You will carry their sides,
>>> Holy companion,
>>> Holy compadre.

Adaptation from J. F. Collier 1968: 165

When the man chosen as embracer finally consents he signifies this by accepting a drink. Theoretically, he can refuse, but no actual refusals have been reported. Once he has accepted, drinks are served by the petitioners; henceforth the embracer, his wife, and anyone their age or older in the house at the time become compadres of all the petitioners and their wives and of all the adult members of the girl's group. The boy and girl enter into the relationship by calling the embracer and his wife TOT and ME?. The network of relationships is diagramed in Figure 80 (from Fishburne 1962: 46).

The petitioners return to the girl's house to report that the embracer has accepted and, after another round or two of rum, stagger home, leaving the boy at the girl's house. The next day the girl's father distributes the gifts of maize and beans among those of his relatives who are present, and the meat is served in a meal.

After this house-entering ceremony the boy is supposed to stay with the girl's family for four weeks and work for his father-in-law. At present, most boys only work for two weeks and make a cash settlement with the father-in-law for the balance of the time. The boy and girl are now allowed more freedom, and in some cases they are even allowed to begin sleeping together.

The Presentation Ceremony. In the three to four months following the house-entering ceremony, both families prepare for the wedding. The girl and her mother weave new clothes and blankets for a trousseau. The boy's

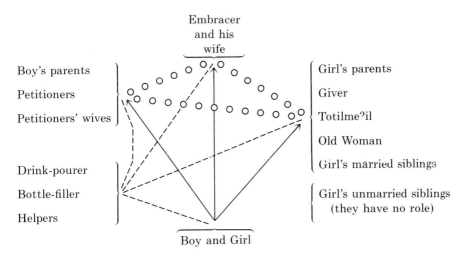

Terms of address used at, and after, the house-entering ceremony:

○ ○ ○ ○ Compadre terms (KUMPARE, KUMALE)

———→ Kinship terms (TOT, ME?). The boy and girl are called by name in return.

– – – – – – Normal terms of address

80. Relationships following the house-entering ceremony

family tries to collect enough money to pay for the wedding, then petitions the girl's father to set the date. The two or three petitions for this are similar to the petitions for the house-entering ceremony.

Once the father of the girl has set a date, both families go together to the house of the embracer to check the date with him. Before the wedding the embracer must find an old woman (HNUP HPETOM or "consort of the embracer") who will accompany the embracer throughout the wedding and become a comadre to both the boy's and the girl's groups. The embracer's wife is usually considered too young to fulfill the ritual duties required.

The two groups meet with the embracer and his consort and all go to see the Catholic priest—either in Zinacantan Center or in San Cristóbal. The young couple present themselves to the priest and tell him they wish to get married. He records their names and ages and questions them; if the two are related, he may demand that they pay for a dispensation. The priest then has time to announce the banns once or twice in church, after which the couple may get married when they choose.

Preparations for the Wedding. The boy's group makes elaborate and careful preparations for the wedding. First, they select a ritual adviser

(TOTILME'IL), usually an older man who has held at least two, or perhaps three, cargos in Zinacantan Center. The boy's father goes to the man with a bottle of rum, asks him to serve, and they discuss the wedding at length. There are several other ritual positions which the adviser and the boy's father must fill. They must name two men as junior and senior HPACHOL (literally, "a person who carries something with both hands"). Another man, called the "bearer of the flowers" (H'IK' NICHIM), is selected to carry a large basket of orange branches and geraniums to be divided among the people who dance at the wedding feast. Two women (BANKILAL and 'ITS'INAL HPATVAH) are chosen to make the special bean tamales that will be served. (This appears to be the only instance in which BANKILAL – 'ITS'INAL terms are applied to women). If a bull is to be killed for the wedding, two men (HK'EL BEK'ET or "meat watchers"), are needed to supervise the butchering and division of the meat. Finally, three musicians are required to play at the wedding—a violinist, a harpist, and a guitarist.

Many tasks are the responsibility of the groom and his helpers. Orange branches and large leaves in which to wrap the bean tamales must be brought up from the lowlands. Three pine branches and three bunches of geraniums must be collected to decorate the house cross.

The bride's group has only to provide one new person for the wedding— the "mother of the girl" (ME' TSEB) who ritually takes the place of the girl's own mother. She helps the bride dress, accompanies her during the ceremony in the church, and attends the feast in the boy's house. Usually the same old woman who accompanied the bride at the house-entering ceremony is asked to serve in this capacity.

A wedding requires huge amounts of food, including at least three jugs of rum, as well as maize and beans, not only to make the special bean tamales, but also to feed all the helpers who gather at the boy's house at least two days before the wedding. Special bread (MUTAL VAH, called "bird tortilla," because it is shaped like a bird's wing) must be purchased in San Cristóbal.

Two days before the wedding the ritual adviser, his wife, and the women who are to make the bean tamales come to the boy's house. Under the supervision of the adviser, the maize and beans are carefully measured out and placed on the fire to cook. This day is called SHLOK' 'ISHIM CHENEK' (removal of maize and beans).

Meanwhile, all the rest of the women (wives of the other assistants) help the boy's mother and sisters make large quantities of tortillas, cook the meat, and make PISIL VAH, a tamale somewhat like the bean tamales, but made of pure maize—to be presented later to the embracer as a gift. In the afternoon the junior carrier, his wife, and the drink-pourer take a gift of meat and rum to the girl's house. Then they return to take a basket of maize tamales, as well as gourds of coffee and gifts of bread to the embracer to ask him to attend the confession the next day.

The day before the wedding (PAT VAH or "making tortillas"), special bean tamales are made (see Chapter 3). The maize and beans are ground, while the musicians, who arrive early in the morning, begin to play; while the tamales cook, the tortilla-makers dance to the music.

Early in the morning the day before the wedding the embracer, his consort, and the girl's entire family, including "the mother of the girl," gather at the boy's house or meet the boy's group near the church. The boy is usually accompanied only by the senior carrier, his wife, and the drink-pourer; the others are back at the house preparing for the wedding. They go first to the town hall where the Secretary records the names of the bride and groom, and asks them to sign (or to thumbprint, if they cannot write). In exchange for 20 pesos, the bride and groom are given a slip of paper saying they have been married by the civil authorities. After the wedding party leaves, the Secretary gives the Presidente 5 of the pesos.

That afternoon the couple present themselves to the priest and give him the Secretary's document. The priest also records their names and collects 10 to 15 pesos for the church ceremony. Then he sends them to a lay sister for catechism instruction. Since very few Zinacantecos take communion before they are married, the sacraments of first communion and marriage are usually combined. At night they usually stay with friends or in rented or borrowed houses in Zinacantan Center rather than returning to their hamlet.

The Wedding. On the morning of the wedding, the bride and groom must be at the church by 5 A.M. The groom usually goes to the bride's house to dress; alternatively, both may meet at the embracer's house and dress there. The "mother of the girl" *must* be present to help the bride. The bride and groom both are dressed as elaborately as they will ever be in their lives. Standing on a bull-hide mat, the groom puts on a pair of knee-length, white cotton pants; then, over his usual shirt, a long-sleeved white cotton shirt that comes to the waist. His outer clothing includes knee-length green velvet pants buttoned up the front, a long, wide strip of white cloth, embroidered at both ends and in the center, which serves as a belt, a square piece of white lace-trimmed cloth, and two long red pieces of cloth that are wound around his neck and head. He carries a wide-brimmed, black felt hat, and looks somewhat like an alférez in the cargo system who is about to go through a change-of-office ceremony.

The bride then dresses, putting on a new blouse and skirt, covered with a long white overblouse (*huipil*) embroidered with white chicken feathers. Her hair is braided in an elaborate and special fashion with a long cloth strip of two colors, and covered with a red scarf. A large square of white cloth practically covers her face and comes down below her hips. Rosaries and scapulars are placed around the necks of both the bride and the groom (Figure 81).

After the bride and groom are dressed, the two older women, the embracer's consort, and the "mother of the girl" dress. They each put on a ceremonial poncho CHILIL, have their hair arranged like the bride's, and cover themselves with large squares of white cloth. The embracer dresses in a black ceremonial robe, wraps his head in his scarf, and carries four large white candles, a two-meter-long piece of pink ribbon, two rings, and thirteen coins for the church ceremony.

At the church, the groom leads the wedding party, followed by the embracer, the bride, the embracer's consort, and the "mother of the girl." The bride and groom kneel together at the altar rail while the embracer and his consort sit behind them, on the first bench. Before the ceremony begins, the embracer lights the candles, giving one each to the bride and groom and one to his companion, retaining one for himself. A lay sister collects the coins and rings from the embracer. The priest arrives, ties a knot in the pink ribbon, and slips it over the heads of the couple. He gives the thirteen coins to the groom, who in turn presents them to the bride, saying in Tzotzil, "I give you this money, wife"; she replies "I receive it, husband," (This is the first time the couple call each other husband and wife.) The bride lets the coins, which are for the church, run through her fingers onto a plate held by the priest's assistant. Next the priest places one of the two rings on the groom's finger and gives him the other to put on the bride. Then the priest says Mass and gives communion to all the couples, following this with a short sermon. The priest tells the grooms to work hard and to refrain from drunkenness and beating their wives; he tells the brides to work hard, not to quarrel, and to feed their husbands when they are hungry. This church wedding ceremony, largely of Spanish Catholic origin, is very similar to the ceremony currently performed in Spain (Foster 1960: 136–137).

After the ceremony, the wedding party marches out in the same order that it entered. A bottle of rum is drunk outside the church.

If the bride and groom live in Zinacantan Center (or nearby), the party goes immediately to the boy's house. But if they live in a distant hamlet,

81. Bride and groom dressed for the wedding

everyone returns to the house where they spent the night to undress the bride and groom so that the heavy clothes need not be worn on the trail over the mountains.

Meanwhile, at the groom's house, preparations are in full swing. The women are cooking out in the patio; the junior carrier and the flower-bearer, each wearing a black ceremonial robe and carrying gourd rattles decorated with pink chicken feathers, are holding orange branches and geranium flowers and dancing to the music. Shortly before the wedding party is due, the junior carrier stops dancing and takes a bottle of rum to meet them halfway. Here he serves drinks to all but the bride and groom to warm them for the remainder of their hike. Then the junior carrier exchanges places with the senior carrier, while the latter rushes ahead to the groom's house to announce the approach of the wedding party. Just before the party arrives, it stops somewhere (perhaps under a tree) to dress the bride and groom again. At this point, all the men and women who have not dressed up before put on ceremonial robes and ponchos.

At the house of the groom, all are inside except the ritual adviser, who meets the wedding party in the patio. One by one its members come forward to greet him, bowing and kissing the rosary he wears. Only the bride and groom do not approach, but stand hand in hand before the decorated house cross in the smoke of the burning incense. Standing in the door, the ritual adviser then says a long prayer asking "if the bride and groom will accompany each other in sickness and in death, if they will not scold each other, if they will mother each other and father each other, and if they will be kind to each other" (J. F. Collier 1968: 177).

When the meal is ready, a table, oriented east-west, is set up in the patio, and the ritual adviser seats everyone. He himself sits at the eastern end, with the bride and groom facing each other in the middle, flanked by the bride's adult male relatives and the embracer. Near the western end sit the two old women, the embracer's consort and the "mother of the girl." This arrangement may vary, depending upon the advice of the ritual adviser, who may place the bride's female relatives, the groom's parents, and the senior carrier at the table. Usually, however, the other women of the bride's family eat apart with their children, and the groom's parents eat inside the house. In any event, the meal is very much like the meal at the house-entering ceremony, when the bride's family served the groom's group; now the situation is reversed, with the groom's family serving the food and directing the ceremony. Although they sit at the table, the bride and groom do not eat or drink. They are served, and at the end of the meal their untouched food is given to the embracer and his wife.

Following the meal, the embracer and his consort take the bride and groom into the boy's house to remove their wedding clothes. The groom sits on a chair, while the bride sits beside him on the mat. This entrance is of crucial ritual significance for it marks the bride's introduction to her new home and new relatives. If she leaves the boy after this, her father will not have to repay him money spent on the courtship. The boy is then dressed in the black ceremonial robe and the girl in the ceremonial poncho—clothes symbolizing their attainment of adulthood. From now on they may take part in the important ceremonial activities where the wearing of these items is required.

The embracer then delivers a lecture:

> He usually tells the groom to work hard, to provide for his wife, and not to get mad at her or beat her. He also warns him that his wife is new in the house and still has many things to learn, and that he should not get mad if she does not behave properly at first. Then the embracer tells the bride to obey her husband, to give him food when he is hungry, and to get up early in the morning and not be lazy. After this, the embracer often turns to the groom's mother to tell her to be kind to her new daughter-in-law and to show her the proper way to do things instead of scolding her. He also reminds the boy's mother that her family had to pay a lot of money for the bride and that all the money would be wasted if the bride was made so miserable that she went home again. (J. F. Collier 1968: 177–178)

After this the embracer asks the musicians to start playing and invites the bride's family into the house where each goes through very careful bowing and releasing behavior with the groom's family. The groom's family serve them rum, and the bride's family invites the groom's group outside to dance. Outside, where the flower-bearer hands out geranium flowers and orange leaves, the dancers form in two lines: men in front and women several feet behind. Often the groom's mother holds the hand of the bride's mother as they dance. The men have one song, the women have another, but all sing at the same time. The embracer and his consort do not dance with the others, but stay ouside the group, dancing around in circles with the consort following behind the embracer. During the dancing the drink-pourers from both groups are very busy, since each group is serving drinks to the other. As the dancing continues, more and more people drop in drunken stupors, until finally there is almost no one left. At this point the dancing ends and the musicians stop playing.

The embracer and his companion return inside of the house to remove the ceremonial poncho and black ceremonial robe from the bride and groom and to undo the bride's hair. She is seated in front of the metate by the companion, told to grind maize, and shown the fire on which she will cook. The musicians leave after being fed and paid, and the bride's family and groom's helpers follow—if able; those who are too drunk stay until the next morning. Meanwhile, the bride and groom spend the night among the drunken relatives and often do not consummate the marriage until the second night.

At the wedding a few more people are taken into the compadre relationship. The ritual advisers, the carriers, the tortilla-makers, and the flower-bearer become compadres of the bride's group and the embracer's group.

> The relations set up at the wedding can be best understood by thinking of the wedding party as consisting of three groups: the bride's family, the embracer's group, and the groom's group. All the responsible adult members of one group become compadres of the adult members of the other two groups, while within a group the younger members address the older men as TOT or TOTIK. The actual bride and groom are in a sense outside this arrangement, because they call the important adult members of every group TOT and ME?. (Fishburne 1962: 86)

These relationships are diagramed in Figure 82.

The day after the wedding the groom leaves the house to return the wedding clothes to the bride's parents, who in turn give them back to the owners. This is the only time during the three days after the wedding that the bride and groom leave the house. The people who normally live in the house remain, but no visitors come and the new couple go outside only to relieve themselves.

After three days the groom returns the rings to the embracer, and the couple usually visits the bride's home. The only things the bride brings to her new home are her clothes and one or two blankets. Equipment such as a metate, pots, and a loom are all provided by her husband's family.

Variations in Courtship and Marriage. The foregoing description outlines the preferred type of courtship and marriage, but in fact many Zinacantecos cannot afford these expensive procedures and are forced to marry in one of three other ways. A proper courtship, even if it is not the most expensive type, can cost as much as 800 pesos and the wedding another 800. A common way of cutting down the expenses is simply to do everything on a smaller scale by reducing the length of the courtship, giving fewer gifts, and involving fewer people in the proceedings.

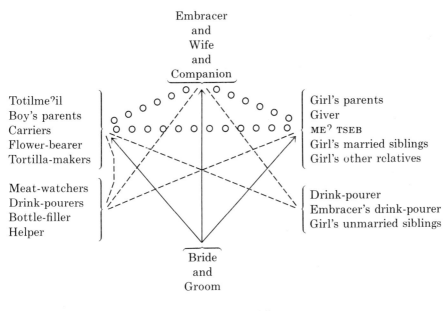

Embracer
and
Wife
and
Companion

Totilme?il
Boy's parents
Carriers
Flower-bearer
Tortilla-makers

Meat-watchers
Drink-pourers
Bottle-filler
Helper

Girl's parents
Giver
ME? TSEB
Girl's married siblings
Girl's other relatives

Drink-pourer
Embracer's drink-pourer
Girl's unmarried siblings

Bride
and
Groom

Terms of address used at, and after, the wedding:

O O O O   Compadre terms (KUMPARE, KUMALE)

————→   Kinship terms (TOT, ME?)

- - - - - -   Normal terms of address

82. Relationships following the wedding ceremony

A second form of marriage, often used by very poor families and even less acceptable than having a "poor" wedding, is to treat the house-entering ceremony as the wedding ceremony. For a second marriage after the death of a spouse, this variation is considered quite acceptable.

The third, and least desirable form of marriage, is an elopement. This is becoming more common and usually has the tacit approval of the boy's family, since it is less expensive for them. A girl simply leaves her house without telling her parents and meets the boy at some prearranged spot from which they go to the boy's house to live. The girl's parents are furious, and her brothers threaten to kill the boy. But the girl's father finally lets it be known how much money he wants for his daughter, usually demanding more than he expects to get, often 600 or 700 pesos. Or the girl's father may take the case immediately to the Presidente and demand that the boy be forced to pay. After much bargaining the agreement reached is usually some 300 to 500 pesos. The broken relations between the families will never be repaired, and the marriage unites two people rather than two families. The girl's family loses more: they receive only money instead of rum, fruit, and bread for two years; and instead of gaining new kin relationships, they lose a daughter.

The Breaking of Courtships and Divorces. Courtships are broken off frequently, but not easily. Such breaks often cause disputes that must be taken to the Cabildo or even to the authorities in San Cristóbal for settlement. The boy's family always demands the return of the money he has spent, while the girl's family tries to reduce the amount. If the boy has not kept a careful record of expenditures, he is almost certain to be cheated. The girl's family is at a disadvantage since they must return cash for the food and rum they have already consumed. Thus, both sides feel cheated and their relations may be strained or hostile for years.

There are many reasons why courtships may be interrupted. At the time of the first petition, the girl's parents are seldom in a position to refuse. Later, if they find they really dislike the boy, they make an effort to get rid of him. If there is a legitimate complaint, the case can be taken to court; otherwise, they have to discourage the boy in other ways—by being rude, sending their daughter away when they know he is coming for a visit, gossiping to the neighbors about how awful he is, and so on. Ultimately the boy realizes what is happening and decides to break the engagement. If a boy asks for a very young girl, her parents may so prolong the courtship that he becomes discouraged and decides to look elsewhere. Or a girl might engage in a flirtation or even an affair with another boy, inevitably producing one of the most bitter kind of dispute in Zinacantan.

Outright divorces are rare, but periodic separations are frequent. Many men beat their wives when they are drunk, after which the wife goes home. If the husband wants her back, he must go to her home with a bottle of rum and beg her to return. Usually she relents and returns. Later in marriage, especially after several children, the relationship becomes more stable. A divorce can be obtained at the Cabildo for 300 pesos. In such a case, the Secretary simply erases his records, so that from the "legal" point of view the marriage never existed. The church is never consulted, and Zinacantecos feel free to remarry. Upon divorce, the property should be divided between the husband and wife. Even the children are supposed to be divided equally, except for nursing babies, who stay with the mothers. Such divisions are difficult and involve even more disputes that must be settled at the town hall.

Courtship, Marriage, and Social Structure. The long courtship and the various marriage ceremonies perpetuate Zinacanteco's social structure in both symbolic and practical terms. The economic transactions and ritual procedures lead to the creation of a stable marriage and to the preparation of the young bride and groom for responsible adult roles.

At the first petition the boy asks his prospective parents-in-law to "measure" him as a man. His future father-in-law responds by telling him, "You are my child. You will become a man." The intrinsic idea is that the boy, through these contacts with his future father-in-law, will learn to become an adult. During the period of gift-giving the boy is symbolically providing for a woman, weaning her away from her own domestic group and into a relationship with himself and his family. The gifts also pay her father for the expenses of rearing her and thereby remove her family's claim for her services and her child-bearing potential. The gifts also represent the first time in the boy's life that he is producing food for a wife, the lifelong task of an adult male. They show the seriousness of the boy's intent and his respect for the girl's father. This show of respect is very important because it can be symbolically extended to a respect for all the elders and more generally for the established order of the society. Throughout the payment of the bride price, the girl also learns her future tasks. She helps prepare the boy's food, hands it to him, and prepares his bed if he stays to spend the night.

At the time of the house-entering ceremony the boy is considered to have fulfilled the major part of his obligations. He has demonstrated that he can work and support a wife and that he has a proper attitude toward people outside his own family. The time has arrived for him to become a member of the girl's group, to be able to talk with his future wife, and in some cases to begin living with her. This change is symbolized in part by the gifts brought at this time. Instead of fruit, bread, meat, and other luxury items, the boy brings maize and beans, the staples of the Zinacanteco diet, symbols of his ability to feed the girl everyday foods, of the everyday relationship of marriage. He brings a blanket, symbolizing the sexual side of marriage, which is not used until the bride and groom start sleeping together.

In the minds of the Zinacantecos, the marriage takes place on two levels. An interaction is set up not just between two groups of people, but also between the souls of the groom and his bride. These souls are symbolically placed in the care of the embracer after the house-entering ceremony. When the petitioners ask a man to serve as embracer, they ask him to "carry for us the souls of our children." He is asked to plant the souls firmly ("as pines and candles") beneath the feet of San Lorenzo and Santo Domingo—two of the important patron saints of Zinacantan. This is symbolized by his carrying candles for them during the marriage ceremony in the church.

The embracer has important practical duties too. He dresses the young couple in the symbols of adult life: the clothes the boy wears at the wedding and the ceremonial poncho and black ceremonial robe that the bride and groom wear later. He gives them advice on their duties in adult life, advice geared to the realities of Zinacanteco life. After the wedding the embracer is charged with keeping both the souls and the bodies of the bride and groom together by mediating any disputes which might threaten the marriage.

If they are to lead to successful marriages, the courtship customs must overcome a lack of trust and avoidance of economic and emotional involvement with others that are especially marked in Zinacantan. The courtship handles this problem on a symbolic level in the theme of entering a house. At the first petition the girl's house is entered violently and there is no trust whatever between the two groups. Then follows the long period of courtship in which more trustful, interpersonal relations are established between the two sides, relations that are gradually cemented by a network of ritual kin ties in the compadrazgo system. By the time of the house-entering ceremony, the boy's group is invited into the house as honored guests by a ritual adviser. Later at the wedding the girl's group is similarly invited into the boy's house and the circle of trust is completed (J. F. Collier 1968: 193–194).

It is significant that after the house-entering ceremony, personal relationships are replaced by ritual ones. The old woman (ME? TSEB) who accompanies the bride replaces her mother, the ritual adviser her father. The groom's parents become nothing more than members of the group of petitioners. The final separation of the girl from her family is thus in the hands of people who have little emotional commitment.

Although, as Jane Collier points out, Zinacanteco marriage can be viewed as an exchange of goods for a woman, it actually consists of a series of economic and ritual transactions that lead up to the final transfer of the bride from her own home to that of her husband. At the first petition the girl's father is almost forced to say he will give his daughter because he can rarely refuse the petitioners' request (1968: 195). The events which follow are a dramatic enactment of what Mauss has called "the system of total prestation"—an exchange of individuals, goods, services, courtesies, entertainment, and ritual, which is at once economic, social, religious, and moral. But, he recognizes, a gift is not merely an inanimate object—it partakes of the essence of the donor, who is not simply giving a thing, but giving himself. The pattern of reciprocal transactions is "a pattern of spiritual bonds between things which are to some extent parts of persons, and persons and groups that behave in some measure as if they were things" (1954: 1, 10). The rum that is exchanged is called the "dew of the gods"; and the interaction of the "souls" of the individuals involved are as important to the Zinacantecos as interactions between the people themselves.

A gift demands a gift, with the donor simultaneously a supplicant. The courtship proceeds. "The two families become involved with each other as if they were cogwheels—tooth filling notch, notch embracing tooth. Groom's party gives rum, bride's party receives rum, bride's party gives bride, groom's party receives bride, groom's party gives groom, bride's party receives groom, groom gives bride's party rum, and so on in dizzying evolution" (Laughlin 1963: 75–76).

Each side becomes increasingly committed, emotionally as well as financially. As the boy's side invests more and more money, its interest in the outcome of the investment grows accordingly. The girl's side accepts more and more consumable goods which would be difficult to return if the courtship were to end. But even at an advanced stage, the girl's father is not entirely committed to giving away his daughter. It is not until the house-entering ceremony that he makes the final transaction, and accepts the boy as part of his family. Then, persons who play ritual roles take over and carry the courtship to completion. At the end, the bride's father is given no chance to break the bargain. The ritual continues until the bride is safely installed in her husband's home. Even after the wedding it is the embracer's task to see that both sides live up to the bargain. "It is his ultimate duty to leave the bride and groom planted together as firmly as two candles beneath the feet of San Lorenzo" (J. F. Collier 1968: 195).

Death

According to Zinacanteco belief, no death results from what we consider natural physiological causes. Rather, it is caused by "soul loss" resulting from "fright" (SHI'EL) caused by the gods, by the death of the animal spirit companion which has escaped from the supernatural corral, or by the sale of the soul to the "Earth Lord." Alternatively, death may result from accidents or from murder.

The Funeral Ceremony. Most Zinacantecos die on their petates (reed mats) on the earthen floors of their houses. The scarf (for a man) or the rebozo (for a woman) is placed over the head, covering the mouth. If the death occurs before sundown, the burial, preceded by an all-night wake, takes place the next day. If the death occurs after sundown, the wake is not held until the following night. An old man (or old woman), with a different Indian surname (from another lineage), is called upon to bathe

the corpse with laurel and myrtle leaves. An elderly person is selected, because there is danger that the soul of the deceased will take others to the grave with him. After the corpse is washed, it is dressed in clean clothes (new clothes in some hamlets) and placed on a petate that is turned upside down and covered with a blanket that is turned wrong-side to the body. The head is placed facing west, and the area around the petate is blocked off with sundry household articles.

A pine coffin is purchased either from the local Ladino carpenter in Zinacantan Center (for 85 to 110 pesos), or from a carpenter shop in San Cristóbal. While awaiting its arrival relatives and neighbors gather in the house to contribute money—ordinarily 50 centavos or a peso—and each coin is placed in a plate by the body. (The money is later used to purchase candles for rituals at the cemetery.) Then, if anyone knows the Pater Noster (few do), it is recited. Three musicians—a violinist, guitarist, and harpist—are summoned to entertain the soul of the deceased. If the death occurs in or near the ceremonial center, two sacristanes may be summoned to recite traditional Catholic prayers in Latin.

When the coffin arrives, the body is placed in it, with head toward the west, unless it is an unbaptized child, in which case the head faces east. A rooster's head is set in a bowl of broth beside the head of the deceased along with some tortillas and salt. Three small bags of money are placed with the body, one tied to the belt where a Zinacanteco purse is normally carried, the other two hidden at the sides. At the foot of the corpse are set a small bowl and a gourd with water; these are the drinking dishes needed by the soul. A small sack of charred tortillas (food unlike that consumed by the living) is added for food. The all-night wake follows, during which the musicians play, rum is served, and a ritual meal is provided at which the rooster (whose head was placed in the coffin) is eaten.

At dawn another ritual meal is served and preparations are made for the trip to the cemetery. All in the house cry openly and loudly to express their grief at the departure of the loved one. The coffin is closed and carried outside where it is fastened to two long poles which will rest on the shoulders of the four pallbearers. If the deceased was a married woman, her husband is expected to state publicly whom he plans to marry as the coffin is being removed from the house. Since there is a strong belief that the soul of the deceased wishes to take family, friends, and possessions with it, there are a number of ritual acts to protect the survivors. The most important is the spitting of salt water on the spot where the coffin has been located during the wake, as well as in all the places around the house and patio where the deceased has worked, walked, and slept, in order to "loosen the soul from the house." In the hamlet of ?Apas, the house cross is also pulled up and set against the fence at the side of the patio when a death occurs, presumably to remove the ritual entrance to the house so that the soul cannot find its way back.

The funeral procession now forms, to the accompaniment of loud wailing. First come the musicians, then the coffin, carried by the pallbearers (who are compadres or friends of the deceased, specifically not brothers or close relatives), next the men, including the assistants who will dig the grave, then the women, led by the widow (if the deceased were male), and finally the young women and children (whose souls are least firmly attached). There are fixed resting places on the way to the cemetery at which the procession stops, the coffin is opened, candles are lighted and prayers said, the corpse is given water to drink by an old woman, either from a geranium or with her finger, and everyone drinks rum.

Upon the arrival at the cemetery, the coffin is set down and another round of drinks is served. The gravediggers start digging the grave; when it is half-finished, another round of rum is served. Any bones encountered from previous burials are kept on the side to be buried again with the coffin. After the grave is finished, the workers drink pozol while the two sacristans (if they have come) recite the Catholic prayers for the dead. A pick and shovel are left crossed on top of the grave so that the deceased will not attract any souls of the survivors into the coffin with him. Every half-hour or so the deceased is given another drink of water to relieve his thirst. The children who are present step up to the open coffin and kick the side so that the deceased will not take their souls with him.

As the coffin is closed for the final time and lowered halfway into the grave, with the head to the west, a round of drinks is served. The coffin is then lowered the rest of the way, and all present throw three handfuls of dirt over it to prevent the deceased from taking their souls. The filling of the grave is done in six "strips." When it is half-filled (three strips), the grave objects are put in, just on top of any bones that have been unearthed. These objects (which have been removed from the coffin before it is closed for the last time) include, for a man, his hat, with the edges burned and the black bands ripped in three places ("so they won't turn into snakes") and his sandals with the high backs cut ("so they won't turn into bull's horns and gore the soul"); The woolen rebozo of a deceased woman is cut at the corners ("so it won't turn into a ram"). Additional grave objects include a cup, a plate, a needle and a ball of thread, a married person's rosary, a woman's hair comb and hair roll, necklaces, blankets, and old clothes and any special mementos prized by the deceased. These objects are all said to possess the soul of their owner.

Finally the grave is completely filled. If the pile of earth accumulated on top from the handfuls of earth tossed in by those attending the burial is large, the deceased should have lived longer and was probably bewitched; if it is small, it was time for him to die. Pine needles are placed over the grave; an unmarked cross is erected and adorned with pine boughs and red geraniums; the three candles are lighted in the pit in front of the cross: two of wax (tortillas for the soul) and one of tallow (meat). The grave is now the "house" of the dead (Figure 83). In ?Apas the people follow an old custom of later erecting a thatched roof over the grave; in other hamlets the pine needles suffice. The burial party moves a short distance away where they have another chicken meal and drink rum. They return to the house of the deceased where they finish the remaining liquor before returning to their homes.

There are several major variations in the pattern described above. A pregnant woman has the fetus removed before burial, "so the soul will not suffer"; a deceased woman's weaving is finished for her for the same reason. If a cargoholder dies, he is buried in the clothes in which he was sworn in, and two regidores come to the house to swear him out of office. Anyone killed violently is buried without grave goods, and without a day of rest before the burial. Unmarried men and women or those in common-law unions are buried with either green or purple ribbons crossed on their chests in lieu of a rosary. Unbaptized babies are buried with heads to the east.

Cemeteries. Interaction with the dead by no means stops after the burial takes place. Ordinarily, the closest survivors make daily trips to the cemetery for nine days after the burial (following the Catholic Novena) during the time the soul is believed to linger. Candles are lighted and prayers said. When a lactating mother loses her baby, she pumps milk from her breasts onto the spot in the house where the baby died in order to feed the soul.

Special rituals are also performed in the cemeteries at Todos Santos and other important ceremonial occasions, such as San Lorenzo and San Sebastián. The graves of deceased relatives are decorated with fresh pine needles on the mounds and with fresh pine boughs and red geraniums on the crosses at the heads of the graves. Each year the souls visit their graves and the houses of their descendants, which they will find even if they have moved. Visiting is done especially at Todos Santos. The souls of children return the Saturday before, adults on Sunday, and both leave on Monday. Those who died a long time before visit for a longer time.

83. Grave covered with pine needles in the cemetery of Paste?; note small cross at head of the grave

Zinacantan maintains a number of cemeteries. The dead from outlying, more distant hamlets are buried in cemeteries located at their outskirts. In many hamlets, such as ?Apas, Paste?, and ?Elan Vo?, the ancestors in these cemeteries appear to be "guarding" the main trail into the settlement. The dead from Zinacantan Center are buried in MUKENAL HOL NA ?ICHIN (top of owl house cemetery), located on a high ridge between Zinacantan Center and Salinas. MUKENAL TSELEH, a large cemetery on a high ridge between the center and Na Chih, is shared by Vo?ch'oh Vo? and Pat ?Osil, with distinct areas for each hamlet. It also contains a section for the combined use of families from Na Chih, Paste?, and ?Elan Vo? who choose to bring their dead to this more distant cemetery instead of burying them near their hamlets. Sometimes aging persons from these hamlets request burial here in order that their souls be able to hear the church bells of Zinacantan Center's churches, and hence continue to participate in fiestas after their deaths.

There are at least two special cemeteries for dead babies. Between KALVARIO and MUKENAL TSELEH is a small cemetery (called BIK'IT

MUKENAL or "little cemetery") where unbaptized babies are buried and between TOCH VITS and the trail to SHULVO?, there is a small cemetery where babies from Na Chih are buried.

The Souls of the Dead. The soul is believed to leave the body in the form of a fly. It lingers on earth for nine days, retracing all of its actions during the two days before death. Then it is carried over a river by a black dog, to whom it gives as payment the unburned tortillas buried with the body. On the other side it follows a trail until it comes to a crossing. To the left is a wide, straight path, and to the right an almost unnoticeable crooked path. At this point, the rooster (whose head was buried with the body) crows, indicating that the soul should take the small, crooked path. It turns out that in this K'OTEBAL ("place of final judgment" in the afterlife), the path to the right leads to "heaven" (VINAHEL), and the trail to the left to "burned bones" (K'ATIN BAK). As the deceased is facing east, "demon" (PUKUH) is on the left shoulder and "God" (RIOSH) on the right.

If the soul goes to the right, it is met on the road by relatives and friends for whom it did favors in life, and is escorted through a gate tended by a Ladino gatekeeper. Other souls steal the money (which is carried openly) and the charred tortillas. Life in VINAHEL is similar to that on earth. There are rectangular houses, and people work; but for those who in life did not work on Sunday the work is easy. Anyone without the appropriate number of callouses is made to work until "the blood pours from his hands." Anyone who has not attended fiestas during his life is locked up during fiestas in VINAHEL. If the person was fussy in life about the water he drank, his soul will drink dirty water, blood, or pus. Those who lived without church marriages are condemned to live in the dark. Widows join their first husbands.

K'ATIN BAK is quite different. It is heated by burning bones and contains various demons. It is peopled by those who mistreated and were too fussy about the "long-suffering maize"; by loose women, who have hot wires put up their vaginas "until they sizzle" and are then forced to eat the surrounding flesh; by the incestuous and murderers, who are alternately eaten and disgorged whole by "demons" and thrown into the fire.

There are a number of special paths for souls with unusual experiences. Those who have been sold to the Earth Lord do not cross the river with the black dog, but go to work for the Earth Lord. Infants who died before baptism become demons, since they have no fixed souls. Baptized babies are passed through a fire once for having kicked their mothers before they were born, then go easily to VINAHEL, where they are changed into flowers and tied on a cross. The soul of anyone who dies on Todos Santos takes the fruits brought to the dead to VINAHEL with him. The soul of anyone who dies within a month of Todos Santos guards the houses of the souls in VINAHEL when they go to visit their graves in Zinacantan.

10 / Relationship Systems

There are two institutionalized kinds of relationship systems in Zinacantan: kinship and compadrazgo.

Kinship

The kin terms used in Zinacantan are shown in Figures 84, 85, and 86 (adapted from J. F. Collier 1967). Table 7 presents a complete list of these terms and their ranges of application to genealogical positions in the kinship system. These are "reference terms," as contrasted with "address terms" (described below), and are the Tzotzil kin terms used to refer to specified relatives when talking to a third person. They represent the response in the sentence frame: "he is my ———."

In the terms for lineal relatives (Fig. 84) all siblings are distinguished according to sex, sex of speaker, and relative age—except the dyad "Elder Sister" ⟷ "Younger Si, Br," where one term is applied to each member. Children, regardless of sex, are referred to by one term by male speakers, and by another by female speakers. Only one term is used for grandchildren. A variant, HMUK' TOT, is used for grandfather in the western part of the municipio; otherwise there was complete consistency in these terms for lineal relatives in the sample of twenty-five genealogies collected by Jane F. Collier (1967).

The terms for collateral relatives (Fig. 85) have been simplified by including only father's sister and mother's brother and their spouses, even though the terms apply equally to father's brother and mother's sister and their spouses, making the system "bilateral." The figure is further simplified by

In this chapter I am especially grateful to Jane F. Collier (1967) and Michelle Z. Rosaldo (1967) who have worked on kinship, and to Elena Uribe (1966) and Gwendoline van den Berghe (1965) who have made field studies of compadrazgo.

placing all cousins older than ego to the left and all cousins younger than
ego to the right of the chart. Since no distinction is made between them,
brother's children are joined with sister's children. Unlike the more stable
terms for lineal relatives, the kin terms for collateral relatives are under-
going change. In the twenty-five genealogies there was a great variation
among the informants. The more traditional system is contained in the
first alternatives; the most important variant terms in the second. For
example, a father's sister traditionally referred to as HHUN ME², is now
commonly called HMUK'TA ME².

On the other hand, the terms presented in Fig. 86 form a core of consistent and stable terms, covering the most important affinal relationships.

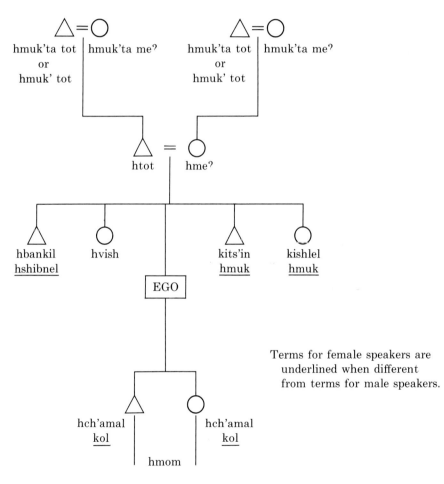

Terms for female speakers are
underlined when different
from terms for male speakers.

84. Kin terms for lineal relatives

85. Kin terms for collateral relatives

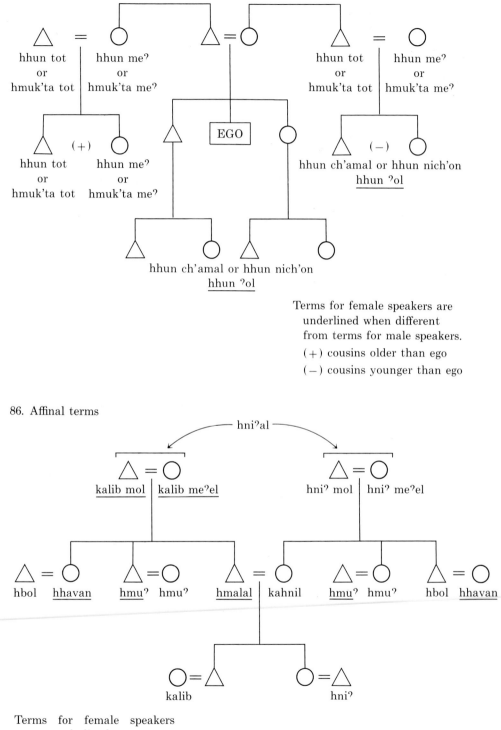

Terms for female speakers are underlined when different from terms for male speakers.
(+) cousins older than ego
(−) cousins younger than ego

86. Affinal terms

Terms for female speakers are underlined.

Table 7. Zinacanteco Kin Terms

Term	Range of application
HTOT	Fa
HME?	Mo
HMUK'TA TOT	FaFa, MoFa; variant for FaBr, FaSiHu, MoSiHu, male cousin older than ego
HMUK' TOT	Variant for FaFa, MoFa
HMUK'TA ME?	MoMo, FaMo; Variant for MoSi, FaSi, MoBrWi, FaBrWi, female cousin older than ego
HHUN TOT	FaBr, MoBr, FaSiHu, MoSiHu, male cousin older than ego
HHUN ME?	MoSi, FaSi, MoBrWi, FaBrWi, female cousin older than ego
HBANKIL	ElBr (male speaking)
HSHIBNEL	ElBr (female speaking)
HVISH	ElSi
KITS'IN	YoBr (male speaking)
KISHLEL	YoSi (male speaking)
HMUK	Younger sibling (female speaking)
HCH'AMAL	Child (male speaking)
KOL	Child (female speaking)
HMOM	Grandchild
HHUN CH'AMAL	Cousin younger than ego (male speaking)
HHUN NICH'ON	Variant for cousin younger than ego (male speaking)
HHUN ?OL	Cousin younger than ego (female speaking)
KAHNIL	Wi
HMALAL	Hu
HNI?	DaHu
HNI? MOL	WiFa
HNI? ME?EL	WiMo
KALIB	SoWi
KALIB MOL	HuFa
KALIB ME?EL	HuMo
HBOL	WiBr or SiHu (male speaking)
HHAVAN	HuSi or BrWi (female speaking)
HMU?	WiSi or BrWi (male speaking), HuBr or SiHu (female speaking)
HNI?AL	Child's spouse's parents

An examination of the terms for consanguineal relatives (both lineal and collateral) reveals that five distinct variables characterize the more traditional pattern. These variables are (1) generation; (2) lineal or collateral; (3) age relative to ego; (4) sex of referent; and (5) sex of speaker. The traditional pattern can be neatly diagramed as shown in Figure 87 (from J. F. Collier 1967: 7).

Note that the two most important components are relative age and lineal versus collateral. Relative age divides the whole system in two, even extending to ego's generation as ego differentiates between older and younger siblings. The lineal–collateral division would be even neater if the terms HMUK'TA HUN TOT and HMUK'TA HUN ME? were added to the upper-left-hand corner; then the diagram would be completely consistent with all the collateral terms containing the root HUN and neatly divided from ego's own

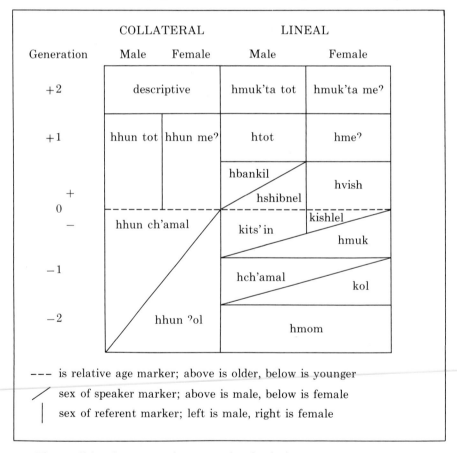

87. The traditional pattern of consanguineal relatives

bilateral line. Jane Collier thinks "it is probably safe to assume that this pattern was in use two generations ago" (1967: 8). The diagram also shows that the sex of referent division is always made for relatives older than ego, but seldom for younger relatives, who are typically distinguished by sex of speaker rather than by sex of referent.

Address terms, except in special cases determined by the compadrazgo and other ritual relationships, follow a simple rule: an older kinsmen is called TOT or MEʔ (depending on sex), and responds by calling the younger person by name. Non-kin are addressed as TOTIK or MEʔTIK. Or, less formally, both kin and non-kin may be addressed as "TOT——" or "MEʔ——" depending on sex (Michelle Rosaldo 1967: 11).

While descent in Zinacantan, represented by the inheritance of the double surname (see Chapter 7), is wholly patrilineal, and inheritance (with an ideal of equal distribution among sons) of land and house sites tends to be patrilineal, the localized patrilineages are shallow, seldom exceeding three generations. This poses a contrast to San Pablo Chalchihuitán, a more isolated Tzotzil municipio north of Zinacantan, which still preserves a Crow-Omaha kinship system (Guiteras-Holmes 1954). In Zinacantan a residential arrangement, which is essentially an ego-specific (rather than a lineage) alliance, seems to be implicit in the terminology (Michelle Rosaldo 1967: 4). By this I mean that the kin terms reflect patterns of behavior that are geared more to sets of dyadic relationships between pairs of kinsmen than they do to alliances among lineages. Whether or not Zinacantan once had a Crow-Omaha system is not known. What is important now are sets of reciprocal relationships that classify kinsmen and designate the appropriate role behavior among them in residential domestic groups.

The reciprocal dyadic relationships assume three forms. In the first, the same term is used reciprocally by two persons standing in symmetrical relationship to each other. A good example is the term HNIʔAL, meaning "child's spouse's parents," which is used reciprocally between the parents of a married couple, and represents the alliance between the domestic groups involved. In a second form reciprocity occurs when the same term covers two kin types that are reciprocals of each other. An example is found in the terms for brothers-in-law and sisters-in-law in the terminology for affinal relatives. A third form occurs in cases when two terms are reciprocals of each other—as, for example, in HMUK'TA TOT-HCH'AMAL, grandfather-grandchild (male speaking).

The reciprocal relationships between ascending and descending generations are of further significance in that the ascending generations are divided by sex (into grandfathers and grandmothers), whereas the descending generations are differentiated by sex of the speaker (with grandfather and grandmother each using separate terms to designate grandchild).

In ego's generation relative age is of overriding importance with male ego making both a distinction between older and younger brother, and between older and younger sister. On the other hand, a female ego differentiates between older siblings by age, but groups her younger siblings together. These differences are congruent with the importance of rank among siblings, especially brothers, to the male Zinacanteco who has constructed a symbolic world that places great emphasis upon "junior-senior" (see below). They are also congruent with the fact that a female ego is less concerned with rank and, perhaps more importantly, that she serves (in the years before her marriage) as a substitute mother for her younger siblings. In this respect, the pair of terms HVISH–HMUK (older sister–younger sibling) parallels the set HME?–KOL (mother–female's child). For, as the mother cares for her children, the older sister cares for her younger siblings.

The affinal terminology not only expresses the alliance between the two domestic groups in the reciprocal term used between the parents of the married couple, but also differentiates clearly between husband's ascending kinsmen and the wife's ascending kinsmen in the terms KALIB and HNI?, respectively. The same terms are applied to son's wife and to daughter's husband, making the system consistent with respect to the alliance between the two lineages. We have been unable to translate HNI?, but KALIB has a common derivation with the verb -ALAH, meaning "to give birth," in which case "son's wife" is appropriately defined as a woman brought into the lineage to give birth to children.

Many of these more traditional kin terms are being replaced in everyday usage by compadrazgo terms, and there is a marked trend of change in Zinacantan in the direction of using descriptive terms for collateral relatives. Younger Zinacantecos are more likely to refer to aunts and uncles, nieces and nephews, and cousins with descriptive terms; that is, instead of referring to an uncle as HHUN TOT, they are more likely to designate him as "my father's older brother." While the lineal and affinal terms are being preserved, the collateral terms are changing rapidly.

Compadrazgo

In meeting and greeting one another many adult Zinacantecos use KUM-PARE (in addressing or referring to a man), and KUMALE (in addressing or referring to a woman), rather than traditional Tzotzil kin terms or first names. These are loan words from the Spanish *compadres* and *comadres,* utilized in the ritual kinship system known by the Ladinos as *compadrazgo.* This ritual kinship system is universally used in the European-derived cultures of Latin America. Mintz and Wolf have traced the historical origins of the system and discussed its cultural importance in medieval times, when it was an essential pattern throughout Europe. They describe how the system gave way before more impersonal modes of organization in countries with advanced industrial development, but continued to survive in areas such as Spain, Italy, and the Balkan countries, "where the development of industrial capitalism, the rise of a middle class, and the disintegration of the feudal order has been less rapid" (1950: 352). It was from southern Europe that the complex was transmitted to the New World.

The system we now observe in Zinacantan was quite obviously adopted from the Spanish conquerors and their Ladino descendants in highland Chiapas during the Colonial period. The Zinacanteco system of compadrazgo has, however, developed a series of extensions and functions that go well beyond those of the institution in local Ladino culture. It binds Zinacantecos into an intricate network of social relationships with important rights and obligations, and hence carries a heavy functional load in contemporary Tzotzil life.

For members of the Catholic and Episcopal churches in the United States, godfathers and godmothers are selected to participate in the baptism (or christening) of a child. Following the sacramental rite, a reciprocal relationship is established between the godparents and the godchild. These terms are often used as reference terms, but seldom, if ever, as terms of address. Following Church doctrine, it is the duty of the godparents to ensure that the godchild has proper religious instruction and is duly confirmed at the appropriate time. Although the parents and godparents of the child are normally either close friends or relatives, they do not address or refer to one another by special terms, nor do they have any very special mutual relationship involving specified rights and obligations. The relationship that continues to be important—if any persists at all—is between the godparents and the godchild.

In southern Europe and in the Latin American cultures derived from them, this system of ritual kinship takes on important new dimensions. The crucial relationship established is not between the godparents and the godchild but between the godparents and the parents of the child. This contrast is displayed in the diagrams of Figure 88. The adults involved in the system, that is, the parents and the godparents of the child, address

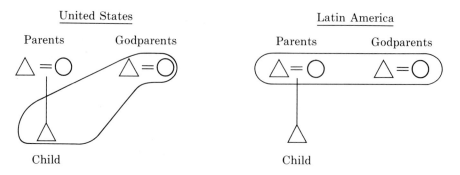

88. Godparental relationships

(and refer to) each other as compadre or comadre. Furthermore, the relationship established normally involves mutual rights and obligations, such as economic, political, or social assistance. The relationship between godparents and godchild is either de-emphasized and/or highly perfunctory, and often ignored except as a reference point for establishing the all-important compadrazgo relationships.

In Ladino culture in San Cristóbal, compadres are acquired not only in the sacrament of baptism but also in confirmations and weddings. The number and importance varies with social class. An upper-class family may have many compadrazgo ties, with compadres selected not only from other families in San Cristóbal but from other towns in Chiapas and even Mexico City; but it tends to depend less upon these relationships for economic and political help. On the other hand, a humble Ladino family living in one of the outlying barrios tends to select compadres from the immediate vicinity and to utilize these ritual kinsmen in coping with crises of many kinds. These humble families lack wide-ranging contacts and distinguished family lineages, and therefore "create" relatives via the compadrazgo system (Gwendoline van den Berghe 1965; Pierre van den Berghe and Gwendoline van den Berghe 1966).

Zinacantecos utilize the ritual kinship system more like the lower-class Ladinos, but have developed it much more fully. Not only can compadres be acquired with the sacramental rites of baptism, confirmation, and marriage performed in the Catholic church, but literally dozens are added, by extension, in the ritual meals at home which follow the rites of baptism and confirmation, and more especially in the house-entering and wedding ceremonies.

Compadres for either baptism or confirmation are selected by Zinacantecos with four considerations in mind. First, the godfather must have a different surname from the father and should be called upon to embrace three children of a family in the ceremony for baptism. Ordinarily, a man must be married in order to serve; and his wife serves with him. The third consideration, normally, is that the compadres live nearby, typically in the same hamlet and often even in the same waterhole group. Unlike the preceding rule, this is not an explicit or formal consideration; it is more a consequence of the fact that most Zinacantecos know people well who live nearby, and are thus much less likely to know or call upon someone in a distant hamlet. (Our data indicate that the cases in which compadres live in distant hamlets tend to occur when a Zinacanteco is serving a cargo and living for a year in Zinacantan Center. If a baby is born during this cargo-holding year, the father often selects the godparents from Zinacantan Center or from among other cargoholders who are also living there just for the year.) The fourth consideration is that the compadres should ideally be both willing and able to provide future economic and political services. This means that they have passed a cargo, are respected members of the community, and are relatively well-to-do. It also means that certain Zinacantecos, especially the more acculturated ones, reach outside the culture to ask either Ladinos in Zinacantan Center or in San Cristóbal to become compadres. Several have, in recent years, asked visiting anthropologists to become their compadres.

Baptism. The Catholic sacrament of baptism is normally carried out in a Church by a priest within two weeks after a Zinacantan baby is born, certainly before the infant is a month old. It may be performed in the Church of San Lorenzo in Zinacantan Center during one of the important fiestas, when the priest has come to say Mass. He performs weddings at about 5 A.M., before the Mass, and baptisms immediately after the Mass. Alternatively, the baptismal rite can be performed in the Cathedral in San Cristóbal; it may occur here any day of the year, since a priest is always on duty, but usually takes place on Sunday.

Well in advance of the day of the baptism, the father of the child goes to the house of the couple whom he and his wife have selected as godparents, presents a bottle of rum to the potential godfather, and asks that he and his wife serve as "embracers" of the new infant. The future *padrino* accepts and serves the drinks if they agree to serve as ceremonial sponsors; then a date is set. The day of the baptism, the father goes to pick up the godparents, and the two couples travel together to Zinacantan Center or San Cristóbal. They must all appear before the Parochial Secretary, who asks if they are Catholics, records their names, and collects 10 pesos for the baptismal service. Two white candles of 50-centavo size are purchased,

89. Baptism of a Zinacanteco child

one to be held by each godparent. The four Zinacantecos, plus the infant, then wait in the part of the church where the baptismal font is located. When their turn comes, they light the candles and move forward. The infant is transferred from its mother to the godparent of the same sex as the infant, while each godparent holds a candle. The priest recites a prayer for the demon to come out from the child's soul, and at the same time places a piece of salt in the infant's mouth. Another prayer follows, while the priest makes the sign of the cross on the forehead, mouth, and chest, and touches the head of the infant with the tip of his stole. He then asks that the godparents recite the Apostles Creed, which contains the fundamental elements of the Roman Catholic faith. (They usually do not know it and have to be prompted.) The ceremony moves to the baptismal font where the priest bathes the infant's head in Holy Water (Figure 89) and finishes by telling the godparents what duties they now have toward their godchild. Henceforth the child refers to his godfather as HCH'UL TOT and to his godmother as HCH'UL ME'; a godfather refers to his godchild as HCH'UL CH'AMAL and the godmother refers to hers as HCH'UL 'OL. The address terms are the same except that the H- possessive prefix is dropped.

The infant has now been through all the necessary ceremony as far as the Catholic Church is concerned, but the Zinacanteco ritual continues. The father purchases the ingredients for a formal ritual meal, and all return to the parents' home. The ritual meal includes rum, pieces of chicken served in a chili broth, tortillas, coffee, and rolls, all served on a small table in a strictly specified order (see Chapter 23 for a full description). The baby's grandparents on both sides and often other relatives and neighbors are invited to sit at the table and share the meal. This ritual meal is one of the means by which additional persons are included by extension in the compadrazgo system. But even if the baby's grandparents cannot attend the ritual meal, they, along with all the other kinsmen of the baby on both sides, become compadres of the godparents. However, these "secondary" compadrazgo relationships, acquired by extension, involve no obligations beyond the use of the address terms. The primary compadrazgo relationships acquired at a baptism that do involve major mutual rights and obligations are fewer in number: the baby's parents; his grandparents on both sides; and perhaps an older brother (and his wife) of the baby's father who become compadres with the godparents.

The other important development, in Zinacanteco thought, is that the soul (CH'ULEL) of the infant has been more firmly fixed in the body, and there is henceforth less danger of the infant losing this soul (see Chapter 16).

There is an exchange of gifts, with the godparents giving their new godchild a full set of new clothes, and in return receiving from the parents two chickens, two pesos' worth of chocolate, a block of brown sugar, sixty tortillas, two bottles of rum, and a kilo of meat. This exchange usually takes place within a six-month period after the baptismal ceremony. The gift of clothes is quite special, particularly the baby girl's blouse, which must be woven by a woman specially skilled in this task. These clothes are usually delivered by the godmother to the house of the child's parents; she may be given a small meal in appreciation. By contrast, the delivery of the gift of food from the parents to the godparents is a much more formal affair. Both parents take this substantial gift (similar in size and content to a wedding gift) to the house of their compadres, where they are given a formal ritual meal. Anyone partaking of this meal becomes a compadre of the parents—hence the parents and an older brother of the godfather may by this means be included in the widening network of compadrazgo relationships.

In theory, the godparents have obligations toward the child, especially to care for him, or even adopt him, in the event the parents die and he has no close relatives to rear him. In practice, their most important obligation is to provide the new clothing for the child.

Confirmation. Although all Zinacanteco infants are baptized, and the ceremony is always performed with dispatch within the first month of the infant's life, not all children, especially those in distant hamlets, are confirmed. This sacrament is taken much less seriously by Zinacantecos.

If parents do take their children to San Cristóbal for confirmation by the Bishop, the ceremony is similar to the baptismal rite. Confirmation ordinarily occurs before the age of ten. It is not preceded by any required religious training, and the novitiate needs no knowledge of the Catechism. Rather, ceremonial sponsors, usually a married couple, are selected by the parents of the child; during a visit in which a bottle of rum is presented them, they are asked to serve. A date is set and the child is confirmed in the side chapel of the Cathedral in San Cristóbal, with the ceremonial sponsors carrying lighted, white (1-peso size) candles. The priest performs the ritual, and the group returns to their hamlet for the ritual meal, which follows the same pattern as that given for a baptism and may also include additional persons, who by extension become compadres and comadres.

Rights and Obligations. The moment a new social link is established through compadrazgo, the persons who address and refer to each other as KUMPARE and KUMALE and consider themselves "primary" compadres acquire special rights and obligations toward one another. The relationship takes on a genuinely "kinship" quality; in fact, in many respects the links are more secure than they are with distant biological kinsmen.

For a man, a compadre can be called upon to loan money for any number of crises—the expenses of a cargo, of a curing ceremony, of seed or tools for farming, of back debts that are owed others, and so forth. He may be called upon for labor—building a new house, helping a cargoholder with his time-consuming ceremonies in Zinacantan Center, or helping as an assistant in a curing ceremony. A compadre can also be counted upon for support in political crises; for example, if a man is charged with theft, molesting a woman, performing witchcraft, and so on, he may turn to his compadres for assistance.

For a woman, a comadre may be asked to loan a small amount of money during an economic crisis. But more important, her comadre is a person to whom she can turn for assistance in tortilla-making for ceremonial occasions when huge amounts of food must be produced. She is also a person with whom the woman can gossip in confidence.

For both men and women the compadrazgo relationship occasionally provides hospitality when they are traveling. For example, when they travel from their outlying hamlets to Zinacantan Center for fiestas and have no house in which to live, they may request living space in the home of compadres. Similarly, many Zinacantecos who have Ladino compadres in Zinacantan Center or San Cristóbal can expect to receive special consideration for credit (if the Ladino is a storekeeper), to be invited into the house and fed, and often to be provided with a place to sleep overnight.

In general, the compadrazgo network provides a pool of people to whom one can turn for money, labor, credit, political support, hospitality, and other services. It creates a security network without which an individual Zinacanteco would be left exposed to the dangers and vicissitudes of his complex world.

Economic and Social Implications. The compadrazgo complex is flexible and adaptable and can be utilized to bind together a wide group of individuals through ceremonial ties (Mintz and Wolf 1950). Paul makes the important point that the mechanism can be used either to enlarge numerically and spatially the number of (ritual) kin, or to reinforce already existing blood or ritual ties. He calls these contrasting motives "extension" and "intensification" (1942: 57).

The current system in Zinacantan utilizes both of these mechanisms. Following from the rule that one may not marry a compadre or comadre and from the rule that compadres must not be selected with the same Indian surname is a basic tendency for "extension." The mechanism brings into the ritual kin network persons who are not previously involved in close relationships with each other. On the other hand, there is also some "intensification" evident in that compadres who are already affinal kinsmen may be drawn into the network by the extensions that occur at the ritual meals in weddings, and following the baptismal and confirmation ceremonies. There is also evidence from ʔApas, where we have a complete genealogy of all residents, that compadrazgo alliances serve to intensify and reinforce marriage alliances between certain lineages.

An especially crucial use of the compadrazgo system is for a successful cargo career, particularly for those men who do not come from large, well-organized lineages. An excellent case has been described by Cancian.

Antun, the *Mayordomo Rey* for 1960, had something approaching an ideal pattern of borrowing. He received 12 loans from fellow Zinacantecos. Three were from a friend and two ritual kinsmen who were aiding him in anticipation of, or in return for, aid he would give or had given them during their cargos; four were from kinsmen; and the remaining five were from ritual kinsmen. He had a large debt with the

Ladino woman who sells drink in the ceremonial center, and a smaller debt with a rancher who sold him a steer on credit. Two features of his borrowing are very close to the ideals described above: (1) he borrowed for the first time on June 20, just a few days short of the middle of his term; (2) all the Zinacantecos he borrowed from were either his relatives or his ritual kinsmen, except for one, a friend who made him the loan on a reciprocal basis.

Antun's pattern of borrowing also has some unusual features. First, his total debt, 4,010 pesos, is relatively small considering the cargo passed. This is explained by the fact that he was very well paid as a schoolteacher for years before his cargo, and made additional profits in agriculture during the same period. He is very rich. Second, he took no loans from siblings. Antun has only one brother, a poor man with whom he does not get on very well. However, because of his wealth, his political power in days past, and his ability to deal with the Ladino world, Antun has more than 100 ritual kinsmen, who make up in part for his lack of siblings. An examination of the auxiliary personnel recruited by Antun for his cargo will also reveal the manner in which ritual kin have replaced siblings for some other support needed by the cargoholder. (1965a: 102–103)

The system also reflects subtle differences in interpersonal relations, especially among the men. Although the women continue to call each KUMALE and to call men KUMPARE, there is a shift in terms of address among men as the relationship grows in confidence and intimacy; KUMPARE is then shortened to KUMPA.

It is evident that the system carries a heavy functional load in contemporary Zinacanteco society, perhaps partly because it is replacing the functions of strong lineages that once must have carried the burden of land control, political help, assistance in cargoholding, and cooperation in farming and house-building.

The Junior–Senior Principle

One of the most crucial principles of discrimination in Zinacantan culture is described in Tzotzil as BANKILAL and ʔITS'INAL. These terms, which serve to distinguish between older and younger brothers, can be applied as well to hills, mountains, waterholes, crosses, cargoholders, shamans, fireworks, drums, and so forth. Since a Zinacanteco refers to his older brother as HBANKIL and to his younger brother as KITS'IN, and sometimes translates

BANKILAL and ʔITS'INAL as *hermano mayor* and *hermano menor,* these translations have been utilized in earlier publications. However, by so translating the terms, I am making an assumption, not really justified by the data, that these concepts ultimately derived from "older brother" and "younger brother" kinship terms and subsequently were extended to other domains in the human and natural environments.

Some obviously important contrasts and oppositions are being expressed in Tzotzil by these terms, but I think it best to assume that the opposition is between "senior" and "junior" in a principle of ranking. One manifestation of this principle occurs in the society's age-ranking system, and a more specific aspect of the age-ranking is the contrast between older and younger brother. But, since the principle is also applied to mountains, waterholes, and crosses, it is better to translate the terms as "senior" and "junior," or perhaps even as "older" and "younger," "more powerful" and "less powerful," or "more prestigeful" and "less prestigeful," rather than to utilize one specific manifestation as a statement of the general principle.

The Zinacantecos are very rank-conscious people and one of their crucial principles of rank is based upon age, or more properly, time elapsed since an event occurred in the life of a person or in the transformation of a natural object, such as a mountain. For example, a man of fifty is senior to one of twenty since more time has elapsed since his birth. A shaman who made his ritual debut twenty years ago outranks one who only became a shaman last year, even if the latter is older, since more time has elapsed since this important event in the lives of the two shamans. A KALVARIO erected for a waterhole a long time ago outranks a cross shrine erected two years ago since, again, more time has elapsed since it was set up. Similarly, a senior saint in a temple is one that the Zinacantecos have had longer than its junior counterpart. So, when Zinacantecos say people or mountains or crosses are senior as opposed to junior, or that a certain man or shaman is "MAS BANKILAL" (more senior) or "MAS ʔITS'INAL" (more junior), they are expressing a principle of ranking that is embedded in the flow of time in their universe, rather than telling us that one is an older brother, the other a younger brother.

Bowing and Releasing Behavior. There are many behavioral ways in which the junior–senior principle is expressed in Zinacantan apart from the kinship terminology and patterns of behavior between kin. For example, when two people meet on the trail, the younger must stand aside and allow the older to pass along the narrow trail first. By far the most important and ubiquitous expression of age-ranking occurs in what I have labeled "bowing and releasing" behavior. The action is quite simple: the younger person bows his head toward the older, who releases the bow by lightly touching the forehead of the younger person with the back of his right hand; the younger person then straightens up again.

Bowing and releasing does not occur in every encounter between people in Zinacantan. Casual meetings on the trails while traveling to and from waterholes or to and from San Cristóbal may involve only a proper greeting. But if the persons involved stop to talk, bowing and releasing is likely to take place. If the situation is formal, for instance, requests for favor or services, bowing and releasing usually occurs. And, if the encounter is one of ritual context, that is, in any kind of ceremony, there is invariably much bowing and releasing. Thus, bowing and releasing is a recurring daily reminder of the age-ranking system in the society, one which is significantly emphasized in the rituals which express so many basic values of Zinacanteco culture.

Seating Behavior. In the ordinary daily life of a domestic group, a man may sit down wherever he likes in his house, on his terrace, or on a rock resting beside his maize field. Although men do not sit close to one of the metates and take up space needed by the women to make tortillas, they may sit anywhere else in no particular order. However, the moment that the situation changes from secular life to a ritual situation, rigid requirements regulate seating order. The basic order at a small table during a ritual meal, which depends upon the senior-junior ranking, is diagramed in Figure 90.

If shamans are seated at the table for a K'IN KRUS ceremony, the most senior sits in position 1, followed by those of lesser rank. In this case, rank ordinarily depends upon the time elapsed since each shaman made his debut. If the male members of a domestic group are seated at the table (for example, in a meal following a baptism), then the general order follows

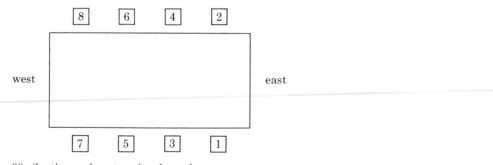

90. Seating order at a ritual meal

the ages of the men. Similarly, groups of musicians, shamans, cargoholders, or civil officials seated on a bench also arrange themselves by rank. The group composed of violin, harp, and guitar always sit in that order, since the violin is the highest ranking instrument, followed by the harp, and then by the guitar.

Drinking Behavior. Ritual events are always accompanied by ceremonial drinking, most commonly of rum, but sometimes of chicha, beer, or even Coke. A drink-pourer, appointed to serve drinks (of rum) from a shot glass, is expected to observe a precise rank order, starting with the most senior and ending with the most junior, serving himself last.

Marching Behavior. In ordinary daily life, walking order generally follows the rules of men before women, and older before younger, with the head of the group going first in order to receive and transmit greetings on the trails as his group meets other people. There is a certain informality about the extent to which these rules are observed. But, the moment the situation becomes a ritualized part of a ceremony, the formal recognition of rank is rigidly enforced. The general principle is that the most junior person is in front and the most senior in the rear. Thus, when a group of shamans are in procession, their rank order can be precisely determined by observing them from the end to the front of the procession. In certain ceremonies in the ceremonial center the 61 cargoholders in the hierarchy arrange themselves in rank order, with the Senior Alcalde in the rear and the lowest ranking mayor in the front; by this, the Zinacantecos are recognizing that the Senior Alcalde has passed through three previous cargo positions and has now reached the pinnacle of ritual power in the municipio. Rank is also expressed in pilgrimages to the sacred mountain dwelling places of the ancestral gods. The shaman always marches in the rear, directly preceded by the patient and then by the flower and candle carrier. The symbolic significance of this type of marching continues to be something of a mystery, especially since the rank order in processions appears to be the reverse of the rank order at a table for a ritual meal when the participants are seated with the most senior occupying the head of the table—toward the rising sun where the principal gods are located.

Order of Marriage and Cargo Positions. Age-ranking is also clearly expressed by the ideal order in which marriages and cargos are arranged for male children. Older brothers are expected to marry before the family allocates its resources to help younger brothers. In a certain sense, marriage is regarded as a kind of "first cargo" or "platform cargo" in Zinacantan, since cargos in the hierarchy normally require that a man be married in order to serve.

Other Expressions. The senior-junior principle applies to a wide variety of phenomena in Zinacanteco life. In the domain of mountains BANKILAL MUK'TA VITS is the majestic volcano that rises just east of Zinacantan Center and is believed to contain the corrals of the animal spirit companions; while ʔITS'INAL MUK'TA VITS is the mountain south of Teopisca, near Rancho Chenekultik, where the shamans go to perform rain-making ceremonies. In Pasteʔ there is a large limestone cave called ʔAVAN CH'EN with two openings—one regarded as senior, the other as junior. The KALVARIO shrines on hills, where prayers are addressed to the ancestral deities of snas and waterhole groups, often come in pairs—senior and junior—and both are visited on the ceremonial circuits in the K'IN KRUS ceremonies. The shamans are organized into senior and junior groups for Year Renewal ceremonies (see Chapter 20). Each of the mayordomo positions attached to saints come in pairs. Similarly, the two mesoneros and the two mayordomos reyes are classified as senior and junior. The two orders of alféreces are senior and junior, and the pairs of special cargos for Easter, the Pasioneros, and for the Fiesta of San Lorenzo, the Capitanes, are similarly classified. The only such classification I have found among women's positions are the HPATVAH in a wedding. These two women, who make special bean tamales for serving at the wedding ceremony (J. F. Collier 1968), are classified as BANKILAL and ʔITS'INAL.

Many of the saints in the temples are classified by senior and junior terms—including two Christ children who appear in the nativity scene at Christmas time! Similarly, many of the specially costumed performers in the Fiesta of San Sebastián carry these terms; there are two magnificent jaguars dancing in the fiesta: senior and junior jaguars.

Ritual paraphernalia and action are classified as senior and junior. The drum and flute combination always contains two drums and one flute; the small drum is junior and the larger drum is senior, and in procession the player of the junior drum marches in front. One particular kind of fireworks is called KAMARO; it consists of gunpowder packed into a metal container and ignited. In various sequences of ritual action, there are two firings of the KAMARO—the first is junior, the second senior.

These data raise the interesting question regarding the social roots of the senior-junior principle in Zinacanteco culture. At least three sources are possible: (1) sibling rivalry between older and younger brothers; (2) the previous existence of senior and junior patrilineages; and (3) the society's age-ranking system, which may have been generalized to become related cosmologically to an important set of conceptions concerning the passage of time in Zinacanteco life.

Hypothesis (1) seems attractive at first, since there is abundant evidence for strong sibling rivalry and conflict between older and younger brothers. On the other hand, there is little evidence for strain between older and younger sisters. Sisters are normally separated, while brothers are kept together in the system of patrilocal residence. Hence there is more potential for strain between brothers, and the stresses become especially acute when there is trouble over the inheritance of resources (particularly land).

The following cases, elicited from an ex-Presidente of Zinacantan, illustrate the kinds of difficulties that occur between older and younger brothers.

> Lol Peres Vots from Nabenchauk had a fight over land with his brother. The land was about 6 hectares in a part of Nabenchauk. Lol's brother wanted to split the land, but Lol didn't. Lol went to the Cabildo to present his side of the case. He said that his brother owed him 300 pesos, and that he, Lol, was keeping the land in payment. The brother, however, said that he should get his share as he was, after all, Lol's full brother and had a right to half the land. Shun, who was then Presidente, asked Lol's brother if he could pay back the 300 pesos. If he could, the land could be divided. So Lol's brother agreed to pay the sum to get his land, and Shun sent the Síndico out to measure the land and divide it equally between the two brothers. (Jane F. Collier, Case 76, 1963)

> Lol K'o of Nabenchauk deeply resented his older brother Manvel's keeping the family land under his sole control after the death of their father. Lol wanted his share to work for himself and his family, but Manvel said that he had had to pay for his younger brother's courtship and wedding and later for curing ceremonies for Lol who had often been sick, and that, although he didn't expect to be reimbursed for those expenses, he was going to keep ownership of the land. When Lol became drunk, he would fight with Manvel about the land, and the situation became so serious that it was brought before the Presidente in Zinacantan Center. The Presidente asked Lol if he were willing to repay his brother for some of his courtship expenses in return for his share of the land. Lol agreed to the sum of 200 pesos, and the land was divided into two equal plots. Both Manvel and Lol were satisfied by the settlement. (Jane F. Collier, Case 76, 1963)

> Shun Tanchak, eldest of four siblings of ?Elan Vo?, kept control of the family's land, in spite of requests by his two married sisters and

his younger brother, Martin, to divide it with them. Martin was bitter about not getting his share and fought with his older brother at every opportunity. Finally Martin and his sisters came to believe that Shun, who was a shaman, was witching them, and Martin became angrier still. One day as Shun was returning from Hot Country, Martin waited for him with a gun and machete. When they met, Martin demanded that Shun divide the land. Shun replied that he would not, because he was the eldest and could best manage the land. Infuriated, Martin then attacked his brother and cut off his head with the machete. The Chamula helper accompanying Shun tried to assist, but Martin turned on him, as well, and killed him. Leaving the dead men on the trail, Martin walked off toward the mountains. He happened to pass the Presidente at that time, and although the Presidente noticed blood on Martin's machete and clothes, he didn't stop to question Martin then. Later, the Presidente was informed that two murdered men had been found on the road not too far from where he had passed Martin, but when the Presidente and others investigated the murders and then went to look for Martin, he was not to be found. Two years passed before Martin was seen again, and during that time the land Shun had held lay unused, although informally in the control of the two married sisters. No one dared to try to take over any part of it through fear of Martin, who had already killed two men. Martin returned when a new Presidente was installed in Zinacantan Center. He presented a bottle to the new Presidente and asked that his past be forgotten. The Presidente agreed, and Martin took over the family land. He divided it fairly into four plots, giving one each to his married sisters and to Shun's ten-year-old son, and keeping one for himself. There has been no trouble over that land since. (Jane F. Collier, Case 80, 1963)

Because we have discovered that BANKILAL and ʔITS'INAL are more properly translated as "senior" and "junior" rather than specifically "older brother" and "younger brother," I am now inclined to view the kin terms for brothers as a specific manifestation of a more general principle of rank that applies not only to people but also to the many other domains illustrated above.

Hypothesis (2) was suggested by Henning Siverts (1964), who argues that if the ancient Tzotzil and Tzeltal had fully developed lineage systems, there may have recurred struggles for power and resources each generation between senior lineages descended from older brothers and junior lineages descended from younger brothers. These events could have led to fissions in the system in which the junior lineages were forced to move to new lands where they would have established their separate ancestral shrines on other mountains. Hence, the splitting off of lineages might have led to the senior-junior distinctions that are made in the domains of mountains, cross shrines, and so on. This hypothesis is also possible, though it does not account for the use of senior-junior terms in classifying domains such as the religious hierarchy.

Hypothesis (3) is perhaps the most likely. If we can assume that the senior-junior distinction is an expression of the importance, broadly conceived, of age-ranking in the society and that the principle can be extended to include elapsed time since the transformation of natural objects, then I think we can explain all manifestations of the principle in the culture. This type of age-ranking also has a built-in potential for strain, for if a man's worth is basically judged by "time in service," there is bound to be conflict with younger men who display intelligence and competence and achieve given goals more quickly. A bright, competent Zinacanteco of twenty-five must normally bow to a relatively incompetent Zinacanteco of fifty, whether he likes it or not; a successful young shaman who made his debut last year must take a lower ranking position in a ritual procession than an elderly shaman who had his dreams thirty years ago and has not cured anybody for the last ten. In the emphasis upon senior and junior, Zinacantecos are both re-enforcing this basic age-ranking system and expressing the dilemma that occurs in a social code of this type.

But, since the principle is applied in many other domains, the formula for rank expressed by senior and junior is more general than "age" in the sense of "years since birth." Anything in the Zinacanteco universe is more senior if more time has elapsed since the discriminating event occurred that places this person or object in rank order. Thus, the discriminating events that transform the statuses of persons or objects may be their births, the debuts of shamans, the establishments of ancestral shrines on top of mountains, or the acquisitions of saints in the temples. In each case, the senior person or object experienced the transformation before the junior person or object. It is relative position on the time scale since the transformation occurred that counts in the rank system expressed by the terms BANKILAL and ʔITS'INAL.

11 / The Cargo System

When a Zinacanteco speaks of ?ABTEL TA HTEKLUM he is referring to the "work" or "service" provided by individuals who hold ritual positions in the ceremonial center. ?ABTEL, which means "work," may be used to refer to the work of carrying a heavy load of maize with a tumpline, but in the context of the ceremonial center this concept is probably related to the Ancient Maya idea of the "Year Bearer," especially since most of the positions are held for a year. Just as an Ancient Maya god was thought to carry the "year" with a tumpline, passing it along to the next bearer at the end of the year, a contemporary Zinacanteco carries the burden of office for a year, after which he passes it along to his successor (see Bricker 1966). In Spanish these positions are known as cargos, meaning office or post.

The cargo system in Zinacantan is enormously complicated, both in its structural and economic aspects as well as in its ritual, for no day passes in the ceremonial center without some ritual's being performed by the cargoholders for the benefit of the community. There is an essentially religious hierarchy of positions that count in the system of advancement; but there are also auxiliary positions occupied by ritual specialists and helpers, many of whom serve for longer than a year. Finally there are the more "political" positions filled by a group of officials who serve in the Cabildo.

I am especially grateful in this chapter to Frank Cancian who has devoted eighteen months of field work in Zinacantan to a study of the cargo system. This chapter is a brief summary of the detailed data that can be found in Cancian (1965a). Additional data can be found in Zabala (1961a).

The Religious Hierarchy

Unlike the civil-religious hierarchies reported for highland Guatemalan Maya communities (see especially Nash 1958; Wagley 1949) and discussed more generally for Mesoamerica by Carrasco (1961), the Zinacanteco hierarchy contains strictly religious positions. Nash points out that, while Guatemalan Indians think of the two ladders as one system, anthropologists separate them for purposes of analysis (1958: 67). The ideal type of highland Maya civil-religious hierarchy is usually presented as in Figure 91, with Indian men alternating between the "civil" and "religious" ladders as they progress through the system. In Zinacantan the Indians make a very clear distinction between those positions that count for progression up the ladder and those which either are auxiliary to the religious hierarchy or are positions in the civil government. Essentially, the important positions are religious cargos; these are arranged in four levels. A man must serve a first-level cargo before he can pass on to a second-, third-, and finally fourth-level cargo—after which he becomes an honored *pasado*. There are forty cargos on the first level, fourteen on the second, four on the third, and three on the fourth. This religious hierarchy is schematized in Figure 92 and a complete list of the cargos is provided in Table 8.

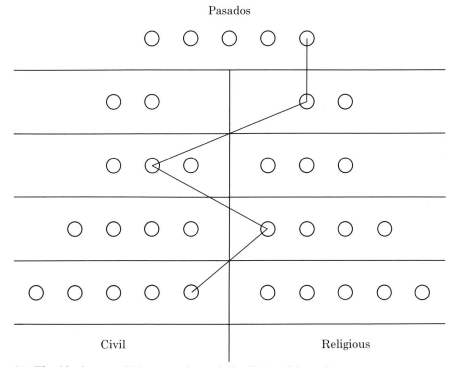

Pasados

Civil   Religious

91. The ideal type of Mesoamerican civil-religious hierarchy

Table 8. Cargo Positions

Level	Title of cargo	Number	Tzotzil translation
Fourth	Alcaldes Viejos[a]	two	ʔALKALTEETIK
	Senior Alcalde Viejo		MUK'TA ʔALKALTE
	Junior Alcalde Viejo		BIK'IT ʔALKALTE
	Terminal Cargo	one	
	Alcalde Shuves		ʔALKALTE SHUVES
Third	Regidores[a]	four	REHIROLETIK
	First Regidor		REHIROL MAYOL
	Second Regidor		SCHAʔVAʔAL REHIROL
	Third Regidor		YOSHVAʔAL REHIROL
	Fourth Regidor		SCHANVAʔAL REHIROL
Second	Alféreces	fourteen	ʔALPERESETIK
	Senior	seven	BANKILAL
	Santo Domingo		SANTOROMINKO
	Divina Cruz		KAHVALTIK RIOSH
	Santísima Trinidad		TRINIRAT
	San José		SAN HOSE
	Virgen del Rosario		ROSARIO
	Virgen de Natividad		NATIVIRAT
	San Sebastián		SHANSHCHOVASHCHAN
	Junior	seven	ʔITS'INAL
	San Lorenzo		SANTORENSO
	Virgen de Soledad		SORIRAT
	San Antonio		SANANTONYO
	San Pedro Martir		SAN PARO MARTIL
	San Jacinto		SAN HASINTO
	Santa Rosa		SANTA ROSHA
	San Sebastián		SHANSHCHOVASHCHAN
First	Mayordomos	twelve	MARTOMOETIK
	Senior	six	BANKILAL
	Sacramento		SAKRAMENTU
	Santo Domingo		SANTOROMINKO
	Santa Cruz		SANTAKRUS
	Virgen del Rosario		HCH'ULMEʔTIK
	San Antonio		SANANTONYO
	San Sebastián		SHANSHCHOVASHCHAN
	Junior	six	ʔITS'INAL
	Sacramento		SAKRAMENTU
	Santo Domingo		SANTOROMINKO
	Santa Cruz		SANTAKRUS
	Virgen del Rosario		HCH'ULMEʔTIK
	San Sebastian		SHANSHCHOVASHCHAN
	Mayordomos Reyes	two	MARTOMOREYETIK
	Senior Mayordomo Rey		MARTOMOREY BANKILAL
	Junior Mayordomo Rey		MARTOMOREY ʔITS'INAL
	Mesoneros	two	MESHONETIK
	Senior Mesonero		MESHON BANKILAL
	Junior Mesonero		MESHON ʔITS'INAL
	Cargos of Hamlet of ʔAts'am	two	
	Mayor		MAYOL
	Mayordomo de la Virgen del Rosario		MARTOMO HCH'ULMEʔTIK

Cargos of Hamlet of Nabenchauk	two	
Senior Mayordomo		MARTOMO BANKILAL
Junior Mayordomo		MARTOMO ʔITS'INAL
Cargos of Hamlet of ʔApas	four	
Senior Mayordomo Rey		MARTOMOREY BANKILAL
Junior Mayordomo Rey		MARTOMOREY ʔITS'INAL
Senior Mesonero		MESHON BANKILAL
Junior Mesonero		MESHON ʔITS'INAL
Cargos of short duration	four	
Easter season fiestas	two	
Senior Pasionero		PASHYON BANKILAL
Junior Pasionero		PASHYON ʔITS'INAL
Fiesta of San Lorenzo	two	
Senior Capitán		KAPITAN BANKILAL
Junior Capitán		KAPITAN ʔITS'INAL
Mayores (policemen)	twelve	MAYOLETIK
Auxiliary Personnel		
Ritual Advisers	forty-six	TOTILMEʔILETIK
Sacristanes	four	PISHKALETIK
Incense-bearers	twelve	HCHIK' POMETIK
Musicians	two	HVABAHOMETIK
Escribanos	two	ʔISHKIRVANOETIK
Women's Advisers		MEʔELETIK
Special Musicians		HVABAHOMETIK

[a] Alcaldes Viejos and Regidores are collectively known as Elders (MOLETIK).

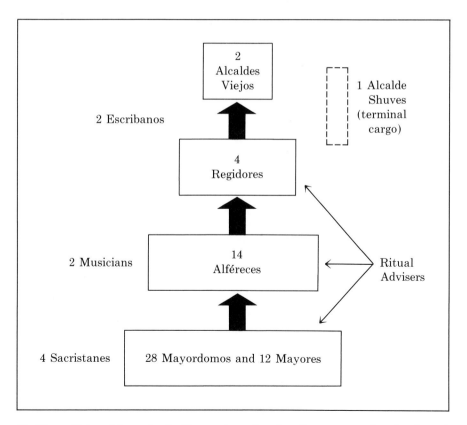

92. The religious hierarchy in Zinacantan, showing 61 cargos on four levels and four types of important auxiliary personnel

The Cargo Positions

The forty first-level cargos are, for purposes of presentation, shown in Figure 92 as twenty-eight mayordomos and twelve mayores, but the situation is actually more complex. The twenty-eight mayordomos include not only the twelve mayordomos who care for saints in the churches of San Lorenzo and San Sebastián, but also the two mayordomos reyes and two mesoneros who serve the saint in the Hermitage of Esquipulas, as well as the eight officials who care for saints in the outlying hamlets of Salinas, Nabenchuk, and ꞌApas and the four officials who serve special roles for the Easter season and for the Fiesta of San Lorenzo. The saint statues served by these first-level cargoholders, with the name of the principal saint in italics, are listed in Table 9.

The burden of performing the day-to-day ritual falls on the cargoholders of the first level in the hierarchy. They change the flowers and light the candles in the six churches and chapels in Zinacantan. They also sweep the floors and tend to the saints' garments. At the more important fiestas they have more complex ritual obligations, but the duties that distinguish them from the higher cargoholders are their everyday ones.

The twelve mayordomos (Figure 93) care for the two churches in Zinacantan Center and all of the saints in them, each junior-senior (BANKILAL–ꞌITS'INAL) pair being assigned to the saints, as listed in Table 9. Not only are these mayordomos subdivided into senior and junior orders, but within each order they are carefully ranked from the "most senior" to the "most junior." Hence the entire group of twelve is supervised by the "most senior," the Senior Mayordomo of Sacramento, when they are performing complex ritual duties, such as flower change in the churches, that require all twelve. Cancian has observed that should this Mayordomo be absent or too drunk to perform, the authority is passed on to the Senior Mayordomo of Santo Domingo and so on down the line (1965a: 35). The Junior Mayordomo of San Sebastián, "most junior" of the junior order, is appointed as drink-pourer for the group on certain ritual occasions. The ceremonial dress of the mayordomos consists of a full-length black wool ceremonial robe (SHAKITAIL) with red, rose, or purple silk cloth decoration around the square neck and ribbons in front. The everyday scarf is tied around the head in a special manner, and ordinary men's hats are worn.

The mayordomo reyes and mesoneros take care of the small chapel called the Hermitage of Esquipulas which houses Señor Esquipulas and a large table where the ceremonies for the religious oaths of office occur. While all four are officially on duty throughout the year, the senior mayordomo rey

Table 9. Saints served by first-level cargoholders

Location	Cargoholders serving	Saints[a]
Zinacantan Center	Mayordomos of Sacramento (Senior and Junior)	*San Lorenzo* (3), Sacramento, Cristo, Sagrado Corazón Menor
	Mayordomos of Santo Domingo (Senior and Junior)	*Santo Domingo* (2), San Pedro
	Mayordomos of Santa Cruz (Senior and Junior)	*Santo Entierro,* San Mateo, Trinidad, Jesús Nazareno, Resurrección, Senõr del Pilar, Cruces (2)
	Mayordomos of Virgen del Rosario (Senior and Junior)	*Virgen del Rosario,* Virgen de la Candelaria, Virgen de Dolores, Virgen de Pascua, Virgen de Santa Rosa, Virgen Purísima, San José
	Mayordomos of San Antonio (Senior and Junior)	*San Antonio,* San Jacinto, San Pedro Mártir, Santa Magdalena, San Juan, Sagrado Corazón Menor
	Mayordomos of San Sebastián (Senior and Junior)	*San Sebastián,* and all other saints in the church of San Sebastián
	Mayordomos Reyes (Senior and Junior) Mesoneros (Senior and Junior)	*Señor Esquipulas*
?Ats'am (Salinas)	Mayor Mayordomo	*Virgen del Rosario* (3), San Antonio, Sagrado Corazón, Cristo, Santa Columba
Nabenchauk	Senior Mayordomo Junior Mayordomo	*Virgen de Guadalupe,* Corazón de Jesús, San Martín, Virgen de Fátima, Santo Niño
?Apas	Mayordomos Reyes (Senior and Junior) Mesoneros (Senior and Junior)	*Señor Esquipulas,* Virgen de Guadalupe, Virgen del Carmen

[a] The name of the most important saint is italicized. The number in parentheses indicates the number of saints by that name in the same location.

93. Mayordomos with flags in procession

and mesonero serve for a month and then give way to their junior counterparts for a month, alternating throughout the year. The two mayordomo reyes and two mesoneros dress like the mayordomos except that they carry a billy club at their belts.

Cargoholders in the hamlets of Salinas, Nabenchauk, and ʔApas, take care of the saint images in their chapels. The chapel in Salinas is old and has a sacred salt well associated with it. While the Mayordomo is mainly in charge of chapel and saint, the Mayor's principal duty is to bring salt from his sacred well every second Sunday to the Hermitage of Esquipulas in the ceremonial center where the salt is divided among the mayordomos reyes, the mesoneros, the alcaldes viejos, the regidores, the escribanos, and the Presidente and Síndico. The other chapels are newer. That in Nabenchauk was built in 1952–53, and cargos were begun in 1954. The chapel in ʔApas was built in 1962; the cargos were established shortly thereafter.

The two pasioneros serve special ritual roles during the Easter season, while the two capitanes are active during the Fiesta of San Lorenzo.

Finally, the mayores (MAYOLETIK), perform duties which tend to be more civil than religious. They sweep the Cabildo and run errands for the Presidente and other Cabildo officials as well as for the Elders (MOLETIK). They serve as policemen, making arrests under orders from the Presidente. They also have ritual duties, especially during the Fiesta of San Sebastián, following their year of service. The mayores dress in ordinary clothes; the only symbol of their rank is a small billy club which they carry in their shoulder bags.

The second-level cargos consist of fourteen alféreces in two orders. Like the mayordomos, the positions are paired into senior–junior positions: Santo Domingo is paired with San Lorenzo, and so on. Like the mayordomos, the Tzotzil names are loan words from Spanish, except for the Divina Cruz who is called KAHVALTIK RIOSH and is known as the Alférez Divina Cruz only by the most Ladinoized Zinacantecos. Unlike the mayordomos, however, the names are not parallel, except for the San Sebastián pair. The alféreces dress in black ceremonial robes, like the first-level cargoholders, but add a red turban covered by a large, broad-trimmed black hat. When they dance, they use gourd rattles decorated with feathers. Alféreces going through a change-of-office ceremony can easily be identified by their long blue capes with white collars, their green or blue knee breeches, their long red stockings, and a peacock feather in their black hats (Figure 94).

94. Alféreces dancing in front of the church

Unlike the incumbents of the first-level cargos, these alféreces do not have major responsibility for saints or buildings. Other than their appearance in processions at the Easter season, they appear to function for only seven major fiestas a year, and at each of these fiestas a pair of them is exchanged for new incumbents. Here the emphasis is really upon change-of-office ceremonies, and it is during these seven major fiestas that they dance in front of the temples, participate in processions, and invite the whole community to drink atole when they enter their cargos. Much of the ritual effort is devoted to meals among themselves and to visiting each other's houses during ceremonial rounds that make counterclockwise circuits of the ceremonial center. Cancian concludes that they are neither the workhorses of the hierarchy, as are the first-level cargoholders, nor are they responsible administrators like the Elders. Rather, their functions seem to be to provide "a major embellishment at major celebrations" (1965a: 38).

The third- and fourth-level cargoholders are known collectively as the Elders (MOLETIK—a term also applied more generally to older men). The third level consists of four regidores, and the fourth level of two alcaldes viejos—these latter being called alcaldes "viejos" (old) to differentiate them in Spanish from the "alcaldes jueces" (judges) who serve with the Presidente at the Cabildo, and from the one interesting terminal cargo, called "alcalde shuves."

The regidores (Figures 95, 96, 97) are dressed like the alféreces, but carry long, plain wooden staffs in their left hands. The two alcaldes viejos dress identically and can be identified by their black batons with silver heads and tips which display a set of red, rose, and purple ribbons attached to a silver half-ring about one-third of the way down from the head. These batons are carried under the left arm of each man in such a way as to permit the ribbons to flap conspicuously in the breeze as they march along (Figure 98).

Even though the regidores and alcaldes occupy different levels in the hierarchy, many of their duties are performed by the group as a whole (Figure 99). Their duties are mainly administrative and ritual. As administrators of the whole cargo system they are responsible for appointing cargoholders and making last-minute adjustments in the event that a prospective or current cargoholder dies. In theory, they serve for alternating periods of fifteen days; the senior alcalde, the first and second regidores, and the senior escribano alternate with the other three elders and the junior escribano; in fact, the senior alcalde must be available at all times to handle problems. Their ritual duties involve an altar and a chest containing a

95. Regidores praying in front of the church

96. Regidor in ceremonial costume

97. Regidores praying at a street corner cross in Zinacantan Center

98. Alcaldes Viejos examining the cargo waiting lists; note baton carried under left arm of the Senior Alcalde

99. From right to left: the senior and junior Alcaldes and four Regidores seated in rank order; note batons of Alcaldes in rack between Alcaldes and Regidores

sacred picture of San Sebastián, which the senior alcalde has in his house. Every fifteen days the flowers decorating the altar are changed; the Elders participate, and the alcaldes provide the candles for the ceremony. All of the Elders have very special ritual roles in the Fiesta of San Sebastián in January following their year in service (see Chapter 22).

The Elders also have duties that combine administration and ritual. For example, at the change of mayordomos they go to the house of the incumbent for the counting of the medallions, to make certain that the number observed when the cargoholder received them is still there. For the change of alféreces, they perform the oath of office. The regidores and escribanos go out to the hamlets to collect money for Masses to be said at important fiestas.

As the ranking official in the hierarchy, the senior alcalde has an additional important obligation. He serves as host for the initial meetings of the three (per annum) Year Renewal ceremonies performed by the shamans for the entire municipio.

Finally, the Alcalde Shuves (ʔALKALTE SHUVES) is a terminal cargo that is served without regard to level. The holder of this position is principally active during Carnaval when he accompanies the pasioneros on their rounds and serves atole to all those who come to his house at a specified time. The position is usually given to an elderly man who is obviously not going to be able to progress to the top of the hierarchy anyway, either because of the expense or his lack of ability.

All of the positions described above are changed annually. But there is also a group of six Holy Elders (CH'UL MOLETIK) who have special life-tenure positions. This group is self-perpetuating; when one dies or retires, the remaining five select his successor, ordinarily from the pool of *pasados*, or men who have passed through the hierarchy and have completed their service in the four levels. Their functions are limited, but of great ritual significance: they nail the Christ image to the Cross on Good Friday. It is possible that these Holy Elders have some kind of symbolic relationship or link with the six elders who are serving at the top of the cargo system. This symbolic link resembles the relationship among the lower three levels of the cargo system, their ritual advisers, and the ancestral deities in the mountains.

The Waiting Lists

While the Holy Elders are self-perpetuating, recruitment for the sixty-one annually rotating positions in the cargo system takes quite a different form. Until about a generation ago cargoholders were appointed by the elders whose responsibility it was to find incumbents for all cargos. They had the power to jail an appointee who refused to accept, if in their judgment he was economically able to pass the cargo to which they appointed him.

More recently an interesting system of requesting cargo positions in advance has evolved. These requests are kept on lists in hard-cover notebooks, and a page or more is devoted to each year in the future, up to the last year for which a cargo has been requested. The escribanos enter the name of a man, the cargo he has requested, and the hamlet in which he lives as each request is made (Figure 100). Before the fiesta of San Lorenzo each year, the escribanos who will serve for the coming year make new copies of the lists. On August 8, at the fiesta, they read out the lists on the north side of the church of San Lorenzo (Figure 101) where a large group of men has gathered to listen. (Usually it is composed of men who wish to make certain that their names remain on the list, and those who wish to ask for a cargo.) All men who are on the waiting list present a

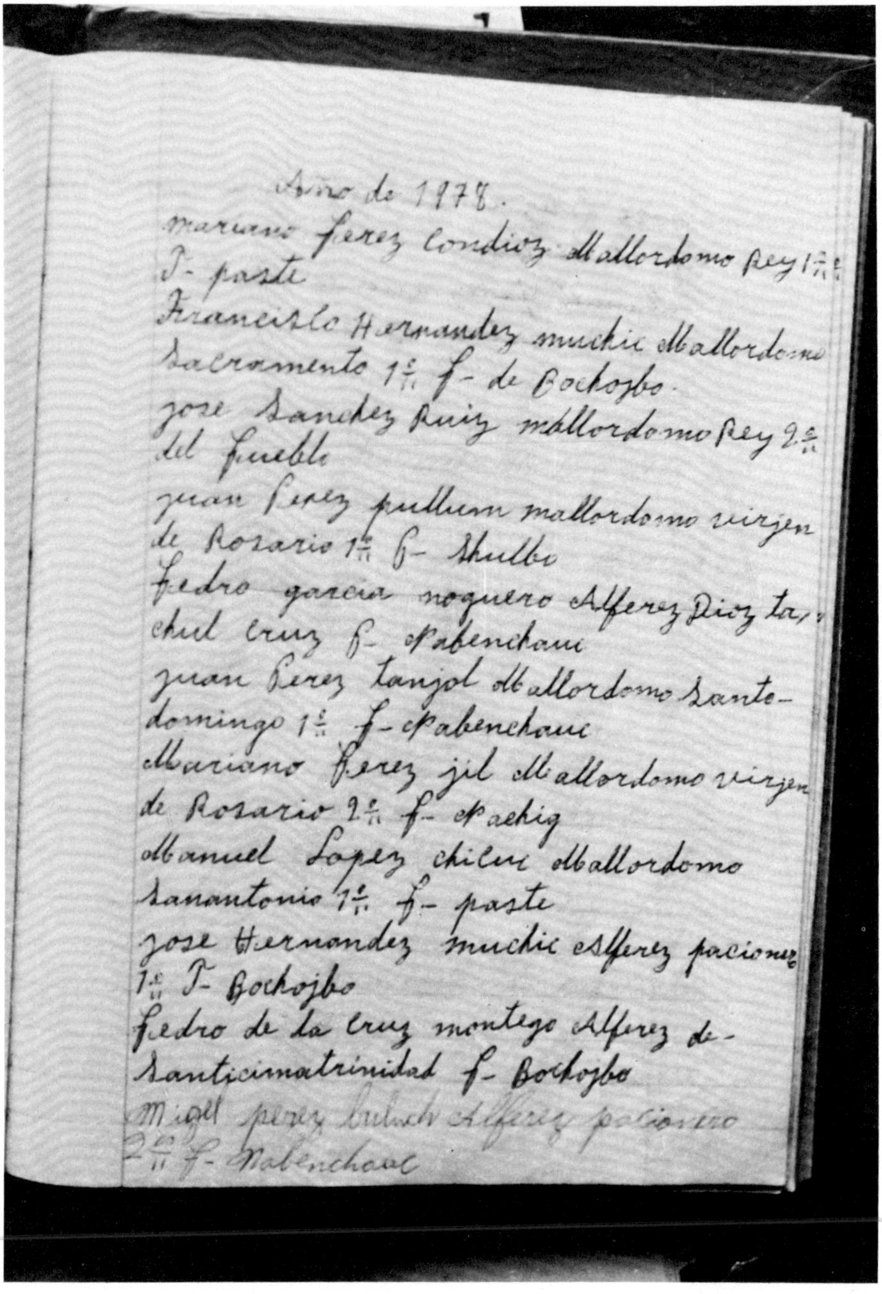

Año de 1978.
mariano perez condioz Mallordomo Rey 1º
P- paste
Francisco Hernandez muchic Mallordomo
Sacramento 1º P- de Bochojbo.
jose Sanchez Ruiz mallordomo Rey 2º
del pueblo
juan Perez pullum mallordomo virjen
de Rosario 1º P- Shulbo
pedro garcia noquero Alferez Dioz ta-
chil cruz P- Nabenchauc
juan Perez tanjol Mallordomo Santo-
domingo 1º P- Nabenchauc
Mariano Perez jil Mallordomo virjen
de Rosario 2º P- Nachig
Manuel Lopez chilui Mallordomo
Sanantonio 1º P- paste
jose Hernandez muchic Alferez pacionero
1º P- Bochojbo
pedro de la cruz montejo Alferez de-
Santicimatrinidad P- Bochojbo
Migel perez bulush Alferez pacionero
2º P- Nabenchauc

100. Sample page from waiting lists for cargos for year 1978

101. Reading off the waiting lists for cargos

bottle of rum to the Elders at this time; if one fails to appear with his bottle and has not made some previous arrangement, it is assumed that he is no longer interested. After notifying him, the Elders and escribanos are free to drop his name from the list and add another. Those who wish to request a cargo for some date in the future also present bottles of rum and ask for a cargo in a year that is not yet taken.

Although the books are considered somewhat sacred, Cancian was able, after great effort, to photograph books for the years of 1952, 1958, and 1961 (Figure 100 displays a sample page). When a senior alcalde leaves office, he takes the list used during his incumbency back to his hamlet and keeps it in his house. This system is a strong check against any major tampering with the lists on the part of any set of cargoholders, for they can always be checked with past cargoholders in various hamlets.

The waiting period, which has been increasing over the years, is now more than twenty years for some cargos. In 1952 the longest waiting period was only ten years; in 1958 it was sixteen. Cancian (1965a: 182) notes a strong correlation between the prestige of cargos, especially on the lower levels, and the length of the waiting period.

The waiting list system does not apply to the mayores, for this cargo has little prestige and few people wish to hold it. These appointments are made mainly from suggestions supplied by the incumbents. A rather ingenious device is used by appointing as policemen and errand boys for the Presidente the young men who have been giving the community authorities trouble. But most cargos have more prestige and involve long waiting periods—more than twenty years for the Senior Mayordomo Rey, eighteen for the Senior Mayordomo of Virgen del Rosario, sixteen years for the Alférez of Divina Cruz, and so on.

In addition to providing a more or less orderly system for filling cargos and for mustering resources for the year of service, the waiting lists have, for Zinacantecos, social consequences which Cancian has called "surplus value." A Zinacanteco may define himself as a person of a certain category simply by having his name on the waiting list for a certain cargo.

> The community cannot blame him for the fact that there is a long waiting list. Certainly being on the list is less satisfactory than actually passing the cargo; he has only demonstrated intention and has not accomplished anything. However, though the knowledge of who is on the waiting list for a given cargo is not nearly as widespread as knowledge of who has passed it, it is sufficiently widespread in the neighborhood and hamlet of a prospective cargoholder to compensate somewhat for his lack of actual achievement. (Cancian 1965a: 183–84)

Costs and Prestige

The costs of serving cargos vary from approximately 50 pesos for the Mayor to more than 14,000 pesos for the senior Mayordomo Rey. These costs, as well as other factors, especially traditional rank or authority, determine the prestige a man derives from serving in a given cargo. Since both the costs and the traditional ranks of cargos are public knowledge, the community has an easy way to assess an individual. From the point of view of the participant, cargos are a clear way of communicating his abilities and his self-image to his fellow Zinacantecos.

The items for which expenditures are made are similar for all cargos. Drink and food for fellow cargoholders and for auxiliary personnel account for most of the budget; rum, meat (chicken and pork as well as beef), maize, beans, rolls, brown sugar, and candles are the major items. Vegetables, eggs, spices, cigarettes, and matches account for a few pesos at any ritual event. Permanent items such as pots, lanterns, and musical instruments may be borrowed or purchased, depending upon the financial condition of the cargo-holder and his plans for future use of the items in other cargos. Table 10 provides data on the details of expenses in two cargos—the very expensive Senior Mayordomo Rey and a moderately expensive Senior Mayordomo of San Sebastián for which Cancian was able to collect exact figures.

Table 10. Detailed expenses of two cargos[a]

	Mayordomo Rey *bankilal* 1960		*Mayordomo San Sebastián* *bankilal* 1952	
Drink	5,880.00		1,400.00	
Meat	3,984.00		497.00	
Bread	529.60		140.00	
Sugar	532.00		142.50	
Candles	250.00[b]		116.00	
Miscellaneous	296.70		little	
Permanent items	533.00		0	
total	6,125.30		895.50	
Corn	1,740.00		367.50	
Beans	220.00		135.00	
Chickens and eggs	129.60		408.00	
Coffee	200.00		135.00[b]	
total	2,289.60	14,294.90	1,045.50	3,341.00

Source: Cancian 1965a: 82.

[a] All figures are in pesos and are calculated at 1960–61 standard prices.

[b] Estimated.

In general, the relative prestige of any cargo can be measured by both normative statements and the observable behavior of cargoholders (for example, who bows to whom); the prestige ranking depends on a number of variables, including the cost of each cargo. For example, in the first-level cargos high prestige is accorded to the mayordomos reyes, the mayordomos of the Virgen del Rosario and Sacramento, and the pasioneros; low prestige is accorded to the mayordomos of San Antonio, the capitanes, and the mayores, with the latter on the bottom of the scale in all respects. In the second-level cargos the highest prestige goes to the Alférez of San Lorenzo and the lowest prestige to the junior alféreces of San Sebastián and San

Pedro Mártir. In the upper two levels, the most prestige rests with the Regidor Primero and the Senior Alcalde. A wealthy and ambitious Zinacanteco might plan his strategy to serve successively, for example, as the Senior Mayordomo Rey, the Alférez of San Lorenzo, the Regidor Primero, and the Senior Alcalde, or come as close to this ideal as possible. A poorer Zinacanteco may aspire only to the lower cargos at each level and be satisfied by finishing as the Junior Alcalde; and of course many Zinacantecos never serve more than one or two cargos before they either give up or die.

To achieve the ideal state of passing up the ladder to the highest prestige levels depends not upon inherited property or money per se, but upon the successful manipulation and management of one's social and economic life. The resources to pay for a cargo costing as much as 14,000 pesos—a figure ten times the annual income of a relatively prosperous Zinacanteco— requires that a man get on well with his kinsmen, both in his domestic group and in his sna, and that he be called upon to serve as godparent in many cases so that he will have many compadres. Once a man has served two or three cargos he is in even greater demand as a godfather, especially for weddings where compadres are acquired in large numbers. Thus, a two-way process is operative for important men: the more compadres, the more prestigious cargos; the more prestigious the cargos, the more compadres. The successful cargoholder must be expert not only in maize farming by his own efforts, but also as an entrepreneur in managing lands that he either acquires from the ejido or rents from Ladinos in the lowlands. He will need to call upon his kinsmen and compadres not only for assistance in maize farming, but also as helpers when he serves in the cargo position. And even if he is a successful entrepreneur in maize farming, he will have to borrow large sums of money in order to meet the expenses of the office. Again, his kinsmen are the ones to whom he will turn most for loans of cash. Even with all these resources he typically leaves office with a series of debts, and it will take some years before he has recouped his resources and is ready for another cargo. In short, the "rest periods" between cargos are necessary to provide Zinacantecos with time to recover from one cargo and get ready for the next.

Auxiliary Personnel

The cargoholders do not perform their ritual duties alone; advisers, musicians, and other helpers form a sizable corps of people in much the same way that a retinue must have assisted Ancient Maya priests. Cancian divides them into two classes: "those who contribute special skills and knowledge," and "those who almost in a perfectly literal sense, lend a hand" (1965a: 42). The former include the ritual advisers, the sacristanes, the musicians of the alféreces, the escribanos, the women's advisers, and the special musicians. The second class includes the ordinary musicians and general helpers, some of whom have special roles.

The ritual advisers (TOTILME²ILETIK) are the masters of ceremonies for the cargoholders. The Tzotzil term for the role is the same as that applied to the ancestral gods who live in the mountains around Zinacantan Center. Just as the supernatural TOTILME²ILETIK give advice and direct ceremonies inside their mountain homes, the living TOTILME²ILETIK give cargoholders technical ritual advice on how to carry out their duties. Each cargoholder (except for the mayores) in the first three levels of the hierarchy recruits a ritual adviser to help him with the complex ritual during his year in office. The man selected must have passed at least two cargos and is chosen for his intelligence and ability to talk and direct ritual. I have repeatedly observed ceremonies in Zinacantan Center in which the ritual adviser of a novice cargoholder has interrupted a ritual sequence when it was being improperly performed. Although these elderly men are not formally organized, they form a pool of ritual talent and knowledge that is regularly tapped by the annual incumbents of the cargo positions. They can be identified by their red turbans, black ceremonial robes, and rosaries.

The duties of the ritual advisers vary greatly with the cargo. For a short cargo, such as capitán, which lasts only four days during the fiesta of San Lorenzo, the cargoholder has little opportunity to gain knowledge or experience and hence is mainly directed by his adviser. For year-long cargos, the ritual advisers accompany the cargoholders only at the most important points in the annual ceremonies; the number of these declines as the cargoholder moves up the ladder and acquires more knowledge himself. A mayordomo is accompanied by his adviser for a few days during each of the following events: when he enters office; when he holds the special celebration of the sacred chest on the altar in his house; when he is sponsor of an important fiesta; when all the mayordomos participate in an annual fiesta that is known as "killing of the saints"; and when he leaves office. An alférez' ritual adviser serves on only three occasions during the year: when he enters; when it is his turn to invite all the alféreces for a meal; and when he leaves office. The regidores have advisers only when they enter office, and the alcaldes viejos do not have them at all.

The major responsibility of the ritual adviser when the cargoholder is entering and leaving office is to go to the sacred mountains to pray to the ancestral gods, asking that the cargo be served well and that the cargoholders be pardoned for inadequacies in the performance. Similarly, he speaks to the other cargoholders when the man he is representing leaves office, again asking pardon and expressing the hope that they are satisfied with the manner in which the duties have been performed. The importance of the ritual adviser as a speech-maker and representative is expressed in the alternative Tzotzil name for the role: HTAK'AVEL, "he who answers." Each of these duties also expresses the crucial link that is believed to exist between those members of the community who are now departed ancestors living inside the sacred mountains—ancestors who have previously served their cargos in Zinacantan Center and are carrying on in the supernatural world—and the cargoholders who are still in office and must carry the burdens before they pass them along to their successors.

The temple of San Lorenzo has four sacristanes (PISHKALETIK) whose daily duties consist of opening and closing the church and ringing the bells at 6 A.M., noon, and 6 P.M. They alternate, each serving every fourth week. In addition, they assist the mayordomos in their ritual duties—and this brings them often into service as a group. They must know how to read the church calendar, which is printed in Spanish, and are responsible for informing the mayordomos on which dates they must perform rituals. (In this respect they are the functional equivalents of calendar specialists found in other Maya communities.) They also know special prayers that must be said on certain occasions, as, for example, when the mayordomos count the medallions they keep in their chests and bring them to church to place around the necks of the saints. Sacristanes serve for a number of years, and their long experience makes them important advisers to the mayordomos when their ritual advisers are not present. They are called (in rank order) the Senior Sacristán (BANKILAL PISHKAL), the Second Sacristán (SHCHA'VA'AL PISHKAL), the Third Sacristán (YOSHVA'AL PISHKAL), and the Fourth Sacristan (SHCHAVA'AL PISHKAL), and dress in regular clothes but wear a large, black wool blanket folded and draped over the left shoulder.

Each mayordomo recruits an elderly woman (HCHIK POM) past menopause to serve as an Incense-bearer and helper in changing the flowers on his house altar. (For additional data on these female ritual assistants see Chapter 21; and see also L. Haviland 1967.)

For second-level cargos—the alféreces—extremely important specialists serve as advisers when the ritual advisers are not present. They are musicians (HVABAHOMETIK), a violinist and a guitarist. The elderly violinist in the current group has served for more than thirty years; the guitarist is a relatively recent appointment made after a previous one was unable to perform properly. Unlike the other cargoholders' musicians, who serve for only one year, the musicians of the alféreces are sworn into their posts and expected to serve for life.

The two escribanos (ʔISHKIRVANOETIK or scribes) are attached to the six Elders. They are chosen for their ability to read and write Spanish, and their duties involve keeping a list of all adult males who must pay taxes for fiestas, writing out notifications of appointments to cargos, and keeping the lists of men who are waiting for cargos. They are appointed for one-year terms coinciding with those of the Elders, but they are often reappointed for second terms and many serve as often as three times. Hence, the escribanos also accumulate knowledge and experience about the performance of rituals that are important to the smooth functioning of the hierarchy. They dress like the sacristanes, except that their folded black blankets do not hang down as far.

Each cargoholder appoints an old woman (HPACHVANEH VEʔELIL) to direct the work in the kitchen which will serve special foods on certain ritual occasions. These women's advisers are responsible for knowing the requirements of food and of etiquette in serving for various fiestas. Each cargoholder has as well a HKʼEL VEʔELIL who oversees the preparation of food for him at larger ritual gatherings.

Finally, there are two special musicians, a violinist and a guitarist, and, although they are not sworn in, their appointments are theoretically permanent. They serve different cargoholders at three important fiestas: at San Sebastián they play for the jaguar performers (BOLOMETIK); during the Easter season they serve with the Pasioneros; and during the Christmas season they serve with the Mayordomos del Rosario, sponsors of the fiesta.

In addition to the specialized auxiliary personnel, each cargoholder must recruit a number of other, less specialized helpers. The most skilled of these are the musicians. The Elders and all of the first-level cargo pairs, senior and junior, who serve on a year-long basis have three musicians (violinist, harpist, and guitarist) who are present to play for flower changes and other rituals at the home of the cargoholders and for almost all the rituals performed in and around the churches. For many occasions the Elders also need a flutist and two drummers; the alféreces need flutist and drummers only when entering and leaving their cargos.

The Elders, the mayordomos reyes, and the mesoneros, all have Special Helpers (HMAKBALAL) who run errands, carry objects, serve food, and pour drinks. Their commitment is stronger than those to be discussed, for if they cannot serve on a particular occasion they must find their own replacements. The cargoholder must inform the civil officials at the Cabildo which two individuals have been designated as his special helpers for the year, and request that they be exempted from any other regular community service during the year—a very special exemption indeed!

Simple helpers are known as HCH'OMILETIK, or alternatively CH'AMUNBILETIK, "borrowed people." Among these helpers there are special roles, but people may be used interchangeably. A man must serve as drink-pourer, and one helper's wife (known as the HCH'OL VO?) must be responsible for pouring the rum from the large container in which it is stored into the bottles carried about by the drink-pourer. Another helper role is generally, but not necessarily, held by the same man all year: this is the HTEN KAMARO, who shoots off the KAMARO, a miniature cannon about 15 centimeters long. Cancian describes the process as follows:

> Powder is packed into the bore with a stick, and a little is fed into a fuse hole. Then the fuse is lighted, usually with a cigarette, and the cannon is held at arm's length until it goes off. The explosion is deafening even at 15 or 20 feet, and the job of the cannoneer requires some skill, a good deal of courage, and strong eardrums. The explosions are often used as signals between groups of cargoholders who are starting off on coordinated ritual rounds from different points. People who live in the ceremonial center are often able to tell what point a ritual has reached simply by listening for the sequence of cannon shots. (1965a: 47–48)

Each alférez also has a series of helpers that must be added to the retinue, such as the boy who holds his hat and rattle.

The recruitment of the auxiliary personnel is quite different from the waiting list procedure for the cargoholders. The escribanos are recruited by the Elders long before they are to enter service, and with the understanding that the senior one is selected first and has the right to choose the man he would like as his junior partner. The sacristanes name the replacement they wish, should any of their number leave his post, but the rum used in requesting the services of the new sacristán is provided by the mayordomos. The alféreces recruit their musicians, and the cargoholders whom they serve recruit their special musicians. All other helpers and regular musicians are recruited by the cargoholders they serve. Kinship is an important factor in the recruitment of the auxiliary personnel for two reasons.

(1) Kinsmen are more readily approachable by the cargoholder, more easily obligated to him, and more likely to enter into a reciprocal

agreement in which they will receive similar aid when passing a cargo
. . . (2) The behavior and capacities of individual kinsmen are likely
to be better known to the cargoholder, and they are more likely to have
already worked together. The probability of disruptive conflict within
the group of helpers is thus reduced considerably, for the interpersonal
relations and the lines of authority have already been tested.

When a man has few kinsmen he can depend on, he retreats to the
second line of defense, his ritual kinsmen, and recruits many of his
helpers from among them. (Cancian 1965a: 48–49)

Still other cargoholders recruit helpers from among their work groups that
farm together in the lowlands.

While the rewards of the cargoholder are quite clear in terms of the
prestige he accrues and the authority he wields while in office, the rewards
for the auxiliary personnel are more the free supply of drink and food they
enjoy at the expense of the cargoholder and the excitement of being in the
ceremonial center during the year. Some of the auxiliary personnel, such
as the sacristanes and escribanos, come to be respected for their ritual
knowledge, but even more important is the fact that they are maintained
year after year while serving the cargoholders.

Functions

The cargo system in Zinacantan Center not only has consequences for
individual Zinacantecos but also performs important functions for the
community as a social system. As Cancian points out, the religious cargo
system "is crucial to the continued existence of Zinacantan as an Indian
community, a community separate and distinct from its Ladino environment" (1965a: 133). It defines the limits of community membership, rein-
forces commitment to common values, reduces potential conflict, and
supports traditional kinship patterns.

The clearest integrative consequence of the system results from the
movement of people from the outlying hamlets into the ceremonial center
to serve in cargo positions and to attend fiestas for pleasure. The presence
of the sacred mountains, waterholes, and temples in the center are perhaps
the most important reasons why Zinacantecos from the hamlets are all
oriented toward the ceremonial center; it is through the cargo system and
through the markets set up for the major fiestas that they make the most
frequent personal contact with each other.

The rituals and the fiestas of the cargo system link Zinacantecos together

in common religious celebration and reaffirm commitment of each participant to the common religious symbols. Since these symbols are in many
important ways unique to Zinacantan, the public rituals involving them
distinguish Zinacantecos from non-Zinacantecos. Individuals are required
to commit themselves to the Indian way of life by service in the cargo
system. Some Zinacantecos are, of course, lost to the community each year
when they refuse to serve in a cargo, but the integrity of the system is
maintained for they are defined as nonmembers and most of them ultimately become Ladinoized and are drained off into the Ladino world. The
cargo system thus permits clear definition of the boundaries of the Indian
community.

The economic expenditures for the cargo system both require and help
to maintain an integrated community.

> Before he spends the great sums required for a cargo, a man must
> feel assured that his doing so will satisfy at least the majority of his
> fellows. If only a few of them were to recognize this achievement, the
> investment would not be adequately repaid. On the other hand, after
> he has made this tremendous investment in the cargo system he is
> required to support the norms of the community that stipulate rewards
> for such behavior. If he does not, he undermines his investment. And
> if he enters the Ladino world, his investment is totally lost, and even
> a detriment to him in some circles. (Cancian 1965a: 135)

The cargo system also serves to rank the members of the community in
a single social structure. Both incumbent and past cargoholder are accorded
respect and prestige from all sectors of the municipio.

Because of the obvious advantages in cargo service possessed by a Zinacanteco with many and close relations with kinsmen, not only in his
immediate domestic group but also in his lineage and with his compadres,
the operation of the system strongly encourages the maintenance of the
traditional kinship system.

Through the expenditure of great amounts of money in the cargo system
Zinacantan is provided with an amazingly effective means of transferring
surplus wealth from the private to the public sector of the economy, thereby
reducing considerably the envy of the rich by the poor (Cancian 1965a:
135). One of the critical features of a corporate peasant community (cf.
Wolf 1955) of the type represented by Zinacantan is a pattern of institutionalized envy directed especially against individuals who accumulate what the culture defines as more than an appropriate share of the
wealth. While Cancian has demonstrated that the Zinacanteco cargo system does not completely level differences between families (1965a: 107–125),

it does pump a great deal of wealth into consumable goods—drink, food, candles, fireworks, and so on—that are shared with other cargoholders and their retinues as the ceremonies are held each year. After serving an expensive cargo and thereby making a great contribution for public and "necessary" ceremonies, even a prosperous Zinacanteco is stripped of enough wealth to bring him back into understandable range, thereby tempering the envy and gossip, and probably even accusations of witchcraft, that might otherwise be directed against him.

The Future

Cancian's analysis of the economic system and demographic growth of Zinacantan as these relate to the cargo system indicates that some drastic changes will have to be made in the system within the next decade or two (1965a: 140–143). For, while the number of positions in the hierarchy has been increasing (for example, the four regidores who were civil officials before 1899 have become assimilated into the religious cargo system, and a number of cargos have been added both in the center and in connection with chapels that have been recently constructed in the hamlets of Nabenchauk and ?Apas), the rate of growth in the cargo system is not keeping pace with the recent demographic explosion. The development of the waiting lists has provided a temporary solution to the problem, but it is doubtful that a man will be willing to wait much more than twenty years for a cargo, especially since the average life span is low by our standards. In addition, greater numbers of Zinacanteco entrepreneurs are growing large maize surpluses on rented lands in the lowlands, and pressures are increasing to expend this wealth in other ways than for a cargo for which one may have to wait two decades.

Several possibilities exist. Cancian predicts that the cargo system will be strained to the point where it will lose its importance as the social institution through which the community is integrated (1965a: 193–194). While I grant this is a possibility, two other possible avenues of change should be considered: the cargos may be markedly expanded in number if one or more of the outlying hamlets with chapels—Nabenchauk, ?Apas, or Salinas—develop full-scale hierarchies, either dependent upon the hierarchy in Zinacantan Center or independent; a system might evolve in which the cargos were served by an elite group of families—that is, families with more surplus wealth—as seems to have happened in Chichicastenango (Bunzel 1952), where the cargo system maintains its cultural integrity with a large, expanding population and a limited set of cargos.

12 / The Political System

Unlike the cargo system which remains much the same year after year, the political system of Zinacantan is in a constant state of change.

The Civil Hierarchy

Although no civil positions (except mayores) count in the system of advancement up the ceremonial ladder of Zinacantan Center, they are of crucial importance in the legal and political life of Zinacantan. The civic offices in the Ayuntamiento Constitucional (municipal government) were established in 1899. Before 1962 these positions, filled by Zinacantecos, included the Presidente, the Síndico, and four Jueces (ranked 1 through 4).

While hearing complaints and judging cases, these six officeholders sit on a long bench to the left of the town hall door (see Figures 102, 103). Occasionally, for reasons discussed later, they are joined by the four regidores from the religious hierarchy. The bench to the right of the door on the porch is occupied by the mayores—also ranked from 1 to 8 on the rare occasion when all were present; ordinarily, however, the order is 1 to 4, since they usually alternate the duty every two weeks (Figure 104). (Since these mayores have the only positions in the civil hierarchy that count for advancement in the ceremonial ladder, and since they have important ritual functions, they were described in Chapter 11.) By 1965 there were twelve mayores, rather than eight and they alternated every two weeks, with six theoretically on duty at any one time. Inside the Cabildo, seated behind a desk with an ancient typewriter, sits the Secretary, the only Ladino to occupy a position in the civil government of the municipio of Zinacantan.

I am especially grateful for material used in this chapter to Stephen B. Young, who made a study of Zinacanteco political structure during the summer of 1965 (Young 1965).

102. Positions of civil officials at the Cabildo (1962)

103. From right to left: the Presidente, the Síndico, and the four Alcaldes Jueces on their bench in front of the Cabildo

104. A Mayor on duty at the Cabildo

There is also a treasurer who collects from local stores a monthly tax based on inventory. He visits each weekly to collect 1.50 pesos for every 100 pesos of goods he calculates are in the store, keeps a list of receipts and expenditures, and places the money in a box kept by the Presidente in the Cabildo. Finally, there are the principales (KRINSUPALETIK), young Zinacantecos appointed for one year from each of the hamlets, whose duty is to act as representatives of the government in their respective hamlets. They collect money for public expenditures and deposit it with the officials in the center; they also carry messages and announcements back to the hamlets. Most of the hamlets have two principales, although some of the smaller ones have only one (see Chapter 8); they are classified as senior and junior, and alternate the duty every two weeks. Most of their duties are civil, but they have an important ceremonial function in serving as hosts for the Year Renewal ceremonies.

A number of committees require the occasional services of many men. Almost every hamlet has a Comité de Educación. The Ejido Committee, which controls the lands given the community under the national land-reform program, is a very powerful independent group that provides many of the important bases of political power in Zinacantan. In addition, there are temporary committees, appointed by the Presidente and his colleagues, among which are committees to collect funds or to direct activities for fiestas and for public works, such as repairing the roads, the Cabildo, or the jail.

In 1962 six civil regidores were added. They do not have clearly established responsibilities, but their addition tells something about the recent history of how Zinacantan has altered its official organization as a municipio, established by the state laws of Chiapas, to conform with the traditions of community service in Zinacantan Center.

Before 1899, the year the Presidente and civil government were installed, Zinacantan was not officially a municipio. Authority for settling disputes among the Indian population was apparently vested in the officials who have since become the four regidores of the religious hierarchy. Up to 1952, all the offices in the civil government were served for one-year terms; in 1952 these terms were extended to two years.

Until 1962 the municipios of Chiapas were divided into three classes. As a third-class municipio Zinacantan was required by law to have only a presidente, a síndico, two regidores and two alternate regidores, and a juez and his alternate, each serving terms of two years. These offices were filled as specified, with two important exceptions. First, the four regidores of the religious hierarchy were nominally appointed to fill the offices of civil regidores and alternate regidores; they served their one-year terms as religious officials and only occasionally served as civil officials. Second, there were four jueces rather than one juez and an alternate. This was apparently an adjustment to the traditional Zinacanteco custom of alternating the duty in a fixed pattern, two weeks at a time. The two jueces and their alternates were ranked 1 to 4; they ordinarily alternated, with No. 1 and No. 3 serving for two weeks, followed by No. 2 and No. 4.

This happy state of affairs came to an end by the combination of a political crisis in 1960 and the new laws of 1962. The Presidente was impeached in October 1960, after a long political struggle described later. Under the law the first regidor would assume the office for the fourteen months left in the term of the impeached Presidente. But this first regidor was a religious official who had intended to serve only during the calendar year 1960. Moreover, he spoke only Tzotzil and had almost no skills for carrying out the presidential functions. The Síndico was accepted as de facto Presidente, but the former religious regidor was still required to settle law cases and be present for contacts with visiting Ladino officials. By the end of 1961, both the man and the community had suffered from this situation, and were forced to comply with the new laws of 1962 which specified that all municipios of Chiapas were to be equal with respect to formal organization of their governments. The law requires that a municipio be administered by a Presidente; a Síndico (in charge of social welfare); six regidores and three alternate regidores, who are heads of various municipio subcommittees; and a juez and alternate juez—all serving for terms of three years each (Cancian, 1965a: 19–20).

To date, not much has happened in the reorganization of Zinacantan except for the addition of six new civil regidores, whose only function is to free the religious regidores of any formal governmental responsibilities.

Duties of Civil Officials

In theory, the officers of the civil government of a Mexican municipio are elected and are concerned with public works, the administration of justice, and the relations of the community to the state and national government. In fact, however, these civil officials in Zinacantan are placed in office by the political boss of the municipio.

While the Presidente, Síndico, and jueces have a variety of functions, including greeting visiting Ladino officials (Figure 105), occasionally collecting money for roads and bridges and supervising their repair, and appointing committees for fiestas, their major civil duties are concerned with disputes

106. A Zinacanteco woman presenting a complaint to the Presidente in front of the Cabildo

among Zinacantecos.* Day after day, the Presidente, Síndico, and at least two of the jueces on duty sit on their bench on the front porch of the Cabildo, weaving their palm hats and waiting for law cases. When all are present, the group listens to cases and settles the disputes. If the Presidente is absent, the Síndico takes the Presidente's staff, moves to the No. 1 position on the bench, and hears the case (Figure 106). If both are absent, then the leading juez (with permission of the Presidente) may move up and hear the case.

*Jane Fishburne Collier is making an intensive study of the Zinacanteco law cases. See her paper in Vogt, ed., 1966.

105. Zinacanteco political meeting with a representative of the Mexican Government

While some Zinacantecos seek out the Presidente in his house at night so that they can have an uninterrupted hearing of their cases, the formal and more common procedure is for the plaintiff to approach the Presidente while he is at his post in front of the Cabildo. The plaintiff bows to the Presidente and other officials in rank order and presents beer and one or two liters of rum for all. The Presidente listens to his complaint, and, if persuaded, summons two of the mayores to go after the guilty party and bring him into Zinacantan Center. The defendant appears, also with rum and beers, bows to the Presidente and other officials, and presents his defense. Often both parties, accompanied by relatives known to be good talkers, who serve as lawyers, all talk at once, and one wonders how in the ensuing pandemonium a judgment is ever reached. Witnesses may be called by both sides to provide additional testimony. The case may have one of three outcomes. First, it may be settled in this Zinacanteco court, with the Síndico and jueces helping by expressing their approval of an argument or hooting with laughter at a defendant who is telling an obvious lie. In this case the culprit will be required to return the stolen property and be fined or jailed (Figure 107) or both. Or the case may prove too serious for the Indian court to handle (murder, for example) and will be passed along to the Ministerio Público in San Cristóbal. Finally, it may be impossible to reach a clear-cut decision, even after all the witnesses and testimony are heard, in which case the Presidente's main efforts are devoted to soothing the two parties so they will not bear grudges against each other.

In addition to helping the Presidente with law cases, the Síndico is given the duty of supervising the work of prisoners on municipal projects (such as repairing roads), supervising public works on schools, and so forth, and collecting taxes. The jueces have special duties in representing the authority of the civil government away from the Cabildo. For example, they carry out investigations of murders and thefts; they accompany a mayor to bring in a culprit to the Cabildo; if witches are forced to return to caves to retract promises they have made to the Earth Lord, a juez goes along to represent the civil authorities; and if a Zinacanteco is missing, the jueces try to find him. They also take prisoners to the Ministerio Público in San Cristóbal. The position of Secretary is maintained in Ladino hands in municipios like Zinacantan with the rationalization that none of the Indians knows how to read and write well enough to keep the official records. Actually, a number of Zinacantecos know how to read and write, and one served in this post for some years. But it is quite clear that by keeping a Ladino in this position, the state department of Indian Affairs manages to maintain basic control over the political situation (Aguirre Beltrán, 1953). Although the Secretary is usually merely engaged in keeping records (births, deaths,

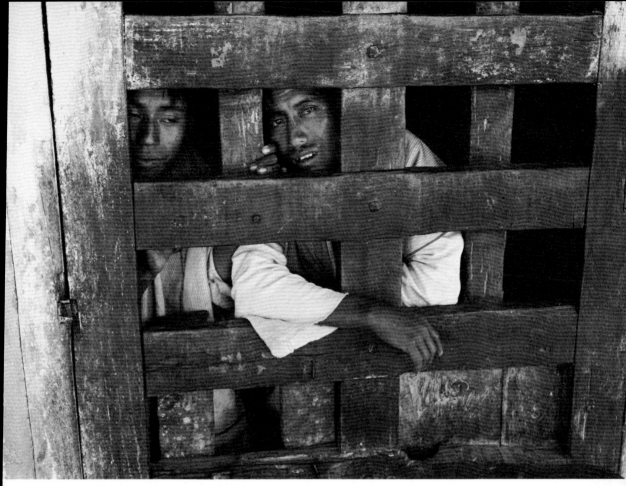

107. Jailed in Zinacantan Center

and marriages), assembling the census, and preparing papers needed by Indian officials, in the event of real trouble he could phone for police from San Cristóbal or for federal troops. The only phone in Zinacantan Center, connecting with San Cristóbal and the outside world, is located by his desk in the Cabildo. Some secretaries in other neighboring municipios have long records of exploiting the Indians by extracting additional cash or food (like eggs or chickens) from the people, or by serving as the recruiter who, for a fee, signs Indians for labor on distant coffee plantations. Our experience in Zinacantan has been that the present Secretary is basically an honest man who operates within the law, at least as it is interpreted by local custom.

The civil officials are compensated in various ways. The highest paid official in Zinacantan is the Ladino Secretary who in 1960 received a monthly salary of 350 pesos from the municipio, 100 pesos a month from the INI, and 50 percent of the fines levied by the Presidente. His municipio salary is collected by the principales who tax each head of family in each hamlet forty centavos on the last day of each month. The money is taken to the Presidente, who pays the Secretary his salary on the first day of each month.

The Presidente has received (since 1960) 100 pesos a month from liquor taxes collected in the center, plus 50 percent of the fines levied. He also receives the taxes levied on merchants at the large markets of fiesta days. These are taken up by the Síndico and Juez No. 1, who make the rounds collecting 5 pesos from each merchant who sets up a stand and $1\frac{1}{2}$ or 2 pesos from the smaller merchants who peddle goods in the open air. This amount totals 100 pesos or more in a large fiesta.

The Síndico receives 1 peso per day for each day that a prisoner is in jail. The legal limit, according to Mexican federal law, that a prisoner may be kept in jail in municipios like Zinacantan is three days (72 hours). But at the end of one, two, or three days, the prisoner or his family must pay the Síndico 1, 2, or 3 pesos before he is released. In some cases fines can be levied and the prisoner kept in jail, thereby providing funds for the Presidente, the Secretary, and the Síndico. There is obviously not much compensation in the system for the Síndico, but he can at times leave his post for as long as two weeks and engage in farming or other work.

The Presidente, Síndico, and jueces also receive some compensation from the rum presented during law cases, for they may either sell it or use it for their own domestic ceremonies.

When there is a murder, one of the jueces goes with a mayor to investigate; he later charges the family of the deceased 25 to 50 pesos for the investigation. Only one juez goes, but by custom he splits the fee with the other three. Like the Síndico, the jueces are not on duty all the time, but may alternate and hence have time to carry on their maize farming and other economic activities.

The mayores are not paid at all, but since the position counts in the first level of the hierarchy, it is not appropriate that they should be. The principales from the hamlets are not paid in any way, nor does their position count in the hierarchy; this is clearly the least attractive post of all, although it exempts them from taxes for a year and provides opportunities to take trips to Zinacantan Center.

Considering the small amounts of compensation involved, even for the top officials in the civil government, it is a wonder that men of any competence are persuaded to serve in these posts. The Secretary is moderately well paid from the various sources, but the Presidente is especially hard-pressed since he has to be at his post more of the time than any of the other Indian officials.

Symbols of Authority

The most important symbols of authority in the various Zinacantan hierarchies are special items of clothing, and various types of staffs of office. The two items of clothing, worn by all top-ranking authorities, which signal special authority are the high-backed sandals (CHAK SHONOBIL) and the long, black ceremonial robe (SHAKITAIL) described in Chapter 5. To these are added special arrangements of the scarf on ritual occasions, and for the top three levels of cargoholders—the alféreces, regidores, and alcaldes—a red turban and broad-brimmed black hat.

Except for the mayordomos and alféreces, every important official in Zinacantan carries a staff of office of some kind. The mayores, mayordomo reyes, and mesoneros carry wooden clubs (TS'ARAM TE?, similar to policemen's billies). A shaman carries a bamboo staff (BISH), in his left hand; a regidor carries a wooden staff (VARA). Finally, and most important in terms of power, are the silver-headed, beribboned, polished wood batons carried by the two top cargoholders, the senior and junior alcaldes viejos, the Presidente and Juez No. 1, and by the Presidente de la Junta of major fiestas. Each staff is believed to possess a "soul" placed in it by the ancestral gods in the mountains. This is especially true of the silver-headed batons, which possess the strongest souls; they are baptized by the Catholic priest to lock the soul within the silver head.

The Presidente and Juez No. 1 can be identified by the silver-headed batons which resemble those carried by the alcaldes viejos but lack ribbons. Other civil officials have no special costuming, except for the mayores' billy clubs. When the Síndico is substituting officially, he uses the Presidente's baton.

The currently powerful cacique, Mol Marian, insists upon keeping the baton of the Presidente of the Ejido Committee on his house altar in Zinacantan Center, even though the current Presidente lives in Paste?. When the Presidente has to carry the baton to a meeting of the ejido members, he must first go to Mol Marian's house to ask for it. Not only is the supernatural power contained in the baton thus kept in Mol Marian's house, but the Presidente is forced to check in with Mol Marian on all important occasions.

The relation of the baton to the living social structure on the one hand and to the supernatural world of the ancestors on the other was illustrated by a series of moves the current Presidente made to increase his power. He first instituted the position of Comandante, designating him as the only man authorized to wear a pistol and one who was to be sent to help the mayores make difficult arrests. He also instituted a ritual held at his house altar every fifteen days for the batons of the Presidente and Juez No. 1. These rituals involve music, dancing, a change of flowers on the altar, and the consumption of rum and a ritual meal to please the ancestral gods and the saints, who are believed to renew constantly the power of the souls inside the batons. The baton derives its power from the supernatural world of the ancestral gods of the municipio and serves as a constant reminder to all Zinacantecos of the authority wielded by its current possessor. As the Presidente stated, "He who doesn't hold a baton, holds nothing" (Young 1965).

Sources of Political Power

The Tzotzil term HYU⁷ELETIK refers to men with special ability to MELTSAN K'OP (settle disputes) the internal conflicts of the community and to cope with the problems that impinge upon Zinacantan from the Ladino world. Such men have not only the ability to "speak well" in handling internal and external political problems but also political power derived from other sources—holding a cargo or having served in the past in the cargo system, being the old and respected head of a large lineage, having many compadres, serving on the Ejido Committee that controls land, and so on. Wealth is important, not so much for its own sake as for the help it supplies for advancement through the cargo system and for the accumulation of compadres who can be called upon for political support. Control of land is important in that it enables a man to give his sons farming land and house plots as they marry and establish independent households, thus keeping his lineage intact and enabling him to muster kinsmen for political struggles.

Some political power in Zinacantan rests in the formal religious and civil positions as well as in the high-ranking shamans. The men occupying the top six cargo positions not only perform crucial ceremonies for the municipio but are also the managers of the cargo system and keep waiting lists for cargo posts; they are highly respected and have great power while in office. Once a man becomes a Pasado, his position is known throughout the municipio, and he is called upon for advice on many matters. Similarly, the high-ranking shamans maintain their own realm of power. They not only direct the important Year Renewal ceremonies, but like all shamans, have power both to cure diseases and (at least by implication) to "give illness" (see Chapter 20). If a man is both a high ranking shaman and has passed through the cargo system, he reaps power from both these prestigious roles.

At the local level in the hamlets, the heads of lineages hold the power; the larger the lineage, the greater the power. These men are frequently called upon to settle disputes in the hamlets and are consulted on all important matters.

There have also emerged in Zinacantan a series of what are best called *caciques*. These are "political bosses," who do not necessarily occupy formal positions of authority but whose opinions on any issue carry great influence in Zinacantan. They are men of energy and vitality who have special ability to speak forcibly. The powerful local caciques who function in hamlets generally have extensive kinship connections, and may train junior men to take over their positions. Bitter struggles for power between rival hamlet caciques often lead to factional disputes until one is defeated (see Dunwell 1965). There may well be regular cycles in these struggles, as old caciques die or become senile and younger men challenge the establishment. The more compact hamlets like ?Apas seem to have only one cacique at a time, while larger and more dispersed hamlets such as Paste? have several.

The municipio-wide caciques have close connections with the hamlet caciques. In the past, extensive lineage and compadrazgo connections may have placed the municipio cacique in a position of power, but in recent decades the most important caciques have drawn their power less from kinship connections than from their ability to speak Spanish and cope with the Ladino world and their relationship to the management of the ejido. The control of ejido lands places them in a position to control an increasingly scarce resource. The most powerful cacique since 1940 is Mol Marian who has in effect controlled the Zinacantan ejido for twenty-five years. His rise to power and his struggle with other caciques makes a fascinating chapter in recent Zinacanteco history.

The Rise of Mol Marian. Mol Marian's name first appears on a petition for ejido land that was filed in 1934, which he signed for those who did not know how to write. He also held a minor position as one of the first officers of the Zinacantan ejido group that was seeking more land. Other Zinacantecos remember him as having been a poor and not very important man, but it is clear from the ejido records that he was extremely active. He worked in at least three hamlets where his ability to write made him invaluable in drawing up documents. It was this skill that allowed Mol Marian to rise higher and higher in the ejido movement as correspondence with Ladino officials grew, until in 1938 he was selected to head the Ejido Committee of Zinacantan Center for a year. From this position he went on to become the municipio Presidente, as had previous ejido heads. In 1940, when Mol Marian's one-year term ended, the ejido situation changed completely. Land was provisionally granted to Zinacantan, and it was announced that all the separate hamlet committees should now be united under a central committee to handle the new lands. The engineer selected Mol Marian, as the ex-Presidente and the man who had handled all the correspondence, to be the provisional head of this central committee. Although there have been "elections" for committee positions every three or four years since, Mol Marian has retained his power and the membership of the ejido committee has changed very little. The "elections" have actually served Mol Marian's purposes in that they have allowed him to drop committee members who no longer support him.

Control of the ejido put Mol Marian in a unique position of power. He was in charge of distributing the newly acquired lands to ejido members and, even after this initial distribution was completed, he retained the power to settle disputes arising over the inheritance of parcels and to reassign any parcels left vacant. He also had the right to collect dues from ejido members and was therefore in charge of a potentially very large sum of money. Nonetheless, the actual ejido organization has proved to be Mol Marian's greatest source of power. There are officers in each hamlet with lands in the ejido who are subordinate to the central committee. This gives Mol Marian a network through which to enforce his will on the hamlet level. The men who are members of the Zinacantan ejido have all become, in effect, Mol Marian's men. They are obligated to appear when he calls a general meeting, and the consensus they form gives an air of legitimacy to his maneuvers.

Mol Marian's most obvious show of power occurred in September 1960, when he arranged for the removal from office of the incumbent Presidente, Yermo Nuh. Yermo had entered office in January for a two-year term with the approval of Mol Marian, but by summer the two were no longer in agreement. The actual crisis came when Yermo released from jail two ne'er-do-well brothers who had been accused of murder. As no witnesses could be produced to testify to the murder, Yermo claimed he was unable to keep them in jail any longer. Wild rumors ran through Zinacantan Center to the effect that the Presidente had accepted a bribe. At this point Mol Marian stepped in and took over. He called for a meeting to take place at dawn in the cemetery above the center and had the principales sent out to notify each household. The Síndico actually conducted the meeting, reciting the Presidente's crimes and suggesting that he be removed from office. In the middle of the morning the group left the cemetery to converge on the Cabildo where they confronted the Presidente with their accusations. The Presidente was finally rescued by some INI officials who arrived and took him away to San Cristóbal in their jeep. There followed a week of political maneuvering on various levels. Mol Marian's group tried to press its advantage and carried their complaints to the Ladino officials. Yermo Nuh spent the week desperately trying to rally support, largely from the Milpería and the Nabenchauk faction opposed to Mol Marian. But the real issue apparently was decided by Ladinos, who felt that for the sake of preserving peace and order in Zinacantan the wishes of Mol Marian's group should be heeded, Yermo removed from office, and a successor appointed. This was done the following Sunday at another general meeting.

Although Yermo Nuh was no longer Presidente, the affair was far from ended. Yermo, a wealthy man and a cacique in his own right, became the leader of the opposition to Mol Marian. This opposition became more and more active, and, in January 1962, filed a complaint accusing Mol Marian of embezzling money from the ejido and from a fund to build bridges in the Center. They also accused him of conspiring to murder several Zinacantecos; a "cave full of bones" was the alleged evidence. Mol Marian went into hiding, but was eventually caught and jailed in Tuxtla. He stayed in jail for four months until his supporters were finally able to obtain his release. When he returned to Zinacantan, there was some question as to whether he would remain in charge of the ejido. A Ladino ejido official came to conduct a meeting of all its members to hear their complaints against Mol Marian. No one voiced any, and, when the official asked for a show of hands, he was forced to conclude that the ejido members wanted Mol Marian reinstated. Mol Marian has kept his old position, but there is now consensus in Zinacantan that his power has been weakened.

Although the extent of Mol Marian's power is unique in Zinacantan, the means he used to obtain it are not. Would-be Zinacanteco caciques often rely on personal self-assertiveness at least as much as on the support of numerous kinsmen and compadres, and usually work their way into some civil office from which they are in a better position to manipulate their followers and eliminate opposition.

Lines of Political Authority

The exercise of political authority in Zinacantan flows along at least three main channels which have important power relationships to both Mexican government officials and Catholic Church functionaries. These complex interrelations are diagramed in Figure 108.

At the local level in the domestic groups, Zinacanteco men have formal authority over women and adults over children. These domestic groups are

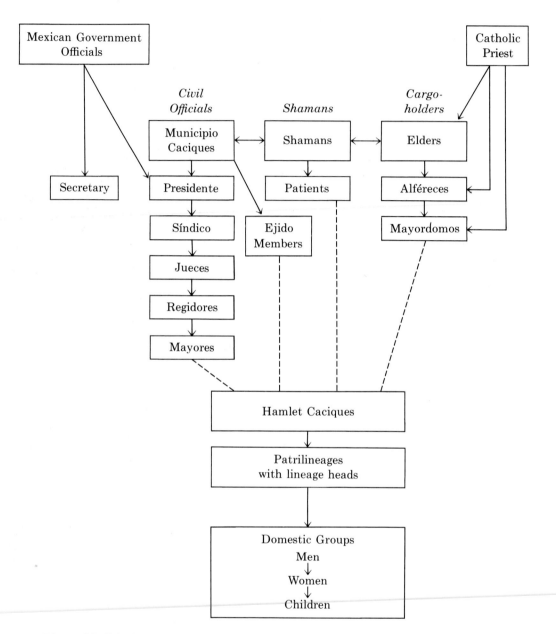

108. Lines of Political authority in Zinacantan

ordinarily embedded in patrilineages in which the eldest male traditionally has authority over the others. The senior members of a lineage now have less formal authority than before, but they are still consulted on important matters and still assume roles in rituals that symbolize this political influence.

Reading upward from the localized patrilineages, we note that each channel of authority has different bases of power and a distinct sphere of influence. The civil authority, controlled by municipio caciques, has two branches: one operates via the officers in the Cabildo, the other through the formal organization of the ejido (the Comisariado Ejidal) with its committee of officials consisting of President, Secretary, Treasurer, and Suplente. The cacique not only wields heavy influence in the election of officials at the Cabildo but also derives power from the Ejido Committee and controls its membership. This channel of authority is of course ultimately controlled and reinforced by Mexican government officials whose influence comes to bear in two ways: the appointment of the Ladino Secretary, who is the main link between Zinacantan and the outside world, and the formal certification of the Cabildo officials, all of whom occupy posts that are technically part of the apparatus of the Mexican government.

A second channel of authority is dominated by the shamans, who acquire power by dreams and exercise authority by directing rituals (especially curing, based on divination) and by holding (at least potentially) the power to perform various types of witchcraft.

A third channel of authority is found in the religious cargo system with its four ranked levels: the Alcaldes Viejos and Regidores, known jointly as Elders, who administer and manage the hierarchy, the Alféreces, and the Mayordomos, including the Mayordomos Reyes, Mesoneros, and Mayores. Since this cargo system manages the cult of the saints, and the saints are housed in the Catholic churches, the Ladino world also impinges upon this system insofar as the priest must say Mass during important celebrations for the saints and also may influence behavior with reference to the church each time he comes to Zinacantan. Note that the Mayores serve in two hierarchies of authority: the Cabildo and the Cargo System.

At the top of the three main channels of authority, there is a formal link between the shamans and the cargoholders (when the former are hosted in the house of the Senior Alcalde Viejo for the Year Renewal ceremonies three times annually) and an informal link between the caciques and cargoholders in that the caciques are in the process of working their way up the cargo system hierarchy.

If there is consensus among the most important cacique, the highest ranking shaman, and the Senior Alcalde Viejo, as well as cooperation from the Mexican government officials in San Cristóbal and Tuxtla and the Catholic functionaries in San Cristóbal, the chances are excellent that most Zinacantecos will go along with the approved course of action. If, however, one or more of these officials (or groups of officials) do not agree, there is likely to be political friction and factional disputes within the municipio.

This system provides an interesting set of checks and balances. If the most important cacique oversteps what are regarded as the legitimate boundaries of his power, he is curbed by another line of authority—the shamans. An illustration is provided by the case of Mol Marian, who owned a small combination store and cantina which specialized in rum and beer for a number of years in the ceremonial center. The cantina was located in a strategic spot, just outside the courtyard of the church. Business was booming, but the shamans complained that the drunks from the cantina wandered into the churchyard to urinate. Pressure against the cantina began to mount, and, when Mol Marian's son defecated in the churchyard, the shamans were able to force him to remove the cantina (Edel 1962).

Decision-Making in Zinacantan

Decision-making in Zinacanteco political spheres bears little resemblance to the kind of parliamentary procedure of debating, taking a vote, and abiding by the rule of the majority to which we have become accustomed in the Western European-American political world. Rather, the process of decision-making is based on the various rank orders according to age, sex, and position in the various hierarchies of authority, and the procedure of endless talking and discussion among interested parties until a consensus is reached. These procedures can best be illustrated by describing how "elections" take place and how Zinacantecos cope with new elements imposed upon them by the Ladino world.

The selection of civil officers for posts at the Cabildo takes one of two forms: the officers may in effect be named by a currently powerful cacique, or they may be "elected" by a meeting of politically important men in front of the Cabildo. Both procedures involve two meetings attended by politically influential caciques from each of the hamlets. One meeting, held in September, is called by the outgoing Presidente in the last year of his term of office; the second is held in November on the day of the Mexican elections.

If the proceedings are dominated by a powerful municipio cacique, this man comes to the September meeting with his candidates in mind. Starting with the choice for Presidente he moves over to one side of the group in front of the Cabildo and says "My candidate is X. If you don't like him, find another." Most, if not all of the leaders present move over and join him, indicating that the case is settled. Then they proceed to "elect" the Síndico with similar dispatch.

If the proceedings are not dominated by a currently powerful cacique, the men stand around while various names are mentioned for consideration. If a man's name is called out and a number of the leaders object to him with good reason, he is dropped from consideration. Then, those men supporting a candidate gather in a group around him, and the man with the largest group wins. In practice, this custom inhibits competition, since the voting is public and most are inclined to stay grouped around the candidate most favored by discussion and by the size of the group supporting him. If additional candidates wish to be considered, they must walk away from the main group and wait to see if individuals break away to form groups around them.

In November the second meeting takes place. Initially the group of politically important people from the hamlets discuss the September choice for Presidente and Síndico. Usually the men agreed upon in September are confirmed by the same group-voting procedure used in November. Then they proceed down the slate to "elect" the jueces and regidores. (The mayores are appointed from a slate of names suggested by the Presidente and incumbent mayores, and hence not included in these proceedings). Because each hamlet suggests one of its citizens for each of the positions, many names are put forward. Leaders from each hamlet praise the merits of their candidates, and finally a consensus is reached by discussion, without a vote (Young, 1965).

An interesting example of the decision-making process in Zinacantan was provided during the summer of 1965 when a group of American students from Loyola University arrived, with the blessing of the Catholic church in San Cristóbal, to repair and repaint the Church of San Lorenzo. There was much misunderstanding about their presence in the community since, as the Zinacantecos put it, "How could anybody in his right mind do something for nothing?" There was gossip all summer—they were going to "steal the saints and take them back to the United States," and so on. A crisis was reached when they dug a well inside the courtyard behind the church and a hole for a septic tank just outside the wall of the church for the purpose of installing a proper toilet for the visiting priest when he comes to say Mass. The students were unaware that the location of the septic tank was exactly the spot where the Elders sit each August to read the waiting lists for cargo positions and add names as new requests are made. Furthermore, there are many legends about buried treasure around the church. And, most importantly, any such holes in the ground are an invasion of the domain of the Earth Lord. What had previously been only rumor and gossip about the Loyola student work program was now translated into action. One Sunday afternoon when the principales had gathered from all the hamlets, a cacique from Na Chih appeared before the Presidente and stated that he objected to the digging of the holes and demanded that the work be stopped immediately. The Presidente responded that the elders from all hamlets should gather the next day to discuss the holes with the Americans. Word was passed to the hamlets by the principales, and the date was changed to Tuesday. On that day at least two older men from each hamlet gathered at the Cabildo. They walked over to inspect the holes while the cacique from Na Chih presented the opposition. The work was defended by the Presidente as harmless at worst and beneficial because a better church would please both men and gods. After hearing both sides, the elders began to comment favorably and all agreed that the work should continue.

However, the following day the five top-ranking shamans arrived at the Cabildo, stating they felt the gods objected to the holes and they wanted to speak with them to ascertain their true opinions. The Presidente agreed that they should speak with the gods about the problem and set the following Sunday as another day for discussion of the problem. At that time, caciques from all the hamlets, the civil officials, the top-ranking shamans, and the Elders of the cargo system were all asked to be present.

On the appointed day the various leaders gathered. First the top-ranking cargoholders were asked for their opinions; they strongly supported the work of the Americans. Then the shamans reported that the gods did not object, but only wanted pardon sought for the trespass. The Presidente asked all the representatives of the hamlets if such ritual action would suit them. They agreed, and the shamans performed a ceremony to ask the pardon of the gods, especially the Earth Lord, for the work that was going on. The case rested at this point and the work was successfully completed.

Relations between Civil and Religious Hierarchies

Civil and religious officials in Zinacantan interact in several ways. At the lowest level, the mayores are integral parts of both hierarchies. At

109. From right to left: the Presidente, the Síndico, the two Escribanos, and the Elders (Alcaldes Viejos and Regidores) on one of the occasions when these latter religious officials come to sit in front of the Cabildo

higher levels, the Presidente, Síndico, and jueces are called upon to perform certain key ritual duties. They not only appoint juntas to administer fiestas, but the Presidente may go to the Hermitage to back up the Elders if they need to threaten a reluctant cargo appointee with a jail sentence. The Presidente and the Síndico attend the swearing-in ceremonies of new cargo-holders at the Hermitage. All of them attend the two large ritual meals that are served for the entire religious and civil hierarchies at the Fiesta of San Sebastián. The Presidente and a delegation from the Cabildo attend the Year Renewal ceremonies of the shamans. The Elders periodically come and sit on the bench in front of the Cabildo—to the left of the Presidente's bench as one faces the Cabildo (Figure 109). And, for the Christmas ceremonies, the Presidente serves as a godfather for the Christ children.

Each of these links serves to intertwine the two hierarchies, and more especially to provide the Cabildo officers with more ceremonial duties each year. It is too early to tell whether this trend to involve the civil officials in the ceremonial life will continue, but it is clear that events in Zinacantan follow directions that are not necessarily planned, projected, or expected by the Mexican government.

Part IV / Religious Beliefs and Rituals

13 / Cosmology and Ancient Gods

The cosmology and deity concepts that emerge from the corpus of myths (see Chapter 14) and from interviews with informants are not entirely uniform and consistent throughout the municipio of Zinacantan. This is not surprising in a culture that has been under acculturative pressure from the Ladinos for almost four and a half centuries and that places more emphasis now upon rituals than upon a systematic cosmology. However, an approximate consensus exists about fundamental features of the cosmos and the ancient gods that inhabit this Zinacanteco universe.

Cosmology

The surface of the earth on which men live is the top of a cube known as BALAMIL (literally, "earth" or "world"). It is composed of a series of mountains and valleys, with Zinacantan Center (HTEKLUM) being in a valley at the very center. This center is precisely located at the small mound known as the "navel of the world" (MISHIK' BALAMIL) which is shown on Map 7. At the lower corners of the cube are four "pillars of the world" (YOKOL BALAMIL) which are conceived of either as animals that hold up the earth on their shoulders (some say on their tails) or as gods called VASHAKMEN. At any rate, when they grow tired, they shift the weight of the earth from one shoulder to another and earthquakes occur.

Above this surface is a quadrilateral space with three layers together called VINAHEL (literally, "sky" or "heavens"). (Some informants describe only one layer.) In the lowest layer the female moon (CH'ULME?TIK) traverses her path every day. In the middle layer are the stars that provide light both below and above. In the third, or upper, layer the male Sun (CH'ULTOTIK or TOTIK K'AK'AL) travels along his path each day.

Below the earth surface is another cube of approximately the same size called the "world below" (ʔOLON BALAMIL). Here lives a race of dwarfs known as KONCHAVETIK, left over from the early creation of people described in the flood myth. It is very hot there, since the sun in passing under the earth, comes very close to the surface of the "world below," forcing the dwarfs to wear mud hats to protect themselves.

Directions are expressed as "where the sun rises" (LOK'EB K'AK'AL) and "where the sun sets" (MALEB K'AK'AL). What we regard as north and south are called "sides of the sky" (SHOKON VINAHEL), that is, the sides of the path of the sun.

Clouds and lightning are both believed to come out of caves. In the dry season the clouds are kept in caves inside the mountains; in the rainy season they travel to meetings in the sky. They also visit the tops of the mountains where they talk to the ancestral gods about their "work," for example, where they should travel and where they should take the rain each day.

Ancient Gods

The crucial aboriginal deity concepts still functioning in the Zinacanteco belief system are TOTILME ʔILETIK (related to the words TOT and ME ʔ, meaning "father" and "mother"), who are ancestral gods; YAHVAL BALAMIL (the "Earth Lord" or "Earth Owner"); and VASHAKMEN, the Zinacanteco version of the four-corner gods that appear throughout most of the Maya area. Additional deities are partly aboriginal but show some Catholic influence: the Sun, called either TOTIK K'AK'AL (the father sun), CH'UL TOTIK (divine father), or CH'UL K'AK'AL (the divine sun), which has associations with RIOSH (Dios or "God"); and the Moon, called CH'UL ME ʔTIK (divine mother), which has associations with the Virgin Mary as well as with the various statues and pictures of Catholic virgins.

The Ancestral Gods

The most important Zinacanteco deities, judging from the frequency by which the people think about them, pray to them, and perform rituals for them, are the ancestral gods (TOTILME ʔILETIK). These are envisioned as elderly Zinacantecos who live inside the sacred mountains surrounding Zinacantan Center as well as in smaller hills above the waterholes and house-clusters in the hamlets; it is believed they went into the mountains to live sometime in the mythological past. A common myth related about the origins of the tribal ancestral deities revolves around the theme of six elders from Zinacantan who were summoned to Mexico City by an Indian king to help the Presidente overcome his enemies who were about to conquer Mexico. These ancient Zinacanteco men were called SHOHOBETIK, and, just as "engineers now look into the distance," they were able to see into the mountains and perceive the Earth Lord. Each of these six culture heroes had specialized powers: one could make fog, a second produce lightning, a third create a whirlwind, a fourth fly like a hawk, a fifth like a butterfly, and the sixth like a fly. They successfully overcame the hidden enemies by laying down a heavy fog and under its cover erecting a series of crosses like a corral around them. After consulting the Sun God (KAHVALTIK TA VINAHEL), they proceeded to destroy their enemies by setting the crosses on fire with lightning and having the whirlwind fill the corral with sea water. The water boiled and all the bodies of the enemies floated to the surface. It was the task of the hawk to make certain that none of the enemies reached the edge of the boiling water, cooled off, and came to life again; the butterfly made certain that no enemy reinforcements arrived; and the fly inspected each of the floating bodies to make certain that they were dead. The Presidente and the Indian king then came to see that all the enemies were dead and gave a large fiesta, lasting six days and six nights, for the elders. Then the elders returned to Zinacantan, but, fearing reprisals by the enemy forces, they asked permission from the Earth Lord to take up residence inside the mountains, rather than returning to their old homes. He granted it, and the six elders took up residence in six mountains. The "most senior" went to ʔOSHYOKET (an archaic term for MUK'TA VITS), while the other five went to mountains called KALVARIO, SAN KISHTOVAL, LACH CHIKIN, ʔISAK'TIK, and NAKLEB ʔOK. At the same time, their wives took up residence in six "female" mountains: MUSHUL VITS, SISIL VITS, NINAB CHILOʔ, NIOʔ, YAʔAHVIL, and TS'AHOB PIK'.* They still live inside these mountains whence they monitor the affairs of their living Zinacanteco descendants and wait for the offerings of black chickens, white candles, incense, and rum which sustain them. An alternative term for VITS (sacred mountain) is TOTILMEʔIL, reflecting the strong identification of these gods with the sacred mountains in which they live. Each of the sacred mountains is believed to have special features inside that are associated with the different ancestral gods who reside in them; see Chapter 17 for list and description.

---

* Other mountains that are added, or substituted, in this list by some informants include: SAK CH'EN, NA HOH, CH'UL TON, LANSA VITS, and YAM TON. See Map 7 for the locations of the most important sacred mountains.

The meeting place of these tribal ancestral gods is at KALVARIO, the sacred mountain immediately above Zinacantan Center, which has the most elaborate cross altar in all the municipio. In the hamlets there are dozens of smaller KALVARIO shrines erected by waterholes and on hills where the ancestral gods of each waterhole group and of each sna convene to watch over the affairs of the living and to await offerings. How and why the Christian concept of Calvary (*calvario* in Spanish) came to be associated with these ancestral shrines we do not know, but it is clear that each unit of the social structure, ranging from sna through waterhole group to hamlet and on up to the municipio as a whole, is symbolized in the KALVARIO shrines and related conceptually to the ancestral gods.

Each of the mountain dwelling places of the ancestral gods is now marked by an ostensibly Christian cross. There are cross altars at both the feet and the summits of the tribal sacred mountains around Zinacantan Center. To Zinacantecos, these crosses are "doorways" to the ancestral gods. When a curing procession arrives at a sacred mountain, its members, led by the shaman, decorate the crosses with pine boughs and flowers, burn incense, light candles, and offer prayers before them. By so doing, they "pass through" the outer doorway of the god's house; they follow the trail to the top of the mountain where another set of crosses designates the inner doorway (really the "house cross") to the place where the ancestral god receives his visitors and their offerings. Here the prayers are repeated, and the curing party proceeds to the next mountain (see Chapter 20).

The conceptions about the behavior of these ancestral gods and the rituals performed for them indicate that they have both rewarding and punishing roles. They are believed to have basic control of all of Zinacantan and its customs, especially by their power over Zinacanteco souls and "animal spirit companions"; further, their ways of life inside the mountains are the model for human behavior. The Zinacantecos who approach them via the ancestral shrines communicate with them (via the soul) and learn about rituals which represent (albeit somewhat imperfectly) how the living descendants should behave. In short, the ideal is believed to be inside the mountain; Zinacanteco rituals approach this model and provide guides for day-to-day living. The day-to-day living approaches, again imperfectly, the guides provided by the rituals. A good example is provided by the ritual meal that accompanies most ceremonies in Zinacantan. The ancestral gods inside their mountain homes are believed to be engaging in the prototype for proper behavior at meals served on small tables—rigidly prescribed seating and eating order by rank, highly patterned etiquette for eating and drinking, and so on. In a ceremonial context the living Zinacantecos do their best to replicate a proper ritual meal. Often there are makeshift arrangements; two or more small tables may have to be placed together to make a large enough table for all the participants; there may not be chairs for everyone; the shaman may be drunk and miss some of the ritual. But a genuine effort is made to approach the model provided by the ancestors. In turn, the ritual meals provide guides for ordinary, everyday meals that are served on the ground rather than on a table. Even then, the "most senior" men are served first, water is provided for washing the hands and rinsing the mouth, and, if rum is served, the proper toasts are observed. (See Chapter 23 for details on the ritual meal.)

The ancestral gods have punitive powers when behavior deviates too far from the norms established by their models. They are especially quick to punish their living descendants for quarreling with kinsmen, failing to bathe and put on clean clothes regularly, mishandling maize, and failing to take ritual duties seriously. Punishment comes in two forms. The ancestral gods may knock out one or more parts of the wrongdoer's soul—most commonly by sending a lightning bolt which leads to "fright" (SHI'EL) involving the loss of parts of the "inner soul." Even more serious punishment may be meted out by letting a person's animal spirit companion out of its supernatural corral inside the sacred mountain of MUK'TA VITS and thereby exposing the wrongdoer to grave danger. In either case, divination must be used to determine the cause of the illness that ensues and elaborate curing ceremonies performed to ask the pardon of the ancestral gods in prayers and to offer them white candles (the "tortillas" of the ancestral gods), black chickens, rum, and incense. If the ceremonies are effective, the gods forgive the transgressor and he recovers from his grave condition. Unlike Larrainzar (Holland 1963; 1964), Zinacantan does not appear to have ancestral gods belonging to specific patrilineages. The closest analogy to this pattern are those prayed to at nearby cross shrines by the snas.

The significance of the twelve sacred mountains that were occupied by the six ancient elders and their wives after they had conquered the enemies of Mexico is still unclear. One possibility is that they formerly had significance for six or twelve different lineages. Another possibility is that they are somehow related to the six elders who currently serve in the two top levels of the cargo system, or to the six Holy Elders who nail Christ to the cross on Good Friday. But, although the numbers are correct, I have been unable to elicit any specific links currently made by the Zinacantecos, except that the ancestral gods are said to convene and deliberate at KALVARIO in the same way the Elders convene and deliberate in Zinacantan Center.

The Earth Lord

Next to the ancestral gods the most frequently mentioned deity of aboriginal origin is the Earth Lord (YAHVAL BALAMIL). He has multiple manifestations in that any opening in the form of a cave or limestone sink or waterhole constitutes a means of communication with him. He is pictured as a large, fat Ladino who possesses piles of money, herds of horses, mules, and cows, and flocks of chickens. He also controls all of the waterholes on which the Zinacantecos depend for household water and for water for their livestock; he controls the clouds that are believed to come out of caves, rise up into the sky, and produce the needed rain for Zinacanteco crops; and he controls all the products of the earth that Zinacantecos use—trees for building houses, mud for the walls, limestone needed to produce lime, and so on. Hence, a Zinacanteco cannot use land or any of its products for any purpose, whether to grow maize in a milpa or to construct a new house, without compensating the Earth Lord with appropriate ceremonies and offerings.

Closely associated with the Earth Lord is the puzzling concept of ʔANHEL. For many years I assumed this was a loan word from the Spanish for angel (*ángel*), but I kept worrying about the fact that the properties of the ʔANHELETIK seemed to have nothing in common with Christian angels except the name. Our informants described the ʔANHELETIK as being like a bolt of lightning that comes out of a cave and added that the thunder was like the skyrockets of the ʔANHELETIK. They also described clouds as coming from the Earth Lord's caves as ʔANHELETIK. Finally in 1965, Alfonso Villa Rojas assembled a body of data from Landa, Tozzer, and Roys which demonstrated that what Landa called *ángel* was in Yucatán a corruption from an Ancient Maya concept of CANHEL, the Spanish chroniclers simply having made a mistake in recording the name. The Yucatec CANHEL appears to have been a ceremonial staff or insignia carried by certain gods or god impersonators, and the associations are clearly with water, rain, and winds (Villa Rojas, personal communication, April 15, 1965). Villa Rojas went on to point out that Guiteras-Holmes (1961) describes the ʔANHEL in Chenalhó as being "rain god and owner of animal life, thunderbolt, etc." It therefore seems most likely that the Tzotzil concept is much like that of Yucatán. If lightning (and associated thunder, clouds, and rain) can be regarded as something carried or sent by the Earth Lord, the parallel is indeed very close.

Still another set of beliefs about the Earth Lord concerns his locomotion underground. He is believed to ride on deer, utilizing iguanas as blinders for his mounts; a snake is his whip; and the shell of the land snail is his powder flask for making skyrockets or shooting off his shotgun. (Informants vary as to whether lightning bolts are his skyrockets or the firing of his shotgun.)

Crosses erected by waterholes or in caves are regarded as means of communication with the Earth Lord. There are formal ceremonies performed at waterholes and in fields in which shamans offer prayers and tallow candles (which symbolize meat), rum, and incense for him so that rains will come and crops will grow; other ceremonies compensate him for materials used in new houses (see Chapter 24).

Communication with the Earth Lord is viewed with ambivalence. On the one hand, there are glorious myths about men's acquiring riches in the form of money or livestock by going to visit the Earth Lord's cave. On the other hand, the Earth Lord needs many workers, and there is danger that a person's soul will get "sold" to him as a servant for years—until the iron sandals given each worker wear out. The "selling" of a soul to the Earth Lord is one of the principal forms of witchcraft (see Chapter 19), and ceremonies to persuade him to release a soul are expensive and arduous.

A major problem exists in unraveling what could have been the symbolic nature of the Earth Lord before the Conquest. The contemporary symbolic representation of the "lord of the earth" as a greedy Ladino seems nicely adjusted to the realities of the bicultural situation in which the Zinacantecos live—but we do not have any information on the Earth Lord's aboriginal character.

VASHAKMEN

The VASHAKMEN of Zinacantan are clearly a manifestation of the Ancient Maya concept of a quadrilateral universe. They are most commonly described as the gods at the four corners who hold up the world on their shoulders. When they tire and have to shift the burden on their shoulder, the earth trembles and earthquakes occur. They are also described as having created waterholes as they walked over the surface of the earth in the mythological past and pushed their walking sticks into the ground; and they helped to construct the Church of San Sebastián.

The exact location of these gods and the translation of their names raise some interesting questions. Since VASHAK means "eight," some informants believe that there are senior-junior pairs at each of the four corners, located at the intercardinal points. These corners (CHIKIN) are emphasized both in ceremonies for new houses and in ceremonies for the milpas. On the other hand, the meaning of MEN is obscure. Could it be related to H-MEN, the ritualists described in Yucatán? (Redfield 1941). Another possibility is that VASHAKMEN is a collective term for the four corner gods and for four gods at the cardinal points, as Holland (1964) has found in Larrainzar. The main flaws in this interpretation are, first, we know of no words in Zinacanteco Tzotzil to describe "north" and "south"; rather, LOKEB K'AK'AL ("place where the sun rises") and MALEB K'AK'AL ("place where the sun sets") are the only named directions, and what we call north and south are merely the "sides (SHOKON) of the sky" or sides of the path of the sun; and, second, we have no data on gods of the cardinal directions. On the other hand, certain interesting similarities exist between the data from Larrainzar and Zinacantan. Holland reports a god of rain in the east, a god of maize in the north, a god of death in the west, and a god of wind in the south (1964). We know that Zinacantecos go eastward to the sacred mountain of ʔITS'INAL MUK'TA VITS from the summit of which they pray toward the east for rain; there is some evidence in myths that the crow is thought to have brought maize from NA HOH, a sacred mountain located north of the ceremonial center; and there are many associations of death with west (the dead are buried with the head to the west; when a chicken is killed over a patient, if the chicken heads toward the west, the patient will die, and so on). Still another possibility is suggested by a variant form of the name of these gods. Some informants insist they should be VASHAKNEN, which would be translated as "eight mirrors" or "eight windows." NEN is a proto-Maya word which Kaufman (1964: 110) translates as *vidrio* (windowpane) or *espejo* (mirror), and I would suggest that the original term applied to some type of pyrite mirror. All of this raises the interesting question of whether there is some belief about these gods either having mirrors or looking through windows at people. Or perhaps there were eight apertures in "heaven" through which the VASHAKNEN surveyed the affairs of men. (Similarly, a shaman is a "seer" who "sees" into the mountains and the principal curing ceremony is MUK'TA ʔILEL "the big seeing"; perhaps men—represented by their shamans—are always looking at the gods, and the gods are looking back at the men.) Finally, there may be some relation to the crystal or mirror possessed by a talking saint which gives the saint the power to "speak."

Demons

Zinacantecos believe in various classes of frightening, evil beings or spirits to which they refer as PUKUHETIK. These spirts are in a different class from the deities already discussed. While the VASHAKMEN hold up the world, the

Earth Lord owns and cares for the earth, and the ancestral gods control the modes of social conduct, these demons are shadowy creatures that come and go. They are permanently inhuman figures, unlike the witches who are living people with powers to transform themselves into frightening and harmful forms.

There are many types of demons, but the ones that most often frighten people are the POSLOM, a ball of fire that travels at night and hits people, causing a bad swelling; and the Blackmen (HʔIK'ALETIK), small, black-skinned, curly-haired men with winged feet who soar out of their caves at dusk searching for food and companions. These latter swoop down into Zinacanteco patios to seek chicken eggs or to carry off fowl and bread (never tortillas). They possess two-meter long, death-dealing penes. So potent is their sexuality that their progeny appear three days after conception. "Though the means for eliminating Blackmen are various, one oft-repeated account claims that it was the women who freed Zinacantan from their nefarious visits, by inviting them to drink a bowl of soup. When their vision was blocked by the up-tilted bowls, the women scalded, then skewered, then roasted them over the fire" (Laughlin 1963: 191). They are believed to be less common now, but occasionally they still appear at night, frightening especially the women.

A demon may also appear in a less defined form and may transform itself during the course of the night, as in the following case, taken from my 1960 field notes:

> One time, long ago, the old woman who lives in the house above ours was sleeping with her daughter. She heard a board hitting below the small window. the daughter opened the window and looked out. It was bright moonlight. She saw a creature with a black face crouching on the ground. She spat on it and shut the window. The creature stood up and it was only a meter high. Then it changed into a horse and started eating the squash in the sitio. The woman and her daughter were shaking all night with fear. At dawn, it changed into something smaller again and tried to get into the door, so the old woman poked it with a stick. It then changed into a squash and rolled away into the ravine near the house. But there are fewer demons like this than there used to be.

Relations with Generic Maya Deities

Like their cultural relatives elsewhere in the Maya area, the Zinacantecos have preserved many ancient concepts of deities (Blanco 1963). The ancestral gods mirror and reinforce the social organization in contemporary

Zinacantan in much the same way that their counterparts function in neighboring Tzotzil and Tzeltal communities (see Pozas 1959; Holland 1963; Guiteras-Holmes 1961; Villa Rojas 1947), in the highlands of Guatemala (see La Farge 1947; Wagley 1949; Oakes 1951; Valladares 1957; Bunzel 1952; Girard 1962; Wisdom 1940), and in lowland Maya communities (see Tozzer 1907; Redfield and Villa Rojas 1934; Villa Rojas 1945). Similarly, the aboriginal Earth Lord is still present, jealously guarding his domain, even though he is now (appropriately) pictured as a greedy Ladino. Beliefs about the four-corner gods are somewhat less vital and more confused, but they obviously represent a local Zinacanteco version of the deification of a quadrilateral universe (Thompson 1934). The relation of the demons (PUKUHETIK) to beliefs elsewhere in the Maya area is somewhat less clear. It is tempting, however, to suggest a relation between the Yucatecan death-god, Ah Puch, and the probably cognate PUKUH in Zinacantan.

14 / Myths

Zinacanteco myths, described locally as ʔANTIVO KʼOP or "talk of times past," defy simple classification into legends, folktales, and myths along the lines suggested by Malinowski (1926). Rather, any event that happened before the lifetime of the teller of the story is "ancient word." Thus, oral narratives about the Mexican Revolution (1910–1920) are real-life events to the older generation who participated in this political and military upheaval; but the same events are ʔANTIVO KʼOP to young Zinacantecos, who regard them in a class with tales about more ancient mythological times, when houses moved around and danced together, rocks were soft like mud, and the various saints were found in the woods or otherwise discovered and brought to Zinacantan to have "houses" (churches) built for them.

The tales vary greatly in subject matter, some expressing beliefs about the nature of the cosmos, others explaining the origins of rituals, and the like. Some mention the gods, the sacred mountains, and the nature of clouds, rain, and lightning; while myths about waterholes typically explain how the first KʼIN KRUS was initiated for each. Other tales appear to have more to do with interpersonal relations in the society or about various kinds of "spooks" or "evil spirits," such as the "Blackmen" (HʔIKʼALETIK) or the "Demons" (PUKUHETIK), or about various "wars" that were allegedly fought at some time in the cultural history of Zinacantan. The more direct correspondence between cosmology (expressed in myths) and rituals that one finds, for example, among the Navaho is difficult to locate in this corpus. Zinacantecos seem to have spent more time and energy systematizing their rituals than their mythology. Nevertheless, I am certain that it will be

I am grateful to Robert M. Laughlin for field data and ideas in the preparation of this chapter, and especially for his permission to use the tales from his collection for illustrative purposes.

possible in the future, as our knowledge of the Zinacantan culture and Tzotzil language increases, to make structural analyses of these myths along the lines suggested by Lévi-Strauss (1955, 1964, 1966) and others. In addition to the work of Robert M. Laughlin who is currently working with Zinacanteco myths, Gary H. Gossen (1965) has set out to collect and analyze a corpus of Chamula myths. When these results are available we shall understand Tzotzil myths far better than we do now. In the meantime, I shall present a series of illustrative types of tales from the Zinacantan corpus and comment briefly on the symbolic meanings expressed. (Appendix IV contains four additional examples with both Tzotzil and English versions.)

Origins

The Flood. This first tale is an example of multiple origins that is characteristic of Maya mythology. In other versions (see Appendix IV) there were other types of beings created before men—dwarfs, for example, who still live in the underworld and wear mud hats to protect themselves from the Sun as it passes close to them each night.

> Long ago, when the world was flooded,
> There were people left,
> Our late grandmother told me,
> She told my mother,
> My mother heard about it and told me, you see,
> The world was flooded,
> Two people fled away;
> There was a large mountain,
> On its top, they were saved, you see,
> There they hid themselves until the water dried up
> They sent away the buzzard,
> The buzzard arrived, you see,
> It didn't return;
> There came the red-bill [Turkey Buzzard] as we call it
> It came too, it didn't return;
> There came the king vulture as we say, white wings,
> It came too, it didn't return,
> It became used to the food,
> There was good food,
> It went too;

The crow came,
It got used to cracking maize;
There came the bonebird [grackle] just the same;
The CHINCHON [rusty-crowned sparrow] came just the same;
It didn't return,
The towhee came, it didn't return;
The quail came, "There is maize, I'll eat," it said,
It didn't return either;
The dove came, it got used to it too,
Whatever there was,
Dead horse,
Dead sheep,
Dead dogs,
Whatever there was,
There they got used to it;
The towhee came,
The sparrow,
The little yellow bird,
CH'IKCH'IK [Wilson's warbler] it's called,
It didn't return either;
"Why is it that not one bird returns,
Returns to say what it's like,
If there are still people,
How the land remained,"
Said the woman and the man who survived, you see;
"Who knows, better wait, you'll just go and die,"
Said his wife, you see;
The man waited three or four days, something like that,
There he waited,
Nothing arrived,
Nothing at all arrived;
They got used to their food,
He sent one of his dogs,
It got used to eating horse,
He sent a, who knows if it was a dove,
I don't know what kind of bird came last, came too;
"Why is it that they don't come back?"
"Eh, who knows," she said;
The last bird came alone, it came;
"Eh, but it looks as if the water hasn't dried up yet,

There is still water,
Forget it, I'm not going yet,
I'll just die," said his wife, you see;
He waited one week, it seems, for it to dry up,
For the earth to be good and dry, you see,
The end of the time was reached for the water to dry up well,
Now the ground can be walked on,
Now he can walk if he comes;
But you see he got hurt,
He came out of, he came out of his house, it seems,
He hurt the calf of his leg,
Slashed, who knows if by a machete,
Who knows if by a knife,
For his leg had a long cut,
He came back:
"Skip it, it's still impossible to walk on the ground,
Look, I just went and wounded my leg," said the man,
He came back;
"Forget it, forget it,
Didn't I tell you not to go yet,
Didn't I tell you?" she said, you see;
He came back,
"I'll wait one or two days,
I'd just be going out to kill myself," he said;
"That's right, it's not worth it,
Not until then shall we go see how it is," she said;
He came out when the however many days that he had said were up,
The man came,
He opened the first house,
Full of water,
Filled with water,
He was soaked, you see,
But it had a smell, a real stench,
Where the dead people still were;
He broke in with a stick
Or a stone
Or whatever to open the house,
Don't you see, the doors were swollen by the water, you see;
"Ah, I shouldn't have come,
It would have been better not to,

The earth stinks horribly," he said;
He saw that at the time he opened,
I don't know if it was three or four houses
Or what he opened that the water came out of,
"Oh well, I'll wait here till the water dries up,
That tree here is the 'thick leaf,'" he said;
It was standing there,
He lit his little fire,
Warmed his tortillas, and ate;
He finished eating and finished his tortillas,
There he slept,
He didn't go back because the trail was very slippery,
He couldn't return now to where he was, it seems,
As the mountain he had to climb was steep, you see,
And there he slept;
"What did you go looking for,
You shouldn't have gone,
Better to wait until the earth was well dried out, you hear,
I'm right when I say that the houses are full of water,
What good did it do that you went," she said;
"Yes, you're certainly right,
It's completely impossible to rest, it seems,
The smell inside the disgusting house, it stinks," said the man,
He told his wife;
"Never mind, wait until the ground has gotten well dried up,
If you see that it is good and dry;
Never mind, let our livestock go,
Whatever animals there are," she said;
"The crow is still going to bring them to us," she said;
Then the crow went,
When the earth seemed dry enough,
Dry now, good now for walking,
Don't you see, it looked where it no longer left its footprints,
Where it was good and dry now;
The bird went to tell them,
"It's fine now, dry now,
I told you I would come to call you,
Come to take you,
Go look at the houses,
Here the mud cracked well where they were shut," it said;

"The others, just the tips of their roofs show,
They're just sunk in the mud." it said;
"Ah," the man said, "How many of the houses are still good?"
  he said;
"There are still maybe six or seven good ones," it said,
"Those which were packed hard," it said;
"Ah," he said, "Never mind, I'm going to look," he said;
He came, you see,
He finished looking at the houses,
He found one house,
He found there, I don't know if it was seventy pesos,
Solid pesos,
The money of long ago, seventy;
Another house twenty-two,
Another house fifteen,
Another house ten, you see;
He just found money;
"But, my God, you can't eat this,
But this, my God, wouldn't be enough if just I stayed,
What can I subsist on?" he said;
"True, here there's still my corn,
There's still my wheat,
I can eat;
But if it runs out,
What can I subsist on?" he said;
Two daughters he had,
And two sons,
One baby;
The baby grew,
I don't know if it had reached four years or what,
Then its mother took sick,
She took sick;
Then they ate some kind of root,
Either fern roots or the root of HOL P'UK,
Whatever it was they ate;
Swelling began,
The woman swelled up,
This big her face,
And as for her belly, horribly big like this;
She had bad stomach cramps, the poor thing,

She died, you see,
She died;
So the man was left alone;
"God, what can my children eat now,
What can I think of,
I haven't any corn,
The corn is finished up,
I have no seed corn,
I haven't found any;
Do you know what I can do, holy crow,
Do you know what I can plant,
I haven't any corn," he said;
"You haven't any corn," said the crow;
"None at all," he said;
"You be quiet still, here at the top of Crow's House
There are two bins of corn," it said;
"There is yellow," it said;
"There is white," it said;
"There is black," it said;
"There is red," it said;
"I'll go steal from there one ear apiece for your seed corn," It said;
"That's where I eat when there's nothing to eat,
So I'll go take them," it said;
"Please be so kind, because there's nothing at all
When this is finished,
Nothing I can subsist on,
There's nothing for my children to eat," he said;
"O.K.," it said;
It finished bringing each ear,
Each equal measure of corn,
Went to give it:
"Here is your seed corn," it said;
Each time,
Each ear it carried off in its beak,
Went to give them to that man,
It said, "See, here is your seed corn."
"That's right, thank you," he said;
"I'm going to bring you the others," it said;
Just the same way it came again holding [the corn in its beak],
Came to give him it again,

Went to bring the other ear,
Went to give him the next one,
When they were complete,
"See here is your seed corn,
Look now, you eat this,
Because they won't let me enter where I took out [the corn],
"'What could you be doing with so much corn,
It isn't because you finished eating up all that,'
The owner of the cave told me."
"Ah," he said,
"Never mind, I understand, I'll just plant this,
Today I've broken my little bit of land,
My heart has nothing to complain about,
I'll plant,
It's good enough if I subsist on the little corn tassel," he said;
So he began to eat the tassel,
Began to eat the tassel;
At that time there arrived,
I don't know if it was the Spanish or who it was long ago,
So then they joined together,
He looked for a wife still,
A Spaniard, the woman whom the man took;
His hour came,
The man died, he died;
Then were left his children . . .
There they stayed,
Long ago they looked at, it was possible to look at Our Lord [the
    Sun],
As many as stayed, stayed;
When they stayed,
Several were saved on the top of the mountain,
They climbed to the top of the mountain,
When it flooded,
The flood long ago;
There they were saved;
Now he went to look, Our Lord himself;
When the Lord arrived,
The men were angry, as many as were saved;
They were angry, angry:
"Where did you save yourselves?" they were asked;

"Ah, we climbed to the top of the mountain," they said,
"We stayed in the woods," they said;
"Ah," he said, "Where, what woods?"
"Wherever they were," they said;
"And your house," he said;
"Ah, so what," they said
"What did you live on, ah, was it corn that you lived on?"
"Ah, I didn't live on anything, I lived on vine berries," said one;
"I lived on nuts," said one;
"Ah, well, good," he said;
"What or how, then, do you still want to live?" they were asked;
They answered angrily now; "Well, look at your backside then,"
They were told;
They look at their backsides here,
Then when they do that, then they turn into monkeys;
Now when they turn into monkeys,
Then they go to the forest;
Now they are turned into monkeys:
Their tails were born,
Their ears were born,
Their hair;
Now their faces look like humans',
Just that here they have hair;
So they didn't become well-made people;
The monkeys are people,
The people of long ago are still monkeys,
Haven't you seen monkeys,
Wherever you've seen them, they have hair, long tails,
Because they didn't accept Our Lord's order;
Now, if you don't believe the command,
Let your hair be born,
Go eat nuts, vines, berries,
Just that for your whole life,
That's why they turned into monkeys;
Those who didn't answer at all,
Those who didn't speak,
Those children, it seems,
Well, they were left as progenitors,
For they didn't answer,
Not even a word did they answer,

The children of the man, they didn't answer,
Not a word did they say;
But those who answered angrily,
They turned into monkeys till this day, you see;
Not till then did they [the children] get married,
His wife was born, her husband,
They have increased in the world till now,
Two families of humans it seems,
The people grew up,
The people increased,
Long age, you don't think there were many who were left,
Who were saved,
For those turned into monkeys,
Went to the woods,
Went to eat in the woods,
Turned into animals to this day,
Animals to this day;
But those who didn't answer Our Lord,
Those who didn't talk back,
They didn't move,
There they knelt,
They weren't guilty;
But those who answered,
"Go," was the command,
They went, went into the woods,
That's why they are like that till now,
Turned into monkeys;
Those who are humans now,
It's because they didn't answer,
Just like us.

(Robert M. Laughlin, Tale 70)

Supernaturals

The following two tales illustrate the ways in which Zinacantecos relate myths about their supernaturals.

The Sweeper of the Path. This tale describes the Morning Star (Venus), who is believed to have been a Chamula girl transformed into a "Sweeper of the Path" for the Sun. The Morning Star precedes the Holy Sun on

his path across the sky and underneath the earth to reappear each day.
This concept may be related to the assistants of a shaman during a curing
ceremony when they are known as "sweepers" as they precede the curing
party and remove the old flowers and add new pine boughs on the mountain
shrines that will be visited (see Chapter 20).

Once the great star came out, as we say,
The sky becoming light everywhere;
"I am the sweeper of the path,
I sweep his path,
I sweep Our Lord's path for him,
For when Our Lord passes he finds it already swept,
For he walks, then the sun comes out,"
Sweeping, we tell ourselves, but how can it be,
For first is the great star,
The great star is a Chamula girl,
She came from Chamula country, you see,
They didn't believe the Chamula girl when they talked about it,
"We'll see what our Chamula girl is like,
So she says she is a star,
Could she know how to be a star,
The awful ugly black Chamula,
And isn't the star beautiful,
It has rays of light,
The star is a beautiful bright red," said the women,
Making fun of that Chamula girl for saying she is a star,
They think she isn't;
"Are you right, I don't understand what you say,
You mock me,
But it is I,
It is I who prepare the path,
I sweep off the path,
When Our Lord is lost,
When the sea dries up,
Then the fish finish coming out,
When Our Lord passes there,
Then Our Lord is lost,
That's why there is monkeys' sunset as we say,
For that's where Our Lord passes over the ocean,
So the cover comes in,

Then far off now is seen the sunbeams;
I am the sweeper of the house,
I sweep off the path,
I walk first,
When the land gets light,
In the dark again,
For I sweep here beneath the world;
When the land gets light again the next day,
I come sweeping again,
For that is my work,
That is what I do,
I haven't any other work,
For that is my work that is,
That's why I am a star;
For early, when it is dark,
The great star comes out, say the people,
But it is me, I,
I sweep the house, his path, Our Lord's path,
It isn't just anyone's path," she said, you see;
She sweeps, sweeps it off so much,
When he is lost, then she walks inside the world again
Where the star is going to come out again on the next day,
She sweeps it off again,
She passes beneath us,
Under the world it seems,
She is going to come out on the next day again,
Just the same way she comes out there;
That is why the star seems to come out first;
"So it is I who sweeps Our Lord's path," she said,
The path of the Holy Sun, you see,
We ourselves didn't believe that it was a Chamula girl,
"If I ever see what it is that sweeps,
It seems to be a star,
But the Chamula, I don't believe her," we told ourselves;
So she heard when we mocked her,
When she was mocked, the poor girl,
If it hadn't been for her the truth then wouldn't have been heard,
But now it is known that that is the way it is.

(Robert M. Laughlin, Tale 79)

Our Holy Mother of Salinas. This tale describes the events that led to the construction of the Catholic chapel in the hamlet of Salinas (?Ats'am), commonly called "Salinitas" as in this myth. The three sisters that have now become important saints in Zinacantan Center, Ixtapa, and Salinas each had to have their "homes" built. The eldest sister is the Virgen del Rosario in the church of San Lorenzo in Zinacantan Center; the middle sister is the Virgin in Ixtapa (a municipio that borders Zinacantan on the west). This left the youngest sister without a house until she persuaded the young Zinacanteco who was out working his small field to assemble his relatives and build a small "cow house" (an old type of Zinacanteco house; see Chapter 4) for her across the river from the present chapel in Salinas. It seems the ground was soggy on this side of the river and there were floods. So the people built a better house for her on dry ground across the river and installed the hollowed-out log on top of the salt well behind the chapel. The myth weaves together the three settlements involved in the salt industry that has been important for the Zinacantecos since before the Conquest.

> Long ago when Salinitas was formed,
> Our Holy Mother arrived there,
> A man saw her,
> Now to the man: "What are you doing, son,
> What are you looking for here?" said our Holy Mother;
> "I'm not doing anything, Mother, I'm taking a walk,
> I am looking at my little bit of land,
> For I would like to clear off my little bit of brush today,
> The time has come, it seems,
> I'm looking to see if the little river that passes here
> Hasn't risen too high,
> I would like to work a little piece of my small cornfield," he said;
> "Ah," she said,
> "Hear what you are doing," she said,
> "If you would like to just ask, chat,
> Tell your companions,
> Those who have the most spirit,
> Those who seem most manly,
> If you want to build my house for me,
> Build for me my church here,
> Because the holy earth appears to me to be very good,
> I feel like living here,

I want to sit here,
If you want to make me my little house here,
That's what I said,
I'll come in fifteen days,
I'll come here to wait for you,
Think about what I've said, son,
Think about it,
If you want to chat here with your companions,
If you want to tell your companions,
If you want I'll come to hear."
"Ah, don't worry, Mother,
Don't worry, I'll tell them,
At least one family I guess,
If I'm answered favorably,
I'll come to wait for you,
That's just if it's favorable;
If I'm not answered favorably, still I'll come wait for you,
Mother, there is nothing for your heart to complain of,
For if they want to I'll come to tell you,
If they don't want to I'll come to tell you,
They wouldn't know yet what we are coming to do,
Where shall I come to sit?"
"I'm coming here to sit beneath the avocado [tree]
Here, beneath the avocado,
There I'll come to sit,
Ah, but you understand,
If they want,
I will bring something,
I want them to make the hollowed-out log for our salt,
Our salt will be born,
You will prepare our salt, you understand,
You will look for your money,
You look for your half *reales*,
I'll help you if you build my house,
Your salt will be born,
You will make your griddles,
You will boil my salt,
There will be nothing to worry about at all,
I am the youngest sister,
My older sister is the one in Hteklum,

My younger sister is in Ixtapa," she said.
[It is the middle sister that is there in Ixtapa,
And the littlest younger sister now in Salinitas. Informant's correc-
   tion.]
"My older sister is content now,
She is living there now,
She has her house now,
Her house is already built,
But the men there accepted her command,
Her house is built,
My older sister's command was accepted right off,
Now I would like,
I want my house too,
If you will be so very kind,
If you will build my house."
"I understand too, if you come, mother,
Don't deceive me,
If it isn't as you say,
You are deceiving me, it seems."
"Why wouldn't I come,
For I want to live here,
If you want to build for me,
Let it just be a little house for me,
For I wish to take out our salt here, it seems,
There is nothing now for you to think about,
Your salt will be born,
You will boil it,
Then you will sell it,
You will eat and drink water,
It won't be necessary for you to buy your salt,
You will have your salt now."
"Ah, I will chat I guess,
You will know what I have been told in fifteen days,"
   said the boy, you see,
The boy arrived home,
He left,
"Until then, son,
Until then take care of yourself,
I'll talk to you in fifteen days," said the lady,
You see, that's just the way he was spoken to,

Just like that;
The boy didn't see where the woman went;
"Ah, was it a real person,
Was it a person who told me she wanted a house,
Couldn't it have been some dirty business,
Something casting sickness on me,
If I were to die of this," said the man.
"Ah, I guess I'll go chat first with my mother and my father,
See what they tell me,
If it's a caster of sickness [a witch],
If they tell me it's something bad,
Then certainly it's terrible,
It isn't good at all," said the awful boy;
You see, he had a grandfather,
It was there he arrived to chat with his grandfather [who said],
"Don't worry, go, wait for her,
Wouldn't that be our holy mother there, you hear,
There is an older sister,
You hear, there is a younger sister,
You hear, she herself is the youngest sister,
But that is known,
That there are three, it seems,
Living where they want,
Where each one desires her seat."
Could it be that I am not conversing properly,
For that is what I saw,
For that is what I heard,
I tell myself, I understand,
Let however many families of men join together,
Come, we'll make, we'll build her house,
Collect the money if that is what they say,
If they come.
Who knows how many years it was when the earth was cleft,
There was a little river there,
That descended from the foot of a cave,
Where the edge of our Holy Mother's house was,
The earth was cleft,
A river now came forth,
But our Holy Mother was under the avocado,
Leaning against it,

Her whole house was completely filled with water, you see,
Now there is "Little River" there as it is now called,
Now a river passes by
The edge of our Holy Mother's house, it seems;
Long ago when she arrived,
There wasn't any;
The church is on open ground now,
The church is big now;
Long ago it was that little "cow house" they made for her,
They built the house,
They have rebuilt the church now,
It is a church now there,
For they say that the earth was cut open,
Water came out, the river;
Our Holy Mother landed and leaned against the root,
The root of the avocado,
But she was hardly our Holy Mother when she talked,
It was a human,
The boy who talked to her, you see;
He had seen that maybe it was our Holy Mother,
For it seems she disappeared;
Now she came to sit down again,
But she left her seat it seems,
There she went to sit on the altar, it seems,
Then she was on the altar, you see,
Then she landed under the avocado, leaning against it;
Our Holy Mother jumped out
When her house was flooded, it seems,
Now there is made one hollow log now;
Long ago the hollow log,
If they don't come,
But then we are good-for-nothings,
I can tell my grandfather, you should have said."
"Ah, I certainly didn't say that,
For that lady set apart a fifteen-day period,
Until fifteen days,
For she wants to come to live,
For she wants her little house,
Wants to come here, you see,
It is alright still for fifteen days,

Think what you want to think,
Tell whom you want to tell,
I guess I'll tell my compadre Marian," he said,
"My compadre, Juan, to see what my compadre Juan tells me,
I'll know I guess, if we make,
If we build a house of whatever size for her to live in,
If they say so,"
You see, he conversed with the compadre,
I don't know if it is true,
That the boy was able to converse with him,
That there was a woman who had come wanting to settle;
"Oh, wouldn't it be our Holy Mother?" said the compadre,
"Oh, how can you think it is our Holy Mother,
If it is a lady who wants to soften wool,
To spin, to weave,
Here in our house,
If we scorn her,
She may cover us with something;
She may wrap us in something good,
Make our clothes, our scarves,
If we scorn her;
Let her settle, the poor lady,
It's worth it to build her a little 'cow house'," they said.
They built her little house,
They got together,
"What else can we do?"
But you see, where she said she wanted her house,
They made the house right away,
Right away they built the house,
The house was built right away,
There was a large hollow log on the other side of the river,
I saw it myself,
It wasn't just anyone who saw it,
It was a good meter in length,
But the water hole was maybe ten or fifteen meters in depth,
Where the salt was taken out;
Once, when I was little,
I was maybe eight years old when I arrived there,
Beneath the feet of our Holy Mother;
You see, the hollow log passed over [to the other side], it seems,

They made a new hollow log here on this side,
For there they took out the salt water,
It is soggy on the other side of the river,
So it passed over here to this side of the river,
So now there is a hollow log there till now;
They hold a fiesta,
There is the Fiesta of the Rosary,
The musicians enter, descend, whatever they do,
Again and again;
There is a fiesta,
For that is what our Holy Mother wants,
All the officers,
The Scribes,
The Regidor,
Alcalde,
Presidente,
The Síndico,
Whoever goes,
They go to hold the fiesta there,
Whoever is the actual holder of the fiesta,
The very owner of the fiesta,
The Mayordomo Rey,
The Mayor,
The servant of our Holy Mother,
Mayordomo of our Holy Mother,
He is the servant of our Holy Mother;
Now the fiesta is entering in,
They cense with the incense-bowls,
They do everything there in Salinitas,
They hold a fiesta now,
For her house is a good one now,
They built her house,
They collected money in the town, it seems,
They built her church,
Now her little church is big;
But long ago it was a "cow house" that was built,
For that's how they began to build her house;
Now they hold a good fiesta,
For now the band arrives,
It enters.

Before it was the little string instruments,
The little violin,
The little guitar.
They hold the fiesta,
They celebrate,
They give food,
They give whatever they give,
As has come down from very long ago, it seems.
It is a good fiesta that they celebrate now,
The earth is well-made there, it seems,
Like that it is left,
Like that.

(Robert M. Laughlin, Tale 83)

Sacred Objects

San Sebastián. Another portion of the corpus of myths describes sacred objects and places of various kinds. In the following tale San Sebastián was believed to have been a Spanish army captain who was attacked by wild animals, shot by Lacandons' arrows, and apparently killed. But the Crows, Blackmen, Squirrels, and Spaniards (all performers at the Fiesta of San Sebastián; see Chapter 22) came, and the Spaniards requested that he be spared since "he is our captain." He was spared and placed in the church of San Sebastián (also called the church of the Martyr) where he still lives.

Long ago the church of the Martyr wasn't built by masons,
Or whatever,
It was built by the VASHAKMEN long ago;
In five nights and five days it was done,
It was built,
The stones and poles and whatever were brought on mules;
It became dark,
There was no day, no night,
Just darkness on the land;
So it was the VASHAKMEN, they're called, who worked long ago,
It was the VASHAKMEN who carried the stones,
It was the VASHAKMEN who carried the lime,
It was the VASHAKMEN who transported the logs,
That's why the land was dark;

The Martyr was built long ago, you see,
The church was built,
The church was built in those five days,
Day and night it was dark,
The land was dark,
It never dawned;
"Why can it be that the land is so dark?
Why can it be that dawn doesn't come?
It's annoying," said the people;
"Eh, who knows why,
Maybe God is punishing us for something,
If we don't win, if what we subsist on is ended,
We'll die of hunger," said the people;
But you see,
When the five days and five nights were completed,
The church was standing,
It was standing,
There was now its building,
It has its tile now;
The bell-tower isn't tall, it's short there,
That's why, for it was built by the VASHAKMEN, that's why;
It's built there now,
It's been repaired,
It was hard to repair it,
It was hard to build,
Because it was not built by people,
Ah, people maybe, but it was the VASHAKMEN who built it,
So long ago;
It wasn't just yesterday,
The building of the church there,
I don't know how many years there,
I don't know in what year,
But long ago;
Our holy fathers, VASHAKMEN, who built the church, you see,
They finished building it, making it;
There was a cemetery there where the church is,
There was a cemetery there,
There were standing white stones and whatever,
There at the head of the graves of the dead,
Where the people were buried, you see,

There by each one, each one of the dead was set a stone;
Where we look at the fiesta there now, it seems, I saw them,
But as my age is, I am forty-six years old, I am,
Now since the church was built;
You scarcely think you would know how many hundred years
The church has been built there;
Long ago, the church,
There isn't anyone who saw it built,
It was the ancestors who saw the church built;
The bell wasn't large either,
Its bells are little;
Don't you see, long ago there weren't any big bells,
There were just very little bells,
Until the ancestors, they had their bells,
But here in the church of our holy father San Lorenzo,
So who knows how they were built;
But holy Martyr there, he was a captain,
Our holy father there, he came from the woods,
They went to throw him in the woods,
I don't know what our holy father's crime was,
They went to throw him in the forest,
Gave him to be killed by jaguars,
Gave him to be killed by coyotes,
Gave him to be killed by whatever animal that was dangerous;
Long ago, our holy father, they fulfilled their desires, where they
    threw him,
They fulfilled their desires where they tossed him;
But he didn't die,
Nothing happened to him,
I don't know if it was the Lacandons,
I don't know what dirty work it was that he was hit by arrows long
    ago,
He was wounded in many places by just arrows,
"Flecha," they're called,
He was wounded many times in his chest,
Wounded in his legs,
Wounded in his stomach,
In his hip, in his ribs,
Wherever the arrows entered, they hit him, they killed him,
For he was an army captain,

We wouldn't have known it was our holy father Martyr,
So it was built there,
The church was made there,
They went to throw him where they went to throw him,
But he didn't die,
Nothing happened to him,
For he found his place,
Like our holy father Martyr there, you see,
He returned there, he came, it seems,
He still didn't die because of them,
So they looked at him, it seems:
"How can it be that he doesn't die,
How can it be that nothing happens to him,
How can he just be there, there indeed,
He didn't die,
I would say he would be killed by coyotes,
I would say he would be killed by jaguars,
Die from whatever animal in the woods,
But he's returned just the same, alive, you see,
It was lies, for he didn't die at all,
Now we'll finish killing him, I guess," said the Lacandons;
Then they hit him with arrows;
Now the Crow came,
The Blackmen came,
Their Squirrels came,
The Spaniards came;
The Spaniards said, "Why are you killing him?" they said when
   they arrived,
"Don't kill him, don't you see, he is our captain," said the Span-
   iards,
"No, don't kill him, he is coming here,
He is coming to live in the house here," they said;
You see, that's the way it was left,
So the Spaniards defended him,
Long ago;
The end.

   The Myth-Teller Corrects Herself:

Long ago they didn't carry the poles and the stones,
They came by themselves,

They worked by themselves,
They already knew where,
Our holy fathers the VASHAKMEN just gave the order,
They did it; they did it,
They just said the command, "You enter here";
If the stones heard, they knew how to get up,
They knew how to build by themselves, and the trees too;
"Let's go," they were told,
They just went on their own,
Dragged themselves away,
Walked by themselves,
They had legs long ago;
That's why it didn't take long to build the church.

(Robert M. Laughlin, Tale 85)

Birth of the Flute. This brief tale describes how the conch horns preceded the flutes as musical instruments in Zinacantan. Now the flute, played with a large and a small drum, is in common use.

Once there was no flute.
The drum was first.
There wasn't anyone who knew how to blow on the flute before.
They just had their horns,
These they played with the drums for a fiesta.
When there was a fiesta they didn't have flutes.
Later the flute was born too,
Later the flute was born,
For the horn was lost,
So the flute was born.
Now there aren't any horns today.
Longer ago they had horns,
These they played with the drums.
Now, today, it's the flute now,
The flute with the drum today;
No longer can we see those horns anywhere.
Tun Kanto was the name of the person who knew how to play
    them,
Dead long ago.
Just his name is left.

(Robert M. Laughlin, Tale 100)

Birds and Animals

Zinacanteco mythology is rich in tales about birds and animals. The following describe some properties of the hummingbird and explain the birth of the fox.

The Hummingbird. The symbolic references to the large size, the whiteness, and the term "one leg" are obscure. We do know, however, that the hummingbird is believed to serve as an important messenger for the ancestral gods—hence the reference to the TOTILME'IL.

The hummingbird is good and big.
So that's the way it is;
There were workers in hot country;
They were burning beanpods,
The fire could be seen well, it was so tall.
The hummingbird came,
It came out,
It came flying in the sky.
Well, it saw the fire;
Its eyes were snuffed out by the smoke.
It came down,
It came down,
It came down so that they saw that it was big.
Don't you believe that it is little, it is big.
Just like a dove, its wings are white,
All of it is white.
I say they tell lies when they say that the hummingbird was little,
The men said it was very big.
Then they recognized how it was,
For none of us had seen it,
We didn't know what it was like.
Yes, it says "Ch'un ch'un" in the evening,
But we didn't know what size it was.
But they, they saw how big it was,
They saw that it was the same as, the same size as a hawk,
Having to do with the father-mother [TOTILME'IL],
"One leg" as we call it.

(Robert M. Laughlin, Tale 93)

The Birth of the Fox. This brief tale describes the origin of the so-called *gato de monte,* a gray fox (*Urocyon cinereo-arenteus*). This animal has retractile claws that enable it to climb trees, a fact that led to its inappropriate local name in Spanish.

> Once there was a cat,
> But it was very evil,
> The awful cat.
> You see, it fled out of its house.
> It fled,
> It went to the woods.
> It stuck itself in a hole,
> The cat did;
> But when it came out,
> Now it was a fox.
> Its house was just left,
> It didn't arrive at its house anymore,
> It became wild.
> Well, that's why when it went into the woods, it became,
> That's why it is now called "gato de monte."
> That's all.

(Robert M. Laughlin, Tale 94)

Transformations

Many tales describe unusual transformations of people—a woman who detaches her head from her body and crunches charcoal by the fire, a man who puts on the wings of a Blackman and flies to Guatemala, and so on.

The Charcoal-Cruncher. In this first grisly tale, salt is used to separate permanently the charcoal-cruncher's head from her body; later the head is enticed off the husband's body (where it has fixed itself) by tempting it with fruit. The head then attaches itself to a deer, which runs off to a cave where the head is eaten by a coyote. The deer is shot and its flesh buried with the charcoal-cruncher's body without the usual funeral ceremony.

> There was a man once
> Who was a companion of the one I just finished talking about,
> There was a woman,
> That woman, you see, became a charcoal-cruncher,

She would get up to go out,
Get up to go out;
"Ah, why do you do that so much, woman,
Ah, what do you get up to look for so much,
What is your business?" he said;
Her head arrives to stick on,
When that man gets up, "Where are you going?" [he says]
Her awful head doesn't answer,
The man only hears her already gnawing the charcoal by the fire-
    side,
She crunches it,
Or if not, you hear her knocking around now behind the house,
If there isn't any charcoal by the edge of her fire,
At whatever house she goes to to crunch the charcoal,
She arrives knocking about to frighten [people] outside the house,
To the side of it;
If she arrives at the house of her comadre,
So she looks for whatever house she knows well,
There she goes to crunch,
Because that is perhaps where they won't kill her, she thinks;
But you see, you see, the awful man was tired of it, you see:
"I don't know what to think, this is annoying me so much." the
    man told his mother,
"I don't think well of that awful woman,
I feel awfully tired of this now,
I'm dying of fright,
Mother, I'm perishing of fright,
Mother, you feel in the evening the awful woman's [headless body],
There's nothing to say to her,
You rest her head on your hand, you say,
Where will you find it,
She hasn't any head, the ugly headless woman,
So her head, who knows where it is sitting," you see:
"But stand watch, son," said his mother;
The man stood watch;
Yes, she went out to crunch charcoal,
Either bumping around outside,
Or at another house where she went to scare people, you see,
Until she returns;

She has a child,
When she had a child she went out seldom,
When she hadn't a child, it seems,
When the baby was big now, didn't nurse anymore,
And seemed to eat well,
Then she left the man embracing his child,
He didn't hear his wife leave;
When the awful woman went,
She went out,
Went to crunch charcoal;
But you see, when that man undid her by witchcraft,
He looked for salt,
He rubbed the salt with his fingers on her tail,
I mean on that woman's neck,
He put the salt on her,
For his mother had told him what she had thought,
For the man was dying of fright,
He was very tired of it,
Night and day,
Night and day,
The woman was no good for company,
Nor when he sat down to chat with her,
She would just nod [her head],
She just nodded,
You wouldn't see good laughing talk,
Just nodding is what she did;
Or if you went to bed,
She would go out in,
In the yard [inside the fence],
Or wherever outside,
To the side of her neighbors' houses,
She enters the house,
Bumping around,
She jumps up and into the top of the wall,
For the roof-ledge of our houses is wide, it seems,
The roof-ledge is big,
Her head enters,
Bumping along it arrives at the fireside,
That owner of the house heard her,
Or if he didn't hear her,

Now he hears her gnawing as she crunches the charcoal;
"Ah, is there a charcoal-cruncher,
Ay, did you hear it over there,
It is crunching charcoal, it sounds, by the fireside,
Man, wake up," her neighbor said to her husband;
"Oh I don't know if that's what it is,"
"Oh that's what it seems to be,
Ay, did you hear it crunching the charcoal!";
They finished striking matches,
They looked,
There the awful head was lying,
What do you think, the awful woman's head was sweeping at the
    fireside, you see;
"What are you doing,
What filthy thing are you?" said the man;
He got up,
He looked,
Oh, bounding it left,
It jumped up and away to the roof-ledge;
When it felt itself outside, it went;
Now they just searched for it,
They didn't find it anywhere;
"But we'll stand watch one night,
Or so to see who, who it could be there," they said;
"If there are still charcoal-crunchers,
For the charcoal-cruncher was buried," they said,
Said the men;
But you see it came down to the fire
At the house of her neighbor in this way;
Don't you see, the man was asleep,
He was befuddled;
When he satisfied himself standing guard,
He rubbed salt on her neck with his fingers,
He gave her the salt,
There she was bumping around,
There she was jumping up,
Thinking she would lie down;
That man was looking, don't you see,
There was nothing the man could do,
Because he had been asleep;

When he got up from his sleeping-place,
It jumped,
It landed on his neck,
The man had two heads,
There it was stuck on his back where it went;
"Ah, why is it good for you, boy,
You think it so good that you have two heads,
Are you a hermaphrodite with your long hair," the poor man was
    told wherever he walked;
He had a man's head and a woman's head,
Two heads, the poor man;
As for the woman,
She had long hair,
But her hair was wild,
For it had been on his body for a long time,
Already the eighth or tenth day perhaps,
That was the number of days the awful woman was stuck there to
    the man's head,
To his shoulder;
He went,
The man was tired of her now,
"I guess I'll go take a walk,
Go look, I guess, where I can leave her by trickery,
Where some kind of nut can be eaten in the woods,
If there is any kind of fruit to eat, mother,
I am tired of this,
My shoulder is tired,
Because she doesn't understand talking:
'Get off, my shoulder is tired,' I was telling her";
"I'm not staying, man,
I'm not staying,
It will annoy me very much if you leave me," said the awful
    woman,
She went,
Went accompanying him to take a walk, you see;
"Look how good they are,
Won't you eat the fruit there," he told her,
"I'll climb to cut it, I guess,
Eat it,
It's very good indeed,

Look how yellow it is," he said;
He climbed up,
He hadn't eaten like that,
He hadn't walked far before, that poor man;
In a moment she jumped up into the pine,
She landed and perched on his shoulder, you see;
He came with her again, you see;
When that poor man had been taught by his mother and his
  father,
"Never mind, but you just aren't winning at all,
For that way you are suffering,
Who knows what the best thing is we can think up for her,
Trickery I guess,
Go, I guess."
Said the man, "Better if I take my gun,
I'll look there if I can find anywhere a deer,
If I find a deer or whatever, I'll shoot it,
But then I'll win," said the man;
The man went;
There was fruit on an awful K'OSHOSH tree;
"Won't you eat it,
Won't you eat it,
Look how thick it is with fruit,
Look how thick the K'OSHOSH tree is with fruit,
[There's] a fruit of the TILIL tree, you see,
The fruit of the TILIL tree."
There she became befuddled,
So she ate it, don't you see;
Then flying along came the deer,
Then it passed in a flash,
[The head] landed and stuck;
"Why are you leaving me," it said to him;
On the middle of [the deer's] spine it landed,
It landed and perched on the deer;
It went, the deer went,
Went to a cave;
It landed,
Squeezed in the cave, you see;
As for the deer, it entered you see,
It jumped into the cave;

The squirrel arrived, you see;
It [the head] thought it would carry it away,
It didn't want to,
The squirrel jumped passing from tree to tree, you see,
The squirrel wouldn't take it away;
Where the man had arrived,
He tricked it by climbing up to the TILIL berries:
"Climb up, climb up,
Eat them,
Let's see if you can do it,
Just the good ones are there,
The little ones are like cherries," he said, you see;
She went to eat the TILIL berries,
Then she became befuddled, don't you see;
The man, her husband, had taken his gun,
For he had said that he was hunting;
He went;
There passed, the deer passed by;
It went away;
He saw his wife;
"Man, wait for me,
Wait for me,
Why are you leaving me behind?" she said;
But it was a deer,
There it landed and stuck on top;
He went,
The deer left;
"What could that be there on my back," said the deer;
When it had nearly arrived at the cave, you see,
He saw the person:
"Stay, get off,
Get off my back,
I'll just hit your head,
I'm entering the cave here,
Because I sleep there," he said;
It stayed;
"You can huddle here,
I'll come take you tomorrow,
I'll carry you out,
We'll go together," [the deer] told her;

But it was because the deer knew a coyote was coming, you see;
The coyote came late in the evening,
Eleven o'clock or midnight it was,
Ah, at midnight it arrived;
"Ooo," said the coyote,
"Ooo," said the coyote;
"Ah, man, come take me,
I'm going to be killed by the coyote tonight, it seems,
That coyote is calling."
"Wait, I'm coming now," he said;
Then that coyote arrived,
For it had heard where the talking was;
In a moment it dragged it out by its hair,
Grabbed it,
Ate it.
That ends the talk of the poor woman,
Eaten, that's the way she was finished;
The deer came out,
Then the man was waiting there,
He shot the deer,
The man had his deer,
One deer,
The deer that he killed was an old stag,
He killed it,
That man who carried his wife away;
That poor woman died because of the coyote,
That's the way she died;
The man found his deer.
He went to eat it with his children,
His heart had nothing to complain of,
Now that he had lost his wife in the woods, it seems;
You see, the words are ended;
They went to bury her body,
They buried her, it seems,
They buried the meat of the deer,
They buried the woman,
They didn't eat chicken,
There wasn't anything,
They didn't buy her a coffin,
They dug her grave for her, you see;

That's how the charcoal-crunchers were gotten rid of long ago,
Until today there aren't any,
We don't hear of charcoal-crunchers at all now.
The end.

(Robert M. Laughlin, Tale 82)

The Blackman. The next tale introduces the Blackman (ʰʔɪ𝐊'ᴀʟ) and relates how a man wounded one, received money, killed him, and then flew off to Guatemala with the Blackman's wings. In Guatemala he received more money and then returned home to tell his adventures.

Well, once there was a man who went to low-country [the low-
   lands],
He returned from low-country.
He had many horses,
He lowered his load halfway up the mountain,
He piled up all his baggage there halfway up the mountain where
   he slept.
Well, the man slept,
And contentedly he ate and slept.
He ate his beans,
He ate well and slept.
Well, he was very scared,
He trembled,
He was quaking a lot, now that night was coming.
Well, "God, my lord, what will I do later on tonight," he said;
Well, he had a gun,
Well, he ate and slept well.
He slept,
He slept in the midst of his baggage,
He set his gun at his side to sleep with.
Well, because he was tired, his soul went [fell asleep];
He slept, and when his soul entered [he woke up],
There was crouched a Blackman eating at the fireside,
Because there were leftover beans hidden away for the night
Which he said he would eat the next day;
When his soul entered, The Blackman was eating well now,
Crouched contentedly he ate.
"Well, no man, but what can I think up for that?" he said.
And in a jiffy he picked up his gun,

In a jiffy he whistled bullets at him.
Well, the Blackman flew away,
Was well-peppered with bullets next to his heart.
Oh, the Blackman flew off now,
He went to the other side of the mountain.
Our Holy Mother was fine [the moon was very bright],
The world was nice and white [it was light];
The man had seen where the Blackman landed;
Well, he went to look,
When dawn came he took up his gun,
He went,
He went to look.
There he was crouched in the middle of a gully,
There the Blackman was crouched in the gully,
Curing his chest.
Well, when the man arrived carrying his gun,
"Ay, don't kill me," said the Balckman;
"Don't do that,
I've already received bullets,
But look at the width of the bullet wounds," he said.
"What a bastard,
Why didn't you receive the bullets, bastard,
Why do you go frightening me in the evening,
What are you looking for?" said the man.
"Well, if you want I'll give you a lot of money,
But not if you kill me,
Just if you'll help me will I give you a lot of money," he said.
"Well, give me however much money your heart desires,
Give it to me,
Then I certainly won't kill you," said the man.
He was given the money,
A lot of money he was given,
The Blackman gave.
First he received the money,
Then he whistled bullets at him again,
He peppered him with bullets again.
Well, he died,
There the Blackman was cut to pieces.
Well, he looked,
He turned him around,

Turned him over,
There was something there on the back of his foot.
"What could that be?" he said.
"Could it be his flying apparatus?" he said, said the man.
He took off from him the thing that was on the back of his foot,
The wing of the Blackman.
He stuck them on the backs of his feet too,
And when he stuck them on the backs of his feet,
For perhaps he wanted to see where the house of the Blackman's
    wings was,
Wanted to return them to their house;
Well, the man stuck them on the backs of his feet,
Thinking perhaps they were good;
Now when he stuck them on the backs of his feet,
He flew,
Gliding away he left.
The wings of the Blackman carried him away.
He left,
He arrived at Guatemala.
Well, "What are you looking for?" said the people there in Guate-
    mala.
"I'm not looking for anything,
It's just like this, and this:
A Blackman went and scared me a little, I don't know why," he
    said.
"Ah, but that one goes fast,
But I saw him standing just at evening time," said the people
    there.
"I don't know at all,
I saw him like that,
He frightened me," said the man,
"That's why I killed him," he said.
Well, and "Go then," said the people,
"Go today,
You have your money,
Return and enter, arrive at your house," they said.
Well, the man was elated now,
He found lots of money.
He came,
He came,

He came.

"Well, well, I'll tell for the little and big to hear
What the Blackman is like,
Look how far they [the wings] brought me," he said.
Well, he came,
He entered his house.
There wasn't any argument, none,
He just entered to let them see his money.
Well, he entered to tell his children what had happened:
"So the Blackman did this and this, like this," he said upon
   entering.
Well, that's the way it was,
So that they still converse about it that way,
That it was true
That a man once got the Blackman with bullets.
That's why it was left that way,
For he conversed about it to his children,
So in that way till now it is like that.

(Robert M. Laughlin, Tale 25)

"Historical" Events

Finally, there are stories about alleged happenings in the past that have affected, or at least are rationalizations for, the political order of things in the Zinacanteco world.

The Indian King. The first tale explains how Ladinos came to be superior to Indians.

Well, do you want to hear about
When the king, the Indian king was born?
Me, I heard,
I was told by my father,
I was told by my grandmother
About when the Indian king was born,
Here at our holy mother MUSHUL VITS,
There a boy would bar the way,
There he was always lying on his back everyday,
Every single day.
The travelers to San Cristóbal he would stop on the path:
"Give me one of your tortillas," he said.

"Give me one of your oranges," he said.
"What do you know, loafer,
Put your hands to work,
I'm buying fruit to eat because I work,
Because I am a man," said the travelers to San Cristóbal.
Whichever friends, "Well, will you eat a tortilla?"
Said the people, whichever people.
"Well, give it to me then," said the boy.
"Will you eat an orange?"
"Well, thank you," he said.
There he played,
There he was digging under a stone,
Under a stone where our holy mother MUSHUL VITS is.
Sir, he was there.
Well, oh, who knows how long he asked for alms,
He asked for tortillas,
Asked for fruit.
There he was given whatever the poor people,
Those who were good,
Could.
Those who were stupid,
Gave him a bawling out.
Well, you see, he was lucky:
The boy, digging there beneath the stone,
[Found] a green ring for his hand,
Very green.
Ha, the boy left,
He left.
He had a house.
Well, the boy had a chest,
Belonging to his mother and father,
But it was a battered chest, sir,
But it was a large battered chest.
The holy land dawned,
Brimful [the chest] at dawn.
There was also a pot,
After the next night,
Brimful at dawn.
A ring,
A green ring,

Just money,
Just money,
In one night;
The old chest,
The chest of the orphan boy's mother and father,
Was filled at dawn.
There were pots there face-down,
He set them up,
They were brimful at dawn.
He went to the houses of whichever friends he had,
Their chests came,
He borrowed them.
"I will buy them," he said.
"Or I'll borrow them," he said.
"No, just borrow them," said whichever of his friends.
Now, it was heard by the people of San Cristóbal here.
They went.
"But where did the lazy Indian come from,
No he won't win,
That money is ours," they said.
But you don't know now how many chests,
How many pots,
How many houses there were now,
There were houses of it now.
Now the lord here went to look.
But they went to match the boy with the money.
God, they didn't even reach a half,
There it was left counted out.
So the gentlemen,
The lords,
Came walking.
Now their messages went as far as Mexico City,
Their messages went everywhere where there were [governments],
To the government in Tuxtla.
Soldiers came,
He was left as king.
The money,
Oh God,
As there weren't cars before,
Who knows how the money went.

He was left as a king,
But an Indian king,
But because he was a man when he arrived in Mexico City.
Then the Mexicans took care of him there.
So they made him a legitimate Zinacantecan Indian king.
Well, now, if the king had stood up,
If he had come to defend us long ago,
Then Zinacantan would be on top here,
The Ladinos face-up.
The Ladinos got on top,
Because the king left,
He went to Mexico City;
That's how the world here lost.

(Robert M. Laughlin, Tale 113)

The Revolution. This last tale relates the encounters between the forces of General Obregón and General Pineda during the battles of the Revolution (1910–1920) in Chiapas.

Will you hear about a war?
There was a war long ago,
Obregón against the Pinedists.
They clashed together in the month of September.
Now the Obregonists didn't win.
Pineda gained the upper hand.
Obregón fled down as far as Tierra Blanca;
Pineda, sticking right behind, descended.
Obregón, oh God, he stopped at Ixtapa.
Obregón went for good in September,
He went far off until April when he came up.
When he came up, Pineda was ready now, Obregón was ready now.
A machine came in the sky,
A red one,
Just one came,
One plane.
Well, then Obregón came up here at, here at Canita:
There they brought,
There arrived four cannons,
But cannons Holy Mary!
Well, then, then Pineda was at Ixtapa;
At the church door,

They brought the cannons.
At first they fired a test shot
To see if he died, or didn't die.
Well, then, they stopped,
Pineda fired a machine gun with bullets.
Well, they stopped half an hour;
The soldiers arrived from First-Field [above Ixtapa],
One group came down,
From Soyalo another group came,
From the San Rafael road came another group,
He was surrounded;
The soldiers fired their cannons,
Obregón fired.
Well, it was one o'clock,
It was one o'clock,
A plane came.
Well, all the Pinedists died,
All of them,
To the ground.
Well, the plane dropped six bombs from above,
It dropped them now,
They came down;
Their souls left,
The people died, one hundred,
One hundred men were taken alive.
They were coming to burn our Holy Mother,
Not until then were the Pinedists going to burn her.
They became angry,
They seized her,
They were going to put cloth there at the door of our Holy Mother.
Well, they didn't,
Didn't burn her;
The soldiers seized them right off,
It was the Obregonists that seized them.
Well, and then the plane returned,
It came in half, just a half hour;
It stopped,
It returned right off,
It came to see how many,
If there were still more enemies coming down,
If there were still more coming from Nut-Tree, from Soyalo.

There were advance groups there.
Well, and then one hundred men were taken,
It was filled there with all the generals,
The lookouts,
All the devils of the headquarters,
The Pinedist generals.
Of the Obregonists there were there,
There were there only the spies,
They were watching there.
They sent an order,
They came to the cemetery.
The soldiers,
A thousand Obregonists,
Because of them they all died,
The blood poured now,
That's all for they were waiting for the time,
As the very generals were here right at the window,
Sitting there.
They gave an order
Because the Obregonists were strong-hearted now.
They won now,
They took the lead,
All the devils had their hands cut off at Point-of-Water.
Now their hands were cut off.
Others were seized by the soldiers.
Well, they came to the cemetery
From wherever they had started out.
They wrote,
They asked a favor,
They wrote how they died;
From just five bullets [bombs]
One hundred men died
There at the cemetery;
They didn't win;
Carried, they went into one grave.
All of them entered one grave,
Very long ago.
Oh, who knows if it was,
If it was fifty years ago,
The war long ago.

(Robert M. Laughlin, Tale 112)

15 / Catholic Churches and Saints

The influence of Catholic theology in Zinacantan began at least as early as the 1540's when the Dominicans established a convent in Zinacantan, but the missionary effort has been sporadic and generally slight compared to many other areas of Middle America. Father Early (1965) points out that even in 1963 there were only 38 parish priests to cover the whole diocese of San Cristóbal. The same priest who serves Zinacantan is also responsible for El Bosque, Mitontic, Chenalhó, Pantelhó, Chamula, Teopisca, Amatenango, and Aguacatenango with a total population of some 75,000. He visits Zinacantan only on the last day of the principal fiestas of the year to say Mass and perform baptisms and marriages. By noon he departs for another town, not to return to Zinacantan again until perhaps four weeks later.

Assisting the Catholic priest when he is in Zinacantan Center, and representing him when he is not present, is a recently constituted group of church officials: President, Secretary, and Treasurer of the church, and two men who look after the vestments and other gear belonging to the priest.

Many formal Catholic concepts and ritual paraphernalia have been incorporated into Zinacanteco culture over the past four centuries. There are six churches or chapels—three in Zinacantan Center and one in each of three hamlets. Approximately fifty-five saints' statues, pictures, and large crosses are kept for the most part in the temples, although some of these are in the houses of incumbent cargoholders and a few in houses in outlying hamlets. A fluctuating number of "talking saints" function in the hamlets. Hundreds of crosses are erected at the feet and summits of mountains,

In this chapter I am especially grateful to John D. Early, S.J., who has made a detailed field study of Zinacanteco religion.

beside waterholes, in caves, at strategic points around the ceremonial center, in the patios of houses, and in Zinacanteco maize fields. Finally, some interesting syncretized ideas are held about the Christian concepts of God, Jesus Christ, and the Virgin Mary.

Churches

The ceremonial center contains three Catholic churches. By far the most imposing is that of the Church of San Lorenzo (SANTORENSO), located in the heart of Zinacantan Center (Figure 110). The main nave is oriented approximately east–west, with the doorway to the west, so that when the people enter and approach the main altar to pray to the patron saint, San Lorenzo, they are facing in the direction of both the rising sun and the principal sacred mountain, BANKILAL MUK'TA VITS. The side chapel opens off at right angles to the main nave and hence runs to the south—the second most important direction in Zinacanteco ritual.

The Church of San Lorenzo has not always been oriented this way. According to elderly Zinacanteco informants, it originally opened the way it does now, toward Ixtapa. The Ixtapanecos became rich, and there was an earthquake signifying the gods' dissatisfaction with the orientation. The church was then rebuilt facing Chamula (as the side chapel is oriented today). The Chamulas subsequently became rich and there was another earthquake; hence, the church was changed back to face Ixtapa, as it remains to this day. In either position, however, the orientation of a person praying to the saints on the altar would be either south or east, never north or west.

In front of the Church of San Lorenzo is a large walled courtyard, containing a set of courtyard crosses (analogous to the KRUS TA TIʔ NA of the individual Zinacanteco house compound) and a kiosk-type bandstand where the imported brass band plays for fiestas. Four gateways, located on four sides of the courtyard, provide entryways to the courtyard.

Near the center of the south wall of the courtyard is the second temple: the small Hermitage of Señor Esquipulas. The present hermitage is a new building, erected in 1962; the older, dating from 1899 and located immediately to the west still has a cross and is used only for occasional prayers by the mayordomos reyes and mesoneros. In the new hermitage the main altar also faces west, so that people praying to Señor Esquipulas are facing the all-important direction of the rising sun.

The Church of San Sebastián is located north-northeast of the northern gateway to the courtyard of San Lorenzo and is reached by a street that

110. The Church of San Lorenzo

traverses rows of fences and across a bridge over the Big River (MUK'TA ?UK'UM). The street connecting the two temples is reminiscent of the causeways between temples in Ancient Maya sites. This church is a much less imposing structure than that of San Lorenzo and is never kept in such good repair. It consists of a single nave, running approximately east–west, with its doorway to the west, so that Zinacantecos praying at the main altar face the rising sun. On the south side of the church there is a courtyard and a set of courtyard crosses.

All three of these churches are of utmost importance to the Zinacantecos, since they are the "homes" of the saints just as the sacred mountains around the ceremonial center are the "homes" of the ancestral gods. For some types of ritual procedures, for example, a curing ceremony which includes a pilgrimage to Zinacantan Center, the churches are treated as a unit, and the curing party visits and prays to saints in all three as it makes the rounds of the sacred mountains. But, in addition, the three churches have quite specialized functions in the ceremonial calendar. San Lorenzo is the major focus of ritual activity for the ceremony of the main patron saint in August; San Sebastián is the stage for the principal ritual performed during the Fiesta of San Sebastián in January; the Hermitage of Esquipulas is where oaths of office are taken by incoming cargoholders in the ranks of alféreces, regidores, and alcaldes.

Three outlying hamlets—Salinas, Nabenchauk, and ?Apas—now also have small Catholic chapels. The chapel at Salinas, dedicated to the Virgen del Rosario and located beside a sacred salt well, appears to be quite old. The chapel in Nabenchauk, dedicated to the Virgin of Guadalupe, was erected in 1957 and seems to have been at least in part a nativistic response to the efforts of the Protestant missionary who lived in this hamlet for about ten years. The chapel in ?Apas is even more recent. It was built during 1961–62 and the first ceremony for its saints, a Señor Esquipulas and two Virgins (Guadalupe and Carmen), was celebrated in April 1962. The motivating force for the establishment of this church came from a dream, and all such outlying chapels may have been motivated by the dreams of elders in the various hamlets.

Saints

The total collection of sacred objects that may be labeled "saints" (SANTOETIK) numbers at least fifty-five, not counting pictures of saints that individual Zinacantecos keep in their houses. Most of these saints have their "homes" in the three churches in Zinacantan Center, which among them contain thirty-six statues of saints, four pictures of saints, and two large sacred crosses, or a total of forty-two saint figures. In addition, eight saint figures are kept in the houses of the incumbent mayordomos in the ceremonial center; the incumbent Senior Alcalde keeps a sacred picture of San Sebastián; there are three or more saint figures in each of the outlying chapels at Salinas, Nabenchauk, and ?Apas; and I know of at least one saint, Virgen del Rosario, kept in a small house in Paste?.

The distribution of the forty-two saint figures is shown in Figures 111, 112, and 113. The statues in the three temples vary in height from one to five or six feet. Most are dressed in long robes that reach the feet, and have items of Zinacanteco dress, such as pink-and-white striped shawls and necklaces with ribbons on the Virgins and Zinacanteco men's ribbons and tassels on male saints. No item of clothing for the saints is ever discarded; when new clothes are placed on the statue, the old clothes are removed and placed in the chests of the mayordomos, which are now bulging with ancient robes. During major fiestas, the ?UAL, a necklace of old coins or medallions, is also removed from the mayordomo's chest, carried in procession to the proper church and placed around the neck of each of the major saints. Although they look like Catholic rosaries, the Zinacantecos attribute to them distinctive properties and functions.

The following eight figures are kept in houses of the incumbent mayordomos: Junior Mayordomo of Santa Cruz, a crucifix with a figure of Christ; Senior Mayordomo of Virgen del Rosario, two statues of Virgen del Rosario and one of Virgen de Candelaria; Junior Mayordomo of San Antonio, two statues of San Antonio; Senior Mayordomo of San Sebastián, three statues of San Sebastián. These are all small (about 15 cms. high), and dressed in at least five layers of clothing woven in the style of Zinacanteco chamarras.

The church in Salinas contains five statues of saints: Virgen del Rosario Mayor, Virgen del Rosario Menor, Santa Rosa, San Antonio, and Santa Columba. Their arrangement is shown in Figure 114. The Virgen del Rosario Mayor is a large statue, about 2 meters high, clothed ornately in robes and decorated with mirrors. At its foot is the tiny 15-cm.-high statue of Santa Rosa. San Antonio, Santa Columba, and Virgen del Rosario Menor are just over a meter high. The Virgen del Rosario Menor is the one which travels: to Zinacantan Center for the fiestas of San Sebastián, Cuarto Viernes, San Lorenzo, and Sagrado Corazón; to Nabenchauk for the fiesta of Guadalupe; and to Ixtapa for the Fiesta of Asunción.

Of the forty-two religious statues in the ceremonial center, there are six with special properties and functions that seem to have particularly distinctive personalities and mythologies attached to them.

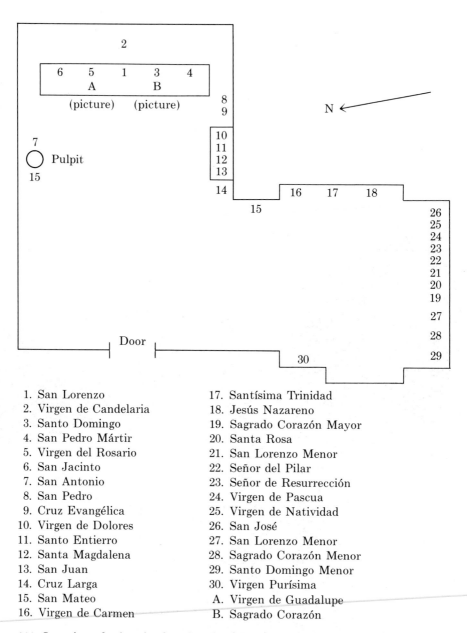

1. San Lorenzo
2. Virgen de Candelaria
3. Santo Domingo
4. San Pedro Mártir
5. Virgen del Rosario
6. San Jacinto
7. San Antonio
8. San Pedro
9. Cruz Evangélica
10. Virgen de Dolores
11. Santo Entierro
12. Santa Magdalena
13. San Juan
14. Cruz Larga
15. San Mateo
16. Virgen de Carmen
17. Santísima Trinidad
18. Jesús Nazareno
19. Sagrado Corazón Mayor
20. Santa Rosa
21. San Lorenzo Menor
22. Señor del Pilar
23. Señor de Resurrección
24. Virgen de Pascua
25. Virgen de Natividad
26. San José
27. San Lorenzo Menor
28. Sagrado Corazón Menor
29. Santo Domingo Menor
30. Virgen Purísima
A. Virgen de Guadalupe
B. Sagrado Corazón

111. Location of saints in the Church of San Lorenzo

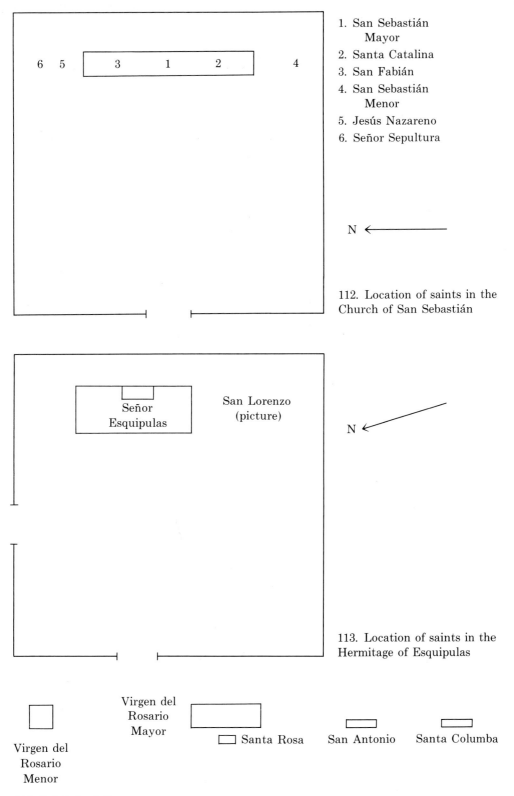

1. San Sebastián Mayor
2. Santa Catalina
3. San Fabián
4. San Sebastián Menor
5. Jesús Nazareno
6. Señor Sepultura

112. Location of saints in the Church of San Sebastián

113. Location of saints in the Hermitage of Esquipulas

114. Saints in Salinas

115. San Lorenzo with his necklace of coins

(1) San Lorenzo (SANTORENSO) is now the main patron of Zinacantan, and his statue occupies the place of honor over the main altar of the principal church (Figure 115). He is also represented by two statues (both San Lorenzo Menores) in the side chapel of the church and by a picture in the Hemitage of Esquipulas. San Lorenzo was allegedly found in the woods long ago; his clothes were torn and he was hungry. He told the Zinacanteco who found him that he wanted to stay in Zinacantan and asked that this request be made to the Presidente at the Cabildo. The request was granted, San Lorenzo brought into Zinacantan Center, and a church built for him. When the church was finished, he entered his "home" where he now lives above the main altar. When he first arrived in the center, San Lorenzo could talk; but the elders do not like "talking saints," so they threw hot water over him and forever silenced him (Early 1965: 36–37).

116. San Sebastián with his necklace of coins

(2) San Sebastián (SHANSHCHOVASHCHAN) occupies the place of honor over the center of the altar in the Church of San Sebastián (Figure 116). He is also represented by a smaller statue (San Sebastián Menor) to the right of the altar. He has the distinction of having a somewhat richer mythology attached to his past and the most complex ritual performed for his fiesta in January. Zinacantecos relate at least three versions of his origins.* In one, San Sebastián was an army officer.

The king of the army wanted him to marry his daughter and San Sebastián refused. This enraged the king who ordered San Sebastián to be killed. San Sebastián fled, but the king's soldiers pursued him to Zinacantan where they killed him with their arrows. He carried two drums with him. At his death one went into the cave at NIOʔ. At times it can still be heard playing there; the other is the one used during the fiesta of the saint. San Sebastián was buried where the church is now. Five years later some children taking care of sheep in the pasture found him sitting on the rock called BOLOM TON. They went to tell the Presidente. The Presidente gathered the shamans, and with candles

* The style and phrasing of these myths have been slightly altered to conform to style of this monograph.

and incense, they went to talk to San Sebastián. When they arrived, he had gone, but he had left a piece of paper saying that he wanted a church built so that he could live in Zinacantan. The shamans placed candles to the ancestral gods and to San Lorenzo to ask their advice. San Lorenzo then came and told the shamans not to worry, that the church would be built, and that the sun would be darkened for three days while the work was in progress. The church was then built in three days, some Zinacantecos say by the VASHAKMEN. Others say that San Lorenzo was the *maestro* of the work, while insects carried the rock, sand, and lime, and Santo Domingo mixed the cement. The Virgen del Rosario cut and carried the wood. The church was finished just as it stands today, and San Sebastián lives in it. (Early 1965: 27–28)

In the second version of the myth San Sebastián was the captain of a group of soldiers in Oaxaca.

The king wanted him to marry his daughter, but San Sebastián refused. His refusal infuriated the king who ordered him to be shot. The soldiers took him outside the city, bound his hands behind him and shot him. But the bullets did not harm him. So they commissioned a group of Aztec or Lacandón Indians for [for the informant, these are two names for the same people] to shoot him with arrows. San Sebastián fell mortally wounded, his body filled with arrows. San Lorenzo and Santo Domingo heard about this and went to Oaxaca to see what had happened to San Sebastián. A Ladino merchant was traveling from Oaxaca to Comitán with his merchandise in an ox cart. He found San Sebastián by the side of the road. He put the saint on his ox cart thinking how fortunate he was to have the protection of a saint on his trip. On the second day of the journey they arrived in Zinacantan, and camped for the night in the north pasture. San Sebastián decided to stay in Zinacantan. The next morning the merchant could not load San Sebastián back on the cart. He weighed too much, much more than he had before, and this was a sign he wanted to remain. The merchant left, but animals came to guard San Sebastián: jaguars, birds, and two other types, one of which is black. San Sebastián expressed his wish to remain. The people consulted San Lorenzo and Santo Domingo who knew what had happened from their visit to Oaxaca. Thus the church in the north pasture was built. The same four types of animals still guard the church against anyone who should try to steal the saint from the church. (Early 1965: 340–341)

In still a third version:

> San Sebastián was a captain of some soldiers. He was about to marry the daughter of the secretary of the king. But one night he had a dream, and in the dream an angel came to him and told him it would be bad fortune to marry this girl. Sebastián, trusting his dream, decided firmly not to marry the girl, and he so informed her. She told her father, who complained to the king, who called in Sebastián and threatened him. Sebastián decided to flee, taking with him some soldiers, a large and a small drum, and a cornet, symbols of his authority as a captain. The large drum is now buried with the cornet at LACH CHIKIN. The small drum is the T'ENT'EN that comes over from ʔElan Voʔ for the fiesta of San Sebastián. San Sebastián was captured and tied to a quince tree that had been partially stripped of its branches, and then shot with arrows. San Lorenzo and Santo Domingo could not help him because it had not been decided that way in heaven, so they just stood alongside him and watched him get shot, Lorenzo on one side, and Domingo on the other. There is a painting on the altar in the church of San Sebastián that shows this. And there are also three crosses to mark the spot where Sebastián was killed. This place is called "el lugar donde bailan los Españoles" [the place where the Spaniards dance].
>
> Three years after Sebastián's death, the Virgen del Rosario was walking along in Zinacantan and she saw Sebastián bathing in a place called NIOʔ. There they had a conversation, in which Sebastián asked the virgin to ask Lorenzo to build him a temple, a home. She went to Lorenzo and told him what had happened; Lorenzo didn't believe it, so he went to see for himself. Santo Domingo went with him. They went to the same bathing spot, but did not find him. They returned to the temple of San Lorenzo. Then, from afar, they heard a whistle. They looked all around and spotted Sebastián sitting on a huge rock, called BOLOM TON. Lorenzo spoke to Sebastián, who said, "build me a temple on top of my grave for my house, nothing more. Meanwhile, said Sebastián, "I will live underneath this stone."
>
> Lorenzo and Domingo wanted to comply with Sebastián's request, but there was not enough money to build the church. Finally, Lorenzo seemed to have an idea. First, he asked RIOSH for three days of darkness, only for Zinacantan, to help in the building of the church. And RIOSH complied. Lorenzo directed the work. Four buzzards changed into men, and stationed themselves at each corner of the building, to work as brickmasons. Domingo's job was to carry the stone and sand for the

walls. The virgin's job was to carry the wood and tile for the roof. Domingo couldn't do all the carting himself, so he called on the ants to help him, and they did. Maria [the virgin] went into the woods with an axe. On her way up, she stopped at KALVARIO to find a companion to go with her. Just like today a woman never goes out alone. Once in the woods, Maria cut a special magic stick, and whenever she hit a piece of wood three times, it went by itself to the construction site. In this way, the church was finished in three days, and thus Sebastián had his home. (Allen Young 1962: 41, 64–66)

(3) Santo Domingo (SANTOROMINKO), whose statue stands just to the right of San Lorenzo over the main altar of the principal church, is a secondary patron. He is also represented by a smaller statue (Santo Domingo Menor) in the side chapel. He was the main patron saint until the end of the eighteenth century, but, for reasons we do not yet know, was replaced by San Lorenzo sometime between 1776 and 1792 (Zabala 1961b: 150). His image represents Zinacantan Center at fiestas in the hamlets of Nabenchauk, Salinas, and ?Apas and in the municipios of Ixtapa and San Lucas, where he is carried for ritual visits. We have been unable to elicit myths about his origins.

(4) Santo Entierro (HMANVANEH or "the buyer [of souls]") is a Christ-in-the-tomb statue kept in an enclosed case, along with San Juan, Santa Magdalena, and the Virgen de Dolores, to the right of the nave in the church of San Lorenzo. According to the Zinacantecos, Santo Entierro used to live on earth. He was chased by the demons, who caught him and put him up on a cross in the ceremonial center to kill him. When the demons went to eat, Santo Entierro came down from the cross. He took a blue rock and threw it high into the air, creating the blue sky. The demons returned and put him back on the cross where he died. In dying, he paid the price for our sins; this is why he is called "the buyer." If he had not done this, we all would have died. Later Santo Entierro came back to life and went up into heaven to live. The Holy Week ceremonies now center around this image.

(5) Virgen del Rosario (CH'UL ME?TIK or "divine mother") is considered the patroness of women in Zinacantan. She is sometimes identified as the moon, and as the mother of Santo Entierro.

(6) Señor Esquipulas (?ISKIPULA) is a Christ on a cross, but his skin is white, not black as is that of the more traditional Esquipulas figures in Central America (Borhegyi 1954). His clothes consist of an intricately designed loin cloth and numerous bright-colored ribbons draped around

the figure until only the head is visible. Ornamental reflecting mirrors are hung on the figure, and a small cap is placed on its head. The ritual dressing of the figure takes place each Sunday and at other important ritual occasions during the year. He is the saint of the Hermitage in which incoming cargoholders take their oaths of office. He is also associated with the salt trade in that ritual salt is delivered to elders in this chapel every other Sunday morning.

Although the most important saints have distinct personalities and clearly defined functions, many of the others do not. All of the fifty-five saints are regarded as highly sacred, judging by the amount of ritual attention they receive and by the resistance of Zinacantecos to the viewing and picture-taking of them by outsiders. No major fiesta occurs in the ceremonial center in which at least one group of tourists is not forcibly evicted from the Church of San Lorenzo for attempting to photograph the saints. More commonly, the sacristanes simply lock the church doors when they see tourists approaching. The saints are regarded as gods of extraordinary power, with souls located in the statues. Their "homes" are the churches or the houses of the official cargoholders. They must be bathed by water from the sacred waterholes and their clothes must be periodically washed and incensed—just as the clothing of a patient in a curing ceremony is purified by being bathed and by having his clothes washed and incensed. Like the ancestral gods, the saints expect prayers and offerings of candles, incense, music, and flowers.

The Catholic Mass is considered by Zinacantecos an elaborate prayer for the saint whose fiesta is being celebrated. For his fiesta he very much wants the Mass with all the elaborate ornaments and vestments of the Catholic priest, and, if it is not celebrated, he will be enraged and will punish whoever is responsible for this failure. Accordingly, the elders always go to San Cristóbal to petition the priest for a Mass for every fiesta. If the priest comes, the saint will have his "prayer"; if he is otherwise occupied and cannot come the Zinacantecos are not upset for the elders have accomplished their duty in requesting the Mass. The saint will still be enraged and send punishment, but he will punish the Catholic priest rather than the Zinacantecos (Early 1965: 287).

The complex rituals performed for the saints by the religious cargoholders will be described in Chapters 21 and 22. But the family prayers to saints during fiestas are also extremely important. Father Early describes how family groups, led by the father carrying the candles and the flowers, with wife and children trailing behind, continuously file into the church during fiesta days. The family approaches as close as it can to the statue of the fiesta saint (which is usually placed in a prominent position); they place their flowers in a basket near the statue or on the altar. Each member of the family takes the hem of the saint's clothes into his hands, touches it to his forehead, and kisses it. Then all kneel, light their candles and place them on the floor in front of the statue, and remain praying for fifteen to thirty minutes. The praying is emotionally intense, in the high-pitched prayer tones, and there is often crying. Sometimes candles are purchased for all the saints in the church and the group moves from saint to saint, lighting candles and praying.

When the Saints Come Marching In

Since the Chiapas project began I have been looking for a certain 78-r.p.m., record to donate to one of the owners of the loudspeakers that blare away during fiestas in Zinacantan Center. These play, for 20 centavos apiece, various well-worn records of *danzones,* cha-cha-chas, and *marchas* that have been purchased through the years in San Cristóbal. My search has been for "When the Saints Come Marching In," which could be played for the amusement of the visiting tourists when a prominent part of the ritual of a large fiesta takes place: the arrival of visiting saints from outlying hamlets and neighboring municipios (Figures 117, 118). In probably much the same way that important idols were exchanged in aboriginal times on certain ceremonial occasions, Zinacanteco saints visit and are visited by those of the neighboring municipios of Ixtapa and San Lucas, the hamlets of Nabenchauk, Salinas, and Tierra Blanca, and Labor Grande, the Ladino-owned ranch at the foot of BANKILAL MUK'TA VITS. They are brought and returned by members of the community which is having its fiesta. For example, during the important fiesta of San Lorenzo (August 10), Zina-cantecos go to each of the above mentioned places to bring the saints to Zinacantan Center and return them after the fiesta. Similarly, when Ixtapa is having its fiesta for the Virgen de Asunción (August 15), Ixtapanecos take the saint from Zinacantan and return it after the fiesta. In each case, however, at least one sacristán from the saint's community goes along to watch over it.

The statue of the saint that goes visiting is in some cases not that of the fiesta's patron—largely because these latter are usually too large for men to carry with tumplines. Thus, Zinacantan is represented at the other communities not by its large San Lorenzo, but by the smaller Santo Domingo Menor. However, when Santo Domingo Menor arrives at the other community, he is addressed as "San Lorenzo." From Ixtapa comes

117. When the saints come marching in

118. A visiting saint in procession

a small Virgin del Rosario, but when she arrives in Zinacantan for the fiesta of Asunción, she is called the "Virgen de Asunción." San Lucas is represented by a small San Agustín, regarded as "San Lucas." From Salinas comes not the large Virgen del Rosario, but the Virgen del Rosario Menor. But the main statues of the other hamlets are smaller and come themselves: Virgen de Guadalupe from Nabenchauk, Señor Esquipulas from Tierra Blanca, and San Sebastián, San Nicolás, and Virgen de Purísima from Labor Grande. No exchanges have yet been arranged with the new chapel in ?Apas.

While this exchange of saints may have some roots in the aboriginal past, it is clear that it has continuing economic and political functions. Since San Lucas, Ixtapa, Salinas, and Tierra Blanca are located in lower ecological zones, the movement is important for the exchange of highland and lowland products. With the saints come not only caretakers, but also many others who trade in the large fiesta markets. There is also an important dimension of social and political integration involved in these visits. San Lucas is a community settled by Zinacantecos within the past hundred years, Ixtapa a highly acculturated town whose former Indian population was also probably derived from Zinacantan. Through these visits Zinacantan Center not only commands ceremonial and political allegiance from the hamlets with chapels and saints of their own—such as Nabenchauk which has been threatening for years to split off from Zinacantan—but it also reaches beyond the borders of the municipio to retain ceremonial links with towns that historically were offshoots from Zinacantan.

Talking Saints

In a quite different category for the Zinacantecos are the so-called "talking saints" (HK'OPOHEL RIOSH). Unlike neighboring municipios, such as San Andrés Larrainzar (Holland 1963) and San Pedro Chenalhó (Guiteras-Holmes 1961), where such saints are apparently respected and consulted by many families, the "talking saints" found in Zinacantan today are not well-regarded. They are usually pictures, but sometimes small statues, kept by families in boxes in their houses. These families claim to have found them in caves and brought them home, where they displayed not only the ability to "talk," but also to diagnose illnesses and prescribe cures. The families that own them have a positive attitude toward their supposedly miraculous powers, and other Zinacantecos on occasion certainly consult them and pay fees to the owners. But the attitudes of the officials in the ceremonial center and the vast majority of Zinacantecos toward them range from ambivalence to outright skepticism, and the "talking saints" frequently are responsible for lawsuits at the Cabildo. A typical case might proceed as follows: A Zinacanteco family consults a "talking saint" in one of the hamlets, the saint provides medical advice about an illness, and the fees are paid. The patient fails to get well, and the family appears before the Presidente to request that their money be refunded by the owner of the "talking saint." The Presidente sends out the mayores, who bring in the owner of the saint—who fails to bring the box containing the saint. The Presidente sends the owner back home with the mayores to bring in the saint. The "talking saint" never talks for the Presidente, whereupon the picture or image is confiscated and the owner thrown in jail until he agrees to give up his saint and refund the fees paid by the plaintiffs.

There is always an unknown and fluctuating number of "talking saints" operating in the hamlets. In the spring of 1960 we knew of at least eight well-known "talking saints," and I suspect there were more. Despite the pressures brought to bear against the owners for these unorthodox practices by the officials in Zinacantan Center and by the generally unfavorable climate of opinion about them, obviously some needs (perhaps persisting from aboriginal times) are being fulfilled by "talking saints." Perhaps, the aboriginal idols (whatever their form) "talked" as the orthodox church "saints" today do not. Further, since during dreams a person's soul can communicate with the souls of the ancestral gods in the mountains, perhaps there is something very compelling about a "talking saint" that finds enough support in the society to keep the practice going. In this connection, it is noteworthy that two highland Chiapas rebellions (1712 and 1869–70) were triggered off by "saints" that were believed to have the power to "talk." It is also important to remember the "talking crosses" in Yucatán (Villa Rojas 1945) and in highland Guatemala (Thompson 1954).

Catholic Sacred Personages

Other than the saints already described, the most important concepts that have become integrated into the contemporary religious thinking of Zinacantan are God (RIOSH KAHVAL), Jesus Christ (HESU KRISTO), and the Virgin Mary (CH'UL ME?TIK).

RIOSH. As an obvious loan word from the Spanish *Dios* (God), the Tzotzil RIOSH appears commonly in prayers. A Zinacanteco frequently begins a prayer: ?AN CH'UL NOMPRE RIOSH HESU KRISTO KAHVAL (In the divine name of God, Jesus Christ, my Lord). Such prayers are said not only by the religious officials attached to the saints in the ceremonial center and by individuals who come into the churches to pray to the saints, but also in prayers used by the shamans for curing illness, dedicating new houses, and promoting the good growth of maize in the fields. RIOSH is commonly coupled with KAHVAL in the phrase RIOSH KAHVAL, or even more frequently in the plural form RIOSH KAHVALTIK. KAHVAL is not a loan word, but a Tzotzil form also meaning "my master" or "my Lord." The same stem occurs, for example, in YAHVAL BALAMIL, the Earth Lord. KAHVAL is also very frequently used by Zinacanteco women as an exclamation of surprise.

The simplest explanation of all these meanings would be that Zinacantecos have adopted the Catholic meanings of "God," "My Lord," or "My Master." However, this interpretation is probably not applicable for several reasons. First, the stem -AHVAL, signifying ownership or control of various domains in the Zinacanteco universe, is clearly an Ancient Maya concept into which the idea of "God" as an "owner" or "master" has been fitted. Furthermore, many informants report that saints are KAHVALTIK RIOSH and that they formerly lived all over the world until the VASHAKMEN made the churches and placed the saints in them. Thirdly, one of the alféreces, the Alférez de Divina Cruz, is called KAHVALTIK RIOSH—for reasons that still escape us.

The clearest identification that can be elicited for RIOSH KAHVAL is with the sun, commonly called TOTIK K'AK'AL (father sun), CH'UL K'AK'AL (divine sun), CH'UL TOTIK (divine father), or sometimes Señor San Salvador. So, it would appear that the Catholic God is most nearly equated with the ancient concept of the sun as a deity. This fact fits with the importance of the direction of the rising sun in Zinacanteco symbolism, and with the belief that RIOSH (as the sun) stops each day at noon—when the sun reaches the middle of "heaven" to "sit down at a desk and make a list of sins of men," as one informant expressed it—as well as with the belief that the demons try periodically to kill RIOSH by letting ferocious animals out of caves, thereby causing an eclipse of the sun.

HESU KRISTO. Another obvious loan word in the prayers comes from the Spanish *Jesús Cristo*. This relates to HMANVANEH (the buyer), or Santo Entierro. However, beyond routine mention in prayers, and the important Holy Week ritual centered around the Santo Entierro image of Christ-in-the-tomb and the nailing of the Christ figure to a cross, I see little important symbolism surrounding HESU KRISTO, except that in some prayers he is referred to as RIOSH HESU KRISTO KAHVAL (Lord Jesus Christ, My Master). He does not appear to be related to the maize god or to the sun, as seems to be the case in other Maya communities. (See, for example, Holland's statement that Christ is identified with the sun in Larrainzar [1963: 75].)

CH'UL ME'TIK. Much more important in the religious symbolism is CH'UL ME'TIK (divine or holy mother). This name is clearly Tzotzil for the moon as an object and as the moon goddess (see Thompson 1939) and is also identified with the Virgin Mary, as well as all of the other female saints— Virgen del Rosario, Virgen de la Candelaria, and so on—and the female sacred mountains, such as SISIL VITS (Santa Cecilia). In addition, CH'UL ME'TIK is believed to be the mother of the sun.

In short, the beliefs about Christ seem to have been overshadowed by those of the Ancient Maya sun god and moon goddess, which represent the more salient male and female counterparts in the symbolic system.

16 / Human Souls and Animal Spirits

It is impossible to understand the world in which Zinacantecos live—how the deities in the celestial order are connected with the social order, how individual Zinacantecos interact with one another and with their natural habitat, or even how an individual becomes ill and then either recovers or dies—without a precise understanding of their two "soul" concepts: CH'ULEL and CHANUL. I use the term "soul" advisedly to indicate that the familiar European concepts of "souls" and "spirits" are inadequate for precise ethnographical description. In a very general way these Zinacanteco "souls" signify that the people are "animistic" in the Tylorian sense of the term; they also signify local manifestations of widespread Middle American beliefs about *tonalism* and *nagualism* that have been discussed by Foster (1944), Correa (1960), and Aguirre Beltran (1963), and more particularly for the highlands of Chiapas by Holland (1961) and Villa Rojas (1963). But these statements tell us little about the complex and subtle meanings implied in the Zinacanteco concepts. Furthermore, there is still a vast amount of ethnographic confusion in the usage of these two Middle American terms. Both *tona* and *nagual* are Nahuatl terms, and neither is used when the Zinacantecos are speaking Tzotzil among themselves. As Correa points out, nagual has come to mean two things in a confusing way in the literature—both the "guardian" or "familiar spirit" and a person who transforms himself into an animal to harm another person (1960: 42). Finally, neither tona nor nagual defines precisely the Zinacanteco concept of CH'ULEL, or CHANUL (Vogt 1965c).

The Inner Soul

The Zinacanteco CH'ULEL is an inner, personal "soul," located in the heart of each person; it is also found in the blood which is known to be connected with the heart. This soul is placed in the body of an unborn embryo by the ancestral gods.

This Zinacanteco soul is composed of thirteen parts; a person may lose one or more and require a special curing ceremony to recover them. But the soul, while temporarily divisible into parts in the various kinds of "soul-loss" that can occur, is believed to be eternal and indestructible. At the point of death the soul leaves the body. According to some informants, it is associated with the grave for a period of time corresponding to the length of the deceased person's life on earth, then rejoins the "pool" or "supply" of souls that are kept by the ancestral gods, to be utilized for another person. While the person is alive, the soul as a unit can leave the body during sleep and go visiting with the souls of other Zinacantecos or with the deities. It can also "drop out" of the body temporarily in periods of intense excitement, such as sexual intercourse. One of the most consistent behavior patterns is a mother's sweeping with her shawl the ground on which she has been sitting to gather up all the parts of the soul of her infant. Parents are expected to treat a small child with utmost care and affection, lest its soul, not yet used to its new receptacle, become frightened and leave. One of the major purposes of baptism is to "fix" the soul more firmly in the child's body.

Even baptism does not prevent "soul-loss" (SHI'EL) from occuring through fright later in life (see Gillin 1948). There are many readily recognized causes for soul-loss, such as falling down suddenly, seeing a demon on a dark night. The Zinacantecos still relate vividly how a large number of people experienced soul-loss when the first aircraft swept low over Zinacantan about twenty years ago; apparently the shamans were busy gathering up pieces of souls for weeks following this event! At a more profound level soul-loss is believed caused by the ancestral gods, who punish bad behavior by making a person fall down, or, more dramatically, by sending a lightning bolt to knock out one or more parts of the soul; or to an evil person who performs witchcraft ritual in a cave to "sell" one or more parts of a victim's soul to the Earth Lord, who uses the victim as a servant.

Without all thirteen parts of the soul, a person cannot be healthy; he feels or possesses "sickness" (CHAMEL). A shaman must be summoned for diagnosis and curing. The diagnostic procedure involves "pulsing" (PIK CH'ICH') of the patient: when the shaman feels the pulse, the blood "talks" and provides messages which he can understand and interpret. If he determines that soul-loss has occurred he performs a ceremony called LOK'ESEL TA BALAMIL (to extract from the earth) to recover the lost parts of the soul and replace them in the patient's body.

The phenomenon of the soul is by no means restricted to the domain of human beings. Virtually everything that is important and valuable to Zinacantecos possesses a soul: domesticated plants, such as maize, beans, and squash; salt (which possesses a very strong soul); houses and household fires; wooden crosses erected on sacred mountains, inside caves, and beside waterholes; saints whose "homes" are inside the Catholic churches; musical instruments used in their ceremonies; all of the various deities in the Zinacanteco pantheon. The ethnographer in Zinacantan soon learns that the most important interaction going on in the universe is not between persons nor between persons and material objects, but rather between souls inside these persons and material objects.

The Animal Spirit Companion

The Zinacanteco CHANUL is a kind of "animal spirit companion" or "spiritual alter ego" that lives in the majestic volcano called BANKILAL MUK'TA VITS (Senior Large Mountain) east of Zinacantan Center. A series of supernatural corrals containing about 8000 animal spirit companions, one for each person in Zinacantan, are located inside the mountain. One corral contains jaguars, a second coyotes, a third ocelots, and a fourth smaller animals such as opossums (see Chapter 17 for details).

These animal spirit companions are watered, fed, and cared for by the ancestral gods, under the general supervision of the supernatural Senior Alcalde, who is the celestial counterpart of the highest ranking member of the religious hierarchy in Zinacantan. His house is located inside the mountain, and his household cross is the shrine that Zinacantecos visit for ceremonies on top of the volcano. Assisting the Senior Alcalde in the care of the animal spirit companions are mayores of two types: HPETOMETIK (literally, the "embracers") and the HKUCHOMETIK (literally, "the carriers"). (These same types of supernatural assistants are reported for Larrainzar, where Holland [1963: 113] describes how the animal spirit companions of more important people care for those of less important people.)

The animal spirit companions of Zinacantan are let out to "graze" each day to the south, and the corrals are believed to have gates toward the south. The ancestral gods "transform" them into cows and sheep so they can graze as far as Totolapa in the lowlands. In the evening they are transformed back into their wild animal forms and herded safely into their corrals.

The connection between people and their animal spirit companions is made in the Zinacanteco belief system by the concept that each person and his animal spirit companion share the same soul. Thus, when the ancestral gods install a soul in the embryo of a Zinacanteco, they simultaneously install the same soul in the embryo of an animal. Similarly, the moment a Zinacanteco baby is born, a supernatural jaguar, coyote, ocelot, or other animal is born. Throughout life, whatever happens of note to the Zinacanteco happens to his animal spirit companion, and vice versa. If an animal spirit companion, let out of the corral and left to wander alone in the forest, is injured or shot, its Zinacanteco "companion" feels the same injury. If the animal spirit companion is neglected by the ancestral deities and allowed to leave the corral, a Zinacanteco is in mortal danger. Such a state may also be diagnosed by the "pulsing" procedure of a shaman, who must proceed with dispatch to perform the proper ceremony asking the pardon of the ancestral gods and persuading them to round up the lost animal spirit companion of the patient and replace it in the supernatural corral.

Ordinarily, sometime during childhood a Zinacanteco discovers what kind of animal spirit he has, usually receiving this knowledge in a dream. His soul, able to leave his mortal body during sleep, may visit the ancestral deities inside the mountain containing the supernatural corrals, and there "see," "recognize," and "visit" with his animal spirit companion. Although informants vary regarding the animals that can be spirit companions, all are "wild"; none are the domestic animals imported with the Spanish conquest, such as sheep, horses, mules, or chickens.

The following creatures and birds have been elicited as potential animal spirit companions (CHANULETIK):

BOLOM	jaguar	CHUCH	squirrel
ʔOK'IL	coyote	SABEN	weasel
TSAHAL BOLOM	puma	NAPACH'	raccoon
TEʔ BOLOM	ocelot	SHIK	hawk
TS'UTS'UNCHAB	anteater	ʔICHIN	horned(?) owl
ʔUCH	opossum	SHOCH'	screech(?) owl
VET	fox		

Most Zinacantecos believe that the "souls" are transmitted in the patrilineage in the same way that first names are handed down. They cannot pass from father to children, since each soul stays at the grave of a dead person for the period corresponding to the length of a person's life on earth. Hence, if a young child dies, the ancestral gods can use the soul and its associated animal spirit companion quite soon again. But if an old person dies, it is many years before the name and soul can be used again. When they are used, however, they are placed with a new member of the same patrilineage. And this transmission of the name and soul makes the new member of the patrilineage a "replacement" or "substitute" (K'ESHOLIL) for the departed ancestor (see Montagu and Hunt 1962 for comparative data on other Chiapas communities).

This concept of a "replacement" is replicated in many other parts of the social and ritual system. For example, when a black chicken is sacrificed during a curing ceremony, it is a "replacement" for the patient to prevent the ancestral gods from carrying away his soul. When an incoming cargoholder in the religious hierarchy takes over his duties from the outgoing cargoholder, he is the "replacement" in this ceremonial system.

Souls, Animal Spirits, and Social Control

The beliefs in the concepts of CH'ULEL and CHANUL are clearly related to social control in Zinacantan. Anything that stirs up the wrath of the ancestral gods against a particular Zinacanteco can lead quickly and directly to punishment by causing the person to experience some form of soul-loss, or, in more serious cases, by having his animal spirit companion turned outside its corral to wander alone and uncared for in the woods. The types of deviant behavior that can lead to these troubles include, significantly enough, the breaking of the important moral codes or the flouting of the central values of Zinacantan: fighting with or mistreating kinsmen; failure to accept community service as a cargoholder in the religious hierarchy; failure to care for maize fields properly; mishandling of the maize after it is brought into the home; failure to wash regularly and change into clean clothes; failure to pay "taxes" for fiestas.

Supernaturally caused sicknesses require immediate curing ceremonies to appease the wrath of the ancestral deities; these in turn have important social and economic effects. In the prayers to the ancestral gods asking for pardon, the patient freely expresses his guilt and is quite obviously relieved psychologically after the ceremony is over. The ritual patterns require the cooperation and good will of the kinsmen with whom the patient may have been quarreling, and stress the respect, the sharing, and the proper etiquette that should always be displayed between individuals in Zinacanteco society.

The economic effects are also important. If the patient is a wealthy man, who has failed to accept or to perform properly a cargo duty, the costs of the ceremony in chickens, rum, incense, and food have the immediate result of relieving him of his surplus. Therefore, if he has not expended his surplus, as he should, in community service, it is in effect "confiscated." For by the time he finishes a series of curing ceremonies, he is economically deprived as much as if he had served his cargo duty in the first place.

Zinacantan, like other closed corporate communities described by Wolf (1955), displays patterns of "institutionalized envy". This envy is frequently focused on one man's possession of what Zinacantecos define as excessive wealth that is not used for community service, such as taking a cargo. Even if the ancestral gods do not punish the wealthy man, his fellow Zinacantecos will, by gossiping about how the wealthy man must have acquired his riches in an unethical way—by selling souls to the Earth Lord. When gossip reaches a sufficient level of seriousness, the wealthy man (who fails to pass cargos) begins to worry about his own actions and his own health. Necessary to the recovering of good health and good relations with his fellow Zinacantecos, will be a series of expensive curing ceremonies that will relieve him of his surplus (distributing it among other Zinacantecos as well as to San Cristóbal shopkeepers) and re-establish him in the eyes of his neighbors as a good (no longer excessively rich and to-be-envied) man.

Souls, Animal Spirits, and the Natural Environment

The concept of the animal spirit companion relates Zinacantecos in a fundamental way to the world of nature. In Tzotzil a clear distinction is made between the areas that are used and controlled by human beings (NAETIK), such as the house, the patios, the waterholes, and the fields, and areas not under human control (TE?TIK), such as the wild wooded slopes of the Chiapas mountains (Acheson 1962: 38). All of the animal spirit companions are CHONETIK TA TE?TIK (animals of the forest). All of the areas designated as NAETIK are enclosed ritually by ceremonial circuits or processions. Beyond these areas are the wooded, mountainous areas where the "animals of the forest" roam and whence come various birds of evil omen to warn the Zinacantecos of impending sickness and death brought from the "forest." The ceremonial circuits annually reaffirm this basic dichotomy in the Zinacanteco world. The concept of the animal spirit companion connects these dichotomous parts of their universe (Acheson, personal communication, 17 November 1963) by creating an intimate relation between the lives of men and the lives of wild animals (compare Lévi-Strauss 1964). In these same high mountains dwell the ancestral gods who survey the affairs of their Zinacanteco descendants and exercise maximal control over their behavior by either care or neglect of the animal spirit companions upon whose well-being the Zinacantecos absolutely depend for continuing survival.

17 / Sacred Places

The visible sacred world of the Zinacantecos is characterized by strong emphasis upon two features of the natural topography of highland Chiapas—VITS (mountain) and CH'EN (cave)—and two types of man-made constructions—KRUS (cross) and KALVARIO (literally, "calvary," but signifying special types of cross shrines).

VITS is a Tzotzil variant of a proto-Mayan word WITZ that still occurs in all Mayan languages (Kaufman 1964: 110) and designates mountain (or hill). CH'EN is likewise a Tzotzil variant of a proto-Mayan word still found in many Mayan languages and designating natural holes in the ground, whether these be caves, limestone sinks, or waterholes. Quite apart from their economic significance for the Zinacantecos, such as places for gathering wood or sources of water, these two basic features of the Chiapas landscape have assumed extraordinary sacred significance. For a VITS is often the home of an ancestral god and a CH'EN is a means of communication with YAHVAL BALAMIL, or "earth god" (see Thompson 1959 for comparative data from other Maya areas).

When Zinacantecos say KRUS they are obviously using a loan word from the Spanish word for cross, *cruz*. But, while to a Ladino the actual KRUS may appear to be a contemporary replica of the classic Christian cross, it is not to the Zinacantecos. Rather, it symbolizes a "doorway" or means of communication with either the ancestral gods who live in the mountains or the earth god who lives beneath the surface of the earth. Similarly, when Zinacantecos say KALVARIO they are using a loan word from the Spanish word for "calvary," *calvario*. But, although this type of cross shrine may look like a contemporary replica of crosses on Calvary in far away Jerusalem, it proves to have no such meaning to the Zinacantecos, but symbolizes, instead, the particular place where one goes to make suitable offerings and prayers to ancestral deities for the various social units (snas, waterhole groups, hamlets) in the Zinacanteco social system.

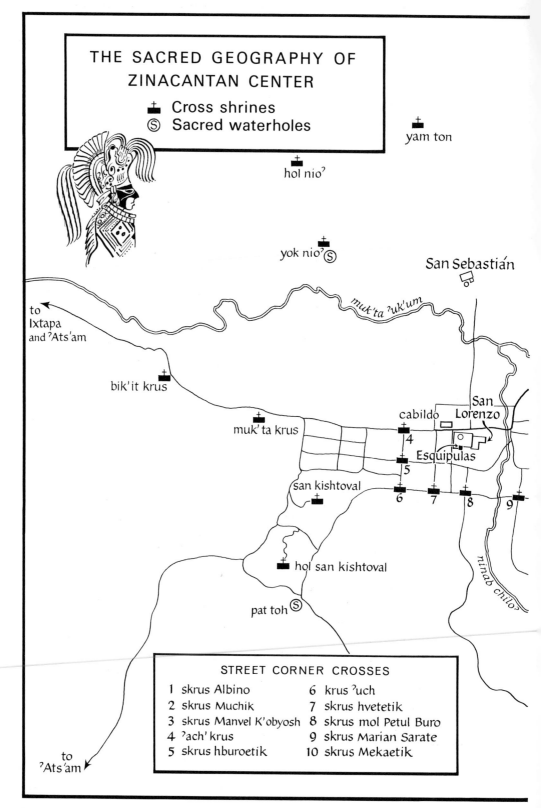

THE SACRED GEOGRAPHY OF ZINACANTAN CENTER

‡ Cross shrines
Ⓢ Sacred waterholes

yam ton

hol nio'

yok nio' Ⓢ

San Sebastián

muk'ta 'uk'um

to
Ixtapa
and 'Ats'am

bik'it krus

muk'ta krus

cabildo

San
Lorenzo

4

Esquipulas

5

san kishtoval

6   7   8   9

niñab chilo'

hol san kishtoval

pat toh Ⓢ

STREET CORNER CROSSES

1 skrus Albino	6	krus 'uch
2 skrus Muchik	7	skrus hvetetik
3 skrus Manvel K'obyosh	8	skrus mol Petul Buro
4 'ach' krus	9	skrus Marian Sarate
5 skrus hburoetik	10	skrus Mekaetik

to
'Ats'am

Map 8

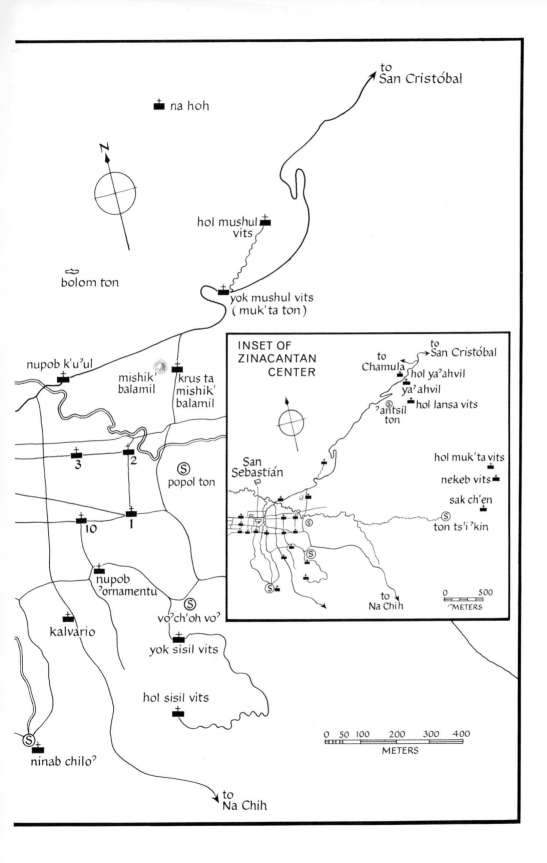

na hoh

N

to
San Cristóbal

hol mushul
vits

bolom ton

yok mushul vits
(muk' ta ton)

nupob k'u'ul

mishik'
balamil

krus ta
mishik'
balamil

3   2

popol ton

(S)

INSET OF
ZINACANTAN
CENTER

to
Chamula

to
San Cristóbal

hol ya'ahvil

ya'ahvil

'antsil
ton

hol lansa vits

hol muk'ta vits

nekeb vits

sak ch'en

(S)

ton ts'i'kin

San
Sebastián

(S)

10   1

(S)

(S)

to
Na Chih

0   500

METERS

nupob
'ornamentu

(S)

vo'ch'oh vo'

kalvario

yok sisil vits

hol sisil vits

(S)

ninab chilo'

to
Na Chih

0 50 100   200   300   400

METERS

The Mountains of Zinacantan

The names and locations of the sacred mountains that surround Zinacantan Center or are associated closely with it may be found in Map 8, "The Sacred Geography of Zinacantan Center." These are tribal mountains in the sense that the ancestral gods who are believed to reside inside them are worshiped by Zinacantecos from all hamlets. Many are impressive in size and appearance (Figures 119, 121) such as BANKILAL MUK'TA VITS (Senior Large Mountain), ʔITS'INAL MUK'TA VITS (Junior Large Mountain), SISIL VITS (Santa Cecilia Mountain) or MUSHUL VITS. But others seem more like "hills" from our point of view. The very important KALVARIO (see Figure 120) is more of a hill, or a step on the way to the top of the higher mountain, Santa Cecilia, located behind it. San Cristóbal Mountain has neither the majestic height nor the steep slopes of the Senior Large Mountain or Santa Cecilia, yet it has profound sacred importance. Each "mountain" is classified as male or female and has special interior features and functions. Table 11, which lists these, includes not only the mountains in or near Zinacantan Center but also the tribal mountains outside the valley in which the ceremonial center is located.

Table 11. Principal sacred places of Zinacantan

Name	Translation	Male/ Female	Interior features and ritual functions
BANKILAL MUK'TA VITS (or ʔOSHYOKET)	Senior Large Mountain (or Three Hearth-Stones)	M	House of the most senior ancestral god; corrals for animal spirit companions
ʔITS'INAL MUK'TA VITS	Junior Large Mountain	M	Large lake of water; site for rain-making ceremonies
SAN KISHTOVAL	San Cristóbal Mountain	M	House of ancestral god; also has inn for visiting gods
MUSHUL VITS	?	F	House of ancestral god; large bell was found in hole on top
SISIL VITS	Santa Cecilia Mountain	F	House of ancestral god; has lake, some say three lakes in layers
KALVARIO	Calvary	M	Meeting place of ancestral gods; major place for sacrificing chickens

Table 11. Principal sacred places of Zinacantan (continued)

Name	Translation	Male/ Female	Interior features and ritual functions
MISHIK' BALAMIL	Navel of World	?	Center of Zinacanteco Universe
NINAB CHILO?	?	F	House where women who carry and care for small children live; also where laundry women live; clothes for patients in curing ceremonies washed here
NIO?	?	F	Bathing place for ancestral gods
YA?AHVIL	?	F	Unknown
NA HOH	House of the Raven	M	House where ancestral gods and ravens live
YAM TON	Pain-reliever Rock	M	House of ancestral god
LANSA VITS	Spear Mountain	M	House of ancestral god
SAK CH'EN	White Cave		Lower doorway to house inside Senior Large Mountain
NEKEB VITS	Shoulder of Mountain		Corner of house inside Senior Large Mountain
LACH CHIKIN	Pricked-up Ears	M	House of ancestral god; contains cornet and large drum left by San Sebastián
NAKLEB ?OK	Turtle Home	M	House of ancestral god; like an "office" for LACH CHIKIN
?ISAK'TIK	Potato Patch	M	House of ancestral god; place to go for curing ceremonies if Senior Large Mountain fails
CH'UL TON	Divine Rock	M	Doorway to ?ISAK'TIK
TS'AHOB PIK'	?	F	Where in mythological times women were bathing vaginas when the soldiers came

119. Aerial view of MUSHUL VITS, with Zinacantan Center in the background

120. Aerial view of KALVARIO (lower right), with SISIL VITS at the upper left

121. A shaman praying for the soul of a patient at a mountain shrine; in the background is Santa Cecilia—note its resemblance in shape to Ancient Maya pyramids

Some of the types of cross shrines that occur at the feet and summits of these sacred mountains are drawn in Figure 122. In each case there is a walled offertory in front of the altar where candles are lighted (inside the walls to prevent the wind from blowing out the flame), pine needles are laid down, and incense burned. Sacrificial chickens offered as K'ESHOLIL (substitute) for the soul of the patient are most commonly left in the special structure on the western side of KALVARIO, but they may also be left for the ancestors at MUSHUL VITS and at Santa Cecilia Mountain, depending upon the particular ritual practices of the shaman officiating at the curing ceremony.

122. Some cross shrines in Zinacantan

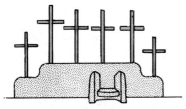

Senior Large Mountain
(BANKILAL MUK'TA VITS)

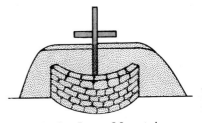

Junior Large Mountain
('ITS'INAL MUK'TA VITS)

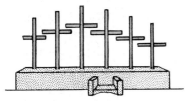

San Cristóbal Mountain
(SAN KISHTOVAL)
(foot)

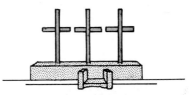

Santa Cecilia Mountain
(SISIL VITS)
(foot)

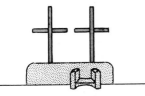

MUSHUL VITS
(foot)

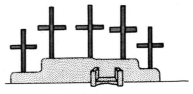

MUSHUL VITS
(top)

Figure 122, continued

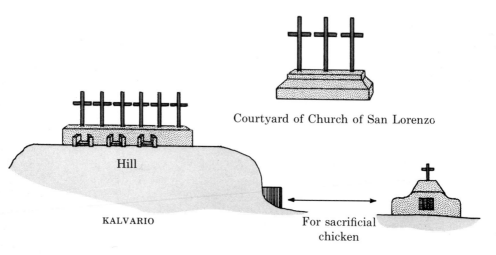

Courtyard of Church of San Lorenzo

Hill

KALVARIO

For sacrificial
chicken

Reports on the sacred geography of Senior Large Mountain (Figure 123) vary, since each shaman whose soul is summoned in a dream to visit the inside of this mountain supplies a different version. Some report only one corral for the animal spirit companions; others report several. Telesh Komis Lotriko, an active shaman from Paste?, had this to report about the interior of the Senior Large Mountain:

> There is a house inside like a Ladino house. It has many rooms, four rooms. In one room is the Senior Alcalde with all the shamans seated along two sides of a large table. They all have their wives with them to cook tortillas and give food to the people. On the north side of the house, there are fruit trees. They get their water from a fountain. On the east side of the house there are four corrals. The first corral by the house has jaguar animal spirit companions; the second one has coyotes; the third one has ocelots and TS'UTS'UNCHABETIK (anteaters); the fourth one has opossums and foxes. Squirrels and weasels run around loose in the courtyard. There is also a large tree in the court-yard in which sits a hawk and two types of owls. There is also a cross in front of the house. This is the house cross of the Senior Alcalde and is the cross you see on top the mountain. The corrals open to the south, and the animal spirit companions are taken out to be fed each day.

I tried to persuade Telesh to draw his conceptions of the supernatural structures inside the mountain. He said he could not draw and preferred to tell me about them. Figure 124 is what I drew, following his step-by-step instructions.

123. BANKILAL MUK'TA VITS

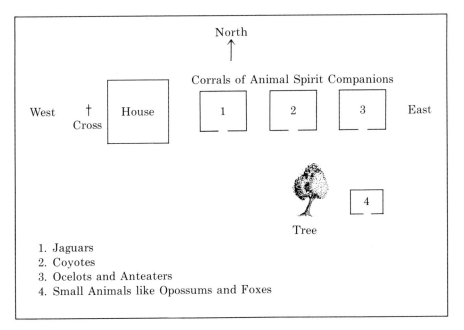

124. The interior of Senior Large Mountain

125. ʔITS'INAL MUK'TA VITS, where the shamans go for rain-making ceremonies (left-hand peak of mountain on the right)

Beyond the municipio borders of Zinacantan to the east lies a special mountain called Junior Large Mountain, ʔITS'INAL MUK'TA VITS, southwest of Teopisca and above a Ladino ranch called Chenekultik (Figure 125). Like its "older brother," it is also a very impressive mountain rising at least 1500 feet above the surrounding terrain (see Map 1). Special HʔILOLETIK make pilgrimages to this mountain by a route passing from Hteklum, through ʔElan Voʔ, and on past Totolapa, to perform rain-making rituals. The top of the mountain, is an important archaeological site, with at least six terraces, 20 to 30 meters wide, near the top and two square rock platforms, one above the other, on the summit. The ancient walls are exposed, and the Zinacantecos have used the rocks from the old ruins to construct an enclosure around their cross on the west side of the top platform (see Figure 122). The enclosure is about a meter and a half high and inside a single wooden cross has been converted into the usual three-cross arrangement by the addition of pine boughs on its arms.

Caves and Waterholes

Although what we could call "waterholes," "limestone sinks," and "caves" have greatly differing economic uses, they are classified together and treated ritually much the same in the ceremonial life of Zinacantan. "Waterholes" are the main sources of household and livestock water; if the "limestone sinks" are not too precipitous, small plots of corn may be planted in them; "caves" give shelter during rainstorms. But in the sacred geography all these CH'ENETIK are "openings" in the earth's crust, hence means of communication with the Earth Lord. Most of them near Zinacanteco dwellings contain cross shrines and are included in ceremonial circuits of one or another type of K'IN KRUS.

The important waterholes from which water is taken for curing ceremonies, shown on Map 8, are: VOʔCH'OH VOʔ (female); POPOL TON (male); NINAB CHILOʔ (female); PAT TOH (male); NIOʔ (female); YAʔAHVIL (female); and TON TS'IʔKIN (male). Just as the ancestral gods living in their nearby mountains are believed to bathe in these waterholes, so the same water is used to bathe both the patient and his "substitute" in curing ceremonies, to wash the sacred chests and clothes of the saints, and so on.

The CH'ENETIK are also important as the sources of lightning bolts and clouds. I have had a number of interesting conversations in which I have attempted to convince Zinacantecos that lightning does *not* come out of caves and go up into the sky and that clouds form in the air. One of these arguments took place in Pasteʔ as I stood on the rim with an informant, and we watched the clouds and lightning in a storm in the lowlands some thousands of feet below us. I finally had to concede, that, given the empirical evidence available to Zinacantecos living in their highland Chiapas terrain, their explanation does make sense. For, as the clouds formed rapidly in the air and then poured up and over the highland ridges in much the same way that the fog comes in from the Pacific and pours over the coastal range in northern California, they did give the appearance of coming up from caves on the slopes of the Chiapas highlands. Furthermore, since we were standing some thousands of feet above a tropical storm that developed in the late afternoon, I had to concede that it was difficult to tell whether the lightning was triggered off in the air and then struck downward to the ground, or was coming from the ground and going up into the air as the Zinacantecos believe. Given their premises and the evidences observable from day-to-day behavior of clouds and lightning, their beliefs were as understandable as mine.

Cross Shrines

Wooden structures in the form of the Christian cross appear in the following contexts in Zinacantan: a small cross about one foot high placed on top the tile or thatch roofs of houses; the KRUS TA TIʔ NA (house cross) varying in size, but usually about a meter high, placed in the patio outside the houses; the cross placed beside, usually above, a waterhole; the cross inside caves, usually at the back if the cave is shallow; the crosses placed at the feet and summits of mountain "residences" of the ancestral gods; crosses placed at the edges of parajes and around the edges of the ceremonial center (see Table 12 and Map 8); crosses placed on top of or, more importantly, in the courtyards or patios of churches; and crosses placed at heads of graves in the cemeteries.

Table 12. Principal cross shrines in Zinacantan Center

Name	Translation
BIK'IT KRUS	Small cross
MUK'TA KRUS	Large cross
SKRUS ʔALBINO	Cross of Albino (family)
SKRUS MUCHIK	Cross of Muchik (family)
SKRUS MANVEL K'OBYOSH	Cross of Manuel con Dios
ʔACH KRUS	New cross
SKRUS HBUROETIK	Cross of Burro (family)
KRUS ʔUCH	Opossum cross
SKRUS HVETETIK	Cross of Fox (family)
SKRUS MOL PETUL BURO	Old Man Pedro Burro's cross
SKRUS MARIAN SARATE	Mariano Zarate's cross
SKRUS MEKAETIK	Cross of Meka (family)

All of these crosses (except those on top of churches and houses) function as "doorways" or "entryways"—as means of communication with sacred places or as boundary-markers between significant units of social space in Zinacantan. The crosses on top of churches and houses that are so important in Christian theology and cosmology seem little emphasized; it is believed they "protect" the house or church, but they appear less important than the other types. On the other hand, the house patio, waterhole, cave, and mountain crosses are strongly emphasized and ritual attention is paid to them in recurring ceremonial circuits, they, in effect, relate people to deities, even in case of the house cross, since it is believed that ancestral gods are present at ceremonies performed in a house. The important crosses at edges of parajes and around the edges of the ceremonial center are also emphasized as boundary-markers of these important units of social space in Zinacantan. Again, ritual respects are paid them whenever a ceremonial pilgrimage passes in or out of a paraje, or in, out or around the edges of Zinacantan Center. Finally, the crosses at heads of graves are means of

126. A shrine with only two crosses converted into a three cross shrine by the addition of a pine bough to the left

communication or linkage between the living and the recently dead members of the domestic group and lineage.

For any kind of ritual activity a KRUS must be triple to be effective. Many cross shrines contain in fact only one wooden cross, as, for example, the house cross; some contain only two wooden crosses, as, for example, many shrines at the feet or summits of the sacred mountains. But they are ritually converted into a triple cross by the addition of pine boughs (STEK'EL TOH) at the sides of the one or two wooden crosses (Figure 126). Further, we have noted that when no wooden crosses exist at some place where a ritual must be performed (for example, a spot where a part of a soul has been lost), the three-cross combination can be created ritually by simply placing three pine boughs in the ground. This has led me to conclude that the wooden cross is for the Zinacantecos a handy structure on which to place the crucial pine boughs and flowers, and that it is the pine boughs and flowers that really provide the needed symbols.

When I initiated my field work in Zinacantan in 1957, I was shown the hill above Zinacantan Center containing a large and elaborate cross shrine and was told it was KALVARIO. Since at that point Zinacantan appeared to me to be a peasant community that had been converted to Catholicism in the 1500's, I was not surprised to find a "calvary" near the churches in the ceremonial center. Later I discovered that black chickens were left as a sacrifice by curing parties at this KALVARIO. I gradually learned that the ancestral gods are believed to have meetings at the KALVARIO just as officials meet at the Cabildo down in the center. By the second and third seasons, it had become more and more apparent that Zinacantecos were not Catholic peasants with a few Maya remnants left in the culture, but rather that they were Maya tribesmen with a thin veneer of Spanish Catholicism. But the final shock came when I discovered in 1960 that there is not a single KALVARIO in Zinacantan, but hundreds of them, located throughout the municipio in all the parajes. Presently, we understand the Zinacanteco KALVARIO as a special type of cross shrine where particular groups of ancestral gods are believed to meet, deliberate about the affairs of their living descendants, and wait for offerings. It has also become clear that they symbolize units of social structure in the system in relation to ancestral deities who were responsible for these units. The original KALVARIO I was shown proved to represent the meeting place of the tribal (or all-municipio) ancestral gods; the others represent in each case a sna or waterhole group. Thus, the KALVARIO shrines mirror the social system, one with apparently deep roots in the Maya past.

Ceremonial Circuits

An important patterned feature of Zinacanteco ritual life may be seen in the ceremonial circuits that take groups of worshipers to these sacred places. Most ceremonial circuits move counterclockwise—whether these be K'IN KRUS participants or cargoholders who proceed from one sacred spot to another and then return to the place where the ceremony began. The evidence is less clear for curing parties since they display a great deal of variation in their movements around Zinacantan Center. Many go to San Cristóbal Mountain, MUSHUL VITS, Santa Cecilia Mountain, and KALVARIO in that order (Vogt 1961). But fewer or more mountains may be included, and the party may also visit the churches and pray to the saints; hence, depending upon the customs of a particular shaman as well as considerations of convenience, these curing party circuits may move clockwise or follow crisscross patterns. However, the data are invariant with respect to the circuits of the cargoholders (for example, the "rounds" of the alféreces), the K'IN KRUS groups, the agricultural ritual groups, and the new-house-dedication ceremonies (see Chapters 20 and 21).

Why the movement should be counterclockwise is a mystery to us, but it is clearly the preferred direction of ritual movement. It also agrees with data on ceremonial circuits from other Maya communities, both ancient and modern. Evidence is provided in the descriptions of the Uayeb rites depicted in the Dresden Codex and described by Landa (Tozzer 1941) for sixteenth-century Yucatán. A recent paper by Michael D. Coe (1965) provides a brilliant analysis of the possible relation of these rites to ancient Maya community structure and makes clear that the ceremonial movements were counterclockwise. Where there is evidence, most ceremonial circuits in contemporary Maya communities move in the same direction (Vogt and Ruz 1964: 391). Alfonso Villa Rojas has suggested (personal communication, November 24, 1964) that the Maya ceremonial circuit might be derived from observations of the wheeling of the constellations in a counterclockwise direction around the Pole Star. While this may have provided the model in the natural world, it does not explain why countless other societies (for example, the Navaho) in the Northern Hemisphere witnessing the same movement of constellations chose a clockwise direction for their ceremonial circuit.

The functions of the circuits appear to involve a set of boundary-maintaining mechanisms in the Zinacanteco social system. When groups of cargoholders make a circuit around Zinacantan Center they are symbolically saying (on behalf of all Zinacantecos), "this is our sacred center through which the holy river flows and around which live our ancestral gods watching over and guarding all of us". When the members of a water-hole group make a circuit that involves the waterhole and the sacred places around the waterhole, they are symbolically saying, "this is our waterhole." When the members of a sna make the K'IN KRUS circuit around the lands they have inherited from their patrilineal ancestors, they are saying symbolically, "these are our lands." When a circuit is made around a maize field it likewise marks off the boundary symbolically, or when a counterclockwise circuit is made around to four corners of a new house, this also says symbolically, "here is our new house in which we are going to live." Hence each circuit symbolically designates property rights and marks off crucial social spaces in the Zinacanteco world.

18 / Ritual Symbols

Certain symbols provide a sacred context for any ritual activity in Zinacantan involving communication with the ancestral gods, Earth Lord, or the VASHAKMEN. These symbolic elements define the situation and set the stage for the performance of "ritual" (as opposed to "technical") activity. Each day Zinacantecos perform many "technical" activities, such as hoeing corn, weaving cloth, and herding sheep. Although these may involve taboos of various types, they are clearly differentiated from "ritual" activities, in which appropriate offerings are to be made to supernaturals (Frake 1964). The three symbolic elements are flowers (NICHIM), incense (POM), and rum liquor (POSH). A fourth, VOBETIK, the playing of music, is added to particular ritual events.

"Flowers"

Although we often gloss NICHIM as "flower," following the lead of Spanish-speaking Zinacantecos who describe these plants as *flores*, it is clear that the Tzotzil category NICHIM covers a quite different set of plants from those we usually refer to as "flowers" (Laughlin 1962). It includes not only flowers, such as TSAHAL NICHIM (red geranium), but also the young, freshly grown tops of pine trees (either from the BATS'I TOH or the ʔAHAN TOH) and pine needles (SHAK TOH) from the BATS'I TOH tree as well as a variety of other plants. In point of fact, except for red geraniums and white roses, the category NICHIM, as used in setting up the sacred context for rituals, includes more non-flowers than flowers.

The Tzotzil word TOH may be glossed as "pine," and the Zinacantecos distinguish three types of pine that are important in their ceremonial life. BATS'I TOH, literally, "the real pine" (called *ocote* by the Ladinos), is a variety of white pine (*Pinus montezumae* Lamb), apparently the most common one in the municipio of Zinacantan. It produces wood with a great deal of pitch, and hence is used by both Indians and Ladinos in small, slender slivers for lighting fires, especially when firewood is green or wet. It was used for torches in the days before kerosene lanterns and flashlights, for, if the point of an ocote is lighted, it will continue to burn, even when held upright. The BATS'I TOH provides four types of greenery that are of crucial importance for ritual. One type, small 3- to 4-foot boughs cut from the tops of these pine trees (TEK'EL TOH), is used to decorate the main stem of the cross. If the shrine contains three or more crosses, a TEK'EL TOH is tied with palm to each cross. If the shrine contains only one cross, it is conceptually transformed into three by tying a TEK'EL TOH upright to each of the two cross arms. If the shrine contains only two crosses (as at the foot of MUSHUL VITS), a third is added by propping up a TEK'EL TOH with rocks beside the two crosses (see Figure 126). If there are no wooden crosses, a shrine can still be constructed simply by sticking three boughs of BATS'I TOH in the ground. These arrangements are usually prepared in advance of the arrival of whatever group is going to perform ritual at the shrine. For example, for the procession of a curing party from one sacred mountain to another the mayores always either cut the TEK'EL TOH in advance, and tie it on the cross shrines then, or leave it beside the trail to be placed on the shrines before the arrival of the shaman, the patient, and the rest of the group. The important point is that these TEK'EL TOH decorations are always on the cross shrines *before* the shaman arrives—the ritual stage is set for communication with the supernaturals.

The second type of greenery from the BATS'I TOH are the long, thin needles stripped by hand from the boughs and called SHAK TOH (*juncia* by the Ladinos). SHAK TOH is placed around the bases of cross shrines of all types just before candles are lighted and also placed on the floors of all the chapels. For proper communication with the supernaturals, people must stand or kneel on SHAK TOH. This custom is also found in Ladino culture in San Cristóbal where whole houses, patios, and sometimes even whole streets are spread with juncia for festive occasions like weddings. It is important that the needles be pulled from BATS'I TOH; none of the other types covers floors as satisfactorily.

BATS'I TOH also provides the material for the wands used by shamans to summon lost parts of the soul (CH'ULEL) of a patient. Sometimes it is mixed with oak boughs when the wand is used for calling the soul and for "brushing" the illness from the patient's body at each of the mountain cross shrines.

The fourth use of BATS'I TOH is to decorate the courtyard in front of the church of San Lorenzo for certain fiestas—San Lorenzo, Virgen del Rosario, Esquipulas, San Sebastián, Cuarto Viernes, and Sagrado Corazón —when small pines are cut and set in the ground around the yard. These are called TS'UNBAL TE?.

The second important species of pine is the ?AHAN TOH (*Pinus oocarpa* Schiede), which is closely related to the BATS'I TOH but has darker bark and shorter, thicker needles. Boughs about a foot long are always cut from the freshly grown tops of these trees to be used in curing ceremonies at the mountain shrines. They are called NI? TOH (literally, "top of pine"), and three are required for each shrine. They are either placed upright against the base of the shrine at the back of the offertory just before the candles are lighted, or they may be placed on the TEK'EL TOH in the bundle along with the red geraniums, laurel boughs, and other plants. In some parajes— such as ?Apas, where BATS'I TOH is now scarce—the ritually used pine needles, SHAK TOH, are now pulled from the ?AHAN TOH.

It is not surprising that most of the small pines near the dwellings of the Zinacantecos look stripped, as whole small trees and tops of large trees are continually cut with machetes for ritual use.

The third species of pine of ritual importance is called K'UK' TOH, or *pinavete* in Spanish, and has been identified as *Pinus chiapensis* (Martinez) *Andresen*. It is used to construct the crèche (LECHOPAT) where the two Christ Children—BANKILAL and ?ITS'INAL— are kept during the Christmas season, and for the construction of crosses and of the sacred boxes kept in mayordomos' houses.

Once the various pine boughs and pine needles have been properly placed on the shrine, the most important flower—a bundle of red geraniums (TSAHAL NICHIM)—is added just before the major prayer begins. To this is often added TSIS ?UCH (laurel leaves), KRUS ?ECH' (a type of bromeliad called *tecolúmete* in Spanish), NI? K'OS (*Synardisia venosa* [Mast.] *Lundell*), as well as white rose petals, which are sprinkled around the base of the shrine (Figure 127).

Incense

Not only must the TI? NA (literally, "door") be readied with the "flowers," but POM must also be burning in a censer for effective communication with the supernaturals. The censer is called a YAV ?AK'AL (literally, "container for burning embers"), and the incense that is burned is of two types: BEK'TAL POM, in forms of nodules of resin, and TE?EL POM, in the form of chips of wood. These types of incense may come from one of two trees,

127. A shaman's assistant ties a bundle of red geraniums on a cross decorated with pine boughs

BATS'I POM (*Bursera* excelsa [HBK.] Engl.), or ʔACH'EL POM (*Bursera bipinnata* [DC.] Engl.), that grow from Guadalupe Shukun on down to the Rio Grijalva in Tierra Caliente. The Zinacantecos much prefer BATS'I POM (real incense) to ʔACH'EL POM. Both types are burned together in the censer, and the incense must be burning at the TIʔ NA before the arrival of the ritual party. For example, a KRUS TA TIʔ NA must be decorated with TEK'EL TOH and SHAK TOH for a curing ceremony, with POM burning before it, when the shaman begins to light candles and pray.

Rum Liquor

With the "flowers" in place and incense burning, the participants must also be readied for communication with the supernaturals. Just as the most important communication or transaction among people (borrowing money, asking a man to serve as godfather, asking for a wife, and so on) is accompanied by the drinking of rum (POSH), so must transactions between men and their supernaturals be accompanied by the proper consumption of this liquor.

When a garrafón is purchased for a large ceremony, it is carefully "measured" into smaller containers by an old woman who is especially designated as the drink-measurer (HCH'OL VO?). The drink is then served to participants in a ritual by a drink-pourer (HP'IS VO?), who pours the liquor into a drinking glass or shot glass of appropriate size for the occasion. The rum may be diluted with half water to make it go further, and watered down even more if it is strong.

A highly patterned sequence of behavior is involved in a drinking ritual; this pattern is followed, with minor variations, whether the occasion is a small curing ceremony within a domestic group or a large change-of-office ceremony performed by the cargoholders in Zinacantan Center. The young man designated as drink-pourer is given the bottle of liquor and a shot glass. He pours a glass full (Figure 128) and hands it to the senior male present. The senior male accepts the glass (Figure 129) and engages in toasting and bowing-and-releasing behavior with all others present. He raises the shot glass and says, KICH'BAN "I receive" (followed by a kin term or name) to each person in rank order, receiving in return the reply, ?ICH'O, "Drink it." The toast is accompanied by bowing and releasing: each of the more junior persons bows his head, and is released as the senior touches the back of his right hand to the forehead of the junior. The senior man then drinks the shot of rum in one gulp (Figure 130), grimaces to show how strong the liquor is, spits on the floor, and returns the glass to the drink-pourer, who serves the next man in rank order. The second man repeats the toast and the bowing and releasing: he bows to the more senior man, but all others bow to him and are released. The sequence is continued, with the rank order following the age of the men, then, starting with the most senior woman present, until all have been served. Finally the drink-pourer takes a shot himself and goes through the toasting and bowing-and-releasing behavior. The rounds of drink normally proceed in threes. If the occasion is the presentation of a bottle of the liquor by a visitor asking for a loan of money, for example, the bottle should be consumed in three rounds. If the occasion is a ritual meal for a curing ceremony or a K'IN KRUS, normally there are three rounds of rum during the course of the meal. It is the duty of the drink-pourer to make careful calculations so that the entire bottle will be consumed in three rounds. While rank order is strictly observed in the serving of the liquor (as in countless other activities), each person present should receive equal amounts, regardless of rank.

129. Drinking ritual in progress at a fiesta
in Zinacantan Center

130. Shaman drinking a glass of rum

If two men are of equal age and cannot be distinguished in rank by service as shaman or cargoholder, they shake hands instead of bowing and
releasing. Informants report an earlier pattern in which two men of equal
rank clasped right hands, then bowed and released each other simultaneously; but we have never seen this in the field and apparently it is no
longer practiced.

There is an interesting pattern for handling excess rum when a person
becomes too intoxicated or does not wish to drink. Men typically carry an
empty bottle, along with a small metal funnel attached by buckskin to
their MORALETIK or net bags carried over their shoulders. They participate
in all the toasting and bowing-and-releasing behavior and touch the glass
to their lips but, instead of drinking the liquor they funnel the drink into
their empty bottles. Women do not carry this equipment, but pour the rum
into a bowl near the metates where they are working by the fire in the
house. Younger men are expected to drink on each round, but older men

may exercise the option of drinking less. As much as a full liter of drink is frequently collected by this method of pouring-off during an all-night ceremony; the rum so collected can be utilized by the person as he chooses.

Viewed in terms of its strictly patterned sequences of action and in terms of the flow of liquor, the drinking ritual provides a neat model of the social structure and dynamics of the situation (Wilson 1963).

Music

Music is not a part of curing ceremonies, new-house dedication ceremonies, or agricultural ceremonies performed for the maize-fields; but for K'IN KRUS ceremonies for the sna and waterhole group, the Year Renewal ceremonies, the Rain-Making ceremonies, and all important ceremonies performed by the cargoholders in Zinacantan Center, it is an essential ingredient.

During a major fiesta in the ceremonial center four types of music are often played simultaneously—an experience jarring to the nerves of visiting ethnographers but which from a Zinacanteco point of view adds gaiety and reflects the fiesta's importance. Two of these types of music are aspects of the more secular side of the fiesta: that blared over loudspeakers from Mexican records, played on battery-powered record players in the cantinas; and the rhythms of a brass band, hired usually in Chiapilla or in San Lucas, which plays in the kiosk while the men dance in the evenings. This band also accompanies groups of *voluntarios* (volunteers) who march from their homes to the church to light candles to the saints. The musicians walk up the trails from Chiapilla or San Lucas, but young Zinacantecos are appointed by the Presidente de la Junta de la Fiesta to carry the instruments for them. It is a startling experience to see a Zinacanteco in full fiesta regalia, new ribbons flowing from his hat, crossing the Pan American Highway with a tuba, for example, on the foot trail from San Lucas to Zinacantan Center!

The other two types of music are much more important ritually (Figure 131). The flute and drum group, always consisting of one flute player and two drums—a large one (Figure 132) and a small one (senior and junior)—accompanies processions of various types, both around Zinacantan Center during major fiestas and in the hamlets during K'IN KRUS ceremonies. Whether the music being played is aboriginal or more probably a type of colonial Spanish music is not known yet. Second (Figure 133, 134, 135), the violin, harp, and guitar combination (with the instruments ranked in that order) plays for certain ceremonial occasions, such as the rituals, including dancing, performed by the mayordomos, for the shamans when they are doing a K'IN KRUS, a Year Renewal, or a rain-making ceremony. This group sometimes also accompanies processions and plays while marching along. For some rituals, such as those of the alféreces, the harp is not used; the tunes required by those rituals reputedly are not adaptable to a harp. The instruments used are made by Chamulas in several of their hamlets (Arbuz 1963). Though based on Spanish Colonial models, they are but crude reflections of the originals. (For example, the violin has three pegs, but only two strings.) The music played appears derived from early Spanish Colonial tunes the Zinacantecos have learned since the Conquest (J. Haviland 1966 gives additional details on music).

131. Drum and flute players on left; violin, harp, and guitar players on right

132. Drum and flute players

133. Violin, harp, and guitar players tune up

134. Tuning up a guitar

135. A harpist tunes up; note small funnel on shoulder bag used for pouring off drinks into empty bottle

The Sacred Context for Rituals

With "flowers" on the cross shrines, incense smoking in a censer, rum consumed by the participants, and (in many instances) music played by Zinacanteco musicians, the stage is set for efficient communication with the supernaturals through appropriate prayers and offerings (Figure 136). The offerings are typically candles (the white wax ones being regarded as "tortillas," the tallow candles as "meat" for the gods) and black chickens, ✓ whose souls are eagerly consumed by the gods. As the candles burn down, it is believed that their souls are providing the necessary sustenance, along with the souls of the black chickens, for the supernaturals, who will be so pleased with these offerings that they will reciprocate by restoring the soul of a patient, by sending rain for a thirsty corn crop, or by eliminating any number of evils in Zinacantan.

Some questions remain to be answered about the specific content of elements of this sacred context. Why is it necessary to have three TEK'EL TOH on the cross shrine? Does this symbol derive from Spanish Catholic concepts of the three crosses on the original Calvary or is it related to an ancient Tzotzil belief that a person's animal spirit companion sits on a stool inside his corral in the mountain and that the stool is surrounded on three sides with pine boughs (Holland 1963: 11)? Is the use of pine needles (shared by Indians and Ladinos in the highlands of Chiapas) of Tzotzil or Spanish origin? What is the effect of burning incense? Does it provide "flavor" for the candles so the gods will accept them, as some claim, or does it purify ✓ space through which communication with the supernaturals is to take place as is suggested by the ritual censing to purify freshly washed clothes for a patient in a curing ceremony? Chickens have probably replaced turkeys as sacrificial offerings, but what did the Tzotzil use in place of candles in pre-Columbian times? Was it pine torches, or some kind of beeswax candles? Do the "flowers" placed on arches over shrines (as, for example, over the altars constructed in the mayordomos' houses) represent the flowered path of the sun across the sky? Could these altars possibly be small-scale models of the Zinacanteco view of the universe, with the sacred chest symbolizing the quadrilateral earth and the reed mats enclosing the underworld (Figure 137)? These are mere speculations. We still do not really understand the full dimensions of these symbols in Zinacantan.

136. A shaman prays for a patient and her husband before a fully decorated cross shrine

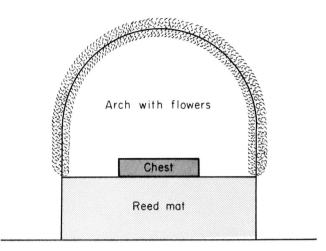

137. Mayordomo's altar

19 / Witchcraft

No generic Tzotzil term applies to the diverse witchcraft beliefs and practices, but for comparative convenience I shall group together a number of patterns in which an "evil" living person is believed to harm a fellow Zinacanteco through various ritual or supernatural methods. These "witchcraft" beliefs and practices have an important relationship to the social structure and to the psychological pressures experienced by individual Zinacantecos.

"Giving Illness"

The most common form of witchcraft, and certainly that most talked about by Zinacantecos is ʔAK' CHAMEL, literally "giving illness." In the Zinacanteco view, there are two kinds of shamans; while both types (TUK'IL Hʔ ILOL and Hʔ AK'CHAMEL Hʔ ILOL) know how to cure illness, the latter also knows how to give illness to others.

Shamans who can give illness are believed to maintain small crosses in secret caves near their hamlets, where they go to perform their evil rituals. Here they are believed to use small candles of the seven colors, which they cut in half and light upside down while they pray "against" their victims; in an alternative practice they cut the small candles into thirteen pieces and burn them as they say their evil prayers. The seven types of candles (all made by Ladinos in San Cristóbal) are white wax (SERA), black wax (ʔIK'), red wax (TSOH), yellow wax (K'ON), blue or green wax (YOSH), multi-colored wax (ʔORO), and tallow (SHEVU). (The same colors are used to erect a "candle curtain" to prevent à passing witch from "seeing" the decorated cross shrine and offerings of white wax and tallow candles in a curing ceremony—see Case 1 in Appendix V).

Once this ritual has been performed, the victim suffers "sickness" (CHAMEL) by one of two mechanisms. The "witch" may enter into communication with the Earth Lord and "sell" him the soul of the victim in a ritual called "selling to the earth" (CHONEL TA BALAMIL). Sometimes the witch sells the souls of an entire hamlet in exchange for a large sum of money, thereby "causing" epidemics. This type of witchcraft can also affect animals, since the soul of a mule or horse, for example, can also be sold to the Earth Lord, who is conceived as a greedy Ladino, always in need of human workers and pack animals for his enterprises. As long as the souls are "owned" by the Earth Lord, the person or animal will be sick and may even die.

To protect against witchcraft, a Zinacanteco must avoid an excess of wealth, social success, or acquisition of power; these make his fellows envious, and envy leads directly to witchcraft. To counteract a case of witchcraft, it is necessary to locate the witch who performed it and force him to return to his secret cave and "take back his words" or undo the "sale" of the soul that he made to the Earth Lord. Such cases often reach the court in Zinacantan Center, and one or more Cabildo officials are sent along to make sure the transaction is retracted. The following case illustrates this type of witchcraft:

> Marian de la Krus Chanmul, accompanied by Marian Peres Tanhol, both of Paste? went to the cave of ?AVANCH'EN to try to borrow money from the Earth Lord. Marian Chanmul presented the requisite candles and was asked by the Earth Lord what he desired. They bargained, and the Earth Lord asked for 300 souls in exchange for the money Marian Chanmul wanted. Later Marian Tanhol told a friend about the cave episode, and the friend, concerned that the shaman (Marian Chanmul) might bring an epidemic upon the community to provide 300 souls, went with another Paste? man to tell the Presidente in Zinacantan Center.
>
> The Presidente sent for Marian Chanmul and assembled the shamans of Zinacantan Center to pulse Marian to determine whether he was guilty. Despite his pleading innocent, he was found guilty and made to return to the cave to retract his evil bargain. The eldest shaman present, ?Antun Montejo, a shaman from Nabenchauk, and an Alcalde Juez accompanied him and watched him light candles and pray in front of a cross there. ?Antun Montejo then asked Marian if he had lit candles in any other spot. Marian replied that he had not, but Antun grabbed and pulsed him, and angrily accused him of lying.

Threatened with "legal" death there in the cave with witnesses if he refused to disclose the other place, Marian finally led the shamans deeper into the cave, through a narrow tunnel and beyond some water to a second cross, green and larger than the first. There Marian was made to light candles and pray again.

The shamans and Marian returned to the Cabildo in Zinacantan to report all that had happened. Marian was jailed and ?Antun Montejo advised that he should be kept there until he had made two more trips with candles to the cave. ?Antun was persuaded to accompany Marian each time to see that the correct rituals were performed, but asked that he be paid 5 pesos a day for the time he was spending. Marian paid him in advance, and Marian's relatives brought the necessary candles to him in jail.

The following day Marian returned to the cave, taking the candles, incense and some flowers, and accompanied by ?Antun, a Juez and two Mayores. He prayed at the first cross, and as they passed the water toward the second cross, the earth shook. Marian finished his ritual, and they all returned to Zinacantan Center. The Alcalde Juez related the earth's shaking to the President, who questioned Marian about its cause. Marian told him it signified the Earth Lord's releasing him from their agreement. After another night in jail and another trip to the cave to light candles and pray, Marian was returned to the Cabildo. ?Antun asked and received 10 pesos more from Marian for his time, and an *acta* was drawn up telling about the crime. Marian was then allowed to go free. (Jane F. Collier, Case 31, 28 March 1963)

A second mechanism by which the victim may actually receive the illness is for the witch to offer the victim food or rum containing "poisonous" substances. The witch may approach his victim at a fiesta and offer him a drink of rum; as he offers it he is smiling and pretending to be a friend, but "in his heart" he is repeating the prayer that he said in the cave to harm the victim. Zinacantecos therefore believe that one must be especially circumspect at fiestas or other large gatherings. It is important to inspect the rum and, if one sees that it is "bad," that it contains a substance that looks like nasal mucous, he merely touches it to his lips and asks the suspected witch to drink first. The poisonous substance may be placed in food or may be transmitted from the soul of the victim in a dream that brings the two souls into contact. One informant described how his father-in-law was destroyed by witchcraft in 1964:

Mol ?Antun, my father-in-law, was very content, because I had my cargo and everything was going well for us. Chep Peres Tanhol of ?Apas was envious of us and wanted to be an elder and in on important events in the hamlet. Chep has his cave near ?Apas on a mountain called SHK'UK'TE?, and there he performed the ritual of cutting up small candles and burning them. This act enabled the witch's soul to transmit illness to Mol ?Antun's soul, especially since Mol ?Antun was drunk at the time and his soul was not watching very well. Just before he died, Mol ?Antun said Chep Peres Tanhol was the one who had given him the sickness. (Vogt: Field Notes, 19 February 1965)

Other substances that can be transmitted this way include worms in rum or oranges, which cause more worms to grow in the victim's nose, and substances which cause balls of string or even lizards to grow in the victim's stomach. The following Cabildo case illustrates this type of witchcraft:

Marian ?Ernantis of Pat ?Osil was accused by Mikel de la Krus of "giving illness." The two men had shared a bottle at the Fiesta of San Sebastián, and shortly thereafter, Mikel found he had worms in his nose and went to the President to ask that Marian be brought to the Cabildo. Mayores were sent that evening to apprehend Marian, who feared they had come to kill him. After being assured of safe conduct, he returned with them to Zinacantan Center where he was put in jail for safekeeping overnight. The next morning the Presidente heard the two men's stories. Marian, at first, protested that he was innocent. Then it was determined that Mikel, who was quite rich, had refused Marian, who was very poor, a loan of money during the fiesta. Marian, in anger, had retaliated by putting worms into the bottle for Mikel. Marian was told by the Presidente that it was a bad thing to get angry and throw witchcraft, that the people he witched might get angry and kill him. Marian was advised to work for the money he needed and not harbor ill will against those who had more money than he. Marian accepted the advice and signed the *acta* to the effect that he would not send worms again. Mikel also signed the *acta,* saying that he would not press further charges against Marian. With Marian's giving Mikel some rum to help pay for the curing of the nose worms, the case was settled. (Jane F. Collier, Case 90 May, 11 1963)

Pending the exact identification of the witch a shaman may be summoned and a ceremony called SA?EL HCH'ULELTIK TA BALAMIL (the search for our souls in the earth) performed in order to try to persuade the Earth Lord to release the soul that has been sold to him. A ritual called VALK'UNEL may also be performed to "return the illness" to the witch who was the source of the patient's difficulties. This ritual is accomplished by using small candles of the seven colors, which are also used by shamans as a kind of "candle curtain" to shield the cross altar from being seen by the traveling soul of a witch who might be passing by or spying on the ceremony. It is also believed that certain types of night-flying insects are messengers arriving from the "evil" ceremony to spy upon the "good" ceremony, and they are carefully killed by the shaman. A specific case may illustrate:

> While the candles were being lighted at the house cross a number of night-flying insects, attracted by the light, flew into the patio and hovered around the candles. There was hushed discussion between Telesh, the shaman, and his assistants. Telesh explained that these insects, called SUPULETIK, were spies from the other ceremony being performed by the witch inside BANKILAL MUK'TA VITS. Telesh carefully proceeded to kill each of the insects, either with the butt of his bamboo staff or by pouring rum on them. He said it didn't make any difference how they were killed as long as they were eliminated and could not take messages back to the witch at his ceremony. (Vogt: Field Notes, 20 July 1961)

There is ample evidence that all of the ritual procedures to prevent and counteract witchcraft, including forcing a suspected witch to go to his secret cave and "take back his words," do in fact occur. On the other hand, there is little verified evidence that any "evil" shaman actually cuts candles in half and burns them upside down or actually places poisonous substances in rum to give to victims. The situation may be similar to that of the Navaho (Kluckhohn 1944), in which such procedures are products of a vivid and suspicious imagination; this of course would make them no less real to the Zinacantecos, who certainly believe that witchcraft takes place and do not hesitate to retaliate.

Witchcraft by Transformation

A second common type of witchcraft is performed by an evil person HVAYHEL who possesses the power to transform himself into an animal, ordinarily a male goat with long horns, and to go about at night seeking victims. Lively stories are told about seeing these goats on the trails and how they attack persons or kill their victims by attaching them to their backs and running off into canyons. Since no goats are kept by Zinacantecos, the sight of one at night is certain evidence of a witch who has transformed himself from human form, allegedly by rolling over three times like a horse.

Some vivid examples have been reported:

> Romin reported that his compadres Marian and his wife, had gone out to look for land last December. They drank rum on the road and came home very late. Above Romin's house they ran into a dark thing they could hardly see, since there was no moon. Marian was frightened and felt his head swell up very large. Then he came home and told us about it. But it's more dangerous when you meet a goat on the road, and he climbs on you and pokes you with his horns. (Vogt: Field Notes, 5 March 1960)

> Shun ʔAkov reported that in 1930 Marian Shimenes Maniʔ was assassinated in VOM CHʼEN (in the hamlet of Pasteʔ) because it was believed that he went out at night and turned himself into a male goat and attacked people. When he went out, his wife reported, he would hang his clothes on the house cross and be gone five hours or more, wandering around as a goat. (Vogt: Field Notes, 13 June 1960)

> Chep ʔErnantis said he saw a male goat one night when taking clothes to Mol ʔAntun, while the latter was in jail in Zinacantan Center. Chep and three other men chased the goat for several blocks, but it disappeared. There was another instance in the ceremonial center, many years ago, when a curing party encountered a goat in the moonlight one night. The shaman hit it with his staff. The goat fell down and began to talk like a person, pleading "Don't harm me, I'm just out taking a walk." The goat later got up, but was wounded and died three days later, thereby killing the man who had transformed himself into this form. (Vogt: Field Notes, 19 February 1965)

"Sticking Pins in Meat"

A third, and apparently rare, form of witchcraft is to cut a piece of beef into the form of the victim, stick pins in the head, and bury it in a cemetery.

> Shun ʔErnantis of Nabenchauk was informed by a friend, Marian Peres of Nabenchauk, that his former wife and her husband, Petul

Martines, were burning candles against him. Shun was frightened, because his former wife and her new husband were shamans, and he debated with his own second wife what they could do to counteract the witchcraft. They burned candles at their house cross one night, cut a piece of raw meat into the shape of a man—to represent Petul Martines—and stuck pins into the figure's head. They took the meat figure to the cemetery and buried it, but dawn was breaking before they finished and they were seen by people passing by on the trail. They were not accosted at the time, but that night a goat appeared at the house of Petul Martines and another at the house of Marian Peres.

Petul and Marian met next morning and compared notes on their goat apparitions. When they heard the rumor of Shun and his wife having been seen in the cemetery, they surmised Shun was witching them and planned to ambush him on his return from Hot Country.

They were waiting at the narrow pass at the edge of Nabenchauk some days later when Shun returned. One of their bullets hit Shun's leg, and Shun's shouts brought people out of their houses to see what was happening. Petul and Marian ran away to escape capture. Shun, fearing another attempt on his life, left his wife and fled to San Cristóbal with his belongings. His wife, also frightened, moved to Muk'ta Hok'. Shun eventually settled in Na Chih with a third wife, but he has never returned to Nabenchauk.

The elders of Nabenchauk said that Petul and Marian were not to be punished for their attempt to murder Shun; because people had seen Shun and his wife in the cemetery, and they had further proved their guilt by running away. They said that Shun received what he deserved, and Petul and Marian were able to resume normal lives in Nabenchauk. (Jane F. Collier, Case 32, 28 March 1963)

Accusations and Assassinations

Our field data indicate that the overwhelming number of witches are male, middle aged or older, and individuals with relatively high wealth, power, and prestige. These data are interesting when viewed in the context of a system which is patrilineal, utilizes age as the basic criteria of rank order, and accords power and prestige to men who are shamans and/or have passed through many cargos.

Since the project began in 1957, we have reports of five individuals who have been assassinated for witchcraft. The witch is ordinarily killed by shooting (with a muzzle-loading rifle) or by blows with machetes. By the time the killing takes place, there is usually social consensus within the hamlet that the man is a witch and must be done away with. Thus, even though the group doing the killing is "unauthorized," it has enough community approval to avoid repercussions. It is quite possible that the witches killed are often outstanding "deviants," who fail to conform to the basic patterns of Zinacantan. This point is well illustrated by the most recent assassination in Zinacantan.

*The Case of Mol ʔAntun.** For years before his murder, ʔAntun Muntishu Krus had been considered an unusual individual by Zinacantecos and anthropologists alike. His own preoccupations also pointed to a confused self-image, which combined extreme arrogance and recklessness in asserting his independence from convention with a haunting fear of death and a pathetic fascination with the Ladino world to which he could never belong.

Certain of ʔAntun's achievements indicated extraordinary success in Zinacanteco society: as a high-ranking shaman he was greatly respected for his supernatural powers; he had augmented his prestige by passing the cargos of mayordomo, Alférez of Trinidad, and Alférez of Santo Domingo (thereby bypassing regidor to go directly to senior alcalde); at the time of his death, he had eighty compadres.

At the same time, ʔAntun often evoked reactions of pity and disgust, and the respect which people granted him as an important shaman shaded into their real fear of him as a powerful witch. By his frequent drunkenness and his acts of blatant disrespect for the rules of his culture ʔAntun further antagonized those who knew him. He was in debt almost constantly, borrowed things without returning them, and begged or demanded drinks from total strangers.

Many of ʔAntun's accomplishments (from his success as a shaman and cargoholder to his reputation as a witch) were motivated by a keen sense of competition and rivalry, aimed most directly at his neighbor, the cacique Mol Marian (see Chapter 12). Though seldom out of debt, he was constantly preoccupied with plans to build a house bigger than Mol Marian's, and ostentatiously made his ritual offerings of candles bigger than anyone else's.

ʔAntun was tormented by his lack of children and, to avert the blame from himself, often boasted of a mistress and an illegitimate child in

---

* This case is drawn from Ellen Hunsberger, "Witchcraft Patterns in Zinacantan," Freshman Seminar Report, June 1965, as well as from field notes by George A. Collier (in 1960), Susan Tax (in 1959), and Vogt (in 1959).

Nabenchauk. He feared he would die without any sons "to take care of his things, to remember him," and wanted "someone to have his face and form when he dies" (Susan Tax: Field Notes, August 1959).

He was fascinated by the Ladino world, especially by its women. During one fiesta, he bypassed a yard where about fifty Indians were dancing Zinacanteco-style and attempted to dance with a number of Ladinas on a porch nearby. He sometimes put on Ladino clothing, and even left Zinacantan for a year, apparently to do roadwork in Tuxtla.

The legends which formed around ʔAntun even before his death poignantly illustrates his most notorious characteristics in the eyes of his fellow Zinacantecos. The legend of ʔAntun's activities during his year's absence from Zinacantan emphasized his potential alignment with the outside (Ladino) world, his willingness to betray his own culture, and the fear that he was capable of unscrupulous acts—even murder—especially in pursuit of his own interests. It is often claimed in Zinacantan that strong bridges require human bodies to be buried in their foundations; some also assert that electric light plants are fueled by the fat of human corpses. At the time of ʔAntun's departure, a bridge was being built over Río Frío, a wide river which would have required many bodies. ʔAntun was allegedly hired to attack people on dark trails, kill them, and deliver their bodies to the bridge-builders. A second story, in addition to placing on ʔAntun the blame for his childless marriage, reflects his reputation as a man both intent on personal power, by whatever means, and disrespectful toward the basic rules of his culture. A few days before his marriage, twenty-one-year-old ʔAntun allegedly drank a bottle of oil, following a procedure recognized by Zinacantecos for increasing physical strength. However, he disregarded the required several weeks of sexual abstinence, which would have given him time for the oil to mix properly with the blood, and had intercourse with his fifteen-year-old bride, passing the oil into her and ruining her reproductive system forever. One final anecdote attributes both sexual deviance and association with supernatural beings to this notorious witch. One day, while looking for rabbits in the woods, ʔAntun is said to have met a jaguar and had intercourse with it, merely to prove that he could.

On November 20, 1964, at the age of fifty, ʔAntun was murdered. He had been drinking for fifteen days, following his abandonment by his wife, who returned to her father's house because of "mistreatment." After he spent all his money on rum, he bought more on credit and begged for it from several cargoholders. Finally, he went to KALVARIO, where he demanded drinks from a curing party that was praying there. In the exchange that followed, he was shot, beaten, and sexually mutilated by the shaman and three ritual assistants who were helping with the curing ceremony. Although the curing party disbanded, these four men continued on their nighttime curing circuit until they were apprehended at BANKILAL MUK'TA VITS, the last point in their circuit. The four were sent to the Ladino authorities in San Cristóbal, where the shaman was fined 4000 pesos, his accomplices 1000 each, and all were let free. From the point of view of the Ladino court, the men who carried out the killing were acting in self-defense. From the point of view of most Zinacantecos, a notorious witch had been assassinated.

20 / Shamanistic Rituals

Zinacantan now has more than 160 shamans (H'ILOLETIK) performing a variety of ritual functions in the hamlets and in the ceremonial center. Approximately 110 are men and 50 women; and are as young as fifteen (Silver 1966a: 24). Since these shamans live predominantly in the outlying hamlets, and since many of their ceremonies are carried out within the privacy of household or neighborhood social groups, they have been infinitely more difficult for ethnographers to study than have the cargoholders, who perform the ceremonies of the religious hierarchy in Zinacantan Center.

Recruitment

The word H'ILOL means, literally, "seer." In the Zinacanteco view of the world, there was an ancient time when all Zinacantecos could "see" into the mountains where the ancestral gods were living. Now, however, only shamans possess the ability to see the ancestral gods and to communicate directly with them.

There are various patterns of recruitment for shamans, but the most common involves a series of at least three dreams which ordinarily begins when a person is ten to twelve years old. In the first dream, the soul (CH'ULEL) of a mayor from the house of the Senior Alcalde—and thus the supernatural counterpart of the highest ranking cargoholder in Zinacantan—approaches the soul of the novitiate. They go together to the house of the supernatural Senior Alcalde, located just west of the corrals of the animal spirit companions, inside BANKILAL MUK'TA VITS. The visible cross

Preliminary descriptions of certain aspects of shamanism in Zinacantan have appeared in Vogt 1965a and Vogt 1966a. I am especially grateful to Daniel B. Silver for detailed field data on shamans (1966a and 1966b).

shrine on top of this Senior Large Mountain is the house cross of the Senior Alcalde inside the mountain. Upon arrival, the novitiate* is ushered into the house where the Senior Alcalde is seated at the east end of a long table; all the shamans of Zinacantan are seated in rank order at the sides of the table. The novitiate kneels at the west end of the table and bows appropriately to all his seniors. He is then asked by the Senior Alcade whether or not he is going to become a shaman and cure people. Zinacantecos claim that he must consent, for if he refuses he will die. The novitiate is given all the types of candles and flowers required for curing ceremonies and instructed on how to use them. Then he is given a black ceremonial robe (SHAKITAIL) and kneels while the Senior Alcalde makes the sign of the cross on his forehead to swear him officially into office. Now a patient is brought whom the novitiate must "pulse" (to diagnose the illness) and cure, while the Senior Alcalde and all the shamans observe.

In the second and third dreams, typically occurring a year or more apart, the process is repeated, but the patients the novitiate is asked to cure are different. If, for example, the patient in the first dream was an old man, the next time the patient is a woman, then a young child, and so on. A fourth dream may occur, but after the minimum three dreams the novitiate feels that he has sufficient power and knowledge to make his debut as a shaman. His debut ordinarily occurs at some point when he becomes ill and knows that he must answer the call to become a shaman. He goes to the highest ranking shaman in the hamlet in which he lives, and presents him with a liter of rum. As they drink together, the novitiate tells all of his dreams to the senior shaman and asks permission to make his debut. The shaman recites a long prayer to all the sacred mountains of the ancestral gods, then gives permission. The novitiate goes to the lowlands to cut a bamboo staff (BISH), which he will carry in his left hand while marching in ritual processions, then finds a senior shaman to perform with him the debut ceremony TA VA?AN SBA H?ILOL (literally, "to stand up for oneself as a shaman"). This formal ceremony is rarely performed now, but when it is, it is similar to a large-scale curing ceremony. It involves a ceremonial circuit of the sacred mountains, crosses, and waterholes in the ceremonial center (and possibly in the shaman's own hamlet), where the novitiate and his mentor pray to the ancestral gods to accept the activities of the prospective shaman (Silver 1966a: 32). Upon returning home, the members of his family and lineage know that he has become shaman and

---

*For purposes of presentation, I shall hereinafter omit mention that all this interaction in dreams involves the souls of living people, but the reader is asked to remember that such is the case.

they begin to call upon him to perform curing ceremonies. It is said that "If the new shaman has just been telling lies about his dreams, he will die right away when he tries to pray to the ancestral gods in the mountains."

Silver has discovered two other types of supernatural recruitment.

> In one, the selection of the individual as a shaman occurs before birth, so that certain individuals are, so to speak, pregnant with their destinies as curers. These may be revealed early or late in life through the medium of illness. The shaman who pulses the patient divines from the blood his destiny as a shaman and informs him that to be cured he must make a debut as a curer himself.

> Another variant has the confrontation with the ancestral gods taking place while the shaman elect is unconscious in the course of an epilectic seizure. The soul leaves the body, as it does in the dream confronta tions, and travels to the sacred mountain to receive instructions. (1966a: 28)

There are alternative patterns for making the debut. One now common seems to be a period of surreptitious practice climaxed by arrest, judicial hearing, and subsequent forced participation in the public ceremonies (Silver 1966: 30). This surreptitious beginning allows one to avoid as long as possible the onerous duties involved in the K'IN KRUS ceremonies in which all shamans in a given social group are required to participate. But eventually this practice is reported to the authorities, who force the shaman to take part in the public ceremonies.

We also have data indicating that in some cases the dreams of the shaman continue after the debut as the ancestral gods give additional instructions in more complex curing techniques.

Organization

Perhaps the most remarkable feature of the shamans as a group is the extent to which they are formally organized. Male shamans are ranked in an order which depends upon time in service, that is, the number of years since public debut. This organizational feature is diagramed in Figure 138. The shamans are carefully sorted out by rank in each localized sna, in each waterhole group, and in each hamlet. In this figure, one of the local living units we call a sna has three shamans, the other four. When they combine in ceremonies for the waterhole group composed of two of the snas, the shamans are ranked from one to seven. The same ranking process takes place for hamlet ceremonies involving shamans from two or more waterhole groups and for municipio ceremonies involving all fifteen hamlets.

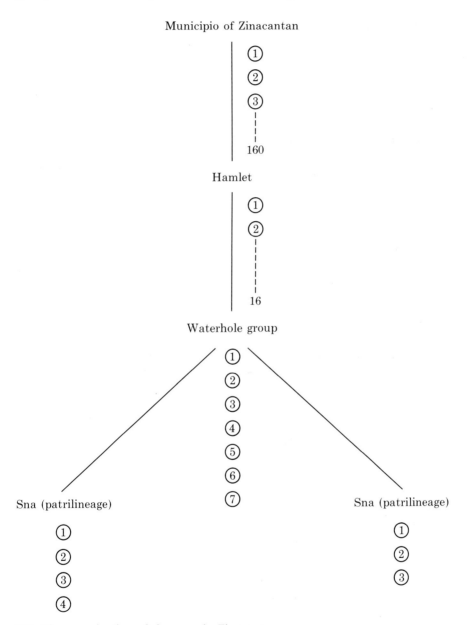

138. The organization of shamans in Zinacantan

Silver points out that rank order for all 110 male shamans is never known, because they never gather as a corporate body with an occasion to sort out all their respective ranks (1966a: 36–37). But rank is known in the snas, waterhole groups, and hamlets and can be calculated when representatives from hamlets gather at the Year Renewal ceremonies in Zinacantan Center.

Fortunately, there are reliable operational measures for determining rank in observing Zinacanteco behavior. Marching order in processions and pilgrimages is always junior man in front, senior man in the rear. Similarly, there is a seating order at the ritual tables when the shamans assemble to eat and pray, and it is followed regardless of the size of the ceremony or of the table (see Figure 90).

The highest ranking shaman of each hamlet, waterhole group, or localized lineage directs its ceremonies. This senior shaman may be assisted by a group of high-ranking colleagues who are also accorded senior shaman terms of reference and status, as opposed to the low-ranking shamans, who are termed junior. In addition, the highest ranking shaman within a hamlet has the function of giving permission to novitiates to make their debuts and of deciding which shamans will represent the hamlet at the Year Renewal ceremonies in the ceremonial center.

Incompetence can lower the position of a shaman in the rank order established for important public ceremonies. A shaman may become too old to carry on his ritual duties; he may begin to drink heavily or to perform incompetently. In these cases, the highest ranking shaman in the hamlet will make the decision to lower his position in the rank order.

There is some specialization. Women shamans perform only curing ceremonies, do not participate in the other ceremonies listed below, and hence, are not included in the public rank order system. Some shamans have special powers to recover parts of a lost soul from the Earth Lord; others specialize in the ceremony which persuades the ancestral gods to round up an animal spirit companion and return it to its supernatural corral; others are specialists in an extraordinary rain-making ceremony that requires a long pilgrimage to the top of Junior Large Mountain; still others are skilled in bone-setting (TS'AK BAK).

Ritual Functions

The problem of listing, classifying, and describing the variety of ritual functions of the shamans is complicated by the fact that there is no general word in Tzotzil designating "ceremony." If the ethnographer attempts to use a Spanish word or concept (as has been common in Middle American research) such as *ceremonia*, his difficulties are compounded and the results distorted. For example, whereas the ethnographer may think a curing ceremony has started when the shaman arrives at a patient's house and chants a prayer at the house cross, my informants do not think a *ceremonia* has begun until they light the candles at the house cross—some two hours after they started performing a whole sequence of complex ritual procedures and prayers! However, the rituals described in this chapter include the six types of ritual activities of shamans as we now understand them: curing ceremonies, K'IN KRUS ceremonies, maize-field ceremonies, new-house ceremonies, Year Renewal ceremonies, and rain-making ceremonies.

Curing Ceremonies

Although there is no generic Tzotzil term for "curing ceremony," there are a number of behavioral sequences and prayers that are focused upon a person or family who has "sickness" (CHAMEL). These include two types of divination and a series of procedures for curing the illness once it has been diagnosed. The types of divination are PIK CH'ICH' (literally, "touch blood") or pulsing, and SAT ʔISHIM. Pulsing is used as a basic diagnostic technique by all shamans to determine whether the cause of illness is due to the inner soul having some of its thirteen parts "knocked out" of the body by the ancestral gods; the animal spirit companion having been let out of its corral; or an evil person having practiced witchcraft against the patient. Upon arrival at the house of the patient, the shaman first prays:

In the divine name of Jesus Christ my lord
How much my father
How much my lord,
Holy KALVARIO, holy father
Holy KALVARIO, holy mother,
Take me unto your presence
Cure the sickness
With one great pulsing
With one small pulsing;

At your feet
At your hands,
Let your son,
Let your son, then, lord,

Walk in your holy sight
Walk in your holy countenance,
   My lord.

The shaman then feels the pulse of the patient (HCHAMEL) at the wrist and on the inside of the elbow, first on the right arm and then on the left. It is believed that the blood "talks" and provides messages which the shaman can understand and interpret. Divining with grains of maize (SAT ʔISHIM) is utilized to discover how many parts of the soul are lost. The shaman uses thirteen grains of each of four colors of maize—white, yellow, red, and black. In sequence they are thrown into a bowl of salt water— thirteen grains of white maize, then thirteen of yellow, followed by the red, and finally the black. The shaman inspects the fifty-two grains, and compares the number resting on the bottom of the bowl; those "standing up" indicate the number of lost parts of the soul. The reason for using fifty-two grains of maize when the soul is reported to have only thirteen parts is puzzling. Several of us have observed the procedure many times during the past years, but by the time the divination is performed so much rum has been consumed that the results are confused, to say the least! The shaman, several of the assistants, and often the ethnographer as well, peer into the bowl of water trying to count the floating or "standing up" grains of maize by the light of flashlights and pine torches. After some discussion, the shaman usually announces that five, six, or seven parts of the soul have been "lost" and proceeds with the ceremony. I am convinced that the use of fifty-two grains is a remnant of an earlier belief that relates to some pattern of numeration, calendrical reckoning, or possibly to multiple animal spirit companions. The latter is to me the most intriguing possibility; perhaps Zinacantecos formerly believed that a person's soul was shared with four "animal spirit companions" located in mountains in the four directions, and that these are represented by the white, yellow, red, and black colors of maize. This hypothesis would conform to the traditional correspondence between these colors and Maya directional colors (see Thompson 1934).

The ritual procedures and prayers also include the sequences focused upon a person who has CHAMEL. We have had major difficulties eliciting a consistent list of these ceremonies, even after a decade of field work in Zinacantan (compare, for example, Vogt 1965a and Silver 1966a). It is now clear that, while the public ceremonies performed by shamans (see below) are quite consistently named and have few variations (at least within the same hamlet), the private curing ceremonies performed for domestic groups show a great deal of variation—both in procedure and in classification in the minds of Zinacantecos. Silver provides an astute analysis of this variation, pointing out that these "private ceremonies are individually revealed to each shaman, in his encounters with the ancestral gods. Any variation he wishes to introduce thus can be attributed to divine revelation" (1966a: 149). In practice, of course, various factors limit variation: the concepts and symbols that are used, the principles of organization in the culture, and the acceptibility of the procedures to the clientele of the shaman.

Taking into account the variations, I can provide a minimum statement of the discriminations made by Zinacantecos in thinking about and naming these ceremonies. A basic distinction can be made between "good" and "bad" ceremonies. The good ceremonies are generally called TUK'IL ʔALEL VOKOL. This class is opposed to "bad" ceremonies involving witchcraft, but there is no term of equivalent status to describe the latter; the best that Silver could elicit was SKUENTA ʔAK'CHAMEL, meaning "on account of witchcraft" (1966a: 153–155). Borderline cases occur, as in the PERTONAL (pardon) type (see below).

"Good" ceremonies include three types. First, K'OPLAEL, a very simple curing procedure, includes diagnosis by pulsing, followed by a short prayer and either the rubbing of salt on the patient, or boiling plants for him to drink or have rubbed on his head. The ritual only takes about an hour, and is performed because an ancestral god is angry with the patient for some minor infraction and has caused a headache, a toothache, or some pain elsewhere in the body.

The second, ʔOCH TA SVOLIM (literally, "entering his ceremonial bed"), is any of a set of ceremonial variations involving a ceremonial circuit to Zinacantan Center, a visit to one or more mountain shrines and the churches, and the decoration of the patient's bed with flowers. In its maximal form it is called MUK'TA ʔILEL, or alternatively MUK'TA NICHIM. MUK'TA ʔILEL is best translated simply as "major curing ceremony," but many informants suggest that it means "great vision" and that the words refer to the large number of gods who will be visited and "seen" in their mountain homes. The same informants suggest that MUK'TA NICHIM means "big flower" and the terms refer to the large number of flowers required for the ceremony. It is performed to sustain the animal spirit companion of the patient, and is the longest and most complex Zinacanteco curing ceremony. Depending upon how far the patient's house is from the ceremonial center, the time required for performance of all the ritual may vary between twenty-four and thirty-six hours. The pilgrimage includes at least four

sacred mountains—SAN KISHTOVAL, MUSHUL VITS, SISIL VITS, and KALVARIO
—as well as the three churches—San Lorenzo, San Sebastián, and the
Hermitage of Esquipulas. In extreme cases it may also include BANKILAL
MUK'TA VITS. Water for bathing both the patient and the two black
sacrificial chickens must be fetched from the seven sacred waterholes
around the ceremonial center. The patient is bathed in the water (which
has been boiled with special flowers) and dressed in freshly washed
(laundered at NINAB CHILO?) and incensed (by holding them over a censer)
clothes. Large quantities of candles, flowers, incense, and rum are required,
and four mayores must assist in the ceremony. One of the chickens is left
as a sacrifice to the gods at KALVARIO or at one of the other sacred mountains. At least three ritual meals are served: one at the house near the
beginning; one at KALVARIO; and another at the patient's house. Upon
return to the house, the patient is placed in a platform bed decorated with
flowers and pine boughs, and the second chicken is killed and thrown in
bed with him. Near the end of the ceremony a ritual called LOK'ESEL TA
BALAMIL (to extract from the earth) may be added to call back parts of
the soul that may have been lost through fright. In a shortened form, a
ceremony called ?O?LOL NICHIM (which many informants translate as "half
flower") is frequently performed when a patient cannot afford the MUK'TA
?ILEL. In this case the pilgrimage to the ceremonial center includes only
two sacred mountains and ordinarily requires only two mayores since there
is less paraphernalia to carry. The other variants—including visits to one
or three mountains—are not named.

The third "good" ceremony, ?ALEL VOKOL TA KANTELA (diagnosing suffering with candles), is a set of rituals much the same as ?OCH TA SVOLIM,
except that the patient's bed is not decorated. It can also occur in variants
that include any number of mountains.

Ceremonies to counter witchcraft are considered dangerous and evil
because they may turn the illness onto another. There are three such procedures. In PERTONAL (pardon) small candles of seven different colors are
set before the cross shrines. The explicit purpose of these small candles is
to "close the eyes" of a "giver of illness" who is causing trouble for the
patient. This ceremony is considered borderline between "good" and "bad"
ceremonies. When it involves a pilgrimage to Zinacantan Center it can be
called ?ALEL VOKOL (diagnosing suffering) and thus classified as a "good"
ceremony. But, since the small candles are utilized, it can also arouse
suspicion. If the "pardon" ceremony is held entirely at the patient's house,
it is called VALK'UNEL (return), meaning that its purpose is to return the
illness to the witch who is the source of the patient's difficulties. In this

case it is unequivocally a witchcraft ceremony (Silver 1966a: 153). The third, SAʔEL HCH'ULELTIK TA BALAMIL, means "searching for our souls in the earth." This ceremony involves pilgrimages to special caves where the shaman can communicate with Earth Lord and persuade him to release a soul that has been "sold" by a process described in Chapter 19.

Ritual Procedures in Curing Ceremonies

Silver (1966a: 159–196) provides an excellent detailed description of the sequence of ritual behaviors occurring in the largest and most complex ceremony, MUK'TA ʔILEL. Zinacantecos recognize at least nineteen steps necessary for the "Great Vision."

Finding a shaman. The patient first seeks a shaman, who pulses him and determines both the nature of the illness and the ritual necessary to cure him. The shaman indicates which mountains and churches should be visited and what quantities of the various ritual materials will be required. He and the patient set a time for the ceremony and agree that someone will be sent to fetch the shaman at the proper time.

Preparations. The preparations involve recruiting ritual assistants and procuring the necessary paraphernalia and food. Four male assistants called HCH'OMILETIK are recruited from the patient's domestic group or, if there are none there, from more distant relatives or neighbors. Four or more female assistants are sought to help prepare food and wash the patient's clothing; these may be the wives of the male assistants or other female relatives, neighbors, or friends. The assistants assemble at the patient's house on the day of the ceremony, ordinarily about 5 A.M. The male assistants go immediately to collect a gourdful of water from each of the seven sacred waterholes around Zinacantan Center (see Map 8) and return to the patient's house. Next they gather the necessary plants in the mountains: pine boughs and pine needles, two types of air plant (KRUS ʔECH' and VOHTON ʔECH'), laurel and myrtle leaves, and VISHOBTAKIL, K'OS, and TILIL. Meanwhile, all but two or three women remain in the house, grinding maize for tortillas; one woman goes out to purchase red geraniums and one or two others (called HʔUK'UMAHELETIK) go to the waterhole called NINAB CHILOʔ to wash the patient's clothing with soaproot. Two men are sent to San Cristóbal for candles, incense, chicken or pork, rum, and rolls for the ceremony. When the men return with the plants they "sweep" the cross shrines, replacing the dried pine needles in front of the cross shrine with fresh needles. Each of the four sweepers (HMESETIK) takes care of one mountain. Meanwhile, the family must procure two black chickens, the same sex as the patient, and construct an enclosure around the patient's bed.

Fetching the shaman. When all is ready at the patient's house, a male assistant (HTAM HILOL, or "escorter of the shaman") goes to the shaman's house and presents him with a bottle of rum and two rolls. The shaman prays to the ancestral gods; the two men drink the rum; and the shaman prepares his staff and his black ceremonial robe. Meanwhile, at the patient's house the men orient a table with the long axis running east–west, and place on it the package of candles, wicks pointing east. Just before the shaman arrives, the "escort" runs ahead to give the signal and two incense burners are lighted; one is placed in front of the house cross, the other at the foot of the table.

Arrival of the shaman (Figures 139, 140). The shaman first stops at the house cross and crosses himself. He speaks to the people, enters the house, kneels, prays at the table, and finally exchanges bowing and releasing gestures with everyone present. The moment the shaman enters the house, the male assistants are considered mayores, rather than "assistants" or "sweepers"; they will be referred to as mayores* in this account of a major curing ceremony.

Inspection of the candles. The shaman seats himself at the table, checks the candles and other materials, and chants a prayer known as K'EL KANTELA (see Appendix V, Case 1).

Preparation of plants. With the aid of the mayores, the shaman censes, then assembles and ties together the bundles of plants for the patient's bed and for the mountain shrines. The bundles are placed around the bed, and an arch is constructed at the entrance to the bed.

Preparation of the bath. The shaman calls for a large pot and puts into it a small quantity of each type of plant, along with water from each of the seven sacred waterholes. The pot is placed on the fire to heat.

Praying over the candles (Figure 141). The shaman prays over the candles (SNUP KANTELA, or adoration of candles). The words he speaks are believed to be received by the gods at the moment he utters them. In addition to the words, the gods receive the candles, the rum, the shaman's gift (given at the end of the ceremony), and the meals at the table and at KALVARIO. After the shaman finishes, he calls forward each of the members of the curing party (including the patient), singly or in pairs, to salute the candles. The patient's prayer is as follows:

*Not to be confused with mayores of the civil hierarchy in Zinacantan Center; compare Chapter 11.

139. Close-up of a Zinacanteco shaman

140. A shaman smoking a cigarette

In the divine name of God my lord
  Who is thought
  Who is measurement,
    Will you stand up in holiness
    Will you stand firmly in holiness
      Behind me,
      Beside me;

If there is a passing by,
If there is a respite from
  Sickness,
  From death
  From illness
  From pain,
Also behind my lowly back, then,
Also by my lowly side, then,
  Will you stand up in holiness,
  Will you stand firmly in holiness,
    Behind my lowly back, then,
    By my lowly side, then,
      Holy KALVARIO, my father
      Holy KALVARIO, my lord,
        If there is a divine cure,
        If there is a divine rest;

See how I suffer
See how I am weak
  In one afternoon
  In one morning
    No longer is guarded my lowly back,
    No longer is protected my lowly side,

Receive these, then, if you will stand up in holiness
If you will stand firmly in holiness,
  If you can understand suffering
  If you can understand hardship,
    If you can still watch over me,
    If you can still see me,
      My lowly back,
      My lowly side.

141. During a curing ceremony the shaman, holding a burning censer, prays over the candles arranged on the ritual table

Bathing the patient. The shaman bathes the patient with the water from the pot that has been heating. A reed mat is held up to shield the patient and the shaman from the view of others. The women cense the patient's newly washed clothing over an incense burner, and he puts it on after the bath.

Bathing the substitute (Figure 142). One of the black chickens is bathed in the same water. Its neck vein is punctured with a needle by the shaman, and into a bowl is drained about a cupful of blood which the patient drinks (Figure 143). The shaman daubs some of the blood on the patient's forehead in the sign of the cross. The wound in the chicken's neck is sewn up and the chicken is placed on a layer of pine needles on a plate. This bird is the "substitute" (K'ESHOLIL) that will be taken to KALVARIO and left as an offering to the ancestral gods in the hope that they will consume the chicken instead of the soul of the patient. The shaman then prepares the other ritual materials for the pilgrimage: candles are placed in upright position in the middle of a basket of red geraniums; in turn this is placed in a carrying net; pine boughs, pine needles, and bunches of plants are loaded into nets, as are the chicken, the bottles of rum, and food for the journey.

142. The shaman prepares black chicken for its bath

143. Blood being extracted from the neck of the live chicken

The ritual meal (Figure 144). A ritual meal (VEʔEL TA MESHA) is eaten by the shaman, the patient, the mayores, and the women who washed the clothes.

144. A ritual meal of tortillas and chicken eaten by the participants in a curing ceremony; note bottle of liquor at the "head" of the table

Departure for Zinacantan Center (Figures 145, 146). The shaman asks for a bottle of rum, which is left on the table "to ensure that those remaining in the house will not sleep while the others are gone" (Silver 1966a: 176). The bottle is called "the table's moisture" (YAʔLEL MESHA). The symbolism is obscure, but the rum apparently serves to keep open the lines of communication between the household and the ancestral gods while the shaman and his curing party are absent. The members of the curing party load for the trip, then kneel and cross themselves at the table, at the hearth, and at the house cross. They line up in rank order: the shaman in the rear, directly preceded by the patient, then the carrier of the candles, then the others.

145. The shaman wrapping the white candles for the pilgrimage to the mountain shrines

146. Holding a burning censer, the shaman prays over the ritual paraphernalia before the curing party leaves for the mountain shrines

The order in which the party visits the mountains and churches in Zinacantan Center varies, depending on both the shaman and the direction by which the party enters the ceremonial center. The most common order is SAN KISHTOVAL (Figure 147), MUSHUL VITS (Figure 148), SISIL VITS (Figure 149), and KALVARIO (Figure 150). The churches are ordinarily included on the procession between San Cristóbal Mountain and MUSHUL VITS. The sequence of behavior is identical at each mountain cross (except for KALVARIO): the mayores prepare the crosses, attaching fresh pine boughs and flowers; the shaman prays (Figure 151), lights candles, and he and the patient pray together; rounds of drink are served at fixed intervals. The prayer may be illustrated by an excerpt from the one chanted at the shrine at the foot of Santa Cecilia Mountain:

147. The first stop on the circuit of mountain shrines is usually SAN KISHTOVAL

148. The second stop is MUSHUL VITS where an assistant is decorating the crosses while the shaman gets ready to pray

149. The third stop is the cross shrine at SISIL VITS

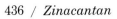

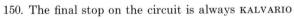

150. The final stop on the circuit is always KALVARIO

151. With incense burning and candles lighted, the shaman prays to the ancestral gods to spare the inner soul of the patient

In the divine name of Jesus Christ my lord
  Take this, then, father
  Receive this, then, lord
    Divine Maria Cecilia, my mother
    Divine Maria Cecilia, my Lady
      Who is so much;

I come kneeling, then,
I come bowing low
  At your lordly side
  At your lordly front,
    Receive this, and let me step
    Let me walk
      To the descents of your feet
      To the descents of your hands;*

You who are thought,
You who are measurement,
  If you will stand up in holiness,
  If you will stand firmly in holiness,
    Receive, then, at your holy back
    Receive, then, at your holy side,
      Your sons
      Your children
        Your flowers
        Your offspring,

If you will accept this graciously,
If you will think well of me,
  This lowly little bit
  This humble amount
    These four lowly pine branches
    These four lowly candles,
      From your son
      From your child,
    This humble bit of incense
    This humble bit of smoke,
        From your sons
        From your children,

* Ritual terms referring to the mountain shrines.

For this I beseech divine pardon
For this I beg divine forgiveness
  That you do not yet lose,
  That you do not yet throw away
    From your lordly back
    From your holy side,
      Your sons,
      Your children
        Who have sickness
        Who have pain
        Who are suffering
        Who are miserable
     In one afternoon
     In one morning
        Who no longer are well
        Who no longer are healthy
        Who no longer receive
        Who no longer possess
          The flower of your divine sunbeams,
          The flower of your divine shade. . . .

The procedure for visiting churches is also standardized: the party salutes the cross altar in the patio outside the church, has a round of drinks at the door of the church, enters the church and kneels in order three times—once inside the door, once halfway to the altar, and finally before the altar. Here the shaman and patient remain on their knees while the mayores rise, set a censer before the altar, and serve a round of drinks. Then the shaman, accompanied by the patient, lights his candles and prays. The assistants then light candles and place geraniums before all saints in the church. The party makes a circuit of the church, genuflecting at each statue. Three genuflections are repeated as the party moves toward the door. Once outside, another round of rum is served, and the party moves on (Figure 152).

At KALVARIO, the ritual sequence is as described above (Figures 153, 154), but the sacrificial chicken is left for the gods at the ʔAK'OB K'ESHOLIL on the west side of the shrine (see Figures 122, 155). The shaman places the chicken inside with the head pointing east, since this is the direction where the sun rises and comes to receive it (Silver 1966a: 183). A 20-centavo white candle is lit and left in the hole also; then the enclosure is walled up with loose stones. The curing party has a meal of cold chicken or pork, and returns home.

152. The shaman rests a few moments before moving on to the next stop on the circuit

153. The shaman prepares the offering of candles at KALVARIO; note Church of San Lorenzo in background

154. View of KALVARIO

155. A black chicken is left in this offeratory at KALVARIO as a meal for the ancestral gods

Return to the patient's house. The party marches home in the same ritual order. Upon arrival they light candles at the house cross, burn incense, and pray.

Entering the decorated bed (Figure 156). When they have finished praying at the house cross, they enter the house, greet first the table, then the hearth, and finally all the people who remained at home. The shaman washes the patient's hands and feet with the same water that was used for the bath, and then the patient climbs through the arch into the bed decorated with pine boughs and flowers (Figure 157). The shaman censes him three times, and prays to the ancestral gods to watch over him. He kills the second chicken (usually by pulling its head) and tosses it onto the patient. If the chicken jumps around a great deal while dying, the patient will improve. If the patient is going to live, the chicken's head will fall to the east; if he is to die, it falls to the west. The chicken is placed, head to the east, beside the patient's head. Later it is hung for a day, head down, on a hook outside the bed enclosure, after which it is eaten by the patient.

"Soul calling." If the "soul calling" ritual (LOK'ESEL TA BALAMIL) is included, it comes at this point. Using a MAHOBIL made of pine needles and/or oak branches (see Chapter 18), the shaman strikes on the ground to summon the patient's soul. Two small gourds with salt water are also necessary. They contain the grains of maize that were used for the grains-of-maize divination, and one is used by a mayor to make a shrill whistling sound that attracts the errant soul. Starting at the house cross, then moving to other locations where fright may have occurred, the shaman lights candles and prays (for a patient named Shun):

> Come now Shun,
> Come from where you have stayed in the earth.
>
> You are not only seated there,
> You are not only huddled there,
>   From where you were frightened,
>   From where you were affrighted,
>   Your feet were frightened,
>   Your hands were frightened.
>
> Near you,
> In front of you,
>   The divine heaven
>   The divine earth

156. Close-up of the decorated bed ("corral") in which the patient will be placed at the end of the ceremony

157. The patient is placed in the decorated platform bed at the end of a curing ceremony

The divine father accompanies you,
The divine mother accompanies you,
  The six divine Mayores,*
  The six divine assistants
    Six divine feet,
    Six divine hands.

Come now Shun
  Not only may you be lying there face down,
  Not only may you be lying there on your side
    The extent to which you were frightened in such a place,
    That you were affrighted in such a place.

In whatever place,
In whatever direction,
  Be it a place below,
  Be it a place above,
    Remember your house,
    Remember your dwelling place.

Your father,
Your lord,
  Your mother,
  Your mother-in-law,
    Get up so you may come,
    Get ready to come.

You come accompanied by the holy father,
You come accompanied by the holy mother,
  Six divine Mayores,
  Six divine assistants.

Come now Shun,
Come.

                   (Silver 1966a: 355–356 with revisions)

    The shaman then strikes the ground with the wand and spits liquor on the ground, while the mayor blows the whistling sound on the gourd. The parts of the soul are assembled and led back into the house and returned to the body of the patient.

*A reference to the assistants of the ancestral gods.

158. Candles are also offered inside the patient's house as shaman prays over a glass of liquor

Final ritual meal. A final ritual meal is eaten at the table by the shaman, the mayores, and the women who have washed the clothes, while the patient eats in his bed. They also drink the rum that has been on the table all this time (Figure 158). The shaman is then escorted home by a mayor, who carries the gift of four bottles of rum, four dead chickens, eighty tortillas, and 2 pesos' worth of rolls.

Postceremonial seclusion. For a period of two weeks or more (depending upon the curer's prescription) after the MUK'TA ʔILEL ceremony, there are strong taboos on the patient and rigid patterns for his care. There must always be a woman in the house watching over him and doing no work. If there are two guardians, one sleeps while the other watches, for in theory someone must always be watching to make certain that the patient does not suffer a "blow" from the ancestral gods and that he is not attacked by demons. When there is only one guardian, she may sleep if a light is kept burning. Neither cabbage nor black beans may be eaten. The patient takes two or three days to finish eating the chicken "substitute." He collects the bones in a pot and saves them for the shaman to take away when the flowers are removed. He stays in bed and cannot talk to the guardians; no visitor can enter the house; and when the patient goes outside to relieve himself, he must be accompanied by someone and another person must sit in front of his bed to guard against demons. It is believed that during this period of seclusion the ancestral gods and their supernatural mayores come to see how the patient is getting along.

Removing the flowers from the bed. At the end of the period of seclusion, the shaman is fetched to remove the flowers from the bed. He first prays at the patient's bed, censing it with three circuits. He rubs the patient with the flowers, then places them in a sack and sends them with two male assistants to be left in the branches of a tree at KALVARIO. The shaman also takes away the gourds of water and the pot of water left from the patient's bath. When the assistants return from KALVARIO, they help the shaman bury the bones and feathers from the chicken "substitute" in a hole, about two feet deep, behind the house cross. The ritual ends with a meal on the table, and the shaman returns to his home.

Postceremonial sweat baths. After the flowers have been removed, the patient still must wait two or three days before he can get out of bed for short intervals to warm himself in front of the fire. He still may not be left alone in the house. The guardians may weave again, but only with black wool, since white objects attract "blows." The patient, accompanied by his wife or mother, takes a series of sweat baths at three-day intervals. After the first bath he no longer requires his guardians but cannot go outside alone. After the second bath he can go outside in the sun and stay there alone. After the third bath he can go out and his bed need not be watched. He gradually resumes his normal activities, and the cure is ended.

Waterhole and Lineage Ceremonies

A second group of ritual procedures at which the shamans officiate are the waterhole and lineage ceremonies. These, unlike curing ceremonies, have a generic name in Tzotzil: K'IN KRUS. The word K'IN designates "fiesta," or a type of ritual procedure that involves many people and is given on specified days in the calendar (see Figure 159). For example, the large ceremonies on saints' days in the ceremonial center are all designated by K'IN, which also means "sun," "day," or "time" in all of the Mayan languages (Kaufman 1964: 111; Léon-Portilla 1968). The word KRUS is a loan word from Spanish *cruz,* meaning "cross," and signifies that the

159. A procession making a ceremonial circuit during a K'IN KRUS ceremony; drum and flute players are followed by the shamans in rank order and then by the string instrument players

ceremonies have been syncretized with the Catholic feast day for Santa Cruz (May 3). But since these ceremonies also occur in some hamlets in October at the end of the rainy season and have little to do with the Christian concept of the crucifixion, it is evident that they involve ancient Tzotzil concepts.

The K'IN KRUS ceremonies are of two types: those for the waterhole group which express symbolically both the rights of its members to draw water from the waterhole and their obligation to care for it properly; and those for a localized patrilineage which symbolize the rights of the sna to lands they now use and which they have inherited from their ancestors.

Waterhole Ceremonies. The basic steps in the ritual sequence of a waterhole group ceremony can be illustrated from the K'IN KRUS for VO? TA PASTE? which I attended on May 2–3, 1960. (A more detailed description is provided in Appendix V.)

Advance preparations were made by the Senior Mayordomo, appointed yearly from among the families using the waterhole, and the ceremony took place at the end of his term of office. Preparations involved recruiting ritual specialists and other helpers and collecting money for and assembling the requisite paraphernalia for the cleaning of the waterhole; the decoration of waterhole crosses with flowers, pine needles, and pine boughs; a ceremonial meal at the house of the Senior Mayordomo; a second sortie to the same several crosses to place and light candles; and a long dancing and drinking session at the waterhole, followed by a final ceremonial meal. The preparations began two weeks in advance, and the ceremony itself involved participants for a 30-hour period (6 A.M. one morning until 10 A.M. the following).

The ritual specialists and helpers included: eight shamans, who wore black ceremonial robes and carried bamboo staffs; four mayordomos, outgoing and incoming senior-junior pairs; two elderly lineage heads, elders or ritual advisers, seated in places of honor; two groups of musicians— violin, harp, and guitar players, and flute and drum players; two groups of fireworks men—camaro men in charge of powder blasts, and skyrocket men; young men or boys as drink-pourers; female helpers (two ritual hostesses who were also in charge of food preparation and the other twelve women cooks, and two women helpers who portioned out the rum liquor); other men, recruited by the mayordomos, who helped assemble the pine boughs and flowers and decorated the crosses.

The paraphernalia, assembled by nonritual as well as ritual specialists within the waterhole group, included: hoes, rakes, pitchforks, and wheelbarrows for cleaning the waterhole; plant materials (roses, red geraniums, pine needles and boughs, and CH'IB); incendiaries, including 1-peso size white candles, incense (wood chips and resin nodules burned in footed clay censers), and fireworks (gun powder and skyrockets) for venerating the cross shrines; and food (atole, meat in chile broth ingredients, and maize for tortillas) and drink (coffee and large amounts of rum liquor) for sustaining the participants.

The ritual activities began early in the morning when the participants gathered at the house of the Senior Mayordomo for a breakfast of atole and rum liquor.

The cleaning of the waterhole openings followed. The work consisted of digging, raking out the dead leaves and twigs, filling wheelbarrows with the debris, and dumping it some distance away. Drinks of rum were passed at intervals, and the two groups of musicians played alternately nearby. The atmosphere was relaxed and friendly. At the end of the cleaning, the shamans and mayordomos lined up in rank order in front of the waterhole crosses to kneel and pray at length.

The next step was the division of plant materials for cross shrine decoration. Rising and maintaining rank order, the shamans, mayordomos, musicians, fireworks men, and others proceeded to the sacred tree near another opening to the waterhole. There they sat down, still by rank, to divide the plant materials into equal piles that were used to decorate the cross shrines beside the waterhole openings, the waterhole KALVARIO and a hill nearby called CH'UL KRUS VITS (Santa Cruz Mountain).

Small groups of men left in rank order to decorate the cross shrines (Figure 159). Pine boughs were carried by the man leading the procession, followed by a man with CH'IB, another with flowers, one with pine needles, and the skyrocket man. The groups were gone for one hour, and as each cross shrine decoration was completed, a skyrocket was set off at that spot to signal the fact. The waterhole cross decorations included the construction of arches of flowers, while the house crosses of mayordomos had only pine boughs and no arches.

While the groups decorating the cross shrines were away, the others remained drinking and visiting. The head shaman held court to reprimand members of the waterhole group who had not contributed to the expenses of this ceremony.

When the decorating parties returned to the waterhole, the assemblage in rank order proceeded to the house of the Senior Mayordomo. Each official prayed at the house cross (two or three shamans, the pair of junior mayordomos, then the two senior mayordomos prayed together). The shamans pray as follows:

> In the divine name of Jesus Christ my lord
>> How much my father
>> How much my lord,
>>> My lowly earth has come
>>> My lowly mud has come [that is, I am in your presence];
>
> How strongly I beseech divine pardon
> How strongly I beg divine forgiveness,
>> So we shall make ready
>> We shall perform it [the ritual],
>
> Receive this lowly little bit, then,
> This humble amount, then,

If you will accept it with good grace
If you will await it with good grace,
  This lowly little bit, then,
  This humble amount, then,
    Receive this lowly splinter of our pine
    Receive this lowly splinter of our candles,

With this we beseech divine pardon
With this we beg divine forgiveness,
  At your holy side
  At your holy front
    Holy gods
    Holy angels
    Holy priests
    Holy earth gods

Will you accept from me
Will you receive from me
  This lowly little bit, then,
  This humble amount, then
    We shall prepare them, then
    We shall place them, then
      Our humble pine branches,
      Our humble candles,

With these we shall beseech your divine pardon
With these we shall beg your divine forgiveness,
  Your holy sun has gone over the hill
  Your holy year has passed;
    Take these for your great fiestas
    Take these for your great Christmases,
      Holy gods
      Holy angels
      Holy priests
      Holy earth gods;

Receive this,

That you let nothing happen to them
That you let them encounter nothing
  All the little ones
  All the great ones

All the round ones
All the perched ones,*
  For this I beseech divine pardon
  For this I beg divine forgiveness
    At your holy sides
    At your holy front;

Here we share your drink
Here we stand in your shade,
  Receive this lowly little bit, then,
  This humble amount, then,
    Into the holy wellspring of your washing-place
    Into the holy wellspring of your bathing-place,
      The wellsprings from your holy feet
      The wellsprings from your holy hands;

For this I beseech your divine pardon
For this I beg your divine forgiveness,
  I cannot beseech if there is no pardon
  I cannot beg if there is no forgiveness
    Do not ignore our crying
    Do not ignore our sobbing,
      We, your sons,
      Your children
      Your flowers
      Your offspring;

For this I beseech your divine pardon
For this I beg your divine forgiveness
  Take this, here is my lowly earth
  Take this, here is my lowly mud,
    Take this, holy cross of my father
    Holy cross of my lord, who is so much

Let me walk in thy holy sight
Let me walk in thy holy countenance,
  My fathers,
  My mothers,
  And my lord.

*"Round one" and "perched one" are ritual terms for "child"; when a Zinacanteco baby is carried about he is "perched" on his mother's back like a papoose.

Then each official was greeted formally by the hostesses; these two women are older, respected relatives of the Senior Mayordomo and are in charge of the food preparation. The male participants took their places on small chairs and benches around a long table (actually two tables placed with ends together) covered with the traditional striped handwoven cloths and were served rum. Water to wash hands and water to rinse mouths was followed by atole in gourd bowls and beef stew in hot chile broth with stacks of tortillas, coffee, and more rum. Before each course the senior shaman said a prayer and the seated guests made the sign of the cross at the end of it. Then they left the table and went into the patio so that the helpers (including the drum- and flute-players, the fireworks men, and others) could be served. The little boys present were the last to be given food and drink; they were served in the patio where they were the target of comments and jokes of the officials waiting there. During this time the women were eating their meal quietly by the fire, having been included, however, in the rounds of drinks served previously.

When the helpers finished their meal, one of the tables was removed from the house, and the officials re-entered to divide the rum, cigarettes, and candles carefully and ceremonially. Two bundles of peso candles were brought out and placed on the table with butt ends toward the west, pointed ends to the east. The rum was poured from a two-gallon jug into liter bottles and then into the empty cuartita bottles each official and helper had for that purpose. The cigarettes were distributed equitably. Finally, and with much more ceremony, the large 1-peso size candles were unwrapped and placed on the table with the same orientation; the paper flowers (put on the candle bundles at the stores in San Cristóbal) and geraniums were symmetrically arranged around the candle points. The shamans then loosened their head scarves and recited long prayers; they took turns, in pairs, leading the prayers and censing the candles. First, the No. 1 and No. 2 shamans led the praying, each holding and rotating (counterclockwise) the smoking censers, held in their right hands, over the candles. Then No. 3 and No. 4 shamans received the censers and initiated the prayers. They passed the censers to No. 5 and No. 6, and so it continued. This full round of praying in pairs was repeated three times before the candles were properly blessed and readied as offerings for the gods. The candles were tied together in threes, with pink-striped cloths around their butt ends and a paper flower attached. Each of the four mayordomos received such a bundle for his house cross, and shamans No. 3 and No. 4 received one for the KALVARIO cross. The rest of the candles (about half remained) were similarly wrapped in threes and laid aside for the moment.

The four mayordomos then knelt at the foot of the table to recite a long prayer.

After the prayer, the mayordomos, each followed by a shaman designated by the head shaman, went to their own house crosses. Each greeted his house cross and an older male host at the house door, but did not enter. The shaman took the candles and placed one each in the ground in front of the three crosses (referred to as one), lighted them, poured rum around them as a further offering, and chanted a long prayer, kneeling. The mayordomo, kneeling to his left, joined him.

Number 3 and 4 shamans, having left when the mayordomos did, and accompanied by the drum and flute musicians and firework men, went to the waterhole KALVARIO. The shamans placed the bundle of candles in an offertory pit, lighted them, and, kneeling in front of the crosses, they rotated the burning censers they had brought from the Senior Mayordomo's house as they prayed.

This description from my field notes (May 2–3, 1960) illustrates the scene:

> As I arrived at KALVARIO, the spectacle that met my eyes was one to excite the interest of even the most jaded anthropologist. Never have I seen a wilder scene calculated to warm the heart of a field worker! Flickering light from the three candles tied as one in the offertory pit and from a small fire the drum and flute players had made to keep warm in the cold night air illuminated the cross with its pine and flower decorations and the shamans were kneeling and praying before it. From time to time, they bowed low until their foreheads touched the ground, chanting continuously. Incense was thick in the air despite the strong wind, skyrockets were being shot off periodically, and the flute and drum music vied with the wind, the chanting, and the fireworks in one's ear. Only the bitter cold and my desire to return with Manvel and Telesh (a mayordomo-shaman pair) finally tore me away.

Three rounds of rum in coffee was served to the mayordomo-shaman pairs by the house crosses before they returned to the Senior Mayordomo's house. Prayers were said by each group on their return. The senior shamans (No. 1 and 2) who had remained, had tied up the remaining trios of candles into two large bundles and placed each in a net with tumpline.

An hour before midnight the shamans and mayordomos with their helpers were ready to take the remaining candles to the waterhole crosses. The incoming mayordomos carried the two nets of candles in the ranked procession, now joined by the KALVARIO group (who had a greater distance to go and return). Upon arrival at the waterhole sacred tree, ranked seating position was again observed and drinking filled the time until midnight. Then the senior shamans lighted the first candles around the cross just below the sacred tree, while the junior shamans lighted others around the cross above the tree. They proceeded to the other crosses until three candles had been placed, lighted, and prayed before in front of each cross.

After more drinking, following the completed candle ceremony at the waterhole cross shrines, the shamans, mayordomos, and helpers climbed the nearby sacred mountain of the waterhole group—SANTA KRUS—to light candles at the cross shrine there.

The ceremonial group descended from their sacred mountain about dawn to dance for an hour, interspersed with rounds of rum liquor.

There was finally a ranked procession back to the house of the outgoing Senior Mayordomo. Here the guests again were served a ceremonial breakfast by this waterhole group official, and he thanked each official and helper individually for aid and cooperation in this ceremony marking the end of his year in office.

Lineage Ceremonies. The basic steps in the ritual sequence of a K'IN KRUS for a sna can be illustrated from the ceremony for SNA CHIKU'ETIK which I attended on May 5–6, 1960. (A more detailed description is provided in Appendix V.) Instead of focusing upon the waterhole, the lineage ceremony focuses upon the cross shrines and sacred objects possessed by the sna.

Advance preparations included recruiting ritual specialists and helpers and collecting money for and assembling the requisite ritual paraphernalia. These preparations began about a week before the ceremony, which extended from about 3 P.M. in the afternoon to about 10 A.M. the following morning.

The ritual specialists and helpers included: all four shamans resident in SNA CHIKU'ETIK; four mayordomos—two senior-junior pairs, outgoing and incoming—who are in charge of the small image of the Virgen del Rosario that is kept in a special house by this lineage; elders or ritual advisers, the two eldest men in the CHIKU'ETIK lineage, who were seated in places of honor during the ritual meals; two groups of musicians—violin, harp, and guitar players, and flute and two drum players; the same types of fireworks men as in waterhole ceremony; young men or boys as drink-pourers; female helpers (two ritual hostesses in charge of food preparation and two women who portioned out the rum liquor, pouring it from large jugs into smaller bottles); other men, recruited by the mayordomos, who brought candles and incense from San Cristóbal, helped gather pine boughs and flowers, and assisted in decorating the crosses.

The paraphernalia used included the same types as in the waterhole ceremony, except that the white candles were 50-centavo rather than peso size, and roses were used only for the arch over the statue of the saint.

The ritual activities began with a ritual meal at the house of the Outgoing Senior Mayordomo. The procession then moved (counterclockwise) through a circuit during the night, stopping at the house crosses of the other mayordomos, three caves, a sacred tree, the small hermitage of the Virgen del Rosario, and a junior and senior KALVARIO for the sna where the shamans lighted candles and prayed. The ceremony ended with a final ritual meal at the house of the Senior Outgoing Mayordomo. (See Case 4 in Appendix V for a list of these cross shrines and a sketch map of the ceremonial circuit.)

The ritual behavior noted during this circuit was distinctive in two respects. In the house of the saint the two most junior shamans and the mayordomos danced for the saint to the music of the violin, harp, and guitar, while the Virgin (a brown-faced statue about three feet high dressed in a Zinacanteco woman's shawl and ribbons and carrying a brown-faced infant) looked out from an arch of fresh red geraniums and white roses. At the crosses at senior and junior "Stomach Cave" the participants were extraordinarily quiet, and there was an aura of fear as the shamans made their offerings especially to the Earth Lord.

Maize-Field Ceremonies

A third type of ritual procedure is performed in the lowland fields along the Grijalva River, as well as in the ejido fields located on the flanks of the highlands. Here the groups of men who are farming together on adjacent fields gather to perform ceremonies at least twice, and sometimes three times, during the maize-growing season. A shaman directs the ceremonies and says the prayers. If the farming group does not include a shaman, one is summoned to perform the ceremony. The ceremonies are similar in ritual procedure to the K'IN KRUS ceremonies for a sna or waterhole group, but the prayers are different, the counterclockwise ritual circuit usually includes the four corners and the center of the field, and the focus is upon rain-making for the growing of the maize.

The following description of a maize-field ceremony (K'IN CHOBTIK) is from the field report of Jack Stauder,* the only member of our research team to have participated in a full-scale ceremony for the fields in the lowlands.

*I am indebted to Jack Stauder for permission to use this description.

"The Lord of the Earth and the Growers of Corn"

Telesh and the LOPIS CHIKU'ETIK, like all other Zinacantecos, celebrate K'IN KRUS early in May, at their waterhole and houses in Paste'.
K'IN KRUS, Telesh says, is "for the people." But when the men go down
to the lowlands a couple of weeks later to plant, there must be another
kind of ceremony "for the milpa": always at planting, often at midyear
and at harvest-time too. It is called "candles for the cornfields,"
SKANTELAIL CHOBTIK, or "alms for the cornfields" SLIMUSHNAIL
CHOBTIK, because they are giving an offering of candles and prayers
to appease "the Lord of the Earth," and the ruler and sender of the
clouds and winds and rain.

The CHIKU'ETIK had already given him one ceremony this year, when
they decided to have a second SKANTELAIL CHOBTIK in July. The milpa
is drying; it needs rain; and if one can afford the cost it is always good
to perform the full number of ceremonies, just to be on the safe side
of YAHVAL BALAMIL. So Telesh and each of the CHIKU'ETIK in the
renting-group contribute 3 pesos and 25 centavos toward the purchase
of the necessary articles for the ceremony—even the three of them who
are not going this time contribute money, because it is for the milpa
of all of them—and all of them go together to San Cristóbal the day
before leaving for the lowlands to buy them.

In Paste' they take some sacred red geraniums from the Chiku'
gardens. And, going down to the lowlands the next day, they stop a
moment near Shukun to run off the trail to cut some juncia (SHAK
TOH), fresh, long pine-needles. Now all the necessary elements of the
ceremony have been gathered.

They reach their fields near Chiapilla at about three in the afternoon,
and spend a little time resting and eating pozol. Manvel Lopis Chiku'
divides the meat carefully into equal pieces, four strips for each person
present. The others crouch on rocks and wooden stools to watch the
division. When Manvel is done, the meat is set in jars by the fires to
cook. Meanwhile, Telesh has been carefully arranging and separating
the ingredients of the ceremony—the juncia, the flowers, the candles.
He divides them among the five crosses the group will visit, crosses
already standing in the fields from the ceremony at planting-time.

The group begins at five with the "ceremonial meal," the only
ceremony in it being the fact that they are eating meat. They eat only
half the meat, saving the rest for later. The meal is like any other,
Telesh and the CHIKU'ETIK sitting around the hot bowl, dipping their

toasted tortillas into the soup, chewing on their small bits of salted beef. When they are full of tortillas, they drink the soup, passing it from one to another, Telesh and the older men first, till the hot chili-flavored broth is all gone.

Telesh, though a young man, is MAS BANKILAL for the ceremony. He is the most respected, treated as if he were the eldest, because he is a shaman and has special powers with the ancestral gods and the Earth Lord. He knows the prayers, and will be the priest for the ceremony, praying to the Earth Lord for the others.

It is evening when the party leaves their shelter and walks into the high corn, the leaves switching their faces. They cross by their small milky waterhole lying in the arroyo basin at the bottom of their fields and they begin to climb. The field is very large and long, a forest of corn, ascending the side of a large steep hill. The hill the CHIKU?ETIK call KALVARIO, because it holds three of their crosses. Soon the hill is too steep for corn and the men climb up a narrow weaving path through the hillside brush. The first cross is almost to the top of the south side of KALVARIO, tucked under an overhanging of earth, an altarlike enclave in the mountain which simulates a cave in the eyes of the Zinacantecos. Under the earth lives the Earth Lord in his big Ladino house—for he is a Ladino—and caves and holes in the mountains are the doors and windows of his house. It is best to speak to him here. Also Telesh had dreams, telling him where to put the crosses. The hillside is so steep the men have to hold on to trees to keep from slipping down into the cornfield.

Telesh takes a stick and digs holes on each side of the cross. In the holes he places pine boughs at the side of the cross: they serve as "crosses" in the eyes of the Zinacantecos, to make an altar of three. The pine boughs are holy, not the wood. He ties a pine bough to the wooden cross, also, and spreads pine needles underneath the crosses. A red geranium goes on the middle cross, and the candle shop's paper flower. Next he digs holes for the candles. He ties them together with a string, and stands them tall and white in front of the crosses. The wind is blowing against the hill. Two of the CHIKU?ETIK hold a rain cape up behind Telesh while he carefully lights the candles and flicks off the excess wick. One of the boys lights the incense. One of the men opens his bottle of liquor and gives the first glass to Telesh. Telesh says a little prayer—the liquor is sacred also—and turns to the group. "KICH'BAN," he addresses everyone in turn by name, "I receive"; "?ICH'O," they reply, "Drink it," He drinks.

Telesh begins praying, kneeling and bowing and crossing himself, chanting in long rapid phrases broken only when he stops to breathe, and begins again in the same swift vibrant monotone. As he prays the rest of the men drink in turn and smoke and talk behind his back. They hand Telesh a cigarette in the middle of his prayers, and he stops to light it from the candles—KOLAVAL, "thank you"—then continues his prayers, interrupting them only now and then for a puff on his cigarette. In fifteen minutes he finishes, and the Zinacantecos have another round of liquor. Telesh closes with a short prayer and crosses himself as he kneels, thumb to earth to head to breast to lips.

Rain is beginning to fall now, as night drops. The men put on their rain capes and pull themselves up to the top of the hill. The top of KALVARIO is shimmering with long grasses whipping pink and white in the strong wind, in the failing half-light. The Zinacantecos go to the center of the hill and descend a little way to the next cross, also tucked into the earth, where again they have to hold to branches of trees to keep from slipping down the slopes, now muddy in the growing rain.

Telesh arranges the cross and pine boughs and candles as he did at the first cross, they begin drinking liquor and he begins to pray. This time the rain and wind will not let him go on. The water blows in and puts out the candle flames. The men again try shielding the candles with their rain capes but the rain is falling so hard that their attempts are useless. So they stand around on the muddy slope, the cold rain blowing down their rain capes. They do not think of postponing the ceremony. They just wait for the rain to stop, making jokes and smoking and drinking. The glass is not used now: the bottle is passed straight from man to man, and to the little boys too, all of them holding on to the slick mountain-side, waiting for the rum liquor to warm their limbs and for the rain to be called away. The air is turned watery white, obscuring the cornfields below in a turbulent mist, leaves and ears of corn roaring with the torrents of wind and rain. The men try for a long time to keep the incense burning. Finally they run out of the wood chips and it is gone for the night.

At last the rain lets up enough so Telesh can carefully wipe off the second batch of long candles and light them. He says the prayers and they move on to the third cross, picking their way through the mud and brush of KALVARIO, using flashlights to find the way. The third cross is on the grassy top of the northern end of the hill. Telesh is able to get the candles lit again, but the rain keeps falling, a steady drizzle. Their cigarettes fall wetly apart in their hands. They are not hurrying at all, but take their time drinking after the prayers and laughing and talking about things of the day.

Down the mountain they go now, slipping and sliding, grabbing the strong stalks of corn that have come to meet them. The leaves give them wet slaps on their faces and shoulders as they walk, weaving single-file, slowly through the rows of dark corn, led only by the two flashlights. The fourth part of the ceremony is at their waterhole cross. The ceremony here is slightly different. Telesh prays now to the Earth Lord not to dry up their waterhole.

Man after man has taken his turn in opening his bottle of liquor, and passing the bottle among the group. Telesh, like the others, is a little drunk, and more than ever smiling and deferential. Kneeling in the mud in front of the waterhole cross he makes a speech, to which they all listen, though he is telling them things they well enough know themselves. Some bullfrogs are booming raucously in the gutters of the arroyo. "That," says Telesh, "is the sound of the guitars of YAHVAL BALAMIL. And that," as thunder and lightning strike in the west, "that is the sound of the YAHVAL BALAMIL out hunting with his shotgun, for fun . . .

"We are having this ceremony for the YAHVAL BALAMIL, that he should order the clouds to come out of the earth, clouds to rain on our corn, so our corn should not die . . . Because if it does not rain and our corn dries up and perishes, we would perish too . . . So we are praying to the Lord of the Earth, and we are offering him good peso candles, for we only gave him fifty centavo candles at planting, but now we are giving him peso candles, so he will let our corn grow . . . We have to pray to him in our old language, as we have always done, because he is accustomed to us praying in our old language, and if we did not pray thus, he would strike us dead with his snake of lightning . . . We do not see the Lord of the Earth, but he is there under the earth . . . And all of us pray to him, for the corn to grow for all the world . . . For there in Zinacantan is the center of all the world, and we must pray for all the world—if we do not, this world will be destroyed, until another better one comes. . . . Some people in San Cristóbal do not believe in our ceremony, they say it is only a *'creencia,'* a 'belief.' But these are the people who come to us with money for corn, and pay for it and buy it. They are not the ones who grow it . . . And now we are having much rain, because there are many ceremonies tonight, not just here, but all over. Remember, we saw Mariano Peres Peres on the road at Zapotal with his candles and rockets, and we saw many other persons . . . So we are not sad because we are wet, for we know that the Lord of the Earth has heard our prayers. I believe it is going to rain all night, yes, I believe it is going to rain till tomorrow."

After Telesh's speech, all the men kneel to the ground and cross themselves before the candles, their thumbs to the earth to their foreheads to their hearts to their lips.

By the shelter is the last cross. The same ceremony as at the crosses on KALVARIO is performed. The rain is only pattering now. The men could sit inside the hut by the fire if they wished, but they prefer to stand outside with Telesh drinking and smoking as he prays:

> Ch'ul rey
> Ch'ul anhel,
>
> Ch'ul chon
> Ch'ul chauk,
>
> Ch'ul vinahel
> Ch'ul loria,
>
> Ch'ul lum
> Ch'ul ?osil.
>
> Holy king
> Holy angel,
>
> Holy snake
> Holy thunder,
>
> Holy sky
> Holy glory,
>
> Holy earth
> Holy world.

But when Telesh has stopped praying, the rain has stopped. He is drunk and sad. "We have ended badly," he says. "It has stopped raining. How are we going to end it right?" But there is no way. The rain is finished, so is the liquor, and the rest of the cigarettes are passed out till every man, even the two little boys, has five or six extra *Alas* [a brand of cigarettes] behind his ears. Telesh leaves his cigarettes before the candles, and the group goes inside to eat the rest of the ceremonial meal. Tomorrow they will have to go back up the mountain to relight the candles that have been extinguished in the rain. Now they lie down on the ground and pass to sleep. As they sleep, long after midnight, the rain commences lightly again.

New-House Ceremonies

With the construction of a new house in Zinacantan, two ceremonies are performed to compensate the Earth Lord for the wood, the thatch, and the mud that have been taken from him.

HOL CHUK. When the walls are completed and the roof rafters in place, an afternoon is taken off to make offerings to the Earth Lord, that he might have a "good heart." A rope is hung from the peak of the house. The end of the rope marks the center of the floor, and a hole about one foot deep is dug at this point. A number of chickens, both roosters and hens, are hung by their feet from the end of the rope, with their heads concealed inside the center hole. Their heads are then cut off with a knife, and their bodies scalded and prepared for eating. The heads, feathers, and left-over scraps are buried in the hole as an offering to the Earth Lord for the building materials that have been taken from his domain. The ends of the rafters are sprinkled with liquor, and a feast of liquor and chickens follows. The services of a shaman are not required for this small ceremony.

CH'UL KANTELA. This "Holy Candle" ritual is performed as soon as possible after the completion of the new house. A shaman performs this ceremony, whose purpose is to give the house a "soul." The participating group includes not only the house owner and his immediate family but also his father and brothers and their wives. The ritual begins with the planting of the house cross. Three stakes are driven into the ground and the shaman lashes the cross to the center one. While violinist, harpist, and guitarist play, three pine boughs are tied on the cross, and sacred red geraniums are attached to the pine boughs. Candles are offered as incense burns in a censer, and the shaman says several prayers.

The shaman continues the ritual inside the house. While he prays at the table over the candles, an assistant hangs a number of chickens by their feet from a rope toward the east side of the house and wrings their necks. These chickens will later be eaten; their number depends upon the economic situation of the house owner. The rope is moved to the center of the house and suspended from the rafters. A black rooster is hung by his feet and his neck wrung by the shaman. The rooster's body is buried in the center of the floor and sprinkled with liquor. The earth is tamped in on top in the same manner used for burying a person in a cemetery. The cross that will later be placed on top the roof of the house is decorated with pine boughs and red geraniums and planted at the east end of the grave.

Each member of the group then comes forward to "meet" the six candles on the table. The house owner, holding the pine boughs that are to be planted at the house corners, prays to the Earth Lord, saying:

> So I am going to plant firmly,
> The holy pine, the holy candle.
> So I beg holy pardon,
> So I beg holy permit,
> With my spouse. . . .   (Warfield 1963: 78)

The shaman then leads the group to each of the four corners, planting pine tips and candles in the corners in the order shown in Figure 160. The shaman also pours chicken broth on the four corners and on the center of the four walls. Assistants climb onto the ceiling joists and "feed" the "meal" to the roof by sprinkling liquor and chicken broth on the beams and rafters. Then the men don black robes and dance in front of the musicians.

Following the dancing the shaman washes the hands and arms of all who are to live in the house. The man and woman of the new house wash their feet and put on newly washed clothes which have been censed over incense. The six candles are planted in the center of the house, and a formal ritual meal follows.

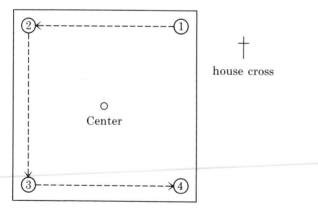

160. Order of CH'UL KANTELA ritual

161. Buying liquor in Chamula for a Year Renewal ceremony

After the meal the shaman leads the man and woman of the new house into the mountains where they make a circuit of four holy mountains—usually SAN KISHTOVAL, MUSHUL VITS, SISIL VITS, and KALVARIO—where candles, incense, and liquor are offered to the ancestral deities. The ceremony ends, as it began, with prayers at the house cross.

For the next three days, the house must be carefully attended to, for it now has a soul and must be cared for "just like a sick person" following a curing ceremony.

Shortly after the CH'UL KANTELA ceremony, the women of the house start placing their hair combings in cracks in the walls. Together with the men, they place this hair in the walls each day as a symbol that they belong to the house, and that they will remain there to cook and to weave.

New Year, Midyear, and End-of-Year Ceremonies

These Year Renewal ceremonies are performed either two or three times a year (Figures 161, 162). For example, in the hamlet of Paste⁹ they are performed for both ⁹ACH' HABIL (new year) and SLAHEB HABIL (end of the year). In the ceremonial center, they are performed three times a year—at new year, midyear, and end of the year. In the hamlets they involve all of the male shamans. These assemble at the house of the Senior Principal, who serves as host for the new year ritual, or at the house of the Junior Principal, who serves as host of the end of the year ritual.

For the hamlets the essential element of these ceremonies is a pilgrimage of the shamans to the ceremonial center, where they burn candles and incense and offer flowers before all of the cross shrines (both at the foot and on top of the sacred mountains around Zinacantan Center) and the saints in the churches.) The ceremony thus appears to be a symbolic way of relating the outlying hamlets to the tribal gods in the ceremonial center.

For the three yearly ceremonies in Zinacantan Center the ritual is performed by the shamans who live in the center plus two shamans from each of the hamlets. Interestingly enough, the shamans from the hamlets are not of high rank but usually relatively new, low-ranking members of the group who are sent to the ceremonial center and also have to make some of the most arduous pilgrimages from the center.

These shamans always gather on Sunday at the Hermitage of Esquipulas, where they are served six liters of rum liquor by the elders and count the money that has been collected for the necessary candles, incense, and liquor. Then they return home. On Monday they gather early at the house of the most senior shaman to drink a bottle of liquor each and to await the arrival

162. Candles and skyrockets being carried into ⁹Apas for a Year Renewal ceremony

of the candles and incense from San Cristóbal. When these have arrived and the pine boughs have been placed on all the cross shrines they will visit, they are notified and march in rank order to the house of the Senior Alcalde, who serves as host for the ceremony and provides the ritual meals. Also present are the elders, the mayordomos reyes and mesoneros from the Hermitage, and a delegation from the Cabildo—the Presidente and Síndico, if they can come, or at least the alcaldes jueces. Violin, harp, and guitar players provide the music.

The seating arrangement of the shamans in this ceremony, and in the Year Renewal ceremonies for some of the hamlets differs in that the shamans are seated with the BANKILAL, or senior, group along the south side of the table and the ʔITS'INAL, or junior group, along the north. This order can be diagramed as shown in Figure 163.

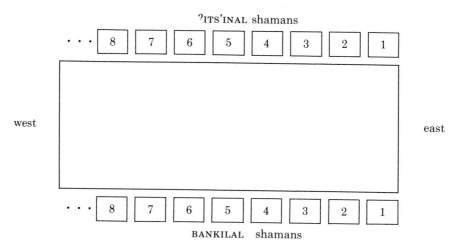

163. Alternative seating arrangement of shamans

At about seven P.M. a long night of praying begins, initiated by four shamans, the two most senior of the BANKILAL group and the two most senior of the ʔITS'INAL group, who stand and pray in unison, holding smoking censers in their right hands. The censers are periodically circled in unison counterclockwise over the flowers and candles on the long table. The first four pray for about an hour, periodically bowing down until their foreheads touch the table, and praying in this position for several minutes. Then the second group of four to the west (two BANKILAL and two ʔITS'INAL) stand, take the censers, and pray in the same manner for about an hour, and so on until about four A.M. When this ritual was observed by Early (8 July 1964), there were four groups of four each, and a fifth group of six.

They pray as follows:

> In the divine name of Jesus Christ my lord,
>> Receive, then, my father
>> Receive, then, my lord
>>> Since I come kneeling
>>> Since I come bowing low;

> We shall beseech divine pardon
> We shall beg divine forgiveness
>> At your sides
>> At your front
>>> To take this unto the place where the feet descend
>>> To take this unto the place where the hands descend
>>>> With the divine Señor San Cristóbal holy father
>>>> With the divine Señor San Cristóbal holy mother
>>>>> With the holy KALVARIO holy father
>>>>> With the holy KALVARIO holy mother,

> To send your holy words,
> To send your holy prayer,
>> To stand in holiness
>> To stand firmly in holiness
>>> Behind us
>>> Beside us
>>>> With all the little ones
>>>> With all the great ones
>>>> With all the round ones
>>>> With all the perched ones
>>>>> All your sons
>>>>> All your children;

> Receive this, that nothing happen to them
> That they encounter nothing,
>> That all be well for a while
>> That everyone feel healthy for a while,
>>> Then stand by the backs
>>> Stand by the sides

Of all the little ones
Of all the great ones
Of all the round ones
Of all the perched ones;

Receive this, if you will accept it,
Take this, if you will receive it
  This lowly little bit,
  This humble amount,
    Take these four lowly pine branches
    Take these four lowly candles,

With these we beseech divine pardon
With these we beg divine forgiveness,
  For this we will step,
  For this we will walk,
    To the descents of thy feet,
    To the descents of thy hands;

Receive this, all you holy fathers
Receive this, all you holy mothers,
  Receive this, all you holy gods,
  Receive this, all you holy saints,
    Will you receive from me
    Will you accept from me,
      This lowly little bit,
      This humble amount;

Grant us divine pardon
Grant us divine forgiveness,
  With this lowly little bit,
  With this humble amount,
    That to all the little ones
    That to all the great ones
    That to all the round ones
    That to all the perched ones,
      That to all your holy sons
      That to all your holy children,
        Nothing happen;
        That they encounter nothing,

That they stay well
That they stay healthy,
   Their lowly backs
   Their lowly sides;

Receive this; for this reason they are worried,
For this reason they speak from their hearts,
  All the little ones
  All the great ones
  All the round ones
  All the perched ones,
    All your holy sons
    All your holy children;

Receive this, then, my father,
Receive this, then, my lord,
  Accept this with good grace,
  Await this with good grace
    This lowly little bit
    This humble amount;

These offerings are not piled high
They are not heaped high,
  It is only a small bit,
  It is only a humble amount,
    But grant us thy divine pardon
    Grant us thy divine forgiveness,
      Receive this humble spray of flowers
      Receive this humble branch of pine
      Receive this humble bit of incense
      Receive this humble cloud of smoke;

With this I beseech divine pardon,
With this I beg divine forgiveness,
  Because all your sons,
  All your children,
    Are anxious,
    Are speaking from their hearts,
      Take unto you all the little ones
      Take unto you all the big ones;

Receive then: your holy sun has gone over the hill
Your holy year has passed
  Take this for the holy end of the year
  Take this for the holy end of the day,
    For this I beseech divine pardon
    For this I beg divine forgiveness
      In the flower of your divine sight
      In the flower of your divine countenance;

All the holy fathers,
All the holy mothers,
All the holy gods,
All the holy saints,
  To you I speak
  To you I pray,
    At the circuit of the holy shrines,
    At the circling
      Of your divine visage,
      Of your divine countenance;

You who are my holy fathers
You who are my holy mothers, my lord,
  Receive this of me,
  Await this of me,
    This lowly little bit
    This humble amount;

For one divine moment,
For a few sacred moments,
  We are kneeling
  We are stooping low
    Beside you
    In front of you,

Receive this at the descents of your feet
Receive this at the descents of your hands,
  And send your holy words,
  Send your holy prayer,
    Stand up in holiness,
    Stand firmly in holiness,

You who are my holy fathers,
You who are my holy mothers,
  Let nothing happen to them,
  Let them encounter nothing,
    All your sons
    All your children;

For this we are kneeling,
For this we are stooping low
  Beside you
  Before you,
    Receive unto you, holy fathers,
    Receive unto you, holy mothers,
    Receive, then, my father,
    Receive, then, my lord,
      So that I may walk in your sight
      So that I may walk in your countenance,
        My fathers,
        My mothers,
          My lord.

At dawn a ritual meal is served, and the groups of shamans take the candles and flowers to the churches and to the mountain shrines associated with Zinacantan Center. Each group has two shamans and their assistants, who carry the candles and flowers. The more junior shamans are given the most arduous journeys to the distant shrines near Salinas, while the more senior shamans divide into six pairs, each of which is joined by one of the six elders, for the easier trips to the churches and nearby mountain shrines. The journeys to the shrines are scheduled for Tuesday, regarded as the best day for communication with the gods. It is the day when the gods are especially "listening" for messages and "waiting" for offerings, and hence the day when they can be "seen" best by the shamans. When all of the sacred mountains, caves, waterholes, and temples have been visited, and the gods have all received the messages and offerings, the entire assemblage meets at KALVARIO. Here all the shamans make offerings and say prayers in unison not only to KALVARIO but also to all of the important mountains around Zinacantan center as they turn counterclockwise in kneeling position (Figure 164). They finish about noon, and all stand. The most junior shaman starts down the line to be released, followed by the next most junior, and so on, and each then marches off to the open space behind the

164. Shamans and Elders praying at KALVARIO during a Year Renewal ceremony

shrine at KALVARIO. This process continues until the only one left in front of the shrine is the Senior Alcalde, the last to join in the meal which is eaten behind the shrine. They then march in formation back to the house of the Senior Alcalde, where a final ritual meal is served. Following this, the shamans disperse to their hamlets. This ceremony has structural significance, because it links together the two peaks of sacred terrestrial power in Zinacantan and relates both to the all-important ancestral deities in the supernatural world.

Some years these Year Renewal ceremonies become occasions on which an important shaman dreams that a new cross should be added or one of the shrines renovated for the ancestral gods. He informs the ranking shaman, and, if the dream is accepted as valid, extra pesos are collected either to have a cross of cedar constructed and painted in San Cristóbal or to purchase cement for the improvement of one of the shrines. These improvements, made during one of the Year Renewal ceremonies, account for the gradual elaboration of the shrines, since the old crosses are always retained along with the new ones.

Rain-Making Ceremonies

Certain specialized shamans perform the sixth type of ritual—the exceptional rain-making ceremony in years of severe drought, which requires four days and is the longest ritual performed by shamans. A pilgrimage is made from the ceremonial center to the summit of ʔITS'INAL MUK'TA VITS (Junior Large Mountain), a peak which the Ladinos call Chenekultik, located some five kilometers north of Cerro Mispia to the southwest of Teopisca, Chiapas. The shrine for this ceremony is located on the summit of Junior Large Mountain, on the west side of a large prehistoric platform mound. When the shamans are praying at the shrine, they are facing east, the most important direction in Zinacanteco cosmology. The mountainside shows evidence of prehistoric terraces, indicating that the summit was an important site in pre-Columbian times. Zinacantecos claim that they originally owned all the land in the lowlands along the north side of the Grijalva River from this mountain to Chiapa de Corzo. Whether or not this is true, this distant peak is an integral part of the ritual system.

We do not yet have a good description of this ceremony, since the specialists in rain-making ritual have been extraordinarily difficult to approach. My data are secondhand from shaman informants who have not themselves participated. According to them, the ceremony begins with a gathering of shamans in the ceremonial center. After gathering for an all-night prayer session, they form a procession at dawn for the trip to Junior Large Mountain. There are normally guitar, harp, and violin players, two candle-carriers, and two shamans, marching in that order. Accompanied by various assistants and two mules loaded with food supplies and with pine boughs and pine needles for the crosses, they proceed from Zinacantan Center, over the mountain pass to Na Chih, and then to ʔElan Voʔ, where they stop at the house of the T'ENT'EN (the sacred drum) for breakfast. They leave the highlands, traveling past Totolapa, and stop at sundown for a few hours of sleep, arriving at the summit of Junior Large Mountain at dawn. They spend this third day offering candles, incense, and prayers at the shrine on the summit. On the fourth day they return to the house of the T'ENT'EN in ʔElan Voʔ, whence they disperse to their various hamlets.

Shamanism in the Social and Economic Systems

The shamans occupy a key role in Zinacanteco society. As Silver points out:

> Illness and curing are inextricably bound up with social relations in Zinacantan. Illness, in Zinacanteco thought, is a major medium of relations among men and between men and gods. Hostility and envy, two prevalent aspects of interpersonal relations in the municipio, express themselves through witchcraft and illness. Transgressions of the social code are punished by divinely sent illness. Even interpersonal conflicts . . . are brought into the purview of the deities, who punish the transgressor with disease. Men and gods, then, are caught up in a three-cornered web of relationships, whose most frequent expression (at least between men and gods) is illness. (1966a: 244)

The shaman functions in a variety of ways in these sets of social relations. The ceremonies (especially curing ceremonies) at which he officiates both express and influence social relations among the participants. At the local level in the hamlets, away from the "official" court at the Cabildo, the curing ceremony serves to mediate disputes and resolve conflicts arising in daily life. The functioning of this mediatory power is based upon three factors. First, the shaman has complete control over the diagnosis, cause, and cure of illness, and speaks with supernaturally endowed authority; his method of divination by pulsing cannot be verified by the patient. Second, the shaman is in a position to be intimately informed about the patient's affairs, including his difficulties within the sna and waterhole group. Finally, the beliefs about causes of illness are well adapted to this mediatory role since most illnesses are believed to be due either to witchcraft, which stems from social disturbances, or to divine punishment for the patient's transgressions (Silver 1966a: 263–264). Hence, many troublesome cases are settled by means of curing ceremonies rather than reaching the court at the Cabildo in Zinacantan Center.

On the other hand, shamans occupy an ambivalent position in Zinacanteco society. They constitute the only channel of communication between the human and supernatural worlds. While the cargoholders, the Catholic priest, and individual Zinacantecos direct their communications to the gods in the form of prayers, sacrifices, and gifts, only the shamans are capable of receiving and offering divine communications. But shamans may also find themselves accused of witchcraft or malpractice, and these cases often result in either counter-witchcraft ceremonies or even litigation at the Cabildo (Silver 1966a: 270–278).

The shaman's relation to the economic system has some interesting aspects. Silver has made a careful analysis of the economic compensations of the shamans and has concluded that their average gross incomes are slightly lower than those of non-shamans. There is a small group of shamans who, exploiting their witchcraft powers, manage to make a fulltime occupation of curing; but most average only one ceremony a week and are compensated by food during the ceremony and gifts of tortillas, liquor, and dead chickens afterward. Since these gifts must be almost immediately consumed, they are not as economically advantageous as would be gifts of live chickens or maize. The food and gifts are also less than could be earned through other activities occupying the same amount of time. Hence, for the vast majority of shamans other gratifications inherent in the role must override economic considerations (1966a: 312).

In attempting to account for why Zinacantecos choose to become shamans, Silver explored a series of both sociological and psychological factors. I originally hypothesized (Vogt 1964a: 31–32) that shamans were likely to be socially displaced Zinacantecos, who were orphaned, living in small, inconsequential lineages, or had some peculiar social experience, and that they were inclined to place more emphasis upon dreaming and introspection. I also thought that perhaps becoming a shaman was an alternative route to the cargo system in leading to a prestigeful or powerful position in Zinacanteco society. Silver's recent work with a sample of fifty shamans, compared with a matched number of non-shamans, proves these preliminary hypotheses incorrect.

Of the various sociological variables explored, Silver found that only two show any difference between shamans and non-shamans: if a person lives in a domestic group with a shaman in the older generation, he is more likely to become a shaman; and shamans tend to have a higher, rather than lower, degree of participation in the cargo system as compared to the non-shamans (1966a: 313).

Silver interprets the importance of the first variable in terms of the amount of information available for the complex procedures in curing and other ceremonies within family lines. The second variable—that shamans have a higher degree of participation in the cargo system—is a more startling discovery. Silver concludes that the role of shaman actually promotes the cargo career of men economically disadvantaged by inheritance or men whose economic performance in farming is hampered either by incompetence or lack of motivation. It is probable that

the H'ILOL (shaman) role itself plays an important part in the establishment of the network of debt relations on which financing a cargo depends. The H'ILOL, through his practice, has a greater opportunity than most Zinacantecos to achieve early in life a large number of relationships with members of his community that carry some sort of obligation with them. It is possible that the H'ILOL is in a position to claim from his patients loans and assistance in the furtherance of his cargo career that the ordinary Zinacanteco can only achieve after a much longer period of himself loaning money and assistance to older men. Similarly, it is possible that the prestige and supernatural power of the H'ILOL insulate him somewhat from strong pressure to repay his loans, so that he can spread his debt relations both farther in time and over a wider social network than the ordinary layman. (1966a: 325)

Silver's study of possible psychological factors in the motivation and recruitment of shamans also contained some genuine surprises. There is an almost complete lack of any discernible mental illness, homosexuality, or other conspicuous forms of deviant behavior—only in a few of the shamans do we observe signs of deviance. The rest might be viewed as "quintessential Zinacantecos" (1966a: 331). Similarly, their psychological characteristics, as explored by Silver, utilizing a modified Thematic Apperception Test, display no strong differences from the non-shamans. We are left with the picture of shamans fitting many of the formal characteristics of classically described "shamanism," but without the bizarre motivations and deviant behavior that supposedly underlie "shamanism." The Zinacanteco case is important in the comparative study of shamanism, "as a demonstration of how shamanistic behaviors that look like expressions of deviance can subserve far less extreme motivations" (Silver 1966a: 344).*

---

* More recently Richard A. Shweder, who did field work in Chiapas in the summer of 1967, has discovered some important differences between shamans and non-shamans in Zinacantan in their cognitive reactions to situations of bafflement and disorder. In a field experiment utilizing photographs that ranged from fully out-of-focus to fully in-focus, Shweder found that his sample of thirty-three shamans: imposed categories and structures on out-of-focus photographs significantly earlier and more often than his sample of thirty-three non-shamans; were more creative in their categorizations; and were less influenced by experimenter-provided alternative categories. In his still unpublished report (Shweder 1968), Shweder's interpretation of these results is that shamans have a much higher cognitive capacity and greater need to impose order upon a potentially chaotic universe. His findings clearly indicate that we are now discovering crucial differences between shamans and non-shamans in Zinacantan.

21 / Cargo Rituals I

By far the most complex rituals in Zinacantan are those performed by the cargoholders in Zinacantan Center. Indeed there are few days in the year when some ceremony is not being performed, and usually several ceremonial sequences are going on simultaneously.

The Annual Ceremonial Calendar

December 14 through January 6. Exceptionally elaborate ritual takes place throughout this period. The Senior and Junior Mayordomos of Rosario are responsible for the special activities.

December 15: Flower change.

December 16: Fiesta of the Virgen de Navidad. Nine days of squash-eating and posada ceremonies commence.

December 23: Crèche built in San Lorenzo church.

December 24: *Torito* (bull constructed of reed mats) constructed. MAMAL-ME'CHUN ten-day cycle begins. Crèche built in San Sebastián.

December 25: Christmas

December 30–31: Cargo change for the mayordomos reyes, mesoneros, escribanos, regidores, and junior and senior alcaldes viejos.

January 1: Torito group visits new cargoholders.

January 4: Flower change.

January 6: Epiphany. Mayordomos of Santa Cruz responsible for fiesta. Cargo change for the Alférez of Divina Cruz and Alférez of the Virgen of Soledad.

In this chapter I am especially grateful to John D. Early, Frank Cancian, Renato Rosaldo, and Manuel Zabala for field data on the cargo rituals and to Catherine C. Vogt for her research assistance in checking, rechecking, and summarizing the complex ethnographic information. More detailed information on the cargo rituals can be found in Early 1965.

January 13. Saints arrive for the Fiesta of Señor Esquipulas. Cargo change of Mayordomos of San Sebastián.

January 15. Fiesta of Señor Esquipulas. Volunteers are responsible for this more recently established fiesta.

January 18 through January 23. Unique ritual surrounding Fiesta of San Sebastián. The Mayordomos of San Sebastián are responsible for fiesta entertainment groups, composed of past year's cargoholders. One of two largest fiestas of the year. Cargo change for the Alféreces of San Sebastián.

January 18: Flower change.
January 20: Fiesta of San Sebastián.
January 22: Last day of fiesta performances.
January 23: Visiting saints depart.

January 25. Articles of office transferred from retired (December 30–31) Senior Alcalde Viejo to new Senior Alcalde Viejo.

February 2. Fiesta of the Virgen de Candelaria. Mayordomos of Rosario are responsible.

Calendar of the Easter Season. (Inserted here arbitrarily, since Easter's changeable date could also place Carnaval before the Fiesta of the Virgen de Candelaria of February 2.) The Pasioneros serve their cargo during the period from Carnaval through the Fiesta of the Sacred Heart. The Alcalde Shuves serves his cargo during the five days of Carnaval.

Carnaval. The five days preceding Ash Wednesday. Continuous ritual activity for the mayordomos, alféreces, and Elders, and for the pasioneros and the Alcalde Shuves who are responsible for the ritual entertainment.

Ash Wednesday. Priest comes from San Cristóbal to say Mass and distribute ashes. After Mass, the mayordomos dance at the house of the Senior Pasionero.

Six Fridays in Lent. Special observances.

First Friday: Saints carried on flower-bedecked platforms through church and churchyard in procession with the pasioneros, mayordomos, alféreces, and elders.

Second Friday: Same ritual occurs, but only the senior cargoholders participate.

Third Friday: Same ritual occurs, but only the junior cargoholders participate.

Fourth Friday: Large fiesta takes place, with the Mayordomos of Santa Cruz responsible.

Fifth Friday: Ritual the same as on the First Friday. Fiesta in hamlet of ˀApas takes place.

Sixth Friday: Ritual the same as on the First Friday.

Saturday before Palm Sunday (Day after Sixth Friday). Flower change by the Mayordomos of San Antonio. Marriages take place. (New cargoholders must be married by priest now, if not already.)

Palm Sunday. Priest comes to say Mass. Procession with palms, encouraged by priest, is avoided by cargoholders. For the most part, only Ladinos participate.

Holy Week. Special ritual takes place between Palm Sunday and Easter, focusing on the HMANVANEH image.

Monday: Mayordomos make preparations.

Tuesday: Small procession, similar to that of the Fifth Friday of Lent.

Wednesday: HMANVANEH image washed ritually by the Alcaldes Viejos and the Holy Elders, placed in bier, and taken in procession (like that of the Fourth Friday in Lent). Two pasioneros and a flutist keep watch by bier through the night.

Thursday: (Maundy Thursday) Ritual re-enactment of the Last Supper. Mayordomos Reyes and mesoneros provide breakfast to all cargoholders—three sittings at two large tables. Procession with large cross announces Maundy Thursday rituals. The priest washes the feet of the mayordomos and one assistant before saying Mass.

Good Friday: Ritual re-enactment of the Crucifixion in San Lorenzo Church, presided over by the Holy Elders. Large attendance.

Holy Saturday: Church interior restored to normal. Priest performs Easter vigil service. Dummy of Judas is burned.

Easter Sunday: Mass. Activity of alféreces and mayordomos similar to fiesta day. Alféreces of Trinidad and San Antonio serve atole to cargoholders.

Minor Litany Days (the three days before Ascension Day).

Monday: (Sixth Monday after Easter) A small procession of the mayordomos and the sacristanes, the latter reciting litanies, around the inside of San Lorenzo church.

Tuesday: Same short procession. Evening chest celebration of the Mayordomo of Santo Domingo by all the mayordomos.

Wednesday: Same procession inside church.

Ascension Day. Always a Thursday and forty days after Easter. Ceremony of raising the dove, in preparation for Pentecost Sunday. Chest celebration in house of the Mayordomo of Rosario.

Pentecost Sunday. Always ten days after Ascension. Ceremony of lowering the dove, representing coming of the Holy Spirit.

One week before fiesta of Corpus Christi. Cargo change of the Mayordomos of Sacramento.

Trinity Sunday. Special ritual. Cargo change for the Alférez of Trinidad and the Alférez of San Antonio.

Corpus Christi. Always the Thursday after Trinity Sunday. Procession when the priest is present. Chest celebration of the Mayordomos of Sacramento who are in charge of the fiesta.

Sacred Heart. Small fiesta with a band coming from Chiapa de Corzo and a visit of the Virgen del Rosario from Salinas.

—End of Easter Calendar—

April 22. Ten days before the fiesta of Santa Cruz. Cargo change for two pairs of mayordomos: Mayordomos of Santa Cruz and Mayordomos of San Antonio.

April 29. Fiesta of San Pedro Mártir. The Mayordomos of Santa Cruz are in charge. Cargo change for the Alférez of San José and the Alférez of San Pedro Mártir.

May 3. Fiesta of Santa Cruz. One-day fiesta with special flower decoration of all crosses. The Mayordomos of Santa Cruz are in charge.

June 13. Fiesta of San Antonio. Small fiesta for which the Mayordomos of San Antonio are responsible.

June 24. Fiesta of San Juan. Small fiesta with the Mayordomos of Santo Domingo in charge. Procession by elders and mayordomos around Zinacantan Center to collect money for the Fiesta of San Lorenzo (August 10)—same as on January 6. Ceremonial meal in Hermitage afterward.

June 29. Fiesta of San Pedro. Small fiesta.

July. A month with no fiestas because of work in the fields.

August 4. Fiesta of Santo Domingo. The change of office for the Mayordomos of Santo Domingo takes two days instead of one.

August 7 through August 11. Activity for and surrounding the Fiesta of San Lorenzo—the most important fiesta of the year in Zinacantan.

August 7: Preparations by many cargoholders. Alféreces active at San Lorenzo church; the elders active in the Hermitage. Mayordomos change house altar flowers.

August 8: Elders greet the visiting saints. The capitanes perform a special dance which is repeated in following days.

August 9: Necklaces placed on saints in church by the mayordomos and left overnight. Horse races (10 A.M.); and elaborate fireworks at night.

August 10: Calendar date for San Lorenzo. Morning horse races. Afternoon church visits by families with flowers and candles for the saints.

August 11: Change of cargo for the Alférez of Santo Domingo and the Alférez of San Lorenzo (the two highest ranking alféreces). Farewells to the visiting saints.

August 31. Fiesta of Santa Rosa. From midnight, August 30, to 8 A.M., August 31, ceremonial visits are paid the saint images in the mayordomo houses, attended by many powder blasts which gave misnomer of "killing of the saints" to this activity.

September 8. Fiesta of the Virgen de Natividad. A large fiesta sponsored by the Mayordomos of Rosario with change of office for the Alférez of Natividad and the Alférez of Santa Rosa.

September 21. Fiesta of San Mateo. Small fiesta with Mayordomos of Santa Cruz in charge.

October. Sunday before October 7 is the celebration of the Fiesta of the Virgen del Rosario in Zinacantan Center. A band is hired for three days by the Mayordomos of Rosario, who are in charge. Statue of the Virgen del Rosario comes up from Salinas. Change of office for the Alférez of Rosario and the Alférez of San Jacinto.

October 7. Actual calendar date for Fiesta of the Virgen del Rosario. Celebrated in the hamlet of Salinas with statue of Santo Domingo from Zinacantan Center attending with the Elders and Mayordomos. The Mayordomos Reyes and Mesoneros help the Mayor and Mayordomo of Salinas in hosting the fiesta. Special ceremony surrounds the Virgen's sacred salt well.

October 18. Fiesta of San Lucas. Statue of Santo Domingo of Zinacantan Center taken to ceremonies in San Lucas Zapotal. The Mayordomos of Santa Cruz are responsible.

November 1. Fiesta of All Saints. Preceded by the chest celebration of the Mayordomos of San Antonio the night before. There are special ceremonies to feed the souls of the dead, with food set out in churches, houses, and cemeteries. Later, the mayordomos gather up the food from cemeteries next day and divide it among themselves.

November 25. Fiesta of Santa Catalina. Small fiesta and chest celebration by the Mayordomos of San Sebastián.

December 8. Fiesta of the Immaculate Conception. Primarily celebrated by Ladinos in Zinacantan.

December 12. Fiesta of the Virgen de Guadalupe. Celebration takes place in the hamlet of Nabenchauk. Santo Domingo statue attends from Zinacantan.

A Major Three-Day Fiesta

Major fiestas occur seven times a year. Zinacantecos believe they should be of three days' duration, the last day falling on the saint's day according to the Catholic calendar.

For three nights before the first day, each alférez who is about to leave his cargo sends out a small party to announce the forthcoming fiesta. The group, consisting of two drummers, a flutist, a drink-pourer (and others interested in the procession and the prospect of free drinks who join the group en route), marches through the streets between 7 and 8 P.M. and again just before dawn, playing special, rhythmic music to announce the fiesta and stopping for rounds of drinks at designated street crosses and at the doorways of the church of San Lorenzo and of the Hermitage. After the evening announcement, the musicians return to the Alférez' house for rum and rest until the early morning announcement begins. The march around the village is repeated, with flute and drum music and stops at the crosses and church doorways; it ends at the house of the outgoing Alférez shortly after dawn.

The events of the fiesta occur in the following order (Early 1965: 283):

A. The Day before the First Day (BALTE? TA NA—"changing the flowers in the house")
   1. Flower Change in the Mayordomos' Houses
   2. Oath of the Incoming Alféreces
B. The First Day (CHUK NICHIM—"tying the flowers in bunches")
   3. Flower Change in the Churches
   4. Coffee at the Houses of the Outgoing Alféreces
   5. Circuits of the Alféreces
C. The Second Day (?ISHPERESH—"vespers")
   6. "Dance of the Drunks"
   7. Mayordomos at the Church
   8. Atole at Outgoing Alféreces' Houses
   9. Circuits of the Alféreces
   10. The Mayordomos Count and Place Necklaces on Saints' Statues

D. The Third Day (SBA K'EL K'IN—"look at the fiesta")
   11. Mass, Baptisms, and Marriages
   12. Aléreces' Dance on Church Terrace
   13. Mayordomos at the Church (cf. 7 above)
   14. Elders at the Hermitage
   15. Mayordomos Return the Necklaces to House Chests
   16. Aléreces' Flag Ceremony, Atole

A. The Day before the First Day

1. *Flower Change in the Mayordomos' Houses.* Each mayordomo leaves four bags of pine needles at San Lorenzo Church in the afternoon. After sunset his retinue of helpers—ritual adviser, musicians, drink-pourers, incense-bearers, fireworks men, and family members (some of whom may take the forementioned roles)—assemble at his house for a simple meat broth meal.

Each senior-junior pair of mayordomos is responsible for a chest altar (kept by the Senior Mayordomo) and an image altar (kept by the Junior Mayordomo). Two of the senior mayordomos by tradition, however, maintain both altars in their houses. Hence, their junior mayordomo partners with retinues join them for the two consecutive ceremonies held in the one house. The account that follows is of such a case.

After the ceremonial greetings of the Junior Mayordomo and his helpers, the Senior Mayordomo puts on his black ceremonial robe and scarf. He and his junior partner then engage in bowing and releasing with their three musicians of violin, harp, and guitar, while reciting the following invocation:

> See then, my older brother
> See then, my younger brother [referring to musicians]
>   In your presence,
>   Before your eyes,
>   We will change the flowers
>   We will change the leaves of the tree [altar decoration],
>   Of Father San Lorenzo
>   Of Father Santo Domingo [saints' names will change with other
>   mayordomos].

> Now we have arrived at his great feast day
> Now we have arrived at his great festival.

For this we are gathered together,
For this we are united,
   On his great feast day,
   On his great festival.

We should do this,
This we shall do.

Now we have arrived at his time,
Now we have arrived at his day,
   My older brother,
   My younger brother.

Lend me the ten toes of your feet,
Lend me the ten fingers of your hands,
   I am going to change the flowers,
   I am going to change the leaves of the tree,
     Of the Lord San Lorenzo
     Of the Lord Santo Domingo
       Oh my older brother,
       Oh my younger brother.

Lend me the ten toes of your feet,
Lend me the ten fingers of your hands,
   For the great feast,
   For the great festival
     Of Father San Lorenzo
     Of Father Santo Domingo.

Lend me your instruments,
Lend me your songs,
   Older brother
   Younger brother,
     For before your eyes,
     For before your face,
       I will change the flowers,
       I will change the leaves of the tree,
         Oh my older brother,
         Oh my younger brother.

Pardon for a moment
Pardon then for a moment [here liquor is passed].

(Early 1965: 225–226, with revisions)

The Mayordomos approach the two Incense-Bearers to be released by them with the same type of invocation, followed by a serving of rum. The Junior Mayordomo places a reed mat in front of the altars of the chest and statue. The Incense-Bearers kneel at the edge of the mat, each with a smoking censer which she places in front of her. The Mayordomos remove the red geraniums and green leaves from the arch over the chest altar and throw them on the mat. Assistants bring in two baskets of red geraniums and several bags of fresh green leaves which are tied into small bouquets by the Incense-Bearers who hand them to the assistants who in turn pass them to the Mayordomos. The Mayordomos tie them on the arch with cord, making a beautiful new decoration (Figure 165).

The same process is repeated for the statue's altar. The Senior Mayordomo places a bottle of rum with the old flowers on the mat and addresses the musicians:

165. Flower decorations on house altar of a mayordomo; note small saint statues under arch

See then, older brother,
See then, younger brother
  Wait for our earth,
  Wait for our ground,
    Here for a moment,
    Here for two moments [that is, wait for us].

I am going to throw away the rubbish of the feet,
I am going to throw away the rubbish of the hands,
  Of the Woman of the Sky,
  Of the Lady of Heaven [the moon].

(Early 1965: 227–228)

The Mayordomos carry the mat behind the house, discard the old decorations, and drink the bottle of rum.

Returning to the house, they proceed to change the clothes of the saint statues—which are about 15 cm. high and heavily clothed. These clothes must be changed every fifteen days and, along with the flowers, before every major fiesta. (See Chapter 11 for list of the saints kept by the mayordomos.) The Junior Mayordomo takes clean clothes from the chest, while the Senior Mayordomo takes the statues out of the case on the altar and stands them on the altar table. He removes the old clothes, while the Junior Mayordomo hands the fresh clothes to the Incense-Bearers who cense them. The Mayordomos place the fresh clothes on the saints, a process that lasts over an hour since each statue has at least five layers of clothing.

After prayers before the two altars by the Mayordomos and Incense-Bearers, each Mayordomo takes four candles and each Incense-Bearer one candle from a rack on the wall. They place these as "food for the saints" in the animal-figure candleholders on the floor in front of the altars and light them. The men then kneel and pray (Figure 166):

. . .
The changing of the flowers is finished,
The changing of the leaves of your tree is done.

Now we have arrived at your great feast day,
Now we have arrived at your great festival.

You will be entertained,
You will be happy,

166. Mayordomos and their Incense-Bearers praying before the freshly decorated
house altar

> On your great feast day,
> On your great festival.
>
> So receive my candle, my father,
> So receive my candle, my lord.
>
> Forgive its being so small,
> Forgive its being so small,
>   My torch is only a twig,
>   My candle is only a splinter. . .

(Early 1965: 230)

167. Mayordomos and their Incense-Bearers dancing before a newly decorated house altar

The last part of the ritual consists of dancing and singing for entertainment of the saints. The Senior Mayordomo opens the glass door of the statue case as the musicians begin playing. The Mayordomos face the musicians, put on their hats, and begin to dance. The Incense-Bearers take positions behind them, and all dance for about an hour to special tunes (Figure 167). At 1 A.M. this ritual is finished.

2. *Oath of the Incoming Alféreces*. During the major fiestas there is a change of alféreces; two of the fourteen finish their year's service and are replaced. The oath ceremony for the new incumbents takes place in the Hermitage of Esquipulas at the same time the mayordomos are changing the flowers on their house altars. The second part, the flag ceremony, takes place on the afternoon of the last day.

About nine P.M. the two Alcaldes Viejos, the Escribanos, and three civil officials from the Cabildo gather at the Hermitage and take their places in rank order at the long center table. The staffs of office are placed on the table with the heads toward the foot of the table, ready to "receive" the new Alférez. The statue of Señor Esquipulas wears its necklace of coins, placed there in the afternoon by the Mayordomo Rey and the Mesonero on duty for the week.

Music and fireworks announce the arrival in the churchyard of the incoming Alférez to the officials gathered inside the Hermitage. Besides his family the new Alférez is accompanied by the four Regidores, a flutist, two drummers, and a fireworks specialist—all of whom had arrived at his house during the afternoon and evening.*

The Regidores lead the new Alférez to the back door of the Hermitage, and the Regidor who has been carrying the peacock feather hat of the incoming Alférez hands it through the doorway to an assistant to take to the Senior Alcalde Viejo seated at the head of the table. The incoming Alférez enters the Hermitage, genuflects, and walks to the foot of the table. Then in order of seniority, the seated officials rise in their places; they turn toward the new Alférez and deliver the following exhortation:

> My venerable father,
>> Now your person has arrived,
>> Now your person has arrived,
>>> Here before the feet,
>>> Here before the hands,
>>>> Of the Lord Esquipulas
>>>>> Oh my venerable father.

> You have come to receive,
> You have come to take,
>> The holy divine oath,
>>> Here before the feet,
>>> Here before the hands,
>>>> Of the Lord Esquipulas
>>>>> Oh my venerable father.

> You must be a good servant,
> You must be faithful to your trust,
>> During the twelve months,
>> During the twelve days.

---

* An account of "The First Days of a New Alférez" may be found in Cancian 1965a: 55–62.

Therefore you must leave your sins,
Therefore you must leave your wickedness,
  Under the feet,
  Under the hands,
    Of the Lord San Lorenzo,
      Oh my venerable father.

For this you are swearing an oath of your person,
For this you are swearing an oath of your being,
  For this you will come to the feast,
  For this you will come to the festival.

You must be a good servant,
You must be faithful to your trust,
  You must leave the cargo in order,
  You must leave the cargo prepared,
    For the two who will succeed you,
    For your two successors,
      For a year in the divine world,
      During a year in the divine earth,
        Oh my venerable father.

Sufficient is our word,
Sufficient are our two words,
  My father,
  My mother.

                    (Early 1965: 238–239)

The incoming Alférez then makes three genuflections, each time moving closer to the foot of the table. He places the tips of the fingers of both hands on the table's edge and bows his head on the table between his hands. The Senior Alcalde Viejo rises, comes to the side of the kneeling figure, and intones the oath:

. . .

He came to receive,
He came to take,
  The holy, divine oath,
  Here under your feet
  Here under your hands,
    Your servant,
    Your rooster.

He must be a good person,
He must be faithful to his trust,
  For twelve months,
  For twelve days,
    Here under your feet,
    Here under your hands.

To no other father of his,
To no other mother of his,
  Will he leave his cargo
  Will he leave any portion of his cargo . . .

Let no one talk against him,
Let no one murmur against him.

May he keep in sight,
May he keep before his eyes,
  His cargo,
  His service . . .

May he see it,
May he watch over it,
  As they saw it,
  As they watched over it,
    His two predecessors,
    His two antecedents.

May he leave it in order,
May he leave it prepared,
  For the two who will replace him,
  For his two successors,
    A year in the divine world,
    A year on the divine earth,
      The worker,
      The servant,
        Of the divine Lord Esquipulas, my father,
        Of the divine Lord Esquipulas, my lord . . .

          (Abridged from Early 1965: 239–240)

As the Senior Alcalde Viejo pronounces the last three lines, he makes the sign of the cross over the bowed head of the Alférez. The new Alférez then goes to the altar of Señor Esquipulas to light a candle, as the Senior Alcalde Viejo turns the staffs around so that the heads face the oath-taker. After praying, the Alférez turns around to the officials for another shorter exchange of prayer greetings. The first exchange is with the Senior Alcalde Viejo who hands him the peacock feather hat to hold during the rest of the prayer greetings. Then the new Alférez' Ritual Adviser comes forward to tie his head scarf in the way denoting a cargoholder. The hat is placed on the table with the hats of the alcaldes. The new Alférez serves rum, coffee, and rolls to symbolize the unity of all present. He takes his place with the seated officials (between the First and Third Regidor) to await the swearing-in ceremony of the second Alférez. The Junior Alférez will take his place across the table from the Senior Alférez and between the Second and Fourth Regidor (Early 1965: 236–240).

B. The First Day

3. *Flower Change in the Churches.* The Mayordomos gather at 8 A.M. in front of the church of San Lorenzo with musicians of violin, harp, and guitar. They don their ceremonial costumes, file into the church in rank order, and kneel in a row across the back of the church to recite a prayer to the saints. The fifteen participants (twelve mayordomos and three musicians), followed by their assistants, rise and pass to the side chapel.

The Sacristanes supervise the flower change that follows, and the general pattern is similar to that of the flower change in the houses the night before. Ceremonial garb is removed for the actual work and put on again before the prayers at the end. Old flowers and pine needles are removed and placed on reed mats, and new ones are arranged with other plant materials in the arch decorations before each saint. Then the Mayordomos place and light candles before the statue of the saint for whom they are responsible, kneeling and praying as their food offering (candles) is consumed.

The Mayordomos rise to form a semicircle around their musicians in the front of the church and dance for the pleasure of the saints. The music and songs are the same as those played and sung at the house flower changes. The dancing and music, with intermittent rum-drinking, continue until the Sacristán rings the tower bell at noon.

Food, brought by the Mayordomos' assistants, awaits them outside in the churchyard. The Mayordomos present their food to the seated Sacristanes, who, in turn, distribute it to the Mayordomos and their assistants, before they themselves eat. Rounds of drinks accompany the meal.

Afterward, the group moves in ranked procession to the church of San Sebastián to change flowers there. The Mayordomos and their assistants stop to greet the two sets of crosses outside the church, enter by the back door, and genuflect three times as they approach the main altar. The Mayordomos each bow before the six saints' statues and remove their ceremonial garments to begin the flower change. Two borders outlining the case of San Sebastián are renewed; old pine needles are swept up and fresh ones strewn on the floor. The Sacristanes place new flowers in the vases, the Senior Mayordomos renew the flower arch over the front door, and the Junior Mayordomos change the one over the side door. Then, in ceremonial garments, the Mayordomos follow the Junior and Senior Mayordomos of San Sebastián as they light candles and kneel to pray in front of the statue of San Sebastián and those of the other five saints.

The Mayordomos sing and dance in front of their musicians to entertain the saints in this church for an hour; after another light meal outside in the churchyard, the group files back to the church of San Lorenzo at 4 P.M. There, on the terrace, they kneel in a line in front of the main door to recite a short prayer, ending the flower-changing ceremonies for the saints of the two churches in Zinacantan Center (see Early 1965: 242–246).

4. *Coffee at the Houses of the Outgoing Alféreces.* This ritual is the first of two farewell gestures to the Elders by the Alféreces leaving cargos. After the flower change, the Mayordomos are joined in front of the church of San Lorenzo by the Alcaldes Viejos, the Regidores, the Sacristanes, and the Civil Alcaldes* from the Cabildo. This group, with the Elders in ceremonial garments and their necklaces outside their blankets, stands on the north side of the church terrace, facing the front of the church, with the Senior Alcalde in first position at the northeast corner of the terrace. The Mayordomos and their musicians line up in order of rank on the opposite side of the patio facing the churchyard (and the Elders); the Senior Mayordomo of Sacramento (highest ranking mayordomo) is directly opposite the Senior Alcalde Viejo (highest ranking cargoholder), and the Junior Mayordomo of San Sebastián (lowest ranking mayordomo) faces the lowest ranking civil alcalde.

The mayordomo line, led by the lowest ranked mayordomo, files by the line opposite them, greeting first the lowest ranked civil alcalde, then the other civil alcaldes, the sacristanes, the regidores, and finally the alcaldes viejos. Greeting and bowing and releasing take place between each individual of the mayordomo line and each official in the elders' line. The Elders themselves are greeted with added ceremony, since the necklaces they wear

---

*Civil Alcaldes are the Alcaldes Jueces described in Chapter 12. They are generally referred to as Civil Alcaldes in this chapter and in Chapter 22 to differentiate them clearly from the Alcaldes Viejos, the two top-ranking religious cargoholders.

must be shown special observance: each cargoholder lifts an elder's necklace with his right hand, touches it to his forehead, kisses it, and releases it before exchanging verbal greetings. Afterward, the cargoholder of lower rank again touches the elder's necklace to his forehead, kisses it, and releases his hold before moving on to the next elder.

After the Mayordomos pass by, the lowest ranking members of the line of Elders fall into line behind the Mayordomos to greet those of higher rank within their own line. The greetings end when the Junior Alcalde Viejo kisses necklaces with the Senior Alcalde Viejo—the only man left in his original position.

Each cargoholder, after greeting the Senior Alcalde Viejo, has followed the man ahead of him in rank to form a line in the center of the terrace. When the Senior Alcalde Viejo joins the line in last (senior) position, the Junior Mayordomo of San Sebastian (lowest rank) leads the long procession to the house of the retiring Senior Alférez.

At the house doorway stand the two (senior-junior) retiring Alféreces, watching the procession approach to greet the house shrine, and joining in the greetings performed as they were at the church. Then the Elders and the two outgoing Alféreces turn toward the San Lorenzo church to recite in unison a prayer to San Lorenzo before the Elders and retiring Alféreces venerate each other's necklaces and speak the formalized greetings.

Seated in rank order on two east-west oriented benches, facing each other, the cargoholders are served a shot glass of rum each. Then two gourds of warm water are passed down the two bench lines for rinsing mouths before each man is served a small gourd of coffee and two rolls covered with a napkin. The food is blessed by the Ritual Advisers; the coffee is drunk and the empty gourds returned to the servers; the rolls are put into shoulder bags to be eaten later. A round of rum is drunk, cigarettes passed around and smoked, and the ceremony is concluded at the house of the retiring Senior Alférez.

The procession moves to the house of the retiring Junior Alférez, and the whole sequence is repeated (Early 1965: 247–252).

5. *Circuits of the Alféreces* (LOK'ESEH VOB or "extracting the musical instruments"). The Alféreces perform a ritual circuit during which they go from the house of one member to that of another, picking up each man in a specified order. This begins on the first evening of the fiesta and is repeated on the second and third days.

They congregate at the house of the second musician (the guitar player), eat a meal, then go to the house of the first musician (the violin player) for another meal. The group continues on the house of the Alférez of San Lorenzo, and, after a round of rum, they all dance to entertain the statue of San Lorenzo there. The assistants then bring a table down from the rafters and set it up for a ceremonial meal. The two Ritual Advisers, seated at the head of the table, bless the food with the customary prayers, and the meal ends with bowls of atole.

The group goes on to the house of the Alférez of Natividad to sit in a circle for drinks of rum and dance for half an hour in honor of the Virgen de Natividad, before being served coffee and bread.

The next house visited is that of the highest ranking Alférez (of Santo Domingo), where the most elaborate activity of the evening takes place. Rum, dancing, and singing to the music of a flute, drum, violin, and guitar precedes more rum and a ritual sharing of one small loaf of bread and a large gourd of coffee by all the Alféreces in rank order before the full ceremonial meal is served.

Following this visit, the Alféreces visit the houses of the two retiring Alféreces (visited by the Mayordomos and Elders in the afternoon) and are served atole. On through the night the group goes to the houses of the rest of the Alféreces, in descending rank order. These are different houses, depending on the fiesta, since the holders of lower-ranking, less-expensive Alférez cargos do not entertain their fellows on each fiesta. At the last house visited, the Alféreces rest from the long night of "entertaining the saints."

C. The Second Day

6. *"Dance of the Drunks."* At about 7:30 A.M. the Alféreces file down from the last house visited during the night to enter the church and pray briefly at the back. Outside again, they sit in rank order on their benches with the two musicians in the middle, separating the Senior Alféreces from the Junior Alféreces. Each alférez is handed a bottle of rum by his assistant and presents it to the first musician, who sets the bottles down on the terrace in two rows of eight bottles each—the first row for the Senior, the second for the Junior Alféreces. Rum, bread, and coffee follow.

The two Alféreces entering cargos arrive separately from their houses, accompanied by their Ritual Advisers. The outgoing Alféreces and the pair about to enter office wear distinctive change-of-office garments (see Figure 41), and usually perform the first dance of the morning—the so-called "dance of the drunks," a stylized, humorous dance that is repeated at intervals. The Senior Alféreces (incoming and outgoing) face the Junior pair several yards apart and in front of the other Alféreces. Periodically they shout, leap forward to change positions with the Alférez facing them, and resume dancing. As the dance progresses, they act increasingly drunk, and their movements become more erratic. After fifteen minutes, they end the dance by falling down near the lined-up rum bottles and taking great gulps of liquor. Then they rise and enter the church to pray:

> God Jesus Christ, my Lord,
> Lord San Lorenzo,
> Lord Santo Domingo,
>   May all be done that is commanded,
>   May all be done that is commanded.
>
> I am confused,
> I have lost my way.
>
> So forgive me, my father,
> Forgive me, my lord,
>   Thy flower [rum] has knocked me down,
>   The leaf of thy tree has taken me off my feet,
>   I have lost my reason,
>   I have lost my way.
>
> Do not completely abandon me,
> Do not cease to protect,
>   My back,
>   My side. . .

(Early 1965: 256)

Rejoining the other Alféreces outside, the four continue their roles by complaining loudly and drunkenly that they have been robbed of their money and their hats. The rest of the Alféreces enter into the resulting hilarious by-play, as the four sob and protest their misfortune.

After a break for rum and cigarettes, dancing begins again with the four Alféreces who are changing cargos lined up in front of the musicians, and the others in a semicircle behind them. The tempo of the music is punctuated by the sound of the rattles they hold and the slapping of their sandals on the stone terrace. Dancing continues with short rests for rum and cigarettes until 11 A.M. During one of the rests, the Alféreces who are leaving their cargos at the next fiesta pass down the line of seated Alféreces with a bottle of rum in their hands, offering drinks and apologizing for any defects in the way they have performed their service during the year.

Sometimes they break into patterned crying to express their sorrow for any misperformance of duties.

In the late morning one of the ritual advisers of the men changing cargos leads all four to the crosses in the middle of the churchyard. They pray, then walk over to the bandstand to present rum to the flutist and drummer seated there. To the music of these instruments, the "dance of the drunks" is repeated during the next two hours with short rests. It differs from the early morning performance only in that the participants remain on their feet the whole time (Early 1965: 254–257).

7. *Mayordomos at the Church:* The Mayordomos gather at about 9:30 A.M. in front of the church—while the Alféreces are drinking and dancing outside it. When all are assembled, they put on their ceremonial garb, enter the church, and genuflect three times. The musicians of the mayordomo pair responsible for the fiesta accompany the group into the church, take their designated place on the bench in front of the statue of San Pedro, and begin to play. The Mayordomos dance in time to the music, swaying and singing, in a semicircle in front of the musicians in order to entertain the saints of the church.

After an hour the mayordomo group moves outside to their benches on the north and east side of the church terrace for a ritual drinking period. Around 11:30 the Senior Mayordomo of Sacramento picks up his empty bottle of rum from the twelve empty bottles at his feet, signaling the end of this activity. The other Mayordomos retrieve their bottles and leave (Early 1965: 258–259).

8. *Atole at the Outgoing Alféreces' Houses.* About 2 P.M. on the second day of the fiesta all religious officials (except the Mayordomos Reyes and Mesoneros) plus the Civil Alcaldes gather in the churchyard in response to invitations made by the Ritual Advisers of the Alféreces who are leaving cargos. The ceremonial lines are formed for the same long greeting ritual as that of the day before, but with the addition of the outgoing Alféreces and their two sets of musicians.

The musicians lead the officials in rank order from the church to the house of the outgoing Senior Alférez leaving—the same house visited first the preceding day—where the Ritual Advisers are greeted. The same two lines of benches have been set up outside the house, and the officials take their specified seats there while the musicians start playing music off to one side.

The ceremony is similar to the one of the day before, but on a grander scale. Two shot glasses of rum are served to each official by the drink-pourers before the first of two servings of atole. The generous serving of atole is barely sipped by each official, who hands his almost full bowl to the small boy (one for each official) standing behind him with a bucket; the atole is later drunk at home. A round of rum follows the atole sipping, and the outgoing Alféreces offer one cigarette to each official, walking down the lines of benches to present them. The second serving of atole is also followed by rum and cigarettes.

The ceremonial group goes then to the house of the outgoing Junior Alférez to participate in a second atole ceremony identical to the first. At both houses the musicians are served a meal inside in appreciation of their providing music during the year-long term of office. The atole ceremony at the house of the Junior Alférez ends the formal fiesta activity of the second afternoon (Early 1965: 260–261).

9. *Circuits of the Alféreces.* The Alféreces move as a group to the house of their second musician to begin another round of Alféreces' house-visiting. Throughout the night they visit the houses of Alféreces, from higher-ranking to lower-ranking, to dance, sing, eat, and drink. At 7:30 the next morning they are once again in front of the San Lorenzo church.

10. *The Mayordomos Count and Place Necklaces on Saints' Statues.* Two hours after sunset the ritual assistants of the Mayordomos make their ways to the several mayordomo houses. A meal of thick chili broth and rolls is served about 9:30, followed by rum. The Junior Mayordomos and their assistants then proceed to the houses of the corresponding Senior Mayordomos to begin the counting of the necklaces belonging to the different saints. They enter the house, where they kneel and pray briefly in front of the chest altar before exchanging greetings with members of the family.

The Mayordomos begin the formal proceedings by bowing to and/or releasing the musicians, assistants, and incense-bearers while reciting the salutation. Two shot glasses of rum are served all the ritual participants. The Junior Mayordomo unfolds the reed mat which is kept on top of the saint's chest, and spreads it on the floor in front of the altar. The two Incense-Bearers take positions at the side away from the altar with their smoking censers. The Senior Mayordomo lifts the chest holding the necklaces out of the main chest and places it on the mat. The Sacristán sits beside it. The Mayordomos untie their scarves to allow the ends to hang down to their shoulders—a symbol of respect to the sacred necklaces—and kneel, one on each side of the mat. The Senior Mayordomo unlocks the necklace chest and opens the lid to remove the large bag that contains the necklaces and their many coverings. He places it in the center of the mat and begins to loosen the drawstrings of the various bags and coverings.* When they are all loosened, the Junior Mayordomo passes the large bag over the censers and, still holding them, offers them for veneration by the Senior Mayordomo, the male assistants, and the Incense-Bearers. He places the large bag on the mat near the chest, and the Senior Mayordomo removes the necklaces (approximately eight in each saint's chest), unties them, and lays them out on the mat.

As the Senior Mayordomo begins the count to determine the value of the coins which make up the various necklaces, the Sacristán records it with kernels of maize (each kernel equals a peso of coin value) which are also kept in small bags in the chest with the necklaces. Each necklace has a bag of maize kernels, which is emptied into the shelf formed by the opened chest lid. The pile of maize is shifted, kernel by kernel, to another pile as the count proceeds. The necklace is held taut by the two Mayordomos—the Senior Mayordomo holding his end in his left hand and moving the coins on their strings from right to left with his right hand while counting aloud. This is done for each of the necklaces. The count varies, sometimes coming out higher (more coins or peso value than maize grains), sometimes lower. If the count is higher, the saint is pleased with the care and service given by his Mayordomo and shows his approval by adding coins to his necklace. The obverse is true when the count comes out lower; the saint shows his displeasure of the service by removing coins between counting periods. Consternation and much discussion follow a low count. When each necklace is counted, the Sacristán recounts the number of maize grains to check against the necklace's total.

The smaller necklaces are hung about the neck of the saint in the house. The rest are tied and replaced in the bags, passed over the incense by the Senior Mayordomo, and stored in the chest with the bags of maize kernels. The chest is lifted onto the altar and the mat folded and placed on top. Two shots of rum are offered to all by the assistants, followed by a cup of pozol and two rolls. Everyone then rests and may even sleep for a while.

About 2 A.M. each pair of Mayordomos sets out for the church with an assistant, usually a young son of the Senior Mayordomo, leading and carrying a censer and pine torch or flashlight. The assistant is followed by the musicians and the Mayordomos. The Senior Mayordomo carries the necklaces in the hollow of his ceremonial blanket, whose lower ends he holds outstretched in front of him. They enter the church, and go to

---

*The necklaces of San Sebastián are encased in at least nine bags.

their saint's altar, after removing their shoes and blankets. The Sacristán climbs onto the altar and ties the necklaces, handed him by the Mayordomos, around the neck of the statue.*

When all the Mayordomos have finished placing the necklaces on the statues they gather in the sanctuary to begin the dancing, which continues for four hours (3 to 7 A.M.). They dance in full ceremonial garb in front of the musicians of the Mayordomos of Sacramento, who are seated on the bench at right side of the sanctuary in front of the Sacramento statue. After an hour, the musicians of the Mayordomos of Santo Domingo replace the musicians of the Mayordomos of Sacramento and the Mayordomos dance to their music. Then the Mayordomos move to the left side of the sanctuary to dance to the music provided by the musicians of the Mayordomos of Rosario—in front of that image. They next dance in front of the statue of San Antonio, to music provided by the musicians of the Mayordomos of San Antonio. Finally they dance for San Pedro, to music played by the musicians of the Mayordomos of Santa Cruz. The music and songs throughout the rotating entertainment of the various statues are the same as those played and sung during the flower-change ceremony (on the day before the first day). During the necklace-placing activity in the church of San Lorenzo, the rituals are being performed in the church of San Sebastián by the Mayordomos of San Sebastián with their musicians and the Sacristanes (Early 1965: 262–265).

D. *The Third Day*

The Mayordomos leave the churches and gather in the churchyard of San Lorenzo where the Alféreces have assembled after their night round of house visits. The Alféreces have had food and drink at the last house where they rested, but the Mayordomos now are served by their assistants at one side of the churchyard. The Mayordomos are then ready to attend Mass.

11. *Mass, Baptisms, and Marriages.* The Catholic priest in San Cristóbal has been asked in advance by the Elders to celebrate Mass for the saint of the fiesta. He arrives in Zinacantan Center around 8 A.M., usually accompanied by two nuns who prepare the altar. Hamlet residents see the priest at this time to arrange for baptisms, marriages, and the blessing of saints' pictures. The priest performs the marriages and hears a few confessions—from Ladinos for the most part, since few Zinacantecos know about confession—before the celebration of the Mass.

---

*The statues not possessing necklaces are Purísima (the Ladino patron), Lord of the Pilar, Resurrection, and the second San Lorenzo Menor. As yet, no one has considered donating necklaces to these less important saints.

The Elders and Mayordomos sit in front on the left side of the church, facing the altar. A scattering of other men are seated behind them and women are on the right side. Ladinos and Zinacantecos are mingled in the congregation. Some of the Alféreces wander in, but they are not required to attend as are the Elders and Mayordomos.

Zinacantecos come and go during the Mass, and some may pray before a saint in the high-pitched prayer tones that often force one of the nuns to ask them to be quiet. This prohibition of praying aloud during Mass is confusing to Zinacantecos who consider a cacaphony of sounds a natural part of ceremonies.

With marriages, confessions, Mass, and baptisms finished, (and perhaps some saints' pictures blessed), the priest and nuns leave in their truck and the church bell signals their departure (Early 1965: 266–267).

12. *Alféreces' Dance on Church Terrace.* Before the priest arrived, the Alféreces had prayed in the church and returned outside to their benches; after he leaves Zinacantan Center, they begin their dancing and drinking on the church terrace as they had the day before, but without the "dance of the drunks." These four Alféreces who are changing cargos still wear their distinctive costumes but remain in the center of the Alférez group dancing with the others throughout the rest of the morning.

13. *Mayordomos at the Church (cf. 7 above).* After Mass, the Mayordomos remain in the church and dance for the further entertainment of the saints, before filing outside to take their places on their L-shaped bench for the drinking ritual which is the same as the day before.

14. *The Elders at the Hermitage.* On important fiestas the Elders file over to the Hermitage after Mass, accompanied by the Mayordomos with the necklaces of Señor Esquipulas, to take care of any cargo business—the same matters that would be brought to them there any Sunday.

15. *Mayordomos Return the Necklaces to House Chests.* Around 11:30 A.M. the Mayordomos with their musicians and the Sacristanes return to the church. The musicians of each pair of Mayordomos take their positions near the saint in their charge and play while the Mayordomos and Sacristanes climb up to untie the necklaces which are handed down one by one to the Mayordomo waiting below with the necklace bag.

Each pair of Mayordomos meets its musicians at the front of the church and departs, winding its separate way back to the house of the Senior Mayordomo of the pair, led by musicians playing en route.

Greeting the house cross at the Senior Mayordomo's, the group enters the house to kneel briefly in front of the saint's altars. The Junior Mayordomo spreads the mat on the floor, and the Incense-Bearers, who have remained at the house, take their places with censers at the foot of the mat. The Mayordomos inform their musicians and assistants that they are returning the necklaces, as they pass by each to bow or release. After two shots of rum have been served, the Senior Mayordomo places the necklace bag on the mat and the chest is removed from the altar and placed next to it. The bag is swung over the incense three times by the Senior Mayordomo before being replaced in the chest. The chest is returned to the altar, the mat folded on top, and after another round of rum the two Mayordomos take their positions in front of the musicians to dance and sing for half an hour. The ceremonial meal for the Mayordomos and musicians which follows marks the end of activity with the necklaces (Early 1965: 268–269).

16. *Alféreces' Flag Ceremony, Atole* (Early 1965: 270–274). The Mayordomos later return to the church of San Lorenzo where the Alféreces are still seated on their bench. The Senior Mayordomos, who are carrying folded flags in their shoulder bags, enter the church to get flagpoles from a corner of the sanctuary, attach their unfolded flags to the poles, and return with them to join the Junior Mayordomos outside the church.

One of the Sacristanes hands a folded red and white blanket to the Mayordomos, and all form a procession and file across the churchyard, greet the cross altar, and move on to a position in front of the Hermitage of Esquipulas. The Alféreces with their musicians file over to the Hermitage and form a line along the front, facing the Mayordomos. The civil officials come over from the Cabildo and fall in next to the Alféreces. The Elders come out of the hermitage and close up the square formed by these four groups of officials. The Mayordomo with the blanket steps out and spreads it on the ground in the middle of the square. Regidores 1 and 2 fall out and kneel at the edge of the blanket near them. The two outgoing Alféreces come forward and take the red flags of the first two Senior Mayordomos. They kneel with the flags at the edge of the blanket facing the Regidores. The two Regidores and two Alféreces crawl on their knees toward each other until they meet in the middle of the blanket where they kiss each others' necklaces and then back up to the blanket's edge. The sequence is repeated a second and a third time. On the third appraoch, the outgoing Alféreces hand the flags over to the two Regidores, saying:

> My venerable father
>> Before your sight,
>> Before your eyes,
>>> The holy divine banner,
>>> Is going to leave my feet,
>>> Is going to leave my hands,
>>>> Oh my venerable father.

Now the time is passed,
Now the time is passed.

I took care of,
I looked after
  My cargo,
  My cargo,
    To no other father of mine,
    To no other mother of mine,
Did I give the cargo,
Did I give the cargo entrusted to me.

It alone did I watch
It alone did I have before my eyes,
  My cargo,
  My cargo,
In the same way they must watch,
In the same way they must have before their eyes,
    During a year in the divine world,
    During a year in the divine earth
      The two who follow me
      My two successors,
        Oh my venerable father. . .

          (Early 1965: 270–271)

The Regidores reply with the same words, but using the third person to refer to the Alféreces. The Alféreces arise and go to the Hermitage to light candles and pray for pardon for any offense committed during their year in office.

    Outside, the Regidores arise and go around to the other side of the blanket vacated by the outgoing Alféreces. The two incoming Alféreces come forward and kneel on the opposite side of the blanket. The four crawl toward each other and kiss each others' necklaces. This is repeated a second and a third time. On the third approach the Regidores hand the flags to the incoming Alféreces as a symbol that they have now taken over their new cargos. The four arise, and the flutist and two drummers come forward. The new Alféreces fall in behind them with the two Regidores in the rear. The group circles the blanket counterclockwise three times while the drums and flute pipe out a lively tune and the new Alféreces shout with joy. They then move over to the Senior Alcalde Viejo at the corner of the square where they are joined by the outgoing Alféreces and the whole group—the old Alféreces with their Ritual Advisers, the new Alféreces, and the two Regidores—passes around the entire square of cargoholders and civil officials, bowing, releasing, and kissing necklaces with all. When the Junior Mayordomo of San Sebastián, the lowest ranking cargoholder present, has been released, they all form a rank and march first to the house of the new Senior Alcalde Viejo and then to the house of the new Junior Alcalde Viejo for a ritual drinking of atole at the two houses (Early 1965: 270–274).

Change-of-Office Ceremonies

A relatively large proportion of the annual ritual activity performed by cargoholders concerns the installation of new cargoholders and the removal of the old. As Bricker has pointed out (1966), there is a striking similarity in conception between these contemporary cargos and the Ancient Maya idea of the "Year Bearer" (see Chapter 11). The point at which the cargo is shifted from the outgoing man to the new incumbent is highly ceremonialized in Zinacantan.

Mayordomos. The six pairs of Mayordomos change five times a year (see Table 13). A few days in advance, the incoming Mayordomos visit the three churches, placing candles before the saints and invoking their help in successfully passing the coming year of cargo service. Some also visit the principal sacred mountains to so petition the ancestral gods.

Table 13. Mayordomo changes

Date of Change[a]	Fiesta (with principal day)	Mayordomos changing
January 14	Señor Esquipulas (January 15)	San Sebastián
Movable Date	10 days before Sagrado Corazón (April 22 in 1962)	Santa Cruz, San Antonio
Movable Date	Week before Corpus Christi	Sacramento
August 3	Santo Domingo (August 4)	Santo Domingo
August 30	Santa Rosa (August 31)	Virgen del Rosario

[a] The Mayordomos complete their change-of-office ritual on the second day of a major three-day fiesta—the third day being the saint's day as determined by the Catholic calendar. There are exceptions: the Mayordomos Virgen del Rosario (whose real day is October 7) change early in Zinacantan Center in order to attend the ceremonies in Salinas which are of greater importance for the Zinacantecos; the Mayordomos of Santa Cruz, San Antonio, and Sacramento also change in advance rather than on the "real" Catholic calendar dates. I cannot explain these latter exceptions unless they are survivals from the ancient eighteen-month calendar that was previously in use in Zinacantan.

The outgoing Mayordomos do not participate with the rest in the flower-changing ceremony of the major fiesta of their cargo change. They are busy with preparations in and around their houses for their change ceremony of the following day. The women of these households go to the sacred waterholes (VOꞋCHꞋOH VOꞋ, NIOꞋ, and NINAB CHILOꞋ) to bring back water for the ceremonial washing of the chests and statues. The young men go out to gather laurel and air plants from the mountainsides.

In the afternoon the outgoing Mayordomos change the flowers of their house altars for the last time. They do not change the clothes on the saint, as they normally would, because this will be done more elaborately the next day. The incoming Mayordomos arrive with their Ritual Advisers to finish dancing with the outgoing Mayordomos. Two Sacristanes also arrive and are served a meal in appreciation for their help during the past year's cargo. After the meal they measure the altar of the outgoing Mayordomos and give the measurements to the incoming pair. Then all visitors depart.

That evening the water from the sacred waterholes is put on the fire to boil, with laurel added to make a fragrant and pleasing aroma for the saint.

On the second day of a major fiesta, when a pair of Mayordomos is changing cargos, there is much ritual at the houses of the outgoing pair. The Sacristanes and the Mayordomos meet at the house of the retiring Senior Mayordomo after midnight, greeting the Ritual Advisers at the doorway. The Sacristanes enter the house, greet those within, genuflect to the saint's chest altar, and share a round of rum while the Senior Mayordomo spreads the altar mat on the floor. The outgoing Mayordomos remove the chests from the altar to the mat and the Sacristanes open them. The Senior Mayordomo passes the necklace bag over two smoking censers, and the bag is venerated by everyone.* The necklaces are transferred to a temporary container, and the regular bags and wrappings are placed in a pile with the clothes of the saint, which the Sacristanes have been removing from the chest and sorting according to whether they are washable (Zinacanteco hand-loomed cotton) or nonwashable (store silks, satins, velvets, or with sewn-on beads or ornaments). The Sacristanes count both piles of clothes and check them against a list kept in the chest; as they sort out and count, they joke about the old clothes. They divide the washable items into two equal stacks, place them in two baskets provided by the

---

*The Junior Mayordomo holds the necklace bag for the Senior Mayordomo to venerate and cry over, signifying his sorrow at ending his cargo and his having to relinquish care of the necklaces.

outgoing Mayordomos, and give them to two women who will take them at dawn to NINAB CHILO? to wash. They are accompanied by a Junior Powder Blastman and a special drink-pourer—the Senior Powder Blastman remains at the house to "answer" the Junior's blasts. The nonwashable clothes are wrapped in a mat and placed on the chest altar.

The rest of the Mayordomos, who have remained outside during the preceding activity, are now called in to help move a large table out by the house cross. There they wash the empty chests with cornhusk rags and the sacred aromatic water and leave them to dry. The incoming Mayordomos have been waiting outside the patio with their musicians until the chest-washing is finished. They join the outgoing Mayordomos in the ritual washing of themselves, as do all present in the household, in order to receive the blessing of the ancestral gods contained in the sacred water. Should any assistant, woman, or child present fail so to do, the gods will punish him with death.

When the last Mayordomo is fully reattired following the body-washing, the Mayordomos begin their usual dance patterns to the music of their musicians, interspersed with frequent drinks. This continues for several hours. Shortly after dawn, a ritual meal of chicken is served inside the house to the Senior Ritual Advisers, the outgoing Mayordomos, and the Sacristanes. Assistants take bowls of broth to the incoming Mayordomos and musicians in the patio. The dancing and drinking resume, continuing until about 9 A.M.

At this time the mayordomos, the sacristanes, and assistants go to the house of the outgoing Junior Mayordomo to perform a shorter version of the above ceremony for the statue and its chest which he has cared for during the past year. The altar is stripped, and the statue and chest taken outside to a table by the house cross where they are washed by the Sacristanes—the statue with geraniums which have been dipped in sacred scented water. The Mayordomos then line up in front of the musicians, who are seated in front of the house, and dance for an hour.

About noon the group of mayordomos (with the exception of one left to guard the drying statue and chest at the house of the Junior Mayordomo) returns to the house of the outgoing Senior Mayordomo for another ritual meal served at a large table in front of the house. The HCHIK' POMETIK (incense-bearers) return from the sacred waterhole with the washed clothes of the saint and are thanked by the outgoing Mayordomos. The Sacristanes wring out the articles and hand them to a mayordomo to shake out and hang out to dry on lines around the patio.

About 1:30 P.M. the group moves in procession to the house of the new

Senior Mayordomo, greeting the house cross and the Ritual Advisers and entering the house to kneel before the newly constructed altar. The Senior Mayordomo unfolds the faded purple cover he has brought along to prepare the new altar for the arrival of the chest. He places one side of the cover at the outside edge of the altar, holding it in position with logs or other weights and allowing the greater part of the material to hang down in front of the altar. The group is seated at a table in the house and served a ritual meal. After this, the group proceeds to the house of the new Junior Mayordomo for another placing of an altar cloth and ritual meal.

At 3 that afternoon the Mayordomos and their retinue leave the house of the new Junior Mayordomo to return to the house of the old Junior Mayordomo for the statue and its chest. Left in the sun to dry, and guarded by a Mayordomo, they are brought back into the house. The Sacristanes then dress the saints in the newly washed and dried clothes—generally four or five miniature Zinacanteco-style full-length cotton garments, one on top of the other.

Prayers are said by the retiring Mayordomos, the Sacristanes, and the Ritual Advisers in front of the altar. The two Regidores, who recently joined the group, approach the altar and pick up the statues and chest and go to the door; there they turn around and kneel facing inside the house and holding the sacred objects as each person in the house comes forward to venerate them. The outgoing Junior Mayordomo cries aloud at this final farewell to his saints (and cargo). Two Civil Alcaldes from the Cabildo and two Mayores also join the group to remain until the end of ritual.

A large procession now forms outside the house for the transfer of the saint and chest to the house of the incoming Junior Mayordomo. First are the musicians, followed by some of the Mayordomos carrying candle-holders, flower vases, and other articles for the altar. Next in line are the Civil Alcaldes with their silver-headed batons, followed by the Regidores 1 and 2 carrying the saints. They are followed in line by the two Incense-Bearers with smoking censers, and last of all come more mayordomos carrying the image cases on their backs.

The members of the procession greet the house cross and the Ritual Advisers at the house of the incoming Junior Mayordomo in the usual manner; but when the Regidores carrying the saint arrive at the doorway, the Ritual Advisers move aside to let them kneel facing inside the house for veneration of the image by the family and others inside. The Regidores give the statues to the Ritual Advisers who place them in the cases on the new altar. Then the Ritual Advisers, the Sacristanes, and two incoming Mayordomos kneel to pray.

The group returns to the house of the outgoing Senior Mayordomo where the saint's clothes and the chest are now dry. The clothes are repacked into the chest and it is placed by the house cross. A mat is unfolded and placed in front of the house cross. The four Mayordomos, the outgoing in front and the incoming in back, kneel by the mat. The Incense-Bearers of the outgoing Mayordomos take up position at the foot of the mat with their censers. The outgoing Mayordomos take the necklaces from the chests and proceed with the counting ceremony for the last time.* The Sacristanes repeat the count with the Mayordomos moving the maize kernels and announce it to the authorities present. The outgoing change places with the incoming Mayordomos at the head of mat, nearest the altar, and the new Incense-Bearers replace the outgoing ones at the foot of the mat with their censers already smoking. The musicians of the incoming Mayordomos take the places of last year's musicians, and new fireworks men replace the old ones. Then the incoming Mayordomos count the necklaces with the help of the Sacristanes and outgoing Mayordomos. This concluded, the necklaces are put away in their wrappings and chest. Ropes are tied around the chests to help lift them to the backs of the Mayordomos who will transport them to the houses of the incoming Mayordomos.

The early evening darkness is pierced by the torches and flashlights of the full procession as it progresses through the lanes to the house of the new Senior Mayordomo where, after greeting the house cross and the Ritual Advisers, the necklace chests are put on the new, awaiting altar.

Following a ritual meal the Mayordomos take their dance positions in front of the musicians and spend the rest of the night dancing, singing, and drinking. Their Incense-Bearers line up behind them and dance also. This is a celebration for the saint and for his new Mayordomo. Although most of the Mayordomos are in various stages of weariness and drunkenness from the twenty-four hours of activity, they will continue dancing until after midnight when their assistants will lead them home.

The Mayordomos who finish their cargo at this ceremony visit the churches a few days later to place candles to the saints and ask forgiveness for any wrong they may have committed during their year of service.

Two weeks after the change ceremony the outgoing Mayordomos perform their final ritual act—the dismantling of their house altars. The ceremony is essentially a flower-changing ceremony, but this time the altar, instead of being redecorated, is dismantled, the parts stored away,

---

* If an outgoing mayordomo wishes to take one of the coins off the necklace as a remembrance of his cargo year, he may do so, but must replace it with a coin of like value. The outgoing Mayordomo often provides a new bag for the necklaces at the end of his term of office. Hence, the great number of wrappings—since they are not discarded.

and the last small paraphernalia for upkeep taken to the house of the new Mayordomo. The activity begins with a meal by each Mayordomo for his family and assistants at about 8 A.M. and ends late in the afternoon at the house of the new Mayordomo. In the following description it is assumed that both altars (of saint and necklace) are in the house of the Senior Mayordomo.

The Junior Mayordomo and his assistants proceed to the house of the Senior Mayordomo. They ritually greet their musicians and dance for an hour or so with interspersing rounds of rum. Around 10 A.M. the Mayordomos remove their ceremonial garb and begin to dismantle the altars. They remove the flowers in the usual way, pull down the mats that form the altar backdrop and rip them apart, and remove from the front of the altar the iron arches that hold the flower decorations. They move the split logs that form the altar, one by one, to a corner of the room and pull up the supporting poles from the earthen floor. The Mayordomos sweep the floor of altar debris, and put the refuse on a mat which they take out into the fields. On their return, the Mayordomos stack the remaining altar parts in the corner of the house where the altar has stood.

The outgoing Mayordomos don their ceremonial garb and light two candles which they place in front of the stacked-up pieces of altar. An hour of kneeling and praying follows, with much forced crying to show their sadness at relinquishing their cargos. The Mayordomos then rise and go through bowing and releasing with their musicians as they say they are going to dance one final time for the saint. With their Incense-Bearers, they dance for an hour with several rum rounds between dancing and in an atmosphere relaxed and jocular. About 2 P.M. a ritual meal is served to all present.

The group then gathers up the small altar articles (candleholders, brooms, other odds and ends) and takes them to the house of the incoming Mayordomo, who greets them and accepts the altar implements and invites the group to be seated for an hour's drinking. About 4:30 the new Mayordomo serves a ritual meal of meat broth to the large group, and it is his Ritual Advisers who now recite the invocations over the cleansing water and food. By 5 the meal is finished and the guests depart. The outgoing Mayordomos, whose real homes are in the hamlets, usually spend one more night in the house they have rented for the year of their cargo service.

Alféreces. In the week before the new Alféreces take over their cargos they visit the three churches (San Lorenzo, San Sebastián and the Hermitage of Esquipulas) to light candles to the saints and pray for their help in the coming cargo year.

The change rituals for Alféreces have already been described in detail in the foregoing section on the major three-day fiesta, since it is during the seven major fiestas of the year that the pairs change (see Table 14).

Table 14. Alférez changes

Date	Fiesta	Alférez pairs
January 6	La Epifanía	Alférez Divina Cruz-Alférez Virgen de Soledad
January 22	San Sebastián	Alférez San Sebastián, Senior and Junior
April 29	San Pedro Mártir	Alférez San José–Alférez San Pedro Mártir
(Movable date)	La Santísima Trinidad	Alférez La Santísima Trinidad–Alférez San Antonio
August 10	San Lorenzo	Alférez Santo Domingo–Alférez San Lorenzo
September 8	Virgen de Natividad	Alférez Virgen de Natividad–Alférez Santa Rosa
Sunday before October 7	Virgen del Rosario	Alférez Virgen del Rosario–Alférez San Jacinto

Other Cargos. While change rituals for mayordomos and alféreces occur at specific fiestas during the calendar year, the rest of the members of the religious hierarchy (mayordomos reyes, mesoneros, regidores, and alcaldes viejos) change their cargos on the same night, December 30–31.

That morning the individual incoming office holders serve a round of drinks, coffee, and bread to their outgoing equivalents and their retinues at their separate houses. The two Mayordomos Reyes and the Senior Alcalde Viejo have altars of saints in their houses, and their consecration takes place on the afternoon of the 30th. The ceremony is the same as the flower-changing ritual—except in this instance there are no old flowers to be removed since the altar is newly constructed in the house of the incoming official in each case. The Ritual Advisers of the Mayordomos Reyes direct the setting-up ceremony. The same ceremony takes place in the house of the Senior Alcalde Viejo with the presence and help of the incoming Elders.

In the late afternoon the outgoing Mayordomos Reyes and Mesoneros take the necklaces, clothes, and chest of Señor Esquipulas to the Hermitage, accompanied by their Ritual Advisers. The Mesoneros place the chest on the altar, and after the saint is dressed the Mayordomo Reyes and Mesoneros dance. While they are dancing, the Elders, Escribanos, and Civil Alcaldes arrive, kneel, pray before the altar, greet the assembled participants, pray at the head of the table, and take their rank order places around the table. The foregoing activity takes place in the same manner as takes place every Sunday morning in the Señor Esquipulas ritual (see below).

A ritual meal is served about 7 P.M. to all the outgoing cargoholders by the Elders' female ritual assistants, wearing their ceremonial blankets. The servings are huge bowls of chicken with hard-boiled eggs and potatoes in thick red chili sauce.

Two hours later the actual change ceremony begins and closely resembles the Alférez oath-taking ceremony described above in its patterns and all-night duration. Processions of the many retiring officeholders now form and leave the Hermitage to visit the homes of the incoming officials for ceremonial hospitality.

Musicians with violin, guitar, and harp accompany the outgoing Mayordomos Reyes, Mesoneros, and their Ritual Advisers as they escort the new officials of like rank to their houses. Upon arrival, the ceremonial visitors greet the house cross and the new incumbent's Ritual Advisers and family and are served a round of drinks.

The group of Escribanos, Regidores, and Alcaldes Viejos, both new and retiring, have a flutist and two drummers to accompany them on their visits to the houses of the new incumbents of these offices. At the houses of the new Regidores and Alcaldes Viejos, three staffs are tied to the house cross. Since none of these officials have Ritual Advisers, the incoming official and his retinue of helpers stand at the doorway to venerate necklaces with the retiring, visiting group. Rum is offered to all at each house, and in addition coffee and bread are served at the house of the Senior Alcalde and warm atole at the house of the Junior Alcalde.

When it is time for all the groups now spread throughout the village to return to the Hermitage, rockets are shot off, and the many processions reform in ranked order and return along the steep narrow lanes to reconvene. The First Regidor takes one of the staffs from the house cross back with him to use in the Hermitage ritual.

The formal change of office for each of these cargoholders varies from the Alféreces' oath-taking ceremony only in the articles used to indicate the transfer of office. The Mesoneros are presented by the Senior Alcalde Viejo with hats and staffs, and these articles are placed in the corner of the large room of the Hermitage at the end of the ceremony. The four Regidores receive hats and staffs; they wear the hats but place their staffs under the large central table. The Alcaldes receive their black hats and silver-tipped batons and place them on the table with the hats and batons of the outgoing Alcaldes Viejos.

The order of taking office is from the least to highest rank in the hierarchy. First, the new Mesoneros and Mayordomos Reyes are sworn in, and their retiring counterparts leave the Hermitage with their musicians to form a dancing line outside where they dance to the music of their musicians. Inside the Hermitage, the new group of Mesoneros and Mayordomos Reyes dance in a semicircle in front of their musicians.

When the four outgoing Regidores escort the last new cargo member, the Senior Alcalde Viejo—highest ranking—to the Hermitage to take his oath, they enter the Hermitage themselves to pray for the last time during their term of office, kneeling in front of the altar of Señor Esquipulas and shedding forced tears of sorrow over ending their cargos. Later, outside, where the fires are still burning for cooking and warmth, the Regidores break their staffs of office and toss them into the flames. They remove their ceremonial garb and resume the attire and role of ordinary Zinacantecos.

After installing the last cargoholder, the two retiring Alcaldes leave the Hermitage and strip off their ceremonial dress. All the new cargoholders are now inside the Hermitage and the large table is prepared with a tablecloth for the ceremonial banquet which follows and is similar to the one served the outgoing officials the previous night. The large meal ends about 10 in the morning, and most of the new cargoholders disperse to their homes, having been formally invested with their offices. Only the Mesoneros and Mayordomos Reyes remain in the Hermitage to be joined by their former counterparts who instruct their successors in performing their duties and rituals for Señor Esquipulas.

The Ritual of Señor Esquipulas*

Another repeated ceremonial sequence of vital importance to the Zinacantecos is that performed for Señor Esquipulas. This figure of the Crucified Christ, according to the Zinacantecos, was first found in a cave, and is, along with San Lorenzo, one of the two oldest holy images in Zinacantan. He was first placed in the Cabildo and remained there for many years, presiding over the oaths of office for new cargoholders. He was cared for

*An intensive field study of the Hermitage of Esquipulas rituals has been carried out by Renato Rosaldo whose data adds much detail to this ethnographic summary. See Rosaldo 1968.

by an old woman, called an "Incense-Bearer," who lit the candles and burned the incense for him, and had the responsibilities that were later assumed by the Mayordomos Reyes. His first Hermitage was constructed and Mayordomos Reyes appointed in 1899 after some soldiers passing through Zinacantan molested the Incense-Bearer in the Cabildo. The present, larger Hermitage was constructed in 1961 and Señor Esquipulas moved into it.

The Mayordomos Reyes and Mesoneros begin their duties as ritual caretakers of the Hermitage of Señor Esquipulas on the weekend following their installation on December 30–31. For the three Sundays in January preceding the fiesta of San Sebastián, all four officials—senior and junior—participate in the ceremonies of drinking, dancing, and counting the necklaces of Señor Esquipulas in the house and at the Hermitage.

On the weekend following the fiesta of San Sebastián, the senior pair take over the ceremonial performance for three weekends without the help or presence of the junior pair. On the fourth weekend, the juniors join the seniors to perform the ritual, and such a weekend may be called a "change-of-duty" weekend. For the following three weekends, the junior officials take over the duties by themselves. Each pair serves six such terms of three weekends interspersed with the weekend of joint service throughout the year. For the remaining one or two weekends of the calendar year (and these officials' cargo year) in December, the two pairs serve jointly.

The change of duty involves the transfer of the bags containing the clothes and necklaces of Señor Esquipulas from the Senior to Junior Mayordomo Rey, or vice versa.* On Saturday morning (around 7) the clothes (mainly cloaks of free-hanging ribbons) are ritually washed in water brought from sacred waterholes by the wife and female helpers who have served for the previous three weekends. Others present are the Mesonero who has had the duty and his wife and/or female helpers who aid in keeping the incense burning, since the clothes are passed over the incense for purification as well as washed.

Every other weekend—on each change-of-duty Sunday and two weeks later—the Mayor of Salinas arrives with his gift of salt. His coming adds excitement as well as greater preparations to the regular weekly ritual activity since he must be given gifts of meat, tortillas, brown sugar, bread, and rum in return for the salt. On Saturday morning the Junior Mayordomo Rey and his drink-pourer go to San Cristóbal to purchase the supplies, while other helpers gather pine boughs and flowers.

---

* Señor Esquipulas has two chests: one kept on the house altar of the Senior Mayordomo Rey, the other on that of the Junior Mayordomo Rey.

At sundown the Junior Mayordomo Rey goes to the houses of his musicians with rum and requests that they come. Before they arrive the house cross is decorated with pine boughs, and incense is started burning in front of the cross. An assistant goes to the Hermitage to light candles and burn incense for Señor Esquipulas.

The flower-changing ceremony which follows has the same sequence as that described for the Mayordomos except that there are no incense-bearers. A folded mat is then taken from the house altar, unfolded, and spread on the floor in front of the altar. The Mayordomo Rey removes from the chest the three large bags, one at a time, passes them over the incense, and places them on the mat in order:

| clothing | necklace | mirror |
| bag | bag | bag |

He and the Mesonero cense them once more, return them to the chest, and shed the forced tears (for turning over the duty to the senior officials) and pray. They light two candles and then bow and release all the participants as they pray aloud. All proceed to the Hermitage to change the flowers on the arch and dance for Señor Esquipulas.

Back at the house of the Junior Mayordomo Rey there is a ritual meal (Figure 168), after which the three large bags are again removed from the chest and placed on the altar. The two officials kneel, one on each side of the mat in front of the altar, and loosen their scarves as a sign of reverence. The Junior Mesonero holds the necklace bag while the Mayordomo Rey unties the drawstrings of the inner bags containing the three necklaces. Each necklace is stored in nine bags, one fitting inside the other. The outer six are made of pink-and-white striped cloth, of the type used for tablecloths in ritual meals; these, replaced by the Mayordomo Reyes each year, are called CHU?IL POK'ETIK. The inner three bags (?AMARA ?UALETIK) are never changed.

The Mayordomo Rey censes each of the three inner bags three times and continues to hold it while the other persons present bow to it. Then he returns the bags to the mat, removes the necklaces, and places them carefully in parallel half-ellipses a few centimeters apart with the center of the necklaces toward the altar and the loose ends away from it.

The necklaces are: ?UAL BANKILAL, comprised of one hundred and thirty-seven 1-peso coins, twenty-four 5-peso coins, and one 30-peso coin, equal to a total value of 287 pesos; ?UAL ?ITS'INAL, comprised of one hundred and four 1-peso coins, twelve 5-peso coins, one 10-peso coin, and one 15-peso

168. Mayordomo Rey, Mesonero, and their musicians eating a ritual meal before counting the necklaces for Señor Esquipulas; bundles on altar contain the necklaces

coin, totaling 189 pesos; and ʔUAL SANTORENSO, comprised of nineteen 1-peso coins, or 19 pesos. Most are recent Mexican coins, readily defined and counted; some are Colonial coins that are by custom defined as being 15 or 30 pesos in value.

The Mesonero takes a small sack from the necklace bag and empties its kernels of white maize onto the mat; there are supposedly the same number of kernels as peso-value of the coins on the necklaces. The Mesonero moves the kernels from one pile to another to record the counting of necklace coins. The counting is done by the Mayordomo Rey (who holds one end of the necklace band in his left hand while the Mesonero holds the other end), using his right hand to draw each coin, dangling on its string, toward him as he counts (see Figures 169, 170).

If the final count exceeds 495 grains of maize (a high count), the necklaces have gained in value since the last count and Señor Esquipulas is pleased. The Junior Mayordomo Rey is delighted. The Musicians and the Junior Mesonero share his glee and make disparaging remarks about the absent Senior Mayordomo Rey's inability to get a high count.

169. Mayordomo Rey and Mesonero counting the necklace of old coins that will be placed on Señor Esquipulas

170. Close-up of necklace of coins

Then the necklaces are replaced in their coverings. All present bow to the large bag resulting from all the separate necklaces and their layers of nine coverings. It is censed again and placed on the altar with the two bags containing the clothes and altar cloths used at the Hermitage. The officials approach the altar, and the Mayordomo Rey places the large necklace bag in his black ceremonial robe—held out in front of him. The Mesonero places the other two bags in similar way in his robe, and the two officials dance to the music of their musicians.

As dawn begins to lighten the sky, which can be glimpsed through the smoke hole, the music and dancing end, and the officials rest as a ceremonial meal is readied for them and the musicians.

After the meal, the officials prepare to leave the house for the Hermitage before SAKUB SHA "dawn." The small procession is led by a helper carrying a smoking censer in his right hand, followed by another helper carrying rum bottles in a net bag by tumpline, then the musicians, and last the two officials with ceremonial bags held before them in their robes. Each individual bows and prays before the house altar and the house cross upon his departure. They enter the churchyard, bow and pray toward the church of San Lorenzo, then make obeisance to the crosses in the center of the churchyard before entering the back door of the Hermitage, whose bells meanwhile are being rung by another assistant. They kneel at the back, middle, and front, and the officials place their bags on the altar as the musicians take their seats along the side wall.

The Mayordomo Rey removes his ceremonial robe and shoes to climb upon the narrow ledges in front of the glass case sheltering Señor Esquipulas and opens its doors. The Mesonero hands him the clothes after turning each article counterclockwise over censers. During the week Señor Esquipulas has two mirrors hanging over his heart, two on each index finger, and one on each elbow, or a total of eight. The Mayordomo Rey now removes the saint's cap and adds seven more mirrors in following order: right index finger, right elbow, left index finger, left elbow, and three over the heart. Then five ribbons (two pink, two purple, and one green) are placed around the neck. The ʔUAL BANKILAL, then the ʔUAL ʔITS'INAL necklaces are added (Figure 171). The ʔUAL SANTORENSO goes on the case of the small statue of San Lorenzo.

The Mesonero takes the two altar cloths from their bag and spreads them on the altar. He also spreads a tablecloth (pink-and-white striped) on the large green central table where the Elders, wearing their red turbans and with staffs of office in front of them, have gathered to carry on their Sunday business of discussing cargo positions with Zinacantecos who come and go.

171. Señor Esquipulas resplendent with his decoration of necklace of coins, ribbons, and mirrors

As the Mayor from Salinas approaches the churchyard the Mayordomo Rey and Mesonero are informed and go to meet him at the northwest corner of the old Hermitage.*

The Mayor enters through the door on the west side of the Hermitage. He prays with his young son (who accompanies him from Salinas), then goes to greet the Elders in order of seniority and is invited to dance.

The salt gift that he has brought is carried into the Hermitage by the Mesonero and later taken to the active Mayordomo Rey's house for distribution to the various officials any time during the next few days. During the fiestas the distribution of the salt is made in the Hermitage and is measured out by a square wooden container (20 x 20 x 5 cm.) by the Mayordomos Reyes to the Alcaldes, and so on, in rank order. Each official who receives a measure of salt, places a quarta of rum in the empty wooden container. It is taken to the Mayor of Salinas, who distributes drinks to the assemblage before measuring salt for the next official.

*During fiestas that the Mayor attends in Zinacantan, a powder blast signals his arrival in the churchyard.

About 2 P.M., after seven hours of intermittent dancing, the Mayordomo Rey removes the necklaces, the ribbons, and the mirrors, and replaces the saint's cap. The figure is left bare of all but this and its painted loincloth. The Mayor continues to dance during the dismantling.

The Mayordomo Rey, with the articles of Señor Esquipulas carefully put away in their coverings and bags, holds the sacred items up for veneration. Then all return to his house, carrying the sacred bags in their ceremonial robes, singing to the music. The Mayor and his son accompany them.

The Mayordomo Rey dances in the house, still holding the necklace bag in his outstretched robe, before replacing the three bags (necklace bag in center, clothing bag on left, altar cloths and mirror bag on right) in the chest. The Mayor then presents a gift of salt to the Mayordomo Rey's wife, saying, "Here is your salt for Saturday and Sunday." In return he receives gifts of meat, tortillas, brown sugar, rolls, and rum liquor from the Mayordomo Rey.

All officials dance once more before making a formal departure to accompany (dancing en route) the Mayor and his son with their gifts as far as MUK'TA KRUS at the edge of Zinacantan Center. Here they ritually bid farewell to the Mayor, who will return with another gift of sacred salt two weeks hence.

22 / Cargo Rituals II

There are five ceremonial occasions each year in Zinacantan Center of extraordinary importance and with highly distinctive features: Christmas, New Year, and Epiphany; San Sebastián; Carnaval, Lent, and Holy Week; San Lorenzo; and the Virgen del Rosario.

Christmas, New Year, and Epiphany

This is a period of very special, elaborate ritual, combining the Christian calendar period of Christmas—including the Virgen de Navidad celebration days of December 15 through 25, the Christmas Eve and Day celebration of the birth of the Christ Child, the *octavo* (eight days) following, and Epiphany (or Day of Kings) on January 6—with activities of an entertainment group of costumed characters, the most important of whom are two owners of (stick) horses, their wives, and the torito they own in common. Their ritual "bullfight" performances begin with the construction of the bull on December 24 and end with the "killing" of the bull on January 6. The cargo changes already described also occur from December 30 through January 1.

Virgen de Navidad Celebrations. These begin with a flower-changing ceremony in the houses of the mayordomos on the evening of December 14. The following day the mayordomos change the flowers in the churches. On December 16, and continuing for nine days (through December 24), the mayordomos gather in front of the San Lorenzo church each morning to perform a ceremony called MISHATIK (Masses). Evidently a novena of Masses once performed in advance and in anticipation of Christmas has been discontinued. But in connection with the Masses, a squash-eating

I am grateful to John D. Early, Frank Cancian, Renato Rosaldo, Manuel Zabala, and Victoria R. Bricker for field data on the rituals and to Catherine C. Vogt for compiling and summarizing their findings.

ceremony was held and continues to take place. The nine days of eating sweetened squash commemorates the nine months of the Virgin's pregnancy—a period when women crave sweet foods.

The mayordomos take turns preparing the squash, whose cooking must begin two nights before it is to be served in the churchyard, as follows:

December 16: Senior Mayordomo of Sacramento
December 17: Senior Mayordomo of Santo Domingo
December 18: Senior Mayordomo of Rosario
December 19: Junior Mayordomo of Rosario
December 20: Senior Mayordomo of Santa Cruz
December 21: Senior Mayordomo of San Antonio
December 22: Senior Mayordomo of San Sebastián and Junior Mayordomo of Sacramento
December 23: Junior Mayordomo of Santo Domingo and Junior Mayordomo of Santa Cruz
December 24: Junior Mayordomo of San Antonio and Junior Mayordomo of San Sebastián

The first night of squash preparation, called SVOK' SMAIL SACRAMENTU or "breaking of the Sacramento's squash," is formal and complicated; the succeeding nights' preparations and cooking are less so. The Sacristanes and the Incense-Bearers of the Mayordomos supervise as helpers remove the rinds with machetes and knives, cut the vegetable into medium-sized pieces, and place the squash in cooking vessels with water and brown sugar to simmer overnight by the fire. Three shots of rum are added to make the squash turn out well. It is believed that the "soul" of the pot receives the "soul" of the rum, and, in turn, blesses the squash and prevents the cooking vessel from breaking.

The next morning some cooked squash is delivered to the houses of the mayordomos, the sacristanes, and the musicians. The second night more squash is cooked, and all of it is taken to the churchyard early the following morning. There it is served by one of the sacristanes to the assembled mayordomos, other sacristanes, the musicians, and any others present. Two tortillas filled with the squash are given each person, followed by a bowl of atole, passed and shared by everyone.

The Posada Ceremony. This ceremony, performed during the same nine-day period, takes place late in the afternoons in the side chapel of the San Lorenzo church and commemorates the Biblical narrative of Joseph and Mary's seeking lodging at many inns just before the birth of the Christ Child.

On the side chapel altar are two turtle-shell drums, a plain drum, and a rattle—instruments played by four musicians in the procession. Three other musicians (violin, harp, and guitar) stand left of the altar, and the statues of the Virgen de Navidad and San José are in front on flower-bedecked platforms.

The Mayordomos enter the side chapel, remove their shoes, and put on their black robes. The procession forms with the four drum-and-rattle musicians at the head. Next come four Mayordomos, carrying the Virgin. Four more Mayordomos follow, carrying San José. Each carrier handle has a small bell suspended from it, and as the procession moves around the chapel, each Mayordomo rings the bell that hangs on the handle in front of him. The rest of the Mayordomos walk behind, followed by two Sacristanes, one of whom reading posada hymns in Spanish from a Catholic hymnal, the other carrying a lighted candle.

The procession moves counterclockwise around the chapel and stops first at the niche of the altar of the Virgen de Purísima. The Mayordomos carrying the statues incline them until they touch heads to represent an exchange of kisses between Joseph and Mary. The procession circles back to the first altar to the continuing accompaniment of drums, rattle, bells, and hymn recitation. The saints are returned to their places in front of the altar, the drums and rattle returned to the altar, and the mayordomos pray in line in front of the statues before going outside onto the church terrace for rounds of rum.

Building the Crèche. On December 23 the Mayordomos, Sacristanes, Ritual Advisers of the Mayordomos of Rosario, the Mayordomos' musicians, and other helpers spend the day building an enormous crèche (LECHOPAT) inside the church of San Lorenzo. The roof, constructed in the morning, consists of a wooden framework, bound together with vines through which pine boughs are laced. The crèche is erected in the niche of the side chapel where the altar of San Mateo stands. Four tiles are removed from the floor to allow insertion of four pine trees, $7\frac{1}{2}$ meters high, which become the corner posts and support the roof. Pine boughs are set along the sides and tied to form the walls, and ropes of red, white, and orange (bromeliad) flowers decorate and delineate the walls and roof. Fruits are hung from the four corner posts, also as decoration. By late afternoon the crèche has been completed and the Mayordomos spend the interval before the posada ceremony drinking rum on the terrace.

The Ritual Bullfight. On December 24 the Mayordomos construct the torito at the house of the Senior Mayordomo of Rosario. The bull and its owners—the MAMALETIK (two husbands), and their wives (the ME?

CHUNETIK), and two boys dressed as angels (the ʔANHELETIK, who are considered their children)—provide entertainment in public places and private homes on December 24–25, on December 31–January 1, and on January 6. Their performances dramatize approved behavior for Zinacanteco men, women, and boys through humorous misbehavior in events concerning the MAMALETIK'S ownership of the bull, their difficulties in taming it, and its "killing" on January 6. Of these characters only the ʔANHELETIK do not behave in a humorous way. Their more passive roles display instead what may be considered the proper behavior for young Zinacanteco boys. They are present for the construction and watch with the others as the four painters from Pasteʔ supervise the making and painting of the bull. Also present are the two men who will take turns manipulating the torito through its strenuous dancing gyrations.

The bull structure is about 2 meters long and 1 meter wide at the bottom front and back, and 1½ meters high. Its framework—2-cm. saplings tied with string and 3 x 9 cm. top runner board—is covered with reed mats, except for the bottom, which is left open to allow the performers to enter (Figure 175).

The rectangles resulting from the junctures of the under-framework, able to be discerned even after the mats have been sewn together and stretched over the frame, are painted red, black, and white. A large "B" painted on the top left rear rectangle represents the Zinacantan cattle brand, and near the bull's head is painted a "bill of sale" in Spanish, such as:

> Zinacantan   1° de
> Enero   1960
> Compraron un Toro
> Valor de 700 Pesos
> de finca de Santo Tomas

The date first written on it is December 24. The bull is repainted on December 31, the day called CHKUSH VAKASH or "revival of the bull," and redated January 1. The price is made even higher than the ridiculously high one painted first on December 24. On the top front is a small triangular bull's head with two tiny horns painted green, red, and white (the colors of the Mexican flag). At the top rear is a tail that appears to be a real bull's tail.

A common Zinacanteco myth about the bull is that it was present when the Christ Child was born. The child was dying from the cold, and the other animals would not stay to warm the hut with their breath and body heat.

The bull, however, at the request of Joseph and Mary, agreed to stay, and this is the reason it is honored at this fiesta.

Between performances the bull is hung in double slings from the porch roof of the house of the Senior Mayordomo of Rosario, and is incensed three times a day. Articles used in rituals are often censed, but Bricker (1968: 249) has suggested that this ritual bull is incensed to keep "evil spirits" from entering it. Yet, the bull itself is considered bad, something to be feared; its performances are accompanied by special music considered bad; and its death on January 6 is signified by the musicians' changing to tunes that the Zinacantecos consider to be good.

The MAMALETIK. When the paint on the torito is nearly dry, two of the senior mayordomos enter the house to dress in their MAMAL costumes. They reappear, each with a scarf (POK') tied around his head in ceremonial style; a very old Zinacanteco hat hanging down in back; a red face mask with black painted beard; a collarless woolen shirt, brown with black stripes, with three-quarter-length sleeves; brown chamois knee-length breeches; and high-backed sandals. They also wear necklaces of small red and yellow crabapples strung on wire. Each holds a 2-meter-long stick horse, made of a brown wooden pole with a hand-carved horse's head with silver metal eyes and forehead decoration and with short red leather reins (Figure 172). In his right hand he carries a gourd rattle with deerbone handle. The gourds are covered with glued-on chicken feathers painted pink. The Senior Mayordomos take turns playing the parts of the two MAMALETIK.

The ME'CHUNETIK. The Junior Mayordomo partners of the senior pair costumed as MAMALETIK then enter the house to dress in their ME'CHUNETIK costumes. These are outfits similar to those of Zinacanteco women: a long, dark blue skirt, pleated at the center front; a red sash; a white blouse hanging loose over the skirt (instead of tucked inside as Zinacanteco women wear them); a large white cotton kerchief with bright pink pom-poms on the corners tied under the chins. (This head scarf is the kind worn by Zinacanteco women at their weddings and is so large that the ends hang down to the waist.) They also wear red and yellow crabapple necklaces, and men's high-backed sandals. The latter provide a visual, comic incongruity with the otherwise feminine costume.

This incongruity is further emphasized by the male gestures and behavior of these female impersonators. They do not attempt an imitation of women's smaller steps or more quiet, modest manners; but by their very large steps and leaps, their loud shouts and masculine postures, they point up the unbecoming picture of masculine behavior for women—and, by implication, any woman's envy, jealousy, or desire for male perogatives.

172. Close-up of the two stick horses of the MAMALETIK

173. The "Angels" that participate in the ritual bullfight

The ʔANHELETIK. The parts of the BANKILAL and ʔITS'INAL, "angel-children" of the MAMALETIK and MEʔCHUNETIK, are played by two boys of ten to twelve years of age, selected on the recommendation of the school principal for their ability to read and write and because they are serious, studious, and interested in becoming sacristanes (Figure 173). Their roles exemplify ideal behavior for young Zinacanteco boys in the presence of adults. They are onlookers (learning adult behavior through observing) and errand boys (passing out cigarettes to cargo officials) during the periods of ritual entertainment. Only a few times do they actively participate, such as when they say the prayers for the bull group in the church, when they touch toes and dance together and/or with their "parents," and on the last day, when they remove their costumes to join in the capture of the bull.

They are present but not costumed during the construction of the bull and the first dance performance that follows the costuming of the MAMALETIK and MEʔCHUNETIK. After the first performance (to be described later), the angels invite the bull construction group to accompany them to their homes while they dress. First, at the home of the senior angel, the guests watch another bull performance in the patio, while the angel dresses inside the house. He appears wearing high-backed sandals, bright pink or red knee socks, blue or green velvet knee-length breeches with small bells at the knee fastenings, a plain red shirt with white bands that cross the chest and tie around the waist, a red turban like those of the alféreces, and, surmounting it, a kind of crown. The crown is 30 cm. high, formed by two bent slim saplings whose arches cross each other at the top and whose ends are held in place (in four equidistant positions) on a sapling circlet that rests on his forehead over the turban. A chin strap secures it (Figure 174). The sapling circlet and arches are painted red, yellow, or green; and paper flowers, red, green, or orange, are attached to the top of the crown where the arches cross. When the angel in costume joins the group waiting in his father's patio, atole is served to everyone. The group then moves to the house of the junior angel, watches another performance as he dresses in his costume, and is served atole by his family.

The ʔANHELETIK follow the performers and musicians whenever and wherever they perform. With arms folded, they walk in the processions or sit quietly watching the bullfight performances. Members of their families accompany them to rearrange their costumes, instruct them from time to time, and look after them.

The Performance. The bull groups give performances of three acts, each with five parts. They form a developmental sequence from the first one, given in the patio of the Mayordomo of Rosario on December 24, to the

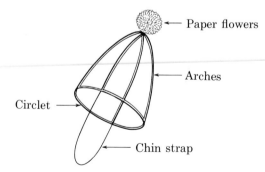

174. The angel crown

last, held in the same place on January 6. Each performance is related to those preceding and succeeding it, and the variations are affected by the physical and temporal settings in which they are performed.

The first part of each act begins with a charge or "fight" between the bull and the horse-riders. In the first act, the MAMALETIK are the riders and stand on the outside ends, in line with their ME?CHUNETIK wives beside them. They are near the house cross, with their backs to it. Twenty feet away, dancing and prancing, the bull waits for the right moment to charge. The MAMALETIK hold their horses in their outside hands (left hand for the MAMAL on the left, right hand for the MAMAL on the right) and the rattles in their inside hands. The ME?CHUNETIK lift their skirts to exhibit their genitalia in an attempt to distract the bull and lessen his chances of "goring" their husbands. The bull charges toward the four dancers as they "ride" and run toward him. Meeting in the middle of the dance area, they turn suddenly and go back to their original positions. On the third charge, the bull gores the horse-riders (Figure 175).

175. The bull "gores" a MAMAL

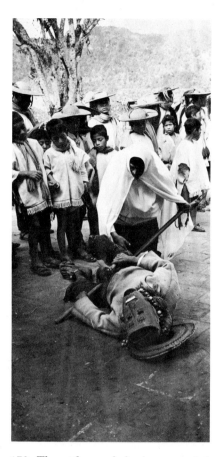

176. The ME'CHUN helps her wounded husband to his feet

177. The masked MAMAL holding his stick horse gets to his feet

The second part includes the agony of the wounded riders and their wives' search for a curer. The MAMALETIK have fallen to the ground, groaning and writhing as if in great pain. The bull retires to one side and stands quietly as the ME'CHUNETIK run to their husbands' sides and hover over them with wails and cries. They use the stick horses to help get their men to their feet (Figure 176), but in doing so they push the poles far up the mens' groins. Remarks with double meanings, obscene and sexual, fly back and forth between the actor couples, as they ascertain where and how severely the husbands are hurt. With their wives' help (Figure 177), the MAMALETIK crawl over to the highest ranking official seated nearby watching.

The third part of the act consists of the wives' beseeching the official to "cure" their husbands, to heal their wounds. The joking and double meanings continue, as illustrated by the following account:

ME?CHUN: Please father, please my patron, mend the bones of my husband, my companion.

Official: Why, what happened to him?

ME?CHUN: A bull gored him.

Official: Well, why did you buy the bull then?

ME?CHUN: He thought it was a good bull and, besides, I wanted it. I thought it would be good.

Official: You shouldn't have bought it, for his goring is causing much suffering. Is anything broken?

MAMAL: Yes, something is broken. Please mend my bones.

Official: I'll try to mend them.

ME?CHUN Please mend them if possible.

Official: I'll recite the [curing] formula:
TONTIKIL PUZUL ?I TONTIKIL CH'ABEN*
Find your place, bones!
Find your place, muscles!
Don't leave your hole muscle!
Don't leave your hole bone!

Good. Try it and see if they are well;
try it and see if they are healed.

[MAMAL jumps in the air three times and repeats following formula]

MAMAL: Stretch out, bone!
Stretch out, muscle!
Remember your place, bone!
Remember your place, muscle!
Don't go to another hole, muscle!
Don't leave your hole empty, bone!

(Bricker 1968: 218–219)

Depending upon the setting, the curer may be the Presidente (or other civil official), when the performance is given in front of the Cabildo; a cargo official or the ritual adviser when the bullfight group is visiting the cargo-

---

*Plant names recited as part of curing formula.

holders' houses; or one of the musicians, when no one of official rank is present. If there are two persons of authority present—for example, both the senior and junior alcaldes viejos—the one of higher rank "cures" the higher ranking MAMAL and the authority of lesser rank "cures" the lower ranking MAMAL.

The fourth part of the act is the curing ceremony itself. The official passes the rattle of the wounded MAMAL three times over each "wound" as he recites the curing prayer. The passes are always made over the patient's genitals, as well as elsewhere on his body. Also in jest, the official "curer" may reach over with the rattle to touch the genitals of one of the ME'CHUNETIK or put the rattle up her skirt. He brings laughter to the watching crowd when he asks the MAMALETIK if their wives are really women. One MAMAL may reach over to touch the other MAMAL's wife on the buttocks and be scolded or hit by the jealous husband, again to the amusement of the onlookers. When the official is asked what payment he wants, he usually asks to sleep with the MAMAL's wife—again provoking laughter—and then requests that the entertainment continue.

The fifth and last part of the act is the dramatization of the recovery of the MAMALETIK who rise from their prone positions on the ground, leap into the air three times to show their full recovery, then jump onto their stick horses to run about with shouts, indicating that they are ready to bait the bull or fight each other again.

A full performance begins with the foregoing "fight" of the MAMALETIK against the bull. In the second act, the bull plays no part; but the MAMALETIK charge each other on their stick horses, whacking the poles in passing, and accompanied by their "wives." In the third act, it is the ME'CHUNETIK who take the stick horses and charge each other, as their husbands run beside them. In each of these acts, however, the parts remain the same: (1) a "charge" or "fight" involving the bull and/or the horses; (2) the wounded horse-riders dramatizing their agony and being helped by their mates; (3) the petitioning of an official or musician to "cure" the wounds; (4) the curing ceremony; and (5) the complete recovery demonstrated by the riders.

Full performances take place inside and in the courtyards of the churches of San Lorenzo and San Sebastián, at the houses of cargo officials, and in front of the Cabildo (on New Year's Day and January 6). An added routine, which occurs in San Lorenzo Church on Christmas Day, New Year's Day, and the Day of Kings (January 6) is a "spinning lesson" by the ME'CHUNETIK, which, with its comic overtones, prescribes the knowledge and behavior expected of a model Zinacanteco wife. On New Year's

Day, another routine occurs in front of the Cabildo, during which the MAMALETIK are jailed by the civil officials for not having the legal papers of ownership for the bull. These routines will be described later.

In the interplay of remarks as the "wives" ask their injured husbands if and how they are hurt, and beseech the "curer" to make them well again, the puns or double meanings are evident, as in "My husband's bone [penis] is broken." In the case of the "wives" thrown by the horses, the husband may say, "Her side [womb] is damaged." They ask that their injured mates be "cured" so that they may have more children. The official adjures the wounded part, either penis or vagina, to stay with its mate after the cure—advising marital fidelity—but also tests these comedian couples when he asks as payment "a prickly squash," referring to the wife's vagina and his wish to use her. He scolds the husbands for buying a bull they cannot manage and bucking horses they cannot tame, and tells the wives they should not even attempt to mount the horses, which women are not supposed to ride. In all the humorous acts of the bullfight group, the underlying thread is one pointing out accepted behavior and illustrating to the watching crowds the injurious results of unaccepted behavior.*

The Birth of the Christ Children. At about 10:30 P.M. on December 24 the ceremonies re-enacting the birth of the Christ Child(ren) begins at the church of San Lorenzo. A procession is led by the bullfight performers and musicians, followed by the Alcaldes, Regidores, Presidente, the Síndico and four Civil Alcaldes. These last twelve officials serve as godparents, and take turns carrying the figures of the Christ Children and those of Joseph and Mary. Next comes a young man with a smoking censer, and, finally, the mayordomos and sacristanes.

The procession moves to the church of San Sebastián to the music and dancing of the bullfight group, the shooting of skyrockets, and the sound of the flute and drums. At San Sebastián the Christ Children are placed in the crèche, and the ritual bullfight is performed for the saints. Then a posada ritual takes place: the Mayordomos carry the statues outside the church, and the doors are shut. They sing petitions to enter and are answered by a group of singers inside, at first refusing, then granting entry. The statues of Joseph and Mary and the two of the Christ Child are brought in and placed in position. The birth symbolically takes place at the moment when the statues of the Christ Child are placed in the crèche. A Ladino girl recites Catholic prayers before the main altar, and sparklers are handed out to the young children observing the pageantry. Sparklers seem to be

---

*A more detailed discussion of the humor in the bullfight episodes is found in Bricker 1968: 202–252.

everywhere as the children run with them inside the church, darting in and out among the crowd.

At one A.M. the procession returns to San Lorenzo Church where the Christ Child figures are placed in the crèche by the Presidente. Then the crowd comes forward to venerate the images in the flickering candlelight and to the resonant sound of the turtle-shell drums.

Christmas Day. The Catholic priest arrives from San Cristóbal to say Mass at 9 A.M. The bullfight group then perform in the church, with the parts of MAMALETIK being played by two other senior mayordomos (replacing those of the day before), and their junior mayordomo partners performing the ME?CHUNETIK roles. The three acts of the full performance are followed by a new routine: the "spinning lesson."

The Spinning Lesson. The ME?CHUNETIK sit down on benches, and, with gourds and cotton yarn on spindles, they demonstrate their skill at spinning and weaving to the many Zinacanteco women present. They ask the women, "Can you spin as well? See how beautiful my work is! If you cannot match this, we pity your poor husband!" The MAMALETIK join in this teasing and joking admonishment to the women, sometimes pointing to specific women whom they scold for being poor spinners and weavers. The women who have been singled out this way, pull back in real dismay and embarrassment, covering their mouths with their hands or pulling their shawls across their faces. A farce it is, and amusing to everyone but the women singled out; yet it is also a pointed lesson, providing guides to Zinacanteco women on how to be good, hard-working, model wives. This routine is repeated in San Lorenzo Church on New Year's Day and the Day of Kings.

New Year's Day. On the evening of December 31 the Mayordomos and the Sacristanes sleep in the sacristy of the church of San Lorenzo and awaken just before midnight. At that time the Sacristanes toll the church bells and set off rockets outside, while the Mayordomos, in pairs, light candles and pray to their saints for protection for the community in the year to come.

The Mayordomos then go to the house of the Junior Mayordomo of Rosario to sleep until time to prepare the bullfight performers at 4:30 in the morning. A full performance is given for the Christ Child figures in San Lorenzo Church from 5 to 6, and the bullfight group returns to the same house for breakfast. They go back to the church for another performance, that may be interrupted by the arrival of the priest coming to recite an 8 o'clock Mass. Such a confrontation is both interesting and disturbing. The priest halts the performance and coerces the watching crowd into quieting down for Mass. The nuns accompanying the priest poke the

Zinacantecos with long sticks to push them toward the altar and into position as a congregation. The Sacristanes are ordered to lock the church doors to prevent people from leaving. The captive congregation has to be told when to kneel and stand, because many of them rarely, if ever, attend Mass.

After the priest's departure, the group resumes the performance, dancing in the back of the church and again near the crèche. They then start on another round of visits to the houses of the new cargoholders, always followed by a large crowd which share in the free rum and atole.

At 4 P.M. the bull entourage visits the Cabildo where the Presidente and other civil officials are seated outside waiting for them. The Presidente requests papers proving ownership of the bull, and the MAMALETIK put on a ludicrous act of horrified chagrin as they try to explain how they have been lost. The crowd enjoys their exaggerated alarm and shouted protests as the Presidente accuses them of having stolen the bull and orders the Mayores to jail them. There follows a lively game of chase and pursuit as the MAMALETIK flee down the road, pursued by the Mayores. They are captured and escape to be captured again, time after time—to the delight of the large crowd watching. The younger boys enjoy the humor and excitement and run to follow the exciting chase. The MAMALETIK are finally caught and put into jail for fifteen minutes. Youngsters gather to peer at them in their comic distress through the barred openings of the jail door. The ME?CHUNETIK plead with the Presidente for their release with wails and excuses, and he finally relents and orders them freed. The bullfight performance is then given in front of the Cabildo for the civil authorities and the Presidente, who becomes the curer when the MAMALETIK and ME?CHUNETIK are gored by the bull or thrown from their horses.

Late in the afternoon the performers wearily return to the house of the Senior Mayordomo of Rosario for an evening meal. The torito is placed in its supporting slings, and costumes are put away until January 6 performances.

The Day of Kings (January 6th). The Epiphany is a large three-day fiesta with a change of two Alféreces. It is the end of the Christmas period, hence, the last time the bull group actors perform the antics of sheer endurance required for the repetitious acts that end near midnight of this day with the "killing" of the bull. Additional features of the group's activities this last day are the presentation of the nombramiento (the special board with lighted candles secured on top and the list of names of the incoming Mayordomos of Santa Cruz and the incoming Mayordomos of San Antonio written on the bottom) which is placed on the main altar of the Hermitage;

the procession around the center with the Escribanos, Regidores, and the Elders with stops at the street crosses where the bull group performs as the Regidores collect money from the surrounding houses for the fiesta of San Sebastián (January 20); the mimicking of the Alférez flag-changing ceremony; and the chasing and killing of the bull.

The Angels' Dance. After the Mayordomos have placed the necklaces on the saints in the church, they assemble at the house of the Senior Mayordomo of Rosario for a meal. The Mayordomos of Santa Cruz and San Antonio who are performing as MAMALETIK and MEʔCHUNETIK dress in their costumes. The ʔANHELETIK arrive in their costumes and join their ritual parents in a dance to carnaval music. The senior MAMAL, MEʔCHUN, and Angel stand in a line on one side, facing their junior counterparts. In time with the music, they slowly raise right legs to touch toes with their opposites; then they raise left legs and touch left toes. This is repeated with right legs and toes, after which the pairs of senior-junior characters cross over, trading positions. After this small dance figure has been done three times, the ʔANHELETIK retire to the sidelines to watch and occasionally pass cigarettes as the regular bullfight performance with its three acts is performed three times. Afterward the bull group and its followers proceed to the San Lorenzo Church.

The priest's arrival to say Mass may again coincide with the bullfight performance, interrupting it and swelling attendance of the Catholic service. But, again, the priest's departure will signal resumption of the bull group acts, performed in front of the crèche, and then in the back of the church, and including the "spinning lesson." The whole performance is given twice in the back of the church, twice in the church of San Sebastián across the valley, and once for the Alféreces as they sit on their benches in front of San Lorenzo Church.

At noon the MAMALETIK and MEʔCHUNETIK, still leaping, shouting, and dancing, take their nombramiento to the Hermitage and place it on the altar of Señor Esquipulas, after greeting the Elders present there. The Senior Alcalde Viejo and the First Regidor give rum to the gathering, as the MAMALETIK and MEʔCHUNETIK distribute coffee and rolls with the help of their assistants.

Returning to the church of San Lorenzo, the bull group joins the Mayordomos as they remove the necklaces from the saints and change the MAMALETIK–MEʔCHUNETIK personnel. The necklaces are returned to the house altars, and after a meal the Mayordomos and the bull group reconvene at San Lorenzo around 2 P.M.

A large procession makes the rounds of the center to collect money for the fiesta of San Sebastián. Leading it is the bull group, followed by the Junior Mayordomos, the Sacristanes, the Angels, the musicians, the Senior Mayordomos with their flags, the Escribanos, and, finally, the Elders. The long file stops at seven street crosses en route, and the bullfight performance is given as the Regidores disperse to collect from nearby houses. At this time, the spectators try to grab for the small crabapples that make up the performer's necklaces as often as they can, and assistants are kept busy replacing them. The procession finally returns to the Hermitage to be joined by the Alféreces, who had danced most of the afternoon at San Lorenzo, and by the Presidente and the civil officials.

Flag-Changing Ceremony and its Parody. The assembled cargoholders then begin the flag-changing ceremony, marking the cargo change for the Alférez of Divina Cruz and the Alférez of Soledad. The bull group is stationed near one side of the Alféreces, who are seriously performing this part of their change-of-office ceremonies. As the Alféreces bow, kiss necklaces, and exchange them, the MAMALETIK and the MEʔCHUNETIK bow, kiss, and exchange their necklaces of apples. When the Alféreces cross themselves and pray, the MAMALETIK and MEʔCHUNETIK cross themselves with rattles in hand, and pray long, loud, and ludicrously. As the Alféreces exchange flags, the MAMALETIK imitate them by exchanging stick horses. The crowd of spectators, witnessing both the serious and comic rituals, is highly amused by the mimics. The ceremonies end with a procession of the important members of the two groups.

The Chase and Killing of the Bull. The bull group rests at the house of the Senior Mayordomo of Rosario after the mock flag ceremony and prepares for the evening sorties to the center of the village that precede the midnight killing of the torito. These trips to the center and back are marked by the high excitement of the crowd and the frantic movements of the bull; the performer makes the torito appear to sense its approaching death. The crowd chases it harder and faster, and the ʔANHELETIK take off their costumes and are given lassos to help rope the bull. He charges madly in the churchyard and the roadway, desperately trying to avoid the nooses which fly at him from every side. A crowd of children runs behind, following his struggles with excited interest. The bull is caught and pulled to the ground. The person who has caught him takes out a bottle and offers drinks to the bull performer. This revives the bull, and it jumps up to go to the closed doors of one of the town bars and pound until the owner opens his cantina and serves the drinks demanded by the bull entourage. They return to the house of the Senior Mayordomo of Rosario to dance and rest before another excursion to the town center.

After the first trip into the center, the bull-painters cut off the bull's bright horns and fasten deer horns in their place. Five more trips are made to the center, as described above. On the return from the last excursion, the bull is caught and tied to a thick post in the patio of the Mayordomo's house. The MAMALETIK and the MEʔCHUNETIK climb on top the bull and plunge wooden knives, covered with silver foil, into its neck; and a clay vessel is held below to catch the "blood"—rum mixed with yerba buena, onions, and chili to color it red. The "blood" is served ceremonially to everyone present by the MAMALETIK. Men then get inside the bull and thrash about in the framework until the reed mats of its body are torn apart. Its mangled remains are put aside to be fully dismantled the next day.

A ceremonial meal, accompanied by more "blood," celebrates the death of the bull. The tortillas are prepared by girls and young women, and the older women supervising them are told by the MAMALETIK:

> Wash the lime-soaked kernels well and take them to the mill! The girls must be accompanied by older women so that no boys will accost them on the path. Watch that the miller doesn't seize their hands! Count your change well, so that he doesn't cheat you. When the corn is ground, return together. When you get home, make a lot of tortillas. People from all the hamlets are going to eat together once we have killed the bull. (Bricker 1968: 247)

The Fiesta of San Sebastián

The fiesta of San Sebastián in January requires more advance preparation, involves more cargoholders, attracts as large crowds, and lasts longer than any other saint's fiesta in Zinacantan. Although the church of San Lorenzo is larger and more often used, and although San Lorenzo is the patron saint of Zinacantan, his fiesta in August does not entail the time in preparation and participation required for that of San Sebastián.

As noted, money for this fiesta is collected on the Day of Kings. Three visits must also be made between January 1 and 15 by two groups of the preceding year's cargoholders with gifts of rum and bread for the owners or custodians of two sacred objects used in this fiesta. The objects are a KʼOLTISHYO, a large red and gold jousting target ring, kept by a family in Pasteʔ, and a TʼENTʼEN, a special slit drum kept by its owners in ʔElan Voʔ. The senior members of the previous year's hierarchy petition for the KʼOLTISHYO from Pasteʔ and accompany it during the fiesta. The junior members of last year's hierarchy ask for, and later accompany, the TʼENTʼEN from ʔElan Voʔ.

While last year's hierarchy prepare for the entertainment aspects of the fiesta, the new cargoholders buy supplies and make arrangements for the ritual aspects entailed in the change of office for the Mayordomos (senior and junior) of San Sebastián and the Alféreces (senior and junior) of San Sebastián. Besides participating in the change-of-office rituals, the new cargoholders will be honored spectators at the afternoon entertainments given by the former cargoholders and will participate on January 25 when the retiring Senior Alcalde Viejo turns over his ritual cargo articles—including the sacred picture of San Sebastián—to the new Senior Alcalde Viejo, who had taken his oath of office on January 1.

Other preparations include visits made before the fiesta of Señor Esquipulas (January 15) to insure the presence of three visiting saints (the Virgen del Rosario from Salinas, Nuestra Señora de Guadalupe from Nabenchauk, and the Señor Esquipulas from Tierra Blanca) for that fiesta in the Hermitage. These three saints remain for the Fiesta of San Sebastián, not returning to their hamlets until January 23.

The fiesta days of San Sebastián are recognized by Zinacantecos to be four in number, instead of three as in other major fiestas. Each of these days has a specific name in Tzotzil: January 19, CHAN K'OBOL or "[day of] jousting"; January 20, BA VE'EL or "[day of] the first banquet"; January 21, MU'YUK VE'EL or "[day of] no banquet"; January 22, SLAHEB K'AK'AL VE'EL or "day of last banquet." These are the core days of the fiesta, which, however, are preceded by days of related ritual as in other important fiestas (see Chapter 21). In addition, on January 16, 17, and 18, last year's hierarchy must make visits to San Sebastián Church to ask forgiveness for any wrongdoing during their cargo year. Thus, cargoholders are participating in ritual activities that are part of the San Sebastián fiesta from January 16 through January 25. The large number of participants, the great amount of time, energy, and resources expended, and the proliferation of costumed entertainers—who may incorporate Mayan mythological figures as well as Spanish-derived fiesta characters—raise questions not yet answered as to the origins and seemingly increasing importance of this fiesta.

The fiesta of San Sebastián gives the new cargoholders the opportunity to celebrate their first major fiesta, and they are garbed suitably in their robes of office. The outgoing officials, however, in their role as "entertainers" (HTOY K'INETIK) are in distinctive costumes. The senior entertainers (MUK'TA HTOY K'INETIK) are six officials of the top three levels of the cargo hierarchy divided into three costumed couples: senior and junior HKASHLAN, the two Alcaldes Viejos; senior and junior HSHINULAN, Alféreces of Santo Domingo and San Lorenzo; senior and junior SAK HOL, First and Second Regidores.

178. The "Senior Spanish Gentle-
man" dances at the Fiesta of San
Sebastián

The HKASHLAN are costumed as Colonial "Spanish Gentlemen " (Figure
178) wearing gold-embroidered red coats and knickers, red knee-socks, and
high-backed sandals. The Senior HKASHLAN carries the San Sebastián
picture in a net bag attached to a leather shoulder strap around his shoulder
and the K'OLTISHYO (jousting target) in his hand. Both men have mirrors
dangling from strings around their wrists and necks.

The HSHINULAN* are costumed as "Spanish ladies" (Figure 179) in embroidered white blouses, red skirts, knee-length red stockings, and high-
backed sandals. Rosaries and mirrors hang from strings around their necks;
on their heads fingertip-length veils of purple (for the senior HSHINULAN)
or red (for the junior) are surmounted by broad-brimmed Alférez hats, of
black felt with gold bands holding a peacock feather upright. They carry
combs in small blue and white enamel bowls.

The two SAK HOLETIK, "White Heads," are dressed in white with red
turbans. They wear white hats, long-sleeved white shirts, white capes that

*The terms HKASHLAN and HSHINULAN are currently in use to designate men and women
Ladinos.

179. The "Senior Spanish Lady" releases a bow from a musician

hang just to below their hips, white breeches, red knee-socks, and high-backed sandals. On their foreheads dangles a large block tinsel "E," turned 90 degrees clockwise so the open side of the letter faces down. Rosaries and mirrors are suspended from their necks, and each carries a small bow and arrow in his left hand and a rattle in his right. (Figure 180).

The junior entertainers (Figures 181, 182, 183) include five costumed groups: four pairs dressed alike, and six in one group costumed similarly. The roles are taken by lower-ranked members of the past year's hierarchy, as follows: senior and junior KAʔBENAL, the Third and Fourth Regidores; senior and junior BOLOM, Alféreces of Trinidad and San Antonio; senior and junior K'UK'ULCHON, two Mayordomos Reyes; senior and junior TSONTEʔ, two Mesoneros; six HʔIK'ALETIK, six Mayores.

The two KAʔBENAL wear purple dress coats and breeches, and the black felt regidor hat from which a long red or purple braid hangs down to the waist. They carry rattles, and bows and arrows tied together.

180. The White Heads with their rattles and small bows and arrows

181. Blackman (foreground) and Crows and Jaguars (background)

182. Spanish-moss-wearers and Crows (with ears of maize in their beaks)

183. Left to right: Spanish-moss-wearers, Crows, and KAʔBENALETIK

The two BOLOMETIK (Jaguars) wear one-piece jaguarlike costumes with black circles and dots painted on orange-brown material and tails and hats of jaguar fur. They carry stuffed squirrels, iguanas, and a coati; also whips and sharp pointed sticks reddened at the tips. The sticks are used as penises when they are poked into the genitals of the stuffed animals. The jaguars make the sound "huh, huh, huha."

Each of the two K'UK'ULCHON (literally, "plumed serpent," but their costumes suggest and many Zinacantecos refer to them as "crows") wears green knee-length trousers, a white shirt with green and red dots, and a white hat with red dots and an attached beak that holds an ear of corn (a large ear for the senior crow, a smaller one for the junior). Small wings are strapped to their backs, and they make the sound "hurr, hurr."

The TSONTE'ETIK (Spanish-moss-wearers, also referred to by informants as "Lacandones")* wear green velvet pants, black ceremonial robes, and black felt hats from which Spanish moss cascades down as a cape.

Five of the H'IK'ALETIK (Blackmen) wear leather pants and jackets; the sixth, dressed like a Ladino woman, wears a blue mask with white rings outlining the mouth and eyes and carries a white doll, her "child." The men's faces and arms are blackened with ashes, and they carry stuffed animals—squirrels, iguanas, or spider monkeys (Figures 184, 185)—and sharply pointed sticks like those of the Jaguars. Their characteristic sound is "ves, ves, ves."

The stuffed squirrels carried by the Jaguars and the Blackmen are painted red on their undersides to emphasize their genitals. Around their necks are draped necklaces and ribbons such as Zinacanteco women wear; indeed, the animals do represent Zinacanteco women, the wives of last year's cargoholders who failed to end their year of office honorably by participating in this final fiesta. The defectors and their wives are named, lewdly joked about, and chastised by the junior entertainer group. For example, on a visit to a new cargoholder's house, an H'IK'AL holds up a stuffed squirrel and pokes its genitals with the stick penis (representing the defaulting official), saying: "Look at Marian Peres from Masan. He's just a fucker who keeps doing it at the foot of a mango tree!" Or, again, he speaks to the women in the house, saying: "Look, my mother; look, my lady, at what Lol ʔUch is doing with Shunka (his wife). How shameless they are, always fucking each other, even when not in their own home!" Then, to the squirrel he says: "Now don't *you* kneel and fuck here. Is this your house here? Yes, you may join the musicans, but don't fuck each other by the fire" (Bricker 1968: 271).

*A tribe of Maya-speaking Indians living in the eastern lowlands of Chiapas.

184. A HʔɪkʼAL with his stuffed animals

185. HʔɪkʼALETIK dancing with stuffed iguana and squirrels

The ridicule of the defaulting cargoholders and their wives centers on their having placed sexuality above cargo responsibility. They are blamed for spending money on ribbons and necklaces for their wives instead of using it for cargo expenditures. They are accused of having intercourse in public places and in unnatural positions. The public shame to which the negligent, though absent, cargoholders are subjected serves a double purpose: their public denouncement and a warning to the new cargoholders of the way they will be ridiculed at the next fiesta of San Sebastián if they do not carry out their duties competently and completely.

The following is an over-all sequence of events for the fiesta:

January 16–18.   Last year's cargoholders visit church of San Sebastián to ask forgiveness for negligence in their cargos.

January 17 (BALTE⁷ TA NA).   Mayordomos renew flowers on their house altars. Assistants prepare the San Sebastián churchyard for the fiesta (see Figure 186).

January 18 (CHUK NICHIM).   Mayordomos renew church flowers. Early morning arrival of the T'ENT'EN, met and accompanied to the owner's relative's house by junior entertainer group. K'OLTISHYO also arrives and is met and escorted by senior entertainer group.

Evening.   Junior entertainer group members gather at the T'ENT'EN house to begin round of visits to new cargoholder houses with T'ENT'EN; visits continue every night until all new officials have been visited. Senior entertainer group gathers at the house of retiring Senior Alcalde Viejo after his house altar flower change, and is present for ritual washing of the San Sebastián picture.

186. Setting for the Fiesta of San Sebastián

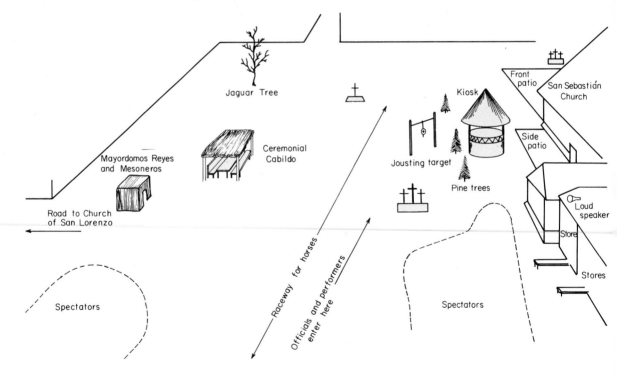

January 19 (ʔISHPERESH and CHAN KʼOBOL).

8 A.M. New Elders meet the San Sebastián picture from Rancho San Nicolás and escort it to San Sebastián Church. They escort the three visiting saints from the Hermitage to San Sebastián. Alféreces dance and drink outside San Lorenzo.

1 P.M. Entertainment at the San Sebastián churchyard by the two entertainer groups (not fully costumed). Program consists of: horse-racing by senior group; KʼOLTISHYO jousting by senior group; dancing to TʼENTʼEN by junior group; and 5 oʼclock finale of more horse-racing by the senior group.

6 P.M. Coffee at houses of retiring Alféreces.

Night. Alférecesʼ oath of office in Hermitage. The two entertainer groups visit houses of new cargoholders to perform.

January 20–22 (SBA KʼEL KʼIN), the general term for main fiesta day, may be used for these three days, as well as their individual names. Events common to all three days are: groups costumed and entertaining the crowds; earlier arrival of officials in churchyard, since visiting saints, already met, are in place in church; Mass recited by Catholic priest; formal afternoon program by entertainer groups for new hierarchy in San Sebastián churchyard.

January 20 (BA VEʔEL, "[day of] first banquet").

Early morning. Mayordomos place necklaces on saint statues.

8 A.M. Mass sung by priest accompanied by organist.

11 A.M. "Dance of Drunks" performed in San Lorenzo churchyard by the four Alféreces of San Sebastian changing cargo. Exchange of drinks with the Mayordomos.

Noon. Gifts of fruit given by Mayordomos to the Sacristanes (each receives three nets full), and by the Alféreces to their musicians.

12:30 P.M. Junior entertainers perform near the Jaguar Tree (BOLOM TEʔ).

1:30 P.M. Junior entertainers divide into two groups: one group goes to Jaguar Rock (BOLOM TON) to perform clowning sequence; the other goes to sacred waterhole (NIOʔ) to light candles, pray, and dance. They reunite at San Sebastián churchyard to provide entertainment during banquet.

2 P.M. Banquet with special food served to new cargo and civil officials at two seatings: first, new Elders and civil officials, second, new Alféreces. They are entertained by junior entertainer group.

2 P.M.   Senior entertainers serve atole to new Mayordomos near San Sebastián church door.

2–4 P.M.   Formal afternoon entertainment by senior and junior entertainer groups.

4 P.M.   After ceremonial leave-taking of saints, crosses, and church, all groups proceed to new Alféreces' houses for atole.

Night.   Circuits of Alféreces. Visits to houses of new cargo-holders by entertainer groups continue.

January 21 (MU'YUK VE'EL, "[day of] no banquet"). Activity is similar to that of January 20, but without the banquet or the ritual at Jaguar Rock and waterhole.

2–4 P.M.   Formal afternoon entertainment.

5 P.M.   Alféreces' flag-changing ceremony in rear section of San Lorenzo Church, followed by atole at the houses of new Alféreces.

Night.   Circuits of Alféreces. Visits to cargoholders' houses by entertainer groups continue.

January 22 (SLAHEB K'AK'AL VE'EL, "day of last banquet"). Activity similar to that of January 20.

Before noon.   Mayordomos remove necklaces from statues of saints and return them to house altars.

1:30 P.M.   Banquet again served to new officials; the junior entertainers active at Jaguar Rock and the waterhole, and then entertain at banquet.

2–4 P.M.   Formal afternoon entertainment by senior entertainers.

5 P.M.   Junior entertainer group lights candles at Hermitage, prays for forgiveness of any wrongdoing in past year's cargo, and dances briefly, before going to house where T'ENT'EN is to honor and guard it during this last night.

January 23.   Visiting saints escorted out to edge of Zinacantan by new Elders. The K'OLTISHYO is escorted similarly by senior entertainer group, and T'ENT'EN by junior entertainers.

January 24.   New Senior Alcalde Viejo erects his house altar.

January 25.   Retiring Senior Alcalde Viejo hands over symbols of office to new incumbent in a special house ceremony. Symbols include: the sacred picture of San Sebastián; two candleholders; a box containing a stamp, a seal, and paper; and the Zinacantan cattle-branding iron: B.

Certain features unique to the Fiesta of San Sebastián and noted briefly in the foregoing list of events will now be described in greater detail. The churchyard of San Sebastián is prepared by the assistants of entertainer groups on January 17. The pasture fence is removed from around the churchyard, and pine trees are placed around the fiesta area in front of the church. Two brush shelters are made at the side of the church—upright posts support pine branches, making a large shaded area. One shelter is used as a ceremonial Cabildo where the civil officials and new Elders sit on long benches to view the afternoon performances and to partake of the banquets served them there on January 20 and 22. The other shelter serves as headquarters for the Mayordomos Reyes and Mesoneros and their families and assistants, all of whom are responsible for preparing the food for the banquets, and who use the shelter as a kitchen (see Figure 186).

Two upright posts with a crossbar are set into the ground at the end of the area where the horses are to charge. The crossbar will hold the K'OLTISHYO for the lance jousting of the senior entertainer group. A tree almost 20 feet high, stripped of its bark, is set securely into the ground to be used by the junior entertainers who will climb it during their clowning afternoon entertainment. This is the BOLOM TE? or Jaguar Tree.

On the afternoon of January 19 a "rehearsal" of the afternoon entertainment for the next three days is held. Shortly after midday the civil officials and the Elders enter the San Sebastián churchyard in ranked procession, pray in the church a short time, and file out to take their places on the benches in the pine-bough Cabildo.

Eight horsemen, sponsored by the senior entertainers and two of the junior entertainers (the Mayordomos Reyes), arrive and line up their mounts at one end of the raceway. A signal is given, they charge down the raceway and return, and the riders dismount and lead their horses away. The charge of galloping horses, their thundering hoofbeats, and the streaming ribbons on the riders' hats provide an exciting prelude and postlude—a similar charge ends each afternoon's entertainment—to the performances.

The senior entertainer group enters now on horseback, led by the musicians on foot and a man, the HCH'AMTE? MOL or "elder bearer of the lances," who carries a pair of black and red wood lances. The senior entertainers wear their black ceremonial robes and red turbans for this rehearsal, but will be in their costumes the next three afternoons' performances. The group dismounts at the bandstand, and, as the band plays, the Senior Alcalde Viejo remounts. Holding the K'OLTISHYO, he rides to the upright posts and ties it with a rope so that it hangs from the crossbar. He rides back to the Lance Bearer to receive one of the lances. Praying to the sun (HTOTIK K'AK'AL), San Lorenzo, and Santo Domingo, he rides between the upright posts striking the jousting target with his lance. Dismounting, he rejoins his group to pray in the church. They return to the churchyard and approach the three crosses, where their musicians settle on the cement base. The Senior Alcalde Viejo removes from his net bag the picture of San Sebastián and places it in a niche at the base of the crosses. To the tunes of their musicians, the senior entertainer group begins afternoon-long dancing and drinking at this spot.

The junior entertainers perform at the west end of the churchyard near the Jaguar Tree. The T'ENT'EN is carried by one assistant and played by another as they make their way through the crowd, dancing forward and then backward, toward the tree. The drum is placed at the base of the western cross nearby, and ritual drinking precedes the afternoon of dancing and joking insults directed at the absent cargoholders represented by the stuffed animals. The entertainment ends around 4 that afternoon with the final thundering gallop of the eight horsemen.

On January 20 and 22 a banquet is served to the new civil and religious officials in the pine-bough Cabildo. The senior entertainers entertain them with banter and serve them bites of sticky jam from small round wood containers, until the junior entertainers come to amuse the officials toward the latter half of the banquet.

The junior entertainers, meanwhile, have divided into two groups, one going to perform at BOLOM TON, "Jaguar Rock," the other to hold a ritual at NIO?, a sacred waterhole. The two Jaguars, three of the Blackmen, and the senior KA?BENAL, K'UK'ULCHON and TSONTE? dance off to the Jaguar Rock, a large limestone boulder, in the nearby pasture but screened from the churchyard by trees. At the base of the boulder is a wooden cross where the KA?BENAL flanked by the two Jaguars places four white candles and lights them. The others join them to pray and then dance. The Jaguars and Blackmen climb the boulder to light three candles in front of the cross on top. They light a fire of corn fodder and grass and shout for help as they toss the stuffed squirrels to their fellows on the ground. Those on the ground toss the animals back up, and the squirrels fly back and forth amid joking and shouting.

The grass fire on the boulder represents the burning of the Jaguars' house, and the two Jaguars descend from the rock to crawl into a cavelike indentation at its base and lie there. The KA?BENAL "shoots" them with his bow and arrow; then, turning to seize two Chamula boys from the crowd, he "shoots" them. Symbolically, the Jaguars are revived by the transference of the souls of the Chamula boys to their animal bodies and leap up, "alive" again, to drink liquor, dance, and cavort with their costumed sub-group on the return to the churchyard.

They meet the other junior entertainers, who have been at NIO⁷ to light candles, pray, and dance. Together they approach the banqueting officials to entertain them. The Blackmen capture Chamula boys time after time and drag them to the officials to bargain for food in exchange for the boys, whom they threaten to castrate and eat. Younger boys are terrified, but those slightly older are amused and pleased at being thus singled out.

The Blackmen take the food they have received to the Jaguar Tree; they climb to its branches and spit or throw food down to their fellows. They offer bits of food to their stuffed animals, which they throw back and forth, poking at their genitals with the pointed stick penises and accusing them of preoccupation with sexuality (see Figure 187).

The officials being served the banquet are numerous enough to require two seatings at the ceremonial Cabildo. The Elders and the civil officials are served first; the new Alféreces are served last. The serving for each official is one whole boiled chicken with hard-cooked eggs and potatoes in a thick chili sauce.

While the junior entertainer group entertains the officials, the senior entertainers serve atole to the Mayordomos in front of the church. After the final horse charge of the afternoon, all of the hierarchy groups file in ranked procession out of the churchyard to go to the two houses of the outgoing Alféreces for the customary serving of atole.

In the evening the Alféreces make their circuits of Alférez houses, and the two entertainer groups visit the houses of the new cargoholders. The groups proceed separately, each with its sacred object—the T'ENT'EN drum with the junior group, the K'OLTISHYO jousting target with the senior.

January 21 continues the fiesta patterns of the market, the carnival rides, the loudspeaker music, and the crowds amused by the entertainer groups in the town center and near San Sebastián Church; but there is no large banquet for the officials on this day, nor do the Jaguar Rock performance and ritual at the waterhole take place. The afternoon performance, opened and closed with the horse charge and presided over by the new officials in the ceremonial Cabildo, does occur.

It is followed in the late afternoon by the Alférez flag-changing ceremony, which takes place in the back part of the San Lorenzo Church. This is the only Alférez change during the year when these officials do not change places as they exchange the flags. After this ritual, the new hierarchy is served atole at the houses of the new Alféreces.

January 22 repeats the sequence of events noted for January 20. But in the late afternoon, the Blackmen leave the San Sebastián churchyard to light candles in the Hermitage and pray for any poor performance of their past year of cargo. They dance one last time for Señor Esquipulas and then proceed to the house where the T'ENT'EN drum is being kept. They guard and honor it during this last night that it is in Zinacantan.

Through the afternoon and evening the crowds begin to thin, as many Zinacantecos leave for their homes in the hamlets. By the following day Zinacantan Center has a deserted air after the departures of the visiting saints, the T'ENT'EN, and the K'OLTISHYO, which are escorted formally to the outskirts of the village by the Elders, the junior entertainers, and the senior entertainers.

There is no recorded data for activities on January 24, but it is assumed that the new Senior Alcalde Viejo sets up his house altar and prepares to receive his articles of office.

On January 25 the past year's officials escort the retiring Senior Alcalde Viejo with the articles of office to the house of the new Senior Alcalde Viejo. An elaborate ritual follows as the chest containing the picture of San Sebastián, the two candleholders, the box with the stamp, seal, and papers, and the branding iron of Zinacantan are transferred to the house altar and safekeeping of the new and highest-ranking cargoholder. With this ceremony, the fiesta period for San Sebastián ends.

Carnaval, Lent, and Holy Week

Carnaval (K'IN TAHIMOLTIK, *"the fiesta of games"*). Carnaval consists of the five days preceding Ash Wednesday. The Alcalde Shuves and the two Pasioneros are in charge of the ritual entertainment, and the H'IKALETIK, or Blackmen, (although their skin is not blackened for this role, and the word has the connotation of "demons" or "evil ones") are the active performers. These roles are taken by young Zinacanteco men who need not be cargoholders. In addition, there is a TOT H'IKAL, "leader of the evil ones," whose part is given to a man known to have the wit and energy for the role. Usually the same man will play the role for five or six years. Finally, all of the religious and civil officials participate during the five days.

The Alcalde Shuves carries out his full cargo duties during Carnaval, and there are increasing difficulties in filling this less important cargo position. It should be held by a man who has passed three cargo levels, but the position is not popular because it is not costly; hence, it has little prestige. Often a man must be pressured to accept the office, and sometimes

187. Jaguars and Blackmen climb the Jaguar Tree

it is not filled. During the fiesta the Alcalde Shuves wears his black ceremonial robe, red turban, a black felt hat, knee-length socks, and high-backed sandals; he carries a red rattle and a silver-tipped baton.

The senior and junior Pasioneros begin their cargo duties during Carnaval, but continue on and complete their service during the Easter season. By contrast with the alcalde shuves, the pasionero cargo is expensive and, hence, important. During Carnaval, the Senior Pasionero must buy two bulls, and the Junior Pasionero one bull, to provide food for ceremonial meals. They must also provide the chicha (the special drink of Carnaval) which is generously served to the officials and to other participants upon request. A Chamula is employed to carry a full cask of chicha on his back; when it is empty, he runs back to the house of the Senior Pasionero to refill it. The Pasioneros must collect huge stacks of wood for the cooking fires and may have to add to the money collected for candles.

The two Pasioneros dress in long-sleeved white shirts with reddish woven bands (that crisscross the shoulders and are tied around the waist), green velvet breeches, red turban, knee-length red socks, and high-backed sandals. This is the traditional wedding outfit worn by a Zinacanteco man. They carry rattles decorated with feathers, and have a special flag as a symbol of office. The woven sashes and flags are provided for them by the Mayordomos of San Sebastián. The TOT H'IK'AL has a blackened face and wears an old black hat, long-sleeved collarless shirt, brown breeches, old brown army coat, and, over the coat, an old blanket with large white and brown patches. He carries a bull's horn full of chicha and a stick as his staff of office. He eats at a separate small table where he is served a double ration. Throughout the fiesta he recites *bombas* (see below). The H'IK'ALETIK wear old, even worn-out, Ladino-style clothing—in combinations that each young Zinacanteco chooses for himself—and participate as "demon" (PUKUHETIK) members of groups that follow different leaders in visits to various cross shrines. One, dressed as a woman, is considered the "wife" of the TOT H'IK'AL.

Music is provided by flute, drums, violin, harp, guitar, and a cornet played to "call the H'IK'ALETIK."

In preparation for the fiesta the two Pasioneros light candles and pray to the ancestral gods at the four sacred mountains (SAN KISHTOVAL, SISIL VITS, MUSHUL VITS, and KALVARIO); the Mayordomos renew the flower decorations on their house altars and on the church altars; and the Regidores decorate their house crosses with new pine boughs.

The fiesta begins late in the afternoon of the Friday before Ash Wednesday when the sacristanes gather at the house of the Senior Pasionero to count the money contributed by the Mayordomos for candles. The Mayordomos, Pasioneros, and TOT HʔIK'AL observe the process. The women make tamales, and a meal is served to all present. Then the Pasioneros don their costumes and go with gifts of coffee, rolls, and rum to the houses of the Alcaldes Shuves, the TOT HʔIK'AL (where he dresses amid many jokes), and the musicians. The gifts are presented and bombas (short, humerous rhymes) are sung. For example:

> A year ago I went to Guatemala,
> From there I brought my white pants,
> To make a brown girl love me,
> To have the eyes of a hawk.
> Bomba!

> In the patio of my house,
> I have a Romero tree,
> It is the time for my girl
> She looks like a blue heron.
> Bomba!

All the Carnaval celebrants then return to the house of the Senior Pasionero to eat, drink, and dance until dawn.

On Saturday morning the carnaval cargoholders—alcalde shuves, pasioneros, and TOT HʔIK'AL—are sworn into office at the Hermitage of Esquipulas by the regidores. As symbols of office, each receive staffs, rattles, and flags, the latter being transferred on the red blanket outside the Hermitage in a ritual similar to the flag-transferral ceremony of the alféreces. A mayor is appointed Keeper of the Flags; he must guard all these cargo symbols while the celebrants are eating and drinking and have left them at the house cross of a cargoholder who is being visited on the ceremonial rounds that will continue for four days.

The same Saturday morning, helpers of the Pasioneros go to San Cristóbal to purchase candles, and atole is served to the Carnaval celebrants at the house of the Alcalde Shuves.

On Saturday afternoon, the celebrants begin a ceremonial round of visits to the houses of all the cargoholders in Zinacantan Center, starting with that of the Senior Alcalde and descending through the hierarchy. At each house they sing, dance, and recite bombas and are given rounds of liquor. This round of visits is continued, with interruptions only for meals served alternately at the houses of the two Pasioneros and for brief sequences of other rituals, until Tuesday night. The Carnaval celebrants are not allowed to sleep during this period, or, the belief is, they would die. The activity is especially wearing for the TOT HʔIK'AL, who is not allowed even the occasional relief of a substitute to take his place, as the other celebrants are.

On Sunday the Catholic priest comes to say Mass in the early morning. The Carnaval celebrants continue their round of ceremonial visits to cargoholders' houses, pausing between visits to entertain crowds in the streets with their comic behavior.

Early Monday morning the celebrants are fed meat, coffee, and tortillas at the house of the Senior Pasionero, along with the Mayordomos, Sacristanes, and a group of young Zinacanteco men who have costumed themselves as HʔIK'ALETIK. After the meal, the group forms a procession to offer candles and prayers, as well as the comic performances of the TOT HʔIK'AL and his HʔIK'ALETIK "children" to various cross shrines in and around Zinacantan Center. They circle each cross shrine three times, either around or in front of the crosses, before they make their offerings. The procession goes first to KRUS MUCHIK, and from here small groups are sent to other cross shrines—two Mayordomos to MUSHUL VITS and two to YAʔAHVIL. Later they rejoin the others at KALVARIO. The next stop is VOʔCH'OH VOʔ where the Alcalde Shuves remains to perform ritual. The others proceed to the summit of SISIL VITS to perform both the sacred candle-lighting and praying, as well as the comic chicha-drinking, dancing, and bombas. They descend to the cross shrine at the foot of SISIL VITS where they are served chicha by the Alcalde Shuves. All reassemble at KALVARIO where the rituals are repeated and a meal is served. The Carnaval celebrants are fed tamales and the bones of the bulls that have been butchered for the fiesta by the Pasioneros, then continue the ceremonial round of visits to cargoholders' houses throughout the day and all night.

On Tuesday the celebrants, along with the Mayordomos and Sacristanes, are fed again at the house of the Senior Pasionero. Candles are lighted and prayers are said at the hermitage, the church of San Lorenzo, and finally at the church of San Sebastián by the Sacristanes. The Mayordomos and Alféreces both dance at the church of San Sebastián while the Sacristanes pray and the HʔIK'ALETIK dance and recite bombas. For an hour the church resounds with the competing voices and music of the four separate groups and the movements of the crowds entering to observe the activity.

Two ceremonial banquets now take place: one at the house of the Junior Pasionero, where the Carnaval performers eat; the other at the Hermitage, where the elders and civil officials (at the first sitting) and the Alféreces (at second sitting) are served.

The TOT H'IK'AL and a few of his H'IK'ALETIK begin three runs with letters exchanged between the Junior Pasionero banquet group and the Hermitage group. These letters, written in Spanish by the Escribanos, contain jokes and charges against the H'IK'ALETIK. The TOT H'IK'AL and his companions shout and joke as they run back and forth and collect a following of young boys on their sorties through the streets.

After the third letter from the Junior Pasionero group to the Hermitage group has been delivered, the TOT H'IK'AL remains at the Hermitage to make his "chocolate"—a mixture of brown sugar, finely ground coffee, and rum. He serves this to the banqueting officials; in return he is given some of their food. He passes it out to his "children," and a near-riot ensues as they fight over each tidbit. The TOT H'IK'AL also may give limes and onions to the officials in exchange for some of the food.

After the exchange of "chocolate" for food has been made with both seatings of banqueting officials in the Hermitage and after their banquet, the Carnaval group amuses the crowds with music, dancing, and bombas at the churchyard. The crowd swells as the time approaches for the chasing and jailing of the TOT H'IK'AL and his "children."

The Presidente orders the Mayores to put the TOT H'IK'AL and H'IK'ALETIK in jail for misdemeanors. The chase and resulting capture and jailing of the entertainers is the high point of Carnaval for the onlookers. The TOT H'IK'AL and his cohorts break away time and again from their cooperative captors to lead them on more wild runs through the crowds. Some of the sub-leaders of the "demon" groups lead their fellows to put up more of a fight against their captors.

When the TOT H'IK'AL, who is the last to be jailed, is safely behind bars, the Carnaval officials (Alcalde Shuves and Pasioneros) plead with the Presidente and Síndico for the prisoners' release. The request is granted, and the "demons," their wrists bound, are led out of the jail in pairs by a mayor. Their wrists are untied, and the "demons" go to the churchyard to "visit the houses," that is, to have rum served them by the cargoholders' wives. This is a short session of heavy drinking by everyone and a time when the women become unusually drunk.

The TOT H'IK'AL is given gifts by the Pasioneros and is finally allowed to go home to rest from his four-day ordeal. The crowds disperse as the rest of the Carnaval officials and the "demons" return to the Junior Pasionero's house to finish off the fiesta food and drink. On the way, the music changes from Carnaval tunes to anything that the musicians feel like playing. At the house the "demons" break up and burn the wooden varas they have been carrying during the fiesta. The musicians remove the flags from the long poles on which the Pasioneros have carried them and hand them to the Mayordomos of San Sebastián who are the flag custodians as well as the providers of the crisscross bands worn across the Pasioneros' chests. Music and bombas accompany the eating and drinking which ends around midnight.

On Ash Wednesday the Mayordomos of Santa Cruz attend Mass with their musicians and remain for the distribution of ashes. During the Mass the Pasioneros go to pay their musicians for the Carnaval playing. The Mayordomos and Sacristanes then go to the houses of the Pasioneros to finish the chicha and drink and dance most of the day.

Lent. Each Friday in Lent a procession forms in the side chapel of San Lorenzo Church with the entombed Christ image (Santo Entierro or HMANVANEH, "The Buyer [of sins]") taken in a slow circuit through the church. This figure is accompanied by other saints appropriate to the season also carried on platforms with bells attached. The tinkling of the bells and a chanting of the *Te Deum* along with incense and lighted candles make a weekly ceremony that attracts many living in Zinacantan Center. Most important is the Fourth Friday in Lent, which is becoming a major three-day fiesta, without, however, a change of Alféreces. A band comes and the Virgen del Rosario from Salinas accompanies the usual Lenten Friday procession. New clothes for HMANVANEH may be bought this week and blessed before being put away until Holy Week. The procession has more images, including the Large Cross, and is joined by the band when it goes outside into the churchyard.

Holy Week. The day before Palm Sunday the Mayordomos renew the church flowers. In the afternoon the priest arrives to marry all unmarried cargoholders who will be participating in the Holy Week ceremonies. Some couples are young and beginning a married life; others are older couples with families who are being officially married for the first time. The marriage ceremony is followed by a Mass.

On Palm Sunday the priest holds services followed by the procession of palms in the church and churchyard. All present are expected to join the procession, but the cargoholders are reluctant to participate.

On Monday of Holy Week the Sacristanes go to San Cristóbal to buy aftershave lotion to be used to wash The Buyer on Wednesday. On Tuesday there is a procession similar to that of the fifth Friday in Lent. On Wednesday The Buyer is washed with aftershave lotion by the Alcaldes Viejos and the Holy Elders (CH'UL MOLETIK). This is accompanied by elaborate ritual, and a red canopy covers the figure as it is moved, undressed, and so on. It is censed, washed reverently, redressed, censed, and prayed over in its bier. A procession like that of the Fourth Friday then takes place. The two Pasioneros, portraying "Los Judios" (the Jews), two, as usual, in black shirts, green breeches, and red stockings, carrying small guns, take positions on each side of the bier to guard it throughout the night. With them, sitting on the floor under the bier, is a flutist who periodically plays short mournful notes.

On Thursday the Sacristanes, Alféreces, Alcaldes Viejos, and the Holy Elders and their assistants remove the Large Cross from San Lorenzo Church and carry it in procession on their shoulders through the village to announce the beginning of the Maundy Thursday rituals. The groups return to the churchyard to be served the banquet of broth, meat, dried fish, snails, and shrimp that commemorates the Last Supper. As each group finishes, the priest hears their confessions, since the cargoholders are expected to receive communion today. In midafternoon the priest washes the feet of the Mayordomos—as Jesus did for his apostles—before he says Mass.

After Mass the Sacristanes prepare the sanctuary for the burial of The Buyer. They spread a reed mat on the floor with a bench on each side and a foot-high crucifix in the center. They empty baskets of rose petals over the crucifix until it is buried in petals. The Alférez of San Lorenzo and the Junior Mayordomos sit to the left of the mat, the Alférez of Santo Domingo with the Senior Mayordomos and a prayer cantor sit to the right. The cantor leads a series of Tzotzil chants which the Mayordomos repeat after him. This group keeps vigil over the rose petals through the night.

In the middle of the main part of the church a larger company surrounds the bier of The Buyer. Many, who have arrived from the hamlets and placed their candles near the bier, may stay there throughout the night. The two Pasioneros and the flutist remain on watch and are joined for several hours by an informal choir of young men who stand at the foot of the bier and sing hymns. The Alféreces enter as a group to place candles by the bier.

In the side chapel there is a regular Catholic Holy Thursday repository arranged in advance by the nuns. White satin drapes the altar of La Purísima, and vases of flowers stand below.

The Large Cross is set up by removing a trap door over a hole at the middle of the sanctuary rail. The foot of the cross is inserted into the hole, and all the officials help raise it into position. Large platforms are set up in front, two wooden staircases are placed leading up to the platforms, and the whole framework is lashed together with rope. Two large pine trees are set up, one on each side of the cross, turning this shrine into one with three crosses (on a grand scale) in the same way that a mountain shrine is converted by the addition of pine boughs. Pine needles and geranium and rose petals are strewn over the platforms.

The Alcaldes and Holy Elders carry the bier of The Buyer to the platform where two Holy Elders lift the figure, with cloth bands and the help of the Alcaldes and the other Holy Elders, up and into position on the Large Cross. As the Christ figure is slowly raised, the Sacristanes sound wooden clappers and a choir chants Lenten hymns. The Mayordomos bring up the figures of La Virgen Dolorosa (The Virgin of Sorrows), San Juan, and Santa Magdalena and place them at the foot of the cross to complete the crucifixion scene. The Sacristanes now hang Judas (a Ladino-dressed dummy with a cigarette in his mouth) over the main church door.

From noon until 2 P.M. the church is thronged with Zinacantecos coming to pay homage and pray to The Buyer. Every cargoholder brings a basket of fresh flowers with lighted candles in it to hand up to the Mayordomos of Santa Cruz who arrange them on the platform—until it becomes covered with a profusion of bright flowers and candle flames. Colored ribbons that have been draped over the cross are cut in pieces and handed to those who request them. Bouquets are handed up to be brushed against The Buyer and returned. Many kneel before the platform to pray and cry.

Around 2 the Alcaldes and Holy Elders return the baskets to their owners, lower The Buyer to the bier, and reclothe the figure. The bier is taken in procession as on Fourth Friday; this time, however, the cross does not accompany the group but remains in its position in front of the sanctuary.

After the procession, through the church and counterclockwise around the churchyard, has returned to the church, the bier is placed on the floor. The red canopy is held over the bier by four men as more people come to pray and venerate. San Juan, La Virgen Dolorosa, and Santa Magdalena are placed at the head of the bier. Small bouquets made from the flowers of the cargoholders' baskets are stroked over The Buyer by the Pasioneros (who sit near the saint statues), the Alcaldes, and two Holy Elders (who sit on the right side of the bier) and the other Holy Elders (on left side of bier) to be handed to Ladinos and Zinacantecos who come to kneel and pray at the foot of the bier.

On Holy Saturday the Mayordomos arrive early at the church to return its appearance to normal. The Large Cross is taken in a short procession around the churchyard before being returned to its usual place inside against the wall; the platform, pine trees and steps are taken away. That evening the priest comes to perform the Catholic Easter vigil service, and at the *Gloria* the dummy of Judas is lowered and burned.

Easter Sunday resembles the third day of a fiesta with the Alféreces drinking and dancing in front of the church, joined by the Mayordomos. At 1 P.M. the cargo officials line up on the church patio to exchange greetings as on an Alférez change day; later they visit the houses of the Alféreces of Trinidad and San Antonio for atole and rum. Variations on the usual atole–rum Alférez ceremony are: after the first rum round the Escribanos rise, stand by the patio cross, and read the names of all cargoholders and their home hamlets; a second rum round follows, but it consists of two full large glasses of rum which must be drunk, not poured off! This ends Easter and the ritual activity in honor of The Buyer.

The Fiesta of San Lorenzo

The fiesta of San Lorenzo (August 7–11), patron saint of Zinacantan, follows in general the pattern of the three-day major fiesta described in Chapter 21. But, because San Lorenzo is the most important saint and must be given more homage, some events occur on the day before the traditional first day, and the change of office of the two most important alféreces (San Lorenzo and Santo Domingo) occur the day after the third day.

By the morning of August 7 activities are well under way. A large market, with rows of stands and booths as well as hundreds of open-air venders, is established on the north and east sides of the church of San Lorenzo. The Alféreces are performing on the terrace in front of the church, and the Elders are seated in the Hermitage of Esquipulas.

In the early afternoon the Junta (a committee of three appointed by the Presidente to manage the fiesta) marches out to the eastern edge of the village to meet the brass band from San Lucas that has been hired to play. The band is escorted to the church of San Lorenzo to play for the saints, then established in the kiosk in the churchyard to play throughout the afternoon. In the late afternoon the Mayordomos renew the flower decorations on their house altars; in the evening they meet at the church to change the flowers on the church altar. They sleep in the San Lorenzo sacristy to be ready to meet the visiting saints early the following morning.

Shortly after sunrise on August 8 all the cargoholders and the two Capitanes (see below) assemble at the church of San Lorenzo to form processions to meet incoming saints and escort them to the church. The visiting saints have arrived well before dawn and are waiting with their Mayordomos at fixed points to be escorted into the Center. The procession moves first to the eastern edge of the Center to greet and accompany San

Sebastián from the Ladino ranch of Labor Grande. On a second trip they go to MUK'TA KRUS to greet the Virgen de Asunción from Ixtapa, Señor Esquipulas from Tierra Blanca (a Ladino settlement near Salinas), and the Virgen del Rosario from Salinas. On the third trip they greet San Lucas from San Lucas and the Virgen de Guadalupe from Nabenchauk. These six visiting saints are escorted back to the church and placed inside on decorated stands where they remain until August 11.

The most characteristic feature of this fiesta are the two Capitanes who dance at the crosses where the visiting saints are greeted and in the procession on the way into the church of San Lorenzo. These Capitanes are cargoholders of the first (lowest) level who fulfill their year's cargos during the main four days (August 8–11) of the Fiesta of San Lorenzo. Hence, the men who hold these cargos must have the physical endurance to perform their dancing and hold their liquor.

The Capitanes wear brown skullcaps from which bright feathers dangle; a rolled red turban tied around their heads with ends falling to their knees; a blue scarf around their necks; an everyday shirt over which is worn an old, torn black suit coat; and blue or green breeches which meet the red stockings below the knees. The two men carry bright scarves in their right hands, and gold paint streaks their faces. They accompany the processions meeting the visiting saints and perform their dance at ritual stops and visits throughout the fiesta. In the dance the Capitanes face each other, making rhythmic hops on one foot while extending the other foot in front, off the ground. At intervals of a few minutes, they raise the scarves in their hands, shout, and exchange places, now hopping on the foot that had been lifted, extending the other foot. As the saints are brought into the village, the Capitanes dance in procession just in front of them.

Also during the morning of August 8 the new Escribanos and Elders sit on benches at tables on the north side of the San Lorenzo Church with the waiting lists for cargos. The reading off of the names of future cargoholders begins before 7 A.M. and continues until after 2 P.M. The petitioners present bottles of rum to the Escribanos and Elders and remain to be certain their names are still on the lists, because according to informants, "at times they lose the names"—a polite way of saying names are sometimes erased and others put in their place through bribery or error.

The escorting of the saints into San Lorenzo Church is accomplished by shortly after noon. The visiting Mayordomos who have brought them are served a meal at the Hermitage by the Elders' assistants who provide the food. During the afternoon volunteer groups bring presents of candles and new clothes for the saints. The alféreces remain in front of the church for their usual dancing and drinking.

188. For important fiestas a brass band is imported from a neighboring Ladino town

In the evening the band is taken into the church to play for an hour in honor of the assembled saints before returning to the bandstand to play for the fiesta crowds (Figure 188). Late in the evening the incoming Alféreces take the oath of office in the Hermitage. The Mayordomos spend the night counting their saints' images necklaces.

Early in the morning on August 9 the Mayordomos place the necklaces on the saints in the church. They are escorted as they approach the church by the fiesta band playing. The rest of the day is one of fiesta and resembles the second day of a three-day major fiesta for the crowds of people whose numbers may reach 5000 and include many Chamulas, and increasing number of tourists (from Mexico, the United States, and Europe), Ladinos from Zinacantan and San Cristóbal, as well as many families from the outlying hamlets.

Around 10 A.M. there is a horse race sponsored by the Alféreces as entertainment along the main street in front of the Cabildo. The fourteen riders assemble with their horses in front of the Cabildo. Each Alférez gives the rider of the horse he has provided a drink of rum, before and after the two back and forth "runs."

In the evening after dark, the fiesta crowds are treated to fireworks. *Castillos* (castles), as many as six or eight of the large framework structures are set up and ignited for the crowd's delight, are interspersed with *toritos*. These firework bulls, that shower the people with sparks from exploding firecrackers and pinwheels, are carried by men, who dart through the crowds like erratic bulls, protected by the mat covering of the framework. Whizzing bombs cross the churchyard on taut wire just above head height. Sometimes there are *globos,* hot-air ballons, a meter or two in diameter made of varicolored tissue paper sections. A small metal disk attached below the opening at the bottom of the balloon holds a kerosene-soaked bit of *pita*, which is ignited to produce the hot air that inflates the balloon and carries it up and away from the bandstand and off into the night sky. The band plays loudly, its music punctuating the showers of sparks from the castillos or the ascent of a globo, or enticing the men to their simple dance step in couples or groups (sometimes arms about shoulders). Rockets are shot off at intervals from the churchyard and church steeple, and music from the cantinas competes with the other noises. The churchyard is crowded with Indian family groups—mothers sitting with the children and ready to care for a drunken husband who is exchanging drinks with friends. Pine torches set up around the churchyard and occasional fires provide soft, flickering illumination of the crowd scene until a castillo momentarily bathes the area with kleig-light clarity.

The Alféreces do not share the celebration, since throughout the night they are again on their cargo-change house visits. The necklaces are left on the saints in the church by the Mayordomos, and the church is left open for visiting Indians to sleep as well as pray during the night.

Although August 10 is the "official" day of San Lorenzo in the Catholic calendar, the morning is like the preceding one with continuing market activity and another race by alférez-sponsored horses and riders. The priest comes to say Mass in the morning, and in the afternoon the church is crowded more than on any other day during the fiesta with the many families bringing candles and flowers as offerings to the saints. Late in the afternoon the Mayordomos remove the saints' necklaces and return them to their house altars.

The ritual activities for August 11 are like those on any other day of a major fiesta. The final ritual for the change of the highest-ranking alféreces takes place this day, beginning around 11 A.M. The cargoholders and the Mayordomos of the visiting saints form a procession in front of the church to visit the houses of the incoming and outgoing alféreces. The Capitanes perform their structured dance step at intervals to the music of the band which accompanies the procession. The procession returns to the churchyard about 3:30 P.M., passing the nearly dismantled fiesta market area. Many Indians have left for their hamlets by this time. The cargo-holders take their prescribed places to watch the Alférez flag-transferral ceremony.*

At 5:30, an hour after the Alférez flag ceremony (the final act of Alférez change) has ended, the red blanket is spread out in the same place for the formal farewells of the visiting saints and flags. The farewells parallel the flag ceremony: in place of the three leaps made by the flag-bearers to the center of the blanket, statues are made to dip three times. The Mayordomos stand on their usual side of the blanket, with the visiting Mayordomos and Sacristanes on the opposite side. First, the eight visiting flags bid farewell to the six Zinacanteco flags separately, then five of the visiting saints say goodbye to the six Zinacanteco flags. Next, the eight visiting flags salute Zinacantan's Junior Santo Domingo—who represents all the Zinacanteco saints at this ceremony. Finally, the five visiting saints exchange farewell "dips" with Santo Domingo.†

With the ceremonial farewells finished by 8 o'clock the visiting officials return to the Zinacanteco houses where they have quartered during the fiesta and gather together their belongings. The departure of the first visiting saint occurs around 11 that evening, and the Elders escort it to the village outskirts. The other saints follow at intervals of about an hour and a half, and by dawn the last has left and the fiesta has ended.

The Fiesta of the Virgen del Rosario

The Virgen del Rosario, a statue of whom is kept in the Salinas church, has a lengthy fiesta which begins in Zinacantan Center the Friday before October 7 (the Catholic calendar date) and continues into the following week in Salinas. This ceremony symbolically interrelates and provides a structural link between the Hermitage of Esquipulas (and its attached cargoholders) and Salinas, whence comes the sacred salt delivered biweekly to Zinacantan cargoholders.

The Virgen del Rosario is brought from Salinas to Zinacantan Center and installed in the church of San Lorenzo during the first part of the fiesta. A band is imported to play during the first three days. There is a change

---

*When it is raining, the ceremony takes place inside the church of San Lorenzo.

†Early notes that "48 farewells done three times each . . . means 144 tippings of the flags" (1965: 376).

of two alféreces in Zinacantan—those of Rosario and San Jacinto. The two Mayordomos of Rosario have changed office during the fiesta of Santa Rosa on August 30–31. The Virgen returns to Salinas on Sunday afternoon after the usual departure salutations.

Many cargoholders from Zinacantan as well as the statue of Santo Domingo attend the celebration in Salinas. They are invited in advance by the Mayordomo (also called the MARTOMO ʔANTS or "woman mayordomo") and the Mayor* of Salinas, who make special house visits with presents of salt asking them to attend and reminding them that by tradition they are expected to appear. Two groups make the house visits: one includes the Mayor of Salinas accompanied by his ritual adviser and helpers and the Senior Mayordomo Rey and Mesonero of Zinacantan Center; the other the Mayordomo of Salinas with his ritual adviser and helpers plus the Junior Mayordomo Rey and Mesonero of Zinacantan Center. The Zinacanteco cargoholders who are invited are the alcalde viejos, the regidores, the mayordomos, the escribanos, and the sacristanes (except for the lowest ranking mayordomo and sacristán, who are left to guard the churches in Zinacantan Center). The alféreces are not invited, since, unlike the other cargoholders, they do not receive salt from Salinas.

The Mayordomo and the Mayor of Salinas are aided substantially in the hosting of the Salinas fiesta by the Mayordomos Reyes of Zinacantan, who assemble their helpers and begin preparations on Sunday evening. The following day (Monday) a group of helpers and horses carry supplies (plates, dried meat, gunpowder, and other items) for the households of the Mayordomos Reyes of Zinacantan (who will be in residence in Salinas for five days) down to Salinas. An HʔAK' PULATU—the name given to the man appointed as supply guardian—accompanies the helpers with his family and remains to take care of the suppliers. He is greeted and given a meal by the Mayor of Salinas soon after his arrival and taken to the house, or houses, he has been able to obtain for the use of the Mayordomos Reyes. Part of the supplies are left at the Mayor's own house—bowls and plates that will be used during the meals he will serve to his official visitors. The other helpers return to Zinacantan. On Tuesday the supplies taken on the second trip include the blankets and more food for the use of the Mayordomos Reyes' families. The helpers leave these supplies in the care of the HʔAK' PULATU and return to Zinacantan—their duties for this fiesta finished.

---

*The mayor is senior to the mayordomo. After a man serves as mayordomo and as mayor in Salinas, he is eligible to serve in an alférez post in Zinacantan Center.

On Tuesday evening the two Mayordomo Reyes, accompanied by their families and helpers in two distinct groups—but with one set of musicians (violin, harp, and guitar) who will precede the two groups on the trail—meet at the Hermitage for three rounds of rum. Both have firework helpers to shoot off three blasts as the separate parties leave their two houses, one blast as they meet at the Hermitage, and one each on their arrival at and departure from the cross shrines along the Salinas trail. This ceremonial trip with its several stops takes all night instead of the usual hour. Fresh pine boughs are placed on and ritual performed at six cross shrines.

The Mayordomos Reyes are met at the Salinas church early Wednesday morning by the Mayor, and the Senior Mayordomo Rey enters the church to pray and light a 50-centavo candle for each adult and a 10-centavo candle for each child in his party. He presents the Mayor of Salinas with flowers which have been carried by an old woman all the way from Zinacantan. After the presentation of the flowers, the Mayor invites the Mayordomos Reyes to his house for a meal. Thus begins the familiar pattern of ceremonial visits among the major characters with heavy drinking and strenuous dancing—in which the women join—for hours on end.

After dancing most of the night they are on hand at the church at 5 o'clock Thursday morning to greet with more dancing the Elders, Mayordomos, Escribanos, and Sacristanes from Zinacantan who also have spent a night en route, making ceremonial stops at the cross shrines. The new arrivals are taken to the houses they are to occupy during their stay in Salinas, and after depositing their belongings they are led by Salinas helpers to MUK'TA KRUS in Salinas for a meal.

As the Elders and others are being fed, the Mayordomos Reyes from Zinacantan Center and the Mayordomo and Mayor of Salinas are preparing two elaborate censers (that have been especially made for this ritual) for the ceremony at the salt well. The censers are large ones similar to those used at Carnaval, made of clay with two arches—like basket handles—that bisect each other at the top. The arches provide four equidistant places above the smoking incense to attach flowers and three 20-centavo candles (twelve in all for each censer). These preparations are made quickly so that the censers are ready when the Elders have finished their meal and arrive at the Senior Mayordomo Rey's house to escort them with the other cargoholders and helpers in the large ritual procession to the salt well.

The procession with the Elders, musicians, powder-blast helpers, and two old women carrying smoking censers marches to the salt well near the Salinas church. Last of all come the Mayordomos Reyes carrying the two decorated censers. The ceremonial participants form a large circle around

189. At the Fiesta of the Virgen del Rosario in ʔAts'am the sacred salt well is given special offerings and the opening covered with reed mats

the salt well, and the Sacristanes prepare the censers to be lowered into it. Ropes, three or more meters in length, are tied to their crossed "handles," the candles and incense are lighted, and the censers are lowered, one lower than the other, into the well. New reed mats are folded over the hollow log opening and tied securely with rope, sealing the salt well from use. The Incense-Bearers place their censers around the well, and prayers are recited by the Sacristanes (Figure 189). Then a fiesta atmosphere prevails as firework "bulls" led and urged on by clown characters circle the well. The heavy ritual drinking which follows may necessitate "relief" men to accept the drinks for a prostrate cargoholder. The Mayordomos Reyes dance in the church, while the Elders and Mayordomos come in to pray and drink before their departure for Zinacantan Center around 5 P.M.

The Mayordomos Reyes ask the Salinas officials to help them remove the censers from the salt well. This petitioning continues through the evening until about midnight when the four cargoholders and their helpers go to the salt well and remove the censers. This takes until daylight, when the group returns to the Mayor's house to deposit the censers which are kept there. The Mayor serves three more rounds of rum and a meal with a bottle of rum, after which there is a further farewell round of drinking. The Mayordomos Reyes go to their borrowed houses to pack their belongings while their musicians remain at the Mayor's house to make their formal farewells to him. Powder blasts signal the departure from Salinas and arrivals at and departures from the cross shrines along the trail.

When the Mayordomos Reyes arrive in Zinacantan Center they go first to the Hermitage to greet and joke with the Mesoneros who have been left to care for the ceremonial objects and perform the weekly ritual. Then they reward their musicians with gifts of rum and money, and another intricate ceremony comes to an end. It will be repeated the following October when a new group of cargoholders from Zinacantan Center will make the long, arduous trip down the precipitious trail to Salinas and ritually express their appreciation to the Virgen del Rosario for providing them with salt from her ancient sacred well.

Part V / Some Principles
and Processes

23 / Replication

Like all cultures, Zinacantan has evolved a network of beliefs, symbols, structural forms, and behavioral sequences that, taken together, form a consistent system. The patterned aspect of Zinacanteco culture that impresses me the most is the systematic manner in which structural forms and ritual behaviors are replicated at various levels in the society, and certain key concepts, expressed explicitly in Tzotzil, are replicated in various domains of the culture. It is as if the Zinacantecos had constructed a model for their social structure, their ritual behavior, and their conceptualization of the natural and cultural world which generates rules for appropriate behavior at each organizational level of the society and for the appropriate conceptualizing of phenomena in the different domains of the culture (see Vogt 1965b).

In my thinking about this principle of "replication" I have been influenced especially by Evans-Pritchard's (1940) description of the concept of *cieng* (home) among the Nuer; by Kluckhohn's (1943) treatment of "patterns" and "configuration" among the Navaho; by Lévi-Strauss's ideas about "models" and "codes" for the analysis of social structure and culture (1953; 1963); by Leach's paper on "Rethinking Anthropology" (1961); and by Turner's (1967) treatment of ritual symbols. I have also come to agree strongly with those of my colleagues who propose that a description of cultural behavior may be attained by a formulation of what one must know in order to respond in a culturally appropriate manner in a given socio-ecological context (see especially Goodenough 1957; Conklin 1962; Frake 1962; Metzger and Williams 1963). If the ethnographer working in Zinacantan could come to understand all the rules of the complex Zinacanteco model, then he would have immediate mastery of the appropriate behavior for the myriad of settings and contexts he confronts in that society.

Structural Replication

Structural replication is manifested in both the social and ritual systems. In the social system, the settlement pattern takes the form of an aggregate of aggregates ranging from the house, or houses, of a single domestic group up to the total municipio with its ceremonial center forming the focal point for tribal activities. Similarly, the social structure consists of units of increasing scale: the domestic group occupying a house compound; the sna composed of one or more localized patrilineages; the waterhole groups composed of two or more snas; the hamlet; and finally the ceremonial center. All social levels are found in the large parajes, but smaller parajes may, for example, consist of a single waterhole group. Figure 190 illustrates the levels in the social structure in the larger hamlets.

The social order of ascending scale is paralleled by a ceremonial order of ascending scale that expresses it in terms of ritual paraphernalia and of ceremonies of increasing size and complexity. In each case the "nodes," expressed by circles in Figure 190, are symbolized by shrines composed of

190. Social structural levels in Zinacantan

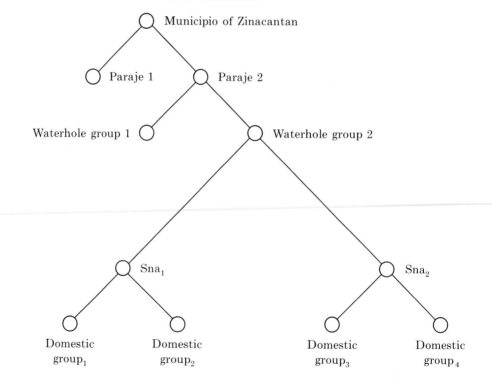

crosses that are conceptualized by the Zinacantecos as "doorways," or as means of communication with the supernaturals: the ancestral deities and the Earth Lord.

Within the context of the domestic group living in its house compound there are a series of ceremonies that involve basically the members of the family and never require the services of more than one shaman. Typical examples are curing ceremonies for individual members of the family and new house dedication ceremonies.

Each sna has K'IN KRUS ceremonies performed in May and in October that involve the services of all of the shamans who live there and the participation of all of the domestic groups. This ceremony appears to be a symbolic way of expressing the rights of the members of the sna in the lands they now occupy which have been inherited from their patrilineal ancestors.

For each waterhole group K'IN KRUS ceremonies are performed semi-annually, typically preceding by a few days in May and in October the K'IN KRUS rituals of the snas. Again, all of the shamans of the waterhole group assemble to perform the ceremony and participation of all of the domestic groups living in the waterhole group is expected. This ceremony appears to express by its ritual forms the rights which the members of this group have to use water from a common waterhole and the obligations they have to care for it properly.

The hamlet unit is ritually expressed by two Year Renewal ceremonies performed by all of its shamans. These ceremonies are called 'ACH' HABIL (New Year) and SLAHEB HABIL (End of Year), and their function seems to be to symbolize the unity of the hamlet and its relation to the tribal ancestral gods in the ceremonial center.

The municipio, or tribal unit, is ritually symbolized by the complex ceremonies performed by the cargoholders (see Chapters 21 and 22).

As one ascends the scale in this ceremonial order it becomes evident that ritual sequences of behavior performed with a handful of people within the domestic group are replicated with increasing number of participants and increasing elaboration in the larger social units. I shall describe first the ritual meal as an example of ritual behavior which appears to exemplify in its details the general rules for appropriate behavioral sequences at various levels in the system.

Ordinary meals in Zinacanteco homes are served on the floor. The men sit on small chairs and eat the tortillas and beans from pottery or gourd bowls. The women eat later sitting on the ground near the fire. For a ritual occasion, however, there is a ritual meal (VE'EL TA MESHA) which follows carefully prescribed etiquette. The important rules are these:

1. The meal must be served on a wooden rectangular table. Every Zinacanteco house contains one or more of these small wooden tables. They vary in size from approximately 30 x 45 cm. to 60 x 90 cm. and are about 30 cm. high. Some are constructed by the Zinacantecos; more commonly they are purchased from the neighboring Chamulas, who specialize in the making of small wooden tables and chairs which they sell in the market in San Cristóbal Las Casas.

2. The table must always be oriented with the long axis running east-west. The importance of the direction east has been noted in various chapters.

3. The table must be covered with a pink and white striped cloth (MANTRESH). The women weave this cloth from cotton thread. The same cloth is used to carry candles from San Cristóbal for the ritual.

4. A bottle of rum and a bowl of salt are placed in the center of the east end of the table. This designates that end as the head of the table.

5. The commensalists must sit in small wooden chairs at the table in strict rank order. The most common rank order is that shown in Figure 90.

6. The meal consists of rum liquor, maize tortillas, and chicken cooked in broth, with chili, coffee, and small round rolls of wheat flour made by Ladinos. Pork, beef, or dried fish may be substituted if the family cannot afford chicken, but such substitution must be noted.

7. The eating of the meal must follow a strictly prescribed sequence which consists of eleven basic steps.

(1) A young man designated as drink-pourer serves a round of rum, using the same shot glass for all participants, serving in rank order. Appropriate toasting and bowing-and-releasing behavior (described in Chapter 18) follow.

(2) The tablecloth is rolled up to the head of the table, or both sides of it are rolled to the middle, and a gourd bowl of warm water is placed on the table. The senior man washes his hands in it, followed by others in rank order.

(3) A gourd bowl of water is passed. The senior man rinses his mouth, spits out the water, and is followed by the others in rank order. The tablecloth is rolled out again to cover the table.

(4) The chicken in the broth is served in individual pottery bowls and a stack of tortillas in a gourd container is placed on the table. The senior man takes a tortilla, tears off a small piece, dips it in his broth, and eats it. The others follow his lead (see Figure 144).

(5) The senior man picks up his bowl and begins to drink the chicken broth. The others follow.

(6) The senior man takes a piece of chicken, places it in a tortilla, and eats it. The others follow. All of the commensalists finish eating at approximately the same time, and they must either eat all of the food served them, or wrap the leftover chicken up in a tortilla and take it home with them.

(7) The drink-pourer serves a second round of liquor. The sequence of behavior is the same as on the first round.

(8) Each commensalist is served an individual cup of coffee (sweetened with brown sugar) with a roll on top. The senior man begins to drink the coffee and eat the roll; the others follow.

(9) The tablecloth is removed from the table, and the hand-rinsing sequence is repeated, initiated by the senior man.

(10) The mouth-washing sequence is repeated, initiated by the senior man.

(11) The drink-pourer serves a third round of liquor. The same sequence of behavior is followed as on the first and second rounds; and the meal is formally over.

These rules of behavior apply to ritual meals at all levels in the social system. In the small domestic ceremonies, such as curing or house-dedication ceremonies, a very small table is used and as few as four or five people eat at it. The shaman sits in position 1, followed by other men, then women, in rank order.

In the K'IN KRUS ceremonies for the sna the table is larger, and more people sit at it. The senior members of the lineage are seated in the honored positions, followed by the shamans in rank order, and finally by the more junior ritual assistants.

For K'IN KRUS of a waterhole group the scale increases. As many as eight to ten shamans have to be seated, along with the ritual assistants; often two or more tables are to be placed together to provide a larger surface for the meal. For the New Year and End of Year ceremonies for an entire hamlet the scale becomes still larger; and as many as fifteen to twenty shamans, plus assistants, are involved.

The maximum scale is reached at the Fiesta of San Sebastián in January when the entire religious hierarchy of cargoholders, plus the Presidente and his assistants, sit down in shifts at an enormous table and are served a whole chicken per person.

Whether the ritual meal involves only one family in a small domestic ritual with a handful of people sitting at a tiny table or the religious hierarchy seated in full regalia at an enormous table the rules of behavior are precisely the same. What is done in the small thatched houses of individual families is replicated in ever-increasing scale for the lineage, the waterhole group, the paraje, and the whole municipio.

The same type of interpretation applies to many other aspects of ritual life in Zinacantan. For example, there is a set of basic rules for ritual processions: the marching order is always junior man in front and senior man in the rear; the movement of the procession from one sacred place to the next is always counterclockwise; the circuit always brings them back to the house where the procession was initiated; and so on. Again, these behavioral sequences are followed whether the procession involves only three or four people or the entire religious hierarchy of cargoholders.

These ritual patterns have important symbolic connections with the Zinacanteco view of the world and the relation of their social system to it. The most important ancestral gods are believed to live in the east, and it is significant that the principal sacred mountain lies east of the ceremonial center. During a ritual meal these ancestral deities supposedly appear and partake of the food and liquor served the living. Their living descendants are arranged in rank order at the table in such a way that the eldest (those closest to becoming deceased ancestors) are seated at the east end of the table—next to the gods. The more junior members, who presumably have more time to live, are seated farther away. It is still unclear why the marching order in processions follows the rank order from junior man in front to senior man in the rear and why processions move around circuits counterclockwise, except that this appears to be an ancient and quite general Maya pattern.

Replication occurs in ritual bathing or washing of people, clothes, chickens, and sacred objects. Water for the washing comes from one or more of the seven sacred waterholes in and around the ceremonial center, waterholes to which the ancestral deities are believed to descend for their baths. In a small curing ceremony water may be collected from one or two of these waterholes for bathing the patient; but in a large ceremony, such as "The Great Vision," it comes from all seven, and not only is the patient bathed but the two sacrificial chickens as well. The same procedures are followed by the mayordomos in a more elaborate ceremony—the washing of the sacred chests which contain the necklaces and old clothing of the saints. Just as clothes for a patient in a curing ceremony are washed by especially appointed laundresses at NINAB CHILO? and later censed over incense and placed on the patient, so are the saints' clothes washed at NINAB CHILO? and later censed and placed on the statues. The flower-changing ceremonies that take place for the mayordomo altars in their homes are replicated on a grander scale when all the mayordomos assemble to change the flowers in the churches. And wedding ceremonies replicate selected aspects of cargo ritual, with the groom being dressed in the same costume worn by alféreces who are changing cargos. In both instances the clothing styles symbolize the significant change in status that is taking place.

Conceptual Replication

The world of the Zinacantecos is segmented conceptually in systematic ways that are replicated in different domains of Zinacanteco culture. There is a word stem in Tzotzil, -PET, which means "to embrace" or "to carry." Thus, for example, HPETOM means "embracer" or "carrier." The concept of "embracing" occurs in at least the following domains of Zinacanteco life: the socialization process in the family, the baptismal ceremonies, the wedding ceremonies, the curing ceremonies, and the ancestral gods inside the mountains.

One of the most important duties of the Zinacanteco father and mother, called TOT and ME?, is to "embrace" a child and care for it well so that it does not lose its "inner soul" composed of thirteen parts. At baptism a child acquires a godfather and godmother, called CH'ULTOT and CH'ULME? (literally, "divine father" and "divine mother"). Their principal duties during the ceremony are to "embrace" their godchild while this important ritual is taking place. And perhaps the most important function of baptism from the Zinacantecos' point of view is to fix the child's soul more securely in the body so that it will not be easily lost. At the wedding ceremony a ritual specialist called HPETOM (embracer) introduces the bride into her new home (the groom's father's house in this system of patrilocal residence). It is his duty to "embrace" or "carry" the bride and groom, or, in other words, to create a new and lasting relationship, one in which the bride will come to like her new home and not run back to her parents' house. The HPETOM goes through a number of ritual sequences, such as taking the bride and groom into the house, removing their wedding clothes, giving the new couple lectures on how they should behave in their marriage, instructing the bride's mother-in-law on how she should take care of her new daughter-in-law, and leading the bride's relatives into the house and introducing them to the groom's parents (J. Collier 1968).

During curing ceremonies a patient who has lost parts of his soul calls the shaman TOT. The ritual TOT in this case is believed to "embrace" the patient in the process of helping him recover the lost parts of his CH'ULEL. In short, all human "embracers" are addressed as TOT by the people they embrace.

Again, the ancestral gods living in their houses inside the Senior Large

Mountain take good care of the 8000 animal spirit companions of the Zinacantecos. They have their MAYOLETIK (assistants) feed and water them, and they "embrace" them. Here the supernatural father and mother "embrace" the alter ego children. However, if a Zinacanteco does something wrong, the ancestral gods stop "embracing" his animal spirit; he may even be let out of his corral and left to wander uncared-for in the forest. In this event, he may be shot at or otherwise injured, and, if so, his human companion will suffer the same fate. The connection between the real world of people and the supernatural world of ancestral gods and animal spirits is made dramatically clear in one ritual sequence in the largest and most complex curing ceremony, "The Great Vision" (see Chapter 20). Toward the end of the ceremony the patient is placed in a platform bed surrounded with pine boughs, just as the corral of his animal spirit inside the mountain is surrounded by pine trees. As the patient passes through the gateway of his decorated platform bed, called a corral, he is like an animal spirit being rounded up and herded through the gate into the supernatural corral within Senior Large Mountain. In this instance, what is done inside the mountain is replicated in the curing ceremony, and in both domains a TOT is "embracing" and caring for a patient or his spiritual alter ego.

In sum, in the socialization process within the family, in the ritual life of the baptismal, wedding, and curing ceremonies, and in the supernatural world inside the mountain "fathers" and "mothers" are "embracing" their children. What is conceptualized in one of these domains appears to be replicated in the others; the result is an amazingly consistent network of symbols that forms a "code" of the type that Lévi-Strauss describes in "The Bear and the Barber" (1963).

The same kind of interpretation holds for other concepts in Zinacantan culture. Another very important word stem in Tzotzil is -IL, which means "to see." Thus, for example, H?ILOL means "seer." In the Zinacanteco view of the world in an ancient mythological time all Zinacantecos could "see" into the mountains where the ancestral gods live. Now, however, only shamans possess this special ability to "see" the gods and communicate directly with them. It follows that shamans are critically important links between ordinary Zinacantecos and the gods for any important ceremony requiring communication and exchange of goods and services with them. Similarly, it is significant that the large curing ceremony is called "The Great Vision" to describe the process by which a patient goes on a pilgrimage to the sacred mountains and "sees" the gods with the aid of the shaman. The same concept appears in the Zinacanteco view of socialization of the young. The long process of education is conceived of as learning "to see," that is, to learn about, understand, and interpret the world in which an adult Zinacanteco functions as a responsible member of his society.

Another crucial concept is the contrast between BANKILAL and ʔITS'INAL, words which mean "male's older brother" and "male's younger brother" in Zinacanteco kinship terminology. These are replicated in so many domains of Zinacanteco culture that they lead us to conclude that something much more generic is involved. Indeed, they appear as a way of classifying phenomena in almost any domain of the universe: there are older and younger brother mountains, crosses, shamans, drums, waterholes, cargoholders in the religious hierarchy. The terms are even applied to the Christ figure, for the Nativity scene in the Christmas ceremonies contains two small Christ children lying in the manger—BANKILAL and ʔITS'INAL!

These words serve as symbols expressing some basic contrasts and oppositions in Zinacanteco life (see Lévi-Strauss 1963: 2); they seem to express the contrasts and oppositions found in the general principle of age-ranking. If this is correct, BANKILAL and ʔITS'INAL are symbolically expressing both the fact (and probably also the stress) found not only in "older" versus "younger" or "senior" versus "junior," but also in "more powerful" versus "less powerful," "more prestigeful" versus "less prestigeful" in the Zinacanteco social system (see Chapter 10).

Another crucial concept replicated in Zinacantan culture is the relation of directors, managers, or initiators of ritual or political action to their messengers, assistants, or "errand-runners." I have in mind here the general concept of TOTILME?ILETIK, a term applied to the ancestral gods inside the sacred mountains as well as to the ritual advisers who tell cargoholders what to do when they serve in office. In the supernatural world the TOTIL-ME?ILETIK have MAYOLETIK (assistants), who water and feed the animal spirit companions and are sent to summon the inner soul of a potential shaman to appear inside Senior Large Mountain and take an oath of office. Similarly, in the real world the Presidente handles disputes in front of the Cabildo. Called TOTIK PRESERENTE, he has twelve MAYOLETIK to call upon to run errands, arrest culprits, and so on. In a curing ceremony the shaman is called TOTIK if male, ME?TIK if female, and the assistants, provided by the family of the patient, are MAYOLETIK to help with the ritual. Similarly, Acheson (1962) suggests that hummingbirds and night-flying moths serve as MAYOLETIK for the ancestral deities. The MAYOL TS'UNUN acts as a messenger and carries out duties like checking on particular families to report back to the TOTILME?ILETIK about the state of their health. The H?AK'CHAMEL TS'UNUN (a type of night-flying insect or moth) is sent by witches to announce impending evil to a household.

191. Cross shrine on San Cristóbal Mountain; note the shape of Santa Cecilia Mountain (in background) which resembles an Ancient Maya pyramid

I have also recently discovered (Zimbalist, personal communication, March 31, 1965) that names for parts of the human body are replicated in the names for parts of houses and for parts of mountains. The walls of a Zinacanteco house are called its "stomach," the corners are "ears," and the roof the "head." The purpose of the new-house-dedication ceremony is to provide a soul for the house just as a human body is provided a soul by the ancestral gods. The same concepts are applied to mountains: the peak is a "head," the base are "feet," and the sides are called the "stomach." Some of the same terms are applied to fields and tables: the corners of a field are the "ears," as are the corners of a table; the top of a table is a "head," and its legs are "feet."

In more general terms, a mountain, a field, a house, a table, and a human body are envisioned as having directional and spatial symbolism that replicate a single model. I have argued that mountains and pyramids may have been conceptual equivalents for the Ancient Maya (see Chapter 25); it would be fascinating to know if the ancient pyramids were conceived as having "heads," "feet," "ears," and "stomachs," and if they acquired "souls" at their dedication ceremonies.

Perhaps the Zinacanteco sacred mountains—residences of the ancestral gods—are the modern equivalent of the Ancient Maya pyramids. If the stone figures carved on the roof-combs and on the stelae erected in front of the pyramids were representations of ancestral deities, it is possible that pyramids had a significance for the Ancient Maya similar to that which the sacred mountains have for contemporary Zinacantecos (Figure 191). If so, the pyramids probably also replicated the quadrilateral cosmos in which the Ancient Maya dwelled and the modern Maya live.

24 / Encapsulation

For a social system like the Zinacantanteco to maintain its cultural patterns in the face of the pressures applied first by the Aztecs, then by the Spanish, and currently by the Mexican government, it must provide itself with mechanisms for handling outside impacts and the imposition of new cultural elements. One of the most important responses to the new elements that are being introduced into Zinacanteco life is a process that might be called "encapsulation": the conceptual and structural incorporation of new elements into existing patterns of social and ritual behavior. This process may be seen as a special form of "syncretism" (see Herskovits 1948) which Zinacantecos have evolved to cope with the new cultural elements injected into their traditional way of life. I shall describe and analyze several examples of encapsulation that have been observed during the past decade in Zinacantan and utilize these data for inferences about how the system may have encapsulated new elements in the historical past of the municipio.

Encapsulation in Contemporary Zinacantan

During the past decade of our field work in Zinacantan we have observed the introduction of a number of new cultural elements in various hamlets and in various aspects of the culture. They have been introduced by INI in its "modernization" program, by other branches of the state and federal government, and, in a minor way, by our group of anthropologists.

The INI School in Paste?. Until 1955 the large hamlet of Paste? had no school, and, although one man from the hamlet had attended a Mexican boarding school for Indians in his youth, the current generation was receiving absolutely no formal schooling. That year INI officials acquired a plot of land, located about halfway between the waterhole of BIK'IT VO? and that of VO? TA PASTE?, and proceeded to build a one-room schoolhouse of rock with a tile roof as well as a small wattle-and-daub house for a teacher. Much of the labor was furnished by the men of Paste⁷ who also helped construct a road which for the first time connected the hamlet with the Pan American Highway near Na Chih. A Cultural Promoter, trained by INI, was appointed teacher. It was his task not only to teach the schoolchildren to read and write Spanish, some elementary arithmetic, and some facts about geography and history but also to promote other INI programs in the hamlet—new crops, a maize-grinding mill powered by a gasoline engine, improvements in the waterholes, and so on. A school committee, organized to help the teacher, consisted of three men, appointed on an annual basis; their duties were to help round up children for school, to guard the schoolhouse, and to watch over and feed the teacher's chickens and hog when he was away. The teacher was none other than Mol Marian, the head of the ejido committee and the cacique of Zinacantan (see Chapter 12). Mol Marian was a very busy man. He not only had to attend to his own farming duties but he also had to carry on political business in connection with ejido and ritual activities since he was still in the process of working his way through the religious cargo system. His permanent home was in Zinacantan Center, and most of his family continued to live there, although from time to time his wife and youngest son would join him in Paste⁷.

Mol Marian is a very astute leader, who quite consciously and explicitly perceives the necessity for change in Zinacanteco culture, but desires change that will not disrupt the system or the existing power structure. Because of his suggestions and an unfortunate event calling for new ritual the INI school became encapsulated into the ceremonial system of the hamlet. In 1957 a man was struck by lightning and killed near the new school. The Zinacanteco interpretation of this event was that the Earth Lord and the ancestral gods were quite angry about the school's presence. With the active cooperation of Mol Marian, a cross shrine defined as a KALVARIO was constructed on the hill just behind the school and a K'IN KRUS ceremony was initiated to appease the gods. The members of the school committee, given the duty of hosting the ceremony, collected a peso from each household head in Paste⁷ to pay for the necessary liquor, candles, rockets, and incense. The ceremony followed the same pattern used in K'IN KRUS ceremonies for a sna: shamans prayed over candles, and a ritual meal was followed by a ceremonial circuit visiting the KALVARIO of the school and other cross shrines and then by another ritual meal. Prominent political leaders in the hamlet participated, and two sets of musicians played for the ceremony: violin, harp, and guitar; and two drums and a flute.

By 1960, the ritual had developed into an established routine. The schoolhouse served as the site for the table altar and the ritual meals, with the table oriented along the usual east-west axis. The candles and flowers were arranged on the table by the two shamans. Everyone, beginning with the shamans and proceeding in rank order, honored the candles with a prayer. After a ritual meal the ceremonial circuit visited two cross shrines known as BANKILAL and ʔITS'INAL ʔAVAN CH'EN, located in a cave about a kilometer from the school; the KALVARIO for the school; and the teacher's house. A final ritual meal was served at the schoolhouse.

The Harvard Field House in Pasteʔ. By the time of the May 1960 K'IN KRUS ceremony for the INI school I had learned enough about ceremonial patterns to bring a contribution of six white candles of the proper size which I presented to Mol Marian. The ranking shaman suggested that my candles be used to pray inside the Harvard field house. I was delighted by this suggestion, and it was arranged that the ceremonial procession would visit the field house after returning from ʔAVAN CH'EN. My notes describe what happened:

> The procession came in through the living room door, and I was very curious as to where they would set up the altar. There was a long discussion as to where the center of the house was, and the shamans were asking Mol Marian where the rooster had been buried when the house was constructed. I had to confess that no rooster had been buried in the floor in the center of the house. They finally decided to set up the altar in the northwest corner of the dining room. Three pine boughs were brought in and set against the wall in the corner, and pine needles were spread in front. The Presidente of the School Committee tied red geraniums to the pine boughs, and all was set, except that Mol Marian approached me at this point and asked if I would provide for two liters of liquor. I gave him 10 pesos and he sent a young man scurrying after the liquor. When the first liter came, Mol Marian briefed me to give it to the senior shaman, saying "this is so you can see." I did so, and it was graciously accepted, and placed by the cross altar. Then the drink-pourer was summoned and he distributed the whole liter—with great ceremony as usual, bowing to everybody, including me to ask permission to serve, and bowing to me again after he had finished. The shamans then set up three candles—with some difficulty because they had to stick them with hot wax to the tile floor (instead of being able to place the butts in the usual type of earthen floor). They then went through their long prayer as the string instruments played inside the

house and the drums and flute played outside. I felt that at last the Harvard field house had been incorporated into Zinacanteco culture. To be sure, we don't have a rooster buried under the floor, nor do we yet have a house cross, but at least we are making some progress. (Vogt, Field Notes, 4 May 1960)

The Pan American Highway in Na Chih. The people of Na Chih tell a myth about the building of the Pan American Highway through their hamlet. It is believed the engineers first planned to place the road south of its present location, passing near a mountain they call TOCH'. The ancestral god who lives in this mountain did not wish to have a highway passing in front of his "home," and so the mountain "shook" and frightened the Ladino engineers into changing their minds. The highway was subsequently built right through the valley in which the hamlet of Na Chih is located.

Many of the people of Na Chih welcomed the convenience of the new highway, for they could ride buses and haul their maize by truck to San Cristóbal or to Tuxtla. But since the highway has a straight stretch for almost a mile passing through the hamlet, the automobiles began to roar through at great speeds. Often they ran into and either frightened or killed sheep; once a car struck and killed a Zinacanteco child.

Finally, in 1960, cross shrines were erected on small hills at locations where the Pan American Highway enters and leaves the hamlet. K'IN KRUS ceremonies are now performed with ceremonial circuits that encapsulate this section of the highway into the ceremonial system and offset its evil influence.

New Government Offices. Another instance of encapsulation is provided by the imposition of new official governmental positions upon the social and political organization of Zinacantan. The trend of events has been for "political" offices gradually to become "religious" offices. Recall that in the history of Zinacantan (see Chapter 2) the alcaldes and regidores had important political functions: in 1704 they were in charge of collecting taxes in the small community and transmitting the funds to Ciudad Real; and until 1899 the regidores had the power to settle disputes that arose between Zinacantecos. Today these cargoholders have almost purely "religious" functions. The alguaciles indios who were functioning in 1592 subsequently became the mayores, who continue to have political functions but are also involved in ritual, and the mayordomos reyes and mesoneros, who still carry billy clubs but have purely "religious" functions in the Hermitage of Esquipulas. Similarly, the alféreces had political control of Zinacantan in

1800; today they too are solely "religious" officials. Although the present Cabildo officers (Presidente, Síndico, and four jueces) continue to serve critical political functions, they have been given an amazing number of ritual duties to perform: for example, the Presidente serves as a "godfather," placing the Christ Children in the manger in the crèche on Christmas Eve. It will be crucial to observe in the years ahead what happens to the six new civil regidores imposed upon the system in 1962.

Encapsulation in the Past

More contemporary instances of encapsulation in Zinacantan culture provide a basis for a series of interesting speculations about how the society probably handled the imposition of new cultural patterns in the past.

The Cross. One of the major symbols of Catholicism—the Christian cross—probably was adopted by the Zinacantecos early in the postconquest period. But it was successfully encapsulated into the ceremonial system by the development of a complex set of procedures for decorating the cross shrines with pine boughs, red geraniums, and other plants to the point that one can hardly see the cross when the decorations are completed. I believe it likely that aboriginal altars were composed of pine boughs and flowers decorating some type of idol, especially since Calnek (1962: 55) provides evidence that various animals and birds were sacrificed to idols outside the door of the houses—where the house cross now stands. There is the further evidence that the pine boughs rather than the wooden crosses are the crucial symbols: cross shrines can be converted into three "crosses" by the addition of one or more boughs; where no crosses exist, three boughs placed in the ground, against the wall of a cave or house, can serve as the "crosses" in a shrine. In the same manner, it is probable that the Christian concept of Calvary became encapsulated as the most important type of cross shrine, the KALVARIO, a meeting place for the ancestral deities who watch over a given waterhole or village.

The Saints. The other item of prominence adopted from the Spanish are the saints, which probably replaced aboriginal idols of some type. Recall how the saints are treated conceptually and ritually at the present time— they were "found" near Zinacantan, had "houses" built for them in the ceremonial center, are clothed in Zinacanteco clothes and ribbons, are honored by having a ʔUAL (necklace of coins) placed on them on important ceremonial occasions, are bathed and have their clothes washed like Zinacantecos are treated in curing ceremonies.

Spanish Surnames. Although it is unknown by what process the so-called Spanish surnames became a part of the Zinacanteco naming system, it is clear that this feature of Spanish culture has been encapsulated into the apparently ancient naming system. The Spanish surname replaced a Tzotzil name, but it now functions as one of two names, both inherited from the father and maintained throughout life by both men and women. The same process occurred when Spanish surnames became established as the second surnames (Gómez Rodríguez, for example); in this case the second name also is regularly inherited patrilineally from the father.

It will be interesting to continue to observe Zinacantan in the future, as the modern world impinges upon its traditional culture, and to determine to what extent the process of encapsulation continues to function as a mechanism for coping with new elements that are injected into its social system at an increasing rate.

25 / Implications for Cultural Change

The ethnographic data on Zinacantan have important implications for the study of Maya cultural development and change. During the decade in which we have been making observations on Zinacantan, we not only have discovered what appear to be a number of ancient patterns with historical roots deep in the Maya past, but we also have observed current trends of change in the culture. We have attempted to project some of these trends forward in time and predict how Zinacantecos will respond to the continuing process of modernization in contemporary Mexico.

Ancient Maya Patterns in Zinacantan

In a series of preliminary papers I have presented a summary of what I think we can infer about the Ancient Maya from current patterns observable in Zinacantan (1961; 1964a; 1964b; 1966a; 1966b). I have also published a methodological note concerning the cautions we should observe in making such inferences (1964d). To utilize field data gathered in the present for inferences about what Maya life may have been like at the time of the Maya Classic period (300 to 900 A.D.) involves a series of assumptions that should be made explicit:

(1) While no Maya ethnographers believe in the existence of survivals of beliefs and patterns of behavior found 1300 years ago, we do assume that the trends of change in Maya culture have been sufficiently regular and systematic to permit us to project the contemporary data back in time and to advance hypotheses about survivals that may profitably be further explored using archaeological, linguistic, and ethnohistoric data.

(2) Since all Mayan languages are unquestionably members of a single family, and since all Maya communities share certain basic cultural patterns, we may assume that the Mayas living today are descended from a

proto-community that existed at some time in the past. The best hypothesis at present is that this community existed in the northwest highlands of Guatemala at about 2600 B.C. (McQuown 1964). Comparative linguistic evidence further suggests that the Tzeltalans emigrated from the proto-Maya community about 750 B.C., and spent some thirteen centuries in the Usumacinta lowlands before moving into the Chiapas highlands where the Tzotzil differentiated from the Tzeltal at about 1200 A.D. These inferences suggest the hypothesis that the ancestors of the Tzotzil-speaking Zinacantecos had some relation to the Classic Maya, most probably on the western periphery.

(3) While we assume descent from a proto-Maya community, we have discovered that each contemporary Maya community is distinct in its beliefs and customs (as each prehistoric Maya community undoubtedly was). There are general themes in Maya cultural patterns, but the precise phrasing of these themes varies not only from one major community to another (such as the municipio units of the Mexican government), but also from one small hamlet to another within each municipio.

Keeping these assumptions and cautions in mind, we can make a number of inferences about elements of Zinacanteco economics, settlement pattern, social structure, religion, and cosmology that may be illuminating for the study of Ancient Maya patterns.

Economics and Settlement Patterns

Every contemporary Maya community is to a greater or lesser extent linked with the national economic system of Mexico or Guatemala, and Zinacantan is no exception. At the same time, a large amount of the daily food comes from aboriginal crops (chiefly maize, beans, and squashes) grown by essentially aboriginal methods. If one could remove certain elements from the economic system (machetes, axes, flashlights, chickens—which probably replaced turkeys—sheep, horses, mules, pigs, fruit trees, and some items of clothing) the system resembles what we can reconstruct for the Ancient Maya. The maize, beans, and squashes are cultivated by what are essentially preconquest techniques, utilizing the digging stick for planting and hand methods for weeding and harvesting the crops.

Clothing types now derive largely from styles that developed during the Colonial period in the contact between the Zinacantecos and the Spanish, but two features seem to be aboriginal. First, in the highlands of Chiapas, each significantly different group (normally those people inhabiting a single municipio) dresses differently, but within the group all men and all women dress alike. Thus, the clothing styles become like uniforms symbolizing the exact social membership of a particular Indian. There is never any doubt as to who is a Zinacanteco as compared to a Chamula or to an Oxchuquero. From our point of view the differences in styles from one municipio to another are often slight, especially in women's dress, but from an Indian's point of view they are symbolically very important. One wonders if the significant units among the aboriginal Maya may not also have utilized differences in clothing style to symbolize their similarities within their group and their differences from their neighbors. Second, some elements in clothing also seem to be quite specifically aboriginal, or at least important replacements for aboriginal elements. For example, Zinacanteco men generally wear footgear, while their women go barefoot. An example of a specific aboriginal element is the high-backed sandals worn by Zinacanteco men. This element closely resembles the sandals represented in Classic Maya monuments, as, for example, at Bonampak (see Figure 48). Finally, the multicolored ribbons on men's hats may be contemporary substitutes for the magnificent feather headgear worn by aboriginal Maya men.

Contemporary Zinacanteco housing is beginning to undergo many changes, especially in the increased use of (Ladino-style) adobe bricks and tile roofs. But close-to-aboriginal housing consisting of wattle-and-daub walls and thatched roofs may still be observed in most areas, and in many hamlets these earlier types are still prevalent. Additional features of interest are the continuing use of manos and metates to process maize, the triple hearthstone arrangement (on the open fire on the dirt floor of the house) to hold the comal and cooking pots, and the presence of household shrines. These cross shrines that are maintained in the patios outside the houses appear to have had their counterparts in Ancient Maya family shrines found in the courtyards. Their antiquity in Zinacantan is suggested by Calnek who has discovered a sixteenth-century reference to the sacrificing of dogs, deer, parrots, and other birds to idols placed outside the house and to the burning of copal incense (1962: 55).

The parallels in settlement pattern between contemporary and Ancient Maya are astonishingly close. The basic Maya pattern appears to be one with a ceremonial center surrounded by dispersed hamlets in a sustaining area where the bulk of the population lives. In the concept of "ceremonial center" I am including here not only the large impressive centers containing the pyramid-temples, plazas, and causeways of the Maya Classic and Postclassic, but also the minor ceremonial centers described by Willey (1956), Bullard (1960, 1964), and others; the *cabeceras* of the modern municipalities, that now contain Catholic churches rather than pyramid-temples but nevertheless continue to function as ceremonial centers; and a variety of waterholes, caves, cenotes, and other sacred places that function today as focuses for ritual activity for small family groups living around them, which probably had a similar function in the past (Vogt 1964b).

We also find contemporary Maya communities that are compact in settlement pattern: for example, the villages located on the shores of Lake Atitlán in the midwest highlands of Guatemala, a number of cases in highland Chiapas such as Amatenango and Aguacatenango, and places in Yucatán such as Chan Kom. Each of these compact communities seems to have resulted either from very special geographical circumstances, such as those existing around Lake Atitlán, or from postcontact political developments with the Spanish directly influencing the establishment of compact, grid-pattern types of communities, such as in Amatenango, Aguacatenango, and Chan Kom. The pattern seems special and atypical compared to the dispersed type of settlement pattern which we find in less disturbed contemporary communities and which was most characteristic of the Maya Classic in the Petén.

Social Structure

Evidence is accumulating, not only from contemporary Maya communities in isolated areas but also from ethnohistoric studies by scholars such as Roys (1943, 1957) and Miles (1957), that Maya social organization was and is based upon a lineage system in which patrilocal extended families are grouped into localized patrilineages. Before the system was shattered in many places by the Spanish conquest, it is probable that the patrilineage system had important corporate functions such as control of land, jural authority in the hands of the senior males of the lineage, and control of marriage. The lineages were also named with a system of patronymics; and this naming system has survived in communities like Zinacantan even after many of the other functions have been lost.

If such a lineage system was a fundamental feature of the Maya in prehistoric times and not just restricted to the upper ruling and aristocratic lineages, as some have suggested, many inferences can be made about the probable patterns of prehistoric life and a number of puzzling problems solved. In Table 15, I suggest an equivalence between prehistoric settlement units observed by the archaeologists and various levels of social structure as we observe them today in communities such as Zinacantan. It is significant, as Bullard (1964) has pointed out, that the order of magnitude in numbers are very comparable between contemporary Zinacantan and the

Table 15. Classic Maya and Zinacanteco settlement patterns

Classic Maya (Petén)	Zinacantan
House group	Patrilocal extended family living within a fenced-in compound
Cluster	Localized patrilineage
Cluster group	Group living around a single waterhole—may have originally been a patriclan or phratry
Hamlet with minor ceremonial center	Hamlet (*paraje*)
Major ceremonial center	Zinacantan Center

Classic Maya in the Petén. For example, the "clusters" he describes as having 5 to 12 houses would equal averages for Zinacanteco localized patrilineages, although in Zinacantan these do range up to considerably larger size, as many as 40 to 50 houses in a few cases. The totals that Bullard estimates for the populations within the sustaining areas of the major ceremonial centers range between 5750 and 8625. It is also significant that the vast majority of dispersed settlement towns that we still have today in the highlands of both Guatemala and Chiapas fall approximately within this range; Zinacantan now has about 8000 inhabitants. Larger units exist, such as Chamula with now some 30,000 to 40,000 or Chichicastenango with over 35,000 inhabitants, but these are rare.

We can, I think, make certain inferences concerning prehistoric Maya social structure. First, the house groups described by the archaeologists were probably patrilocal extended families living around courtyards. These units would have been composed of a man and his married sons who cooperated in agricultural work; their wives would be imported from other lineages living nearby. We can also infer that groups of these extended families lived together in small clusters which were localized patrilineages that controlled and transmitted rights to land. In turn, the localized lineages were probably grouped into larger units which one might call patriclans or phratries, that probably controlled and transmitted rights to important waterholes, cenotes, or other sources of water. Finally, a series of the patriclans would have shared a ceremonial center with pyramids.

The precise arrangement of this hierarchy of social levels in the system probably varied from one part of the Maya area to another and at different periods, but, judging by the contemporary patterns, I think we can infer definite relationships between sizes of settlements and levels of social structure (Sanders 1962–63; Vogt 1964c).

Religion and Ritual

What can contemporary Zinacanteco ethnography add to our knowledge of the meanings of Ancient Maya religious symbols and rituals? Much attention has been devoted in the existing literature to Maya gods that developed from the personification of nature (the gods of rain, maize, wind, sun, and moon, and those that presided over units in the Maya calendar). I shall return to this type of symbol after dealing with another type that looms important in our ethnographic data: symbols that represent or are correlated with various units and levels of Maya social structure.

In Zinacantan important symbols and appropriate rituals are associated with each important unit in the social structure. In fact the most important deities (for whom rituals are being performed almost daily) are the ancestral gods (TOTILME'ILETIK). Each level in the system, from patrilocal extended family living in a single compound on up to the whole tribe or municipio, has shrines of crosses by means of which Zinacantecos "communicate" with the ancestors and engage in propitiatory rituals for them. Families have cross shrines in their courtyards; localized lineages and waterhole groups have them on hills near their homes; hamlets have them on more distant hills; and the whole tribe has a set of sacred mountains (in which the tribal ancestral gods are believed to live) and sacred waterholes (in which tribal ancestral gods bathe) around the ceremonial center. A given social unit—for example, a localized lineage—performs ceremonies at least twice each year that involve counterclockwise ceremonial circuits around the lands belonging to the lineage and passing by and performing rituals (prayers and offerings of copal incense, rum, and white candles) at the shrines of the lineage ancestors. Through these rituals, not only does each lineage pay respects to its ancestors, but the ceremony also links together their descendants as common worshipers and members of the same lineage, and hence symbolizing the unity of the localized lineage as an important unit in Zinacantan society.

The inferences that may be drawn from these data have crucial implications for understanding the composition of Ancient Maya society and the manner in which dispersed hamlets may have been related to their ceremonial center. It is difficult to name the units and levels with precision, but I think a legitimate inference can be made that each ceremonial center, minor or major, found in areas like the Petén (Bullard 1960, 1964) represents a focal point for an important social unit in the society. If one presumes a lineage system built up from patrilocal extended families to patriclans or phratries, then I think it likely that each unit or level in the system may have had a shrine. Perhaps the best hypothesis that can now be advanced is that the large pyramids in the major ceremonial center were somehow associated with tribal ancestors, or at least with the ancestors of maximal lineages in the system. I call them "maximal lineages" to indicate that they would have been the largest units in the system based upon kinship ties—that is, supposed descent from a common patrilineal ancestor. Whether these units are called patriclans, patrilineal clans, or phratries (the latter composed of a series of clans that are believed to be interrelated) is less important than the principles involved: that the Ancient Maya may have had social units that were the forerunners of the modern municipios, and that these units were segmented into a series of patrilineages. In segmentary systems there are always units of ascending size as one moves up in the levels in the system from the small localized extended family to the "maximal" lineage. The important inference is that the various archaeological manifestations that have been called major and minor ceremonial centers give ritual expression to the levels in the lineage system.

The inference that pyramids may have been related to lineages is based upon a series of recent discoveries made in the Maya highland communities. We have long known from ethnographic work in highland Guatemala (see, for example, Oakes 1951; Bunzel 1952) about the importance of sacred mountains, but our more recent work in Chiapas (see especially Holland 1963; Vogt 1964b) has shown that the important ancestral gods are believed to live inside these sacred mountains. In Zinacantan localized lineages worship particular ancestors inside specific hills and mountains near their homes; when, however, their ceremonies take them to the major ceremonial center, they make the rounds of all of the sacred mountains. I have, therefore, interpreted the ancestral gods living in mountains around the ceremonial center as being "tribal" symbols to which the entire municipio owes allegiance. In Larrainzar, however, Holland (1963) found evidence that particular lineages are linked mythologically to particular mountains around the ceremonial center. Furthermore, while in Zinacantan all of the animal spirit companions of the population are now believed to live inside one Senior Great Mountain, Holland found in Larrainzar that the animal spirit companions of members of a given lineage are cared for by the ancestors of that lineage who live in a particular mountain. In both cases, however, it is believed that the ancestral gods are caring for animal spirit companions that take the form of jaguars, coyotes, ocelots, and so on, and that the welfare of living people depends very fundamentally upon this care by the gods inside the mountains.

Since in various types of ceremonies observed today (such as curing ceremonies, and rituals for renewal of the year), the contemporary (Zinacanteco) Maya make ritual pilgrimages to these sacred mountains, it seems highly likely that the Ancient Maya also came from their hamlets into the ceremonial centers either to pay homage to the pyramid associated with their particular lineage or to make the rounds, paying homage to all of the pyramids that represented their tribal gods. Since we have further evidence that Maya men were actually buried inside many if not all of the pyramids (Coe 1956), and that stelae were erected in front and roof combs carved on top, both depicting particular men, I would also make the inference that the stelae with their associated round altars were utilized by the Ancient Maya in ways similar to those in which the cross shrines at the foot of and on top sacred mountains are now utilized by Zinacantecos.

Holland has made the further suggestion, based upon his evidence from Larrainzar, that there is a rank order among the animal spirit companions living inside a lineage mountain. He indicates that the animal souls of the common people live in the bottom layers and that those of the "elite" (curers, heads of lineages) live in the higher layers of thirteen layers of the sacred mountains. He states that these sacred mountains are symbolically equated with the thirteen layers of the sky, as in Ancient Maya belief, and suggests that the steps and layers in pyramids are also representations of basic Maya ideas about the layers in the sky (1963: 110–114). If these inferences are correct, sacred mountains on the one hand and pyramids on the other are both manifestations of a basic Maya cosmological idea about the thirteen layers of the sky. I hasten to add that these hypotheses have yet to be confirmed in Zinacantan or in other Maya communities. We have elicited some data about "layers" inside the sacred mountains, but rarely more than three, and nothing as complex as Holland presents for Larrainzar.

Assuming, however, that mountains were believed the dwelling places of ancestral deities by the early Maya living in the highlands, the movement to the flat lowlands presented a religious and ceremonial problem that may have been solved by the construction of steep-sided pyramids which became the dwelling places of the ancestral gods. This line of speculation is buttressed by an observation of Thompson (1959) that caves may have been the prototype of the dark recesses created by the corbeled vaults in the lowland sites. In other words, there appears to be a significant conceptual parallel between the sacred mountains (in which the ancestral gods reside) with their caves on the sides (which are means of communication with the Earth Lord) in highland Maya communities such as Zinacantan, on the one hand, and the steep-sided pyramids with their corbeled vault passageways in lowland Maya archaeological sites, on the other.

While one important line of inference concerns the relation of outlying hamlets to ceremonial centers as expressed in units of social structure and associated rituals, the other focus for investigation is the ceremonial center itself. Today all Maya communities have some type of cargo system functioning in the ceremonial center and consisting of a ranked series of offices or cargos occupied by men as they ascend a ceremonial ladder. In Zinacantan the hierarchy or cargo system consists of four levels of priestly officials: mayordomos, alféreces, regidores, and alcaldes. While the present form of this system was obviously established by the Spanish in the early Colonial period (Carrasco 1961), it is possible that prehispanic elements were blended into the structure of the hierarchy.

I have suggested that the Ancient Maya ceremonial centers may have been at least partly staffed by priests who served on a rotating rather than a permanent basis (Vogt 1961). This hypothesis provides a possible explanation as to how dispersed hamlets were structurally linked to ceremonial centers. More recently Cancian has offered what I regard as a very important refinement to this idea (1964). He observes that in Zinacantan today the prestigeful cargo positions are filled by men from the outlying hamlets who can accumulate enough of a surplus from the maize farming to devote a series of years to the expensive offices; and that a number of more permanent ritual specialists serve the hierarchy of priestly cargoholders. These ritual specialists are the sacristanes, who know special prayers for certain rituals associated with the care of the images of the saints which the mayordomos themselves do not normally know when they enter their cargos and who ring the bells and open and close the doors of the churches; the musicians, who play for the alféreces and are given lifetime tenure, hence accumulating specialized knowledge of the alféreces' ritual duties; and the scribes, who know how to read and write and have the duty of keeping the sacred books containing the names of Zinacantecos scheduled to assume cargo positions at given years in the future. None of these ritual specialists has much formal power as compared to the cargoholders, but by virtue of the fact that they tend to serve in the same roles year by year, they have exclusive control of a great deal of specialized ritual knowledge and instruct the cargoholders on the details of complex ceremonial procedure. Further, as they serve the cargoholders at the ceremonies during the course of the year they are fed and given liquor at the expense of the cargoholders.

These patterns suggest the interesting possibility that Classic Maya centers contained permanent ritual specialists and artisans but that, rather than holding power at the top of a hierarchy, they served and were supported by men coming in from the outlying hamlets to serve in rotating ceremonial positions and in the process expending their economic surpluses in ceremonial activity. As Cancian puts it, "The rich peasant as economic patron and the ritual specialist as a priest with limited prestige may have been on the scene in the Maya Classic" (1964: 343).

These hypotheses have recently been challenged by Ruz (1964), who feels strongly that Ancient Maya society was aristocratic with permanent priest-rulers, and that today's rotating cargo systems developed wholly during the Colonial period. There is also impressive evidence from the work of Proskouriakoff (1960, 1963–1964) and Kelley (1962) that the figures depicted on Maya stelae at Piedras Negras, Yaxchilan, and Quirigua may have been portraits of reigning lords rather than ancestral deities.

More recently Coe has presented a model of ancient community structure in the Maya lowlands based upon an examination of the Uayeb Rites in northern Yucatan, as described in detail by Landa (Tozzer 1941). He concludes that

> the Uayeb rites describe a model which could be replicated on increasingly higher levels. The ideal Maya community probably was conceived as divided among four endogamous *tzuculs* or calpulli, which were wards consisting of exogamous patrilineages. Each ward was associated with a cardinal direction and with a color. Offices within the divisions were ranked like the terraces of a stepped pyramid, the aspirant to office bearing the *cargo* of any level for one year at great personal expense; the leaders at the top of the pyramid of *cargos* within each calpulli would have been *ah cuch cabs*—rich old men, all of whom made up the town council. On the commoner level, the ritual and political leadership of the community rotated through the four divisions in a four-year counter-clockwise cycle based upon the permutations of the 52-year time count; the chosen man, called *holpop,* enforced the authority of the *batab* or *halach uinic.*

On the level of a large city (like Mayapan) or sizeable ceremonial center, the four quarters would then have been equivalent to the Aztec *altepexexeloliz,* themselves made up of endogamous wards. Here the model has been projected so that political authority of the settlement as a whole is in the hands of the nobility. Over all would have been the *halach uinic* or king (*ahau*), as hereditary ruler of the territorial capital. In each quarter would have been a *batab,* related to him agnatically or by marriage; it is probable that the practice of ward and quarter endogamy applied only to the commoners, and that the aristocratic rulers of a territory consolidated their power by exogamous marriages with real or fictive cross-cousins in other quarters or even in other states. (Coe 1965: 107–108)

Coe goes on to concur with my suggestion that temple-pyramids of the great ceremonial centers could have functioned as residences of ancestral deities. He suggests that since most, if not all, of these structures were funerary monuments erected to house the remains of some great man, the pyramid could have been the focus of a cult dedicated to the royal patrilineage of which the man honored by the monument became the ancestral deity. Finally, he suggests that the Maya managed to evolve a community model that was unique. He writes that

> they alone seem to have hit upon a permutating time count as a kind of automatic device to circulate power among the kin groups of the primitive state. By combining the principles of the *cargo* pyramid, exogamous patrilineages, endogamous wards, quadripartition, a system of four social classes, and calendrical permutation, they evolved an ideal pattern of community life which was well adapted to the dispersed pattern of settlement imposed on them by the practice of shifting cultivation. (Coe 1965: 112).

In my judgment, Coe has produced an impressive synthesis of available data, taking into account our contemporary ethnographic data and interpretations from Zinacantan, and the findings of Proskouriakoff and Kelley, as well as meeting the objections posed by Ruz. Further, his model poses intriguing questions for future research in contemporary communities such as Zinacantan. To what extent does the calendrically based cargo system and its associated ceremonies serve to circulate power? Does the periodic movement of the saints' necklaces from the houses constitute a contemporary system of integrating ritual power in cargoholders' house with the central temples in a manner reminiscent of the ancient Uayeb rites? What was the relation of exogamous patrilineages to endogamous hamlets before the lineages underwent changes?

William A. Haviland (1966a, 1966b) has entered the argument with his settlement pattern and skeletal data from Tikal. He makes three important points in his two papers. He estimates that the minimum population of the Tikal ceremonial center and its sustaining area must have been 20,000 to 22,000, a figure nearly three times the population of Zinacantan (1966a: 628). He has discovered that the principal individuals buried in the "tombs" seem to have had a mean physical stature in excess of 170 cm. compared with a mean of 158 cm. for the rest of the male population (1966a: 626). He states that tentative figures on life expectancy suggest that the principal individuals in the "tombs" lived longer on the whole than the ordinary men at Tikal (1966a: 626). On the basis of these data he argues that the population of Tikal was too large to have been organized by any system of rotating cargo positions, and that the skeletal data from the "tombs" indicate that the men buried in sumptuous "tombs" had been very well cared for in life and hence that they "occupied permanent, and perhaps hereditary, positions of the greatest importance" (1966a: 626).

A minimum population of Tikal of 20,000 to 22,000 does not in itself effect the inferences that Ancient Maya ceremonial centers may have had some system of rotating positions. For, although this population is nearly three times that of Zinacantan, it is only approximately half the population of Chamula which is now approaching 40,000 and which continues to function with a cargo system similar to that of Zinacantan.

The skeletal data from the sixty-two household burials and the six "tomb-type" burials of Early and Late Classic times at Tikal are potentially much more interesting for solid inferences concerning Ancient Maya social organization. Unfortunately, Haviland has not yet published his skeletal data and, although he states there are sixty-two household burials, he does not indicate how many individual skeletons were measured from the "tomb-type" burials which contained "principal individuals" and presumably other burials. However, if these preliminary findings prove to be statistically significant, it is probable that there were at least some well-cared-for Maya men occupying permanent positions in the ceremonial center at Tikal and that Cancian and I will be forced to revise our hypotheses and concede that some kind of hereditary and aristocratic rulers were occupying the top positions in the ceremonial centers. It may be that the Classic Maya socio-political organization was more like that suggested by Coe (1965) than that inferred by Cancian (1964) and myself (1966b). In short, some rotating positions may have existed in the organization of the ceremonial centers, but these may have been located at lower levels of power and authority, rather than at the top of the system. I await further archaeological evidence on this point with much interest.

Cosmology

All Mayas today consider themselves Catholics (except for insignificant minorities here and there which have joined Protestant churches), but this certainly does not mean that their Catholicism has obliterated aboriginal cosmological ideas. We have found a number of Ancient Maya concepts about the nature of the universe and of the gods in nearly every community in which the ethnographic research has been penetrating.

The deification of important aspects of nature continues as a crucial feature of the religious symbolism: the sun, the moon, rain, and maize are all prominent in most contemporary Maya belief systems. There are also usually one or more types of underworld earth gods. The sun is often associated with "God" in areas where Catholic influence is very strong in the theology. Even more common is an association of the Virgin Mary with the moon goddess as in Zinacantan. Rain is believed to be controlled by various types of essentially aboriginal gods—for example, YAHVAL BALAMIL (the Earth Lord) in Zinacantan. It is rare to find a special maize god expressed in the pantheon in contemporary communities, but maize everywhere is treated with great ritual respect.

The belief that the universe is formed of layers is found in nearly all communities, but the most interesting data are from San Andrés Larrainzar where Holland (1964) reports a conception that is diagramed in his book (Figure 192).

Holland says of this conception of the universe:

> The heavens, formed by thirteen levels, are conceived as a cupola or cup over the earth: six layers in the east, six in the west, and the thirteenth one in the zenith, heart of the heavens.
>
> Seen from a distance, this sphere looks like a huge mountain or pyramid. The concept of "the mountain of the earth" is often symbolized in the prehispanic codices.
>
> Some of the Tzotzil Indians still keep the Ancient Maya belief [Tozzer 1907: 154] in the *ceiba,* which ascending from the center of the earth, penetrates and connects the thirteen levels of the heavens. This central point is, for that reason, of a green color. Beneath the earth there exist nine, thirteen, or even an undetermined number of layers that form the underworld or *Olontik.*
>
> At dawn the sun rises in the east preceded by Venus, the morning star, a large plumed serpent called MUKTA CH'ON by the Tzotzil. As it was conceived in the prehispanic times, Venus is the precursor and the herald of the sun, and the Tzotzil still identify it with the serpent deity, as it was among all Middle-American Indians.
>
> The sun ascends the thirteen layers of the heavens, which form a path ornamented with flowers, as if it were carried in a two-wheel cart. Ascending a layer every hour, it reaches at noon the thirteenth one,

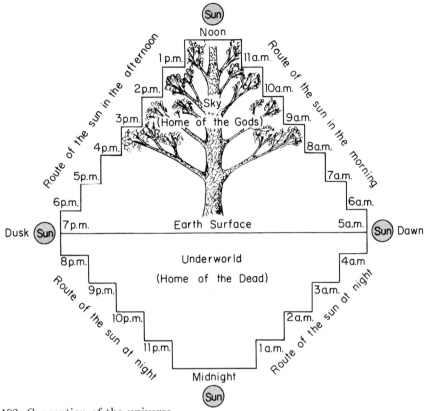

192. Conception of the universe

this is the heart of the heavens, where the sun remains one hour, this being the time when he watches the happenings on the earth. In the afternoon, it descends the western layers, and disappearing into the sea, gives way to the evening. During the night it passes by under the layers of the OLONTIK. When it is night on the surface of the earth, the home of the living, it is day in the domain of the dead, and vice versa. At the next dawn the sun reappears in the east, and gives birth to the new day. (My translation from the Spanish, Holland 1964: 14–15)

Although these data have not been confirmed for other highland Maya communities, we do have data of relevance from Zinacantan on the problem of Maya directional and spatial orientations. It is quite clear that east is the most ritually important direction. For example, much of the most important praying to gods in Zinacantan takes place with the person facing east—toward Senior Large Mountain, where the animal spirit companions are being cared for by the ancestral gods, and toward Junior Large Mountain, where the all-important rain-making ritual takes place. Furthermore, the east–west axis is important and is expressed in the ceremonial life by the orientation of the table every time there is a ritual meal.

Directional symbolism is also strongly expressed in the concepts that express a quadrilateral model of the universe. In most Maya communities there is a belief in four corner gods who are believed to hold the sky and/or the earth on their shoulders. Common expressions of this quadrilateral model are found in rectangular ritual tables, in rituals performed at the corners of square or rectangular houses and maize fields, and in the ritual recognition of four important sacred mountains around the ceremonial center as in Zinacantan. I suggest that Ancient Maya pyramids were also expressions of this quadrilateral model.

There is still a major problem to be solved, however, about whether the most important four corners were the cardinal points, the intercardinal points, or the solsticial points in the east and in the west. Thompson emphasizes the cardinal points (1934), but data from Villa Rojas, from Quintana Roo (1945), and data from Zinacantan and Larrainzar (Holland 1963: 92) place more emphasis upon the intercardinal points. Girard's data from the Chorti (1962) indicate that the solsticial points may have been the most important. Still another possibility is that both cardinal and intercardinal points are important, especially in symbol systems like that of the Tzotzil, where the eight four-corner gods are called VASHAKMEN (probable translation, "eight-doers") and have reference to both the four cardinal and four intercardinal points.

Another aspect of Maya spatial orientation is the counterclockwise ceremonial circuits performed today in processions around ceremonial centers or around the lands belonging to localized lineages. These circuits appear to have a function not only of emphasizing the ownership of given lands but also of purifying sacred territory within the boundaries that are being ritually drawn. Donald Bahr has suggested the interesting hypothesis that the Maya work with boundaries, both ceremonial and supernatural, that describe areas of "purity" or "safety" within the rest of the world (1962). He further suggests that the boundaries tend to be square, linked with cardinal and intercardinal points; that the boundaries are ritually articulated by groups of men walking to or around them; that the area to be purified has greenery spread on its "floor" (pine needles in the highlands, green boughs in the lowlands); and that copal incense is burned inside the "pure" area. This interpretation would fit both data described by Landa (Tozzer 1941) for Yucatec Maya at the time of conquest and ceremonies that we observe today. All of this is relevant to Coe's interpretation that the Uayeb ceremonies moved counterclockwise around four segments of a community (1965).

There is abundant evidence for the survival of the Ancient Maya calendar in many contemporary communities (see Miles 1952; Nash 1957), and these data have great potential for inference about the function and meaning of the Ancient Maya systems. Although the ancient calendar is apparently no longer in use in Zinacantan, we do have data on the solar year calendar that was in use in 1688; there are no data on the divinatory calendar. Data on the solar calendar in use in 1688 (see Table 16) was taken from a manuscript in the library of Casa Blom in San Cristóbal. This manuscript was originally written by Juan de Rodax in Huitiupan in 1688 and copied by Dionicio Pereira in Comitan in 1723. It is reported as the calendar used by "tzotzlem" or "tzinacanteca." With the assistance of Terrance Kaufman, I have converted the original script into the orthography we are now using for Zinacanteco Tzotzil and have added some tentative translations pro-

Table 16. Zinacanteco calendar in use in 1688

Month	Tentative translation	Dates
1. MUK'TA SAK	?	3 March–22 March
2. MOK	fence	23 March–11 April
3. ꞋOLALTIꞋ	?	12 April–1 May
4. ꞋUꞋLOL	?	2 May–21 May
5. HOK'IN ꞋAHVAL	?	22 May–10 June
6. HꞋUCH	drinker	11 June–30 June
7. HꞋELECH	?	1 July–20 July
8. NICHIL K'IN	flower ceremony	21 July–9 August
9. HUN VINKIL	first twenty-day period or month	10 August–29 August
10. SHCHIBAL VINKIL	second twenty-day period or month	30 August–18 September
11. YOSHIBAL VINKIL	third twenty-day period or month	19 September–8 October
12. SHCHANIBAL VINKIL	fourth twenty-day period or month	9 October–28 October
13. POM	incense	29 October–17 November
14. YASH K'IN	green ceremony	18 November–7 December
15. MUSH (or MUY?)	?	8 December–27 December
16. TS'UN	to plant	28 December–16 January
17. BATS'UL	?	17 January–5 February
18. SISAK	?	6 February–25 February
19. CH'AY K'IN	lost ceremony	26 February–2 March

vided by a contemporary Zinacanteco informant. The only possible vestige we find of this calendar is the belief that the five days from February 24 through 28 are "very bad days." This period corresponds closely with the five unlucky days in the old nineteenth month, CH'AY K'IN.

Even more interesting, however, for this book are the recent findings and hypotheses of Bricker (1966) concerning the relation of the Ancient Maya concepts of time and space to the contemporary Zinacanteco cargo systems. She suggests that the "burden theme" in the contemporary cargo system is intimately related to Ancient Maya concepts of time and space. She takes off from Thompson's (1960) suggestion that the Maya conceived of divisions of time as burdens which were carried through all eternity by relays of bearers. Stela D at Copán has a scene showing a number of people (or gods) letting down their burdens in order to rest. The burdens are units of time carried by tumplines; other glyphs show men carrying burdens of time walking along a road. Thompson thinks the road may represent eternity stretching back into the past and forward into the future and that the burdens represent time being carried on a journey through eternity. Bricker suggests that relations between the officials in the contemporary cargo system are analogous to the relations between the time periods of the ancient calendar—in the world of the gods, the gods have the duty of carrying the burden of time through eternity, while in the social world of Zinacantan, the cargoholders have to carry the burden of celebrating the religious ceremonies for the community throughout the year. She offers evidence from the prayers and rituals that accompany change of office and from words used in contemporary Tzotzil that the concepts involved in the "cargos" and in the ancient "burdens" are closely related. For example, there are a number of words in Tzotzil which have both spatial and temporal meanings. The word NOPOL means both "near" and "soon"; K'AL means "as far as" and "until"; and TS'AK'AL both "behind" and "afterward." These words suggest that the Zinacantecos, like the Ancient Maya, view time and space as quantities which may be measured in equivalent units and that both may be thought of as lineal quantities.

Finally, there is accumulating evidence in the contemporary Maya communities for a "ranking," or at least a "pairing," principle that may be important to an understanding of the Ancient Maya. In Zinacantan much of the universe is divided into BANKILAL and ʔITS'INAL. These terms mean "male's older brother" and "male's younger brother" in Zinacanteco kinship terminology, but since they are applied not only to kinship but to such diverse phenomenon as mountains, crosses, fireworks, saints, and cargoholders, it becomes apparent that we have a more general principle involved that focuses upon some system of ranking or pairing of phenomena (see Chapter 10). Certain archaeological findings, such as the pairs of dancing figures (men impersonating jaguars, depicted in the murals of Bonampak) or the twin pyramids in many Ancient Maya sites may well be related to this BANKILAL and ʔITS'INAL principle.

Current Trends of Change

In a preliminary paper (Vogt, 1967) I have summarized the major trends of change that we have observed in Zinacantan over the past decade (1957–1967). In a few aspects of culture the data collected by Sol Tax's expedition to Zinacantan during December 1942 and January 1943 provide an earlier baseline for the study of trends of change. These trends may be grouped into three types: responses to the direct forces for modernization that reach the Zinacantecos from the Ladino world; responses to indirect (or unanticipated) consequences of modernization, especially the local Indian population explosion that has followed from the introduction of selected aspects of modern medicine; and intensification and growth of certain indigenous patterns that suggest the system is in the throes of a "nativistic" or "revitalistic" phase of development (see Wallace 1956).

Highland Chiapas has been a fundamentally bicultural world since the founding of Spanish towns shortly after the Conquest, and pressures for change in the Indian cultures have been continuous over the past four centuries. There is, however, impressive evidence that the intensity of this pressure had increased markedly in the twenty-five-year period since 1940 as the forces for modernization have reached the Indian communities. Since then Zinancantan has received its first ejido land under the agrarian reform program, has seen the paved Pan American Highway built through the municipio, and has encountered the Instituto Nacional Indigenista (INI) with its program of health clinics, schools, agricultural experiment stations, roads, and cooperatives. It is clear that the Zinacantecos not only welcomed, but fought hard for their ejido lands (Edel 1966). On the other hand, they were ambivalent about the Highway when it was completed in 1950, and have only gradually come to accept some of the INI programs.

We have noted a number of strong trends of change in Zinacanteco material culture during the past decade. In housing there is a strong shift from the more traditional house with wattle-and-daub walls and thatched roof to Ladino-style houses with adobe walls and tile roofs. Changes are also underway in men's clothing styles, replacing the traditional short pants with long store-bought trousers. In 1957 only five men wore Ladino clothes regularly (De la Fuente 1957). For many years the men have been wearing long trousers to protect their legs from mosquitos when they are working in the lowlands; now they continue to wear trousers when they return home to the highlands. On the other hand, women's clothes show very little tendency to shift to basically Ladino styles. There is a slow, but quite evident increase in household equipment purchased in Ladino markets: flashlights, metal dishes, maize-grinders, tortilla-presses, wrist watches, gasoline lanterns, transistor radios. The most important contribution of new technology in farming operations promises to be the use of spray-on weed killers, begun in 1964, which may ultimately supplant hand labor with hoes in the weeding of fields. Transportation patterns have undergone a virtual revolution from mainly foot travel (carrying loads by tumpline or pack horses and mules) to the use of commercial buses and trucks along the Pan American Highway and its branches (Cancian 1965b). With the help of funds borrowed from INI, Zinacantecos now own and operate four large trucks themselves. A new industry, the growing and selling of flowers, has become important to three hamlets (Bunnin 1966). Whatever their earlier ambivalent feelings, Zinacantecos have accepted the Highway and the advantages it brings.

There has been selective acceptance of the INI health programs. The most successful have been the mass innoculations against smallpox, typhus, and other diseases that formerly reached epidemic proportions. The use of an ingenious puppet show in Tzotzil which explains the need for innoculations was apparently very important in this case. The control of epidemics has led to a marked decrease in the death rate, and the Indian populations are increasing at an alarming rate. The least successful medical program is that which attempts to persuade Indian women to have their babies in hospitals or clinics. There is not a single documented case of a traditional Zinacanteco woman who had her baby anywhere but at home with a midwife.

In most hamlets of Zinacantan there has been a notable increase in school attendance and in bilingualism. In the 1930's there was much resistance to schools and in 1934 the people in Nabenchauk actually petitioned *not* to have a school (Tax 1943). In 1942–3 the Sol Tax expedition members estimated that less than 20 percent of the men were bilingual but even among this small group the control of Spanish vocabulary was very slight. By the 1950's most of the hamlets had schools. In Paste', where we have accurate counts from the INI school, the 1958 enrollment was 33, all boys. By 1965 the number of pupils had increased to 72, including 28 girls. The incidence of bilingualism is, however, still much greater among men than women. The Mexican government has recently established a boarding school for girls in Zinacantan center in order to enroll pupils from various Tzotzil and Tzeltal municipios and to make a full-scale effort to teach the girls some Spanish.

The agricultural program of INI has had its major impact upon Zinacantan in the distribution of fruit trees, especially apple and peach. We detect little change in the types of maize, beans, and squash or in the patterns of animal husbandry—chickens, sheep, horses, and mules. One of the problems in attempting to introduce improved breeds of chickens in the early days of the INI operation was that it was trying to promote white leghorns. White leghorns are good for egg production, but are worthless for a major use of chickens in Zinacanteco ritual: the sacrifice of black chickens to the ancestral gods in curing ceremonies.

A much more important trend has been the increased renting of land from Ladinos in the lowlands along both sides of the Grijalva River south of the Chiapas highlands. While the acquisition of ejido lands in 1940 doubled the landholdings of the Zinacantecos, it did not solve the problem of insufficient milpa land for the growing population. It was necessary to search for and rent additional land in the lowlands which now supplies most of the maize consumed by the Zinacantecos, as well as the surpluses sold on the market.

In the area of social and religious organization and its ideological components we detect much less change over the decade as a result of direct Ladino pressure. The naming system is slowly shifting from the traditional pattern (each person inheriting patrilineally two surnames from the father) to the Ladino system of the surname of the father, followed by the surname of the mother's father. The pressure for this change has come both through the schools and through the census-takers, who insist upon the Ladino system. The major result has been a vast amount of confusion for all concerned since increasing numbers of individuals are ending up with the same name. I would hesitate to guess how many men in the municipio are named Mariano Pérez Pérez! Although there are about twenty names that include Pérez as the Spanish component, under the older system one could at least separate a Mariano Pérez Tanhol from a Mariano Pérez Tsintan, as each man acquired a Spanish and an Indian surname from his father.

There has been an increased attempt on the part of the local church to make "better Catholics" of the Zinacantecos. But the priest still only appears about ten times a year to say Mass and perform baptisms and marriages.

Except for a few peripheral individuals, working either for INI or for the anthropologists, we detect little change in basic ideology or world view. For example, while modern medicines are often accepted when offered or available, it is clear that disease is ultimately traced to punishment by the ancestral gods, causing loss of part of the inner soul, to the escape of one's animal spirit companion from its supernatural corral in the mountain, or to various types of witchcraft performed by envious neighbors. (Aspirin, penicillin, or antibiotics are believed extremely effective in cases of soul-loss or witchcraft.)

Much more profound trends of change are observed as a result of indirect consequences of modernization. Since they are indirect, and often unanticipated, they are difficult to spot and to analyze precisely. It is, for example, clear that the combination of rising expectations for material goods and economic opportunities made available by the improvement in the transportation network have led to at least two types of social displacement: emigration from Zinacantan; and the emergence of various types of middlemen or what Wolf calls "cultural brokers" (1956), such as maize-sellers, flower-sellers, and INI employees.

We do not have precise figures on the emigration rates from Zinacantan. These are difficult to obtain, since once a man has left the municipio permanently, he tends to sever his connections completely and to be forgotten. We do know that emigration is stimulated by two kinds of situations. The first, increased economic opportunities and the "bright lights" of Ladino towns, surprisingly enough provides relatively little motivation. The second, and much more common incentives, are various social and psychological pressures from which individuals may be forced to flee. Witches are still assassinated in highland Chiapas, and emigrants often had become vulnerable targets for witchcraft gossip and had left to save their lives. Once away, the transition to Ladino life is relatively easy, as they learn more Spanish, change their styles of dress, acquire jobs, and soon disappear into the lower-class Ladino world. It can be argued that this pattern of emigration has the effect of draining off the individuals who have become highly deviant, leaving behind a conservative pool of Zinacantecos to carry on the traditional culture.

More interesting in terms of potential for change in Zinacantan are the astute middlemen, those who make their living, for example, by buying maize from the Zinacanteco producers and reselling it in the market in San Cristóbal (see Chapter 6). These middlemen continue to farm maize themselves and to wear Indian clothing because these are prime symbols of belonging to Zinacantan. By maintaining these fundamental ties with

Indian culture, they retain the respect of their fellow Zinacantecos, keep the supply of maize flowing into their operations, and at the same time make relatively large profits (Capriata 1965). The middlemen are increasing slowly in numbers as well as in types. They merit further close observation.

An indirect consequence of modernization even more potent for the trends of change is the rapid population increase that has followed in the wake of modern medicine. The population of Zinacantan is increasing at the rate of at least 1.2 percent, and Cancian (1965b) projects a population of over 9,200 in 1970, over 11,200 in 1980. But while the population is growing rapidly, the number of positions in the prestigious religious cargo system is increasing at a very slow rate (see Chapter 11). Cancian's careful analysis of this increasing discrepancy indicated that, if full male participation in the cargo system is maintained, the average age of men holding their first cargo will be 44.2 years by 1980; or, if men take their first cargos at the preferred age of 35 or so, only 52.7 percent of those eligible could serve in the system in 1980. In recent decades approximately 90 percent of the male population has participated. Needless to say, something fairly dramatic is going to have to change in this key feature of social structure in the municipio.

A third type of change is the intensification and growth of certain indigenous patterns that suggest the system is in the throes of a "nativistic" or "revitalistic" phase. By indigenous patterns I do not mean preconquest survivals, but refer to traditional patterns developed during the Colonial period. Ancient Maya elements syncretized with Spanish patterns are now regarded as "Indian" as opposed to "Ladino" and clearly antedate the current modernizing trends in the system.

We have clear evidence of a rapid increase in the numbers of practicing shamans. Each year proportionately more and more Zinacantecos have dreams which compel them to become shamans; there are now at least 160 shamans in the municipio (Silver 1966a). Whether or not there is a comparable increase in the incidence of curing ceremonies is not clear, but the greater number of shamans does involve more people in native ceremonial life, since each lineage and waterhole group ceremony is performed by the entire group of shamans resident in the local group concerned.

We have unequivocal evidence that the ceremonies being performed by the cargoholders in Zinacantan Center are more elaborate and more complex than they were a decade ago. For example, the ritual performed by the mayordomos reyes and mesoneros for Esquipulas has become markedly more elaborate and time-consuming in recent years. One of the key elements in the ceremony are the necklaces, composed of coins on ribbons, that are removed from sacred bundles kept on the altars in the cargo-holders' houses, ritually counted, danced with, and then taken in procession to be placed each Sunday around the neck of the saint in the Hermitage of Esquipulas (see Chapter 21). From a field study of this ceremony made by Renato Rosaldo in the summer of 1965 we know that Esquipulas was kept in the Cabildo until 1899, when he was moved to a Hermitage constructed especially for him. The custom of having musicians play for a Sunday ceremony for the saint was added shortly thereafter. First there were only a harp and a guitar; in 1910 the violin was added. Previously only two mayordomos reyes were in charge of the ceremony; in 1938 two mesoneros were added to the ritual activities. The weekly counting of the ritual necklace was instituted in 1944. By 1960 there were two necklaces, and a third necklace with new coins added each year has become part of the complex within the past two years (Rosaldo 1968). What began as a set of simple rituals for a single saint has developed into a complex cult and shows indications of becoming more elaborate each year. Trosper (1967) has provided other examples of how the Zinacantecos have elaborated their traditional ceremonial life as their wealth increases.

Some Predictions for 1984

I shall now set down some predictions for 1984—a date already singled out by another author interested in trends of the future! Since my present plans call for a continuation of the Harvard Chiapas Project at least through 1984, we shall have an opportunity to evaluate these predictions with continuing field research.

First I would like to speculate on the future of the Ladino town of San Cristóbal Las Casas. Given the various pressures for modernization at work in southern Mexico, I anticipate that it will undergo a number of transformations. The streets will be broadened and paved; there will be fewer small stores and many more large modern stores selling goods to Ladinos and Indians alike; tourist travel en route to Guatemala along the Pan American Highway will have increased manyfold; the Ladinos will own more automobiles, and those without cars will have motor scooters. Most important, the electric power lines from Mal Paso (a dam now being completed on the Lower Grijalva River) will have reached the valley of San Cristóbal and there will be beer, furniture, and textile factories in operation with Ladino managers and foremen and Indian laborers.

My predictions for Zinacantan can best be summarized in a series of statements about the municipio:

(1) The population will exceed 12,000.

(2) Zinacantecos will be living within the municipio according to the basic settlement pattern that exists in 1965—with ceremonial center and outlying hamlets—except that those hamlets located on automobile roads will increase in population at the expense of the more remote hamlets.

(3) All-weather roads will lead to all the major hamlets.

(4) The vast majority of Zinacantecos will be living in houses with adobe walls and tile roofs.

(5) Zinacanteco men will wear long trousers and Ladino-style shirts and hats but will retain traditional costumes for ritual occasions. Only a few women will have switched to Ladino dress.

(6) Maize, beans, and squash will continue to be basic foods, but tortillas will be made completely by hand- or power-grinders and by tortilla-presses.

(7) The majority of Zinacanteco children will be enrolled in schools, and the incidence of bilingualism will be something on the order of 80 percent for men, 30 percent for women. The basic language at home will continue to be Tzotzil. A San Cristóbal radio station will have at least one program in Tzotzil that will beam out to transistor radios and will serve as an important medium for news, for advertisements by merchants, and for playing Tzotzil music.

(8) Most Zinacantecos will utilize modern medicine for diseases such as dysentery and for injuries such as lacerations and broken bones, but shamans will still be using native curing rituals to cope with psychosomatic disorders.

(9) The office of Presidente Municipal in the Cabildo will have greater powers to cope with problems of law and order, of community development, and so on.

(10) There will be a choice of three basic occupations: maize farming; merchandizing (operators of stores and sellers of maize, salt, flowers, and so forth); or working as laborers in the projected beer, furniture, and textile factories of San Cristóbal. Some of the factory workers will live in or on the edges of San Cristóbal and will be in the process of becoming Ladinoized, but the majority will live in their hamlets and commute to work.

(11) The occupational choice available will have weakened the patrilineages that exist in 1967. Young men will be able to acquire jobs in merchandizing or in the factories and build their own houses as soon as they marry rather than having to live with their fathers.

(12) The naming system will have shifted almost completely to the Ladino pattern.

(13) The combination of weakened patrilineages and Ladino naming patterns will shift the social structure further in the direction of a bilateral system.

(14) There will be a resident Catholic priest in Zinacantan, and the Zinacantecos will have greater knowledge of orthodox Catholicism.

(15) The traditional cosmological system with ceremonies for the ancestral gods, the earth god, and belief in the soul and animal spirit companion will still be a vital part of the culture.

(16) The religious cargo system will exist as a key institution, but will have evolved in one of two ways: the number of cargo positions will have undergone a substantial increase either through the establishment of more posts in the present ceremonial center or through the development of separate hierarchies in the outlying hamlets that have their own Catholic chapels and saints; or the cargo positions will be held by an economic elite, with others enjoying ritual prestige by becoming shamans.

(17) The patterns of institutionalized envy leading to witchcraft accusations will continue, but the incidence of assassinations will decrease under the influence of Ladino systems of law and order.

(18) The system of compadrazgo will continue to be important, but will take new forms, such as an increased seeking out of important Ladinos (such as merchants or factory managers) as compadres.

In much that I have observed and predicted there are no surprises or mysteries. The sequence of events both in present trends and in projections for the future can be replicated in many parts of the world where essentially tribal peoples are being integrated into the modern world. But three points merit special comment and have some implications for our thinking about social and cultural change and development.

Redfield's characterization of the process of change in Yucatán along a continuum of communities from the tribal Indians, to the peasant village, the town, and finally the Ladino city, which are progressively less isolated and homogeneous and more secularized, disorganized, and individualized (1941) does not fit the situation in highland Chiapas. Rather, as one moves through mountain passes only some 10 kilometers from the Ladino town of San Cristóbal las Casas, one moves immediately into profoundly Indian worlds in the municipios of Zinacantan, Chamula, and Huistán. While these Indian societies have daily contact with San Cristóbal, use Mexican pesos for their economic transactions, and have increasingly important political links with the Ladino government officials, they still maintain themselves as prime examples of Wolf's "closed corporate communities" (1955). (There has in fact been more change observed in recent decades in more remote communities, such as Oxchuc in the Tzeltal area.) I think it highly probable that the Indian communities closest to the Pan American Highway and to the centers of Ladino power and influence (Zinacantan, Chamula, and Huistán, as well as the Tzeltal community of Amatenango) are clinging to and even further developing certain "native" aspects of their culture precisely because they have been subjected recently to such heavy Ladino influence.

My prediction that Zinacantecos will remain in their hamlets and commute to the factories in and around San Cristóbal rather than move en masse to the town is perhaps brash to say the least. I make it because Zinacantecos already have the kind of value-orientations toward time and work that will enable them to make a relatively easy adjustment to factory work; and Zinacantecos are already geared to commute to San Cristóbal, often two or three days a week, to spend the better part of the day in the market, going to the Cathedral for a baptism, or tending to other business. The Zinacanteco value-orientations toward time and work are particularly relevant for trends of change in the future. Unlike the local Ladinos, Zinacantecos place strong emphasis upon the future and are punctual in keeping appointments. They are constantly thinking about future goals, and individual Zinacanteco men are already looking forward to and planning for cargo positions that they will occupy over twenty years hence. The busy shamans have appointments to perform ceremonies often for more than two weeks in advance. (I once tried to make an appointment with a shaman informant who was booked for particular ceremonies for sixteen straight days and had his entire appointment schedule carefully stored in his head.) With ordinary Zinacantecos it is possible to count on an appointment two to three weeks in advance. This tendency is all the more remarkable when one considers that San Cristóbal Ladinos, even of the professional classes like doctors, will not schedule their activities for the same afternoon, much less know what they will be doing the next day.

The orientation toward work is equally remarkable. Except for fiestas, keeping busy, either in the instrumental activities of farming, weaving, cooking, and so on, or in ritual activities is highly valued. Zinacanteco men are constantly occupied—farming, tending horses and mules, building houses, repairing fences, and so on. Most of them carry strands of palm leaves and weave hats as they walk along the trails. The women keep busy cooking, carrying wood and water, tending children, and weaving on backstrap looms that can be carried into the woods, allowing them to work as they tend their sheep (Susan Tax 1964). In short, in important respects Zinacantecos appear to have "the Protestant Ethic" without being Protestants.

With some intelligent management on the part of the Mexican government and industrial managers, I see no reason why the Indians cannot remain in their hamlets (where they already have their "suburbs," so to speak) and thereby bypass a whole phase of the industrialization process of moving into town, becoming a depressed proletariat, and creating vast problems of sanitation, law and order, and so on. They could begin by walking to the nearest buses, as they do now, without spending more than an hour or so of travel each way. As expectations rise, the means of transportation could be shifted to bicycles, then motor scooters, and eventually small cars.

Finally, it may also be brash to predict that the traditional cosmological system with its shamans and cargo system will continue as a key feature of Zinacanteco culture. I make this prediction because, while modern medicine, sanitation, and improved water supplies will help with the problems of disease, and increased emphasis upon orthodox Catholicism will begin to occupy a larger role in the belief system, I cannot foresee that modern doctors, engineers, teachers, political administrators, and Catholic priests can in less than two decades come to handle the problems of psychosomatic disorders, or provide the Zinacantecos with a full sense of meaning and value in their lives. I would guess that the Zinacantecos will maintain the essence of their traditional religious system (albeit in altered form) for some generations. While my colleague Frank Cancian predicts the destruction of community integration based upon the religious cargo system under the pressure of the growing population and the increase in economic surplus (1965b), I will predict—at least for 1984—that the cargoholders will still be chanting, dancing, and drinking for the gods in the ceremonial center and that the shamans will still be dedicating new houses, performing waterhole and agricultural ceremonies, and leading patients on pilgrimages to the mountain shrines to offer sacrifices of white candles and black chickens to the ancient ancestral gods. A number of forward-looking Zinacantecos are already preparing for cargo positions in 1984; our long-range project will allow us to see if their implicit confidence in cultural continuity is, as I suspect, justified.

Appendixes, Bibliography, Glossary, Index

Appendix I / Harvard Chiapas Project Field Workers, 1957–1968

Arden Aibel
Nicholas H. Acheson
Mary H. Anschuetz
Georges Arbuz
Adelaide Pirotta Bahr
Donald M. Bahr
Jordan P. Benderly
William N. Binderman
Merida H. Blanco
T. Berry Brazelton
Victoria R. Bricker
Nicholas F. Bunnin
Francesca M. Cancian
Frank Cancian
Susan Carey
Carla P. Childs
Nancy J. Chodorow
Benjamin N. Colby
Lore M. Colby
George A. Collier
Jane F. Collier
Claude de Chavigny
Roger M. Dunwell
John D. Early
Matthew D. Edel
Nancy Locke Ettrick
Mary Lowenthal Felstiner
Susan Tax Freeman
Gordon A. Gilbert
Benedicte F. Gilman

Antonio Gilman
Harvey E. Goldberg
Eleanor A. Gossen
Gary H. Gossen
Stephen F. Gudeman
John B. Haviland
Leslie K. Haviland
Jonathan Hiatt
Lois M. Hinderlie
Phyllis M. Kazen
Stephanie L. Krebs
Miriam W. Laughlin
Robert M. Laughlin
Susan T. Levine
Siegwart Lindenberg
M. Haven Logan
Barbara Strodt López
Ronald Maduro
Maryvonne Menget
Patrick J. Menget
Judith E. Merkel
Barbara Metzger
Duane Metzger
Frank C. Miller
John M. Miyamoto
Abigail S. Natelson
Ana Elsa Montes de González
Francesco Pellizzi
Carolyn C. Pope
Richard S. Price

Sally H. Price
Eric Prokosch
Todd D. Rakoff
John S. Robey
Michelle Z. Rosaldo
Renato I. Rosaldo
Mark L. Rosenberg
Rand Rosenblatt
Diane L. Rus
Jan Rus, III
Peggy Reeves Sanday
Charles S. Sabel
Diana M. Scott
Carol W. Shweder
Richard A. Shweder
Daniel B. Silver
Jack Stauder

John D. Strucker
Phillip G. Stubblefield
Ronald L. Trosper
Gwendoline van den Berghe
Pierre L. van den Berghe
Catherine C. H. Vogt
James P. Warfield
Maxine M. Warshauer
Frederick G. Whelan, III
George Carter Wilson
Elena Uribe Wood
Henry E. York
Allen Young
Stephen B. Young
Manuel T. Zabala Cubillos
David A. Zubin

Appendix II / Tzotzil Phonemes

The following notes on Tzotzil phonemes are drawn from Lore M. Colby (1960) and Robert M. Laughlin (1963). The letters used in this book for each Tzotzil phoneme are followed in parentheses by the equivalent phonemic symbols that are used for the same phonemes by the linguists in their more technical publications. Where no symbols appear in parentheses, the common letter and phonemic symbols are the same.

a	low, central, open, occasionally closed vowel
e, o	mid, front, and back, opened, fluctuating between rounded and unrounded
i, u	high, front, and back, closed, unsounded
b	voiced bilabial stop. The phoneme "b" presents particular problems discussed by Weathers (1947)
ch (č)	voiceless, aspirated alveo-palatal affricate
ch' (č')	glottalized "ch"
h	voiceless glottal spirant
k	voiceless aspirated stop more strongly aspirated in final position
ʔ	glottal stop
k'	glottalized "k"
l	voiced alveolar lateral with voiceless offglide in final position
m	voiced bilabial nasal
n	voiced alveolar nasal
p	voiceless, aspirated, bilabial stop, more strongly aspirated in final position
p'	glottalized "p"
r	voiced alveolar flap

s	voiceless alveolar spirant
sh (š)	voiceless alveopalatal spirant
t	voiceless, aspirated alveolar stop, more strongly aspirated in final position
t'	glottalized "t"
ts (¢)	voiceless, aspirated alveolar affricate
ts' (¢')	glottalized "ts"
v	voiced labiodental spirant freely variable to bilabial w, with a voiceless offglide in final position
y	voiced alveopalatal spirant with voiceless offglide in final position

Appendix III / Zinacanteco Names

Table 1. Patronymics in Zinacantan

Contemporary surname		1749 surname[b]	Probable translation
Spanish[a]	Tzotzil		
PEREZ			
PERES	TAN HOL	sotanhol	ashy or limey head
	BULUCH[c]	buluch	eleven
	ꞋASYENTO	asiento	from the Spanish *hacienda*
	K'OBYOSH	—	from the Spanish *con Dios*
	PULAN	pulano	probably from the Spanish name Fulano
	HIL, HILIꞋAT	jiliat	long penis
	P'UYUM	puium	?
	ꞋAMALISH	amalis	?
	KULANTU	—	coriander
	SHUT	sut	a type of wild bean and also an archaic word for snail
	ꞋOKOTS	ocot	lizard
	MOCHILUM	muchilum	?
	KONKORON	coscorron	?
	TSOꞋ T'UL	sotul	rabbit feces
	HOLOTE	joltuluk (?)	contemporary name probably from *guajalote* (turkey); 1749 version means "head of turkey"
	TSOTSIL	soquil	strong
	SHULUBTEꞋ	—	?
	MANTUHANO	—	from the Spanish name Mandujano
	VOTASH	—	boots
	TASAHO	tazajo	dried meat
	VOTS	—	?
	SHUK'UMTE	—	?
	SHIK' MUT	—	bird wing
	TAKI BEK'ET	—	probably means dried meat
	CHECHEV	—	a type of mushroom
	KAVRIT	—	from the Spanish *cabrito* (kid)

HERNANDEZ
ˀERNANTIS

MENTIRA	memira	lie	
LANTU	—	?	
HERONIMO	gerónimo	from the Spanish name Gerónimo	
MUCHIKᶜ	—	?	
MIN	minero (?)	from the Spanish *minero* (miner) (?)	
SAPOTE	zapote	from the Spanish *zapote* (sapota)	
SARATE	zazate (?)	from the Spanish name Zarate	
NUH	nog	?	
PROMASH	—	probably from the Spanish name Bromas	
K'Oᶜ	cahogh (?)	?	
HOL CH'O	jolchoc	rat head	
CH'UCH'UKUN	chuchum (?)	?	
ˀINAS	—	from the Spanish name Ignacio	
LEK'SIM	—	lick spit	
KIRIBIN	—	?	

DE LA CRUZ
KRUS

ˀOK'IL	oquil (but combined with PEREZ)	coyote	
CHAMULᶜ	chalmul (?)	?	
TONTOB	toton (?)	snail	
ˀAKOV	—	wasp nest	

LOPEZ
LOPIS

CHIKUˀᶜ	chic (?)	?	
TSINTAN	sinttan	?	
TAN CHAK	tanchac	limey ass	
KITS'	quiz	?	

SANCHEZ
SANTIS

ˀES	etz	?	
NE ˀUCH	neus	opossum tail	
PULIVOK	—	ground dove	
VELYO	—	?	

MONTEJO
MUNTISHU

KONTE	conde	from the Spanish *conde* (count)	
TAS VET	tazuet	nest of grey fox	
TIL HIL NUK'	tizinuc	?	
K'Aˀ MOK	—	old fence or corral	

JIMENEZ			
SHIMUNES			
	TANTIV	—	?
	MANI?[c]	mani	hooked nose
GARCIA			
KASYA			
	NOKERO	—	?
	TSU	—	a type of gourd
GOMEZ			
KOMIS			
	LOTRIKO	rodrigo	from the Spanish name Rodríguez
	BURO	burro	from the Spanish *burro*
VASQUEZ			
VASKIS			
	SHULHOL	soljol	?
RUIZ			
RUIS			
	ROSHYO	roxillo	a color term from the Spanish *rosillo* (roan)
MARTINEZ			
MARTINIS			
	KAPITAN	—	from the Spanish *Capitán* (captain)
ARIAS			
?ALIASH			
	KELEM CHITOM	kolonchiten (?)	rooster-pig
DE LA TORRE			
TERATOL			
	CHOCHOV	—	acorn (?)
MENDEZ			
MENTIS			
	PATISHTAN	—	?
GONZALEZ			
KONSARES			
	PAKANCHIL	pakanchib	"to mend a chil," a type of chamarra worn by old women in certain rituals

[a] The Tzotzil version of the Spanish surname is provided below the Spanish spelling of the name.

[b] The 1749 data are from a census of tributaries collected by Calnek from the Archivo General de Guatemala (Calnek, personal communication, December 26, 1961).

[c] These names may have been derived from calendrical names in use in Chiapas in the sixteenth century (Baroco 1958).

Table 2. First names used in Zinacantan

MEN		WOMEN	
Spanish	Tzotzil	Spanish	Tzotzil
Agustín	ʔAkushtin	Agustina	ʔAkushtina
Andrés	Telesh	Andrea	ʔAntel
Antonio	ʔAntun	Antonia	Tonik
Caspacio	Kash	—	—
—	—	Catalina	Katal
Celestino	Tino	Celestina	Tinik
Dionisio	Nishyo	—	—
Domingo	Romin	—	—
Eduardo	Lukarto	—	—
Fabian	Papian	—	—
Felipe	Pil	Felipa	Pil
Francisco	Palas	—	—
—	—	Guadalupe	Lupa
Guillermo	Yermo	—	—
José	Chep	Josefa	Chepa
Juan	Shun	Juana	Shunkaʔ
Lorenzo	Lol	Lorenza	Lolen
Lucas	Lukash	—	—
—	—	Magdalena	Matal
Manuel	Manvel	Manuela	Manvela, Manuʔ
Marcos	Markush	—	—
—	—	María	Maruch, Mal
Mariano	Marian	—	—
Martín	Maltil	—	—
Mateo	Matio	—	—
Miguel	Mikel	—	—
Nicolás	Mikulash	Nicolaza	Mikul
Pablo	Pavlu	—	—
—	—	Pascuala	Pashkuʔ
Pedro	Petul	Petrona	Petuʔ
—	—	Rosa	Losha
Sebastián	Shap	—	—
Tomás	Tomash	—	—

Appendix IV / Tzotzil Texts

The following Tzotzil texts—four Zinacanteco myths collected by Robert M. Laughlin in 1960—are presented in Tzotzil with English translations to provide a sample for the interested reader as to how these tales are related in the native language.

The Flood

This brief tale is a variant of that presented in Chapter 13.

ʔA ti voʔne ʔital nohel,	Once a flood came,
ʔIcham ti konchaveetike,	The dwarfs, the first people,
ti baʔyi krishchanoe,	Half died,
Cham hʔoʔlol,	Half died,
ʔIsbah sbaik ta kahon hʔoʔlol,	Half shut themselves up in coffins,
ʔImuyik ta teʔ hʔoʔlol,	Half climbed trees;
ʔIskushik sat teʔ,	They crunched nuts,
ʔIyipanik chochob;	They lived on acorns;
ʔInoh ti balamil voʔnee	The world was flooded once,
Bveno, ʔik'ocholah,	Well, they changed form,
ʔIayan sne,	Their tails came out,
ʔIayan stsatsal,	Their hair grew,
ʔIpasik ta mash;	They became monkeys;
Bveno, ʔilah ʔo yech ti	Well, just so the world
balamil voʔnee,	ended once,
ʔEntonse ʔital ʔotro hk'esh	Then came another change
krishchano,	of people,
Haʔ sha li voʔotik ʔune,	Now it was ourselves.
ʔA ti konchavetike,	The dwarfs
Teyik ta ʔolon.	Are down below,
Pero ta la sk'oponik ta hmek	But they come to talk a lot
Li kahvaltike,	With our lords,

ʔItavan sha la shaʔiik ti
    ʔolone,
Porke tol la k'ush k'ak'al,
ʔItavan sha la slapel labal
    ʔach'el,
Ta la sk'an chmuyik tal liʔtoe;
Yech ʔo ti poʔot sha la shlah
    li balamile.

They are already tired of the
    underground
Because it is too hot,
They are tired of dressing just
    in mud,
For they want to come up here;
For this reason the world is
    about to end.

(Robert M. Laughlin, Tale 7)

The Stealing of the Bell

This myth describes how the large bell that once hung in the tower of the church of San Lorenzo and could be heard as far as Chiapa de Corzo and Tuxtla Gutiérrez was given away to the Chiapanecos by the foolish elders of Zinacantan.

Bveno, ʔa li voʔne cheʔe,
ʔA li totil meʔile
Mas ʔotro hkoh moletik,
ʔA li kampana yuʔun hc'ul San-
    torensoe cheʔe,
Muʔyuk sha liʔe,
Pero hipiem.
K'usi ʔune, ti k'al pas bala-
    mile cheʔe,
ʔIskomtsan ti htotik vashakmene,
ʔIskomtsan hun kampana
Yuʔun hch'ul totik Santorenso,
Pero hun kampana,
Pero shvinah to k'al Soktom,

K'al Tushta,
Ti shtih ti kampana.
Bveno, hipil li ch'ul kampana
Yuʔun totil meʔil,
Yak' komel htotik vashakmen.
Bveno, vaʔi ʔun,
ʔA li shok hsoktom ʔune,
Komo naka tsots k'obetike,
Shohobetik . . .
Bveno, bveno, ʔa li htsinakantae,

Well, long ago,
The ancestral gods,
Another generation of elders,
The bell of our holy father
    San Lorenzo,
Isn't here now,
But it was hanging.
You see, when the world was
    made,
Our holy fathers, the VASHAKMEN,
Left a bell
For our holy father San Lorenzo,
But it was a bell,
But it could be heard as far as
    Chiapa,
As far as Tuxtla,
When the bell rang.
Well, the holy bell was hung
By the ancestral gods,
Left by our fathers, the VASHAKMEN.
Well, you see,
The spotted Chiapanecs
As they were just strong-hands,
Light-rays . . .
Well, well, they said to the
    Zinacantecos,

"Ba kich'tik tal li kampanae, "Let's go bring the bell here,
Tal hok'an li? toe," shi la ?un. Bring it and hang it up here."
?Ik'oponat ti mas sonso moletik The more foolish elders were
 ?une. spoken to.
Hna?tik k'u yepal ?imanbat, Who knows for how much it was
  bought,

K'usi ?ak'bat ya?el, How it was given,
Mi manbat If it was bought
?O mi matanal, Or if it was a present,
Hna?tik k'u yepal shchon i Who knows how much they sold
 kampana, the bell for,
Ti mas moletike ?une. The men long ago
?Ishchon, ?a li moletike che?e. They sold it, the elders.
?A li htsinakantae che?e, The Zinacantecos,
?Oy shohob, There was a light-ray,
?Oy chauk, There was thunder,
?Oy ?ik'. There was wind.
Bveno, va?i ?un, Well, you see,
?A li hsoktometike, The Chiapanecs
Naka tsots k'obetik, Were just strong-hands,
Naka tsots k'ob. Just strong-hands.
?A li htsinakanta che?e, The Zinacantecos,
?Oy chauk, There was thunder,
?Oy ?ik', There was wind,
?Oy vaknab, There was rainbow,
?Oy pepen, There was butterfly,
Htsinakanta ?une. The Zincantecos.
?Isk'opon sba ti sonso moletik, The foolish elders talked
  together,

?Antivoetik ?une. The ancestors.
?Ibat ti kampanae, The bell went,
?Ibat ta Soktom, Went to Chiapa,
?Albat pavor ba yak' ?un, They asked the favor to go leave it,
I, ?a li shch'amal totik Santorenso The children of San Lorenzo.
 ?une.
Hna?tik k'u cha?al ba Who knows how they went
Sch'aybeik i skampana ti Santorenso And lost San Lorenzo's bell;
 ?une;
Yech ?o ?oy kastiko k'al tana, That's why there is punishment
  until now

K'u cha?al bik'it muk'e, For the small and the great,
Pero muk' bats'i parehouk sha, But they are not all alike now,
Hlom, Half,

Hlom sha shve?,
Hlom sha mu shve?,
Porke muk' yiloh.
?A ti moletike che?e,
Ba sk'opon sbaik shchi?uk i
    tsots k'obe,
Chapanekoe, ?a li hsoktome.
"Avokoluk ?abolahan," shi.
?Ibat,
Ta ?ik' ?ibat,
?Imahe ta chauk,
Bat un.
?Itame ?un,
?Ikoti li vaknabe,
?Ibat ta Soktom,
?Ihipi ?un.
Bveno ?ihipi ya?el . . .
Hayib ?ora k'ot ta Soktome,
Ch'abal ?isakub,
Li? sha ta tsinakantae,
Te sha shkananet ti ch'ul
    kampana ?une.
?Otro hmoh
Ba yak'el noshtok ?un.
Bveno, ?i ch'abal sakub
Li? sha ta slumal ?une.
Vokol ?inop i ch'ul kam-
    pana le?e.
Bveno, ta yoshibal bvelta ?une;
"Bveno te k'el ?avilik che?e
Ti k'elo k'u sh?elan chabatik,
Mala ?abaik hset'uk,"
Shi li hch'ul totik, kampana ?une.
"Shaval chihipie," shi ta Soktome.

Muk' hipil ?un,
Te pasbat ?un sna ?a li hoybil.
?A ti shba k'ele che?e,
Hlikel
?I ch?at'esvan talel;
K'al tana ?un,
K'al tana mu shu?
Hk'eltik ch'ul kampanae,

Half now eat,
Half now do not eat,
Because they didn't see it.
The elders
Went to talk together with the
    strong-hands,
The Chiapanecs.
"Please, do us a favor," they said.
It went,
It went in the wind,
It was hit by thunder,
It went,
It was picked up,
The rainbow stood up,
It went to Chiapa,
It was hung.
Well, it was hung, it seems . . .
Whenever it arrived at Chiapa,
It wasn't there at dawn,
It was here now in Zinacantan,
There the holy bell was
    ringing now.
Another time
They went to leave it again.
Well, and it wasn't there at dawn,
Here now in its country.
With difficulty the holy bell
    became accustomed to there.
Well, the third time:
"Well, watch out there,
See how you fare,
Wait a little,"
Said our holy father, the bell.
"You say I'll hang," it said at
    Chiapa
It isn't hung,
There its house was made around it.
If you go look,
In a minute
It sprinkles water;
Till now,
Till now we can't
Look at the holy bell,

Nuhul k'al tana,
Mi ʔo bu hok'iem cheʔe,
ʔIyak' sk'ak'al yoʔon.
ʔOra mu sha tots tal ʔun.
ʔIch'ay i ʔik'e,
ʔIch'ay i vaknabe,
ʔIch'ay i chauke,
Haʔ ʔismulinik ʔun
Ti bat ti ch'ul kampana.
ʔIspas mantal ʔun,
ʔIch'ay i shohobetike,
ʔIch'ay vaknabe,
Yech ʔun ti ch'ul kampana leʔe,
Ti li kampana yuʔun htotik,
Santo Rominko ta Soktom;
Pero maʔuk,
  Muk'aʔa muk',
Pero maʔuk.
ʔA leʔe cheʔe
Shvinah k'al Tushta,
Shvinah k'al Komitan,
Shvinah k'al Soktom,
Chtih i kampana;
Tspas misha
I htotik palee,
Pero shaval kampana,
Pero muk'.
Vaʔi ʔun leʔe pves
Muʔyuk bu hok'iem ʔun,
Ta ʔosh s-hok'an ʔun
ʔA li ʔa li shok hsoktome,
Naka s-hok'an tsots k'obetik,

Totil meʔiletik;
Tsots i hsoktometike
Pero mi haʔuk muk' shhok'i
  yuʔunik.
Solel no'osh te nuhul
Li ch'ul kampana k'al tana leʔe.
Mi haʔuk shak'el;
Shabat ta k'elel,
Hlikel ch'at'esvan tal,
K'el ʔaba ta voʔ.

Face-down till now,
It wasn't ever hung
It was angry.
Now it won't lift up.
The wind lost,
The rainbow lost,
The thunder lost,
So it was their fault
That the holy bell went.
They gave the command,
The light-rays lost,
The rainbow lost,
So the holy bell there,
The bell is for our father,
Santo Domingo in Chiapa;
But that isn't the same,
It is surely big, big,
But that isn't it.
That one [formerly in Zinacantan]
Was heard as far as Tuxtla,
Heard as far as Comitán,
Heard as far as Chiapa,
When they rang the bell;
He held Mass,
Our father, the priest,
But you say it was a bell,
But big.
You see, then,
It was never hung,
They were going to hang it,
The spotted Chiapanecs,
They were just going to hang it,
  The strong-hands
The ancestral gods;
The Chiapanecs were strong
But even they couldn't hang
  it.
So just face-down there
Is the holy bell till now.
Nor can you look at it:
You go to look,
In a minute it sprinkles [you],
Watch out for the water.

Bveno, yech ʔiyak' sk'ak'al yoʔon
  li ch'ul kampana leʔ ʔune.

Bveno, pero muk' shkom ta lek
  i hsoktom ʔuk ʔune.

Hlom povre,

Hlom hmak be,

Hlom mu k'u saʔ, chak veʔuk
  yaʔi.

ʔIyak' sk'ak'al yoʔon
  ch'ul kampana,

Yech ʔikom i tsinakantae povre
  kom,

ʔA li Soktom ʔuk ʔune,

Komo likem ta stohol,

Ti k'u spas,

Tal yelk'an ch'ul kampanae.

Bveno, pero ʔoy kastiko
  k'al tana ʔun.

ʔA li kampana cheʔe

Maʔuk sha leʔe,

K'osh kampana,

Ti mol kampanae cheʔe,

Shal ti hmuk'ta meʔe,

Shal ti htote,

Pero mas mol ʔicham.

Pero haʔ to yaloh komel
  ti k'u shʔelane,

Pero mu sha buy yil
  noshtok ʔun,

Haʔ to ti hmuk'ta tot

Yaloh komel ʔune,

Stot i htot ʔun.

Moletik, mas moletik,

Hnaʔtik s-hay k'eshel

Li ch'ul balamil liʔe.

Pves bveno, yaʔi ʔun,

ʔIyil yaʔel

Ti bu bat ti ch'ul kampana ʔun,

Ch'ayem k'al tana leʔe.

Hlom sha stsak ʔants,

Hlom sha smak be,

Hlom sha stih votsina,

Hlom sha kantinero:

Well, so the holy bell there
  was angry.

Well, but the Chiapanecs didn't
  fare well either.

One group poor,

One group murderers,

One group wants to eat and
  can't find anything.

It was angry,
  the holy bell,

So Zinacantan stayed poor,

And Chiapa too,

As it was begun by them

With what they did,

Came to steal the holy bell.

Well, but there is punishment
  till now.

"The bell

Isn't that one,

It is the little bell,

The old bell,"

Said my grandmother,

Said my father,

But he died long ago.

But he left it said
  what it was like,

But he never saw it
  either,

It goes back to my grandfather

Who left it said,

My father's father.

Older, older,

Who knows how many changes

Of the holy earth now.

Well, then he heard,

He saw, it seems,

Where the holy bell went,

Lost till now.

One group now grabs women,

Another group murderers,

Another plays the loudspeaker,

Another barmen:

Ke bruto,
Mu sha k'u puta bal ?o.
Mu k'u sha ?onosh shu? yu?unik,
Hlom sha no?osh ?un
    tsinakanta,
Ha? ti sok ?o chkaltike.
Ha? k'u spasulanik ta hmek,
Ha? skastiko li ch'ul kampana
    k'al tana le?e.
?A li kampana che?e
Naka s-hok'an,
I hsoktometike,
Naka s-hok'an,
Htsots k'obetik,
Shohobetik,
Ha? no?osh tsots k'ob,
Ha? no?osh shohob
I hsoktometike.
?A li tsinakanta che?e
?Oy hun ?ik',
?Oy hun vaknab,
?Oy hun pepen.
Bveno, ?oy hkot supul
Pero hun supul, muk'ta supul.
?A ti k'al ?iyu? pletue che?e
K'al chmile sha li Mehiko che?e,

Ha? tal stotse li tsinakanta.
Bveno, ?itots ?osh vo?,
?Ibat ?a li hun ?ik',
?Ibat hun vaknab,
?Ibat hun pepen.
?A li chauke muk' shtots,
Ha? no?osh hun ?ik',
Ha? no?osh hun vaknab,
Ha? no?osh hun pepen ?ibat.
?Ital sha li pletue,
Komo chcham sha li mehikoe,
?Ital stotsel li tsinakantae.

?Ora bat ?osh vo?,
?Ital li heneraletike,
Tal snupel ta be.

How brutish,
They're not worth a whoring damn.
They just can't do anything,
One half of
    Zinacantan,
So it was ruined, as we say.
Because of all that they did
So it is the punishment of the
    holy bell till now.
The bell,
They just hung,
The Chiapanecs,
They just hung it,
The strong-hands,
Light-rays,
Just the strong-hands,
Just the light-rays,
The Chiapanecs.
In Zinacantan
There was a wind,
There was a rainbow,
There was a butterfly.
Well, there was a moth,
But a moth, a big moth.
When there was a war,
When the Mexicans were being
    killed,
Zinacantan rose up.
Well, three men rose up,
A wind went,
A rainbow went,
A butterfly went.
The thunder didn't rise up,
Just one wind,
Just one rainbow,
Just one butterfly went.
The war came,
For the Mexicans were dying now,
There came an uprising in
    Zinacantan
Now the three went,
The generals came,
Came to meet them on the path.

"ʔEe ke chinga,
K'usi ta hk'an yuʔun me hun krupo,
Yuʔun me hayib syento ta hk'an.
K'usi bal ʔo ʔosh voʔ?"
"ʔAa, bveno kon mucho gusto stak'
   shisut.
Mu ta hpak'alin hba,
Vaʔi, mu shak'anotikotike,
Haʔ noʔosh ʔosh voʔ litalotikotik
   ʔun."
Sut talel ʔun.
ʔIk'ot yal mu k'u bal ʔo
   ʔosh voʔ.
"Ke sonso,
Mu sha bats'i ʔun,"
Shʔutat ta Mehiko ti moletik
   ʔune.
Hii, ta stael ta be,
ʔIkehi li mehikoe,
Kehi li ronetike,
ʔIslok' spishol.
Bveno, ʔisut ʔun,
Ba sk'el li buy ʔa revolusyone.
Ba sk'el i
Bu li ʔa li k'ok' chtale.
Bveno vaʔi ʔochem sha ta barko
   ʔun
ʔA li yolel shveʔik.
K'ot sta li pepene,
Shk'iet ta tiʔ barko,

Shk'iet,
Ta sk'el yolel veʔel yuʔun
   i soltaro,
Pero yuʔun sha chʔoch bala,
Yuʔun sha segido ta hmek,
Yuʔun sha chapal.
ʔA li ʔik'e chapal sha,
ʔA li vaknabe yuʔun sha chkoti.
Bveno, bat tal yal li pepen
   ʔune.
"Yolel veʔel," shi.
"Bveno, haʔ lek," shi.

"Oh how stupid,
What I want is a group,
I want several hundred.
What use are three men?"
"Ah, well, with great pleasure
   we can return.
We won't offer ourselves,
Since you don't want us,
Just three of us came."
They returned.
They arrived to say that three
   were of no use.
"How stupid,
You are good for nothing,"
They were told in Mexico, the
   elders.
Oh, at the meeting on the road,
The Mexicans knelt,
The lords knelt,
They took off their hats.
Well, they returned,
They went to look where the
   revolution was,
They went to look
Where the war was coming.
Well you see they had entered a
   boat,
They were in the midst of eating.
The butterfly arrived,
Spreading [its wings] alongside
   the boat,
Spreading [its wings],
It saw that the soldiers were
   eating.
But bullets were flying now,
Every few seconds,
They were ready.
The wind was ready now,
The rainbow was standing now.
Well, the butterfly came to tell
   them
"They are in the midst of a meal,"
"Well, that's good," it said.

?A li vaknabe hlikel ?ik'ot
Ta ti? barko ?un shi.
?A li ?ik'e
Pero hun ?ik' Maria Santisima,
?A li barkoe nuhul sha ta mar.

Yeva la chingadas te ch'ay ?o.
Bveno, va?i ?un,
Lah ?o k'op ?un,
Te to chkechi.

In a jiffy the rainbow arrived
At the edge of the ship over there.
The wind,
But a wind, Holy Mary,
The boat was face-down now in
 the sea,
Hell, there it was lost.
Well, you see,
The word is ended,
There it is left.

(Robert M. Laughlin, Tale 115)

Rabbit Tricks Coyote

This amusing tale presents the rabbit as a trickster who tantalizes a coyote with the promise of a girl, then binds him to a treetrunk, burns him with a grass fire, and finally destroys him by having him try to drink up all the water in the waterhole.

?O la hkot t'ul
Tal la shk'ot yelk'an lo?bol;
?Ik'ot yahval ti lo?bole,
?Itsake,
?Ichuke ti t'ule,
"?Ok'ob shtal yich' milel,"
Shi la ti yahval lo?bole;

?Ital la hkot ?ok'il,
"Mi latal ?ok'il?"
Shi la ti t'ule;
"Lital," shi la.
"?Aa, k'usi chapas?"
Shi la ti ?ok'ile;
"Mu k'usi ta hpas,
Yu?un litsake,
Lichuke," shi la ti t'ule.
"Mu k'usi hpas,
Ch'abal hmul,
Chi?ak'bat hun tseb,
Yu?un chik'elanbat hun
 tseb,

There was a rabbit,
Who came to steal fruit;
The owner of the fruit came,
The rabbit was caught,
He was tied up.
"Tomorrow I will come to kill
 him,"
The fruit owner said;
A coyote arrived,
"Have you come coyote?"
Said the rabbit;
"I've come," he said.
"Ah, what are you doing?"
Said the coyote;
"I'm not doing anything,
I was caught,
I was tied up," said the rabbit,
"I didn't do anything,
I'm not guilty,
They're giving me a girl,
For they're presenting me with a
 girl,

Pero yuʔun, mu hk'an li voʔon
  ʔune,"
Shi la ti t'ule;
"Mi shak'an voʔote,
Koman ta hk'eshol,
Chahpech' komel lek,
K'u chaʔal pech'bilon voʔone,
Mi shak'an shavik' voʔot ti tsebe,"
Shi la ti t'ule.
"ʔA li voʔone ta hk'an,"
Shi la ti ʔok'ile.
"ʔA ti mi chak'ane cheʔe,
Chahtiman komel liʔ ta
  yok teʔe,
Te shamala lalekom ʔune,
Te shtal yak'belot ʔun,"

Shi la ti t'ule.
"ʔMi yech ʔaval?"
Shi la ti ʔok'ile.
"Yech kal,
Bats'i lek lek la sba ti tsebe,
Tek malao ʔun,"
Shi la ti t'ule.
"Bveno, teyuk cheʔe,"
Shi la ti ʔok'il ʔune;
Te timil ʔikom ta yok teʔ,

ʔItal ti yahval loʔbole,
Stamoh tal smachita.
"ʔOra si, ʔa li hʔelek' loʔbole,
Liʔ ta shlah ʔune,"
Shi la ti vinike;
Pero bats'i shiʔ la ti ʔok'ile,
"Dios, liʔ sha chilah ʔune,
ʔIhch'un sha li loʔloele,
Mi haʔ tseb leʔ ʔune?"
Shi la ti ʔok'ile;
ʔIshipulan la sba,
ʔIkol ta vokol li ʔok'ile,
ʔIbat la ʔlhatav.
ʔOtro hun bvelta
ʔIsnup la ta be ti ʔok'ile;

But me, I don't want her,"
Said the rabbit:
"If you want her,
Stay in place of me,
I'll leave you well tied up,
Just as I'm tied,
If you want to take the girl,"
Said the rabbit.
"Ah I do want to,"
Said the coyote.
"Ah if you want then,
I'll leave you bound here to the
  treetrunk,
Wait there for your girl friend,
Then they'll come to give her to
  you,"
Said the rabbit.
"Are you telling the truth?"
Said the coyote.
"I'm telling the truth,
The girl is very beautiful,
Wait then,"
Said the rabbit.
"Alright then,"
Said the coyote;
There he was bound to the
  treetrunk,
The owner of the fruit came,
Holding his machete.
"Now for sure that fruit-stealer
Will be finished here,"
Said the man;
But the coyote was really scared,
"God, I'm finished here,
I believed the story,
Is that a girl there?"
Said the coyote;
He struggled wildly,
He freed himself with difficulty,
He left, he fled.
Another time
He met the coyote on the road:

"Bu k'al chabat?"
Shi la ti t'ule.
"Kavron, ta to shak'oponon?
Lek ?alo?loon,
Bu li tseb
Chtal yak'ele?"
Shi la ti ?ok'ile.
"K'u ?ora lakalbe?"
Shi la ti t'ule;
"?A li ?alo?loone che?e,"
Shi la ti ?ok'ile.
"?Aa pero yiyil lahuk
  lavo?onc,
Mu shahpas yech,
Mu shati?on,"
Shi la ti t'ule;
"Mi shak'an ba k'elo k'in
Yu?un chinupun,"
Shi la ti t'ule.
"K'u ?ora chanupun?"
Shi la ti ?ok'ile.
"?Aa shmal tana
  chinupun,"
Shi la ti t'ule.
"Chibat che?e,"
Shi la ti ?ok'ile;
?Ilah la yo?on;
"Buy lek chanupun?"
  shi la.
"?Aa le? ta ?o?lol
  hobeltike,"
Shi la.
"Bveno, hmoh me ?un?"
Shi la ti ?ok'ile.
"Bveno, hmohuk,"
Shi la ti t'ule;
?A ti t'ule
Ba la sa? tal serio,
Ba la shoyin ta k'ok'
  ti hobeltike;
?Ii, te la k'ak' ti ?ok'ile,
Te la sh?avet,
?Ihatav la ti t'ule,

"Where are you going?"
Said the rabbit.
"Cabrón, you still talk to me?
You tricked me well,
Where is the girl
They were going to bring?"
Said the coyote.
"When did I tell you?"
Said the rabbit;
"You tricked me,"
Said the coyote.
"Ah, but never mind, don't be
  angry,
I won't do it again,
Don't eat me,"
Said the rabbit;
"If you want, come see a party,
For I'm getting married,"
Said the rabbit.
"When are you getting married?"
Said the coyote.
"Ah, I'm being married late this
  afternoon,"
Said the rabbit.
"I'm going then,"
Said the coyote;
His anger was over;
"Exactly where are you getting
  married?" he said.
"Ah, there in the middle of the
  tall grass,"
He said.
"Alright, is it certain?"
Said the coyote.
"Well, certain,"
Said the rabbit,
As for the rabbit,
He went to bring matches,
Went to encircle the grass with
  fire;
Iih, there the coyote got burned,
There he was screaming,
The rabbit fled,

Stse'in sha la ta hmek 'ech'el,
'Ikol to ta k'ok' k'ak'etik
   'ech'el,
Stsatsal ti 'ok'ile;
"Pero muk' bu shbat,
Ta hti' ta persa,"
Shi la ti 'ok'ile;
'Isnup la ta be 'otro hun bvelta:
"'Ora si li' chahti' 'une

K'u yu'un lek 'alo'loon,"
Shi la ti 'ok'ile.
"K'u cha'al,
Mu vo'nikon,
Muk' bu shakil,
Muk' bu shahnup ta be,
Yan 'o nan,
Li'e, k'elavil vo'one,
Htos 'o hk'u',"
Shi la ti t'ule;
"'Mi yech 'aval 'un?"
Shi la ti 'ok'ile.
"Yech kal,
Mu vo'nikon,
Parte nan bi 'a,
Vo'one mu shakohtikin,
Vo'one lek ko'on,"
Shi la ti t'ule.
"Mi yech 'aval?"
Shi la ti 'ok'ile.
"'A li vo'one,
Vinik shik'opoh;
Mi shak'ane ba hlahestik kik
   vo' le' ta shch'enale,
'A ti me lah kuch'tike,
'O la te lek tseb,
Te la ta htatik,"
Shi la ti t'ule.
'Iyuch'ik la ti vo'e;
"'A li vo'one linoh sha,
'A li vo'ote mas muk' 'ach'ute,
'Ak'o pversa,
Laheso li vo'e,"

Away he went laughing hard;
The coyote escaped from the
   fire,
He got away, his fur afire;
"But he won't go anywhere,
I'll surely eat him,"
Said the coyote.
He met him again on the road:
"Now certainly I'm going to eat
   you
Because you tricked me well,"
Said the coyote.
"What do you mean?
It's not me,
I haven't seen you,
I haven't met you on the road,
Maybe another,
Here, look at me,
My clothes are different,"
Said the rabbit.
"Are you telling the truth?"
Said the coyote.
"I'm telling the truth,
It's not me,
Perhaps it's someone else,
I don't know you,
Me, I've a good heart,"
Said the rabbit.
"Are you telling the truth?"
Said the coyote.
"Me, I speak
Like a man;
If you want to, let's go drink
   the water there in the well,
If we drink it all up,
There is a pretty girl
We'll find there,"
Said the rabbit.
They drank the water;
"As for me, I'm full already,
You, your stomach is bigger,
Try harder,
Finish up the water,"

Shi la ti t'ule.
?Iyak' la pversa ti ?ok'ile;
"Mu sha sh?och ?o hch'ut,
Linoh sha."
"?Ak'o sha persa,
Yu?un ?avu?un li tseb
Ti mi lah ?av?un li vo?e,"
Shi la ti t'ule.
?Inoh ta hmek ti ?ok'ile,
Mu sha stak' shanav;
Pero stse?in la ta hmek li t'ule;
"Pero bu to li tsebe?" shi la;
"Po?ot sha, ?ak'o pversa,"
K'alal yu?un sha cht'om li
   sch'ute;
?Ihatav la ti t'ule;
"?Ah, ?ah, ?ah,
Yech chahlo?lo,"
Shi la ti t'ule;
?Ibat ?o.
Yech ?ilah ?o ti k'ope.

Said the rabbit.
The coyote tried hard:
"It won't enter my belly anymore,
I'm full now."
"Try harder,
For the girl is yours
If you can finish the water,"
Said the rabbit.
The coyote got really full,
He couldn't walk any more;
But the rabbit laughed hard.
"But where is the girl?" he said:
"Almost, try harder,"
Until his belly
   exploded;
The rabbit ran off;
"Ha, ha, ha,
So I fooled you,"
Said the rabbit;
He went away.
So the word is ended.

(Robert M. Laughlin, Tale 20)

The Arrival of the Chiapanecos

This tale describes the coming of the Chiapaneco soldiers who were apparently invading Zinacantan, following the ancient route which passes through the hamlet of Salinas and then passes a series of important sacred places before it reaches Zinacantan Center. The soldiers kept coming until they were swept away in the waters of the "Roaring River."

?Oy to ?osh la bats'i tsots
   viniketik ti vo?ne,
?Oshvo?ik la li viniketike,
?Isk'opon la sbaik, bveno, ?a li:
"K'ushi shana?,
Mi ?u k'u shana? li vo?ote?"
Shut la ti hun schi?ile.
"Mu?yuk,
Mu k'u hna?," shi la.

Once there were very strong
   men,
There were three men,
They were talking together, well:
"What do you know,
Is there anything *you* know?"
He said to one of his companions.
"Nothing,
I don't know anything," he said.

"Vo'ote k'u shana' li vo'ote?"
"Vo'one hna' hts'uh chavok,"
Shi la.
"'Aa shana'."
"Hna'."
"'A li vo'ot 'une k'usi shana'?"
"'A li vo'one hna',
Pepen no'osh li hna' li vo'one,"
Shi li hune.
"'A li vo'ote k'usi shana'?"
'Iyalbe la sbaik li 'osh-vo'ik
   'une:
"'A li vo'one hna' sutum 'ik',"
   shi la;
"'Ik'al vo' hna'," shi la 'un;
'Aa 'entonse,
'Ayik ta Tabasko,
Ta shanbal ta Tabasko,
Chpashiahik,
Hkomersianteetik;
Smanik moy;
'Ora 'iyalik la 'un,
"Pero mi yech te hk'eloh

Hba chilah 'un,
Chtal sha li soltero,
   hmilvanuk 'une,
'A ti 'u k'usi,
K'usi ta hnoptik 'un,
Mi mu shu' ti shba kak'betike?"

Shiik la 'un.
"Batan, 'ak'o batan vo'ot che'e,"
Sh'utat 'a li pepen 'une;
Ba la sk'el 'un:
Lakal la hun perol
Ve'elil 'un ta Soktom 'une,
Va'i 'un;
Li pepene te la shhoyet,

'Istsa'ta la komel 'a li ve'elil
   'une,
'Ipas ta shuvit 'un,

"You, what do you know?"
"Me, I know a little thunder,"
He said.
"Ah, you know."
"I know."
"You, what do you know?"
"Me, I know,
I know only butterfly,"
Said the other.
"You, what do you know?"
They asked among the three:

"Me, I know whirlwind," he said;

"I know hurricane," he said;
Ah then,
They went to Tabasco,
They went walking to Tabasco,
Traveling,
Merchants;
They bought tobacco;
Now they said,
"But if it's true we'd better
   watch out,
We're going to be finished off,
Soldiers, murderers are
   coming now,
What is there,
What can we think up now,
Can't we go to give them
   something?"
They said.
"Go, you go then,"
The butterfly was told;
He went to look:
A cauldron of food
Was cooking in Chiapa,
You see;
Then the butterfly was circling
   around,
He shit on the
   food,
It turned into worms,

Te stik' komel shuvit ta ve?elil
　　?une,
Mu?yuk sha shve?ik solteroe,
Mu?yuk sha slahes li ve?elil ?une,
Komo yu?un ?oy sha shuvit ?un,
Muk' slahes sve?elik la ?une;
Bveno, ?italik la ?un,
Muy tal ?un,
Yu?un sha shtal,
Hmilvanuk ?osh chmuy tal ?une;
?Italik la ?un,
Ha? ta, ?a li ?oy Vok'em Sets'
　　sbi ?une;
Te la lamal ?ep ta hmek li
　　sets' ?une,
Pulatuetik ?une,
Lekik la sba ta hmek,
Te lamal ta be ?une,
Yo? ti mi tsk'anik
Ti me shch'ay ?o yo?one,
Yu?un la ha? te ta shlah ?osh,
Ti yu?un ch'ayuk yo?one,
Pero mu la bu ch'ay yo?on,
Mu la bu sk'elik ?un,
Helavik la tal ?un;
Bveno, ?iyulik tal ta hun ts'el
　　?a li Burero noshtok un:
Te ?une, ?o la te ?a li ?Ik'al Vo?
　　sbi ?un,
Pero yu?un la te tahinik te yo?
　　?une,
?Iyak' la hun ?ik' shchi?uk vo?,
Hset' la mu teyuk ?icham,
Solteroetike,
Pero muk' bu shcham ?un,
Pero ?ihelavik la tal ?un,
Muk' la bu shi?ik ?o tah
　　sh?elan ?iyak' ?ik',
?Ik'al Vo? ?une;
Bveno, ?iyul tal ta Pets toh
　　?une,
Ha? la li toh,
Ta la sh?ak'otah i toh ?une;

There he deposited worms in the
　　meal;
Now the soldiers don't eat,
Now they don't eat the meal,
As it had worms already,
They didn't eat their meal;
Well, they arrived,
They came up,
For already they were coming,
The would-be killers;
They came up, they arrived
At, Broken Bowls it is
　　called;
There there were spread out many
　　bowls,
Dishes,
Very very beautiful,
There spread out on the path,
So that they would want them
And be distracted,
For there they would have died
If they had been distracted,
But they weren't distracted,
They didn't look at them,
They passed on;
Well, they entered near Burrero,
　　too,
There there is a Hurricane,
　　it's called,
But because there they played,

They gave a wind with rain,
They nearly died,
The soldiers,
But they didn't die,
But they passed on,
They weren't afraid of that wind,

Of the hurricane;
Well, they entered Pine Tree
　　then,
The pine tree,
The pine tree danced;

Bveno, muk' bu ch'ay yo'on nosh-
  tok 'un,
Muk' la bu sk'elik 'un,
Muk' la bu sk'elik 'un,
Muk' bu ch'ay 'o yo'on,
Helavik la tal noshtok 'un;
Bveno, 'iyul tal ta, li' ta
  ts'el Vo' Bits 'un,
'O la te hun 'ants noshtok 'un,
Yolel ta shhalav la 'un,
Melel slekil hun 'antse,
Te ch'abteh 'un,
Chhalav la 'un;
Pero mu la bu ch'ay 'o yo'on,
Mu la bu sk'elik noshtok 'un,
Tal la noshtok,
Helav tal 'un,
Li' ta yak'ol sha li 'Ats'am 'une,
Te li, 'o te hun krus 'un,
'O te la hun ch'ivit te yo' 'une,
Pero hun ch'ivit,
'Animal yepaluk:
'Oy la lo'bol,
'Oy la k'utikuk ta hmek,
Ve'elil,
K'utik la chchone 'un;
Pero mu la bu slahesik
  'un,
Porke ti slahesike che'e,
Yu'un te chkom skotol 'osh,
Ti sk'oplale,

Ti'n smanuk,
Smanuk lo'bol,
Smanuk k'u slahes ta ch'ivite,

Yu'un te kom skotol,
Muk' yu'un ha' sch'ay 'o yo'on,
K'usi 'oy ta shchone,
Pero muk' 'onosh bu sman,
Mu la bu sk'elik 'un;
Bveno, tal sha noshtok 'un,
'Oy te 'oy sha li' ta 'ak'ol tal
  Ts'ahom Pik' sbi 'une,

Well, again they weren't
  distracted,
They didn't look at all,
They didn't look at all,
They weren't distracted,
They passed on again;
Well, they entered here near
  Five Pieces,
There was a woman there too,
Weaving,
She was very beautiful,
The woman working there,
Weaving;
But they weren't distracted,
Again they didn't look,
They came on again,
Passed on,
Here above Salinas,
There there is a cross,
There there is a market there,
But a market!
Loads of things,
There's fruit,
There's everything,
Meals,
Whatever is sold;
But they don't eat anything at
  all,
For if they had eaten,
They would have all stayed there,
That was what was supposed to
  happen,
If they had bought,
Had bought fruit,
Had bought what is eaten at
  market,
Then they all would have stayed,
They weren't distracted by
Whatever was for sale,
But they never bought anything,
They didn't look at all;
Well, they came on again,
There there is up here a place
  called Submerged Vagina,

ʔO la te hun ʔants chʔatin ʔun,
Chʔatin ta,
ʔOy te ʔunen nab ti voʔne la
    ʔune,
ʔOy te nab,
Pero hun la yoʔon te chʔatin li
    ʔantse,
Ta shʔatin s-hunleh ta yut voʔ
    ʔune;
Mu la bu sk'elik noshtok,
Mu la bu sk'elik;
Bveno, tal la, tal ʔun,
Yuʔun sha chʔoch tal ta Hteklum
    ʔune poʔot sha;
Bveno,
"Tal sha me li pukuh ʔune,
K'usi ta hnoptik?"
Shi la li viniketik ʔune.
"ʔEh, pero k'usi,
Mu sha k'u stak' hnoptik,
Mi, komo ʔech' sha tal skotol,
Li k'u shʔelan ʔihch'aybetik
    yoʔone,
Muk' bu sch'ay yoʔonik,
K'u ta hnoptik sha ʔun?"
Shiik la ʔun;
"Mu hnaʔ mi haʔ lek ta hnoptik,

Ta hnohestik li ʔuk'ume,"
Shi la ʔun;
"ʔEh, haʔ bi sha haʔ shuʔ,"
Shi la li yan ʔune;
Bveno,
"ʔAk'o nohuk cheʔe," shi;
ʔIvak' la bɘnos voʔ

There is there a woman bathing,
Bathing in,
There was a little lake there
    once,
There was a lake,
But happily the woman is bathing
    there,
Bathing her whole body in the
    water;
Again they didn't look,
They didn't look;
Well, they came, they came on,
For already they are about to
    enter Zinacantan Center,
Well,
"Already the devils are coming,
What'll we think of?"
Said the man.
"Eh, but what,
There is nothing else to think of,
If, they have all come ahead
Where we would have distracted
    them,
They weren't distracted at all,
What will we think of now?"
They said;
"I don't know if it would be a
    good idea,
To fill the river,"
He said;
"Eh, yes indeed, that we can do,"
Said the others;
Well,
"Let it fill then," he said;
He gave a terrific rainstorm
    right away,
In a minute he gave it, the
    river flooded,
In a minute all the soldiers were
    taken away,
Gone;
Not until then was their business
    finished,
In that way the talk ends,

Porke tame ta ʔukʼum ʔun,
Haʔ to te kuch yuʔunik ʔa li
　moletike voʔne la ʔune,
Haʔ to kuch yuʔun,
ʔA li ʔukʼume cheʔe,
Pumlahan ʔUkʼum sbi,
Shlokʼ Yoʔon Ton
　shalbeik,
Yuʔun la ʔoy to ʔosh yoʔon i ton
　noshtok ʔune,
Lek sha la yoʔon li tone,
Pero mukʼ bu skʼelik noshtok,
Helav tal,
Ke yuʔun sha chʔoch sha tal ta
　Hteklum sha ʔun,
Haʔ sha tah ʔukʼum sha snopik
　ʔune,
Noh li ʔukʼum ʔune,
ʔEchʼ sbekʼel ʔechʼel skotol,
Bat skotol,
Bat skotol ʔun,
Haʔ to te lah ʔo skʼoplal ʔun.

For they were taken by the river,
Not until then did the elders
　win long ago,
Not until then did they win,
The river,
It is called Roaring River,
The Stone's Heart Appears, they
　call it,
For the stone there had a heart
　too,
It was a good heart, the stone's,
But they didn't look at it either,
They passed on,
For now they were entering
　Zinacantan Center.
That was the river they thought
　of,
The river flooded,
They were all brushed away,
All gone,
They all went, then,
Right there ended their business.

(Robert M. Laughlin, Tale 56)

Appendix V / Case Descriptions of Shamanistic Rituals

The four ceremonies described here were performed by shamans in Zinacantan between 1960 and 1963. The descriptions are edited versions from my field journal. The cases contain ethnographic details essential for a fuller understanding of the shamanistic rituals but which would have made Chapter 20 tediously long had they been included there.

Case 1. A VALK'UNEL *and* LOK'ESEL TA BALAMIL *Ceremony for Telesh's Daughter (July 20–21, 1961)*

In July 1961 one of my Zinacanteco informants, Telesh Komis Lotriko, a shaman who lives in the hamlet of Paste?, came to me with a story of a complicated interpersonal struggle in which he was involved. Some months before, the fifteen-year-old daughter of his neighbor Pil Lopis Chiku? had complained of a stomach-ache, and the father summoned Telesh to pulse the girl, Shunka?. The pulsing disclosed that Shunka? did not have stomach trouble but was pregnant, and that she had been impregnated by her own brother, Manvel. Pil agreed with the diagnosis, admitting that his son had slept with his daughter while he and his wife had been away; he forthwith whipped both Manvel and Shunka? with a leather strap. As a result, Manvel was furious with Telesh, and on one occasion in June had attempted to stab him during a drunken spree. Manvel carried the grudge further by making several trips to mountain caves to light candles for the ancestral gods, praying that they punish Telesh and protesting his own innocence. This has caused sickness for various members of Telesh's family, the latest victim being his youngest daughter, ?Akushtina.

Telesh invited me to participate in a curing ceremony for his daughter which he was going to perform that night. Since it was the first curing ceremony to which I had been invited—even after four seasons of field work in Zinacantan during which time I had worked hard to develop rapport—I quickly accepted. We set out for Telesh's house in the project Landrover about 5 P.M. At 6 o'clock we managed to become impossibly stuck in a mudhole, and had to abandon the car and walk to the house, arriving about an hour later.

The all-night ceremony took place first inside Telesh's house, then outside by the house cross in the patio, and ended inside.

Participants. The participants included Telesh, his wife, their four daughters, Telesh's wife's father and brother and their wives and children. The genealogical relationships have been diagramed (Figure 193); note that Telesh, an orphan, was living matrilocally, which is rare in Zinacantan.

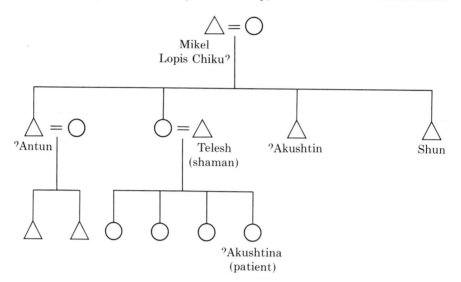

193. Participants in a 1961 curing ceremony

The following assumed the ritual roles necessary for the curing ceremony: Shaman (and father of the patient): Telesh Komis Lotriko; patient: ?Akushtina Komis Lotriko; candle-carrier: ?Antun Lopis Chiku?; pine-bough-gatherer: Mikel Lopis Chiku?; drink-pourers: ?Akushtin Lopis Chiku?, Shun Lopis Chiku?; clothes-washer: Mikel's wife. Telesh's wife also participated ritually by holding the small (age three) patient in her arms, helping dress her in fresh clothes, and praying for her.

Paraphernalia. The paraphernalia, assembled in advance by the assistants, included the following:

Shaman's bamboo staff (BISH) which Telesh carried only when he led the small procession outside.

Shaman's black ceremonial robe (SHAKITAIL) which Telesh wore throughout the ceremony.

Candles purchased in San Cristóbal: six 50¢ (centavo) white wax; four 20¢ white wax; three 10¢ tallow; three 10¢ white wax; one 20¢ greenish-blue; one 20¢ black; one 20¢ multicolored; one 20¢ yellow; two two-for-5¢ greenish-blue; two two-for-5¢ multicolored; two two-for-5¢ yellow; two two-for-5¢ red; two two-for-5¢ white wax; two two-for-5¢ tallow.

Plant materials, including three boughs from white pine trees to decorate the house cross; needles from white pine trees to place in front of the house cross; a bundle of longer needles from the ʔAHAN TOH pine to make a foot-long wand for calling the soul; and a small basket of red geraniums.

Incense of two kinds: BEK'TAL POM, purchased in San Cristóbal; TEʔEL POM, collected in the lowlands.

A ceramic censer, which was placed under the west end of the table and kept burning throughout the night.

Two small (10-cm.) gourds used in calling the soul.

A white enamel bowl, approximately 20 cm. in diameter, used in the maize divining procedure.

Four ears of maize of different colors—white, yellow, red, black—which were placed in a large gourd on the table and covered with the pine needle wand; later, thirteen grains were removed from each ear for divining.

Two baskets, one to contain the geraniums and candles, the other to place over the smoking incense to cense the patient's clothes.

Small table, oriented east–west, which served as an altar, holding the ritual objects; later the ritual meal was served on it.

Two of Telesh's chickens that were cooked and eaten at the end of the ceremony.

Salt from Ixtapa that was used for maize divining and for calling the soul.

Rum liquor, five liters purchased in San Cristóbal.

Two packs of Mexican "Delicado" cigarettes that were first placed on the table, but later distributed to the male participants.

Preceremonial Activities. When Telesh and I arrived at his house, the women were already busy cutting up the two chickens and placing them in a pot for cooking, and various members of the group were eating tortillas and MUM, the latter being a type of wasp's nest containing live larvae. The procedure was to heat the MUM by the fire until the larvae oozed out and then extract them and eat them with tortillas. I only discovered this procedure after I had been handed a chunk and had made the mistake of eating the whole business, nest and all! Aside from this I was offered no food in a formal way, but was asked twice by Telesh if I would like to eat. I foolishly declined thinking that a ritual meal would be served soon. It turned out that food was not served formally until 4 A.M. when the chicken was served in a ritual meal.

The Ritual Sequence. From a combination of my observations during the night and from Telesh's explanations a sequence of ten separate ritual events were noted in this ceremony.

(1) The arrival of the shaman was simplified in this case because Telesh was performing in his own house. Telesh entered his house, without stopping at the house cross, and prayed at the table. He also omitted the formal bowing and releasing gestures with everyone present.

(2) The inspection of the candles (K'EL KANTELA) was performed with great care. After a round of rum liquor, Telesh opened the package of candles, counted them, and then set up the table as an altar whose arrangement is shown in Figure 194.

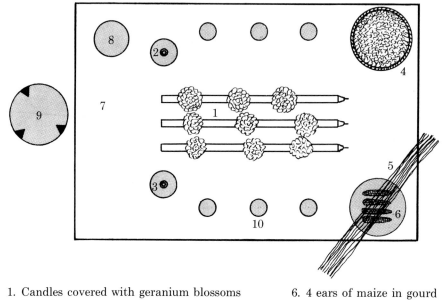

1. Candles covered with geranium blossoms
2. Gourd$_1$
3. Gourd$_2$
4. Basket of geranium blossoms
5. Wand for calling soul
6. 4 ears of maize in gourd
7. Cigarettes
8. Incense
9. Censer
10. Liquor in cuartas

194. An arrangement for a curing ritual

Telesh then chanted the following prayer for the candles on the table altar:

?En ?el ch'ul nompre yos hesukristo kahval,
    K'usi yepal ?un htot,
    K'usi yepal ?un kahval,
        Ta hk'an ti ch'ul pertonale,
        Ta hk'an ti ch'ul lesensiae,
            Ti ta ch'ul ba meshae,
            Ti ta ch'ul chak meshae;

In the divine name of Jesus Christ my lord,
  So much my father,
  So much my lord,
    I beseech your divine pardon,
    I beg your divine forgiveness,
      At the holy head of the table,
      At the holy foot of the table;

Mi shavaʔan ʔabaik,
Mi shatek'an ʔabaik,
  Ta yo spat ʔun,
  Ta yo shokon ʔun,
    Tavalabike,
    Tanich'nabike,
    Tanichike,
    Tak'elomike,
      Ti ʔoy ta hun ʔipe,
      Ti ʔoy ta hun k'ushe,
      Ti ʔabol sbae,
      Ti ʔuts'uts' sbae;

Will you stand up,
Will you stand firm,
  Behind,
  Beside,
    Your sons,
    Your children,
    Your flowers,
    Your sprouts,
      Who have sickness,
      Who have pain,
        Who are suffering,
        Who are miserable;

Ti ta hun shmale,
Ti ta hun sakube,
  Ti mu sha bu slekil,
  Ti mu sha bu yutsil,
    K'usi yepal ti mu sha bu ta shich',
    Mu sha bu ta shuʔunin,
      Tanichim shohobale,
      Tanichim nak'obale;

At dusk,
At dawn,
  They are no longer well,
  They are no longer healthy,
    For how long will they not receive,
    For how long will they not possess,
      Your beautiful sunbeams,
      Your beautiful shade;

Te no la likel,
Te no la kahel,
  Ti hun ʔipe,
  Ti hun k'ushe,
    Ta yo spat ʔun,
    Ta yo shshokon ʔun,
      Mi chavaʔan ʔach'ul baik,
      Mi chatek'an ʔach'ul baik,
      Ta yo spat ʔun,
      Ta yo shshokon ʔun,
        Tavalabike,
        Tanich'nabike;

Then it is just beginning,
Then it is just flowering,
  The sickness,
  The pain,
    In their humble backs, then,
    In their humble sides, then,
      Will you stand in holiness,
      Will you stand firm in holiness,
        Behind them,
        Beside them,
          Your sons,
          Your children;

Ch'ul kalvario, ch'ul totil,
Kalvario ch'ul meʔil,
  Ch'ul kalvario ch'ul yih,
  Ch'ul kalvario ch'ul k'on,
    Ch'ul maretik,
    Ch'ul ʔahvetik,
      Ch'ul tsoblebal,
      Ch'ul lotlebal,
        Ch'ul kolebal,
        Ch'ul kushebal,

Divine Calvary, divine father,
Calvary, divine mother,
 Holy Calvary holy ancient ones,
 Holy Calvary holy yellow ones,
  Holy seas,
  Holy ancient ones,
  Holy gathering-place,
   Holy meeting-place,
    Holy place of recovery,
    Holy place of rest,

K'usi yepal
Ta hk'an ch'ul pertonal ʔun,
Ta hk'an ch'ul lesensia ʔun,
 Chahtaik ta k'oponel,
 Chahtaik ta tiʔinel,
  Ta shoylemal ʔun,
  Tsutlemal ʔun,
   Tach'ul baik ʔune,
   Tach'ul satik ʔune;

This much,
I beseech divine pardon,
I beg divine forgiveness,
 I speak to you,
 I pray to you,
  At the circuit [of shrines],
  At the circling
   Of your holy countenances,
   Of your holy faces;

Ta hhok'an hutuk ʔun,
Ta htsoyan hutuk ʔun,
 Ta sba yol ʔavok,
 Ta sba yol ʔak'ob,
  Tavalabike,
  Tanich'nabike,
  Tanichike,
  Tak'elomike,
   Haʔ ta hk'an ʔo ch'ul pertonal,
   Haʔ ta hk'an ʔo ch'ul lesensia;

I shall visit your shrines a little,
I shall entrust my soul to you a little,
 To your feet,
 To your hands,

For your sons,
For your children,
For your flowers,
For your sprouts,
For these I beseech divine pardon,
For these I beg divine forgiveness;

K'usi ti nopbil tana,
K'usi ti p'isbil tana,
Mi ʔo to nan ti ch'ul kolele,
Ti ch'ul kushel ʔune kahval,
Chahtaik ta k'oponel,
Chahtaik ta tiʔinel,
Ta hlikel ʔun,
Ta chaʔlikel ʔun,
Ta shoylemal ʔun,
Tsutlemal ʔun,
Ta ch'ul baik ʔune,
Ta ch'ul satik ʔune;

What will be thought now,
What will be considered now,
Is there yet holy recovery,
Is there yet holy rest, then, lord,
I speak to you,
I pray to you,
For a moment, then,
For a few moments, then,
At the circuit,
At the circling
Of your holy countenances,
Of your holy faces;

Mi chach'ambekon,
Mi chavich'bekon,
Ti yo hset' ʔune,
Ti yo hhuteb ʔune,
Ti chanib yo stoh,
Chanib yo skantela,
Tavalabe,
Tanich'nabe;

Will you take this for me,
Will you receive this for me,

This lowly little bit,
This humble amount,
    These four lowly torches,
    These four lowly candles,
      From your son,
      From your child;

Ha? ta hk'an ?o ch'ul pertonal,
Ta hk'an ?o ch'ul lesensia,
    Ha? ta sti? yo sna,
    Ta sti? yo sk'uleb,
      Ta skushobil yo?on,
      Ta svik'obil sat,
        Tavalabe,
        Tanich'nabe,
          Kahval.

For this I beseech divine pardon,
I beg divine forgiveness,
    At the entrance of his humble house,
    At the entrance of the place of his humble wealth,
      At the resting-place of his heart,
      At the place where his eyes open,
        Him, your son,
        Your child,
          My lord.

(3) Following another round of drinks served by the drink-pourers, who always served Telesh first, and then proceeded in rank order with all the men, then the women, and served themselves last, Telesh proceeded with the maize divination (SAT ?ISHIM). The white enamel bowl was half-filled with water, and salt was added. Telesh, using his left thumb, removed thirteen grains of corn from the ear of white maize, counting carefully. Holding the thirteen grains in his right fist, he blew on his fist, and then dropped them gently into the bowl of water. He repeated the procedure with the yellow, red, and black maize. He shook the bowl very gently back and forth to see which grains floated or moved back and forth. Telesh asked me to look into the bowl also. We saw five grains clearly moving; a sixth appeared doubtful to me, but Telesh decided there were six, which indicated that six parts of the soul were missing, and he announced VAKIB, "six," to the others. He removed the six moving grains, plus seven others and placed them in one of the small gourds, adding salt water from the enamel bowl. The remaining thirty-nine grains and the remaining salt water were placed in the second small gourd.

There was another round of liquor. Each time the shaman was served, he said a brief prayer over the liquor before he drank it:

> ʔEste kich'ban cheʔe totik,
> Kich'ban cheʔe meʔtik,
>   Kolavalik hutuk.

> Well, then, I drink first, father,
> I drink first, then, mother.
>   Thank you a little.

> ʔA ch'ul nompre yos hesukristo kahval,
>   Tsauk ʔune htot,
>   Tsauk ʔune kahval,
>   ʔO to la hset' ʔun,
>   ʔO to la hhuteb ʔun;

> In the divine name of God, Jesus Christ my lord,
>   Take this, then, father,
>   Take this, then, lord,
>   There is still a little left,
>   There is still a drop left;

> Ti sts'uhulal yol ʔavee,
> Sts'uhulal yol ʔatiʔe,
>   Ta hmakita,
>   Ta hkevuta;

> Of this dew of your holy mouth,
> Of this dew of your holy lips,
>   I will share with you,
>   I will stand in your shadows [under your cover];

> Ta shkich' yo hset',
> Ta shkich' yo hhuteb,
>   K'usi yepal chik'opoh ʔo,
>   Chitiʔih ʔo;

> I take this little bit,
> I take this small amount,
>   With which I speak to you,
>   With which I pray to you;

> Ta hk'an ch'ul pertonal,
> Ta hk'an ʔo ch'ul lesensia,
>   Yuʔun tavalabike,
>   Yuʔun tanich'nabike,

With this I beseech divine pardon,
With this I beg divine forgiveness,
  For your sons,
  For your children,

Mi ʔo to yet'esel,
Mi ʔo to s-helubtasel,
  Ti hun chamele,
  Ti hun lahele,
  Ti hun ʔipe,
  Ti hun k'ushe;

Is there still avoidance,
Is there still transference,
  Of sickness,
  Of death,
  Of disease,
  Of pain;

Ta yo spat ʔun,
Ta yo shshokon ʔun,
  Tavalabe,
  Tanich'nabe,
    Mi shavaʔan ʔaba,
    Mi shatek'an ʔaba,

Behind him, then,
Beside him, then,
  Your son,
  Your child,
    Will you stand up,
    Will you stand firm,

Ch'ul kalvario ch'ul totil,
Ch'ul kalvario ch'ul meʔil, kahval,
  Ta to la shkich',
  Ta shkuʔunin,
    Ti hset' ʔune,
    Ti hhuteb ʔune kahval,
      Helavkon tabaik ʔun,
     Tasatik ʔun,
        Kahval.

Divine Calvary holy father,
Divine Calvary holy mother, lord,
  I receive this now,
  I will take unto me,
    This little bit, then,
    This small amount, then, lord,
      So that I may pass in your sight,
      In your countenance,
        My lord.

(4) In this ceremony the small patient was not bathed, but she was dressed in freshly washed clothes at this point. The censing of the clothes was done by Mikel's wife (who had washed the clothes during the day). Embers were pulled from the fire on a broken piece of a comal; incense of both types was added; and a basket was placed upside down over the top of the smoking incense. The fresh clothing was held briefly over the incense, piece by piece. Her mother awoke and dressed the little patient in the washed clothes. The patient cried throughout the process.

(5) There occurred the paying of respect, or bowing to, the candles, a procedure called SNUP KANTELA. First the shaman said a long prayer; then, in rank order, the other adult participants knelt in pairs at the west end of the table and prayed, placing their heads on the table at intervals. First, old Mikel and his wife, followed by ?Antun and his wife. Next the patient's mother holding the child and ?Akushtin (who took Telesh's place) prayed. (See Chapter 20 for the translation of this prayer.) Since I did not know the proper prayer in Tzotzil, I followed with a version of "The Lord's Prayer," chanted three times, each in a different tone of voice, so that it would seem long enough to be respectable! Another round of liquor followed.

(6) The next procedure involved drinking rum liquor from six cuarta-size bottles which Telesh had prepared when he set up the table as an altar. Instead of full bottles, he poured only a three-finger measure in each. He explained that the ancestral gods had told him liquor was to keep people warm when it's cold and not to make them drunk. The seating arrangements around the table for the drinking were as follows:

	Telesh	Telesh's wife	?Antun's wife	
east			Drink-pourer	west
	Mikel	Mikel's wife	?Antun	

The shaman handed cuartas to the drink-pourer who carefully measured out two shots at a time for each person in rank order. When one cuarta was finished, he went right on to the next. When it did not come out even in the end, he added some from a liter bottle. Telesh explained that these two shots each from each of the six bottles were being drunk because his enemy, Manvel, was up in the mountains again praying against him. All evening Telesh kept saying to me "Let's see who wins"—in this type of counterwitchcraft ritual that was going on.

(7) The next step was to decorate the house cross out in the patio and to light candles before it. A small procession formed with ?Antun carrying the basket of candles, the geranium blossoms, and the smoking censer, and followed by Telesh carrying his bamboo staff. ?Akushtin also went along to serve as the drink-pourer. Telesh first tied a bundle of geranium blossoms on each cross; then he set up the candles, using his staff to make holes in the ground in front of the crosses. The final product took the form shown in Figure 195. When he was not using his staff, Telesh rested it against the right-hand cross piece of the cross.

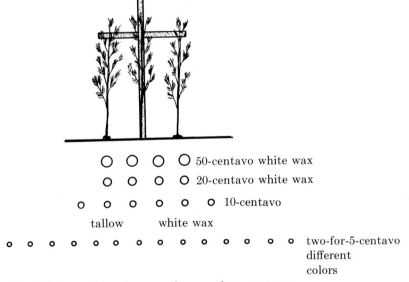

195. The decoration of a cross for a curing ceremony

The action took the following form. Telesh first lighted the candles of 50- and 20-centavo size, and there was a round of liquor. Next he lighted those of 10-centavo size, and there was another round of liquor. Finally, he lighted the small two-for-5 centavo candles, and a third round of liquor followed. While the candles were being lighted, a number of night-flying insects, attracted by the light, appeared. There was a hushed discussion about them, and Telesh explained that they were spies from the Manvel's ceremony which was going on in the mountains. He carefully killed each insect, either with the butt of his staff or by pouring rum on it, so they could not take messages back to Manvel at his ceremony.

Telesh then knelt before his beautiful cross shrine and prayed as follows:

> ʔAn ch'ul nompre yos hesukristo kahval,
> > Tsauk ʔune htot,
> > Tsauk ʔune kahval,
> > > Mi chalekil-ch'ambekon,
> > > Mi chalekil-ʔich'bekon ʔun,
> > > > Ti yo hset' ʔune,
> > > > Ti yo hhuteb ʔune;

> In the divine name of God, Jesus Christ, my lord,
> > Take this, then, my father,
> > Take this, then, my lord,
> > > Will you receive this in good grace,
> > > Will you accept this in good grace,
> > > > This lowly little bit,
> > > > This humble amount;

> ʔAk'o nosh ch'ul pertonal,
> ʔAk'o nosh ch'ul lesensia,
> > Yuʔun ti yol ʔavalabe,
> > Ti yol ʔanich'nabe,
> > > Haʔ ta hhok'an ʔo,
> > > Haʔ ta htsoyan ʔo ʔun,
> > > > Ta sba yol ʔavok ʔun,
> > > > Ta sba yol ʔak'ob ʔun;

> Only grant thy holy pardon,
> Only grant thy holy forgiveness,
> > To your sons,
> > To your children,
> > > For this reason I visit shrines,
> > > For this reason I entrust my soul
> > > > To your feet,
> > > > To your hands;

Mi chavaʔan ʔabaik,
Mi chatek'an ʔabaik,
  Ta yo spat ʔun,
  Ta yo shshokon ʔun,
    Tavalabike,
    Tanich'nabike,
    Tanichike,
    Tak'elomike;

Will you stand up,
Will you stand firm,
  Behind the humble back of,
  By the lowly side of,
    Your sons,
    Your children,
    Your flowers,
    Your sprouts;

Ti ʔabol sbae,
Ti ʔuts'uts' sbae,
  Ti ʔoy ta hun ʔipe,
  Ti ʔoy ta hun k'ushe,
  Ti yo spate,
  Ti yo shshokone,
    Ti mu sha bu slekil,
    Ti mu sha bu yutsil,
      Huhun tanichimal ch'ul ba,
      Tanichimal ch'ul sate;

Those who are suffering,
Those who are miserable,
  Those who have sickness,
  Those who have pain,
    In their lowly backs,
    In their lowly sides,
      Who no longer feel the well being,
      Who no longer feel the goodness,
        Of each of your divinely beautiful countenances,
        Your divinely beautiful faces;

Haʔ ta hk'an ʔo ch'ul pertonal,
Ta hk'an ʔo ch'ul lesensia,
  Haʔ ch'ul kehelon ʔo tal,
  Ch'ul patalon ʔo tal,

Ta sti? yo sna,
Ta sti? yo sk'uleb,
  Tškushobil yo?on,
  Tsvik'obil sat;

For this I beseech divine pardon,
For this I beg divine forgiveness,
  For this I come respectfully kneeling,
  For this I come respectfully bowing low,
    To the entrance of their humble home,
    To the entrance of the place of their wealth,
      To the resting-place of their hearts,
      To the place where their eyes open;

Tavalabike,
Tanich'nabike,
  Ti yol ?anichike,
  Ti yol ?ak'elomike,
    Ti mu to ?ach'aybekon,
    Mu to ?atenbekon;

Your sons,
Your children,
  Your flowers,
  Your sprouts,
    So that you will not lose him,
    Will not abandon him;

?Ok to yet'esel,
?Ok to s-helubtasel,
  Ti hun chamele,
  Ti hun lahele,
    Ti hun ?ipe,
    Ti hun k'ushe,
      Ta yo spat ?un,
      Ta yo shshokon ?un;

Let there still be avoidance,
Let there still be transference of,
  Disease,
  Death,
    Illness,
    Pain,
      From their lowly backs,
      From their lowly sides;

Ch'ul kalvario ch'ul totil,
Kalvario ch'ul meʔil,
  Kalvario ch'ul yih,
  Kalvario ch'ul k'on,
    Tsauk ʔune htot,
    Tsauk ʔune kahval;

Divine Calvary, holy father,
Divine Calvary, holy mother,
  Calvary, holy ancient ones,
  Calvary, holy yellow ones [ancestor gods],
    Take this, then, father,
    Receive this, then, lord;

Mi ta komon k'op tana,
Mi ta komon tiʔ tana,
  Chavaʔan ʔach'ul baik,
  Chatek'an ʔach'ul baik,
    Ti ta yo spate,
    Ti ta yo shshokone,
      Tavalabike,
      Tanich'nabike,
      Tanichik ʔune,
      Tak'elomik ʔune;

Unitedly now,
In unison now,
  Will you stand up in holiness,
  Will you stand firm in holiness,
    Behind the lowly back of,
    By the lowly side of,
      Your sons,
      Your children,
      Your flowers,
      Your sprouts;

Tsauke mi chach'ambekon tana,
Mi chavich'bekon tana,
  Ti yo hset' ʔune,
  Ti yo hhuteb ʔune;

If you will accept this for me now,
If you will receive this for me now,
  Take this lowly little bit,
  Take this humble amount;

Ha? chahtaik ?o ta k'oponel,
Chahtaik ?o ta ti?inel,
  Ta shoylemal ?un,
  Tsutlemal ?un,
    Tanichim ch'ul baike,
    Tanichim ch'ul satike,
      Yu?un ti yo spate,
      Yu?un ti yo shokone,
        Tavalabike,
        Tanich'nabike;

For this I speak to you,
For this I pray to you,
  At the circuit [of shrines],
  At the circling
    Of your divinely beautiful countenances,
    Of your divinely beautiful faces,
      On behalf of the lowly backs,
      On behalf of the lowly sides,
        Of your sons,
        Of your children;

Tsauke chahtaik ta k'oponel,
Chahtaik ta ti?inel ?un,
  Tshoylemal ?un,
  Tsutlemal ?un,
    Tach'ul baike,
    Tach'ul satike;

Take these my words,
Take these my prayers, then,
  At the circuit,
  At the circling
    Of your divine countenances,
    Of your divine faces;

Tsauke ch'ul senyor san kishtoval, ch'ul totil,
Senyor san kishtoval ch'ul me?il,
  Tsauke ch'ul ninab chilo? ch'ul totil,
  Ch'ul ninab chilo? ch'ul me?il,
    Tsauke ch'ul maria sisil,
    Ch'ul maria mushul;

Receive unto you, holy señor San Cristóbal, holy father,
Señor San Cristóbal, holy mother,

Receive, divine wellspring of the holy fathers,
Divine wellspring of the holy mothers,
   Receive, divine Maria Cecilia,
   Divine Maria Mushul;

Tsauke ch'ul chanib ch'ul totil,
Chanib ch'ul me?il,
   Ch'ul chanib ch'ul yih,
   Ch'ul chanib ch'ul k'on,
     Ch'ul sak ch'en ch'ul totil,
     Sak ch'en ch'ul me?il,
       Tsauke ch'ul muk'ta vits ch'ul totil,
       Muk'ta vits ch'ul me?il;

Receive, four holy fathers,
Four holy mothers,
   Four holy ancient ones,
   Four holy yellow ones,
     Holy white cave, holy father,
     Holy white cave, holy mother,
       Receive, holy great mountain, holy father,
       Holy great mountain, holy mother;

Mi ta komon k'op to,
Mi ta komon ti? ?un,
   Chava?an ?ach'ul baik ?un,
   Chatek'an ?ach'ul baik ?un,
     Ta yo spat ?un,
     Ta yo shshokon ?un,
       Tavalabike,
       Tanich'nabike,
       Tanichike,
       Tak'elomike;

United,
In unison,
   Will you stand up in holiness,
   Will you stand firm in holiness,
     Behind the lowly backs of,
     By the lowly sides of,
       Your sons,
       Your children,
       Your flowers,
       Your sprouts;

Ti mu to ʔach'aybekon,
Mu to ʔatenbekon,
  Mi ʔo to ti ch'ul kolel tana,
  Mi ʔo to ti ch'ul kushel tana,
    Ta yo spat ʔun,
    Ta yo shshokon ʔun,
      Tavalab ʔune,
      Tanich'nab ʔune;

If you will not yet lose him for me,
If you will not yet abandon him for me,
  If there is still divine recovery now,
  If there is still divine rest now,
    For the lowly back,
    For the lowly side,
      Of your son,
      Of your child;

Haʔ ta hk'an ʔo ch'ul pertonal,
Hk'an ʔo ch'ul lesensia,
  Ti ch'ul kehelon tale,
  Ti ch'ul patalon tale;

For this I beseech divine pardon,
For this I beg divine forgiveness,
  I come respectfully kneeling,
  I come respectfully bowing low;

Tsauke ta hk'an ch'ul pertonal ʔun,
Ta hk'an ch'ul lesensia ʔun,
  Ta yol ʔats'elik ʔun,
  Ta yol ʔavichonik ʔun,

Receive this, for I beseech divine pardon,
I beg divine forgiveness,
  At your holy sides,
  At your holy front,

Mi chach'ambekon tana,
Mi chavich'bekon tana,
  Ti chanib yo stoh,
  Chanib yo skantela,
    Hp'eh yo snichim,
    Hp'eh yo syanalteʔ,
      Ti hp'eh yo spom,
      Hp'eh yo shch'ail;

Will you receive this for me now,
Will you accept this for me now,
  These four humble torches,
  These four humble candles,
    A lowly flower,
    A lowly leaf,
      A humble bit of incense,
      A humble bit of smoke;

Ta hhok'an ʔo hutuk,
Ta htsoyan ʔo hutuk,
  Ta sba yol ʔavol,
  Ta sba yol ʔak'ob;

I will visit your shrines a little,
I will entrust my soul to you a little,
  To your feet,
  To your hands;

Tavalabike,
Tanich'nabike,
  Tanichike,
  Tak'elomike,
    Kahval, haʔ chahtaik ʔo ta k'oponel,
    Chahtaik ʔo ta tiʔinel;

For your sons,
For your children,
  For your flowers,
  For your sprouts,
    Lord, for these I speak,
    For these I pray;

Skotol ch'ul totil,
Skotol ch'ul meʔil,
  Skotol ch'ul riosh,
  Skotol ch'ul santo,
    K'u yepal ta htih yo ʔaniʔ,
    Ta htih yo ʔachikin,
      Yuʔun ti hun chamele,
      Yuʔun ti hun lahele,
      Yuʔun ti hun ʔipe,
      Yuʔun ti hun k'ushe;
        Mi ʔo to yet'esel,
        Mi ʔo to s-helubtasel;

All the divine fathers,
All the divine mothers,
  All the divine gods,
  All the divine saints,
    With this I touch your holy noses,
    I touch your holy ears,
      Because of disease,
      Because of death,
      Because of sickness,
      Because of pain;
        Is there still avoidance,
        Is there still transference;

Ch'ul totiletik,
Ch'ul me?iletik, kahval,
  Ha? tahk'an ?o ch'ul pertonal,
  Hk'an ?o ch'ul lesensia ?un,
    Kahval.

Divine fathers,
Divine mothers, lord,
  For this I beseech divine pardon,
  For this I beg divine forgiveness,
    My lord.

(8) Telesh then told me he was going to perform LOK'ESEL TA BALAMIL, "extracting the soul from the earth." He stood up, held the pine needle wand in his right hand, blew salt water on it from the second small gourd, faced in a given direction, whirled the wand around 360 degrees, and prayed, interspersed with chanting LA? ME, LA? ME, "come, come," and hitting the ground at his feet with the wand. He faced different directions where parts of the soul had been lost—being reminded of locations by the people shouting out instructions from inside the house—and repeated the process six times. At the same time, Antun stood at Telesh's right and blew into the first small gourd, making a low whistle, "so the soul will hear and return." The soul was then led into the house, past the fire, and over to the patient, where (using more salt water in his mouth from the second gourd) Telesh sucked noisily in four places on the patient's arms, "to call the blood to receive the soul": under the right elbow, inside the right wrist, under the left elbow, and inside the left wrist. Using dry salt, he made a cross on the forehead and on the areas where he had just sucked. This procedure was followed by a round of liquor.

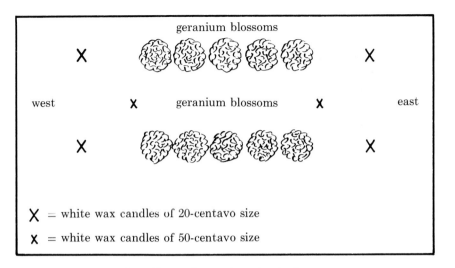

196. Arrangement of candles and geraniums in the house

(9) Next Telesh set up the remaining candles inside the house, using a knife to make holes in the dirt floor in the very center of the house. The final product is shown in Figure 196. Telesh then chanted a long prayer. He explained that the candles lighted at the house cross out in the patio were for the ancestral gods, and those inside the house for the Earth Lord. There should have been three pine boughs to make a cross shrine on the east side of the candles inside the house, but old Mikel forgot to bring the pine boughs for it.

(10) The final procedure was the ritual meal which the women served only to Telesh, old Mikel, and myself. At about 3 A.M. ʔAntun had gone outside, vomited, and then came back inside and collapsed. The young drink-pourers had also gone to sleep. During the previous prayer for the candles inside the house, Telesh himself fell asleep, but was awakened by old Mikel and finally finished the prayer.

Before the meal a *media* of liquor and a large shot glass was placed on the east end of the table, and a round of liquor was served. At this point I was so close to being drunk beyond repair that I staggered over to my shoulder bag, extracted my empty bottle and funnel (which I always carry in Zinacantan), and poured off the liquor into the empty bottle after going through the proper toasting etiquette. We were passed gourds of water for washing our hands and mouths, and were served chicken in chili broth and hot tortillas. It tasted wonderful at 4 in the morning.

Postceremonial Activities. The ceremony was now officially over. I suggested that I return to my field house nearby and sleep before we returned to San Cristóbal, but Telesh suggested that I sleep with them, saying it was only an hour or two before dawn. He moved the two drink-pourers off a reed mat, spread it out for the two of us, gave me a wooden headrest covered with a clean cloth, and covered me with a black, woolen robe. It was very gentle and wonderful treatment. The next thing I knew it was broad daylight and people were up and moving about the house. After a quick meal of tortillas and coffee, Telesh mustered six men to help us extract the Landrover from the mudhole where we had abandoned it the night before. We walked back to get it out and returned to San Cristóbal in time to wait for the arrival of President López Mateos. In checking with Telesh later, I learned that the cost of this ceremony (not counting tortillas) had been: liquor, 20 pesos; candles, 5 pesos and 55 centavos; incense, 1 peso; cigarettes, 1 peso and 20 centavos; chickens, 20 pesos—a total of $47.75 Mexican pesos.

Apparently all the economic costs, time, and energy were worthwhile, for Telesh reported later that he had won his contest with Manvel and that his small daughter had recovered from her illness.

Case 2. A PERTONAL *Ceremony for Romin's Son* (*July 19–20, 1963*)

Romin Teratol's small sons, Shun (age two years and four months) and Chep (age seven months), had whooping cough during an epidemic of that disease in Zinacantan in the summer of 1963. Romin was concerned because Shun's condition had not improved, even after inoculations and medicines recommended by the druggists in San Cristóbal. He finally summoned a woman shaman, Maruch Peres, who pulsed Shun and diagnosed the continuing illness as "soul loss" and advised a curing ceremony called PERTONAL. Romin invited me to participate, explaining that two mountain shrines (San Cristóbal Mountain and KALVARIO) would be visited between the beginning and ending rituals in his house.

Participants. The participants included the woman shaman, Maruch Peres; Romin Teratol and his wife, Matal, and their two small sons; Romin's father and stepmother; Matal's mother; a neighbor woman, Maruch ʔOk'il, and her son Shun Peres ʔOkots; and, at the end of the ceremony, my two sons, Terry and Eric Vogt (see below). Ritual roles assumed by the participants were: Shaman: Maruch Peres, who lives near Romin's father's house; patient: Shun Teratol, who was carried by Romin's stepmother on the pilgrimage to the mountain shrines; candle-carrier: Romin's father, Marian Teratol Chochov; drink-pourers: Romin, Shun Peres ʔOkots, and the observer; clothes-washer: Romin's stepmother. The women all helped Matal in the cooking and participated in the ritual of praying and bowing to the candles.

Paraphernalia. The paraphernalia which had been assembled in advance included:

Plants for the ritual baths: laurel leaves, TSIS ʔUCH (*Litsea glaucescens*); leaves from highland tree, ʔAHATEʔES (*Gaultheria ovata*); highland plant, VISHOBTAKIL (scientific name unknown); highland bromelaid, ʔECH' (scientific name unknown); leaves from highland tree, NIʔTILIL (*Rapanea guianensis*).

Plants for decorating the cross shrines: nine pine boughs TEK'EL TOH, three for each cross shrine (the house cross, San Cristóbal Mountain, and KALVARIO).

Twenty-one pine bough tops, NIʔ TOH, which were used in this way: three for San Cristóbal Mountain; three for KALVARIO; three for the house cross; three for the sacrificial cave of the chicken at KALVARIO; three for the head of the bed of the patient; six for brushing the body of the patient.

Two-pesos worth of red geranium blossoms.

Twenty-two liters of rum liquor: sixteen liters purchased in Chamula for 20 pesos; six liters purchased in San Cristóbal for 18 pesos.

Candles purchased in San Cristóbal: ten tallow of 50-centavo size (three for San Cristóbal Mountain; three for KALVARIO; three for house cross; one for head of the bed of the patient); two tallow candles of 20-centavo size for sacrificial cave of chicken; six white wax and two tallow candles of 10-centavo size, for calling the soul; twenty-one two-for-5-centavos size small candles (three groups of seven colors) for "closing the vision of the witches," each combination used at San Cristóbal Mountain, KALVARIO, and house cross.

Food, including 6 kilos of pork at 10 pesos a kilo, 5 pesos of rolls, and salt.

Two black roosters, one left at the sacrifical cave at KALVARIO, the other killed over the patient and eaten later by the patient.

Two kinds of incense: 1.50 pesos of BEK'TAL POM and 3 pesos of TEʔEL POM.

Four ears of maize (white, yellow, red, and black) for the maize divination.

Two censers—for the house cross and the table.

White enamel bowl for maize divination.

Baskets, nets, and tumplines for carrying paraphernalia on the pilgrimage to the mountain shrines.

Small table that served as an altar inside the house.

The Ritual Sequence. The ceremony began at about 10 A.M. on July 19 with the arrival of the shaman, and ended at 2 A.M. on July 20 with her departure. The sixteen-hour sequence may be a longer period than usual for this kind of curing ceremony, in that we were caught in the rain on KALVARIO and spent some time drying out on our return to the house, and it seemed to me that the woman shaman was more talkative between ritual events than a male shaman might have been. On the other hand, the rain prevented our going to more distant locations from the house to call the soul, so perhaps the time involved was evened out and was about average. Based upon my observations and Romin's explanations a sequence of twenty ritual procedures were noted in this ceremony:

(1) The shaman arrived at about 10 A.M. Romin went to fetch her at 9:30, and when he returned he told the others in the house that she was on her way. Matal had forgotten to have the incense burning in front of the house cross, but rushed out with the censer in time to have it burning well by the time the shaman arrived and prayed briefly at the house cross. I noted that the shaman was not carrying a bamboo staff, and Romin could not explain why she was without one.

The shaman entered the house and went directly to the west end of the ritual table to kneel and pray. Already placed on the table were the bundle of candles, the geranium blossoms, the four ears of maize, the two small gourds, the pine bough tops, and other plants. Another censer burned vigorously on the ground at the west end of the table. The shaman next prayed at the hearth and then turned to ritually greet each person present.

(2) To "inspect the candles" (K'EL KANTELA) the shaman sat down on a small chair at the west end of the table and prayed to the ancestral gods. Then she took plants from the table and placed them in the bath water, which was being warmed in a pot by the fire. The water had been collected from two sacred waterholes. She chanted another prayer to the gods, and carefully sorted the correct number of candles and plant materials that were to be carried later to the mountain shrines into two separate piles on the table. One of the small (two-for-5 centavos) candles was missing and this elicited much comment, but the ritual continued anyway.

(3) The shaman proceeded with the ritual of praying and bowing to the candles, SNUP KANTELA. All of us, except for the little patient and his parents, went to the foot of the table to kneel and pray aloud.

(4) The patient's clothes that had been freshly washed were censed over a basket that had been turned upside down over smoking incense.

(5) Then the shaman bathed the head, arms, and legs of the patient with the special bath water. Romin held little Shun while the shaman bathed him. Shun was then handed to his mother and Romin's stepmother to be dressed in the clean clothes.

(6) The shaman turned to the task of bathing the two black roosters. The first one was brought from under the overturned basket that secured it. She placed it between her thighs, gently stroking its head and neck in a way that seemed almost sexual to me and that quieted the rooster, so that the shaman could pour some of the bath water down its throat. She bathed the rooster by scooping up water with her right hand and letting it run down its back and wings. The rooster's legs were tied together and it was placed under the basket again. (This rooster was destined to be left

as a sacrifice for the ancestral gods at KALVARIO). The second rooster was bathed in the same manner and placed under a basket at the head of the patient's bed. (It would later be killed and placed on the patient's bed.) After each bath, the remaining bath water was poured on the earthen floor under the patient's bed. Blood was not extracted from either of the roosters' necks, as is done by many other shamans in Zinacantan.

(7) Romin changed into clean clothes and carried the patient around the house, having him bow and be released by each of us. Romin and Matal prayed to the candles, with little Shun between them.

(8) A formal ritual meal was served. Shun was served first, seated on a tiny chair in front of his separate little table (the round stool on which Matal pats out her tortillas). I noted that by this time Shun realized he was receiving special treatment and had ceased demanding his mother's constant attention with nagging cries. During the rest of the long day and night ceremony, he behaved exceptionally well. As he sat eating his meal, somewhat self-consciously under the eyes of all of us in the house, Matal commented "ʔACH' VINIK," "A new man!" When, by accident, he spilled pork gravy on his clean clothes, there ensued a general flurry to clean it off, and to put a bib around his neck, so that he would be clean for the ancestral gods on the trip to the mountain shrines. He was given warm words of encouragement during his meal and advised to "have no fear to visit the gods in the mountains for this will make you well again." He was promised that on the return from the mountains he was to have a whole chicken, cooked for him alone, and that he could sleep with his mother. After Shun had finished eating, the others of us were served the ritual meal on the table.

(9) Preparations were made for the pilgrimage to the mountains. The shaman supervised the stowing and packing of the bundles of candles and plants for the trip, and designated who should carry what. We all prayed at the hearth, bowed and released with those remaining at the house, and then prayed at the house cross outside. Romin, Shun ʔOkots, and I led the procession carrying the food and liquor; we were followed by Romin's father carrying the candles and black rooster; behind him came Romin's stepmother carrying the small patient; and last of all was the shaman.

(10) The first stop was the cross shrine at San Cristóbal Mountain. Romin's father added geraniums to the three crosses already decorated with pine boughs, and scattered fresh pine needles on the cement base of the crosses, inside the offertory where the candles would be placed, and some in front where the participants would kneel. The shaman placed three points of pine branches at the back of the offertory and set and lighted three large tallow candles and one group of the seven small candles of different colors on the cement ridge in front of it. She knelt, with Romin, Shun, and Romin's stepmother kneeling in line to her right. The prayer

chanted by the shaman was a long one, and Shun exhibited remarkable patience for a two-year-old during both the prayer and later when he had to bow his head to the ground and remain that way for several minutes while the shaman "swept away the illness" with strokes of laurel and pine branches that she passed from Shun's head down his back. Shun ʔOkots served as the drink-pourer at set intervals.

(11) We made our way to KALVARIO, and the same procedures were repeated at this large cross shrine. The shaman then killed the black rooster by pulling its neck. Romin, his stepmother, and Shun remained to pray by the KALVARIO crosses.

(12) The shaman, accompanied by Romin's father and me, carried the rooster to the sacrificial cave at the side of the hill. (I was pressed into service as the drink-pourer at this point, since Shun ʔOkots had to remain on top the hill with the others.) The shaman first cleaned out the cave, removing the twigs and dead leaves from the floor, and then sprinkled fresh pine needles. She placed three pine bough tops upright at the back of the cave to serve as a cross shrine. The dead rooster was on a plate covered with pine needles; red geranium petals were added around the edge of the plate; and the offering (K'ESHOLIL) was ready for the gods. She placed the plate with the rooster's head toward the east on the cave floor. After setting two candles (one on each side of the plate) on the floor and lighting them, the shaman walled up the cave entrance. There followed a long prayer with three rounds of drinks before we rejoined the others in front of the KALVARIO cross shrine, where the shaman chanted another prayer.

(13) On the lower slopes of KALVARIO, below the cross shrine, we stopped for a meal of tortillas, pork, and coffee, with rum liquor before and after. We made our way back to Romin's house in pouring rain, arriving just at dark. Ritual respects were paid to the house cross and the hearth upon arrival.

(14) Romin and his father set the requisite number of candles up in front of the house cross and lighted them, after rigging up an ingenious shelter of lashed poles covered with a rubber poncho to keep the candles from being snuffed out by the rain.

(15) Shun was placed in his decorated bed with his head to the east. The floor at the head of the bed became the site of a shrine, with three pine boughs stuck in the ground and geranium blossoms tied to them and three tallow candles lighted, in order to bring the ancestral gods to visit the patient.

(16) The shaman pulled the neck of the second black rooster then threw the dying body of the fowl on the bed. Its jerking movements were carefully watched. It "danced well"—a good sign that the patient would recover. It was hung by a string around its feet to the rafters above the bed. It would be cooked and served to the young patient the following day.

(17) The maize divining procedure followed, very confused because the small gourd used as a whistle leaked and had to be replaced. As a result, the shaman became confused and lost track of how many colors of maize she had blown on and thrown into the enamel bowl of salt water. None of us (the shaman, Romin, nor I) could determine the number of maize kernels that were moving or floating, thereby indicating how many parts of the soul were missing.

In the midst of this confusion, my sons, Terry and Eric, arrived to take me back to San Cristóbal. Since I wanted to see more of the ceremony, I asked and received permission from the shaman for them to enter the house and to participate in the rest of the ceremony.

(18) The candles were set up and lighted in the center of the house.

(19) The "calling of the soul" followed—a procedure that was really exciting. I was pressed into service to carry a lamp. Romin, his father, the shaman, and I all made three counterclockwise circuits around the house cross "to give the soul a chance to hear and come back." The shaman lighted small candles—one white wax and two tallow—in front of the candles set up previously. Since Romin and his father were busy running in and out of the house asking Matal about all the places where Shun could have lost parts of his soul, Terry was pressed into service as the drink-pourer and Eric as blower of the whistle (the gourd with salt water). Later on, Terry, Eric, Romin, and I took turns on the whistle because it is an exhausting procedure.

To call the soul, the shaman would take a shot of liquor in her mouth, blow it on the candles, then pound the ground with a wand of oak and pine branches, and shout LA? ME, LA? ME, "come, come!" She kept repeating the procedure heading in different directions where the soul was reportedly lost. Finally, the shaman led the parts of the soul back into the house and back into little Shun's body.

(20) The final ritual meal followed—an elaborate and lengthy procedure of feeding all the participants and thanking the shaman at the table and then by the hearth. We finally left at 2 A.M. just before the shaman was given her parting gifts and escorted home. This was bad manners on our part, but my sons and I were completely exhausted and we hoped the Zinacantecos and their gods would forgive. Apparently, they did for little Shun was markedly improved when I saw him a few days later.

Case 3. The K'IN KRUS *Ceremony for the* VO? TA PASTE? *Waterhole Group in the Hamlet of Paste? (May 2–3, 1960)*

My involvement in the K'IN KRUS ceremony for the VO? TA PASTE? waterhole began at 9 on the morning of May 2, when I presented two dozen skyrockets and six 50-centavo candles at the house of the Senior Mayor-

domo de Santa Cruz; it ended at 1 A.M. on May 3. The ceremony had not
ended then—I just couldn't take any more after sixteen hours of liquor,
processions, and chilling cold. But during these hours I had a deeper and
more complete look at the ceremonial life in the hamlet than I had ever
had before. As is by now usual in my field work in Zinacantan, everything
was more complex than I had anticipated. Instead of trying to reconstruct
the long night's events—unfortunately I did not have any opportunity to
jot down field notes during the night—I shall try to recapture them through
summaries.

Preparations for the Ceremony. I gave a great deal of thought to what
I should take as gifts to the ᴋ'ɪɴ ᴋʀᴜs, especially since I had had repeated
invitations from Manvel Vaskis Shulhol to attend. I finally decided it would
be most appropriate to take two dozen skyrockets and a half-dozen white
candles. I believe this worked out well, except that I should have arrived
with the heads of the skyrockets wrapped in a Zinacanteco-style necker-
chief, and the candles wrapped in a pink-striped cloth. Also, the candles
should have been 1-peso size, instead of 50-centavo size, to conform with
the others that were used. I also took along a bottle of liquor, but it was
a kind of yellowish Comiteco rum instead of white aguardiente with the
result that my first offering of drinks was regarded somewhat suspiciously.
One should always stick to plain white rum. Also I should have taken at
least a media, rather than just a cuarta. But in the end I had plenty of
the right kind of rum to dispense because I started using my funnel in the
middle of the night.

Rapport in Paste'. Rapport could not have been better. During the entire
sixteen hours there was nothing but warmth, respect, and at times even
gentleness in the treatment I received. I decided that the countless visits,
Landrover rides, meals we had served to people, and so forth had at last
paid off. I was no longer a stranger in Paste', even though I still confused
names and faces, and probably always will in a population of this size,
except for those people I see on a more intensive basis. Some concrete
evidence of the state of rapport: when I took the candles and skyrockets
to the house of the Senior Mayordomo, I was immediately offered a chair
and served atole. When the procession returned from the waterhole, I was
not only invited right into the house but given a special chair and fed at
the table with the shamans and the mayordomos. When I looked cold
during the night, Manvel Vaskis Shulhol brought me an extra black blanket
to wear. I was included in all the rounds of rum and cigarettes. I was invited
to return to Paste' on May 5 for another ᴋ'ɪɴ ᴋʀᴜs. People sought me
out to talk with me all during the night. To the best of my knowledge,
I had never met the No. 1 shaman, 'Antun Shimunes, before, but he went
out of his way to be friendly and to include me in the proceedings.

Ceremonial Roles. Shamans were, of course, the key figures in the ceremony. There are at least eight in vo? ta paste?. When the ceremony began seven were involved; one got drunk and dropped out, but rejoined us about sundown. An eighth appeared also about sundown and took his place in rank. The rank order was as follows:

(1) ?Antun Shimunes Mani?, who is the owner of the talking saint. I had not met him before, but found him to be an impressive character—quite tall and lean, with a very prominent nose (MANI? means "hooked nose"), and a small mustache. I thought him quite handsome, and he is obviously bright and able. He never drinks rum, just goes through the toasting procedure and pours the rum in a bottle to be distributed later. He drinks only soda pop. He directed the whole ritual, most competently, I thought.

(2) Marian Lopis Chiku? looks quite young to be No. 2. He has a square-looking face with large teeth. He is also impressive when he prays, especially as drunkenness sets in.

(3) He is a wild-looking man with very long black hair and black full mustache. I didn't catch his name, but he was so drunk by 10 A.M. that he fell down in the procession and the other shamans had to go on without him. He reappeared and took his place at the table about sundown. He was one of the two who prayed at KALVARIO when the group split up to visit various crosses at about 9:30 P.M.

(4) This man arrived late and I didn't catch his name. He is short, small, and wiry-looking with a small, pointed nose. He went with No. 3 to K ALVARIO which is apparently visited by No. 3 and No. 4, while No. 1 and No. 2 remain at the house waiting for the others to return.

(5) Manvel Patishtan Kelemchitom is Romin's compadre, about whom there is much in Bob Laughlin's notes. It was he who performed the series of ceremonies for Romin and his in-laws during this past year.

(6) I don't have his name, but he is so young that it is incredible to believe he is a shaman. I am sure he is less than twenty, and may be as young as fifteen, but he is a handsome young man who prays well.

(7) He too is young, though not as young as No. 6 by any means. I do not have his name.

(8) My old Paste? friend Telesh who was on the School Committee in 1958 was the eighth shaman. Nothing could have surprised me more than seeing Telesh in this role; he apparently made his debut as a shaman recently. He was as handsome and as friendly as ever in this new role. His praying is definitely weak yet.

Each of the eight carried a staff while marching from one point to another. These bamboo staffs were placed together in the northeast corner of the Mayordomo's house and were also placed together against the sacred tree by the Paste? waterhole. When a shaman visited a cross, the staff was placed resting against the decorated cross. All eight shamans either carried or wore black ceremonial robes. Another characteristic of dress is that the scarf is worn loosely over the head and untied during ritual prayers involving the incense.

Four Mayordomos are involved, senior and junior outgoing and senior and junior incoming ones. The waterhole group unites and is fed in the house of the Senior Outgoing Mayordomo, but I was told that the Junior Outgoing Mayordomo has to share cost of the food. They march in the processions and visit the crosses in company with the shamans.

Three musicians played the violin, harp, and guitar. They sat and played by the waterhole and in the house of the Senior Mayordomo but did not go to visit crosses elsewhere. A flute and two drum players played at the waterhole and at the house of the Senior Mayordomo, and with the group that went to KALVARIO.

There were helpers in charge of two kinds of fireworks—skyrockets and the small cannon called a KAMARO. About fifteen women helped with the cooking in the Senior Mayordomo's house. And special mention should be made of Petul and Mikel Lopis Chikuʔ, the two old brothers who are the most senior members of the large Chikuʔ lineage which seems to dominate this waterhole group. They were seated at the ritual meals in positions that outranked the shamans, a fact which symbolized their advanced ages and their positions in the lineage.

Ritual Paraphernalia. All crosses were made into a three-cross shrine by the addition of pine boughs. The waterhole crosses and crosses at KALVARIO were decorated with fresh pine boughs, the leaves of a plant called CH'IB on top of the pine boughs, then an arch with alternating red geraniums and white roses. The ground in front was covered with loose pine needles, and geranium and rose petals were strewn on top. The decorations were beautiful by anyone's standards. The house crosses are decorated in the same manner, except they lack the arches—the geraniums and roses are tied in bunches onto the crosses.

All the candles used were of white wax, 1-peso size. Three were lighted for each set of house and waterhole crosses. At KALVARIO three of them were tied together and lighted.

Incense was of two types—chips of wood (TE'EL POM) distributed from a basket, and nodules of resin (BEK'TAL POM) distributed from a package wrapped in newspaper. The censers had three prongs and each of the prongs had two teats.

Sacred Places. The ceremony moved between the Senior Mayordomo's house, the waterhole, and crosses at other houses and on hills.

The marching order for the procession, from the waterhole to Senior Mayordomo's house and back to waterhole was as follows—from front to rear: flute player; large drum player; small drum player; guitar player; harp player; violin player; Junior Incoming Mayordomo; Senior Incoming

Mayordomo; Junior Outgoing Mayordomo; Senior Outgoing Mayordomo; shamans, with the junior man in front and senior man in rear.

The seating order in the Senior Mayordomo's house is shown in Figure 197. The sacred geography of the total scene of the ceremony is depicted in Figure 198. And the seating order of the ritual specialists around the sacred tree by the waterhole may be seen in Figure 199.

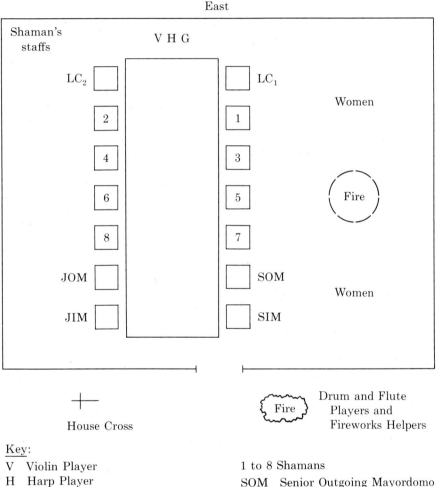

Key:

V   Violin Player
H   Harp Player
G   Guitar Player
LC$_1$ Petul Lopis Chiku²
LC$_2$ Mikel Lopis Chiku²

1 to 8 Shamans
SOM   Senior Outgoing Mayordomo
JOM   Junior Outgoing Mayordomo
SIM   Senior Incoming Mayordomo
JIM   Junior Incoming Mayordomo

197. Seating order in the Senior Mayordomo's house

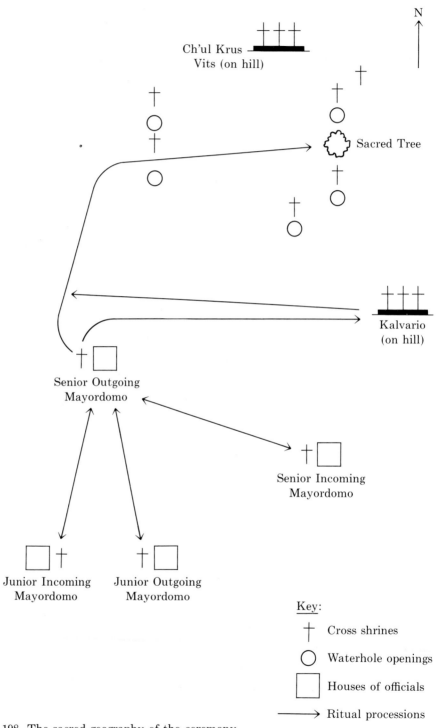

198. The sacred geography of the ceremony

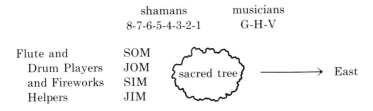

199. The seating order of the ritual specialists

Major Ritual Events. When I arrived in Pasteʔ the men were already at the waterhole, but I drove on past and delivered my skyrockets and candles at the house of the Senior Outgoing Mayordomo. I was immediately ushered into the house where the women were grinding and cooking, given a chair, and handed a bowl of atole which I drank. I was then asked if I wanted more to eat, but I replied that I was going down to waterhole to join the men and work.

At the waterhole the men were digging dirt out from around the square cement casing which INI had built, presumably to keep additional soil from sliding down into one of the waterhole openings during the coming rainy season. Four men were digging with hoes and shovel, and two wheelbarrows were in action. I greeted the men I knew and shortly took a turn on the wheelbarrow, hauling three loads of dirt out—to the amusement of all concerned! I noted that the shamans were working also, including the head shaman, ʔAntun Shimunes. The musicians were seated in rank order to the right of the waterhole, the drums and flute players to the left. Both groups were playing off and on, and rum was being passed around. Almost as soon as I arrived ʔAntun came up to offer me rum, and others followed suit. A little later I offered ʔAntun rum and was surprised when he only touched the bottle to his lips with his eyes changing for a fleeting instant from the usual boldness to fear—as if I were trying to poison him! Then Manvel Vaskis Shulhol whispered to me on the side that ʔAntun never drinks anything stronger than soda pop.

About 10:30 A.M., ʔAntun signaled a change in the proceedings. At this point the seven shamans present and the four Mayordomos formed in rank order and prayed in front of the cross.

The procession moved to the sacred tree near the other waterhole openings and sat around it in fixed order (see Figure 199). Under ʔAntun's direction the shamans divided the pine boughs and needles, the CH'IB, and the geraniums and roses among eight groups who went out to decorate the six crosses for the waterholes and for CH'UL KRUS VITS and KALVARIO. The groups left in fixed order which I reconstruct as follows: man carrying three pine boughs; man with CH'IB; the flowers; the loose pine needles. This process took about an hour and a skyrocket was shot off as the job was completed at each cross.

While the groups decorating crosses were gone, the others stayed and drank and visited. At one point ʔAntun held court, listening to trouble cases. One described to me by Manvel was that various men have failed to pay the 2-peso contribution for the ceremony. One group came forward to complain, another sat back on the hill looking glum (apparently representing those who hadn't paid). After a long talk the affair was finally settled. It was interesting and significant to see ʔAntun serving as a kind of Presidente, hearing trouble cases for the waterhole group.

About 2 P.M. we marched in procession from the waterhole to the Senior Mayordomo's house where the whole group was fed. Each official prayed at the house cross before entering the house. The shamans in groups of three (there were only six at this time); the Mayordomos in groups of two each, and I remember these as being junior and senior pairs, that is, two juniors and then two seniors. Then the officials entered the house, bowing and chanting to two old women hostesses. I was invited in by the host, the Senior Outgoing Mayordomo, and eventually, at ʔAntun's suggestion, placed in a chair at the foot of the table opposite the musicians.

Rum was served in rank order. Two tables were placed end to end and covered with two cloths. The ritual meal proceeded as follows: water to wash hands, water to rinse mouth, atole in gourd bowls, beef stew in hot chili broth with stacks of tortillas, more rum. Then we all went outside while helpers were fed inside the house, including the drum and flute players, the fireworks men, and so on. The last to be fed were the little boys, who were served outside squatting on the ground and observed with much comment by the officials who were at this point mainly standing around watching and waiting. The women ate quietly by the fire afterward, but the drink-pourers always included them in the rounds of drinks. Before each round of the meal, ʔAntun said a prayer, and the rest of us crossed ourselves at the end.

One table was taken away and two bundles of peso candles were placed on the table with butt ends toward the west, pointed ends to the east. There followed a very careful distribution of all the other materials: a two-gallon jug of rum was poured into liter bottles and from these into cuartas and distributed to all the officials and all the helpers, each of whom provided his own bottle. Cigarettes were distributed to everyone equitably, including me.

Later the candles were unwrapped and placed on table with the same orientation, and the paper flowers, plus geraniums were symmetrically arranged around the points of the candles. A long prayer over the candles followed. For this the shamans put on their black ceremonial robes and placed their scarves hanging untied over their heads. The praying was started by No. 1 and No. 2, who held smoking censers in their right hands and periodically rotated the incense over the candles. They passed the censers to No. 3 and No. 4, who took the lead, which went next to No. 5 and No. 6, then back to No. 1 and No. 2. The process was repeated at least three times; all prayed, but a given pair always led the prayer.

About half the candles were distributed among the Mayordomos in bundles of three candles each—with a pink-striped cloth around the butt ends of the candles and a paper flower included. These four Mayordomos, each accompanied by a shaman as designated by ʔAntun, went to their respective house crosses. No. 3 and No. 4 shamans also took three candles and went to KALVARIO, accompanied by drums and flute. I went with Manvel, who was serving as the Senior Incoming Mayordomo, and Telesh to the former's house. Manvel marched in front carrying the candles; Telesh marched behind carrying his staff. Upon arrival at the house, both greeted the cross. Then Telesh placed three candles in the ground in front of the three house crosses, lighted them, and poured rum around them as an offering. Telesh said a long prayer, kneeling, while the Manvel knelt on his left and tried to follow it—not very successfully. The entire ceremony took place outside.

At this point I slipped away in the dark to see what was going on at KALVARIO (see Chapter 20). Here No. 3 and No. 4 shamans were chanting a long prayer.

> ʔAna ch'ul nompre yos hesukristo kahval,
>> Tsauk ʔune htot,
>> Tsauk ʔune kahval,
>>> Ch'ul totiletik,
>>> Ch'ul meʔiletik,
>>>> Chahtaik ta ch'ul k'oponel,
>>>> Chahtaik ta ch'ul tiʔinel,
>>>>> Yuʔun ti yo hpatikotik,
>>>>> Yo hshokontikotik,
>>>>>> Ti yol ʔavalabotikotik,
>>>>>> Yol ʔanich'nabotikotik;

> In the divine name of God, Jesus Christ, my lord,
>> Take these, then, my father,
>> Take these, then, my lord,
>>> Holy fathers,
>>> Holy mothers,
>>>> These my words,
>>>> These my prayers,
>>>>> For our humble backs,
>>>>> For our humble sides,
>>>>>> We who are your lowly sons,
>>>>>> We who are your lowly children;

Ch'ul kalvario ch'ul totil,
Kalvario ch'ul me?il,
  Ch'ul kalvario ch'ul yih,
  Ch'ul kalvario ch'ul k'on,
    Ch'ul maretik,
    Ch'ul ?ahvetik,
      Ch'ul tsoblebal,
      Ch'ul lotlebal,
        Ch'ul kolebal,
        Ch'ul kushebal;

Holy Calvary holy father,
Calvary holy mother,
  Holy Calvary holy ancient one,
  Holy Calvary holy yellow one,
    Holy seas,
    Holy ancient ones,
      Holy meeting-place,
      Holy gathering-place,
        Holy place of recovery,
        Holy place of rest;

Tsauk ?une htot,
Tsauk ?une kahval,
  Tsauke san kishtoval ch'ul totil,
  San kishtoval ch'ul me?il,
    Tsauke ch'ul ninab chilo? ch'ul totil,
    Ninab chilo? ch'ul me?il,
      Tsauke ch'ul maria sisil,
      Ch'ul maria mushul,
        Ch'ul chanib ch'ul totil,
        Chanib ch'ul me?il;

Receive this, then, my father,
Receive this, then, my lord,
  Receive, San Cristóbal holy father,
  San Cristóbal holy mother,
    Receive, divine wellspring of the holy fathers,
    Divine wellspring of the holy mothers,
      Receive, divine Maria Cecilia,
      Divine Maria Mushul,
        Four holy fathers,
        Four holy mothers;

Mi ta komon ti ch'ul k'ope,
Mi ta komon ti ch'ul ti?e,
  Chava?an ?ach'ul baik,
  Chatek'an ?ach'ul baik,
    Ta yo spat ?un,
    Ta yo shshokon ?un,
      Tavalabike,
      Tanich'nabike,
      Tanichike,
      Tak'elomike;

In divine unison,
In divine accord,
  Will you stand up in holiness,
  Will you stand firm in holiness,
    Behind the lowly backs of,
    By the lowly sides of,
      Your sons,
      Your children,
      Your flowers,
      Your sprouts;

Ti mu to ?ach'aybekon,
Mu to ?atenbekon,
  Tsauke ti yo spate,
  Ti yo shshokone,
    Ti yol ?avalabike,
    Ti yol ?anich'nabike;

If you will not yet lose them for me,
If you will not abandon them for me,
  Take unto you the humble back,
  The humble side,
    Of your lowly sons,
    Of your lowly children;

Tsauke ch'ul sak ch'en ch'ul totil,
Sak ch'en ch'ul me?il,
  Shchi?uk li muk'ta vits ch'ul totil,
  Muk'ta vits ch'ul me?il,
    Muk'ta vits ch'ul yih,
    Muk'ta vits ch'ul k'on,
      Tsauke ch'ul ?oshyoketal ch'ul totil,
      ?Oshyoketal ch'ul me?il,
        Tsauke k'usi yepal ?un htot,
        K'usi yepal ?un kahval;

Receive, holy white cave, holy father,
Holy white cave, holy mother,
  With the great mountain holy fathers,
  With the great mountain holy mothers,
    Great mountain holy ancient ones,
    Great mountain holy yellow ones,
      Receive, three holy hearthstones, holy fathers,
      Three holy hearthstones, holy mothers,
        Receive, then, this much, my father,
        This much, then, my lord;

Mi ta komon ch'ul k'op,
Mi ta komon ch'ul ti?,
  Chava?an ?abaik,
  Chatek'an ?abaik,
    Ta yo spat ?un,
    Ta yo shshokon ?un,
      Ti yol ?avalabike,
      Ti yol ?anich'nabike . . .

In holy unison,
In holy accord,
  Will you stand up,
  Will you stand firm,
    Behind the lowly backs, then,
    By the lowly sides of
      Your humble sons,
      Your humble children . . .

Ch'ul lachikin ch'ul totil,
Lachikin ch'ul me?il,
  Tsauke ch'ul nakleb ?okal ch'ul totil,
  Nakleb ?okal ch'ul me?il,
    Shchi?uk li ch'ul maria rosario,
    Ch'ul vinahelal ?ants,
    Vinahelal sinyora;

Holy ears-standing-up, holy father,
Ears-standing-up, holy mother,
  Receive, holy tortoise-house, holy father,
  Tortoise house, holy mother,
    With the divine Maria of the Rosary,
    Divine woman of the sky,
    Divine Señora of the sky;

Ta komonuk ti k'ope,
Komonuk ti ti?e,
   Shchi?uk li ch'ul ?isak'tikal ch'ul totile,
   ?Isak'tikal ch'ul me?il,
      Ch'ul tonal ch'ul totil,
      Ch'ul tonal ch'ul me?il;

In unison,
In accord,
   With the holy potato patch, holy father,
   Potato patch, holy mother,
      Holy stone, holy father,
      Holy stone, holy mother;

Ta komonuk k'op ?un,
Komonuk ti? ?un,
   Va?an ?abaik ?un,
   Tek'an ?abaik ?un,
      Ta yo spat ?un,
      Ta yo shshokon ?un,
         Tavalabike,
         Tanich'nabike,
            Tsauke tanichike,
            Tak'elomike, kahval;

In unison,
In accord,
   Stand up,
   Stand firm,
      Behind the lowly back of,
      By the lowly side of,
         Your sons,
         Your children;
            Take to you your flowers,
            Your sprouts, my lord;

Tsauk ?une htot,
Tsauk ?une kahval,
   Shchi?uk li santorenso,
   Chi?uk li santorominko,
      Chi?uk li ch'ul maria rosario,
      Vinahelal ?ants,
      Vinahelal sinyora;

Receive, then, my father,
Receive, then, my lord,
  With San Lorenzo,
  With Santo Domingo,
    With the divine Maria of the Rosary,
    Woman of the sky,
    Señora of the sky;

Mi ta komon ch'ul k'op ʔun,
Mi ta komon ch'ul tiʔ ʔun,
  Chavaʔan ʔach'ul baik ʔun,
  Chatek'an ʔach'ul baik ʔun;

In divine unison,
In divine accord,
  Will you stand up in holiness,
  Will you stand firm in holiness;

Tsauke k'usi yepal shchiʔuk li ch'ul hmanvaneh,
Chiʔuk li ch'ul htohvaneh,
  Chiʔuk li sinyor ʔiskipula htot,
  ʔIskipula kahval,
    Shchiʔuk li ch'ul martil htot,
    Ch'ul martil kahval;

Receive this much, you who are with our holy purchaser,
With our holy payer,
  With the Señor Esquipulas, my father,
  Esquipulas, my lord,
    With the divine martyr, my father,
    The divine martyr, my lord;

Mi ta komon ch'ul k'op,
Mi ta komon ch'ul tiʔ,
  Vaʔan ʔabaik ʔun,
  Tek'an ʔabaik ʔun,
    Chiʔuk ʔoʔlol ch'ul vinahel,
    Chiʔuk ʔoʔlol ch'ul loria;

In divine unison,
In divine accord,
  Will you stand up,
  Will you stand firm,
    With the center of the divine sky,
    With the center of the divine glory;

Tsauke ch'ul sinyor santo san meriko htot,
San meriko kahval,
   Chiʔuk li sinyor vashakmen htot,
   Ch'ul vashakmen kahval;

Receive holy Señor, holy healer, my father,
Holy healer my lord,
   With the Señor saintly divine VASHAKMEN, my father,
   Holy VASHAKMEN, my lord;

Chotoloshuk ʔun,
Vuts'uloshuk ʔun,
   Ta ʔoʔlol ch'ul vinahel,
   Ta ʔoʔlol ch'ul vinahel,
   Ta ʔoʔlol ch'ul loria;

You are seated then,
You are on bended knees,
   In the middle of the holy sky,
   In the middle of the holy sky,
   In the middle of the holy glory;

Ta hk'an ti ch'ul pertonale,
Ta hk'an ti ch'ul lesensiae,
   Yuʔun ti yo spate,
   Yuʔun ti yo shshokone,
     Tavalabike,
     Tanich'nabike;

I beseech divine pardon,
I beg divine forgiveness,
   For the lowly backs,
   For the lowly sides,
     Of your sons,
     Of your children;

Ch'ul vashakmen htot,
Ch'ul vashakmen kahval,
   Mi ta komon ch'ul k'op ʔun,
   Mi ta komon ch'ul tiʔ ʔun,
     Vaʔan ʔach'ul baik ʔun,
     Tek'an ʔach'ul baik ʔun,
       Ta yo spat ʔun,
       Ta yo shshokon ʔun,

◡

    Tavalabike,
    Tanich'nabike,
    Tanichike,
    Tak'elomike;

Holy VASHAKMEN, my father,
Holy VASHAKMEN, my lord,
  In divine unison, then,
  In divine accord, then,
    Will you stand up in holiness,
    Will you stand firm in holiness,
      Behind the lowly backs, then,
      By the lowly sides, then,
        Of your sons,
        Of your children,
        Of your flowers,
        Of your sprouts;

Ti mu to la ʔach'aybekon,
Mu to la ʔatenbekon,
  Tsauk ʔune htot,
  Tsauk ʔune kahval,
    K'usi yepal ʔun htot,
    K'usi yepal ʔun kahval;

Do not yet lose them for me,
Do not yet abandon them for me,
  Take this, then, my father,
  Take this, then, my lord,
    This much, my father,
    This much, my lord;

Vashakmen ch'ul totil,
Vashakmen ch'ul meʔil,
  Tsauk ʔune htot,
  Tsauk ʔune kahval,
    K'usi yepal voʔot ʔakomtsanoh,
    Voʔot ʔaviktaoh,
      Ta spasel ch'ul ʔoɓil,
      Ta spasel ch'ul balamil,
        Ti sninab yol ʔavokike,
        Sninab yol ʔak'obike;

VASHAKMEN, holy fathers,
VASHAKMEN, holy mothers,
  Receive this, then, father,

Receive this, then, lord,
  This much that you have left,
  This much that you have abandoned,
    When the holy earth was made,
    When the holy world was made,
      The wellsprings of your holy feet,
      The wellsprings of your holy hands;

ʔAchotanoh komel,
ʔAvuts'anoh komel,
  Ti ch'ul rioshe,
  Ti ch'ul ʔanhele,
    Vaʔan ʔabaik ʔun,
    Tek'an ʔabaik ʔun,
      Ta yo spat ʔun,
      Ta yo shshokon ʔun,
      Tavalabike,
      Tanich'nabike;

You left seated,
You left kneeling,
  The holy gods,
  The holy angels,
    Stand up,
    Stand firm,
      Behind the lowly backs, then,
      By the lowly sides, then,
        Of your sons,
        Of your children;

Ch'ul vashakmen htot,
Ch'ul vashakmen kahval,
  Chiʔuk li ch'ul sinyor santo san salvador,
  Muk'ta ch'ul vinik,
  Muk'ta ch'ul hkashlan,
    K'usi yepal ʔun htot,
    K'u yepal ʔun kahval;

Holy VASHAKMEN, my father,
Holy VASHAKMEN, my lord,
  With the holy Señor San Salvador,
  Great holy man,
  Great holy Ladino,
    For how long, my father,
    For how long, my lord;

Ta komonuk k'op ʔun,
Komonuk tiʔ ʔun,
  ʔOyuk ʔavokolik,
  ʔOyuk ʔavik'tiʔik,
    Chihlanik to tal,
    Hoylanik to tal,
      Hch'amuntik to tal,
      Hmakitik to tal,
        ʔA li ch'ul krasiae,
        ʔA li ch'ul bentisyone;

In unison, then,
In accord, then,
  Do the favor,
  Take the trouble,
    Observe us here ever,
    Encircle us here ever,
      That we borrow still,
      That we share still,
        Your holy grace,
        Your holy benediction;

Tsauke ta yo spat ʔun,
Ta yo shshokon ʔun,
  Skotol li bik'ite,
  Skotol li muk'e,
  Skotol li p'ehele,
  Skotol li luchule,
    Skotol yol ʔo ʔavalab,
    Skotol yol ʔanich'nab;

Take unto you all the humble backs,
The humble sides of
  All the small,
  All the great,
  All the round ones,
  All the perched ones,
    All your sons,
    All your children;

Haʔ ta hk'an ʔo ch'ul pertonal,
Ch'ul lesensia ʔun kahval,
  K'usi yepal helavkon tach'ul baik ʔun,
  Tach'ul satik ʔun,
    Kahval.

For this reason I beseech divine pardon,
I beg divine forgiveness, then, my lord,
    For as long as I may pass before your holy countenances,
    Before your holy faces, then,
        My lord.

When I returned to Manvel's house, rum mixed with coffee was being distributed all around. I accepted one drink, but asked for just coffee on the second and third rounds. I think this is the only thing that got me through the night, because we hadn't eaten since about 3 P.M.

We reassembled back at the Senior Mayordomo's house. I noted that No. 1 and No. 2 shamans had remained there, and during our absence had tied up the remaining candles in two bundles and placed them in nets with tumplines.

Prayers were said by each pair as they reported in, so to speak, to the two senior shamans. The only ones who did not return were the pair who visited KALVARIO; they met us on the trail on the way to the waterhole.

By about 11 P.M. the group was ready to leave for the waterhole. But here let me diverge to explain three matters.

First, my relation with others in terms of bowing and releasing pattern were interesting. I had noted at the waterhole and again at the eating and praying table that the rank order of the shamans in terms of their marching and seating order is broken in terms of bowing and releasing: younger shamans bowed to older shamans even though the younger ones outranked the older ones as shamans. I also noted that, when ages were the same, three loose handshakes substituted for bowing and releasing. ?Antun never failed during the night to include me in toasting procedure, or in the bowing and releasing behavior. He was forcefully correct in going down the line and signaling the others to come forward and bow, but when he got to me he offered his hand. I took his hand and then bowed; but I decided this was a mistake and went back to the handshake which he had initiated in the first place. Later in the evening it was significant that Telesh bowed to me at one point.

Before we left to visit the house crosses I brought out my new flashlight (made in Hong Kong) which is a combination flashlight and cigarette lighter. This delayed the ceremony for half an hour while each shaman and Mayordomo and musician took time to examine it carefully and to light a cigarette with it. There was much, much discussion about how much it cost, where I bought it, what the brand name was, and so on. ?Antun took it apart and tried to figure out what made it work. (?Antun also carried an ancient pocket watch and constantly checked his time with my watch; others continually asked me the time. I did not see that any of this was functional, that the ceremony went any faster or was in any way scheduled by the watches, but there seems to be a real curiosity about new manufactured articles and a fascination with time as measured by watches; the latter may hark back to an Ancient Maya concern with time.)

At another point, with Telesh serving as interpreter, there was a long interrogation of me by the various shamans, and especially ?Antun, about ocean widths. "Are they wider or narrower than the land?," they wanted to know. When they found out that I had crossed the Pacific, they wanted to know if the sun were close to the surface of the earth over there where it goes down or where it rises. When I explained that the sun was just as high in the sky when it sets, they were amazed. Then they wanted to know what makes the ocean salty. I tried a long geological and meteorological explanation of this, but they became bored and went back to the ceremony.

About 11 at night the group left the Mayordomo's house, formally thanking the hostesses and praying to the house cross as they left. We went in rank order to the sacred tree at the waterhole; here the officials grouped themselves at the tree in the same rank order as before. There was drinking until about midnight when the rest of the candles (which had been carried in two bundles in the nets by tumpline by the incoming Mayordomos) were divided up to be lighted at waterhole crosses. They began at the crosses which are immediately below and above the tree. Since ?Antun worked on the cross immediately below the tree, and more junior men worked on the cross above the tree, I gather that the waterhole and cross immediately below and close to the tree must be the most important.

By now it was 1 A.M. and I was exhausted. I was told that they would continue the ceremony by lighting three candles at each waterhole cross and praying. Finally the group would go to the cross atop CH'UL KRUS VITS, and, about dawn, would return to the waterhole to dance. Romin says the dancing is the same as that seen during major fiestas in Zinacantan, when people dance to the music emanating from the bandstand. Eventually the whole group would return to the Mayordomo's house for its final ceremonial meal.

Case 4. The K'IN KRUS *Ceremony for* SNA LOPIS CHIKU?ETIK
(*May 5–6, 1960*)

This ceremony involved only the families living on the rim just south of the VO? TA PASTE? waterhole. This sna group seems to be centered around the LOPIS CHIKU? lineage, but includes also VASKIS SHULHOLETIK, MARTINIS KAPITANETIK, and KOMIS LOTRIKOETIK. The unit is compact and cohesive. Its members cooperate in performing this ceremony which is given in May and repeated in October. This sna was originally a patrilineage composed of the LOPIS CHIKU?ETIK, but it now includes the minor lineages listed above who have married into the unit and acquired lands neighboring the LOPIS CHIKU?ETIK.

Ceremonial Roles. All of the shamans belonging to the sna participate in this ceremony. There are four, in rank order: Manvel Lopis Chiku?, the same man with big teeth and square face who served as No. 2 shaman in the waterhole ceremony two nights before; Manvel Patishtan Kelemchitom, who was No. 5 in the waterhole ceremony; Manvel Martinis Kapitan, who is young and quite round with a fat face; I had not seen him before so far as I could remember, and do not know why he did not take part in the waterhole ceremony; Telesh Komis Lotriko.

The number of shamans in this group is increasing. I was told by one old man that a few years ago there was only one shaman, but three recently made their debuts. Such an increase is impressive and it would be interesting to know if it is an important manifestation of nativistic reaction in the acculturation situation.

There were four Mayordomos (two outgoing and two incoming) serving Rosario—the Virgin in the small house in the middle of LOPIS CHIKU?ETIK. The Senior Outgoing Mayordomo, Shun Chechev, was the host for the ceremony. A curious-looking man with small beady eyes and small nose, he lives just above the road in the turnaround for the car at the rim. His house is miserably small and badly constructed. For this reason he constructed a square oak-covered brush structure for the ceremony—though even this was very small and we all fell over each other. Some cooking was done in Chechev's house, but there didn't seem to be enough room, so more cooking was done in the ceremonial structure as well.

The Junior Outgoing Mayordomo was a pleasant gray-haired man who lives to the left of the road, below where we park the car, and often comes up to visit when I take visitors to the rim.

It was puzzling that the carrier of the candles and censer was a very young boy who knelt and prayed in the middle of the shamans at the house of the host. I asked repeatedly about him and was told that he was the Senior Incoming Mayordomo for Rosario. I found it hard to believe, but I was assured that every older man had served his tour of duty as the Mayordomo for Rosario and that they had selected this young boy for next year. He was very cute praying and bowing to his seniors, but had a hard time consuming all the rum.

There were the usual violin, harp, and guitar players, plus two drums and a flute player. Again in this ceremony the two elderly men—Petul and Mikel Lopis Chiku?—were much in evidence, sitting at the head of the table by the musicians, Mikel giving instructions as to how the skyrockets should be divided up for the various sacred places to be visited. They clearly were serving as ritual advisers, TOTILME?ILETIK, in these ceremonies.

Other roles included those in charge of skyrockets, the drink-pourers, two women who poured the rum from two-gallon glass jugs into smaller bottles, and a man who walked ahead of the musicians with a lantern and showed them where each cross was.

Ritual Paraphernalia. The most important sacred object for this ceremony is CH'ULME'TIK ROSARIO. This saint occupies a mysterious little house
by the large tree in LOPIS CHIKU'ETIK. The statue is about a meter high
with a very brown face; the tiny brown face of her baby peeks out from
the folds of the shawl. Long colored ribbons stream down her front and
she wears a Zinacanteco woman's shawl, white with pink stripes. The
1-meter platform on which she stands is decorated with three pine boughs
and CH'IB in front; and surmounted by an arch of geraniums and roses.
The small hermitage has wattle-and-daub walls and a thatched roof. There
are benches along the two side walls inside, and pine needles had been
placed on the floor. Four candleholders were on the floor in front, three
plain and the fourth (in the middle) in the shape of a bull.

Candles for the ceremony were of the 50-centavo size. This time the six
that I had brought were right and were included by the shamans along
with the others to make a total of fifty-two.

The flowers included CH'IB that was tied on all crosses on top the pine
boughs. Red geranium blossoms were used on all crosses, and white roses
were added for Rosario.

Sacred Places. The ceremony began with a ceremonial meal in Shun
Chechev's house. A prayer was said at his house cross, and the procession
moved to the following places (see Figure 200) in succession during the night
and the following early morning: (a) the house cross of the Junior Outgoing
Mayordomo; (b) a sacred rock called SCH'UT TON (Stomach Rock); (c) the
house cross of the Senior Incoming Mayordomo; (d) a sacred tree called
YOLON 'AHTE' (Matazano tree); (e) the house of the Virgen del Rosario;
(f) the junior KALVARIO for the sna; (g) the senior SCH'UT CH'EN (Stomach
Cave); (h) the senior KALVARIO for the sna; (i) the junior SCH'UT CH'EN;
(j) the house cross of the Junior Incoming Mayordomo; (k) the house of
the Senior Outgoing Mayordomo where a final ritual meal was served.

Major Ritual Events. Because I did not arrive until 4 P.M. I am not
certain what events preceded my arrival, but since I was immediately
ushered into the brush house and served atole and then chicken with chili
(with of course the usual handwashing, mouth-rinsing, and salt ritual), I
assume that they had just finished the ritual meal. About 5 the candles
were placed on the table—just one bundle this time, with mine placed
beside it. The shamans said a short prayer, then the candles were unwrapped, and flowers arranged around their tips. The wooden slats which
were wrapped with candles were placed under the tablecloth, and the
incense wrapped in newspaper was placed on the table. Then the shamans
said their long prayer, waving the censers in the usual counterclockwise
pattern, passing them from Nos. 1 and 2 to 3 and 4 and back again.

About 6 P.M. Manvel Vaskis Shulhol No. 2 appeared to invite me to his
house and to talk about hauling his corn to San Cristóbal the following

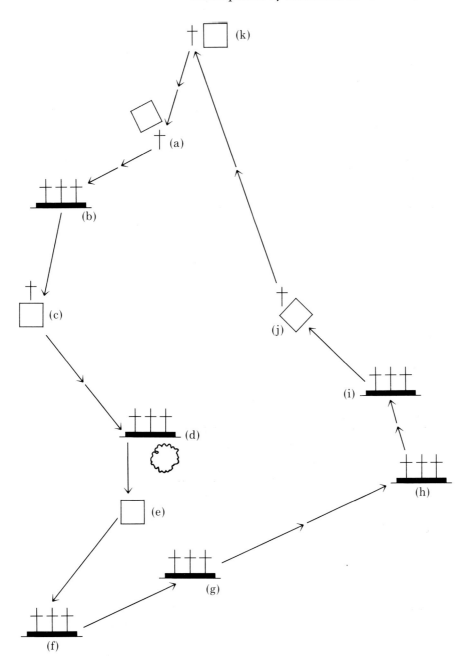

200. The sacred places visited

day. At his house, he offered coffee and lent me a black blanket to wrap myself in during the night—and did I need it before morning!

At 7 there was a prayer at the house cross of the Senior Outgoing Mayordomo before the group started on its ceremonial circuit. We passed by the house of the Junior Outgoing Mayordomo and said a prayer at his house cross, then went to a shrine at "Stomach Rock," located in the limestone sink just below a rather prominent rock defined as SHCH'UT TON.

From here we went to the house cross of Mikel Lopis Chiku? where chairs and benches were very well arranged for the seating of people around the patio. At the time I could not understand why Mikel, rather than Petul, his older brother, was acting as host. I later discovered that we visited this cross not because Mikel and Petul are ritual advisers but because Mikel's grandson, ?Akushtin Lopis Chiku?, is the Senior Incoming Mayordomo.

The next stop was at a cross under a very large tree, Matazano Tree, YOLON ?AHTE?, located between here and Rosario.

It was now midnight and I was becoming more and more eager to have the procession move on to the mysterious little house. Manvel had told me the saint there was Rosario. I wondered if I would be allowed inside.

I had heard skyrockets going off from another group over the hill and had heard talk about our meeting another group. I wondered if our arrival at Rosario would coincide with those of processions from other parts of VO? TA PASTE?, or indeed even from VOMCH'EN, SHULVO?, or some other place, arriving to pay homage to this saint—thinking that perhaps this was the ceremonial focus for the whole paraje.

Finally, about 1 A.M. we moved on to Rosario. There was no question about my presence. I simply went in with the procession, paid my respects to the Virgin along with the others, and took a seat on a bench on the left side. The shamans entered and went through their long prayer. From about 1:30 to 2:30 the two junior shamans and about four others danced for the Virgin. The dance differed from those I had seen before: bodies rotated back and forth while the feet made less marked movements. I was invited to dance, and did so, with the black blanket wrapped around me, for about half an hour.

Shortly after 3 A.M. the procession moved on to junior KALVARIO, which is on the hill south of Manvel No. 2's house. Much more use was made of pine torches at this point, probably because we were traveling over rugged country. A long time was spent at these crosses, and several times I drowsed by the fire momentarily, covered up with the black chamarra. One old man lit his kerosene lamp and spent an hour weaving on a net bag while the shamans were praying and he was waiting for the procession to move on. This was the most extreme case I have observed of the Zinacanteco value emphasis upon not wasting time!

At about 4:30 we went down the trail to Senior Stomach Cave, BANKILAL

SCH'UT CH'EN, which is at the side of another deep limestone sink, south and a little west of Manvel No. 2's house. Here the ritual had some unusual aspects. The people seemed quieter and there was almost an aura of fear hovering over the procession. The candles were tied together in threes and stuck up in a natural hole in the limestone rock. Manvel Patishtan was the shaman who had said the longest prayer; he seemed to initiate the ritual activity here. Since he is a specialist in the ceremony for people who have had their souls sold to the Earth Lord, I am sure that this sacred place is very intimately connected with this powerful god—it may be his stomach that is sticking out at this place!

Dawn broke at 5:30 A.M. About 6 I went to Manvel's house for breakfast and to see if he had his maize ready to go to San Cristóbal. I knew that Bob Laughlin needed the Landrover to go to Zinacantan Center at 8 A.M., and I was really tired. But before I left the procession had moved to Senior KALVARIO (about 100 meters west of the waterhole KALVARIO). As I drove off about 7:30 A.M. the procession had moved to Junior Stomach Cave, ?ITS'INAL SCH'UT CH'EN. I was told that it completed the circuit by passing by the house of the Junior Incoming Mayordomo, and ended by returning to the house of the host, the Senior Outgoing Mayordomo.

I had had to drink very little during the night. My status had reached the point where I had an option as to whether to drink the liquor or pour it in my bottle. I poured most of it in my bottle and collected over half a liter during the course of the night which I distributed the next morning to the drum and flute players.

The ceremony definitely turned out to be a ceremony for the small group that lives in SNA LOPIS CHIKU?ETIK, rather than a ceremony for the whole hamlet as I had anticipated.

Glossary

agrarista	a petitioner for or participant in the ejido system
aguaciles	lowest-grade officials in municipal government; originally assistants of the Regidores in the Spanish Ayuntamiento who maintained the public buildings and attended to the needs of travelers
aguaciles indios	low-ranking Zinacanteco officials of the late 1500's; later probably became the mayores, mayordomo reyes, and mesoneros of today
aguardiente	POSH; sugarcane rum liquor
alcalde mayor	head official of towns; until 1790 appointed by the Spanish government in Chiapas
alcaldes viejos	highest-ranking cargoholders in present-day Zinacantan
alcaldía	system (and building) of governing by alcalde(s); replaced in 1790 by the Intendencia, a government headed by an official called an Intendente
alférez	second-level cargoholder in the religious hierarchy of Zinacantan
almud	a dry measure of maize; equals 3 *cuartillas* or 15 metric liters; see Table 2
atole	ʔUL; drink made of boiled maize dough and water, spiced with various condiments, especially *panela;* always served on festive occasions
ʔATS'AM	salt
ʔATS'AM	the hamlet of Salinas—the only hamlet to have a Spanish as well as Tzotzil name, because it was on the old main road from Tuxtla Gutiérrez to San Cristóbal
audiencia	hearing to settle disputes
ayuntamiento	municipal government set up in accordance with The Laws of the Indies to maintain order and administer justice; still the main form of municipal government, tailored to local Indian political patterns and needs
BALAMIL	world, land, surface of the earth
baldiaje	Indian labor without remuneration three or four days a week for landlord in exchange for the privilege of remaining on the land that previously belonged to the Indian
BANKILAL	senior, older brother

barranca	ravine, gorge, or gully
barrio	ward, quarter, precinct, or neighborhood
BISH	bamboo staff carried by a shaman
BOLOM(ETIK)	jaguar(s); also two performers in the Fiesta of San Sebastián
caballo	horse
cabecera	administrative center of a municipio
cabildo	town hall
cacique	political boss
caldera	dry measure equal to 1 metric liter
cántaro	the Amatenango pottery jugs used in the Chiapas highlands to carry water from the waterholes to the houses of the Indians by tumpline
capitanes	costumed characters in the Fiesta of San Lorenzo
cargo	burden or weight; also used to denote a position held in the civil and religious hierarchies in Zinacantan
Carnaval	fiesta period (five days) preceding Ash Wednesday
chamarra	POK' K'UʔUL; sleeveless, thigh-length pullover garment of wool or cotton, worn over shirt or blouse by an Indian man
CHAMEL	sickness
CHANUL	animal spirit companion
CH'EN	cave, limestone sink
chicha	YAKIL VOʔ; intoxicating drink made of fermented fruit (especially pineapple) and sugar (also from maize); made and used especially during fiestas of San Sebastián and Carnaval
CHENEK'	bean(s), bean plant
CHILIL	woman's stole or shawl; also the special ceremonial robe worn by older women ceremonial helpers such as incense-bearers
CHOʔ	metate; three-legged basalt stone used for grinding maize
CH'ULEL	soul
cohete	skyrocket
coheteros	makers and/or shooters of skyrockets
comadre	KUMALE; co-mother; term of address and reference in the ritual kinship system
comal	SEMET; round earthenware or metal griddle for baking tortillas
Comisariado Ejidal	official in charge of distribution of ejido land
compadrazgo	system of ritual kinship
compadre	KUMPARE or KUMPA; co-father; term of address and reference used in ritual kinship system
Consejo de las Indias	Law of the Indies, under which Spain administrated the New World
cuarta	liquid measure equal to one-half pint

cuartilla	dry measure equal to 5 calderas
ejidatario	man who holds rights to land under ejido system
ejido	communal farmland resulting from 1917 land reform laws, whereby large Ladino-held estates were given to Indian groups and communities
encomenderos	recipients of land grants from the Spanish crown, including the lands and the services of the Indians who lived and worked thereon
encomienda	system of land ownership established by the Spaniards; abolishment begun in 1720
escribano	ʔISHKIRVANO; scribe
fanega	dry measure equal to 12 almudes (also called fanega chica), equal to 1.58 bu. in Spain; weight approximately 130 kilos
fanega-litro	dry measure equal to 12 liters
finca	farm or ranch; refers also to lowland coffee plantations
finquero	owner of farm, ranch, or coffee plantation
garrafón	large glass bottle or jug, holding from 17 to 20 liters
gobernador	governor
hacendado	owner of a hacienda
hacienda	large Ladino-owned ranch supported by Indian labor; many now under ejido management
HCHAMEL	patient in a curing ceremony
HʔILOL(ETIK)	shaman(s)
HKASHLAN	Ladino; from Spanish *castellano*
HOBEL	grass, thatch; also Tzotzil name for San Cristóbal Las Casas
HPʔIS VOʔ	drink-pourer
HTEKLUM	Zinacantan Center
huipil	woman's blouse
ʔIKʔ	black
indio	Indian
INI	Instituto Nacional Indigenista (National Indigenous Institute)
Intendencia	Spanish provincial government, headed by official called Intendente; replaced alcaldías in 1790
Intendente	head governing official of the Intendencia in Chiapas from 1790 until Independence in 1917
ʔISHIM	maize
ʔISHKIPULA	*Esquipulas;* Spanish saint, Señor Esquipulas; also name of small hermitage in Zinacantan Center
ʔISHKIRVANO	*escribano;* scribe

?ITS'INAL   junior, younger brother

juncia   SHAK TOH; pine needles, stripped from branches, used to cover the floor or ground in churches and in front of shrines for ritual occasions

junta   meeting or conference

KALVARIO   from Spanish *Calvario* (Calvary): major sacred mountain in Zinacantan; also refers to the cross shrines maintained by the individual snas as a means of communication with deities

KAMARO   loud powder blasts set off at fiestas; also the cannon used

KANTELA   candle

K'IN   ritual or fiesta

K'IN KRUS   ceremony performed in May and sometimes October

K'OB CHO?   *mano;* grinding stone, held in hands, used to grind maize kernels into tortilla dough

K'ON   yellow

K'OSHOSH   large tortillas, baked until crisp, as long-lasting food for trips

KRINSUPALETIK   *principales;* municipio government representatives in each hamlet in Zinacantan

KUMALE   *see* comadre

KUMPARE, KUMPA   *see* compadre

Ladino   term used to refer to Mexicans (*blancos* and *mestizos*) as opposed to Indians

latifundio   large, Ladino landholdings

límite   unit of liquid measure equal to 1 quart; thus any bottle holding 4 cuartas

litro   dry measure equal to 4 cuartillas; also called *doble decalitro;* also liquid measure equal to 5 *cuartas* or 1 liter

LOK'EB K'AK'AL   "where the sun rises," that is, east

madrina   CH'UL ME?; godmother, term of reference

MALEB K'AK'AL   "where the sun sets," that is, west

MAMALETIK   masked, male figure dancers (two) who perform with the torito during Christmas season; "owners" of torito and husbands of ME?CHUNETIK

mano   *see* K'OB CHO?

masa   PICH'BIL ?ISHIM; maize dough

mayordomos   lowest-ranking cargoholders, charged with caring for the two churches in Zinacantan Center and saints therein

mayordomos reyes   MARTOMOREYETIK; two cargoholders of the lowest rank, who with two mesoneros (MESHONETIK) carry out weekly rituals of the Hermitage of Señor Esquipulas

mayores	MAYOLETIK; policemen, errand-runners; twelve in number who are cargoholders of the first (lowest) level
ME?CHUNETIK	wives of owners of torito; *see* MAMALETIK
mesoneros	MESHONETIK; two cargoholders of first level who aid mayordomos reyes in the weekly rituals of the Hermitage of Señor Esquipulas
metate	CHO?; three-legged basalt stones used for grinding maize
media	liquid measure equal to a pint
milpa	field, usually of maize
municipio	municipality; political unit (e.g., land and people within territory designated for Indians of Zinacantan by Mexican government)
NA	house
nixtamal	PANIN; soaked and lime-boiled maize kernels ready for grinding
ocote	pitchy pine; cut pieces used as kindling and for torches at night
?OLON BALAMIL	the "world below"
padrino	CH'UL TOT; godfather; term of reference
panela	unrefined (brown) sugar from sugar cane; formed into cakes and sold in markets, it is used to make aguardiente and to flavor food and drink
PANIN	*see* nixtamal
paraje	PARAHEL; hamlet; largest subdivision of municipio
pasados	older men who have passed cargos of all four levels
pasioneros	PASHIONETIK; two cargoholders whose special ritual roles are carried out during Easter season
petate	POP; woven reed mat of many uses
POK'	blue-and-white checkered scarf with bright pink wool tassels, worn by men, tied around neck or head
POK' K'U?UL	*see* chamarra
POM	incense
POP	*see* petate
POSH	*see* aguardiente
pozol	?UCH'IMO; ball of uncooked maize dough carried by travelers; small piece, pinched off and mixed with water, provides nourishment
principales	*see* KRINSUPALETIK
PUKUH	evil spirit
regidores	REHIROLETIK; originally members of ayuntamiento responsible for collecting tribute, maintaining cleanliness in public places, and seeing to the general welfare; now refers to third-level cargoholders

SAK	white
SEMET	*see* comal
SHAK TOH	*see* juncia
SHOKON VINAHEL	"sides of the heaven" or sides of the path of the sun (i.e., the directions north and south)
SNA	"the house of"; used to denote social grouping composed of one or more localized patrilineages
subdelegados	Spanish officials who replaced tenientes in the change from alcaldías to the intendencia in 1790
sumidero	limestone fissure
tecolúmete	red and green air plant (or bromilead) used in decoration of altars and shrines
tecomate	TSU; squash (shaped like figure 8) from which gourd water containers are obtained
tenientes	Spanish government officials under alcaldes mayores, heads of important towns under the alcaldía system
T'ENT'EN	small ceremonial slit drum used in the Fiesta of San Sebastián; kept by its owners in ?Elan Vo?
TOH	pine tree
TON KASHLAN	chicken (duck, turkey) egg (from TON, stone, and KASHLAN, chicken)
torito	reed-mat bull used in the Christmas fiesta; also used to refer to the bull-shaped firework structures that provide excitement at other large fiestas
tortilla	VAH; thin, unleavened pancake-shaped maize "bread," the staple of the Zinacanteco diet
TOTILME?ILETIK	ancestral gods; also ritual advisers
TSOH	red
TSU	*see* tecomate
?UAL	saints' necklaces of wide ribbon, from which old coins are suspended
?UCH'IMO	*see* pozol
?UL	*see* atole
VAH	*see* tortilla
VASHAKMEN	the four gods who support the four corners of the world on their shoulders
VE?EL	meal or dinner
VE?EL TA MESHA	ritual meal; banquet
VINAHEL	heaven, sky
VO?	water; well; waterhole
YAHVAL BALAMIL	"The Earth Lord," ruler and sender of clouds, wind, rain
YAKIL VO?	*see* chicha
YŎSH	blue or green (Zinacantecos do not differentiate between the two colors)

LAUGHLIN, ROBERT M.
   1960. "To the People of the Bat," *South Kent School Alumni Magazine* (Winter; special supplement).
   1962. "El símbolo de la flor en la religíon de Zinacantan," *Estudios de Cultura Maya,* 2:123–129.
   1962. "Through the Looking Glass: Reflections on Zinacantan Courtship and Marriage." Ph.D. Dissertation, Harvard University.
   1966. "Oficio de tinieblas: cómo el zinacanteco adivina sus sueños," in *Los Zinacantecos,* Vogt, ed., pp. 396–413.

LEACH, E. R.
   1961. *Rethinking Anthropology.* London School of Economics, Monographs on Social Anthropology, 22:1–27.

LEON-PORTILLA, MIGUEL
   1968. *Tiempo y realidad en el pensamiento maya.* Mexico.

LEVI-STRAUSS, CLAUDE
   1953. "Social Structure," *Anthropology Today,* A. L. Kroeber, ed., Chicago: University of Chicago Press, pp. 524–553.
   1955. "The Structural Study of Myth," *Journal of American Folklore,* 78:428–444.
   1963. "The Bear and the Barber," *Journal of the Royal Anthropological Institute of Great Britain and Ireland,* Henry Myers Memorial Lecture 1962, 93:1–12.
   1964. *Le cru et le cuit.* Paris: Plon.
   1966. *Du miel aux cendres.* Paris: Plon.

LOCKE, NANCY
   1964. "A Case Study in Mexican Conservatism: Why the capital of Chiapas was moved from San Cristóbal to Tuxtla Gutiérrez in 1892." A.B. Honors Thesis, Smith College.

LOWE, GARETH W.
   1959. *Archaeological Exploration of the Upper Grijalva River, Chiapas, Mexico.* Papers of the New World Archaeological Foundation, 2, Provo, Utah.

LOWENTHAL, MARY
   1963. "The Elite of San Cristóbal." Unpublished MS., Harvard Chiapas Project.

McBRIDE, GEORGE M.
   1923. *The Land Systems of Mexico.* American Geographical Society Research Series 12, New York.

McQUOWN, NORMAN
   1964. "Los orígenes y la diferenciación de los mayas según se infiere del estudio comparativo de las lenguas mayanas," in *Desarrollo Cultural de los Mayas,* Vogt and Ruz, eds., pp. 49–80.

McVICKER, DONALD E.
   1965. "Cultural Change and Ecology in Prehispanic Central Chiapas." Ohio, Bowling Green State University, mimeographed.

MALINOWSKI, B.
  1926. *Myth in Primitive Psychology.* New York: W. W. Norton.

MAUSS, MARCEL
  1954. *The gift,* trans. I. Cunnison. Glencoe, Ill.: Free Press.

MEADOW, RICHARD H.
  1965. "Modern and Ancient Maya Settlement Patterns." Unpublished seminar report, Harvard University.

METZGER, BARBARA
  1959. "An Ethnographic History of Zinacantan." Unpublished MS., Harvard Chiapas Project.
  1960. "Notes on the History of Indian-Ladino Relations in Chiapas." Unpublished MS., Harvard Chiapas Project.

METZGER, DUANE, and GERALD E. WILLIAMS
  1963. "Tenejapa Medicine I: the Curer," *Southwestern Journal of Anthropology,* 19:216–234.

MILES, SUZANNE W.
  1952. "An Analysis of Modern Middle American Calendars," in *Acculturation in the Americas,* ed. Sol Tax. Chicago: University of Chicago Press, pp. 273–284.
  1957. "The Sixteenth Century Pokom-Maya: A documentary Analysis of Social Structure and Archaeological Setting," Transactions of the American Philosophical Society 47, part 4.
  1965. "Summary of Preconquest Ethnology of the Guatemala-Chiapas Highlands and the Pacific Slopes," in *Archaeology of Southern Mesoamerica,* vol. 2 of *Handbook of Middle American Indians,* ed. Robert Wauchope and G. R. Willey, Austin: University of Texas, pp. 276–287.

MINTZ, SIDNEY W., and ERIC R. WOLF
  1950. "An Analysis of Ritual Co-Parenthood (Compadrazgo)," *Southwestern Journal of Anthropology,* 6:341–368.

MOLINA, CRISTÓBAL
  1934. "War of the Castes: Indian Uprisings in Chiapas, 1867–70" (translation). *Middle American Series,* New Orleans: Tulane University, pamphlet 8, publication 5.

MONTAGU, ROBERTA, and EVA HUNT
  1962. "Nombre, autoridad y el sistema de creencias en Los Altos de Chiapas," *Estudios de Cultura Maya,* 2:141–148.

MÜLLERREID, FEDERICO K. G.
  1957. *La geología de Chiapas.* Tuxtla Gutiérrez, Mexico: Gobierno Constitucional del Estado de Chiapas.

NASH, MANNING
  1957. "Cultural Persistences and Social Structure: The Mesoamerican Calendar Survivals," *Southwestern Journal of Anthropology,* 13:149–155.
  1958. "Political Relations in Guatemala," *Social and Economic Studies,* 7:65–75.

OAKES, MAUD
  1951. *The Two Crosses of Todos Santos.* New York: Pantheon Books.

PANIAGUA, FLAVIO A.
  1876. *Catecismo elemental de história estadística de Chiapas.* San Cristóbal de las Casas, Chiapas.
  1908–1911. *Documentos y datos para un diccionario etimológico, histórico, y geográphico de Chiapas.* San Cristóbal de las Casas, 3 vols. Contains excerpts from Fray A. de Remesal, *História de la Provincia de San Vicente de Chiapas y Guatemala* . . . (Madrid, 1619).

PAUL, B. D.
  1942. "Ritual Kinship: With Special Reference to God-parenthood in Middle America." Ph.D. Dissertation, University of Chicago.

PEÑAFIEL, ANTONIO
  1885. *Nombres geográficos de México: Católogo alfabético de los nombres de lugar pertenecientes al idioma nahuatl.* Mexico: Secretaría de Fomento.

PINEDA, VICENTE
  1888. *Historia de las sublevaciones indígenas habidas en el estado de Chiapas.* San Cristóbal de las Casas, Chiapas.

PITT-RIVERS, JULIAN
  1967. "Words and Deeds: The Ladinos of Chiapas." *Man,* 2:71–87, London.

POZAS, RICARDO
  1952. "El trabajo en las plantaciones de café y el cambio sociocultural del Indio," *Revista Mexicana de Estudios Antropológicos,* 13:31–48.
  1959. *Chamula, un pueblo indio de los altos de Chiapas,* Memorias del Instituto Nacional Indigenista 8, Mexico.

PROSKOURIAKOFF, TATIANA
  1960. "Historical Implications of a Pattern of Dates at Piedras Negras, Guatemala," *American Antiquity,* 25:454–475.
  1963–1964. "Historical Data in the Inscriptions of Yaxchilan," *Estudios de Cultura Maya,* 3:149–167; 4:177–202.

RAKOFF, TODD D.
  1965. "Time Patterns in Zinacantan." Unpublished MS., Harvard Chiapas Project.

REDFIELD, ROBERT
  1941. *The Folk Culture of Yucatan.* Chicago: University of Chicago Press.

———— and ALFONSO VILLA ROJAS

1934. *Chan Kom: a Maya village*. Chicago: University of Chicago Press (abridged ed., Chicago: University of Chicago Press, 1962).

REMESAL, FRAY A. DE

1908. *1619 historia de la Provincia de S. Vicente de Chiapas y Guatemala* . . . Madrid.

ROSALDO, MICHELLE Z.

1967. "Ever-changing Kinship." Unpublished MS., Harvard Chiapas Project.

ROSALDO, RENATO I.

1968. "Metaphors of Hierarchy in a Mayan ritual," *American Anthropologist,* 70:524–536.

ROYS, RALPH L.

1943. *The Indian Background of Colonial Yucatan*. Washington, D.C.: Carnegie Institution of Washington, Publication 548.

1957. *The Political Geography of the Yucatan Maya*. Washington, D.C.: Carnegie Institution of Washington, Publication 613.

RUZ, ALBERTO

1964. "¿Aristocracia o democracia entre los antiguos Mayas?" Universidad Nacional Autónoma de México, Instituto de Investigaciones Históricas, *Anales de Antropología,* I: 63–76.

SANDERS, WILLIAM T.

1962–1963. "Cultural Ecology of the Maya Lowlands," *Estudios de Cultura Maya,* 2:79–121; 3:203–241.

SILVER, DANIEL B.

1966a. "Zinacanteco Shamanism." Ph.D. Dissertation, Harvard University.

1966b. "Enfermedad y curación en Zinacantan—esquema provisional," in *Los Zinacantecos,* Vogt, ed., 455–473.

SIMPSON, EYLER N.

1937. *The Ejido: Mexico's Way Out*. Chapel Hill: University of North Carolina Press.

SIVERTS, HENNING

1960. "Political Organization in a Tzeltal Community in Chiapas, México," *Alpha Kappa Deltan,* 30:14–29.

1964. "An Exploratory Note on the Seniority Principle (the *bankilal its'inal* Concept) in Maya Political Thinking," in *Desarrollo cultural de los Mayas,* Vogt and Ruz, eds., pp. 380–384.

SMITH, A. L.

1962. "Residential and Associated Structures at Mayapan," in *Mayapan, Yucatan, Mexico,* H. E. D. Pollock, R. L. Roys, T. Proskouriakoff, and A. L. Smith, eds. Washington D.C.: Carnegie Institution of Washington, Publication 619.

STAUDER, JACK
  1961. "Zinacantecos in Hot Country." Unpublished MS., Harvard Chiapas Project.
  1966. "Algunos aspectos de la agricultura zinacanteca en Tierra Caliente," in *Los Zinacantecos,* Vogt, ed., pp. 145–162.

STRODT, BARBARA S.
  1965. "Household Economy in Zinacantan." Unpublished MS., Harvard Chiapas Project.
  1967. "A Reconsideration of the Study of Culture Contact." A.B. Honors Thesis, Radcliffe College.

TAMAYO, JORGE L.
  1949a. *Geografía general de México.* Mexico, 2 vols.
  1949b. *Atlas geográfico general de México.* Mexico.

TAX, SOL
  1943. Notas sobre Zinacantan, Chiapas. University of Chicago Library, Microfilm Collection of Manuscripts on Middle American Cultural Anthropology, number 20.
  1944. "Information about the Municipio of Zinacantan, Chiapas," *Revista Mexicana de Estudios Antropológicos,* 6:181–195.

TAX, SUSAN
  1959. "Weaving and its Social Context in Zinacantan." Unpublished MS., Harvard Chiapas Project.
  1964. "Displacement Activity in Zinacantan," *América Indígena,* 24:111–121 (translated and reprinted as "Actividad de desplazamiento en Zinacantan," in *Los Zinacantecos,* Vogt, ed., 298–312).

THOMPSON, J. ERIC
  1934. *Sky Bearers, Colors and Directions in Maya and Mexican Religion.* Washington, D.C.: Carnegie Institution of Washington Publication 436, pp. 209–242.
  1939. "The Moon-Goddess in Middle America." Carnegie Institution of Washington, *Contributions to American Anthropology and History,* 5:120–173.
  1954. *The Rise and Fall of Maya Civilization.* Norman: University of Oklahoma Press.
  1959. "The Role of Caves in Maya Culture," *Mitterlungen aus dem Museum für völkerkunde,* Hamburg, Sonderdruck, 25:122–129.
  1960. *Maya Hieroglyphic Writing: An Introduction.* Norman: University of Oklahoma Press.

THOMSEN, EVELYN R.
  1966. "How to Handle an Earth Lord: An Analysis of the Myths, Prayers, and Rituals Which Focus on the Waterholes of Zinacantan." A.B. Honors Thesis, Vassar College.

TOZZER, ALFRED M.
  1907. *A Comparative Study of the Mayas and Lacandones.* New York, Archaeological Institute of America, Report of Fellows in American Archaeology
  1902–1905.
  1941. *Landa's relación de las cosas de Yucatan.* Papers of the Peabody Museum
  of American Archaeology and Ethnology, vol. 18. Cambridge, Mass.: Harvard
  University.

TRENS, MANUEL B.
  1957. *Historia de Chiapas desde los tiempos más remotos hasta la caida del
  Segundo Imperio.* Mexico.

TROSPER, RONALD L.
  1966. "Lending and Borrowing in ?Apas." Unpublished MS., Harvard Chiapas
  Project.
  1967. "Tradition and Economic Growth in Zinacantan: Gradual Change in
  a Mexican Indian Community." A.B. Honors Thesis, Harvard College.

TURNER, VICTOR
  1967. *The Forest of Symbols.* Ithaca, N.Y.: Cornell University Press.

URIBE, ELENA
  1966. "Algunas consideraciones sobre el compadrazgo en Mesoamerica." Unpublished MS., Harvard Chiapas Project.

VALLADARES, L. A.
  1957. *El hombre y el maíz.* Etnografía y Etnopsicología de Colotenango, Guatemala.

VAN DEN BERGHE, GWENDOLINE
  1965. "Compadrazgo Among the Ladino Population of San Cristóbal de las
  Casas." Unpublished MS., Harvard Chiapas Project.

VAN DEN BERGHE, PIERRE L. and GWENDOLINE
  1966. "Compadrazgo and Class in Southeastern Mexico," *American Anthropologist,* 68:1236–1244.

VILLA ROJAS, ALFONSO
  1945. *The Maya of East Central Quintana Roo.* Washington, D.C.: Carnegie
  Institution of Washington, Publication 559.
  1947. "Kinship and Nagualism in a Tzeltal Community, Southeastern Mexico,"
  American Anthropologist, 49:578–588.
  1963. "El nagualismo como recurso de control social entre los grupos mayances
  de Chiapas, México," *Estudios de Cultura Maya,* 3:243–260.

VOGT, EVON Z.
  1961. "Some Aspects of Zinacantan Settlement Patterns and Ceremonial Organization," *Estudios de Cultura Maya,* 1:131–146.
  1964a. "The Genetic Model and Maya Cultural Development," in *Desarrollo
  cultural de los Mayas,* Vogt and Ruz, eds., pp. 9–48.
  1964b. "Ancient Maya Concepts in Contemporary Zinacantan Religion," *VI*ᵉ

Congrès International des Sciences Anthropologiques et Ethnologiques, Paris; Musée de l'Homme, 2:497–502.

1964c. "Some Implications of Zinacantan Social Structure for the Study of the Ancient Maya," *Actas y Memorias del XXXV Congreso Internacional de Americanistas,* 1:307–319.

1964d. "Ancient Maya and Contemporary Tzotzil Cosmology: A Comment on Some Methodological Problems," *American Antiquity,* 30:192–195 (translated and reprinted as: "Cosmología Maya antigua y Tzotzil contemporánea: comentario sobre algunos problemas metodológicos," *América Indígena,* 24:211–219).

1965a. "Ceremonial Organization in Zinacantan," *Ethnology,* 4:39–52.

1965b. "Structural and Conceptual Replication in Zinacantan Culture," *American Anthropologist,* 67:342–353.

1965c. "Zinacanteco 'Souls,'" *Man,* 29:33–35.

1966a. "H'iloletik: The Organization and Function of Shamanism in Zinacantan," in *Summa Anthropologica en Homenaje a Roberto J. Weitlaner,* Mexico: Instituto Nacional de Antropología e Historia, pp. 359–369.

1966b. *Los Zinacantecos: un pueblo Tzotzil de los Altos de Chiapas,* Evon Z. Vogt, editor. Colección de Antropología Social, vol. 7, Mexico: Instituto Nacional Indigenista.

1967. "Tendencia de cambio en las tierras altas de Chiapas," *América Indígena,* 27:199–222.

n.d. "Chiapas Highlands," in *Ethnology of Middle America,* vol. 7 of *Handbook of Middle American Indians,* ed. Robert Wauchope (in press).

———— and ALBERTO RUZ L., editors

1964. *Desarrollo cultural de los Mayas.* Seminario de Cultura Maya. Universidad Nacional Autónoma de México.

WAGLEY, C.

1949. *The Social and Religious Life of a Guatemalan Village.* American Anthropological Association Memoir 71.

WALLACE, A. F. C.

1956. "Revitalization Movements," *American Anthropologist,* 58:264–281.

WARFIELD, JAMES P.

1963. "House Architecture in Zinacantan." Unpublished MS., Harvard Chiapas Project.

1966. La arquitectura en Zinacantan, in *Los Zinacantecos,* Vogt, ed., pp. 183–207.

WEATHERS, KENNETH

1946. "La agricultura de los Tzotzil de Navenchauk, Chiapas, México," *América Indígena,* 6:315–319.

WEATHERS, NADINE

1947. "Tzotzil Phonemes with Special Reference to Allophones of B," *International Journal of American Linguistics,* 13:108–111.

1950. "Morphological Analysis of a Tzotzil (Mayan) Text," *International Journal of American Linguistics,* 16:91–98.

WEST, ROBERT C.

1964. "Surface Configuration and Associated Geology of Middle America," in *Natural Environment and Early Cultures,* vol. 1 of *Handbook of Middle American Indians,* ed. Robert Wauchope and Robert C. West, pp. 33–83.

WILLEY, GORDON R.

1956. "The Structure of Ancient Maya Society: Evidence from the Southern Lowlands," *American Anthropologist,* 58:777–782.

1964. "An Archaeological Frame of Reference for Maya Culture History," in *Desarrollo cultural de los Mayas,* Vogt and Ruz, eds., pp. 137–178.

WILSON, GEORGE CARTER

1963. "Drinking and Drinking Customs in a Mayan Community." Unpublished MS., Harvard Chiapas Project.

WISDOM, CHARLES

1940. *The Chorti Indians of Guatemala.* Chicago: University of Chicago Press.

WOLF, ERIC

1955. "Types of Latin American Peasantry: A Preliminary Discussion," *American Anthropologist,* 57:452–471.

1956. "Aspects of Group Relations in a Complex Society: Mexico," *American Anthropologist,* 58:1065–1078.

XIMÉNEZ, FRANCISCO

1929–1931. *Historia de la Provincia de San Vicente de Chiapas y Guatemala de la orden de predicadores.* Guatemala; Biblioteca Goathemala, I, II, III, LXXII.

YOUNG, ALLEN

1962. "Mexico's Federal Corn Warehouses in Highland Chiapas." Unpublished MS., Harvard Chiapas Project.

YOUNG, STEPHEN B.

1965. "Their People's Servants: Political Officials in a Highland Maya Community." Unpublished MS., Harvard Chiapas Project.

ZABALA, MANUEL T.

1961a. "Sistema económico de la comunidad de Zinacantan." Escuela Nacional de Antropología e Historia, México, mimeographed.

1961b. "Instituciones políticas y religiosas de Zinacantan," *Estudios de Cultura Maya,* 1:147–158.

ZIMBALIST, MICHELLE

1966. "La Granadilla: un modelo de la estructura social zinacanteca," in *Los Zinacantecos,* Vogt, ed., pp. 275–297.

ZUBIN, DAVID A.

1963. "The San Cristóbal Corn Market: a Discussion of Vendor–Buyer Interaction." Unpublished MS., Harvard Chiapas Project.

II. *Other Works of the Harvard Chiapas Project*

ACHESON, NICHOLAS H.
1966. "Etnozoología zinacanteca," in *Los Zinacantecos,* Vogt, ed., pp. 433–454.

ANSCHUETZ, MARY H.
1966. "Childbirth in Zinacantan." Unpublished MS., Harvard Chiapas Project.

BAHR, ADELAIDE PIRROTA
1961. "The Economic Role of Women in San Felipe." Unpublished MS., Harvard Chiapas Project.

BAHR, DONALD M.
1962. "An Exploration of Men's Use and Views of the Physical World in Two Highland Maya Municipios." A.B. Honors Thesis, Harvard College.

BRAZELTON, T. BERRY, JOHN S. ROBEY, and GEORGE A. COLLIER
n.d. "Infant Development in the Zinacanteco Indians of Southern Mexico," in *Pediatrics* (in press).

BRICKER, VICTORIA
n.d. "The Pattern of Interaction between the Computer and the Ethnographer in the Field." International Symposium on Mathematical and Computational Methods in the Social Sciences, Rome, July 4–8 (in press).

CANCIAN, FRANCESCA M.
1964. "Interaction patterns in Zinacanteco families," *American Sociological Review,* 29:540–550 (translated and reprinted as "Patrones de interaccíon en las familias zinacantecas," in *Los Zinacantecos,* Vogt, ed., pp. 251–274).
1965. "The Effect of Patrilocal Households on Nuclear Family Interaction in Zinacantan," *Estudios de Cultura Maya,* 5:299–315.
1967. "Categories of Good and Bad Behavior in Zinacantan." Paper presented at the 66th Annual Meeting of the American Anthropological Association, Washington.

CANCIAN, FRANK
1963. "Informant error and native prestige ranking in Zinacantan," *American Anthropologist,* 65:1068–1075 (translated and reprinted as "El error de los informantes y la graduación nativa del prestigio en Zinacantan," in *Los Zinacantecos,* Vogt, ed., pp. 327–336).
1964. "Population Pressure and Social Structural Change in a Highland Maya Community." Paper read at the 63rd Annual Meeting of the American Anthropological Association, Detroit.
1965. "Equilibrium Analysis and Conflict: A Problem in the Study of the Maya of Zinacantan, Mexico." Paper presented to the Annual Meeting of the Southwestern Anthropological Association, Los Angeles, April.
1967. "Stratification and Risk-Taking: A Theory Tested on Agricultural Innovation," *American Sociological Review,* 32:912–927.

1967. "Political and Religious Organizations," in *Social Anthropology of Middle America,* vol. 6 of *Handbook of Middle American Indians,* ed. Robert Wauchope and Manning Nash, pp. 283–298.

CHAVIGNY, CLAUDE E.

1965. "Les Tisserands: dans le quartier des Mexicanos San Cristobal de Las Casas." Unpublished MS., Harvard Chiapas Project.

COLBY, BENJAMIN N.

1960. "Social Relations and Directed Culture Change among the Zinacantan," *Practical Anthropology,* 7:241–250.

1964. "Elements of a Mesoamerican Personality Pattern," *Actas y Memorias del XXXV Congreso Internacional de Americanistas.* Mexico, 1962, 2:125–129.

1967. "Mesoamerican Psychological Orientations," in *Social Anthropology of Middle America,* vol. 6 of *Handbook of Middle American Indians,* ed. Robert Wauchope and Manning Nash, pp. 416–431.

COLBY, LORE M.

1964. "Zinacantan Tzotzil Sound and Word Structure." Ph.D. Dissertation, Harvard University.

COLLIER, GEORGE A.

1963. "Color categories in Zinacantan." A.B. Honors Thesis, Harvard College.

1967. "Familia y tierra en varias communidades mayas," *Estudios de Cultura Maya,* 6:301–335.

1967. "Land Use and Tenure in a Zinacanteco Community." Paper presented at the 66th Annual Meeting of the American Anthropological Association, Washington.

COLLIER, JANE F.

1967. "The Economics of Divorce and Remarriage in Zinacantan." Paper presented at the 66th Annual Meeting of the American Anthropological Association, Washington.

FLØYSTRUP, BENEDICTE

1964. "Waterhole Groups and Settlement Patterns." Unpublished MS., Harvard Chiapas Project.

GILBERT, GORDON A.

1965. "Indian-Ladino Relations in Restaurants in San Cristóbal." Unpublished MS., Harvard Chiapas Project.

GILMAN, ANTONIO

1964. "Municipio Organization." Unpublished MS., Harvard Chiapas Project.

GUDEMAN, STEPHEN F.

1960. "Some Aspects of the Economic System of Chilil." Unpublished MS., Harvard Chiapas Project.

1961. "Toward a Model of the Highland Maya Economies." A.B. Honors Thesis, Harvard College.

HAVILAND, LESLIE K.
  1967. "Women in Ritual in Zinacantan." Unpublished MS., Harvard Chiapas
    Project.

KREBS, STEPHANIE L.
  1967. "A Woman's Life in Zinacantan." 20 minute, 16 mm. color film (in process).
    Harvard Chiapas Project.

KROECK, RICHARD M.
  1966. A manual for users of aerial photographs of the Highlands of Chiapas,
    Mexico.

LAUGHLIN, ROBERT M.
  n.d. "The Tzotzil," in *Ethnology of Middle America,* vol. 7 of *Handbook of
    Middle American Indians,* ed. Robert Wauchope (in press).
  n.d. Tzotzil-English Dictionary (in preparation).
  1967. "Truth or Consequences: Being the Definitive Travails of a Lexicographer
    in Chiapas, Mexico," Paper presented at the 66th Annual Meeting of the
    American Anthropological Association, Washington.

LOGAN, M. HAVEN
  1966. "The process of Ladinoization in San Cristóbal Las Casas, Mexico."
    Unpublished MS., Harvard Chiapas Project.

MADURO, RONALD
  1962. "Schools in San Cristóbal Las Casas, Mexico." Unpublished MS., Harvard
    Chiapas Project.

MENGET, PATRICK J.
  1968. "Death in Chamula," *Natural History,* 77:48–57.

MILLER, FRANK C.
  1959. "Social Structure and Medical Change in a Mexican Indian Community."
    Ph.D. Dissertation, Harvard University.
  1959. "What Happened to Name Groups in Huistan?" Paper presented at the
    58th Annual Meeting of the American Anthropological Association, Mexico
    City.
  1960. "Acculturation and Social Mobility in a Tzotzil Community." Paper
    presented at the 59th Annual Meeting of the American Anthropological
    Association, Minneapolis.
  1960. "The Influences of Decision-making on the Process of Change: The
    Yalcuc," *Alpha Kappa Deltan* (special issue on the Social Anthropology of
    Middle America), pp. 29–34.
  1964. "Tzotzil domestic groups," *The Journal of the Royal Anthropological
    Institute of Great Britain and Ireland,* 94:172–182.
  1965. "Cultural Change as Decision-Making: a Tzotzil example," *Ethnology,*
    4:53–65.

MIYAMOTO, JOHN M.
  1967. "Ritual Objects: Their Pre-Fiesta Logistics." Unpublished MS., Harvard
    Chiapas Project.

NATELSON, ABIGAIL S.
  1967. "Clothing Norms in Zinacantan and Chamula." Unpublished MS., Harvard Chiapas Project.

POPE, CAROLYN C.
  1967. "Food for the Soul: Cemeteries in Zinacantan." Unpublished MS., Harvard Chiapas Project.

PRICE, RICHARD S.
  1968. "Land Use in a Mayan Community," *International Archives of Ethnography,* 51:1–19.

——— and SALLY H. PRICE
  n.d. "Principles of Social Organization in a Mayan Hamlet," *Estudios de Cultura Maya* (in press).

PRICE, SALLY H.
  1966. "I Was Pashku and My Husband Was Telesh," *Radcliffe Quarterly* (May–June), pp. 4–8.

PROKOSCH, ERIC
  1963. "Chamula Government." Unpublished MS., Harvard Chiapas Project.
  1964. "Court Procedure in the Settlement of Disputes in Chamula." Unpublished MS., Harvard Chiapas Project.

REEVES, PEGGY
  1960. "The compadrazgo in Aguacatenango." Unpublished MS., Harvard Chiapas Project.

ROSALDO, MICHELLE Z.
  1965. "Tzotzil Ethnoanatomy." Unpublished MS., Harvard Chiapas Project.

ROSALDO, RENATO I., and MICHELLE Z. ROSALDO
  n.d. Zinacantan ritual language (in preparation).

ROSENBERG, MARK L.
  1967. "Zinacantan: Which Doctor?" Unpublished MS., Harvard Chiapas Project.
  1968. "Zinacantan: Which Doctor?" *Harvard Medical Alumni Bulletin* (Winter), 42:12–15.

ROSENBLATT, RAND
  1964. "Law and Ideology in Chamula." Unpublished MS., Harvard Chiapas Project.

SCOTT, DIANA M.
  1965. "The Candle Industry of San Cristóbal." Unpublished MS., Harvard Chiapas Project.

STRUCKER, JOHN D.
  1964. "Ten days in the INI School in the Paraje of Yalichin, Chamula." Unpublished MS., Harvard Chiapas Project.

SHWEDER, RICHARD A.
  1968. "Cognitive Aspects of Shamanism: Experimental Results." Unpublished
  MS., Harvard Chiapas Project.

STUBBLEFIELD, PHILLIP G.
  1962. "Folk Medicine in Two Mayan Towns." A.B. Honors Thesis, Harvard
  College.

VAN DEN BERGHE, PIERRE L., and BENJAMIN N. COLBY
  1961. "Ladino-Indian Relations in the Highlands of Chiapas, Mexico," *Social
  Forces,* 40:63–71.

VOGT, EVON Z.
  1960. Review of *Chamula, un pueblo de los Altos de Chiapas,* by Ricardo Pozas,
  American Anthropologist, 63:707–708.
  1962. Review of *Perils of the soul: The world view of a Tzotzil Indian,* by C.
  Guiteras-Holmes, *American Anthropologist,* 64:649–651.
  1965. Review of *Medicina Maya en los Altos de Chiapas,* by William R. Holland,
  American Anthropologist, 67:524–526.
  1966a. "Some Implications of Weather Modification for the Cultural Patterns
  of Tribal Societies," *Human Dimensions of Weather Modification,* University
  of Chicago Department of Geography Research Series, W. R. Derrick Sewell,
  ed., 105:373–392.
  1966b. "Ancestor worship in Zinacantan." *Actas del XXXVI Congreso Internacional de Americanistas,* Madrid, 3:281–285.
  n.d. "The Maya," in *Ethnology of Middle America,* vol. 7 of *Handbook of Middle
  American Indians,* ed. Robert Wauchope (in press).
  1967. "The Harvard Chiapas Project." Paper read at the 66th Annual Meeting
  of the American Anthropological Association, Washington, D.C.
  n.d. "Introduction," in *Ethnology of Middle America,* vol. 7 of *Handbook of
  Middle American Indians,* ed. Robert Wauchope (in press).
  n.d. "Recurrent and Directional Processes in Zinacantan." Actas del XXXVII
  Congreso Internacional de Americanistas, Mar del Plata, Argentina, September 1966 (in press).
  n.d. "Human Souls and Animal Spirits in Zinacantan," Lévi-Strauss Festschrift,
  edited by Pierre Maranda and Jean Pouillon, Paris (in press).
  n.d. "Penny Capitalists or Tribal Ritualists?—The Relationship of Ritual Life
  to Market Behavior in a Modern Maya Community." Tokyo, Proceedings of
  the 8th International Congress of Anthropological and Ethnological Sciences,
  1968 (in press).

———— and GEORGE A. COLLIER
  1965. "Aerial photographs and computers in the analysis of Zinacanteco demog-
  raphy and land tenure." Paper presented to the 64th Annual Meeting of the
  American Anthropological Association, Denver, Colorado, November 18–21.

———— and ALBERTO RUZ L., eds.
  1964. "Summary and Appraisal," in *Desarrollo Cultural de Los Mayas,* Seminario
  de cultura Maya, Universidad Nacional Autónoma de México, pp. 385–403.

———— and A. KIMBALL ROMNEY

n.d. "The use of aerial photographic techniques in Maya ethnography." Moscow, Proceedings of the 7th International Congress of Anthropological and Ethnological Sciences, 1964 (in press).

———— and MARK L. ROSENBERG

1968. "People of the Bat Country," *Harvard Alumni Bulletin,* 70:12–25.

WHELAN, FREDERICK G. III

1967. "The Passing of the Years," Unpublished MS., Harvard Chiapas Project.

WILSON, GEORGE CARTER

1966. *Crazy February.* New York: J. B. Lippincott.

YORK, HENRY E.

1960. "The Kinship System of Yalcuc," Unpublished MS., Harvard Chiapas Project.

ZIMBALIST, MICHELLE

1963. "The Corn Fields: A Study of the Social Structure of the Granadilla. A Milpería Paraje," Unpublished MS., Harvard Chiapas Project.

Index